Oracle Press™

MySQL Workbench: Data Modeling & Development

About the Author

Michael McLaughlin, Oracle ACE, is a professor at BYU – Idaho in the Computer Information Technology Department of the Business and Communication School. He teaches courses on IT management, databases, and systems analysis and design. Michael is the author of *Oracle Database 11g PL/SQL Programming, Oracle Database 10g Express Edition PHP Web Programming,* and *Oracle Database 11g & MySQL 5.6 Developer Handbook.* He is the co-author of *Oracle Database 11g PL/SQL Programming Workbook, Oracle Database 10g PL/SQL Programming, Expert Oracle PL/SQL,* and *Oracle Database AJAX & PHP Web Application Development.* Michael worked at Oracle Corporation for more than eight years, most recently as the senior applications upgrade manger in E-business Suite Release Engineering.

About the Technical Editor

Scott Mikolaitis is an applications architect at Oracle Corporation and has worked at Oracle for over 15 years. He works on prototyping and standards development for the Fusion Middleware technologies in Oracle Fusion Applications. Scott also enjoys working with web services in Java as well as Jabber for human and system interaction patterns. He spends his spare time on DIY home improvement and gas-fueled RC cars.

Oracle Press™

MySQL Workbench: Data Modeling & Development

Michael McLaughlin

New York Chicago San Francisco
Lisbon London Madrid Mexico City Milan
New Delhi San Juan Seoul Singapore Sydney Toronto

Cataloging-in-Publication Data is on file with the Library of Congress

McGraw-Hill books are available at special quantity discounts to use as premiums and sales promotions, or for use in corporate training programs. To contact a representative, please e-mail us at bulksales@mcgraw-hill.com.

MySQL Workbench: Data Modeling & Development

1 2 3 4 5 6 7 8 9 0 DOC/DOC 1 0 9 8 7 6 5 4 3

ISBN 978-0-07-179188-5
MHID 0-07-179188-4

Sponsoring Editor
Paul Carlstroem

Editorial Supervisor
Janet Walden

Project Manager
Sheena Uprety,
Cenveo® Publisher Services

Acquisitions Coordinator
Amanda Russell

Technical Editor
Scott Mikolaitis

Copy Editor
Lisa McCoy

Proofreader
Susie Elkind

Indexer
Karin Arrigoni

Production Supervisor
George Anderson

Composition
Cenveo Publisher Services

Illustration
Cenveo Publisher Services

Art Director, Cover
Jeff Weeks

Cover Designer
Pattie Lee

To Lisa, my eternal companion, inspiration, wife, and best friend; and to Sarah, Joseph, Elise, Ian, Ariel, Callie, Nathan, Spencer, and Christianne, who supported me like the champions they are throughout the writing process.

Contents at a Glance

PART V
Appendixes and Glossary

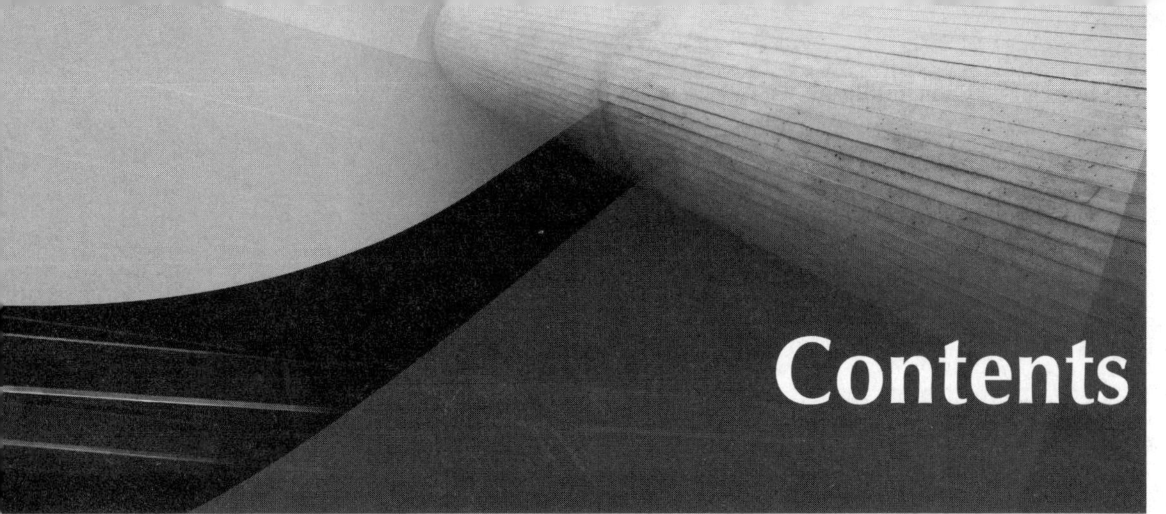

Contents

PART II
Data Modeling

PART III
SQL Development

PART IV
Server Administration

PART V

Appendixes and Glossary

Acknowledgments

Many thanks go to Wendy Rinaldi, who got the project approved, and Paul Carlstroem, who oversaw it, and Ryan Willard and Amanda Russell, who kept me on pace. Their tireless work on this project helped make the book a reality.

Special thanks go to Scott Mikolaitis for his technical editing, Dave Stokes of the MySQL Product Management for his support on the project, and Alfredo Kojima of the MySQL Workbench Development team for his support on the product features.

Thanks to Michael Stokes, Jordan Smith, Rex Barzee, and Kent Jackson for reviewing parts of the manuscript. In addition, thanks to Art Ericson, my CIT department chair, for his support on the project.

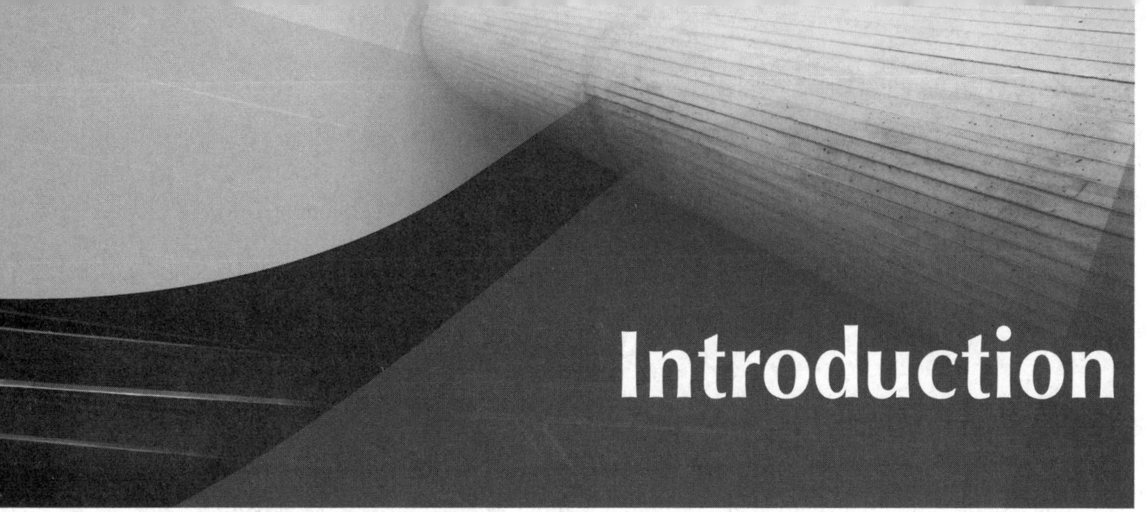

Introduction

MySQL Workbench is a fantastic tool that supports DBAs, developers, and data architects to visually model, generate, and manage databases. Unfortunately, not all features are immediately intuitive. This book demonstrates how to use MySQL Workbench by showing how to use the features.

Who Should Read This Book

Developers, data architects, and DBAs should read this book to learn how to use the MySQL Workbench features. This book should help them speed up their learning curve on the product.

Developers can create data models quickly to deploy new applications. Data architects can use MySQL Workbench to reverse- or forward-engineer data models. DBAs can migrate MySQL 5.0, 5.1, 5.5, and 5.6 to a MySQL-compatible SQL script file. They can also migrate Postgres 9.1, Sybase 15.7, and Microsoft SQL Server 2000, 2005, 2008, and 2012 to MySQL Server instances or into compatible SQL script files.

What This Book Covers

This book introduces how to install and configure the MySQL Workbench product and how to create and maintain connections to MySQL databases. Then, the book explains the concepts of data modeling; how you create and edit tables, relations, and routines; and how to reverse-engineer existing MySQL databases.

This book also covers how you edit and manage SQL scripts. It covers how to administer MySQL Server instances, users, and groups and how to import and export MySQL Server instances, databases, and tables. It also covers the migration tool, which lets you migrate Postgres, Sybase, Microsoft SQL Server, and other MySQL Server instances.

How to Use This Book

You have three options on how to use this book. You can read it from cover to cover, read a section to learn a set of skills, or read a chapter to learn how to use a feature of the product.

Full screen shots walk through all major product features. Descriptions accompany the illustrations to help you walk through the features.

How This Book Is Organized

This book is organized to support reading from cover to cover, by section, or by chapter as a reference.

Part I: Configuration

Chapter 1 covers the installation and configuration of MySQL Workbench.

Chapter 2 covers how to set up, configure, and manage database connections.

Part II: Data Modeling

Chapter 3 covers how to model data, with emphasis on the principles of good design.

Chapter 4 covers how to create tables, views, and relations in the Data Modeling component.

Chapter 5 covers how you create and deploy routines, which may be stored functions or procedures.

Chapter 6 covers how you can reverse-engineer an existing database into a data model when the source is an InnoDB database. InnoDB is required because relationships are determined by the foreign key constraints.

Part III: SQL Development

Chapter 7 covers how to edit data in a database, which includes a grid-like interface that lets you insert, update, and delete data.

Chapter 8 covers how to manage and use SQL script files from within the MYSQL Workbench.

Part IV: Server Administration

Chapter 9 covers how you administer MySQL Server instances.

Chapter 10 covers how you administer users and groups in the MySQL Server instance.

Chapter 11 covers how to import and export MySQL database instances; databases; and tables, views, and routines.

Chapter 12 covers how you migrate other MySQL 5.0, 5.1, 5.5, and 5.6 databases; Postgres 9.1; Sybase 15.7; and Microsoft SQL Server 2000, 2005, 2008, and 2012 to MySQL Server instances or into compatible MySQL SQL script files.

Part V: Appendixes and Glossary

The appendixes provide the answers to the mastery checks at the end of each chapter, explain how to extend MySQL Workbench with Python scripts, and explain how to set up a Microsoft SQL Server. In addition, a glossary of data modeling terms has been included.

Example Code with This Book

You can download the VideoStore.zip file from McGraw-Hill's Oracle Press website, www.OraclePressBooks.com. The zip file contains one file, video_store.sql. You should run it as a non-super user account after you create a storedb database in MySQL. You must edit the video_store.sql script when you want to use another database.

PART I

Configuration

CHAPTER 1

Installing and Configuring

MySQL Workbench runs on Linux, Unix, Mac OS X, and Windows. The installation, configuration, and use of MySQL Workbench are very similar on Linux, Unix, and Mac OS X, which makes sense when you know that Mac OS X is a Unix derivative. The Windows platform offers different interface behaviors because of its dependency on the .NET framework. These differences between platforms are highlighted throughout the book.

This book uses Fedora as the generic Linux and Unix distribution along with Windows 7 and Mac OS X (Snow Leopard). While many screen shots are similar, they're provided for each MySQL Workbench platform in this chapter.

This chapter covers the installation and configuration of MySQL Workbench by platform:

- Fedora Linux
- Mac OS X
- Microsoft Windows

The installation of MySQL Workbench doesn't require a pre-existing MySQL Server installation on the same machine, but it's more useful with one on the machine or network. MySQL Workbench stores its design repository in a proprietary file format on the local file system. Since the query features aren't available without a MySQL Server instance, both the MySQL Server and Workbench installations and configurations are shown in their respective sections. That way you can experiment with Windows, Linux, or Mac OS X.

The installation of the MySQL Server can be on the same machine when you're working on a laptop or desktop development environment. While the MySQL Server is typically on a discrete server when you work in a company, the book assumes generally you're working on development workstation.

The next sections cover the installation and configuration of both products.

Fedora Linux

Fedora Linux is the open-source version of the Red Hat Enterprise Linux. It is also the most like the Oracle Unbreakable Kernel Linux. CentOS is also another Red Hat clone, and it is very similar to Red Hat Enterprise and Oracle Unbreakable Kernel Linux. These Red Hat distributions use the Red Hat Package Manager (RPM) and `.rpm` files to install and upgrade software. This means software is distributed in packages, which include software executables, shared libraries, image files, and configuration files. While openSUSE isn't a Red Hat clone, it adopted the RPM for its package management of software components. Mandrake Linux distributions are a fork or derivative of Red Hat. Mageia is the current major distribution, and it uses Rpmdrake to manage .rpm files.

Debian, LinuxMint, and Ubuntu are Debian Linux distributions. They support the Debian Package Manager (DEB) and `.deb` files. You must convert .rpm files before you can run them on a Debian Linux distribution.

Most Linux software is readily available in `.rpm` or `.deb` formats. When software is only available in `.rpm` or `.deb` formats, you must convert it to the other format. Also, it's important to note that with distributions (or release management forks) the dependencies among packages can be complex. As a result of that complexity, Linux platform *users* are strongly advised to use packages from the Linux distribution where possible. These are available through menu navigation and web searches in either the Gnome or KDE desktops, which are graphical user interfaces (GUIs) like Windows or Mac OS X.

The book uses Fedora 16, which was the most current version available at the time of writing. It also supported the Oracle release of MySQL 5.5 through the GUI package management utilities. Installation of development versions of MySQL or other software generally requires substantial experience with Linux, and is best left to books about the specific Linux distribution.

Converting RPM Files to DEB Files

It's important to know how to convert RPM files to DEB files when you've opted for a Debian Linux Distribution like Ubuntu (a very popular distribution). The following command-line syntax lets you download an RPM package from Fedora's site:

```
wget http://download.fedora.redhat.com/pub/.../package_name.rpm
```

After downloading it, you can convert it to a `cpio` archive with the `rpm2cpio` utility. The `cpio` archive is more or less a common translation file structure, and the `cpio` utility lets you extract from the `cpio` archive into an uncompressed file structure.

The general recommendation is to combine the `rpm2cpio` and `cpio` command in a single command-line step by using a Linux pipe. A Linux pipe takes the standard out from one command and redirects it as standard into another command. It is represented as vertical line symbol (|). You typically perform this in a deployment directory, and some system administrators like to do this in the temporary directories provisioned in the `/tmp` directory. The command syntax to explode (the technical word for uncompressing an `.rpm` file) and write a `cpio` archive into a Linux file system is:

```
rpm2cpio package_name.rpm | cpio -mivd
```

(Continued)

The processing options for Linux programs are preceded by a single or double-dash. The example in this book uses single-dash syntax. The options to the `cpio` command mean the following:

- Preserve the date-time stamp of the original file
- Extract the files
- List each file, which is known as verbose (wordy) processing
- Create leading directories where appropriate

It is also possible to combine the download (a URI is the URL plus any hidden HTTP/HTTPS header information), conversion, and exploding of files in a single command-line statement. You could do the previous command in a single line by combining them. The *uri* string represents the URI from the previous command:

```
wget uri | cpio -mivd
```

This is generally the way many system administrators (SAs) inspect the contents of packages or troubleshoot dependencies that have failed due to missing libraries, files, or symbols. It's a good practice to understand what you're installing before applying the packages.

Install and Configure MySQL Products

The first installation step requires downloading the software. The approach on Linux differs from Windows or Mac OS X. You don't download through a browser and then launch the application. Current Linux distributions provide the ability to add or remove software from the GUI menu or through a command-line launch of the same PackageKit toolkit.

Fedora 16 uses PackageKit's suite bundled into the GNOME 3 GUI, and it makes use of the YUM utility (no joke—these are the names of the software). GNOME 3 is the default windowing environment for the Fedora distribution and many others. The YUM utility comes from the Yellow Dog Linux distribution (another derivative work from the Red Hat distribution), and it stands for the Yellowdog Updater, Modified. The YUM utility has a Python application programming interface (API) that facilitates queries that simplify installing, updating, and removing packages. The book uses the GNOME GUI, but you can also use the KDE GUI if you prefer.

The navigation to launch the GNOME PackageKit interface is Application | System Tools | Add/Remove Software. Figure 1-1 shows you how it will look in the GNOME GUI.

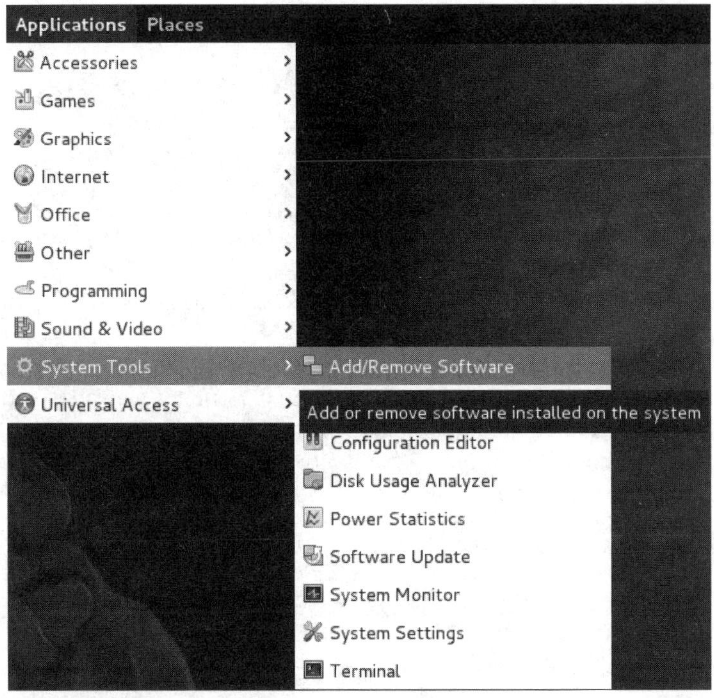

FIGURE 1-1. *GNOME Add/Remove Software navigation*

Launching the GNOME Add/Remove dialog display lets you choose from package collections or package components, like Office, multimedia, or programming components. You also have the ability to perform a search by name for types of available packages.

The next two subsections demonstrate how to install and configure the MySQL Server and MySQL Workbench.

Install and Configure MySQL Server

You search for software packages by using a fully qualified package name or a substring from the package name. After entering the search value, you click the Find button. PackageKit's Add/Remove Software utility will then search the Fedora site for matching packages. Unavoidably, the search sometimes returns more than you need and a couple of packages that aren't relative to the search key.

The following illustration shows a search for MySQL. It returns many packages, but you need only check the box for *The MySQL server and related files* package.

MySQL 5.5 was the current community edition at the time of writing, and the packages are typically the current community edition or open-source version of products.

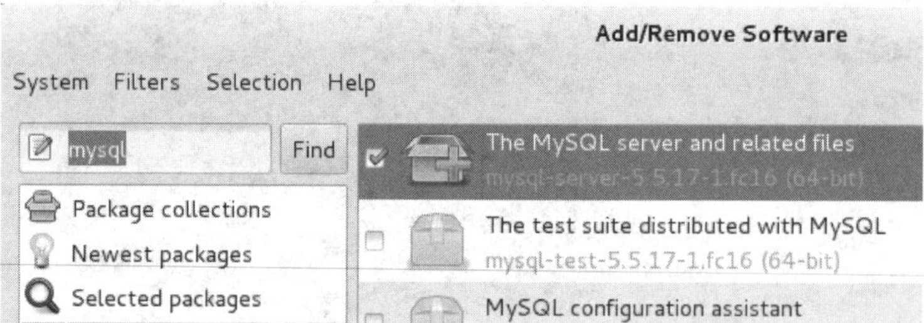

In most cases, packages require other packages to be installed. Fortunately, the Add/Remove Software utility helps by finding all the dependent packages and offering to install them alongside the chosen package.

The next screen shot shows you the scrollable list of packages. You can't install your selected package without also installing these dependent packages. Allow the installation of the dependent packages by clicking the *Continue* button.

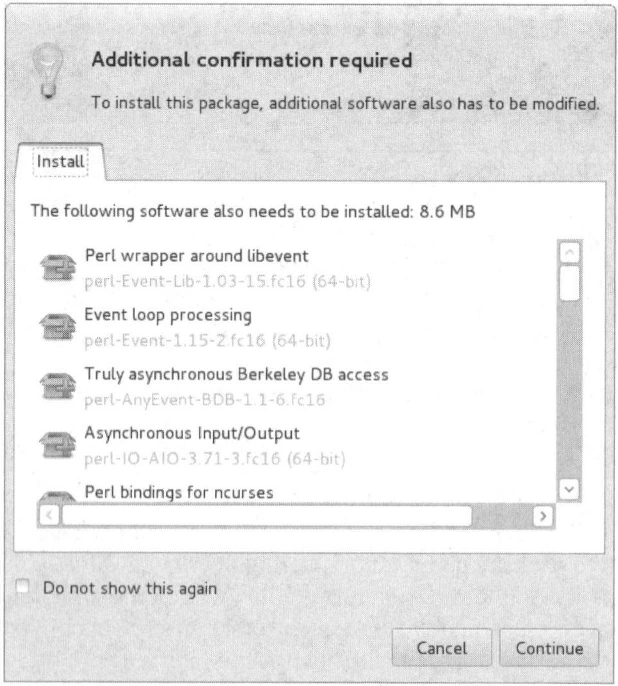

As long as the user that launched PackageKit's Add/Remove Software utility is in the wheel group (the administrator group for sudoers, a group for those who act with rights like super users), you can proceed. Check the "Configuring Sudoers on Linux"

sidebar for instructions on configuring the sudoer privileges. You'll be prompted for the root user's password, as shown in the next screen shot.

Configuring Sudoers on Linux

Granting *sudoer* privileges to a user requires some steps. You should probably grant these privileges to the user that will configure the MySQL Server and MySQL Workbench. There are six steps to enable your user with the sudoers permissions and four others to configure the standard installation:

1. Navigate to the *Applications* menu choice in the upper-left corner. You'll get the following drop-down menu. Click the *Other* menu item to launch a dependent floating menu.
2. The following floating menu displays to the right. Click the *Users and Groups* menu item at the bottom of the list.
3. The choice from the floating menu prompts account validation. Enter your password and click the *OK* button.
4. After validating your password, the *User Manager* dialog opens. Click the single user that should be installed—*your_user_name*. Click the *Properties* button to change the groups assigned to the user.
5. The *User Properties* dialog opens with the default *User Data* tab displayed. Click the *Groups* tab to add the user to the wheel group as a property of your user.
6. Scroll down through the list of groups and click the wheel group check box. Like the Mac OS X, the wheel group provides *sudoer* privileges. Click the *OK* button to assign the group to the user.

After installing the packages (that can take a few minutes), you'll see the choices with check boxes enabled. The installation process doesn't come with a progress bar, which can make determining completion difficult. Just be patient and don't click for a couple of minutes, or more with a slow Internet connection. After it completes, you can install other packages or dismiss the utility.

After installing the MySQL packages, you need to complete some manual configuration steps. These steps let you fix the MySQL configuration file.

You fix the `my.cnf` file in the `/etc` directory by editing the file. The default `my.cnf` file installs with a standard socket configuration like the following:

```
[mysqld]
# Settings user and group are ignored when systemd is used.
# If you need to run mysqld under different user or group,
# customize your systemd unit file for mysqld according to the
# instructions in http://fedoraproject.org/wiki/Systemd
datadir=/var/lib/mysql
socket=/var/lib/mysql/mysql.sock
# Disabling symbolic-links is recommended to prevent assorted security risks
symbolic-links=0

[mysqld_safe]
log-error=/var/log/mysqld.log
pid-file=/var/run/mysqld/mysqld.pid
```

You should edit the `my.cnf` file and replace everything except the `[mysqld_safe]` section with the following:

```
[mysqld]
# Settings user and group are ignored when systemd is used.
# If you need to run mysqld under different user or group,
# customize your systemd unit file for mysqld according to
# the instructions in http://fedoraproject.org/wiki/Systemd

# Default directory.
datadir=/var/lib/mysql

# The TCP/IP Port the MySQL Server listens on.
port=3306
bind-address=127.0.0.1

# The Linux Socket the MySQL Server uses when not using a
# listener.
# socket=/var/lib/mysql/mysql.sock

# Disabling symbolic-links is recommended to prevent assorted
# security risks
symbolic-links=0
```

```
# The default storage engine that will be used when creating
# new tables.
default-storage-engine=INNODB

# Set the SQL mode to strict.
sql-mode="STRICT_TRANS_TABLES,NO_AUTO_CREATE_USER,NO_ENGINE_SUBSTITUTION"

# Set the maximum number of connections.
max_connections=100

# Set the number of open tables for all threads.
table_cache=256

# Set the maximum size for internal (in-memory) temporary tables.
tmp_table_size=26M

# Set how many threads should be kept in a cache for reuse.
thread_cache_size=8

# MyISAM configuration.
myisam_max_sort_file_size=100G
myisam_sort_buffer_size=52M
key_buffer_size=36M
read_rnd_buffer_size=256K
sort_buffer_size=256K

# InnoDB configuration.
innodb_data_home_dir=/var/lib/mysql
innodb_additional_mem_pool_size=2M
innodb_flush_log_at_trx_commit=1
innodb_log_buffer_size=1M
innodb_buffer_pool_size=25M
innodb_log_file_size=5M
innodb_thread_concurrency=8

[mysqld_safe]
log-error=/var/log/mysqld.log
pid-file=/var/run/mysqld/mysqld.pid
```

Next, you start the MySQL service, which can be done at the command line by any user authorized in the *sudoers* list.

The Fedora syntax would be:

```
[username@hostname ~]$ sudo service mysqld start
```

The Ubuntu or Debian prompt and syntax are:

```
username@hostname:~$ sudo /etc/init.d/mysqld start
```

Checking for the Most Current Version

You can ensure that the installed package is the most current by running the following command as the root super user:

```
yum install mysql mysql-server
```

If it returns the following (naturally, your package numbers will increase over time), you're ready to start the service and install the database:

```
Loaded plugins: langpacks, presto, refresh-packagekit
Setting up Install Process
Package mysql-5.5.18-1.fc16.x86_64 already installed and latest version
Package mysql-server-5.5.18-1.fc16.x86_64 already installed and latest
version
Nothing to do
```

After starting the service, you need to secure the MySQL Server. This can be a manual task, or you can simply run the provided script file to secure the installation, which is located in the `/usr/bin` directory:

```
[username@hostname ~]$ mysql_secure_installation
```

This script requires you to interactively reply to a few prompts. The first prompt asks for the `root` password, and initially it's null. That means you reply by pressing the RETURN key. The next question asks if you want to set the `root` user's password. Press Y and press the RETURN key. The script prompts you for the `root` user's password twice.

You're then asked whether you want to delete the anonymous user, which is a must-do item. Press Y and press the RETURN key. The next question asks if you want to disallow `root` login. If this is a development machine, you should press Y and press the RETURN key to restrict `root` login to the local host. That's because it's wise to do so.

The script then asks if you want to remove the `test` database. It's really not important whether you remove it or not, but I'd recommend you do. Press Y and press the RETURN key to remove the test database. The last question asks if you want to reload the privileges table, and the answer should be Y with the RETURN key. This flushes security privileges and reloads them with any changes made during your connection to the MySQL database. The alternative requires you to disconnect, shut down the MySQL instance, and restart the MySQL instance.

After securing the database, you should create a `student` user and `studentdb` database. Please refer to the "Create Default MySQL User" sidebar for instructions if you need them.

Create Default MySQL User

The sample code depends on you creating a `student` MySQL user and `studentdb` database. You want to grant all permissions to the `student` user to work in the `studentdb` database.

You connect to the MySQL Monitor command line with the following syntax as the root super user:

```
mysql -uroot -pyour_root_password
```

You or your database administrator (DBA) can create a `student` user and `studentdb` database with this syntax as the root user:

```
CREATE USER 'student'@'%' IDENTIFIED BY 'student';
```

This account has access to nothing at this point. All the user can do is *connect* to the database from anywhere. `localhost` restricts access to the same machine and an IP address; domain or subdomain restricts it to one or a set of TCP/IP addresses. The % lets the user connect from anywhere. A user with these permissions can see only the `INFORMATION_SCHEMA` database with the following command:

```
SHOW DATABASES;
```

The `INFORMATION_SCHEMA` database is a snapshot of the MySQL database instance. Any user with access to the `INFORMATION_SCHEMA` database can query and discover information about databases that they can't see when they issue a `SHOW DATABASES;` command. This appears to be a security hole in Oracle MySQL 5.6 that Oracle will certainly fix in subsequent releases.

After creating the user, you should create a `studentdb` database. The command syntax for that is:

```
CREATE DATABASE studentdb;
```

Alternatively, an administrator can create a `SCHEMA` instead of a `DATABASE`. The words are interchangeable because `SCHEMA` is a synonym for `DATABASE`, as of MySQL 5.0.2.

This `GRANT` command gives all permissions on the `studentdb` to the `student` user:

```
GRANT ALL ON studentdb.* TO 'student1'@'%';
```

The grant enables the `student` user to use the `studentdb` database. The student user must tell MySQL which database it wants to work with after

(Continued)

connecting because a connection by itself does not connect the user to a work area. You do that with the following command:

```
USE studentdb
```

You should note that the `USE` command doesn't require a semicolon. It's like a SQL*Plus command in an Oracle Database 11*g* instance.

You can change databases at any time, but you must disconnect and reconnect when you want to change users. This is less convenient than the Oracle solution, which lets you connect as another user without leaving the SQL*Plus environment.

You have successfully configured the MySQL instance. The next step requires that you download and install MySQL Workbench.

Install and Configure MySQL Workbench

Downloading, installing, and configuring MySQL Workbench follows the same route that you took with MySQL Server. You search for a string in PackageKit's Add/Remove Software utility. It will search and find the matching package for Fedora.

The best search string for MySQL Workbench is *mysql-workbench* because it returns only one package. Click the check box, and a plus symbol superimposes itself over the open box, which represents a package. Click the *Apply* button at the bottom-right corner of the dialog screen. YUM identifies all dependencies and presents you with a supplemental dialog box requiring you to confirm that additional software will be installed. There's not really a choice, other than to abort. Therefore, click the *Continue* button at the bottom-right of the dialog box.

Having clicked the *Continue* button, you are prompted for the `root` password to install the packages. Enter the password and click the *Authenticate* button. The installation should take a couple of minutes, like the MySQL Server installation. If everything went well, you'll see the *Run New Application* dialog box for MySQL Workbench, as shown in the following illustration:

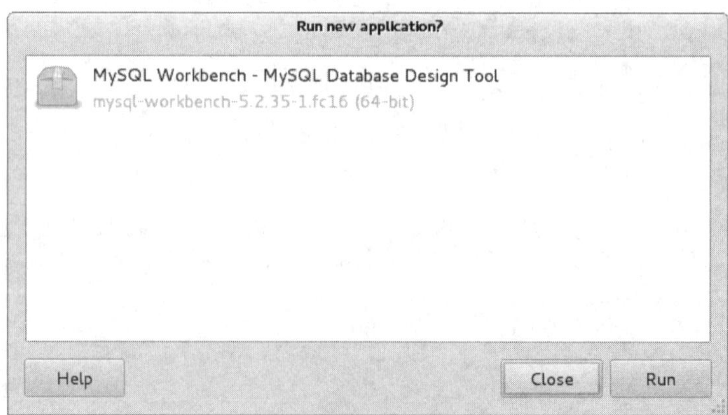

Click the MySQL Workbench inside the white frame, and then click the *Run* button to test the installation and you should see the following screen:

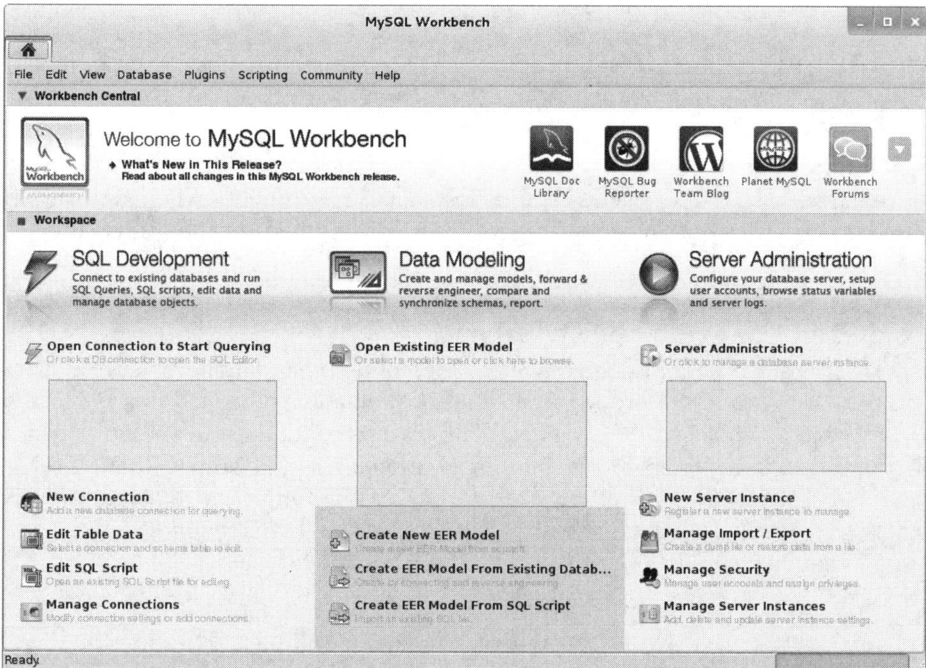

Congratulations! It works—at least it should. How do you get back to it later when you close it? That's easy because MySQL Workbench has been added to your menu. You can navigate to it by clicking Application | Programming | MySQL Workbench.

Now that you've completed a generic Linux installation available as open-source software, the next section shows you how to use a proprietary Unix variant—Mac OS X.

Mac OS X

The Mac OS X is a Unix distribution based on the Mach kernel and BSD (Berkeley Software Distribution), and it is also a proprietary distribution of Unix. The original version of the operating system was the object-oriented operating system NeXTSTEP, which was developed with Objective-C at NeXT Corporation. Its second-generation product name was OPENSTEP. Apple acquired NeXT in 1997 and leveraged the software with GUI look-and-feel components to produce Mac OS X.

The differences between Mac OS X and Linux are substantial, but much of the Unix-lineage approach is preserved in file structures and operating system commands. Most operations can be successfully managed through the GUI interface, and Mac OS X uses Apple Disk Image (`.dmg`) files to install software.

More commonly referred to as DMG files, they manage software installations easily like Microsoft's MSI files. DMG files handle the package management and configuration components.

Install MySQL Products

The first installation step requires downloading the software. The approach on Mac OS X uses a browser download. After downloading the DMG file, you launch the application.

The next two sections discuss how to install and configure the MySQL Server and Workbench. A working knowledge of basic Mac OS X navigation is helpful in these sections.

Install and Configure MySQL Server

This section guides you through the installation and configuration of the MySQL Server. It uses screen shots from an actual installation at the time of writing. Naturally, you may see differences with future installation screens, but hopefully these screen shots give you a way to anticipate items in the installation and configuration.

The first step after you download the MySQL Server Community Edition software requires you to launch it from the Downloads area. You'll see the following illustration when you double-click the MySQL DMG file.

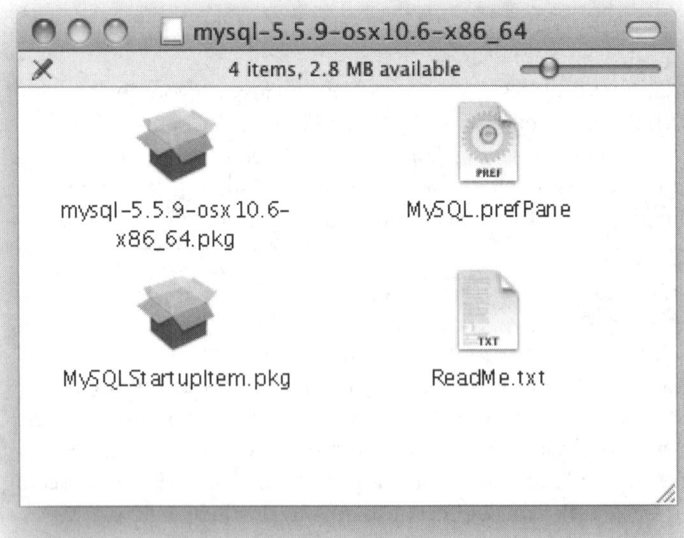

You double-click the package icon to launch the installer. It will provide the following introduction dialog. You click the *Continue* button to proceed.

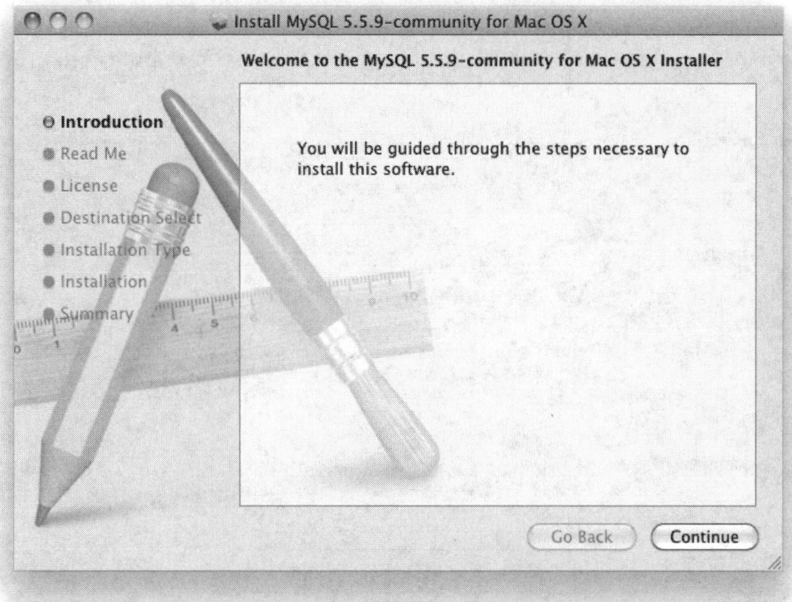

The next dialog is the *Read Me* file for any given version of the MySQL Server. You should read this to understand any changes or potential gotchas that you may encounter with the MySQL software release. Click the *Continue* button to proceed.

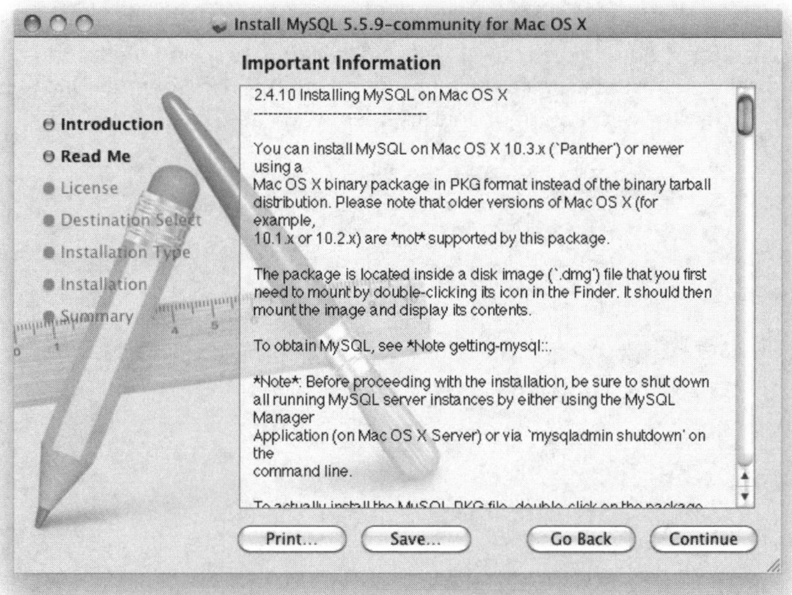

The next dialog is the license disclosure and presents the terms governing your use of the MySQL Server. You should read the license disclosure to ensure you'll be in compliance with your use of the product. Click the *Continue* button to proceed.

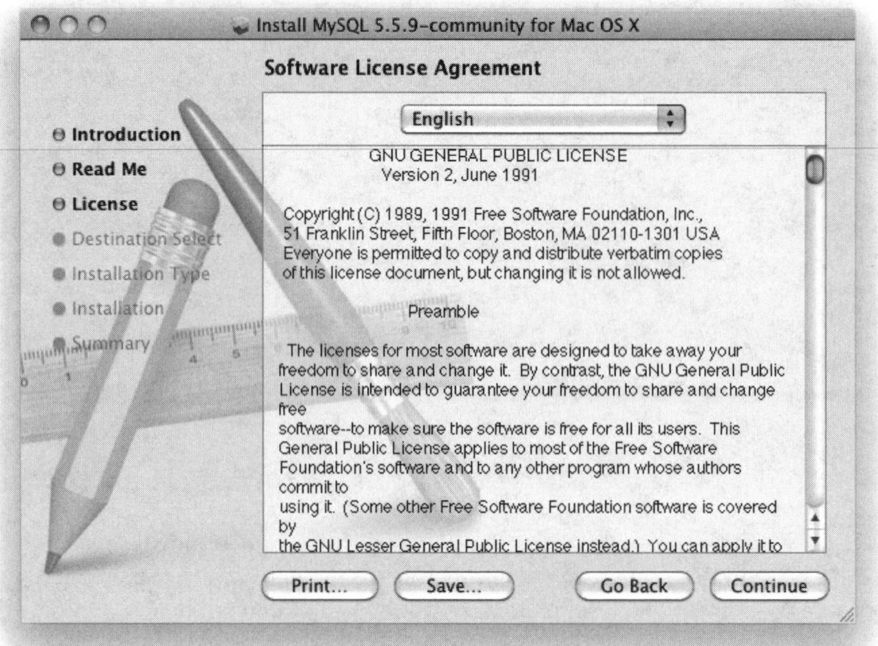

The Mac OS X doesn't let you off with just clicking the *Continue* button of the license disclosure. You must also click the *Agree* button in the overlay dialog before proceeding with the installation. If you disagree, you can't install the product.

To continue installing the software you must agree to the terms of the software license agreement.

Click Agree to continue or click Disagree to cancel the installation and quit the Installer.

Read License | Disagree | Agree

This dialog is where you can change the installation location, which I'd discourage because MySQL is typically only a development tool on the Mac OS X. Click the *Install* button to proceed.

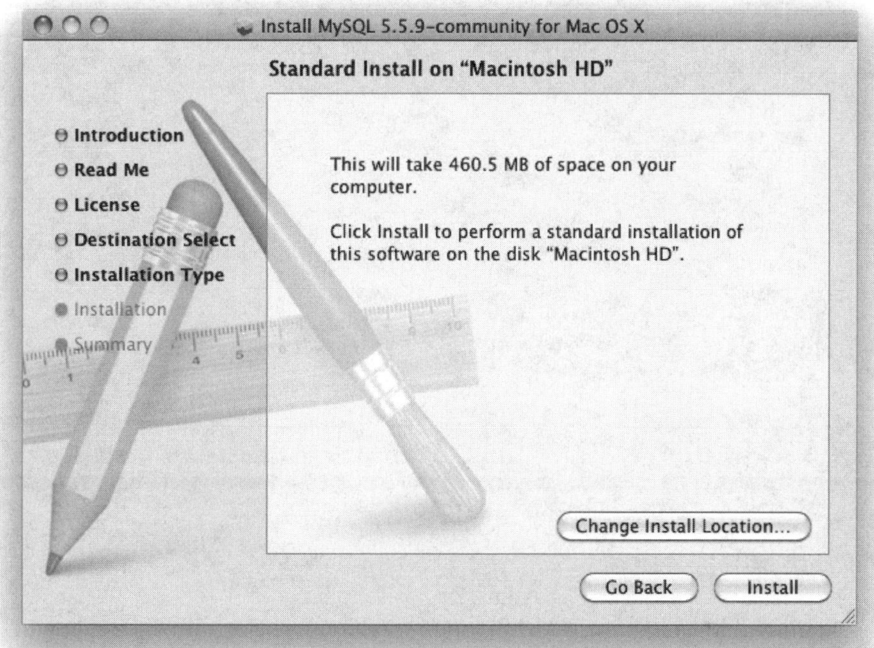

The next dialog requires you to authenticate against the `root` user's account. Enter the `root` user's password and click the *OK* button to proceed.

This is the progress dialog for the installation; it can take a couple of minutes to install, depending on the concurrent load on the machine. The *Continue* button will be grayed out until the installation is complete.

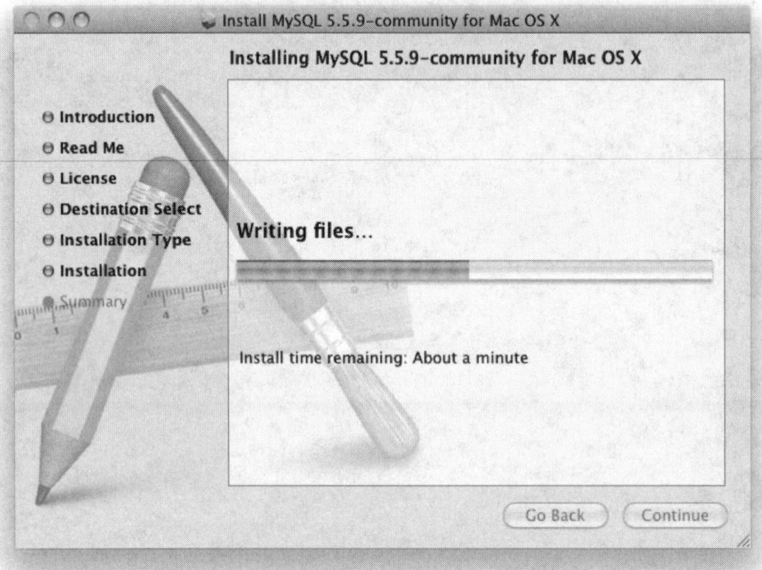

The following dialog displays after the package application completes. Click the *Close* button to proceed.

After successfully installing the product, you need to install the MySQL Startup package. It's that second open box icon in the DMG file. You double-click it to launch the installation program, and this dialog appears. Click the *Continue* button to proceed with the installation.

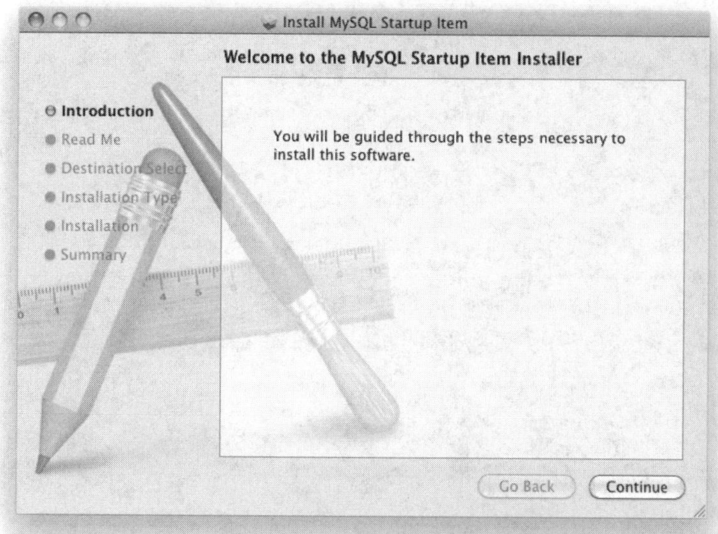

The read me dialog is next. It's always a good idea to check out any last-minute instructions from the development team. Click the *Continue* button when you've reviewed the instructions.

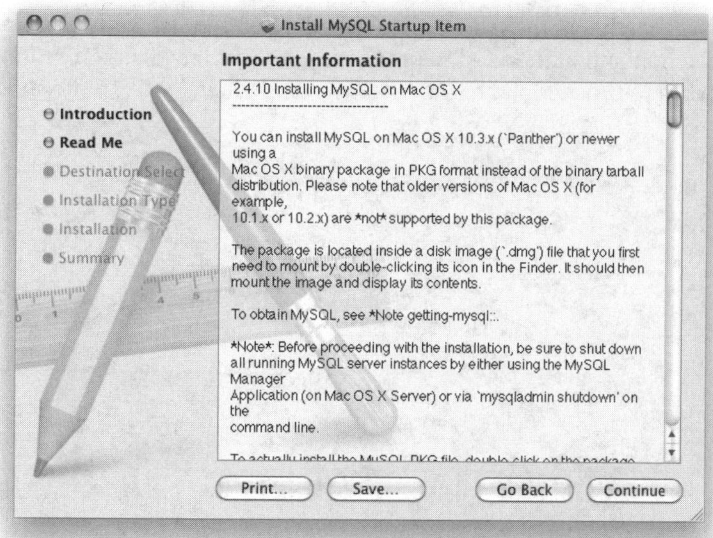

There's no license with this package because it's just installing software that lets you access the MySQL Server. You have the opportunity to install this someplace other than the default, but doing so is even less meaningful than overriding the location for the MySQL Server. I'd suggest you skip it and accept the default location. It's always easier to troubleshoot that way.

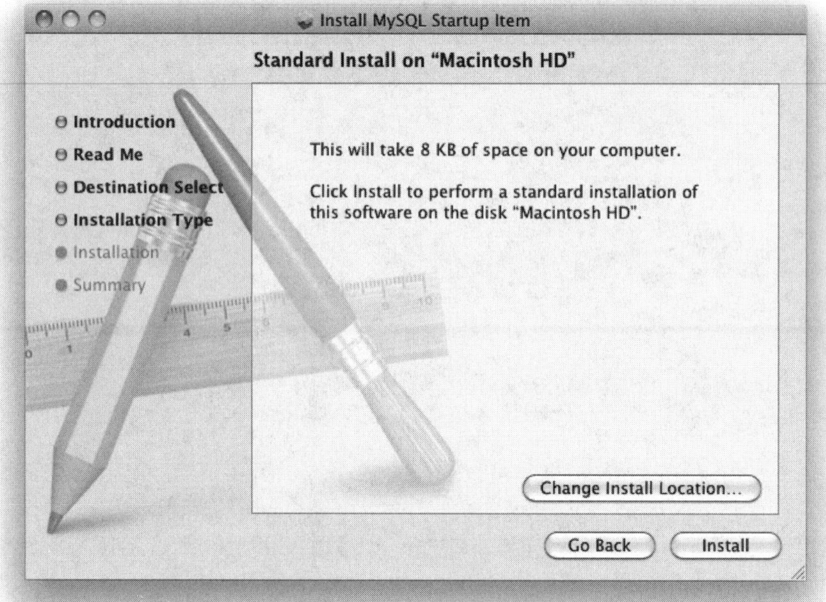

Before you can begin the installation, the Mac OS X must verify that you're in the sudoers group and authorized to proceed. You'll get this dialog requiring the root user's password to proceed. Enter the password and click the *OK* button to continue.

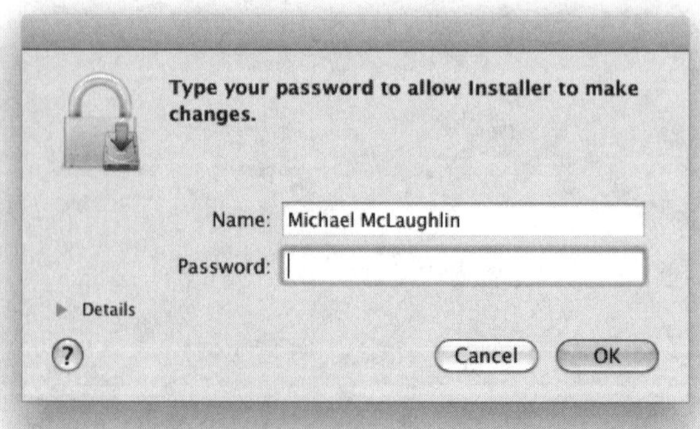

The installation occurs too quickly to capture the in-progress dialog. Good news on two fronts—it's quick and not very meaningful to display. After a brief appearance of that nondisplayed dialog, you get the following telling you that the product installed successfully.

That concludes the installation. You launch the System Preferences to start the MySQL Server. The icon is placed in the Other category at the bottom of the System Preferences dialog.

With the product installed, there are some manual steps to customize your Mac OS X experience. These steps require you to launch a Terminal session. It would be easy to run the `mysql_secure_installation` script file, like Fedora. Unfortunately, the script won't run natively on the Mac OS X operating system at the time of writing. Rather than try to teach readers how to write script files, it seemed better to walk through the configuration steps. It also provides the opportunity to help you configure your environment.

Assuming you accepted the defaults, you should be able to copy the required instructions directly into a `.bash_login` file, if one exists. Unless you've created one before, there won't be a file. Mac OS X doesn't automatically create the file. If you don't have the file, you can create one with the following syntax:

```
touch .bash_login
```

You can open the `.bash_login` file with the vi editor or a text editor of your choice. MySQL 5.5.16 forward installs in `/usr/local/mysql-version` as noted next. You can copy the following contents into the file for the MySQL 5.5.16 release, but most likely you'll need to update the version information to your later releases:

```
# Set the MySQL Home environment variable to point to the root
# directory of the MySQL installation.
export set MYSQL_HOME=/usr/local/mysql-5.5.16-osx10.6-x86_64

# Add the /bin directory from the MYSQL_HOME location into
# your $PATH environment variable.
export set PATH=$PATH:$MYSQL_HOME/bin

# Create aliases that make it easier for you to manually
# start and stop the MySQL Daemon.
alias mysqlstart="/Library/StartupItems/MySQLCOM/MySQLCOM start"
alias mysqlstop="/Library/StartupItems/MySQLCOM/MySQLCOM stop"
```

You need to save the file and close and restart a new Terminal session to place these environment variables in scope. You could also run the following to put them in scope without closing and opening the terminal:

```
. ./.bash_login
```

The preceding command sources the environment file into active memory. This should configure your environment. After restarting the shell, you should be able to run this command to confirm the new environment:

```
which -a mysql
```

It should return:

```
/usr/local/mysql-5.5.16-osx10.6-x86_64/bin/mysql
```

The problem with the mysql_secure_installation script makes it necessary to manually secure the database or modify the script file. As mentioned earlier, we'll manually secure the database because it's a one-time task and much better to understand it thoroughly.

You need to connect to the database as the privileged super user, root user. This is simple because the installation doesn't set any passwords. You open another Terminal session to make these changes, or you could install MyPHPAdmin or MySQL Workbench. The tools work as well in fixing the majority of issues.

You can start the mysqld background process, which is the MySQL Server, by using the aforementioned alias or direct syntax like this:

```
/Library/StartupItems/MySQLCOM/MySQLCOM start
```

You can connect with the following syntax after successfully starting the `mysqld` background process. This works because MySQL installs on the Mac OS X operating system without a password for the `root` super user.

```
mysql -uroot
```

Once connected to the database as the `root` user, you can confirm that passwords aren't set and an insecure anonymous user account has been previously configured. You do that by connecting to the `mysql` database, which is the database catalog for MySQL, and running the following command:

```
USE mysql;
```

You can query the result set with the following query:

```
SELECT USER, password, host FROM USER\G
```

You should see the following output plus the user's name preceding the `MacPro.local` (or `iMac.local`) `hostname` value:

```
*************************** 1. row ***************************
    user: root
password:
    host: localhost
*************************** 2. row ***************************
    user: root
password:
    host: MacPro.local
*************************** 3. row ***************************
    user: root
password:
    host: 127.0.0.1
*************************** 4. row ***************************
    user: root
password:
    host: ::1
*************************** 5. row ***************************
    user:
password:
    host: localhost
*************************** 6. row ***************************
    user:
password:
    host: MacPro.local
```

You now need to change the password for the `root` user. I would suggest that you do this with the SQL command rather than a direct update against the data dictionary tables. The syntax to fix the `root` user account requires that you enter the user name, an @ symbol, and complete host values, like this:

```
SET PASSWORD FOR 'root'@'localhost' = password('cangetin');
SET PASSWORD FOR 'root'@'MacPro.local' = password('cangetin');
SET PASSWORD FOR 'root'@'127.0.0.1' = password('cangetin');
SET PASSWORD FOR 'root'@'::1' = password('cangetin');
```

You should be able to drop both `anonymous` user rows with the following syntax, but I did encounter a problem. Assuming you may likewise encounter the problem, the fix follows the first commands you should try:

```
DROP USER ''@'localhost';
DROP USER ''@'MacPro.local';
```

If either of the anonymous accounts remains in the `user` table, you can manually drop them from the database catalog. This syntax will get rid of them:

```
DELETE FROM USER WHERE LENGTH(USER) = 0;
```

You've completed the configuration and can now type `quit;` to exit the MySQL Monitor. Also, don't forget to use a real password. The one shown here is trivial, which means it is easy to hack. Use something that others might not guess.

To reconnect, you'll now need a password, like this:

```
mysql -uroot -pcangetin
```

You can manually start the database server with the following command, which you defined as aliases in your `.bash_login` shell script. Once started, it will remain awake and active as a process until you manually shut it down. The natural sleep (or hibernation) cycles of your Mac OS X won't shut down the database.

```
mysqlstart start
```

Stopping it is also straightforward; you do this:

```
mysqlstop stop
```

The next section shows you how to install and configure MySQL Workbench.

Install and Configure MySQL Workbench

Downloading, installing, and configuring MySQL Workbench follows the same route that you took with MySQL. You use your browser to download it from the server and launch it from the browser's Download area. It should look like this:

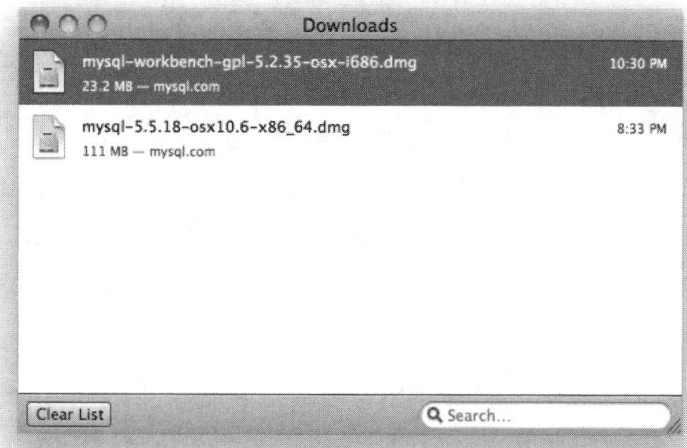

Double-clicking the MySQL Workbench DMG file launches a different type of screen shot, one that you see frequently when you work on Mac OS X. This is known as a drag-on dialog box. You click and hold down the button or two-finger click the *MySQL Workbench* icon inside the *Drag the Icon* box and drag it on to the *Applications Folder* icon.

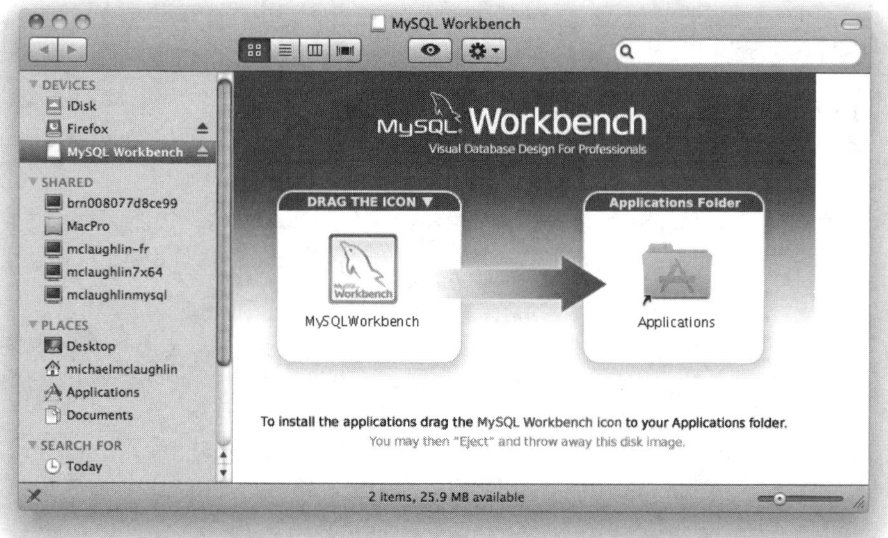

After dragging *MySQL Workbench* icon on top of the *Applications Folder*, you're prompted with a dialog, shown next, requesting that you acknowledge the risk of downloading files across the Internet. Click the *Open* button to launch the *MySQL Workbench* application.

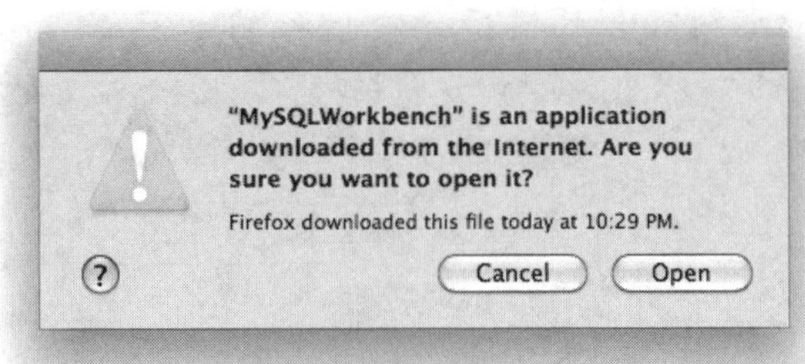

The last instruction launches your application, and you'll see the initial screen shown for all platforms. You should note that MySQL Workbench provides you with three options—they are SQL Development, Data Modeling, and Server Administration.

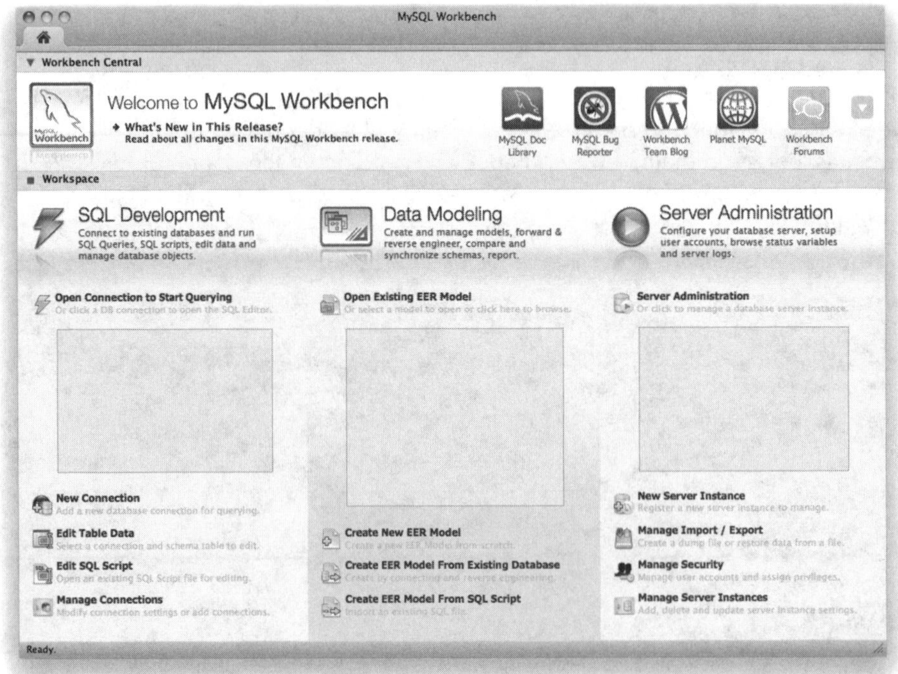

This completes the instructions for installing and configuring MySQL Server and Workbench on the Mac OS X platform. The last set of instructions is for the Windows platform.

Microsoft Windows

Microsoft Windows installation is fairly straightforward to most users because you download the software through a web browser as a Microsoft Software Installer (`.msi`) file and launch it from the *Downloads* window. Rather than call them

`.msi` files, the convention simply calls them MSI files, and we'll use that convention throughout the book.

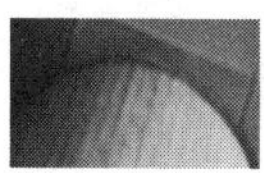

NOTE
Windows 7 was used for all testing for this book.

Two features can present challenges during a Windows installation. One is that MySQL runs as a Windows service, and the other is that MySQL Workbench has a dependency on the .NET redistributable libraries.

Windows services are background processes started automatically when the operating system launches or manually by an Administrative user. After you've installed and configured the product, we'll return and discuss the available Windows services options. More can be found in the "Windows Services" sidebar.

Windows Services

All background processes run as Windows services on the Windows operating system. These services are like daemons (pronounced dee-*muhn;* that is with a long e sound) on Linux and Mac OS X systems.

Each version of Windows has its own set of navigation steps to get to the Services dialog window. The shortcut is to go to Start | Run and enter the following:

```
services.msc
```

That launches the Services dialog, which looks like this:

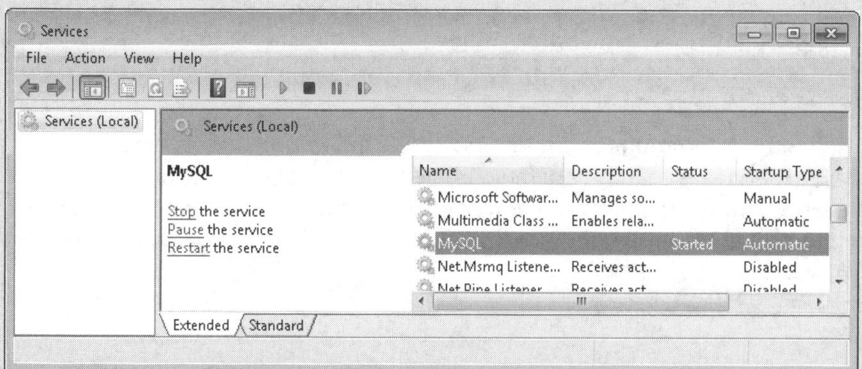

You have the option to stop, pause, or restart the running service. If you stop it, then you'll have only the option to start it. Right-clicking the MySQL name gives you a context menu. Click *Properties* to launch a menu that lets

(Continued)

you configure the MySQL service. The most frequently configured option is whether the service starts automatically with the operating system or manually.

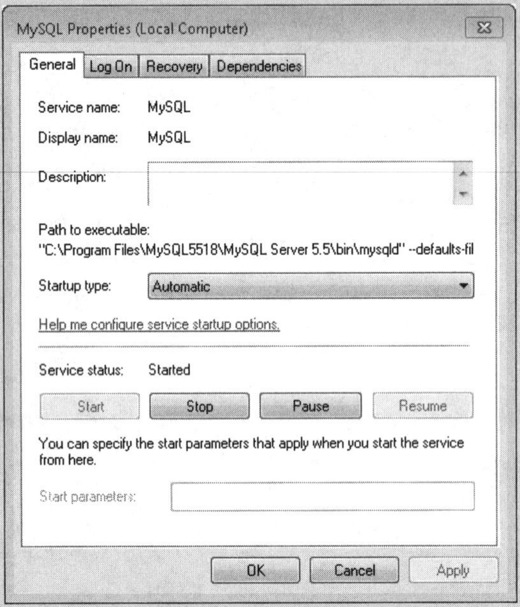

You also have the ability to start and stop Windows services from the command line. You start the service with the following syntax:

```
C:\> NET START mysql
```

Stopping the service works as follows:

```
C:\> NET STOP mysql
```

The most common reason for converting an automatic service to a manual service is that the operating system's resources are required for other activities. That's the most common case on developer machines that also support other development tools, databases, and productivity applications like Microsoft Office.

MySQL Workbench's dependency on the .NET redistributable libraries means many readers will need to perform pre-installation steps. The pre-installation steps are installing the Microsoft Visual C++ 2010 redistributable libraries and the Microsoft .NET 4 redistributable libraries.

Like the Mac OS X software, you download the MySQL Server Community Edition MSI files from Oracle's MySQL web site. My suggestion is you download both before you start. You should also download the Microsoft Visual C++ 2010 and .NET 4 redistributable libraries unless you've already installed the Microsoft Visual Studio 2010.

NOTE
Sometime in the future, downloads may migrate to Oracle's core servers and may become unavailable on the older MySQL web sites.

Pre-install Microsoft Redistributable Libraries

Finding the right libraries could be a challenge without a URL. MySQL conveniently provides them for you when you try to run the MySQL Workbench MSI file. Running the MSI installer to find them is tedious, and you can also simply Google for them.

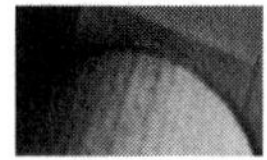

NOTE
Microsoft Visual C++ 2010 and .NET frameworks have different dependencies and patching levels on various Windows installations.

The search strings would be

- Visual C++ 2010 Redistributable Package (x86)
- .NET 4 framework

After downloading the Visual C++ 2010 Redistributable Package (x86), click the *Run* button to launch the MSI file.

This brings you to the Microsoft Visual C++ 2010 Redistributable Setup dialog. You need to click in the check box that you have read and accept the license terms of the software. It's up to you whether or not you want to send information to Microsoft Corporation. If you're inclined, you may check that box, but leaving it unchecked doesn't affect the installation. That check enables the *Install* button, which you click to proceed.

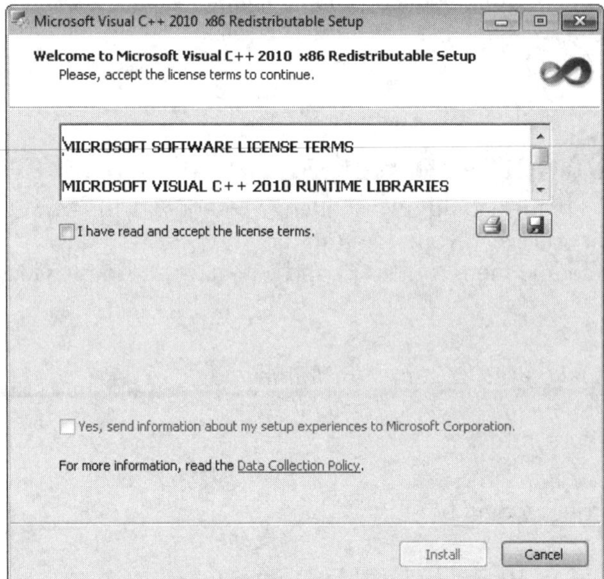

The next dialog is a progress bar. It generally takes a couple of minutes to install these libraries. Don't click the *Cancel* button unless you want to stop the whole process.

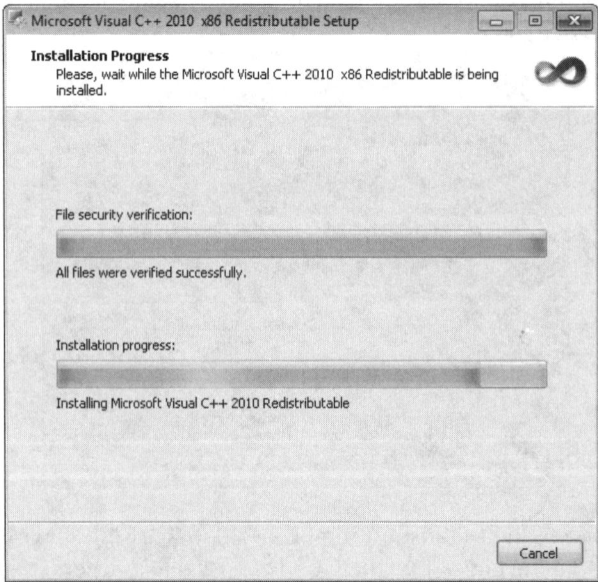

The MSI automatically proceeds to the next dialog after deploying the package to your Windows environment. Click the *Finish* button and rejoice that you don't need to reboot your system to apply these changes.

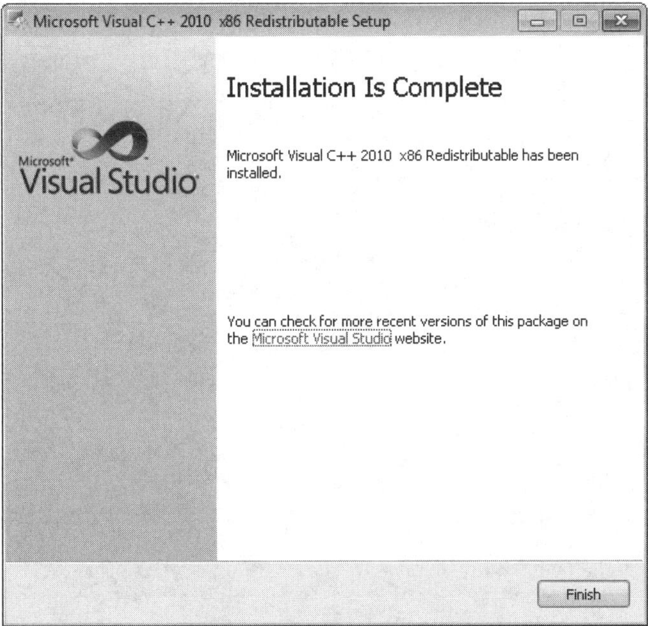

Installing the .NET 4 framework is the next pre-installation step. When you double-click the downloaded MSI file in your browser window, you'll see the following dialog. Click the *Run* button to install the software.

This brings you to the Microsoft .NET Framework Setup dialog. You need to click in the check box, as has already been done. The check acknowledges that you have read and accept the license terms of the software. The Install button became active when you checked that you read and accept the license terms. Click the *Install* button to proceed.

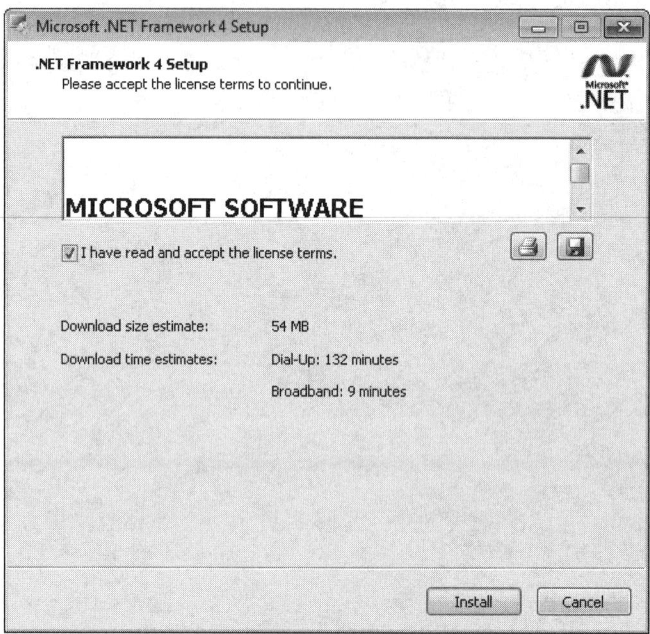

The next dialog is a progress bar. It closes by itself after installing the software.

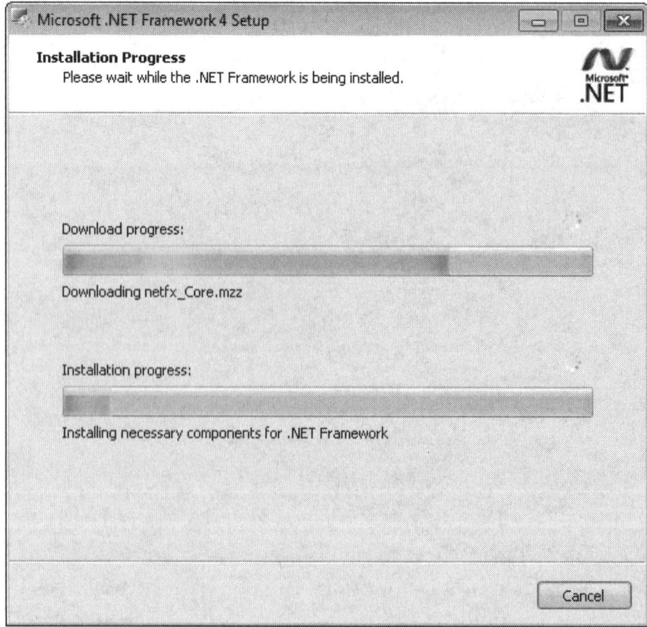

The last screen waits for you to click the Finish button. With that, you've completed the pre-install components.

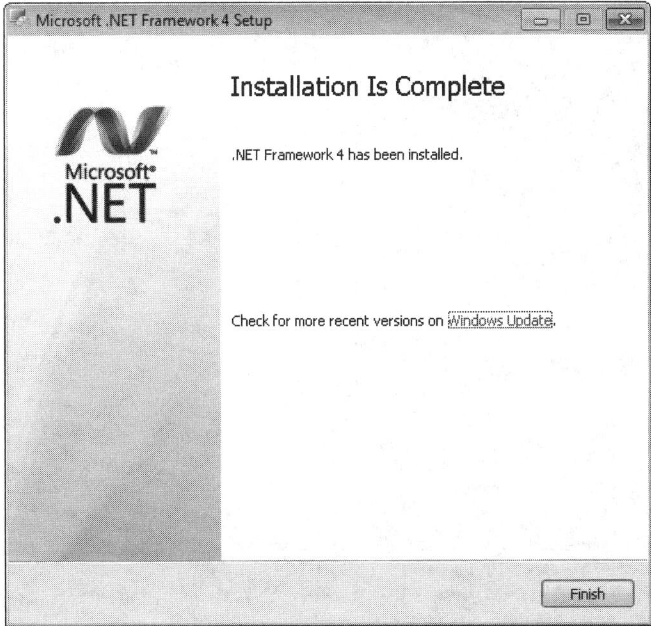

After completing the pre-installation steps, you should reboot your operating system before proceeding. The next section deals with installing and configuring the MySQL Server.

Install MySQL Products

Like the other installation, the first step requires downloading the software. The approach on Windows is somewhat like Mac OS X because it leaves the MSI file in the browser's Download folder. Unlike Mac OS X, however, the MSI configuration tool takes care of most of the setup steps for you.

The next two sections discuss how to install and configure the MySQL Server and Workbench. A working knowledge of basic Microsoft Windows navigation is helpful in these sections.

Install and Configure MySQL Server

This section guides you through the installation and configuration of the MySQL Server on the Windows platform. It uses screen shots from an actual installation at the time of writing. Naturally, you may see differences between this installation and future installation screens of the product. The screen shots should give you a way to anticipate items in your actual installation and configuration of the product.

Having seen two of the dialogs for launching software on Microsoft, we'll skip it and start with the first dialog of the MySQL Server installation. Click the *Next* button to proceed.

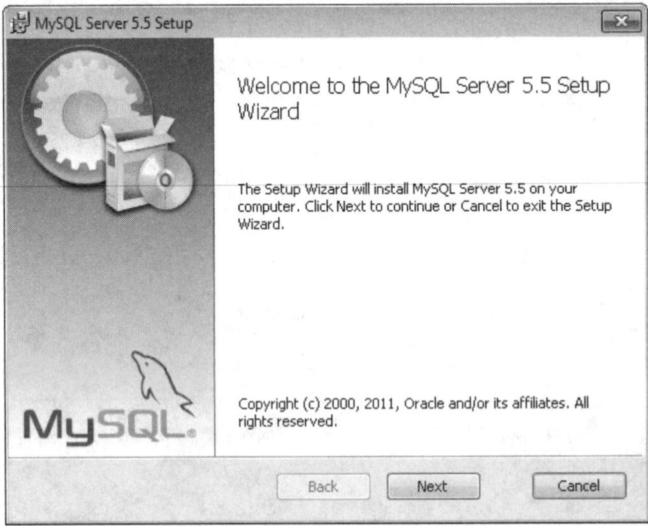

The next dialog is the license. You must click in the check box to accept the terms of the license agreement before the *Next* button becomes enabled. Then, click the *Next* button to proceed.

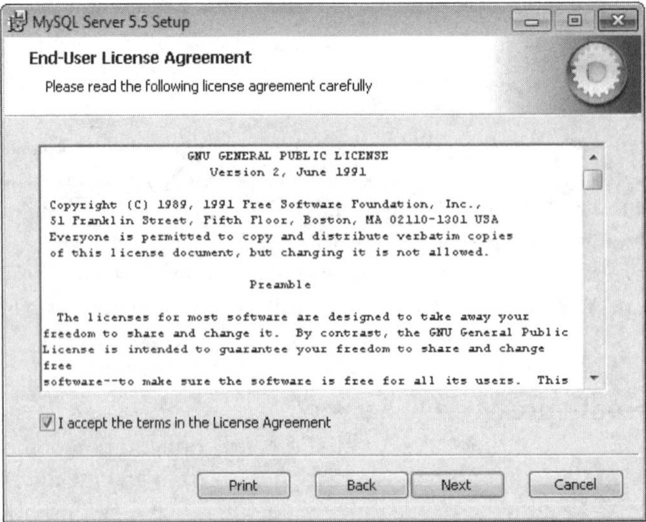

This dialog asks whether you want to install a typical, custom, or complete version of the product. A complete install is the easiest if you only plan to have one installation on the machine. A custom install lets you install multiple copies of the MySQL Server into different directories. A typical install makes a series of assumptions that generally work, but I'd suggest you install it as a custom or complete installation.

For the purposes of the screen shots, click *Custom* to follow the choices in this chapter. That triggers the *Next* button, which you should click to proceed.

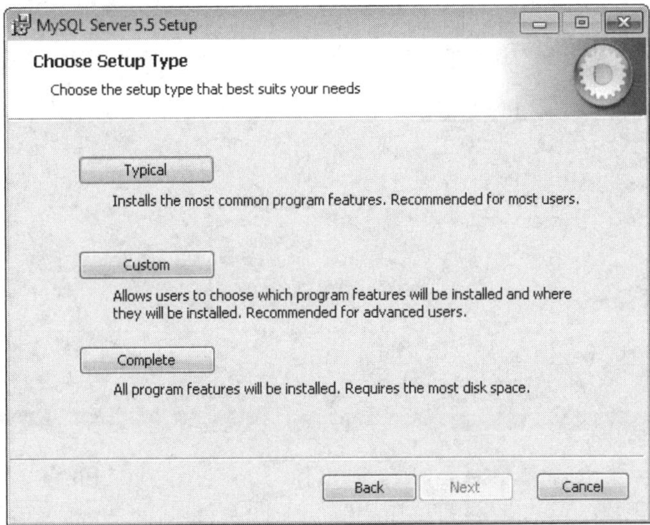

You should note that in a custom installation, the *Development Components* are grayed out. Click the *Development Components* item and choose the first option, "This feature will be installed on local hard drive," in the pop-up dialog.

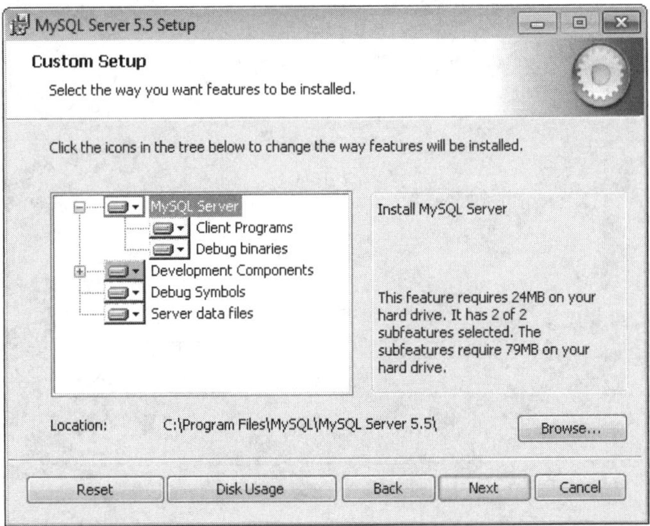

After enabling the *Development Components* item, the dialog should look like the one shown next. Click the *MySQL Server* item, and then click the *Browse* button to customize the installation directory.

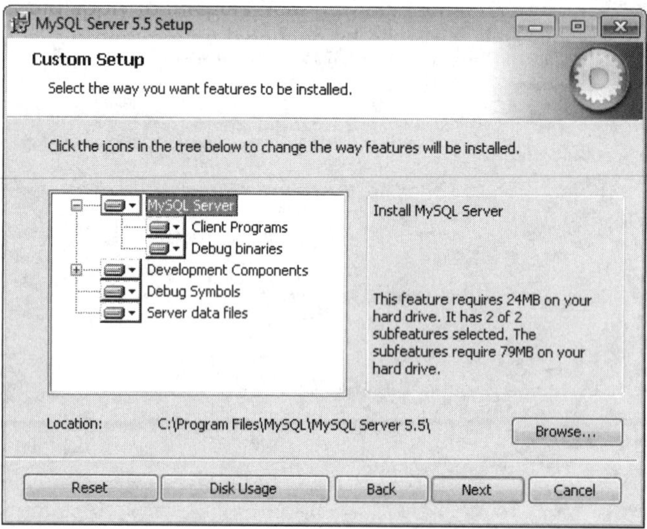

You change the destination folder for all but the server data files by entering a fully qualified path in the *Folder name* field, like the one entered where the folder MySQL is changed to MySQL5518 (for the version of the product). Click the *OK* button when you've entered the complete folder path.

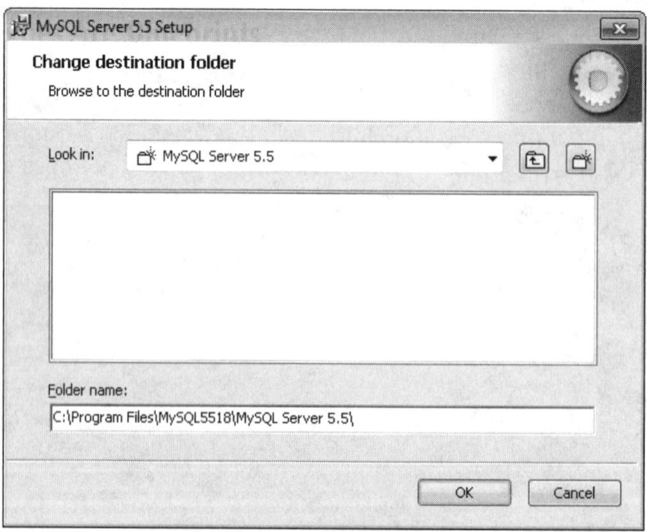

You return to the original screen, but you should note that the *Location* value shows the new destination folder. This changed target folders for the executables but not the server data files. These files are the MyISAM files. They contain the information for the `mysql`, `information_schema`, and `performance_schema` databases. All other databases are created as InnoDB engine files by default and stored in a location covered later in the installation. Click the *Server data files* option.

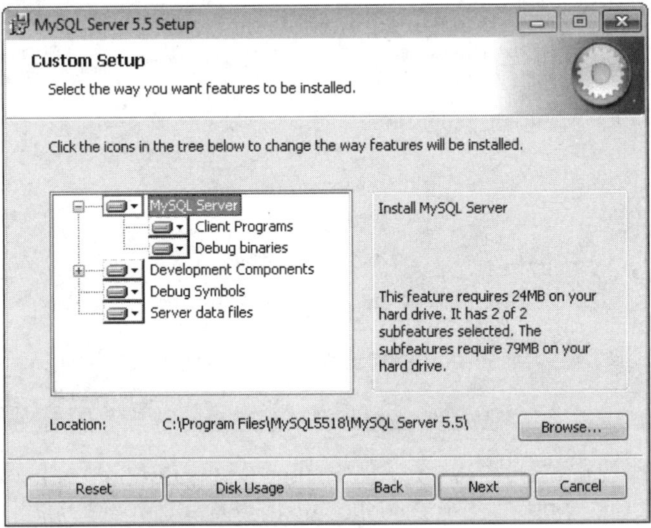

With the *Server data files* item category highlighted, click the *Browse* button to change the MyISAM data folder.

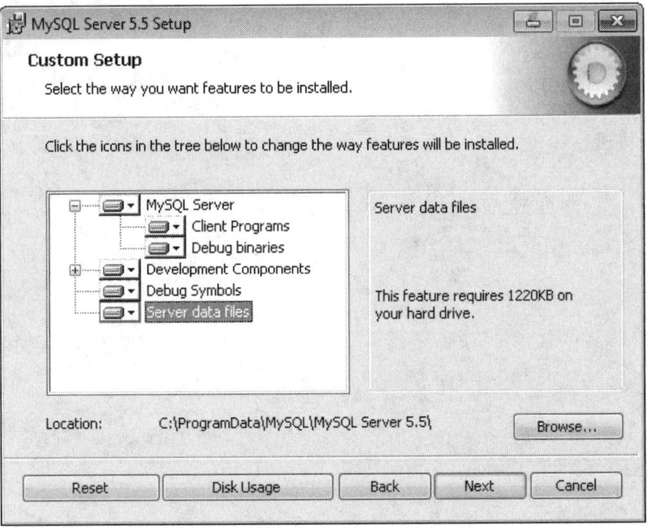

The *Browse* button returns you to the *Change destination folder* dialog. Make the same change here, replacing MySQL with MySQL5518 in the *Folder name* field. Click the *OK* button when you're done making the change.

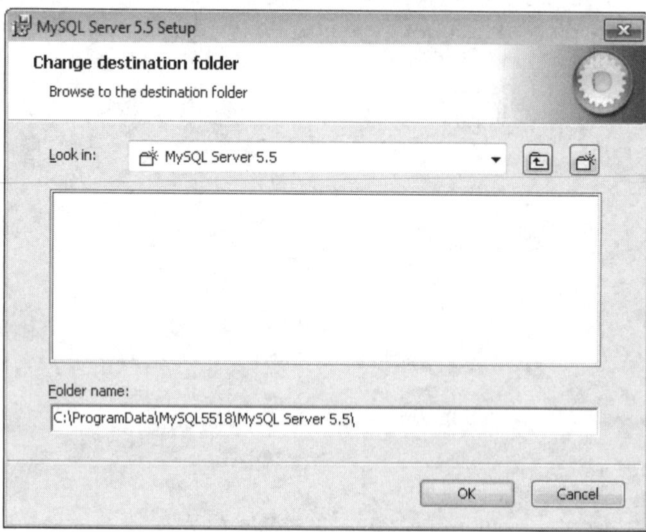

This returns you to the *Custom Setup* dialog, and you should note that the *Location* field now contains a version-specific folder path. You're finally done with this dialog and can click the *Next* button to proceed.

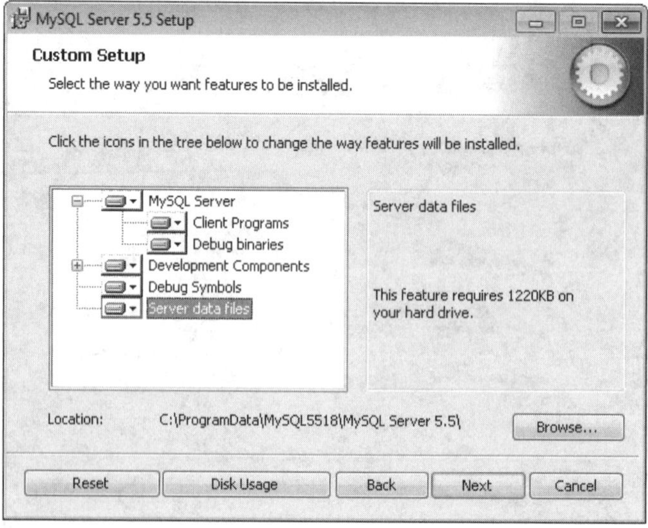

You have arrived at the dialog where you actually install the MySQL Server. Click the *Install* button to proceed or *Cancel* to abort.

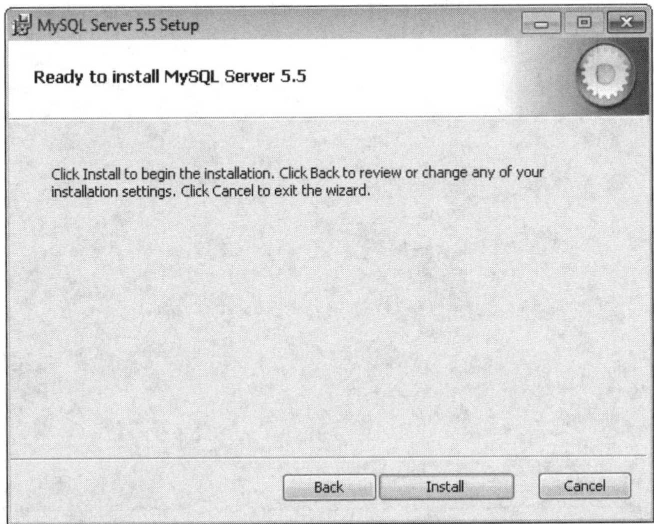

This is the progress bar dialog. It takes about a minute on most laptops. When completed, click the *Next* button to proceed.

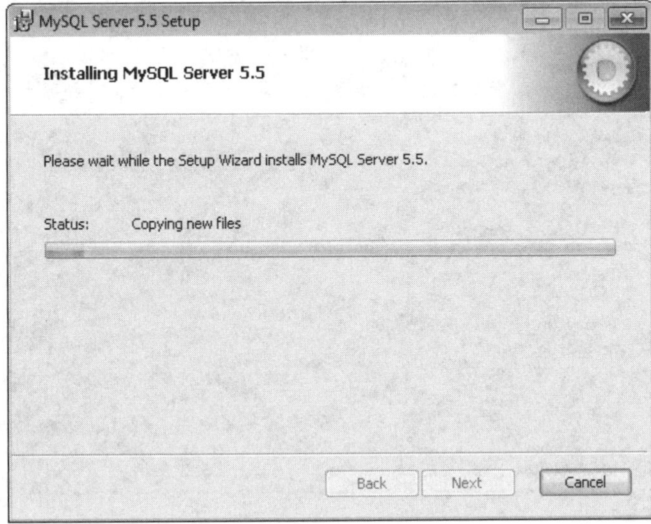

The next screen is a marketing screen that tells you about the MySQL Enterprise subscription. Click the *Next* button to proceed.

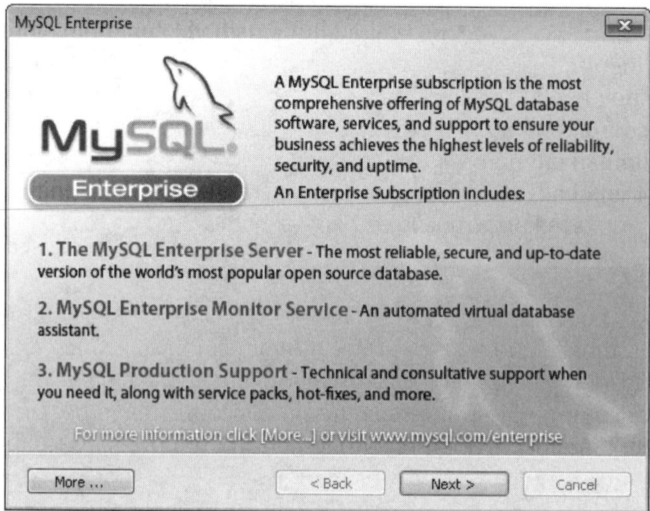

This is the second marketing dialog on the MySQL Enterprise Monitor Service, which is used typically on production databases. Click the *Next* button to proceed.

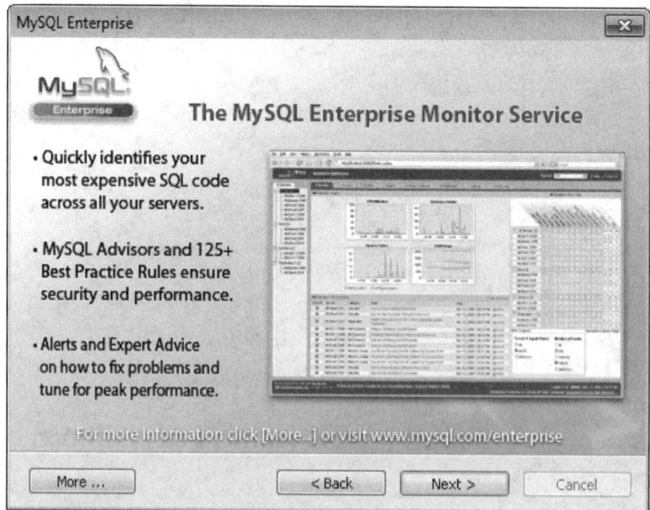

This is the final dialog of the MySQL Server installation. The *Launch the MySQL Instance Configuration Wizard* check box is selected; don't uncheck it! The MySQL Instance Configuration Wizard is the easiest way to configure your newly installed

MySQL Server. It would be awesome if there was one for Linux and Mac OS X, but as you saw earlier in this chapter, they don't have one. Click the *Finish* button to end the MySQL Server installation and begin configuring it.

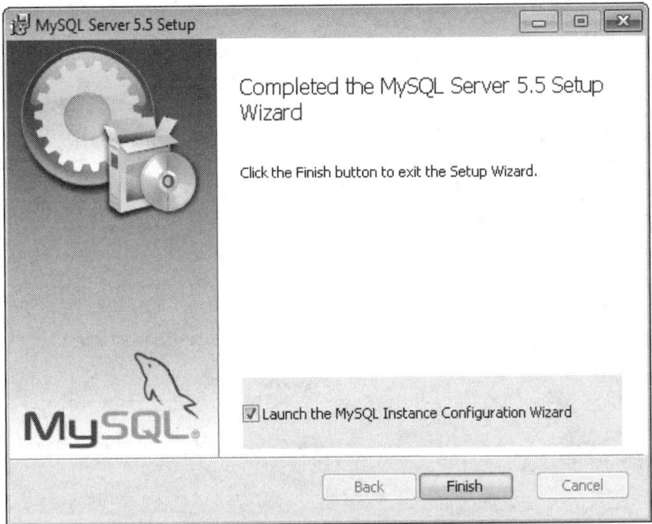

The *MySQL Instance Configuration Wizard* helps you figure out what should be in your `my.ini` file. It's a great utility, and not having it for Mac OS X and Linux makes those installations more complex.

The first dialog is the welcome screen. Click the *Next* button to proceed.

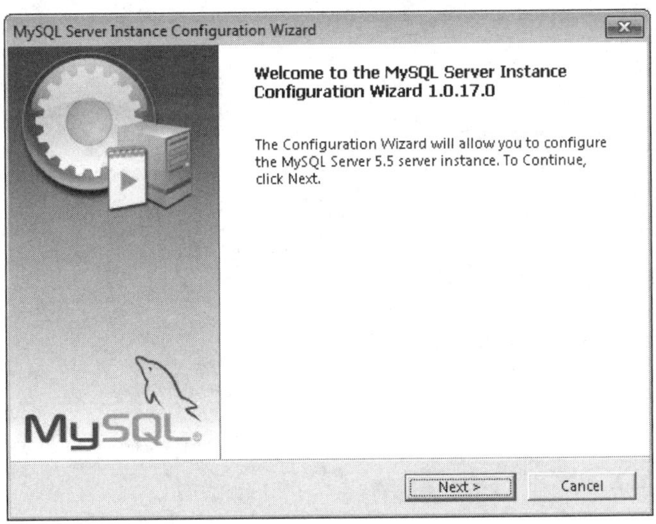

If you're new to this, clicking *Standard Configuration* is the easiest way to go, but we're going to choose the *Detailed Configuration* route. You need to click the radio button for *Detail Configuration* and then the *Next* button to proceed.

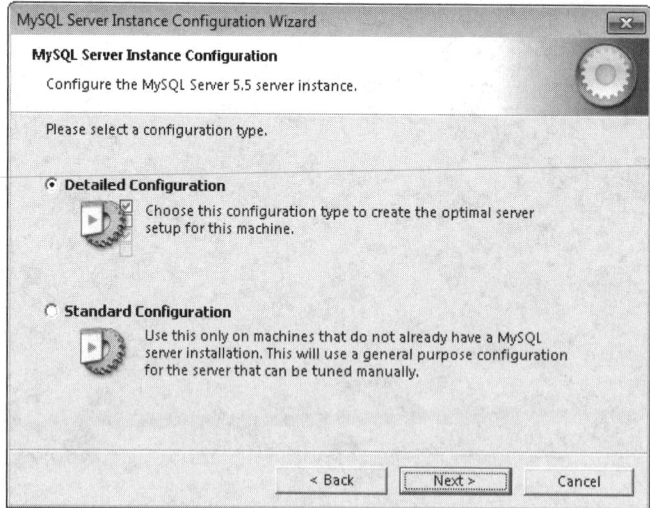

The next dialog lets you designate the machine as a developer, server, or dedicated MySQL Server machine. Since most readers are developers, click the *Developer Machine* radio button and the *Next* button to continue.

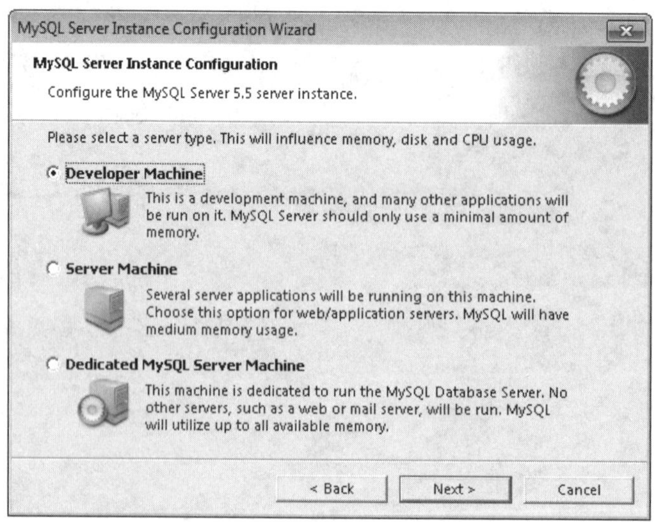

The next dialog lets you choose the primary purpose of the database instance. The most flexible choice is *Multifunctional Database*. Click *Multifunctional Database* radio button and then the *Next* button to continue with the configuration process.

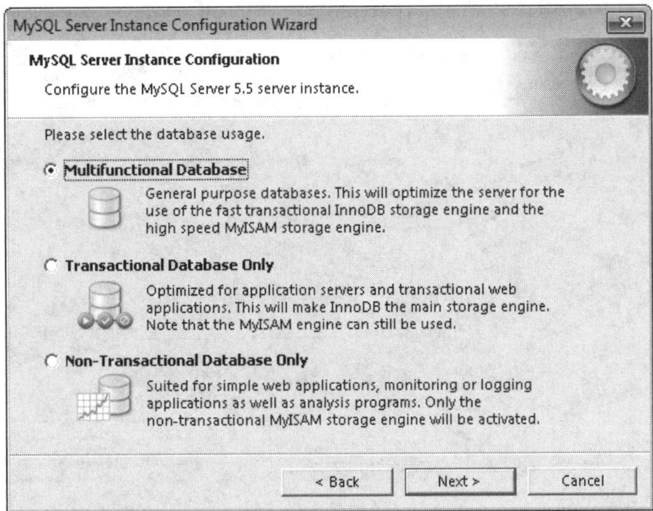

This dialog lets you choose the path for the InnoDB tablespace. Click the drop-down Installation Path combo box and choose the `\MySQL InnoDB Datafiles\` option from the list.

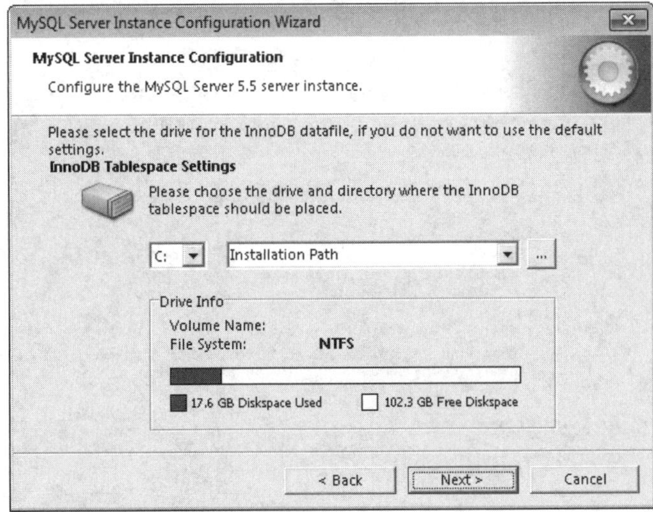

Edit the option within the combo box to include a release number, like this:

```
\MySQL 5518 InnoDB Datafiles\
```

It should appear like the next screen shot. Click the *Next* button to continue the configuration.

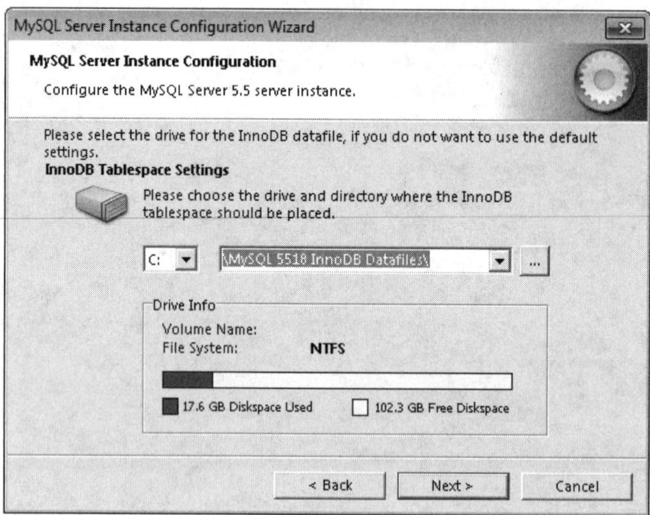

The next dialog lets you choose how many concurrent database connections you want to authorize. The *Decision Support (DSS)/OLAP* and *Online Transaction Processing (OLTP)* choices assign a small fixed number of open channels. Only the *Manual Setting* choice lets you choose the number of concurrent connections.

Set the number of concurrent connections to 50 when you create the instance as a development tool. Click the *Next* button to proceed.

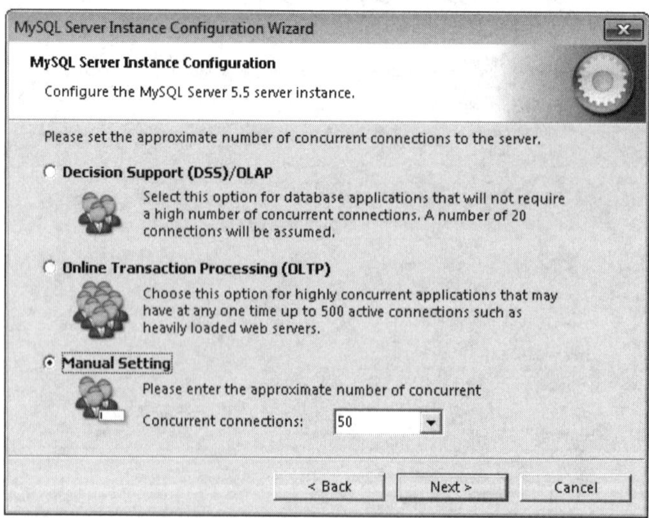

The next dialog sets up your TCP/IP networking. The default port number is 3306, but you may also choose 3307, 3308, or 3309 for your MySQL listener port. Unless you have another MySQL Server running on the machine, 3306 is fine. The port number will be written to the `[CLIENT]` and `[MYSQLD]` segments of the `my.ini` file. This file is read every time the service starts or you call the client MySQL Server software to connect to a database. Click the *Next* button to continue.

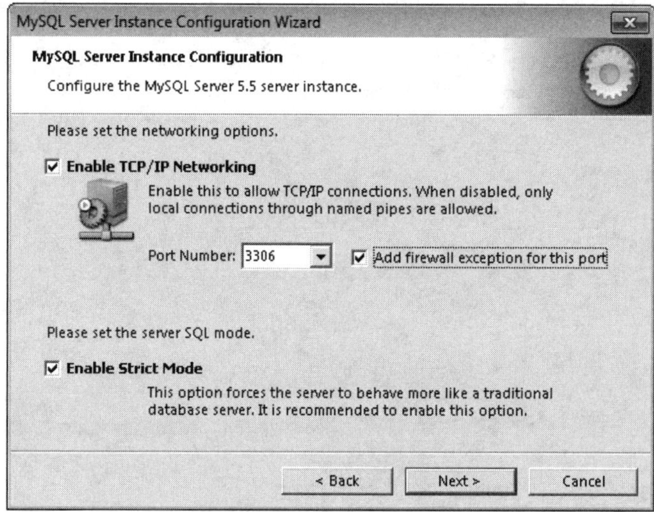

The *Standard Character Set* is latin1 (or ISO 8859-1). *Best Support for Multilingualism* supports Unicode. You can also choose *Manual Selected Default Character Set/Collation*. You should choose a character set that works for your situation; the *Standard Character Set* works in most English-speaking countries.

Click the *Next* button to continue.

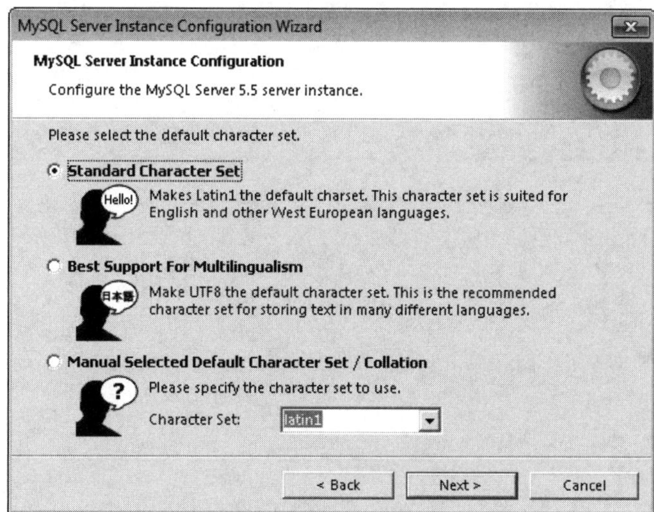

The next dialog asks whether you want to install MySQL Server as a Windows service, which is the best practice. You may pick from the service names in the combo box. Leave the *Launch the MySQL Server automatically* check box enabled when you want the service to start automatically when you start the operating system. Uncheck the box if you only want to run the MySQL Server when you enable it.

Check the *Include Bin Directory in Windows* PATH check box if you only plan to have one instance of MySQL running on the server. Leave that check box unchecked if you plan to have more than one instance running at any given time. This is a more complex option and requires that you create Windows shell scripts to set the `%PATH%` environment variable in a command shell.

The following would be an example of a command shell for MySQL 5.5.18 that dynamically prepends the MySQL path to the operating system's generic `%PATH%` environment variable. You can also type this manually in a command shell each time you want to work with MySQL, but that becomes tedious quickly.

```
SET PATH=C:\Program Files\MySQL5518\MySQL Server 5.5\bin;%PATH%
```

Click the *Next* button to continue the configuration.

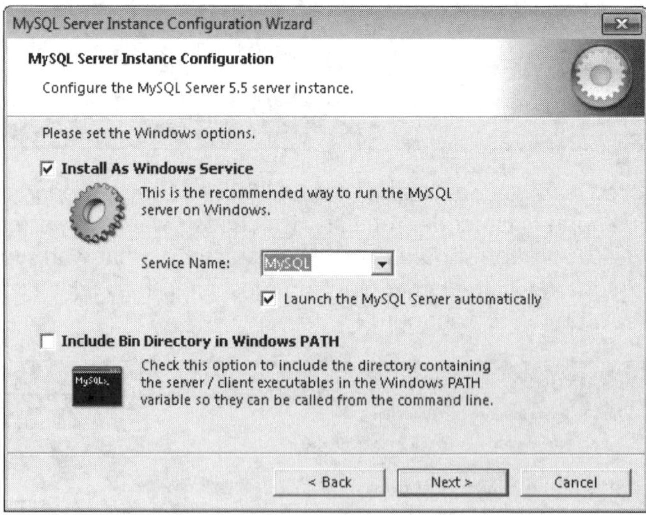

The next dialog sets the root user password for the MySQL instance. You should make sure it's something you won't forget. At the same time, you shouldn't make it too easy to guess. For the sake of the book examples, we use `cangetin`, which is the old Sun Solaris System Administrator's default `root` password for training class. You should not create an anonymous account because it's a horrible practice and a security nightmare. Click the *Next* button to continue configuring the MySQL instance.

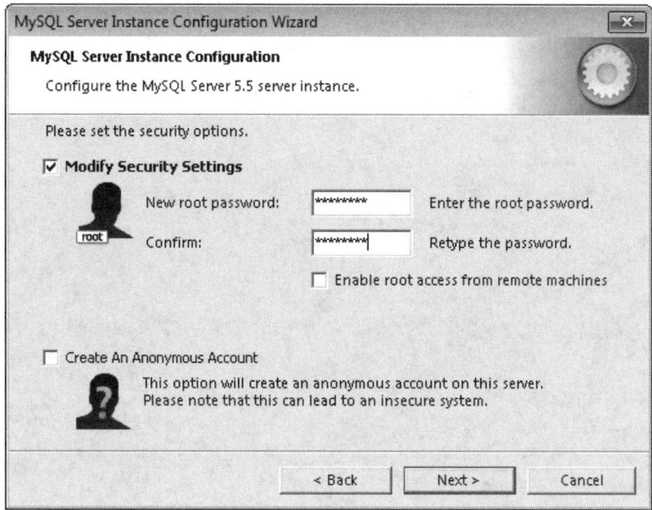

If you do forget the `root` user's password, you can reset it by making a temporary manual change to the `my.ini` file. More on resetting the MySQL root password is in the "Resetting MySQL Root User's Password" sidebar.

Resetting MySQL Root User's Password

Sometimes the MySQL installation goes great, but students forget their root password. It's almost like the DBA who has the only copy of the root user's password getting hit by a bus. How do you recover it? It's not terribly difficult on Linux or Windows.

Linux and Mac OS X Process You shut down the mysqld process:

```
sudo service mysqld stop
```

Then, you start it with this command (the ampersand lets your Terminal session remain in the foreground while starting MySQL Server in the background):

```
sudo mysqld_safe --skip-grant-tables &
```

You connect as root without a password, like this:

```
mysql -uroot
```

(Continued)

Connecting as the super user, root, you perform the following at the mysql> prompt:

```
use mysql;
UPDATE user
SET    password=PASSWORD("new_password ")
WHERE  user = 'root';
flush privileges;
quit
```

You shut down the mysqld process again:

```
sudo service mysqld stop
```

Then, you start it with this command:

```
sudo service mysqld start &
```

Windows Process Windows presents two ways to perform these tasks. The first is quick and easy but risks letting others into the database through the network. The second requires a bit more work but ensures that network is shut down while you disable security to reset the root password. We'll focus on the latter, which is the recommended way.

You add the following parameter to the my.ini configuration file in the [mysqld] section to disable security and reset the root password. You can find the my.ini file in the C:\Program Files\MySQL\MySQL Server 5.x folder for the 32-bit MySQL Server version on a 32-bit Windows operating system (OS) or the 64-bit version on a 64-bit Windows OS. The my.ini file is in the C:\Program Files (x86)\MySQL\MySQL Server 5.x folder for a 32-bit MySQL Server version running on a 64-bit Windows OS.

While you're editing the configuration file, you should also enter the other two because they limit connections to the local server machine. Connections to the MySQL Server can only be made across the local operating system pipe, and network access is closed for the duration of your root user's password reset activity.

```
[mysqld]

# These let you safely reset the lost root password.
skip-grant-tables
enable-named-pipe
skip-networking
```

After you've saved these changes in the my.ini file, you should stop and restart the mysql service. If you named the Microsoft service something else, you should substitute it for mysql in the sample statements. The command-line steps are as follows.

Stopping the service:

```
net stop mysql
```

Starting the service:

```
net start mysql
```

Now you can sign on as the root (super user) without a password and change the password, as qualified earlier with setting the skip-grant-tables option in the my.ini file.. However, you can't do it through the normal command:

```
SET PASSWORD FOR 'student'@'%' = password('cangetin');
```

If you attempt that normal syntax, MySQL raises the following exception (the special formatting of the error message guarantees readability in the final text):

```
ERROR 1290 (HY000): The MySQL server IS running WITH the
  --skip-grant-tables option so it cannot execute this
    statement
```

You need to first connect to the mysql database, which holds the data dictionary or catalog. Then, you use a simple UPDATE statement to reset the root password:

```
-- Connect to the data dictionary.
USE mysql

-- Manually update the data dictionary entry.
UPDATE USER
SET    password = password('cangetin')
WHERE  USER = 'root'
AND    host = 'localhost';
```

At this point, you've done all you need to do. Exit the MySQL Server and remove the additional parameters. Stop and restart the MySQL Server service, and the changes that you made will now be in effect. You should be able to connect with the following syntax:

```
mysql -uroot -pcangetin
```

There weren't any errors if that works. This should also teach you the importance of securing the my.ini file from nonprivileged users.

The next dialog applies the configuration options that you've selected. As a rule, the Prepare configuration and Write configuration steps don't malfunction. The Start service step is notorious for having failures. Those failures aren't typically caused by a defect in the MySQL Server software. They typically occur when somebody didn't uninstall a previous MySQL Server installation correctly. A failure configuring and starting the service typically means your Windows Registry requires recovery to a prior clean state. If you can't recover to a prior state, you have two options. You can manually attempt to clean the registry (not a good idea for a beginner), or you can reinstall the Windows operating system. The latter is the safest bet.

Rarely, the Apply security settings can fail. These failures are fairly simple to fix by manually connecting and fixing the `root` user's password. You can use the instructions from the "Resetting MySQL Root User's Password" sidebar to fix this type of problem.

Click the *Execute* button to configure and start your new MySQL Server instance.

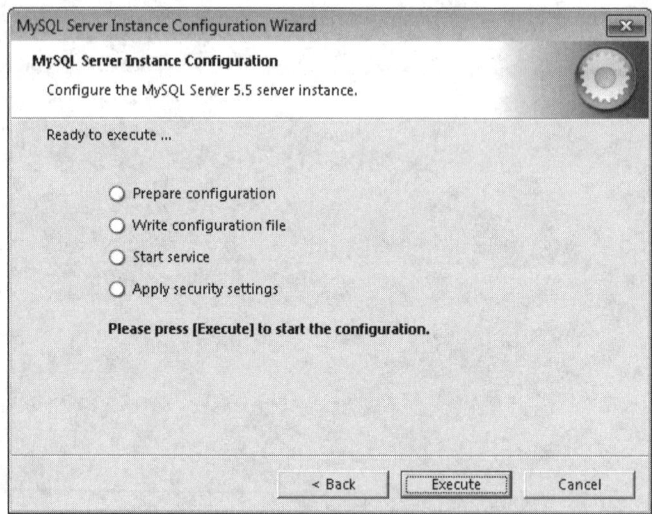

The last dialog for the configuration either reports the errors discussed or the successful installation of the product. The following dialog shows a successful installation with the configuration options shown in this section. Click the *Finish* button to complete the configuration operation of the MSI file.

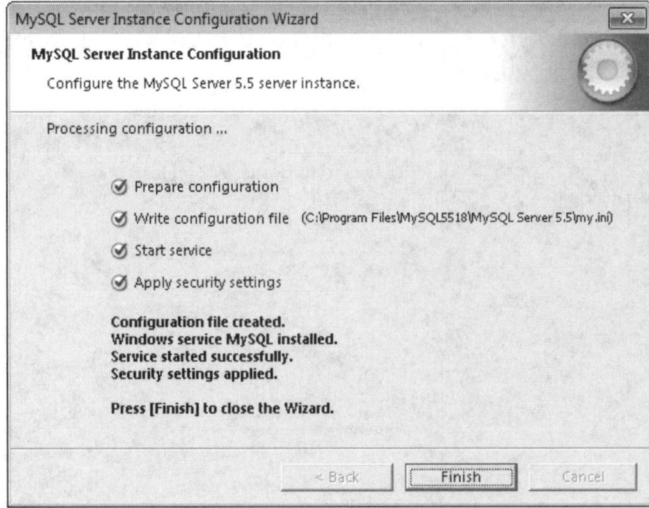

This section has shown you how to configure the database, and it's quite useful to use a Microsoft installation to capture the proper `my.ini` configuration options. You can then modify them slightly and port (technology buzzword for moving from one computer to another) the `my.ini` configuration options to a `my.cnf` file for Linux or Mac OS X. The only real changes are those that require adjusting the file system syntax.

Once you've configured and started the instance, you can create a `student` user and `studentdb` database. The `student` user and `studentdb` database are used in examples throughout the book. You can find the instructions for setting up the user and database in the "Create Default MySQL User" sidebar (borrowed from my *Oracle Database 11g & MySQL 5.6 Developer Handbook*).

Install and Configure MySQL Workbench

Like Mac OS X and the MySQL Server installation, you download, install, and configure the MySQL Workbench Community Edition. If you skipped the installation of the Visual C++ 2010 Redistributable package and .NET 4 framework, you must install them before you install MySQL Workbench. Without the pre-requisites, the MySQL Workbench installation fails.

Like the MySQL Workbench, we'll skip displaying the dialog for running MSI files and start with the welcome dialog of the MySQL Workbench installation. Click the *Next* button to proceed.

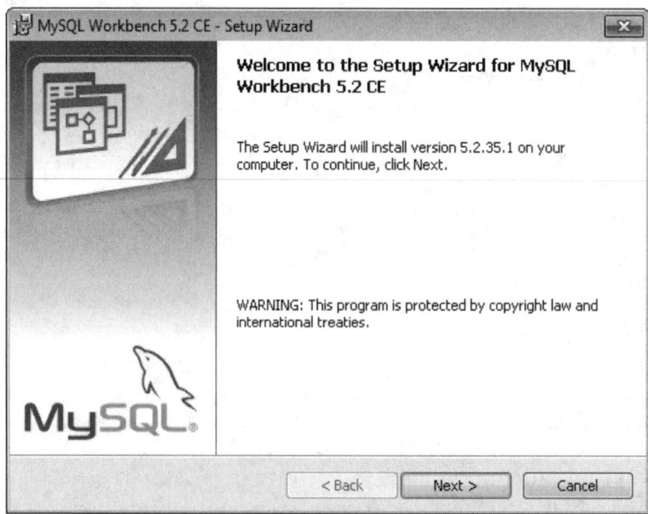

The next dialog gives you the option of changing the folder destination for MySQL Workbench. I'd recommend that you simply install it in the default location. Click the *Next* button to proceed.

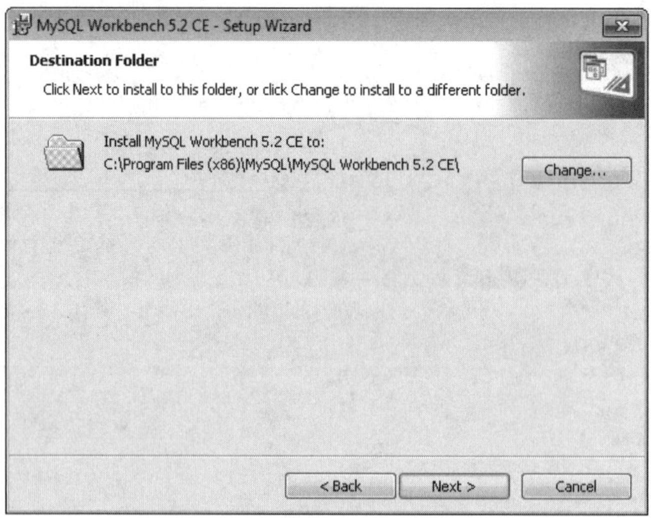

The next dialog gives you an option of installing it completely or installing only some features. I'd recommend you click the *Complete* radio button. Click the *Next* button to continue with the installation.

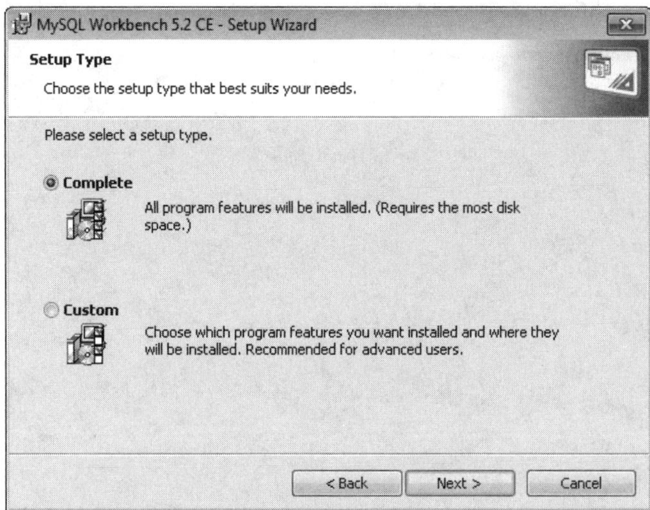

The next dialog confirms the *Setup Type* and *Destination Folder* and asks if you want to install MySQL Workbench. Click the *Install* button to continue.

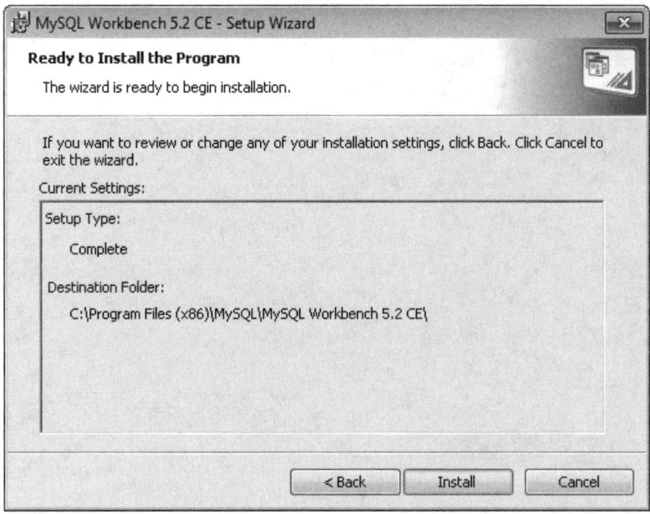

The next dialog displays the progress bar. It doesn't take very long to complete. It should advance to the next dialog without any action, but you may need to click the *Next* button to install the MySQL Workbench.

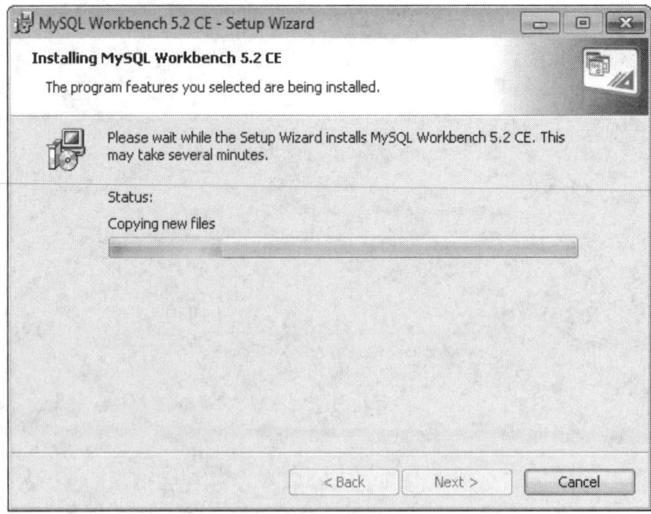

The last dialog of the MSI file lets you check *Launch MySQL Workbench* after you complete the product installation. You should click the check box and the *Finish* button.

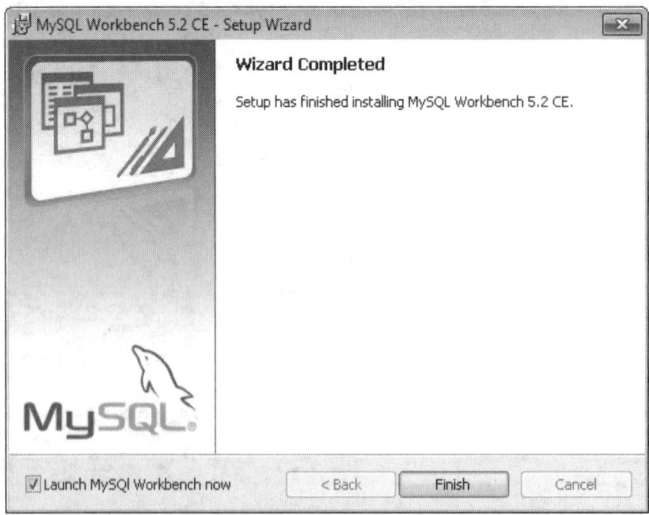

Having launched the MySQL Workbench, you should now see the following initial dialog of MySQL Workbench. It appears exactly like those in the Linux and Mac OS X, which is terrific since they're compiled programs.

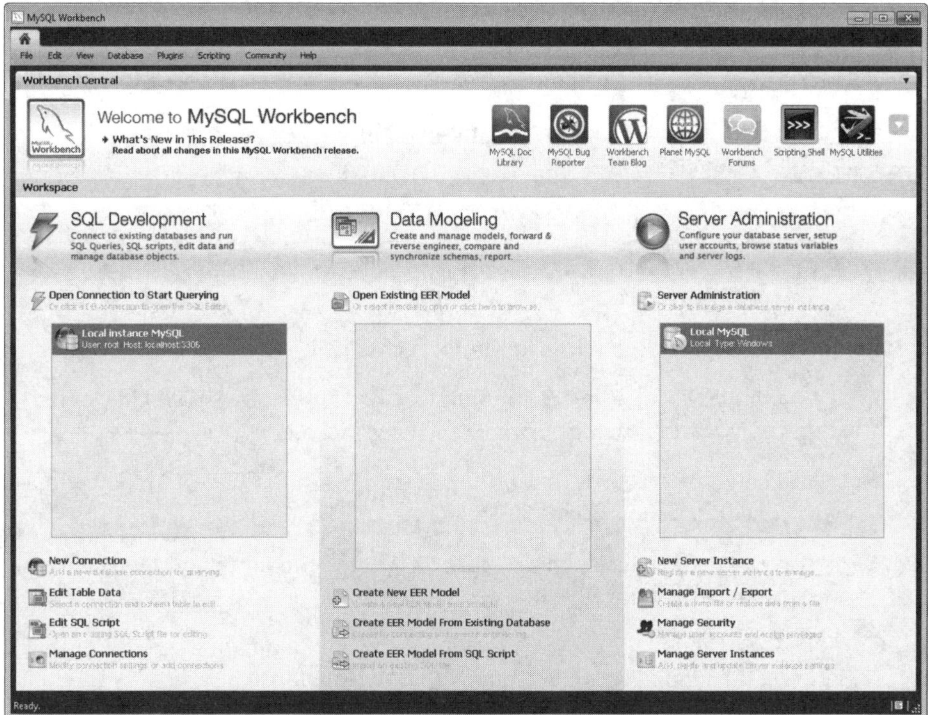

This completes the MySQL product installation section.

Summary

This chapter discussed how you install and configure the MySQL Server and MySQL Workbench on Linux, Mac OS X, and Windows. The chapter also showed you how to secure the MySQL Server and set up users and databases.

Mastery Check

The mastery check is a series of true or false and multiple choice questions that let you confirm how well you understand the material in the chapter. You may check Appendix A for answers to these questions.

True or False:

1. ___You use a Linux socket by default in a Linux MySQL Server after the default installation.
2. ___You configure a listening port when you use the MySQL Windows configuration tool.
3. ___The default service name for Windows is `mysql`.
4. ___The default service name for Linux is `mysqld`.
5. ___You should check the *Include Bin Directory in Windows Path* check box when you want to install two or more MySQL Servers on a Windows platform.
6. ___You can create aliases in a `.bash_rc` file in Mac OS X, and they're read every time you open a Terminal session.
7. ___You can create aliases in a `.bash_login` file in Linux, and they're read every time you open a Terminal session.
8. ___The look and feel of MySQL Workbench's initial dialog menu differs between the Linux, Mac OS X, and Windows platforms.
9. ___The Linux installation of MySQL Server lets you dynamically choose where to install the MySQL product.
10. ___The MySQL Workbench installation puts a menu choice in the Application | Programming menu of the GNOME interface.

Multiple Choice:

11. Which platform provides a configuration wizard that manages the product setup?

    A. Linux

    B. Mac OS X

    C. Windows

    D. All of the above

    E. None of the above

12. Which platform supports running the `mysql_secure_installation` script without modification?

    A. Linux

    B. Mac OS X

    C. Windows

    D. All of the above

    E. None of the above

13. Which platform supports loading a customized package for the MySQL Server?

    A. Linux

    B. Mac OS X

    C. Windows

    D. All of the above

    E. None of the above

14. Which platform supports a Linux or Unix pipe or socket for communication? (Multiple answers are possible.)

    A. Linux

    B. Mac OS X

    C. Windows

    D. All of the above

    E. None of the above

15. Which are the generic ports for a MySQL installation? (Multiple answers are possible.)

    A. 3306

    B. 3307

    C. 3308

    D. 3309

    E. All of the above

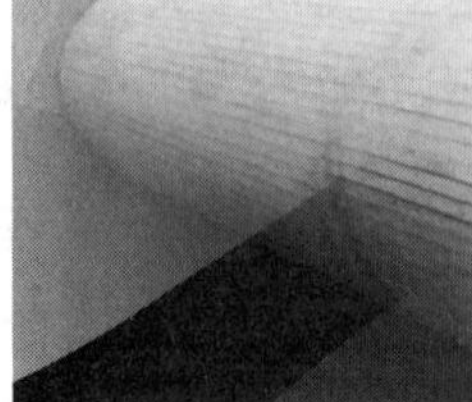

CHAPTER 2

Creating and Managing Connections

fter installing MySQL Workbench, you have three options available for product use. They are SQL Development, Data Modeling, and Server Administration.

The SQL Development and Server Administration tools require connections to the database. This connection works through a socket. A socket can work through a Unix or Linux pipe or through an ephemeral port (that's a short-lived port) where a listener actively listens for incoming requests.

You configure, test, and run connections from within MySQL Workbench. The process is the same across the Mac OS X, Linux, and Windows environments. As mentioned in Chapter 1, this book uses Fedora and the GNOME desktop as representative of Linux in general because they work more or less the same way.

This chapter shows how to create, test, and configure connections to support SQL development. They're covered in the following order:

- Fedora
- Mac OS X
- Windows 7

It's important to understand that MySQL Workstation can reverse- or forward-engineer relational data models and that it maintains modeling data externally from the database. These data models are stored in a proprietary file format.

The next three sections show you the installation of MySQL Workstation and configuration of connections by platform. After the installation issues, there are virtually no differences between how you use the product, which make using the tool simple across operating system platforms. Only the Windows section contains the instructions for Server Administration instances, which are managed the same way across all three platforms. This choice lets me show you the user interface across each platform and how to configure the Server Administration features only once.

Fedora

After installing and configuring MySQL Workbench on Fedora, you may have closed the application. If so, you may wonder how you reopen it. That's simple, because the installation places a menu choice in the GNOME desktop. The navigation to launch the GNOME PackageKit interface is Applications | Programming | MySQL Workbench.

The following screen is the initial display for MySQL Workbench when you launch it. The initial display is also known as the home page.

In this section, we're working with the *SQL Development* features. Click the *New Connection* link in the SQL Development column.

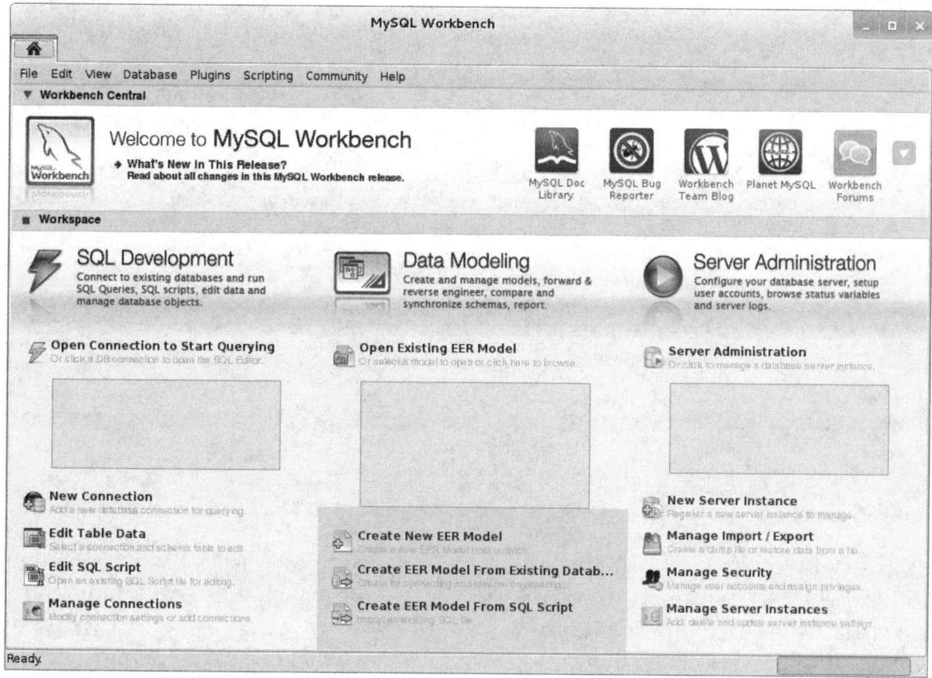

It launches the *Setup New Connection* dialog. Enter **MySQL Administrator** in the *Connection Name* textbox. Everything else should match the values in the following screen shot. The default user is `root`. That means the connection you create will have access to everything because it acts in the role of the `root` super user.

Before you click the *OK* button to create a new connection, you should click the *Test Connection* button to check whether the connection works. Sometimes the default 3306 port isn't the listening port for the MySQL Server. The other standard values are 3307, 3308, and 3309.

You can check the port used by looking in the `my.cnf` file found in the `/etc` directory—that is, if you fixed it by using the instructions in Chapter 1.

The password entry dialog should display. Enter the `root` user's password in the textbox, which is `cangetin` if you're using the book's example. Enter it or the one you chose as the `root` password.

You should never check the *Save password in keychain* check box because that provides a nonauthenticated path to act as the `root` super user. Even in a sample database like this, it's a bad practice.

After entering the password, click the *OK* button to proceed.

Behaviors of Users Without Passwords

Chapter 1 instructs you to run the `mysql_secure_installation` script in Linux, manually configure the database in Mac OS X, and enable a password while running the configuration tool in Windows. These ensure that the `root` super user has a password and disables the ability for you to connect to the database with just a user's name.

Any user without a password may connect to the database without a password. This user effectively becomes insecure to all users on the operating system. Many think of this as an anonymous user because the anonymous user, when enabled, typically doesn't require a password. Although this type of user behaves like the anonymous password, it is simply an unauthenticated user account.

There should never be any unauthenticated users in your MySQL Server. Your user connection won't prompt for a password when the account is unauthenticated.

You get a success dialog screen when everything works and the following failure dialog message when some connection component fails.

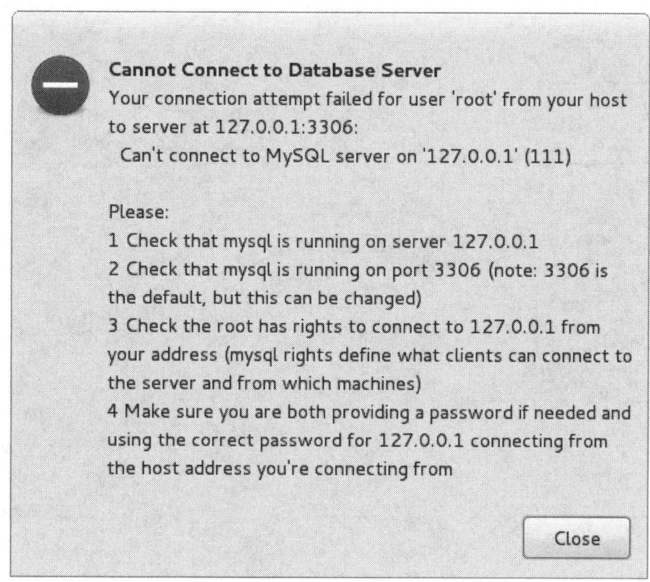

Error messages typically occur because you forgot to start the MySQL Server, which is the case for the previously shown error message. You can dismiss the error message, start the MySQL service, and retest the connection. Chapter 1 shows you how to start and stop the MySQL Server service from the command line.

The error message can also manifest itself when you change the MySQL Server's listening port in the `my.cnf` file. A change in the `hosts` file (found in the `/etc` directory) can also raise this exception. Generally, relaunching MySQL Workbench clears the error when you previously made a `hosts` file or any network file changes.

Click the *OK* button to proceed.

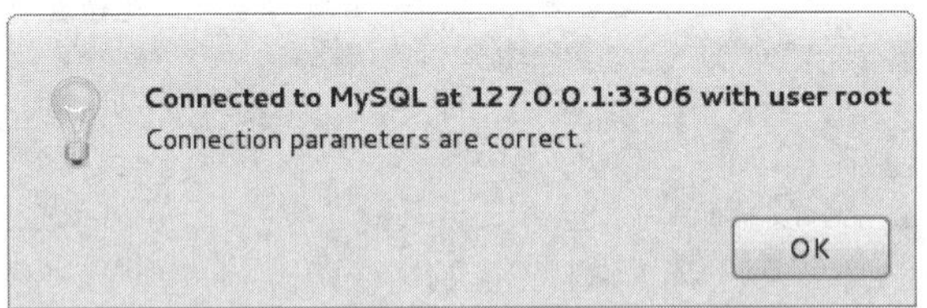

This returns you to the *Setup New Connection* dialog. Click the *OK* button to create the new connection since you know it will work. You're returned to the home page dialog, but you now have a connection in the *Open Connection to Start Querying* box.

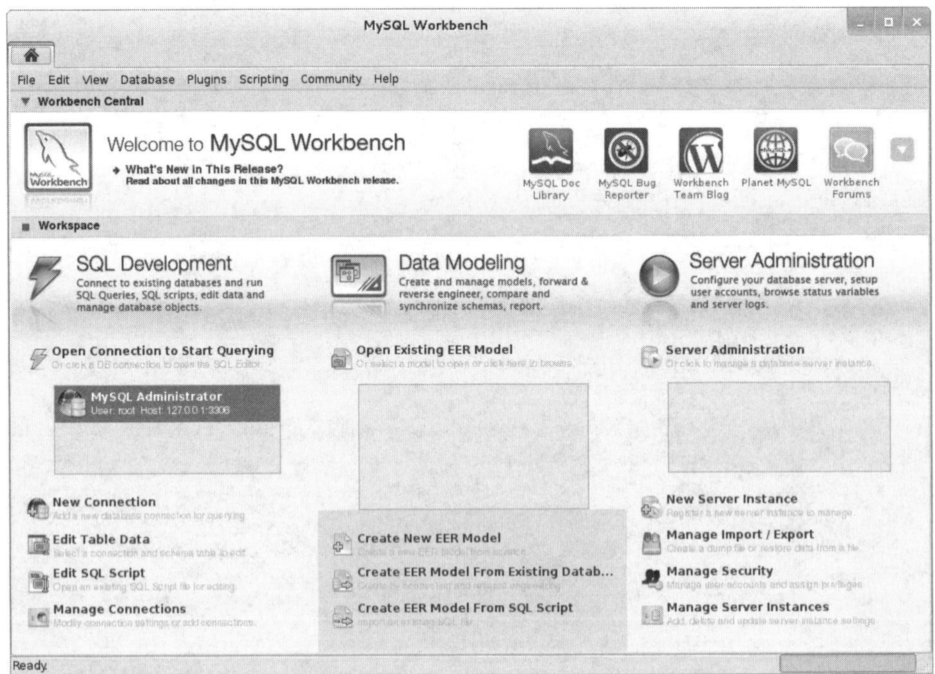

Let's repeat the process for a user with restricted privileges. Enter **MySQL Student** in the *Connection Name* textbox of the *Setup New Connection* dialog.

This example uses the `student` user and `studentdb` database created in Chapter 1. While you don't have to enter a default schema (or database), it's a good idea to create a connection for each unique combination of user name and database. These specific connections let you test exactly how your application code will work in the database, and thereby let you mimic the application context in a connection.

Click the *Test Connection* button to validate the connection before creating it. A connection like this lets you check if the `student` user has access privileges to the `studentdb` database.

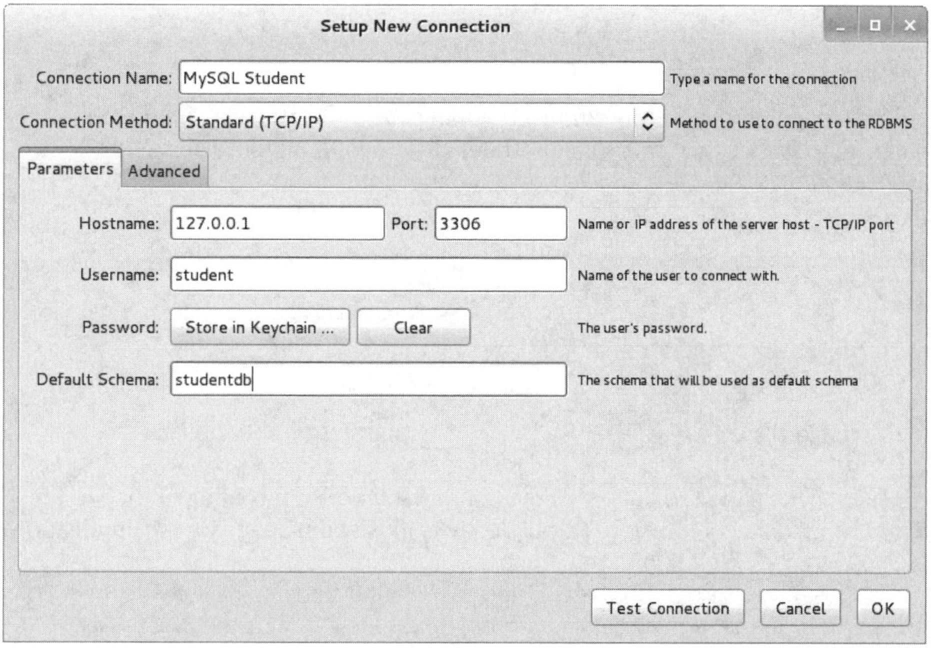

This displays the same password dialog, but the user name is `student`. Enter the `student` user's password in the textbox. The book uses a trivial `student` password, which you may use without too much risk because the data we use is easy to replace and holds no proprietary or monetary value beyond supporting the book. However, I'd be remiss not to suggest secure passwords should always be used generally.

The *Save password in keychain* check box can be checked for the `student` user. This simplifies your connection to the `studentdb` database as the `student` user because it skips the password entry dialog in the future. Click the *OK* button to validate the connection.

The validation dialog confirms everything works. Click the *OK* button to return to the *Setup New Connection* dialog. Then, click the *OK* button in the *Setup New Connection* dialog to create and save the connection.

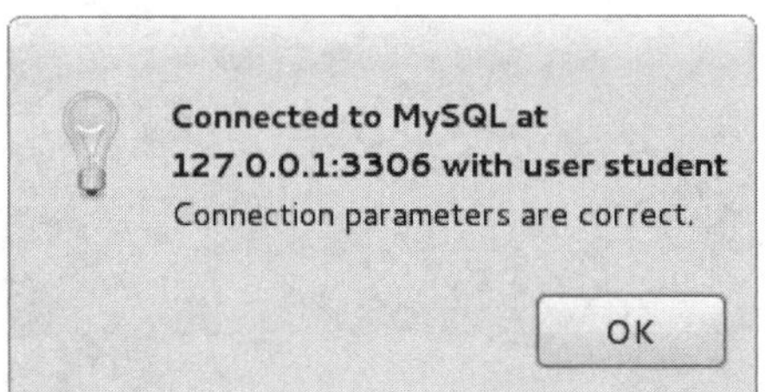

After clicking the *OK* button on the confirmation dialog, you're returned to the *Setup New Connection* dialog. This dialog acts like a home page for the application. You need to click the *OK* button here too.

That last click returns you to the home page dialog, and you have two connections in the *Open Connection to Start Querying* box. One supports the `root` user and super user privileges without a default schema or database. The other connection supports the `student` user with restrictive privileges against the default `studentdb` schema or database.

The home dialog should look like the following screen shot.

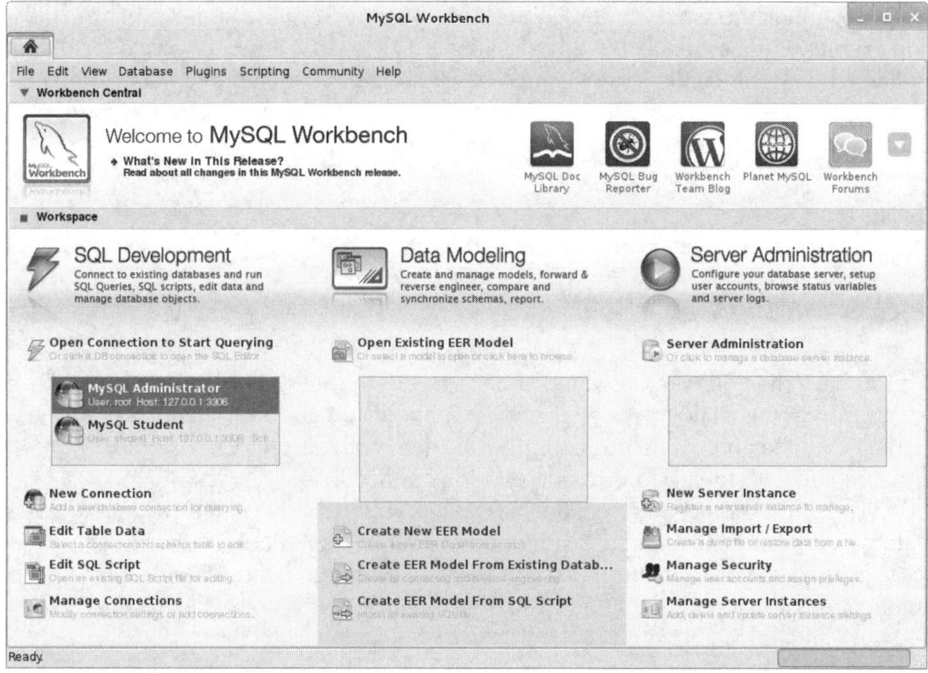

You also have the ability to inspect and manage connections. Navigate in the MySQL Workbench menu to Database | Manage Connections, and you see the following dialog. It allows you to edit, delete, and change the order of connections.

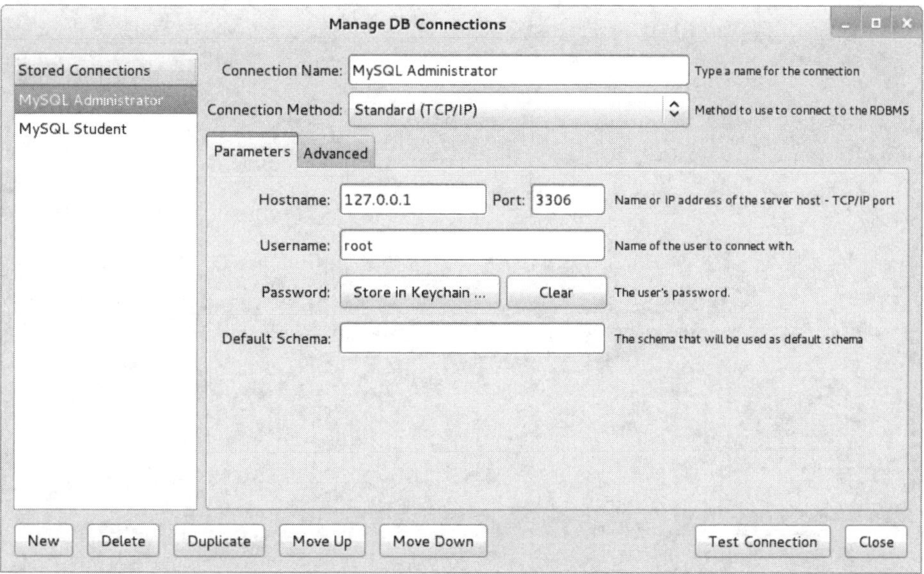

This is much more access and control than you get from the context menus. Context menus are available by right-clicking (on Mac OS X a two-finger click on a multitouch keypad) on any connection. Those choices are limited to *Query Database*, *Start Command Line Client*, *Move Up* (meaning move up the connection in the list), *Move Down*, *Delete Connection*, or *Delete All Connections*.

NOTE
You enter the password for the connection that your mouse is hovering over when you launch the command-line client.

You have the ability to view and change any of the setup behaviors of a database connection in this dialog. It's very handy, but adding an *Edit Connection* option would make the context menu more useful. The *Manage Connections* option provides you with the options to edit existing connections.

Clicking the *Manage Connections* link brings you to the *SManage DB Connections* dialog. The panel on the right lets you choose a connection that you want to edit.

Clicking a valid connection displays the *SQL Editor* console. The version numbers in the bottom left naturally change as MySQL Server moves forward in release numbers.

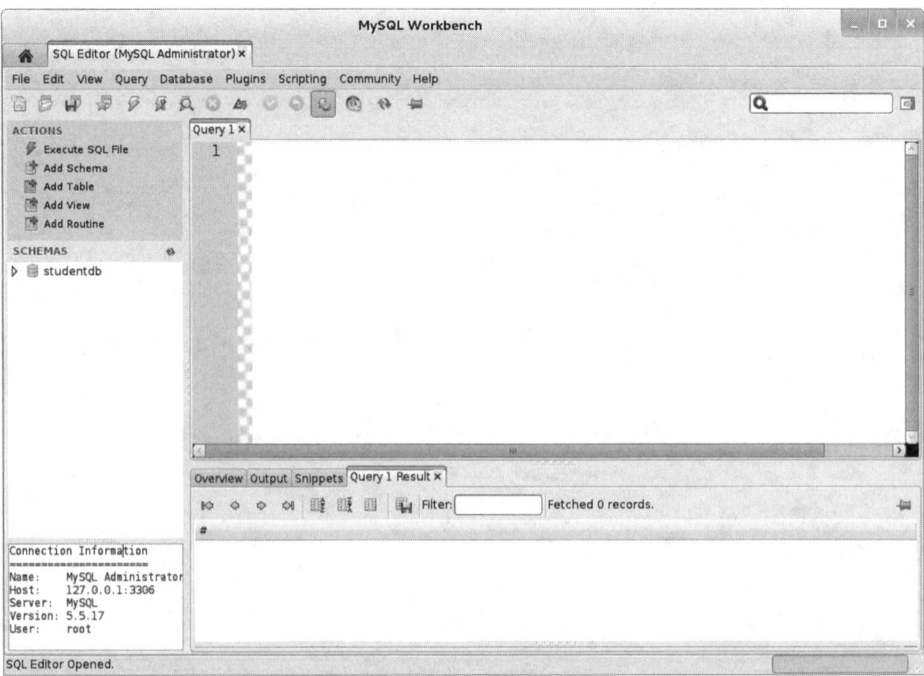

This concludes the Fedora section; the next section shows you how to use the same screens on the Mac OS X operating system.

Mac OS X

After you close MySQL Workbench the first time, you can reopen it like any other Mac OS X application. You click the Spotlight (a finder) window in the upper-right corner or simply press COMMAND-SPACEBAR. Within the Spotlight, type **MySQL Workbench** and click it when displayed in the drop-down list.

Like the Linux installation, you see the same initial display for MySQL Workbench when you launch it. The major difference is that the Windows controls are in the upper-left corner on a Mac OS X display, whereas they're in the upper-right corner in a Linux or Windows display. Click the *New Connection* link in the SQL Development column to create a `root` user stored connection.

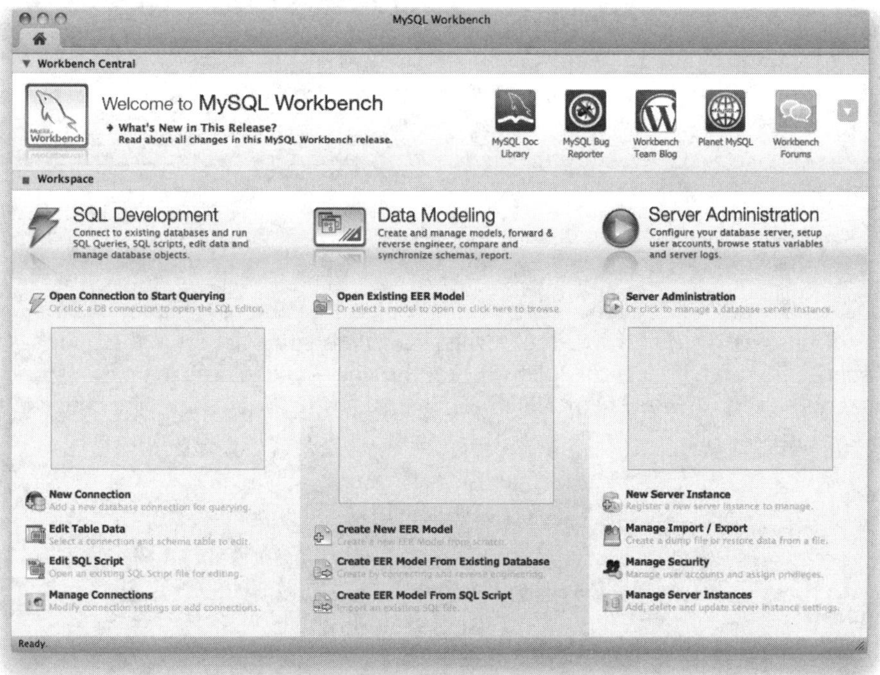

Clicking the *New Connection* link launches the *Setup New Connection* dialog. Enter **MySQL Administrator** in the *Connection Name* textbox, as done in the earlier Linux example. Everything else should match the values in the next screen shot.

The default user is `root`. That means the connection you're creating will have access to everything because it acts in the role of the `root` super user.

Before you click the *OK* button to create a new connection, you should click the *Test Connection* button to verify the connection works.

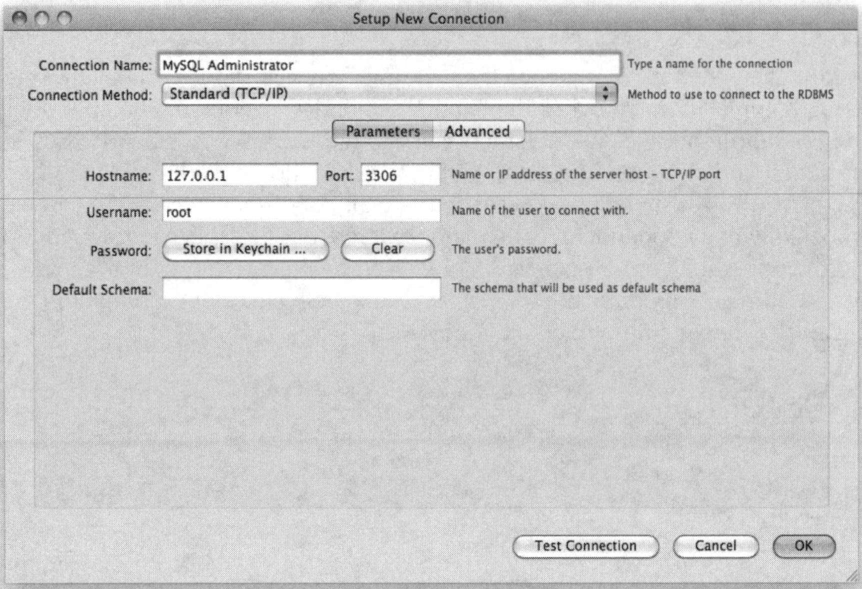

The password entry dialog displays with the service and user name. Enter the `root` user's password in the textbox, which should be `cangetin` in the book's examples. If you've changed it, please enter the one you chose as the password.

As a rule, the *Save password in keychain* check box should never be checked for the `root` super user. After entering the password, click the *OK* button.

You get the following acknowledgment dialog when everything works. If something doesn't work, you get an error dialog.

Errors are typically caused by forgetting to start the MySQL Server. You can dismiss the error message, start the MySQL service, and retest the connection. You'll find instructions for starting and stopping the service in Chapter 1.

Click the *OK* button to proceed.

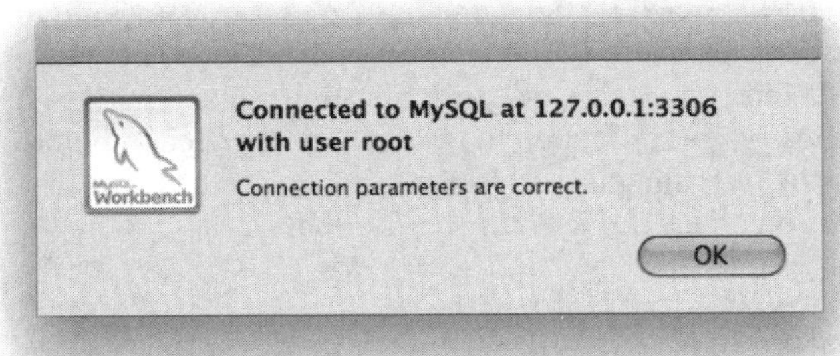

Clicking the *OK* button returns you to the *Setup New Connection* dialog. Click the *OK* button to create the new connection.

You're returned to the home page dialog. You should see a *MySQL Administrator* connection in the *Open Connection to Start Querying* box, as shown here:

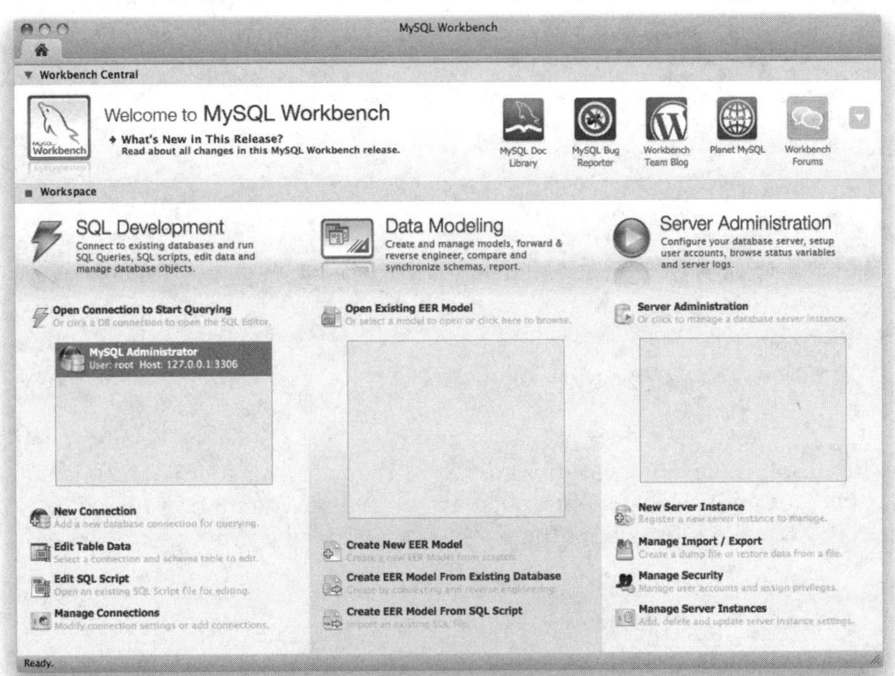

As done in the Linux section, we'll repeat the process and create a connection for the student user. This is a restricted privilege connection. Enter **MySQL Student** in the *Connection Name* textbox of the *Setup New Connection* dialog.

You need to have created the `student` user and `studentdb` database before attempting this step. If you haven't done that yet, please return to Chapter 1 for instructions on creating the user and database.

While you don't have to enter a default schema (or database), it's a good idea to create a connection for each unique combination of user name and database. These specific connections let you test exactly how your application code will work in the database, and thereby let you mimic the application context in a connection.

Click the *Test Connection* button to validate the connection before creating it, but first check that everything looks like the following screen shot. This type of connection lets you check if the `student` user has access privileges to the `studentdb` database.

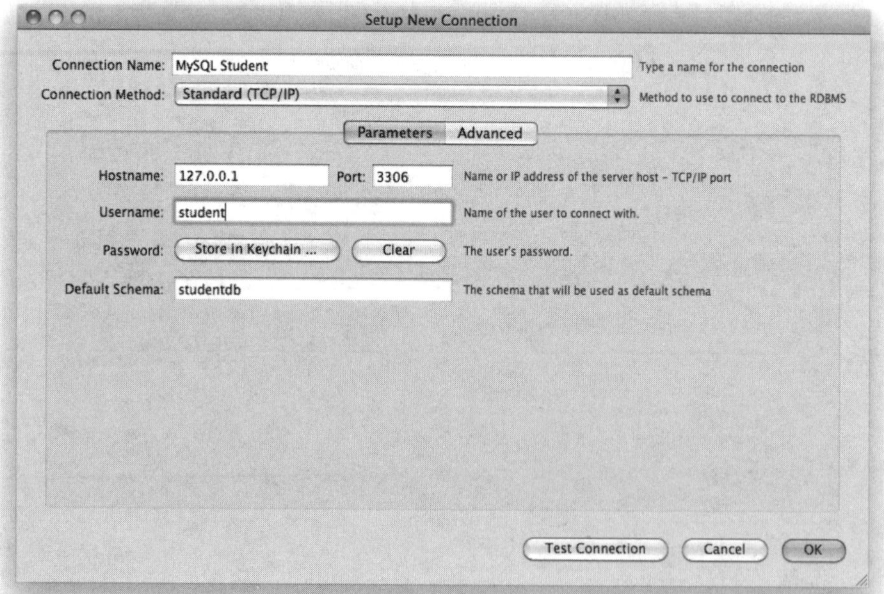

This displays the familiar password dialog. The only change from the prior Mac OS X example is that the user name is `student`. Enter the `student` user's password in the textbox. The book uses a trivial password of `student`.

Enter **student** as the password unless you've changed it. If you've changed it, enter the password you chose.

You can check the *Save password in keychain* check box for the `student` user. Doing so simplifies your connection because it skips the password entry dialog in the future. You should recognize that this option is less secure than requiring a password for each connection. Click the *OK* button to validate the connection.

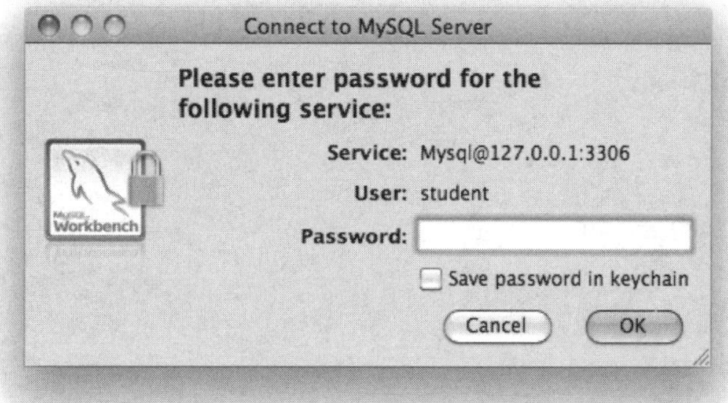

If all the values worked and the MySQL Server service is running, you'll get the next confirmation dialog. You'll need to troubleshoot any error message. Assuming there's no error, clicking the *OK* button returns you to the home page dialog.

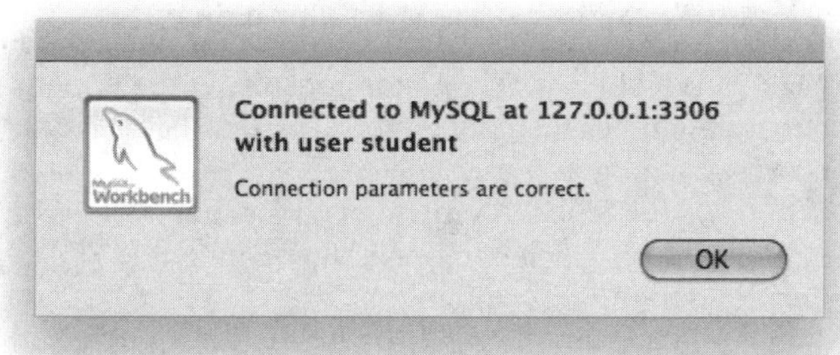

You should have two connections in the *Open Connection to Start Querying* box. One supports the `root` user with super user privileges and without a default database. The other supports the `student` user and their restricted privileges against the default `studentdb` database.

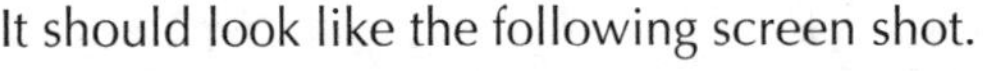

It should look like the following screen shot.

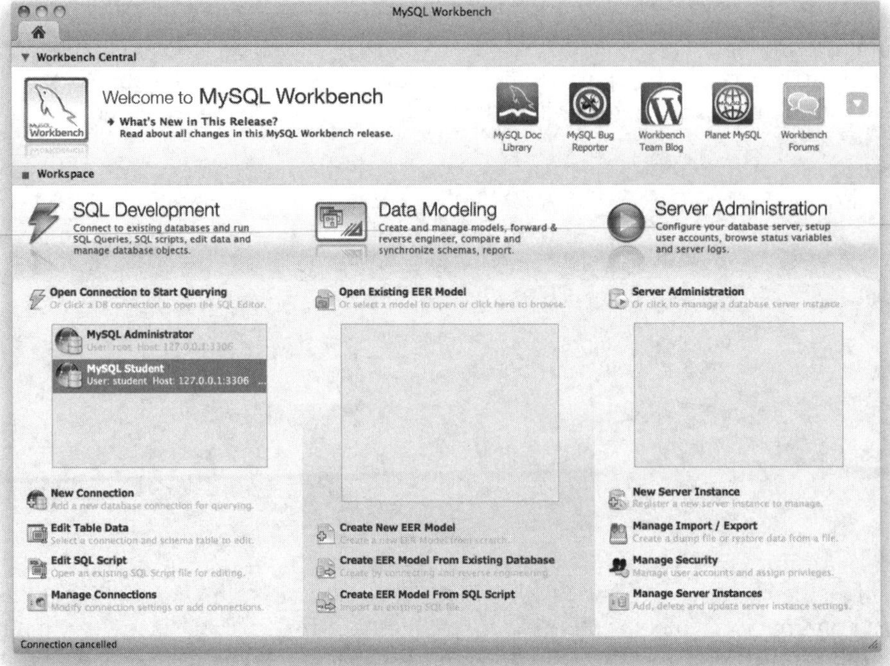

A last confirmation exercise requires you to click the *MySQL Student* connection. It launches the MySQL Workbench *SQL Editor* console. In the upper-left corner, you'll note a tab that designates the connection you're using. This can help you ensure you don't do something as the wrong user.

On the left of the working SQL Development connection, you have the home tab, which resembles a little house. Click it to open other concurrent SQL Development connections or Server Administration instances.

You should see the following dialog, but clearly the version information of the server changes over time. Subsequent chapters teach you how to use this interactive console.

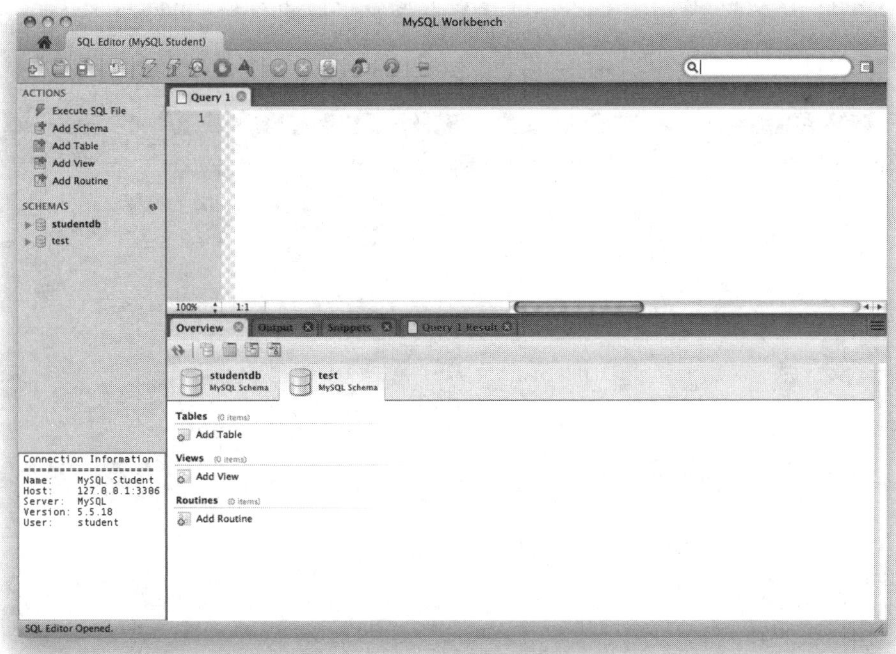

This concludes the Mac OS X section; the last section shows you the same screens from the Windows rendering agent.

Windows 7

The Windows 7 section includes coverage of connections that support sections for SQL Development and Server Administration. All the rules governing configuring Server Administration apply to Linux and Mac OS X.

Configuring MySQL Workbench Connections

Like Mac OS X, you can reopen MySQL Workbench like any other Windows application. You navigate by clicking Start | All Programs | MySQL | MySQL Workbench 5.2 CE. The version number will change over time, but there should only be one MySQL Workbench in your menu. At the time of writing, MySQL Workbench is a 32-bit Windows application and runs from the C:\Program Files (x86)\mysql directory.

It launches the welcome screen, which is the same as the others in Linux and Mac OS X. It's shown in the following illustration. You should note that MySQL Workbench preconfigures your SQL Development and Server Administration connections. These are preconfigured for `localhost` resolution.

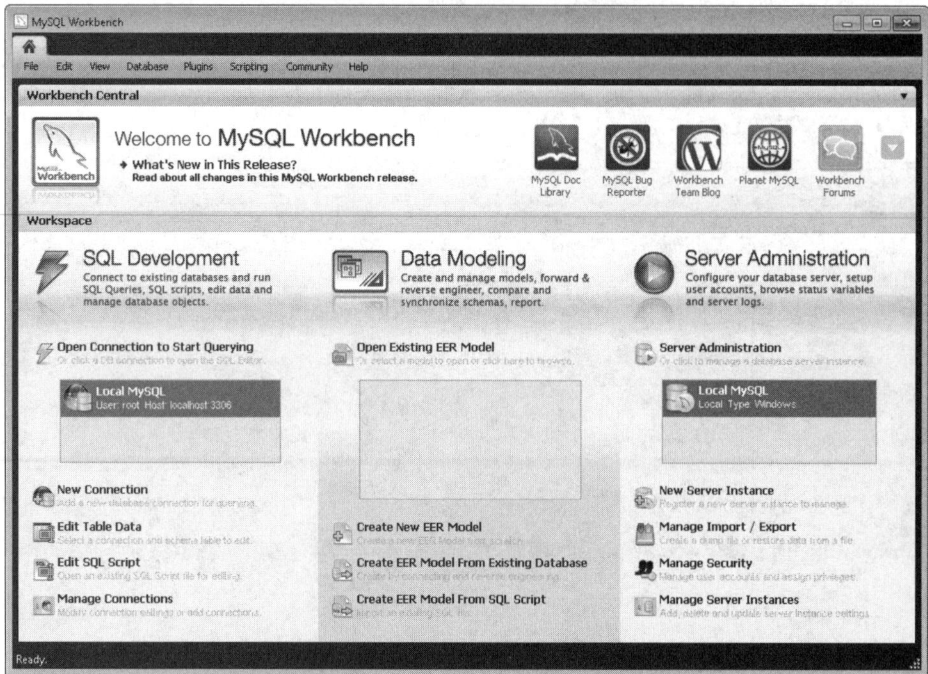

The default connection uses `localhost`, instead of 127.0.0.1, because it assumes that the `hosts` file on Windows hasn't been configured. This decision can result in the following error message appearing the first time you attempt to use the default connection after configuring the `hosts` file.

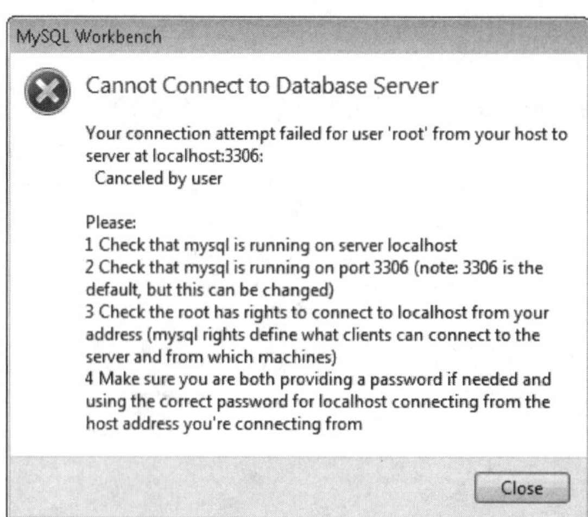

Like Linux, relaunching the connection typically fixes the problem. In some cases, you may need to delete and re-create the connection. You do that by clicking the *New Connection* link and creating a new connection. The screen shots are the same as those for Linux and Mac OS X, except for some trivial rendering elements.

You also have the ability to inspect and manage connections. Navigate in the MySQL Workbench menu to Database | Manage Connections and launch the *Manage DB Connection* dialog. You can create new connections, delete connections, move their relative position in the menu, change configuration options, and test the connection.

You can create connections to remote servers a number of ways, but so far we've opted to configure connections for the local machine. Here we set up another local host connection but one that mimics what you would do to create a remote connection. The only real difference between a local and remote host is the host name value in the connection. This means we replace the `localhost` value with the localhost's `hostname` value.

You can find a machine's hostname by opening a command shell in Windows (or Terminal session in Linux or Mac OS X). You open a Windows 7 command shell by clicking *Start* and then entering **cmd** in the *Search programs and files* text entry box (or on Windows XP by clicking Start | Run, and then typing **cmd**). Inside the shell, type the following keyword followed by the ENTER key:

```
C:\Users\UserName> hostname
```

In my test machine, the `hostname` is `McLaughlinMySQL`. Naturally, it is likely something different on your machine. Make sure to use your machine's hostname, not the sample one.

This section demonstrates that behavior by using a Windows machine as a local server. You configure your `hosts` file to support named resolution and map the computer name to a network node.

You find the hosts file in this Windows 7 (or earlier releases) folder or directory:

```
C:\Windows\system32\drivers\etc
```

The hosts file is in a restricted-access directory on Windows 7, which means you need to know how to work with Windows 7 restricted files. This requires that your user has permissions as the administrator of the Windows operating system and you understand a navigational trick in Windows Explorer. The "Configuring the Windows hosts File" sidebar provides those instructions, and you should perform them before attempting to create this connection.

A text editor allows you to open and save the `hosts` file when you're an administrator. If you forget to open the file as the administrator, the editor won't let you save changes to the `hosts` file.

Configuring the Windows hosts File

Configuring the Windows `hosts` file isn't tricky, but it isn't simple either. This is a file that Microsoft Windows 7 tries to protect from configuration by hiding it. It is also a critical file that must be configured when you want your Windows operating system to mimic a server.

The `hosts` file is in the C:\Windows\System32\drivers\etc directory, which isn't visible until you make it visible. You do that by navigating to the directory in Windows Explorer shown in the following illustration.

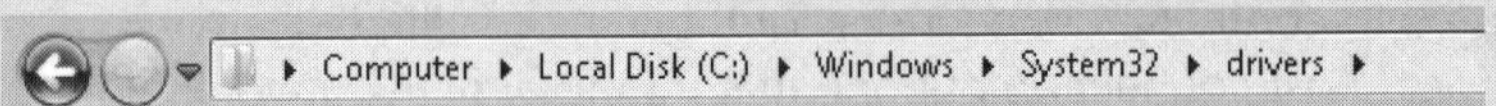

Click in the navigation path, and it changes to a traditional file path, like this:

```
C:\Windows\system32\drivers\
```

Add the missing path element so that you have the following in the Windows Explorer navigation path:

```
C:\Windows\system32\drivers\etc
```

Click anywhere else in the window, and you'll see the following path:

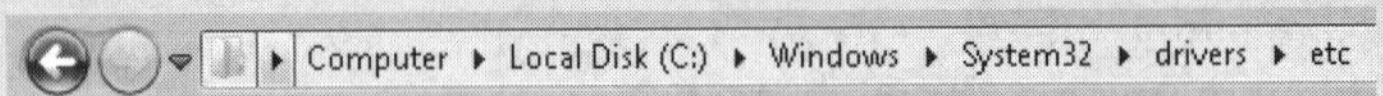

You can use this technique when you attempt to navigate to the directory with an editor, like Notepad++. At least, you can if you launch it by right-clicking and opening the program as an administrator. This lets you open the file as the master owner of all files.

The file is a shell without any network configuration by default. You need to add four lines at the bottom of the header information, which are the comment lines prefaced by a hash (#) symbol.

The first two lines set up `localhost` resolution through the *loop back domain*. The third line links your `hostname` to the loop back domain, and the fourth line links a static IP address to the loop back domain.

You can find your IP address by typing `ipconfig` in a Windows command shell (or `ifconfig` in Linux or Mac OS X), provided you have Administrator rights on the Windows operating system. The IP address is four numbers separated by dots or periods, and the values are between 0 and 255. You can exclude line four when you

User Access Control

Microsoft Windows uses User Access Control (UAC) to manage ownership of files and access privileges. This is the part of the Windows operating system that asks you to confirm actions, prompts you for the administrator password, and so forth.

You can disable UAC through the Windows interface if you have appropriate privileges, but Microsoft discourages that. Microsoft would prefer you open programs as the privileged user when you want to access files you don't own.

You must right-click menu items and program icons when you want to install them as the privileged user—Administrator. This is important because failure to do so limits your ability to alter the contents of core configuration files or libraries.

use Dynamic Host Configuration Protocol (DHCP) to resolve your `hostname`. That's because DHCP licenses may change the assigned IP address from time to time.

```
# Copyright (c) 1993-2009 Microsoft Corp.
#
# This is a sample HOSTS file used by Microsoft TCP/IP for Windows.
#
# This file contains the mappings of IP addresses to host names. Each
# entry should be kept on an individual line. The IP address should
# be placed in the first column followed by the corresponding host name.
# The IP address and the host name should be separated by at least one
# space.
#
# Additionally, comments (such as these) may be inserted on individual
# lines or following the machine name denoted by a '#' symbol.
#
# For example:
#
#      102.54.94.97     rhino.acme.com          # source server
#       38.25.63.10     x.acme.com              # x client host

# localhost name resolution is handled within DNS itself.
#  127.0.0.1       localhost
#  ::1             localhost
127.0.0.1       localhost
::1             localhost
127.0.0.1       McLaughlinMySQL McLaughlinMySQL.techtinker.com
172.16.123.131  McLaughlinMySQL McLaughlinMySQL.techtinker.com
```

It's a good practice to configure the hosts file when you're working with database servers. Name resolution of the `hostname` lets you test web applications more naturally this way—that is, like production servers with real URLs, not `localhost` URLs. It also allows you to call web pages as if your domain were a named server on the Internet or an intranet.

Rather than repeat what we've done on Fedora and Mac OS X, let's start this process from the *Manage DB Connection* dialog. If you closed it, navigate to the MySQL Workbench menu and click Database | Manage Connections to relaunch it. When you click the *New* button, the following *Manage DB Connections* dialog should be the same, but the stored connections may differ.

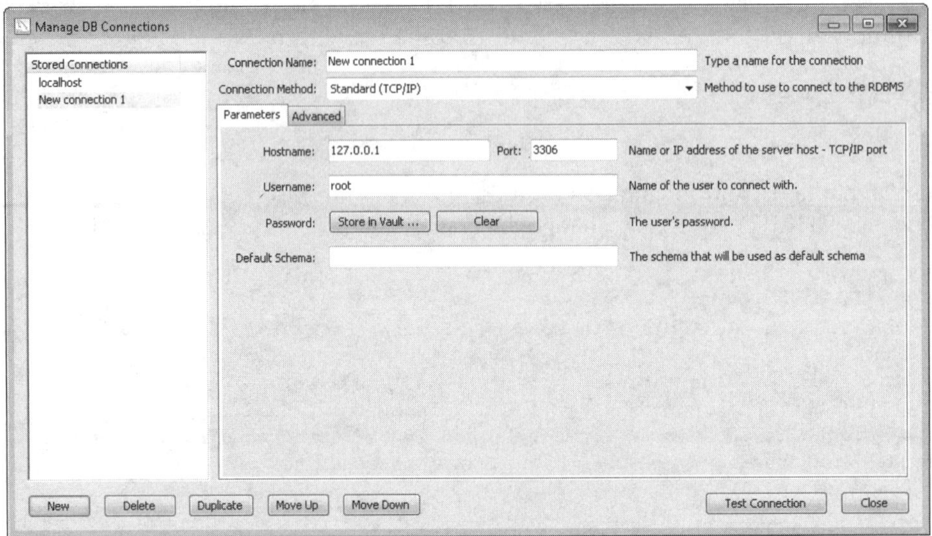

Make the following changes in the new connection dialog's initial values:

- Click in the *Connection Name* text field and type **Student@StudentDB**.
- Click in the *Hostname* text field and enter your `hostname` value, which in this sample is `McLaughlinMySQL`.
- Click in the *Username* text field and enter **student** as the user name (this was a setup feature introduced in Chapter 1).
- Click in the *Default Schema* text field and enter **studentdb** as the default database (this was also a setup feature introduced in Chapter 1).

After making those changes, you should see the following values in the *Manage DB Connections* dialog, as shown in the illustration:

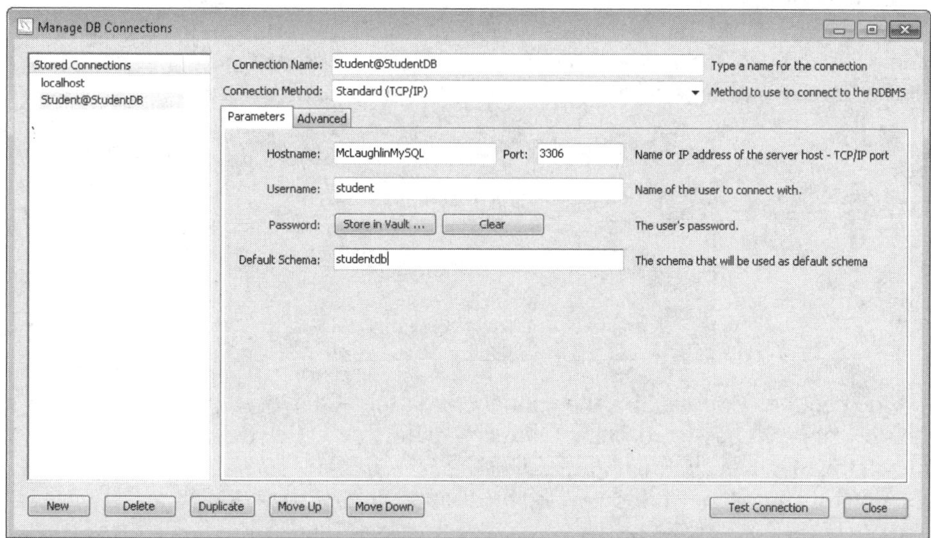

Click the *Test Connection* button to ensure the connection works. That prompts you for the password to the `student` user in the following dialog, which should be `student` if you followed the instructions in Chapter 1. Security-conscious users would enter something else when they set up a demonstration account, and please enter that in lieu of the trivial student password default value if you did.

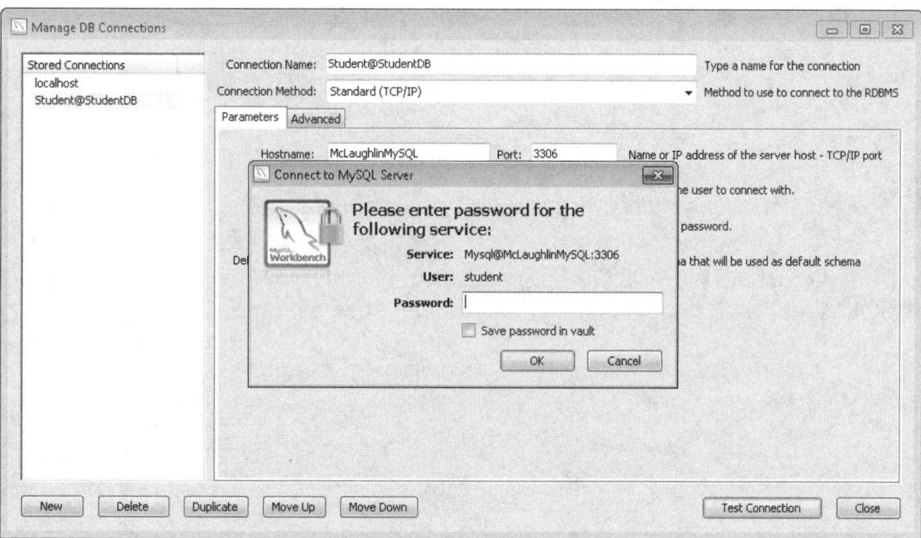

The following confirmation dialog displays when the connection is successful. Click the *OK* button to return to the *Manage DB Connection* dialog and then the *Close* button to complete the creation of a new connection that uses a machine's hostname.

In an ideal world, the machine's hostname should be available via a Domain Name Service (DNS) server with DHCP IP resolution. Sometimes we mimic this convention by file name resolution in the `hosts` file, as described earlier.

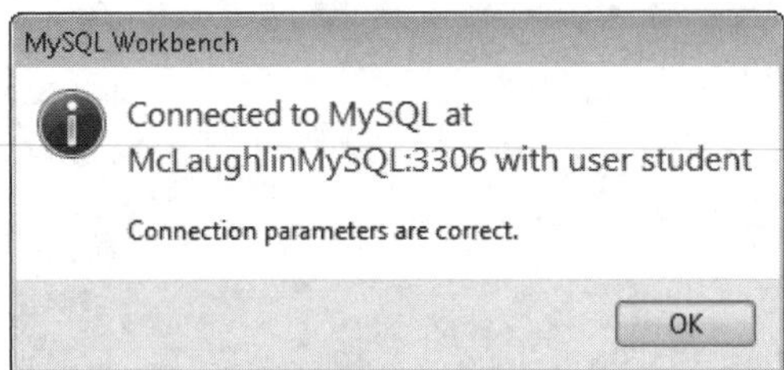

You can then double-click the connection in the SQL Development area, enter the student user's password in the following dialog, and click the *OK* button to launch the SQL Development tool. Click the *Save password in vault* check box if you don't want to type your password each time you use the connection.

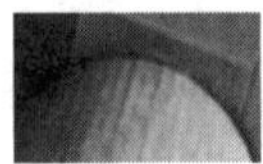

TIP
Security-conscious developers never save passwords.

After launching the SQL Development connection, you'll see the following MySQL Workbench dialog. Notice that you can click the home symbol to return to the main menu at any time. You can also have more than one connection and database modeling connection open at any given time.

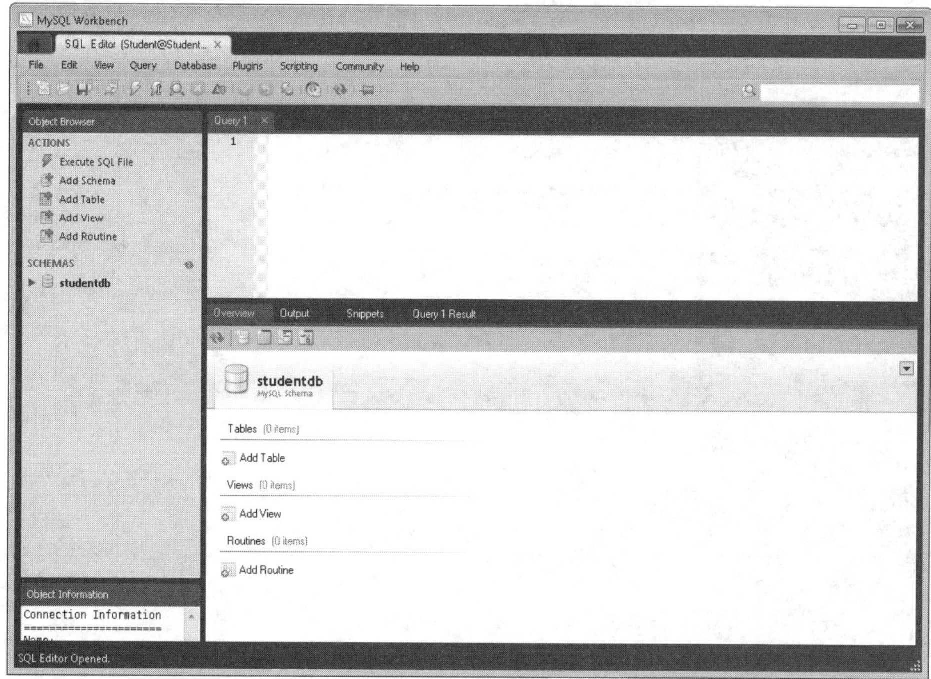

This concludes the MySQL Workbench SQL Development connections as stand-alone components. The next section relies on SQL Development connections to perform MySQL Server Administration.

Configuring Server Administration

Server Administration is an important feature of MySQL Workbench, and it depends on the availability of SQL Development connections. This chapter shows you how to configure Server Administration and discusses its dependency on SQL Development connections. Chapters 9 through 12 explains how to use the Server Administration features.

You click the *New Server Instance* link on the home page to launch the wizard that helps create new Server Administration instances. As you can see in the following dialog, you have three options in the first step that specifies the target host machine. They are local host, remote host, or an existing connection. The default is local host, and that's the radio button you should select before clicking the *Next* button to continue.

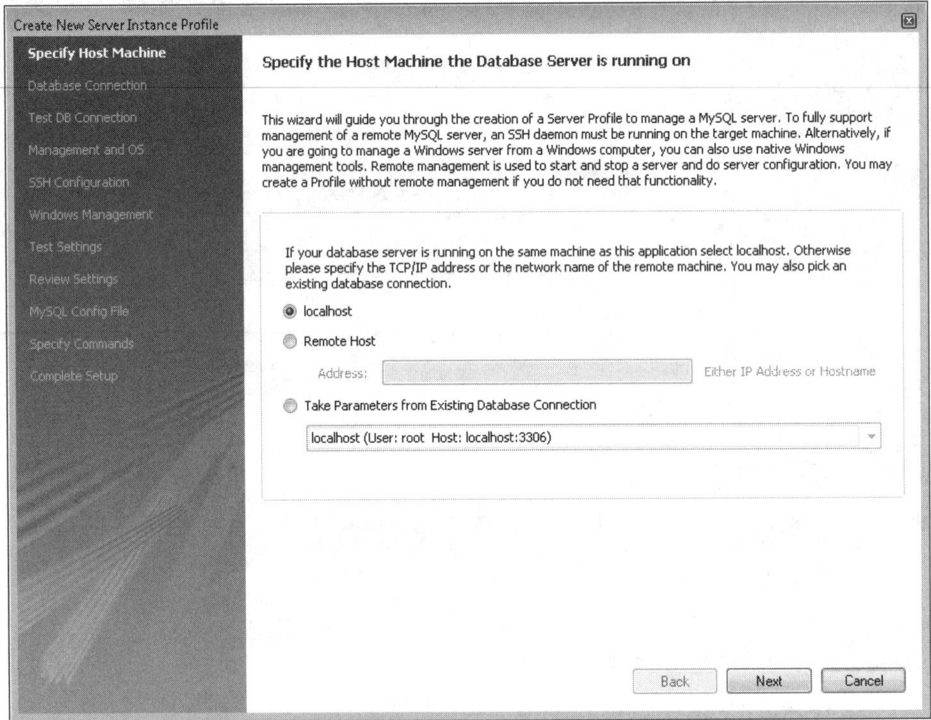

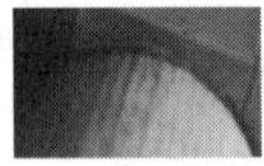

NOTE
Remote administration is more complex and discussed in Chapter 9.

Server Administration is a super user role, which means you must configure these by using the `root` user's account (or user name). Accepting the defaults for the database connection values in the following dialog screen, click the *Next* button to continue.

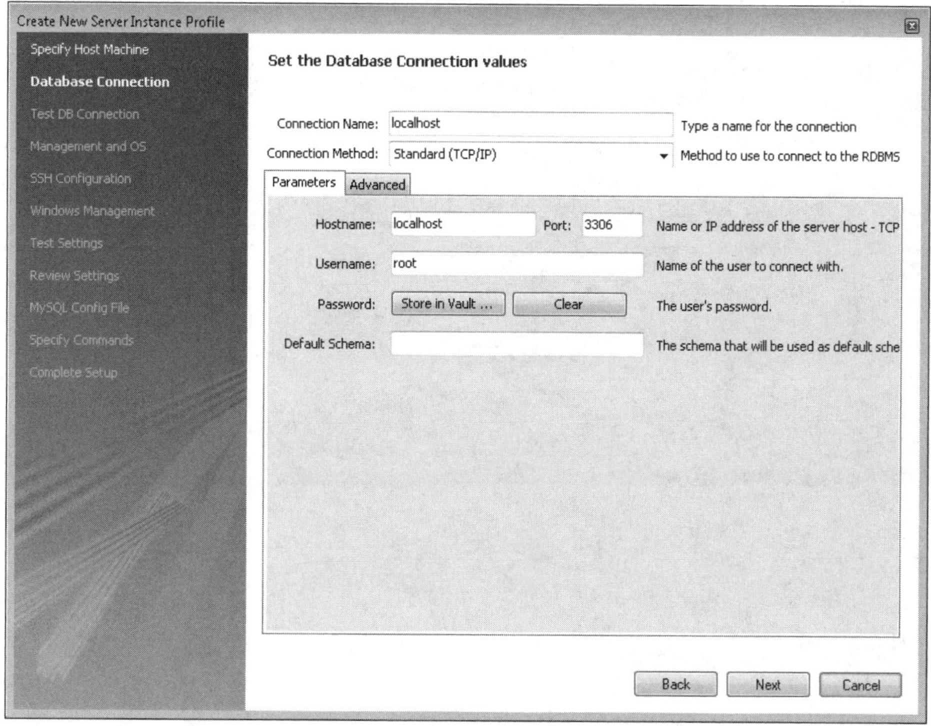

Testing the connection isn't left to chance, and the following modal dialog box overlays the next dialog in the wizard. Enter the `root` user's password and click the *OK* button to proceed.

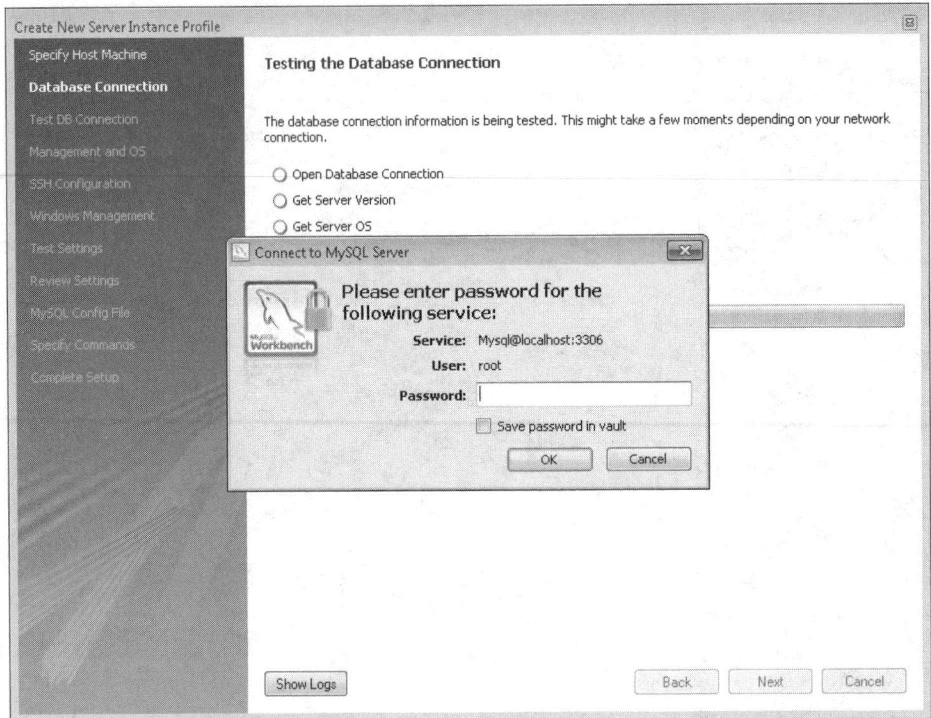

The following complete *Testing the Database Connection* dialog screen displays when you enter the correct password and a connection can be made to the MySQL Server. Click the *Next* button to proceed.

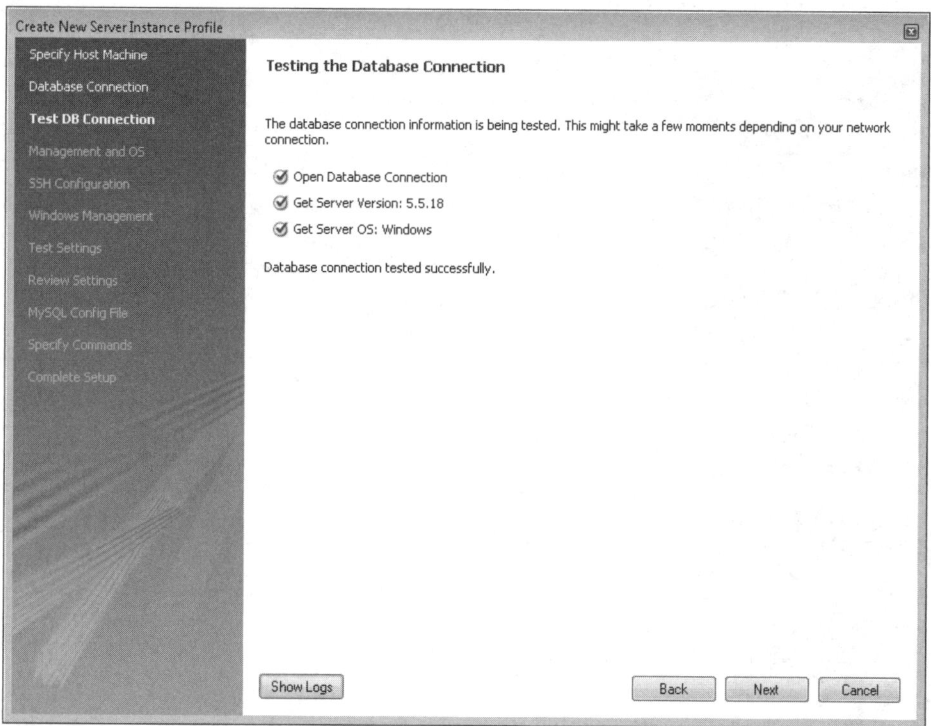

The following dialog screen lets you choose a service to manage and sets the location of the `my.ini` file on Windows (or the `my.cnf` file on Linux or Mac OS X). After checking that you have indicated correct values, click the *Next* button to proceed.

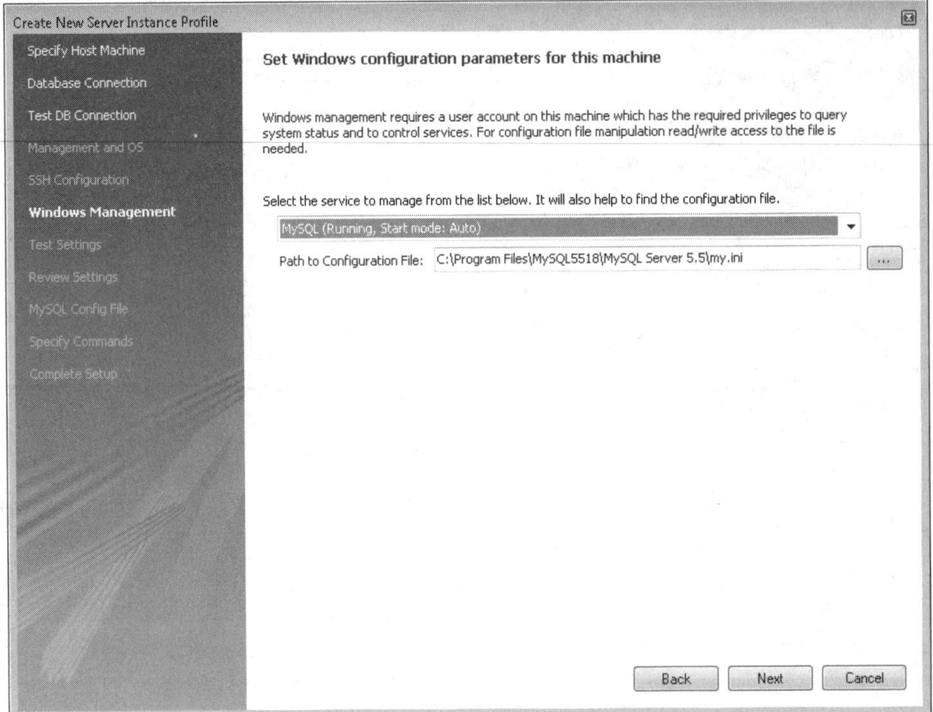

The following dialog screen confirms access to the host server, location of the start and stop features of the service, and the viability of the MySQL configuration file. Click the *Next* button when you get a blue check mark in the *Check MySQL configuration file* radio button.

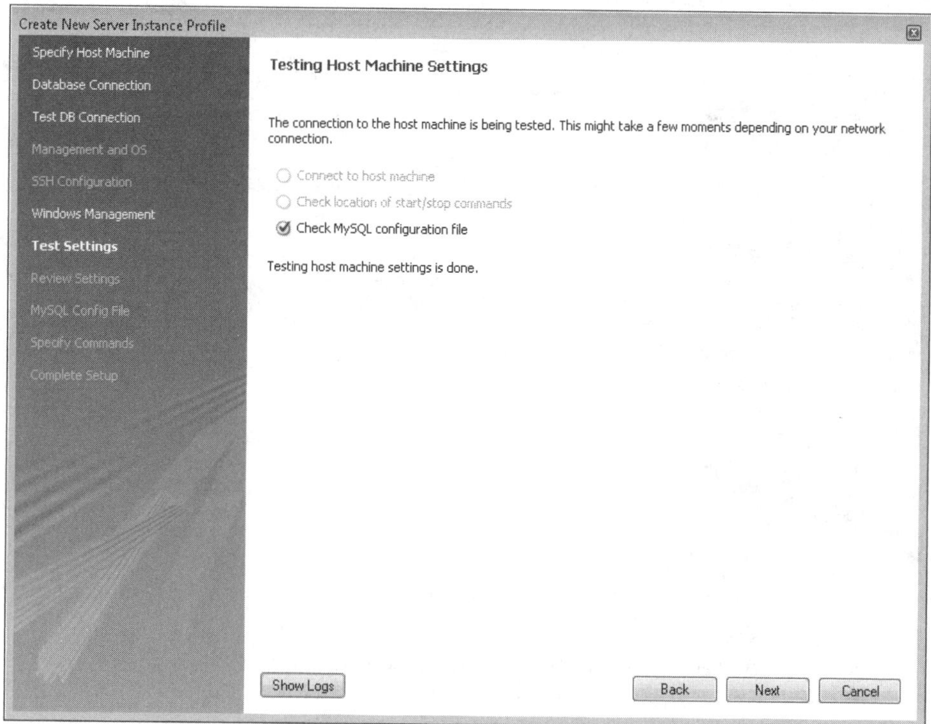

The next screen shows you've completed the process. Click the Next button to continue.

Another modal control dialog box superimposes itself in the following screen shot. Click the *Continue* button when you're comfortable with your preselected choices or the *I'd like to review the settings again* link if you're not sure. I knew they were right, so clicking the *Continue* button is the path that I've chosen.

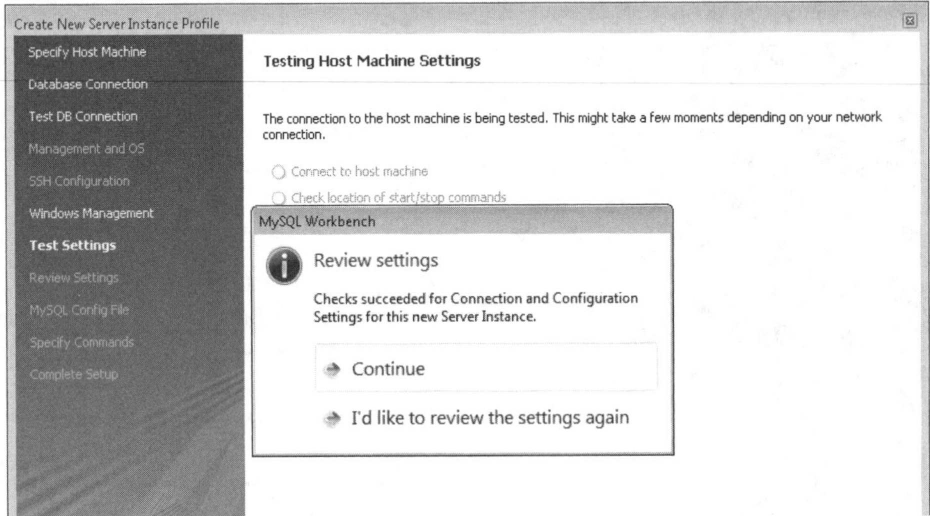

This screen is where you can give the server instance a name. The following displays the default server instance name: *mysqld@McLaughlinMySQL*. The first part represents the MySQL daemon (or background process that runs the MySQL Server), (at) @ symbol, and the valid hostname of the machine. Click the *Finish* button at the bottom of the screen to create the Server Administration widget and complete the process.

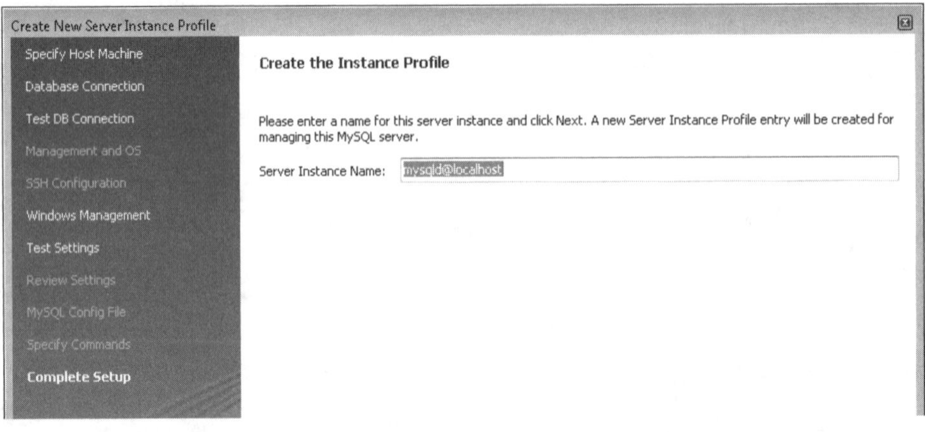

After completing the wizard, you're returned to the home page. Double-click the highlighted server instance to launch a Server Administration console.

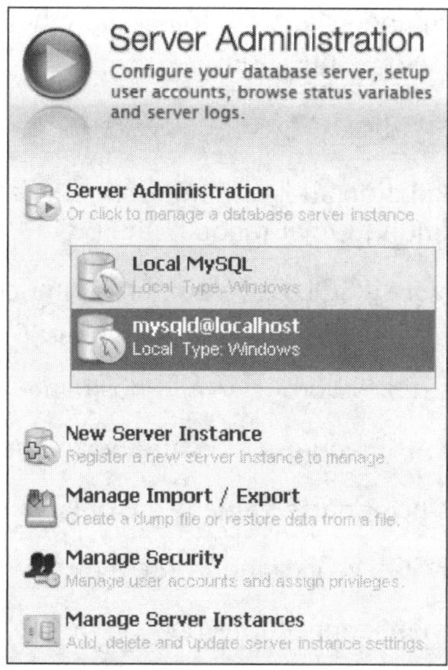

This is what you'll see as the server instance console. Chapter 9 covers how you use this console to manage server instances, including how it can let you start and stop the MySQL Server instance on a local or remote machine.

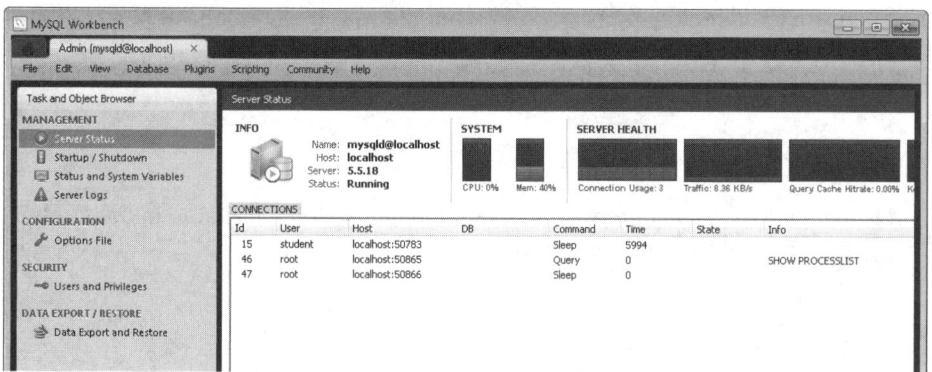

Summary

This chapter discussed how you configure SQL Developer connections on Linux, Mac OS X, and Windows operating systems. It also showed you how to configure Server Administration instances.

Mastery Check

The mastery check is a series of true or false and multiple choice questions that let you confirm how well you understand the material in the chapter. You may check Appendix A for answers to these questions.

True or False:

1. ___The Linux installation adds a menu option to launch MySQL Workbench under the Application | Other menu path.
2. ___You can configure a SQL Development connection that only allows access to a specific schema (or MySQL database).
3. ___The `localhost` keyword is a valid hostname.
4. ___The `127.0.0.1` IP address is a valid hostname.
5. ___The machine's `hostname` value is the only valid hostname.
6. ___You launch MySQL Workstation from a drop-down menu in Mac OS X.
7. ___SQL Development connections depend on the values in the hosts file on all platforms.
8. ___The look and feel of MySQL Workbench is virtually identical across Linux, Mac OS X, and Windows platforms.
9. ___Editing the hosts file on Windows 7 requires the ability to work with restricted directory paths and open an editor as the administrator.
10. ___MySQL Workbench lets you start and stop MySQL Server instances on local and remote servers.

Multiple Choice:

11. Which SQL Development connection features aren't available in the context menu? (Multiple answers are possible.)

    A. Move up

    B. Move down

    C. Edit

    D. Delete connection

    E. Delete all connections

12. Which SQL Development connection feature lets you change configuration options of a SQL Development connection from the MySQL Workbench menu?

    A. Manage

    B. Configure

    C. Edit

    D. All of the above

    E. None of the above

13. On the Windows 7 platform, what is the default hostname for a SQL Development instance?

    A. 127.0.0.1

    B. localhost

    C. hostname

    D. All of the above

    E. None of the above

14. Which platform preconfigures a SQL Development connection and Server Administration to a local instance?

    A. Linux

    B. Mac OS X

    C. Windows

    D. All of the above

    E. None of the above

15. Which of the following is the standard deployment port?

    A. 3306

    B. 3307

    C. 3308

    D. 3309

    E. All of the above

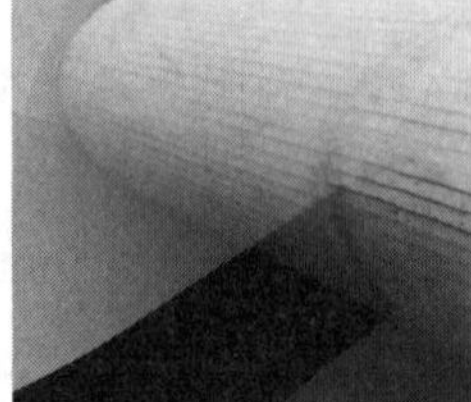

PART II

Data Modeling

CHAPTER 3

Data Modeling Concepts

ata modeling is a process that helps you organize data into relational tables or object types. Together, we'll focus on how to model data into relational tables because MySQL is a relational database.

MySQL Workbench supports SQL development, modeling, and server administration. This chapter moves beyond SQL connections and discusses the modeling component of MySQL Workbench. Here I introduce terms, definitions, and historical details that support how you perform database modeling. Where possible, sidebars hold the historical asides about database modeling and design.

While I considered leaving the asides out as so much baggage, they are in the book for a purpose. They provide key background that supports concepts and ideas of the chapter and details that a number of readers may lack.

This chapter covers the following:

- Data modeling theory
- Data modeling systems
- Classic normalization

It's important to understand that MySQL Workbench can reverse- or forward-engineer relational data models. MySQL Workbench maintains modeling data externally from the database in a single proprietary file format. Data models are stored in this proprietary file format with an `.mwb` file extension.

The three sections of this chapter define concepts for the rest of the book. I strongly encourage you to read this chapter before moving on to the specifics of how to use MySQL Workbench features.

Data Modeling Theory

Data modeling deals with how you organize information into subjects, known as tables. It follows rules that come from academic disciplines, like measurement science, linear algebra, and relational calculus. These are subdisciplines in mathematics. The traditional math approach often makes data modeling too hard for most people who simply want to solve practical problems. My solution to that is working through these concepts with words and analogies.

This section breaks data modeling theory down into a series of questions and answers. It introduces the rule of one, which is critical to modeling data correctly. This section also intends to lay a foundation that lets you understand symbol sets. Symbol sets are how you draw pictures to represent data models. Symbol sets define relationships in math and both classic and domain key database normalization.

The questions for this section are

- What is data modeling?
- Why is data modeling important?
- How do we accomplish it?

After we examine these questions and their answers, the mechanics throughout the rest of the chapter should make logical sense. They should also encourage you to think about data before you rush to organize it.

What Is Data Modeling?

Data modeling is finding *"the one"* in every aspect of information that runs your business. The one means one thing, theme, or subject. You find the one because relational models require that we decompose (break down into little pieces) information into its smallest parts. Only the smallest parts ensure that you can read and write data without the risk of insertion, update, or deletion anomalies, which cause errors or data corruption.

Data modeling is the process of analyzing data required to perform tasks. Let's examine the task of mailing a package to someone. It includes the process of choosing a carrier (the post office, FedEx, or some other carrier) and tracking the package to a delivery point. If we're mailing a gift to a friend, the data may be simple and not worth tracking, but if we're in the business of shipping goods sold by our business, we have a cost to many aspects of this process. That makes the details of the process very important to the data model. For example, one aspect of shipping a package as a vendor is an RMA (Return Merchandise Authorization). RMAs implement a business process when the customer decides they don't want one or more items you've already shipped. An RMA isn't something you consider when mailing a gift to a friend.

Each aspect, characteristic, or attribute of a business process is a task within a shipping process. These characteristics are objects when you analyze a problem using Object-oriented Analysis and Design (OOAD) methods; they are tasks when we apply project management skills. Like most project management tasks, they are composed of subtasks; and the collection of subtasks defines the domain of the task.

A domain defines all the process facts and their relationships. The individual facts become attributes (or columns), collections of related attributes become table structures, and collections of related tables become our domain of knowledge for a relational model. An OOAD approach would also qualify the methods that act on the data. Fortunately, these methods don't fit in the data models of a relational database, and you won't have to model them in the examples of this book.

Scalar Data Types

Scalar data types hold one thing among a set of like things. This means a scalar data type could apply to integers, real numbers, characters, dates, or date-time values. The Java programming language labels scalar data types as primitives.

Attributes are indivisible facts stored as scalar data types. That means you store a single string in a single-variable-length string data type or column, not a list of comma-delimited names in a single column. Indivisible facts are often expressed as atomic data, which means it can't be broken up into parts. That having been said, atomic is a poor word choice because you can now break atoms apart into quarks. When database modelers chose it, atomic was both a descriptive label and the smallest irreducible piece of matter. That's why indivisible fact substitutes for atomic.

Tables define a group or collection of related facts, which are also known as attributes. This makes the table into a structure of a single subject.

The structure defines an object type, and each table can contain many rows that meet the table definition or implement the object type. This makes each row in a table an instance of an object, and the table as a whole an unordered list of objects. It's important to note that tables are unordered lists because the SQL definition says there should be no ordering of rows in a table.

The rule of no ordering covers how databases store and access rows. It doesn't prohibit the ordering of result sets from queries. In fact, the purpose of the `ORDER BY` clause is to order result sets.

Object Types Are Blueprints

Object types are definitions of structures, which are typically a collection of attributes and related methods in OOAD. As such, they serve as a blueprint for building instances of objects, just like a blueprint serves to let builders assemble a Lego set, a ready-to-assemble piece of furniture, or a home.

Following the *rule of one* (finding "the one") means each column holds one fact, each row of a table holds one instance of a subject, and all rows in the table are distinct or unique instances of the subject. Data modeling applies the rule of one to our domain knowledge of a task, like shipping a package. Discovering the domain of knowledge for a table is hard and not a natural task for most people. You need one or more subject matter experts when you define subject domains, and at least one skilled business member on the team to assist you as you qualify the details of a business domain subject into an individual subject—that is, where the individual subject is a fact, or table's definition.

Subject-facts or table definitions are the positive outcome of data modeling. Sometimes subject-facts are subdomains of some business object, like negative, positive, and zero integers are a subset of all integers.

A subject-fact approach ensures that the table holds only one thing, which means it follows the rule of one. As you model to achieve the rule of one, you find that unique subjects fit into a table to hold like subjects. Tables like these contain rows with descriptive data that isn't duplicated in the table because of a natural key.

Organizing the subject-facts into tables is the first and certainly the hardest part of data modeling because as humans we sometimes have an imperfect knowledge of the subject domain. That's also true for business executives who have worked in an industry for years or even decades. This incomplete knowledge can lead to designs that may evolve over time, and data modeling practices should anticipate evolutionary understanding of the domain at hand.

Why Is Data Modeling Important?

Data modeling is the key to organizing data so that you avoid insertion, update, and deletion anomalies. Technically, anomalies like these are deviations from the *common* rules. There are three common rules for good design (check the glossary if these terms are new to you):

- Natural keys should always define unique rows in a table.
- Nonunique keys (like foreign keys) should always access a list of valid primary keys from another table or a copy of the same table (that would be a self-referencing join).
- Foreign keys should always reference the correct primary key.

When you don't follow these common rules, insertion, update, or delete anomalies add, change, or remove data differently than expected. These deviations from the common rules corrupt data because they violate the rules that underpin how you should organize data.

Good data modeling prevents anomalies by ensuring that *unique* rows or object instances are always managed properly by data manipulation commands. This means data modeling guarantees the structure of any object type (or row) and adheres to the rule of one.

The rule of one ensures that every attribute contains either one thing or nothing, and every row ensures that the record structure (or collection of attributes) is unique among all rows in the table. The rule of one also ensures that every table defines a single subject or has qualified a subject-fact.

A subject-fact differs from a subject because it is an irreducible fact, like a datum—one fact. Let's examine the components of a subject-fact. It contains the

External Identifier	Internal Identifier	External References	Non-Key Data
Surrogate Primary Keys	*Natural Keys*	*Foreign Keys*	*Single Fact Data*

FIGURE 3-1. *Data modeling subdomains*

following four subgroups (or more specifically subdomains) when modeled well, as shown in Figure 3-1:

- **External identifiers** These are typically surrogate keys, which are generated from auto-incrementing sequences. A surrogate key stands in for the natural key; and the natural key is a column or set of columns that uniquely describes each row in a table. Surrogate and natural keys are both candidate keys, which are candidates for selection as the primary key. You should always choose the surrogate key as a primary key provided the surrogate key maps to *one and only one natural key* value. A database sequence is a numbering schema that acts like a counter where the first row insert is 1 and the next is 2 and so forth. Surrogate also describes the fact that a sequence isn't descriptive of anything in a table. Surrogate keys should never determine uniqueness that the natural key doesn't. Any attempt to do so means you don't understand the table's domain and can't identify an internally unique identifier (or natural key) among the table's columns. Recognizing this fact, you should have two unique indexes. One should start with the surrogate key and include all natural key columns, and the other should include all the natural key columns. A good design should always elect the surrogate key as the primary key.
- **Internal identifiers** These are typically natural keys, which can be a single column or set of columns that naturally defines unique rows in the table. The idea is that a natural key holds column values that describe the row's data. It should be the values you look for when you want to update a single row in the table. The natural key should also become a unique index by itself, as covered in the external identifier bullet.
- **External references** These are foreign keys, which should reference to primary keys. The only problem with foreign keys typically occurs when they are valid possible foreign keys but incorrect references. This happens through application programming interface (API) errors, where a value is inserted that may reference the wrong primary key value. This type of error occurs when the development team is overly reliant on foreign key

constraints, which don't guarantee the right foreign key—only a possibly correct foreign key. Any value in a list of primary keys is a valid possible value for the foreign key because it meets the typical foreign key constraint rule, but it doesn't guarantee that a correct foreign key exists in any row. You must use the internal identifier to guarantee the correct foreign key in any row when you insert or update data.

- **Non-key data** These are descriptive columns that don't participate in uniquely identifying rows in the table and don't reference other rows in another table (or another row in the same table in a self-referencing relationship).

External identifiers are the surrogate keys or artificially unique numeric identifiers assigned to all rows. Internal identifiers should be the natural key or set of columns that uniquely qualifies an instance (or row) in the table. External references are foreign key columns, and they hold references that link one subject-fact table to another related subject-fact table. Non-key data are all the other columns that come along for the ride.

Primary, Surrogate, and Natural Keys

A *surrogate key* is an artificial numbering sequence that uniquely identifies every row in a table externally to other tables. A *natural key* is one or more columns in a table that uniquely identify every row, and it allows you to find any row inside a table. Natural keys are also called unique keys. It is a good practice to ensure that a surrogate key matches each unique or natural key. Failure to ensure that match means you invite *insertion, update, and delete anomalies* because the design fails to achieve a minimum of third normal form (3NF).

3NF is the third level of normalization. There are eight levels currently in the normalization process, which organizes data in relational models. 3NF requires two things: no transitive dependencies should exist between attributes—that is, no dependency exists between non-key columns; and the table must already be in second normal form (2NF). 2NF also requires two things: All non-key attributes must depend on all of the *natural keys,* which means a natural key defines uniqueness for all rows in a table. Also, the table should already be in first normal form (1NF). 1NF is the basic foundation layer of normalization and requires that all columns together uniquely define an instance of the table, or row, and that every column is atomic. Atomic columns have a single data type and no more than one value of that data type.

Both surrogate and natural keys become candidates for selection as the primary key because they guarantee unique row selection. You should choose the surrogate key as the primary key because its role is external identification,

(Continued)

which supports join operations to other tables. Then, you create an index composed of the surrogate and natural keys to help the database engine find rows in a table more quickly than a full table scan.

This practice is important for normalization, because occasionally design teams may evolve their understanding of the natural key. When you've based joins on a surrogate key and index, you can simply drop and re-create the index with the new knowledge. However, joins based on the natural key often require rewriting all SQL join statements between tables. The latter is simply too expensive and can be avoided by the use of surrogate keys.

The next subsections examine the roles of these subgroups and how they should work together to create a valid data model. After reading them, you should be in a position to avoid some of the most common pitfalls of design. You can think of the external identification as your published phone number, the internal identification as the listing information in a directory, the external references as your place of business or residence, and the non-key data as descriptive entries somebody may or may not maintain in an address book.

External Identification

External identification is the easiest subgroup to discuss when the table uses a surrogate key. A surrogate key is a single column with a unique identifier, typically generated by a database sequence. The identifier is known as a sequence, and in MySQL, sequences are conveniently properties of tables. It's commonly called a surrogate key because it *stands in* for the natural key and contains nothing about the subject-fact in the table. In other words, sequence values don't describe anything about the table except the unique row number.

These columns are typically defined using an unsigned integer data type. Unsigned integers are recommended because they take less space and meet the identification need. The column's data type changes to an unsigned double as the data approaches the maximum range of unsigned integers.

Unsigned Numbers as Primary Keys

Unsigned integers or doubles are the best solution for positive numbers because you can use twice as many of them as signed integers, but that doesn't mean you can't use a signed integer or double to manage positive numbers.

It's important that you use the same data type for primary and foreign key values in MySQL. Failure to match unsigned primary key numbers with unsigned foreign key numbers raises an `ERROR 1005 (HY000)` when using an InnoDB database engine.

The external identifier should always enjoy a one-to-one relationship with the natural key. That means the surrogate and natural keys are qualified as candidate keys. A candidate key has only one requirement—it must uniquely identify all rows in the table.

You choose the table's primary key from the list of candidate keys. Typically, there's only one natural key, but in some rare situations, two or more may exist. My recommendation is simple: Always pick the surrogate key because, over time, your knowledge of the domain may evolve and change the definition of the natural key!

I'd like to leave it at that, but here's the pro and con of the argument for using surrogate keys.

Pro Argument You should choose the surrogate key as the primary key because it becomes an immutable single point of reference to other tables that hold a foreign key value. This works, provided each surrogate key maps to a unique natural key and you create an index that prepends the surrogate key to the natural key. SQL joins between tables are unaffected by changes to the index when the natural key evolves (or adds a column).

Con Argument Surrogate keys are overhead because the natural key holds the values you need to find a unique row in the table. While natural keys evolve (add columns) over time, changes to the natural key should be made to all foreign keys and joining statements.

If you don't see the benefit of the pro argument, please note that it's almost a guarantee that any natural key changes over time. That's true because your knowledge of the table's domain increases over time and enables you to discover better ways to qualify the data. Clearly, the cost of changing SQL joins between tables disappears when you use surrogate keys as the primary and foreign keys. Surrogate keys abstract or hide the natural key from the join operation, which enables you to make alterations to the table structure without impacting joins.

Internal Identification

The internal identification columns are the natural key. The natural key is a column or set of columns (also known as attributes) that uniquely describe instances (or rows) of the table. The natural key columns contain business information that allows programmers and business users to identify instances of data in a table.

When you select, update, or delete a unique row in a table, you use the natural key columns in the `WHERE` clause to isolate a row instance (or record). The natural key should always map to one surrogate key value, and that guarantees that the surrogate key identifies a naturally unique row.

Over time, it is possible that your understanding of a table's subject, or domain, may evolve. Let's take a look at how you model a table. First you choose a subject, like an application user's information. Having chosen the subject, we qualify all the attributes that belong in the subject and then we pick attributes that uniquely identify each row. The collection of attributes defines a natural key.

Somebody in the design group might suggest first and last name as the composite natural key before somebody interjects that there may be two people with the same first and last name. Adding a middle name doesn't solve the problem because two individuals could have all three names in common. While this type of discussion typically happens in early design and by beginners, it illustrates that what we think may be a unique key isn't always a complete key. Adding a middle name to the first and last names evolves the natural key by adding an attribute to it, but it stills fails to guarantee uniqueness. A more involved iteration of this problem occurs when you globalize names, because various countries follow different naming conventions, patterns, and character sets.

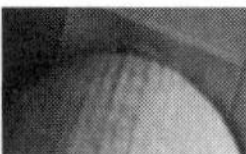

NOTE
The best solution in the application user case requires creating a user-defined user name attribute. This user name can be constrained as unique in the table, which means only one person can ever use it. It becomes a unique, natural, and candidate key all at once.

As your understanding evolves, the set of columns that defines the natural key changes and defines a new candidate key. If you opted to use the natural key as the primary key, all foreign keys must change to reflect the new primary key column set. On the other hand, you need drop and re-create only the table's unique index when you choose the surrogate key as the primary key.

The only problem with evolving natural keys occurs when the set of columns isn't unique with an existing data set. This type of change may mean that the natural key's set of columns must grow by including one or more columns to qualify uniqueness. On occasion, it also may mean that you need to change a column data type to qualify uniqueness. The most frequent change is adding columns to the natural key's set of columns. Sometimes you can simply change a column's data type to increase precision, like changing a `DATE` to a date-time data type, like `DATETIME` or `TIMESTAMP`. This type of change to a natural key column works when no two records may occur within the same date-time but can occur on the same day. The change from a discrete date to a continuous date-time data type shouldn't require a change to existing joins when a natural key is chosen as the primary key, provided you make the same change to any referencing foreign key columns. The change will also require rebuilding the index on the natural key whether or not you use a surrogate key as the primary key.

External References

The external references section can be empty in some tables, but that's usually not the case. That's because there are few tables that are independent of other facts. Most tables have external reference columns, known as foreign key columns, and they point to the primary key of other tables. Some foreign keys point to the primary key found in the same table, and that behavior makes their relationship recursive or self-referencing.

Foreign key columns hold copies of a value from the primary key column. A join between the foreign and primary key columns lets you link the facts from two tables into one result set. Joins like this are made on the basis of equality between the values of the shared column and are called equijoins (a formal word for equality joins).

Many rows in a table may share the same value in a foreign key column or set of columns (for example, when the primary key uses a natural key). Natural and surrogate keys are unique, but foreign key columns frequently hold values that repeat across many rows. The fact that foreign keys hold repeating values helps identify that their purpose isn't to describe the subject of the table. Therefore, the purpose of foreign key columns is to associate the values in one row to another row in that table or a different table.

Non-key Data Non-key data is the easiest to create and the hardest to describe for two reasons. One is that non-key columns hold descriptive values that aren't part of the unique natural key, and the other is that they don't point to other columns inside or outside of a table.

There are three classifications for non-key columns. One class describes something beyond the subject-fact of the table that doesn't merit being placed in a table of its own. An example of this classification type would be a product type column that holds a product's type, a product column that holds a product's code, a product label column that holds a product's language-friendly label, and a product definition that describes the product. Although you could define a table for these four columns and populate the table with a finite set of rows, this type of information fits a common information pattern like a VIN (vehicle identification number). VIN or manufacturing serial number columns contain keys to unlocking product information typically stored in another database model. You shouldn't actually model your product information into tables because it creates the risk of insertion and deletion anomalies.

Another common information pattern, the *common lookup table*, lets you group several small tables into a large lookup table by recognizing that they follow a generalized pattern. This type of generalized pattern is a common reference or lookup table of product type, code, language-friendly label, and definition (or meaning). I'd strongly recommend this information pattern when you need to describe product or item descriptions and leave an external reference (or foreign key) in its place.

A second class of non-key columns would be descriptive columns. For example, the table may contain gender and gender description columns. The two columns would hold, respectively, an abbreviation, like "M" or "F," and description of gender, like "Male" or "Female." They would qualify the same attribute of the fact-subject table, and when gender is required as part of the primary key, you would most likely choose the abbreviation column over the description column.

Another class of non-key columns describes details of the subject-fact table that aren't part of the primary key because presently they're unnecessary to qualify unique rows in the table. These non-key columns may become part of the natural key as your understanding of the domain increases, but in some cases, they're simply related content that doesn't merit its own table. These types of columns are often optional values when inserting rows; and those columns that belong in the natural key evolve into it as your domain understanding increases.

A Common Lookup Table

A common lookup table contains a collection of small tables that describe common values, like gender and other frequently used values. A common lookup table is a generalization of little tables, and you create it by using a three-column natural key. The natural key columns are table name, column name, and a column type value.

The set of possible table and column name column values would qualify rows within a specialization or small logical table. The combination of table, column, and type column values should uniquely identify every row in the design, like that in the next illustration.

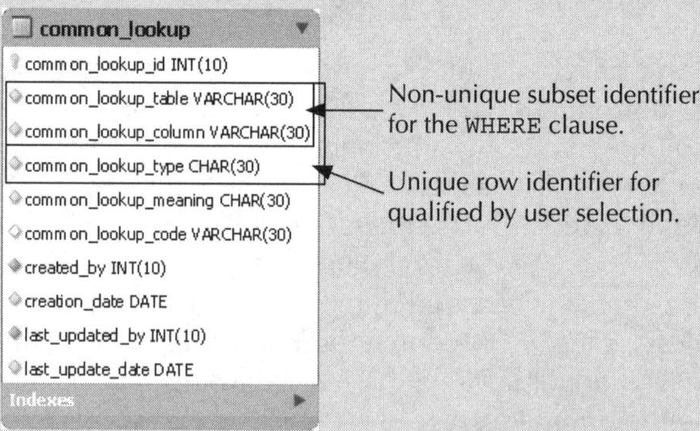

In addition, you generally have non-key columns for the lookup code, language-friendly label, and description columns. These non-key columns are the ones displayed while your programs use the key columns to gather the rows for display.

This section has explained the four subdomains of external identification, internal identification, external reference, and non-key data. It also examined how they interact and work. The next section discusses how you guarantee good data modeling design by applying the rule of one.

How Do We Accomplish It?

This section discusses how you can design an effective database. There are three phases to effective design. They are creating an Entity Relationship Diagram (ERD) or Entity Relationship Model (ER Model), creating a business interaction model, and validating the business interaction and ER models are mutually supportive.

The terms ER Model and ERD are really synonymous terms, and their use is interchangeable in this chapter. MySQL Workbench uses Enhanced Entity Relationship Model (EER Model), and the book uses that term when describing product functionality. That means you have three acronyms that you should associate in your mind to make reading easier—ERD, ER Model, and EER Model.

Create an ER Model

Creating an ER Model is essential to designing how a database supports a business process. You need to create an ER Model as the first step in working with business users.

The key element of a good design for an ER Model (or ERD) requires that you have a team of individuals who have a deep, or profound, understanding of the business process and the data that supports it. You also need to have a data-modeling person who has a solid understanding of how to design normalized tables and relationships between tables. Together, you create a map of tables and their relationships, which is known as an ER Model.

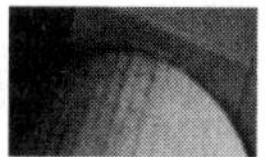

NOTE

Entity is another word for table, as is object type. MySQL Workbench takes the less formal approach and simply calls them tables.

Create a Business Interaction Model

After completing the model, you should invite developers into the forum and create mockups of the user-interface (UI) forms and reports. These mockup sessions are more or less what is sometimes called a *blue sky* exercise. *Blue sky* indicates that there are no limits technologically or financially to developing the envisioned solution. The blue sky design, or first pass through designing mockups, should not attempt to verify that the fields from the UI and reports correlate to the ERD Model; rather, it should be considered a brainstorming session. A brainstorming session records ideas without criticism that may discourage recording the information.

Business interaction models like these help engage the business user in qualifying what may subsequently become the Unified Modeling Language (UML) use cases. It is always more engaging for business-centric people to work with the UI and report mockups over UML diagrams, and the UML can be derived from the UI and reports later by a technical-only staff during the unified process (UP) or Scrum Agile Development project plan. (Both of these are Agile development methodologies associated with iterative System Development Life-Cycle (SDLC) processes.)

Validate the ERD Supports the Business Interaction Model

Validating the ERD isn't very difficult when you recognize that you can walk through the data by using the business interaction model's UI and reports. You simply walk through the logic from data entry to support for Management Information System (MIS) reports.

This step is where you have to ensure that your team has a stake holder, someone with profit and loss (P&L) responsibility for the business process. The stake holder is also called the product owner in a Scrum project management method. You'll also need to have a Scrum Master who oversees the process.

Agile Manifesto Rules

There are four key principles involved in Agile Software Development, and they prioritize:

- Individuals and interactions over processes and tools
- Working software over comprehensive documentation
- Customer collaboration over contract negotiation
- Responding to change over following a plan

The principles state what should be first in four areas but they don't say disregard process and tools, documentation, contract negotiation, or following a plan. How an organization chooses to prioritize and balance these areas indicates the SDLC maturity. A healthy balance between these ensures more frequent success than failure, and a fully documented and budgeted solution at product release.

Together, the teams validate whether their models are mutually supportive by qualifying test cases from a business perspective. The Scrum Master should have these translated into UML activity diagrams, which support how the quality and assurance (QA) teams build test cases. However, it should be noted that UML diagrams are not a hallmark of success and may be avoided by project teams because they create communication hurdles between the business users and data modelers. That's a choice of working software over complete communication from the Agile Manifesto (see the "Agile Manifesto Rules" sidebar).

During the development of the business interaction model, the real domain analysis occurs. That domain analysis decides what tables should exist, how columns should define tables, and what relationships exist between tables. You'll find that the natural keys of tables evolve here, and hopefully they will support the real-world application. The more accurate the natural key at this level of the project, the fewer changes required later in the project. Although a natural key can contain all columns in a table at the 1NF level, good natural keys typically hold between three and eight columns. Natural keys with more than eight columns typically indicate that you have more than a single subject in the table.

It would be terrific to say that this process is smooth and always consistent, but it isn't, and this validation process is often an iterative process until enough is understood to build a small prototype of the application. Initial prototypes tend to evolve throughout each cycle of an iterative process, especially in an Agile software development process.

This completes the basics of data modeling and positions you with a foundation of what it is, why it's important, and how to accomplish it. The next section shows you how to create the ERDs using traditional information engineering and UML.

Data Modeling Systems

Data modeling system sets are numerous. Here, you'll only cover the basics of Chen's modeling system, the modified Chen-Martin modeling system, Martin's Information Engineering, and UML notation. Reviewing these three systems, however, will help illustrate the basic concepts of data modeling.

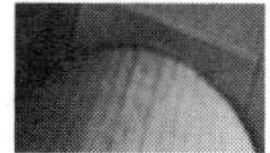

NOTE
MySQL Workbench uses Information Engineering symbols when rendering EER Models.

These modeling symbol sets let you examine the table, its columns, and the relationship between tables in your database model. A relationship can be logical or physical and can exist between two tables or more than two tables. Relationships between two tables are binary relationships; relationships between three tables can be called ternary, but they are usually treated as n-ary relationships. An n-ary relationship exists between *n* number of tables, which traditionally is three or more tables.

There are three possible *binary* relationships between two tables: one-to-one, one-to-many, and many-to-many. This can be confusing because the *one* and the *many* have nothing to do with the two tables. They describe the number of rows involved in a relationship between two tables, and you could more aptly say binary relationships describe how many rows in one table share values that match values in the rows of another table. Binary relationships can also describe how many rows in one copy of a table share values that match rows in a copy of the same table. The binary relationship between rows of the same table is self-referencing because one copy matches against another copy of the same table.

One-to-One It means one row in a table relates to one row in another table through a relationship in its simplest form. In the case of a self-referencing relationship, it means one row in a copy of a table relates to one row in another copy of the same table through a relationship. The relationship may be between two copies of the same row, or one row and another row or set of rows, in a self-referencing table, and the relationship is between a primary and foreign key.

One-to-Many It means one row in a table relates to many rows in another table through a relationship. The one side holds the primary key (which is always unique) and the many side holds foreign keys that map to primary key values. Self-referencing or recursive relationships may also exist in one-to-many binary relations, as well as when one copy of a table holds the primary key and the other side holds copies of rows with foreign key values that match the primary key value.

Many-to-Many It means many rows in a table relate to many rows in another table through a relationship, but it's not a direct relationship like primary-to-foreign key relationships. That's why many-to-many binary relationships are *logical*, not physical, realities. Many-to-many relationships are always logical data models, and that means you must convert them to physical models before implementing them. MySQL Workbench is designed to support physical not logical models.

A physical implementation of a many-to-many relationship would require a primary key column with a scalar value and a foreign key column with a list of values to exist in both tables. The list of values enables mapping between the two tables' primary key values. For example, you start in the scalar column that holds primary keys, then map through a set of foreign keys in the list column to the primary key scalar column in the other table, and vice-versa. The problem is that introducing lists makes it a nonrelational solution to the problem.

It's nonrelational for two reasons. First, relational models don't contain lists, arrays, or serialized values because they're not atomic values. Atomic values means that they hold one thing, like a scalar variable. Second, relational models hold one column value or a null in each row of a table, and a scalar column with a list is unbalanced.

The solution requires you to decompose (break into smaller pieces) many-to-many binary relationships into two one-to-many relationships. That requires you to create an intermediary table called an association table. It holds a foreign key from each table that allows you to connect many rows from one table with many rows from another table.

Like many-to-many binary relationships, n-ary relationships follow the same pattern and require you to break them down into smaller parts. You break the logical n-ary model into two or more sets of one-to-many or one-to-one relationships. For example, an n-ary model of three tables would have an association table that holds three foreign key columns. That means there's one foreign key column in the association for each subject table in the logical n-ary model. This creates three physical one-to-one or one-to-many binary relationships where the one side is always the subject-fact table and the many side is always the association table (which infrequently may also be the one side).

This means ER Model implementations require physical data models, and all physical data models only work with binary relationships. MySQL Workbench is a great tool to use when creating physical ER Models.

Binary Relationships

One-to-one relationships are rare, but may exist. A one-to-one binary relationship between tables identifies one table as unconstrained and the other as constrained in a relationship. The unconstrained table holds a primary key that uniquely identifies each row, and the constrained table holds a primary key of its own and a foreign key that holds a copy of the unconstrained table's primary key.

You pick the unconstrained and constrained tables during your ERD design. You control which table fills which role because there's only one copy of the primary key held as foreign key in a one-to-one relationship. This means you could switch the roles by changing which table holds the foreign key. SQL joins the two related rows from different tables by comparing the values in the primary and foreign key columns.

The *flexibility* of one-to-one relationships is a two-edged sword because one-to-one relationships frequently evolve into one-to-many relationships. In one-to-many relationships, the foreign key is always held by the many side and the primary key by the one side of the relationship. This means you should ask yourself which table is the driving or key table in the business relationship because that table is less likely to evolve into the many side of the relationship. If you chose the wrong driving table during design, fixing the mistake can be expensive, and progressively more expensive to fix as the process continues.

Assume you're new at data modeling and you want to map a customer to an address. You have two options. One assumes the customer has only one address, and the other assumes the customer may have two or more addresses. You choose a one-to-one relationship when the business model states you only care about the customer's current home address and a one-to-many relationship when the business model states you want the current and past addresses of the customer. In both cases, you assign the primary key of the `CUSTOMER` table as a foreign key in the `ADDRESS` table because it works for either model because a SQL statement can join on matches between the primary and foreign key columns.

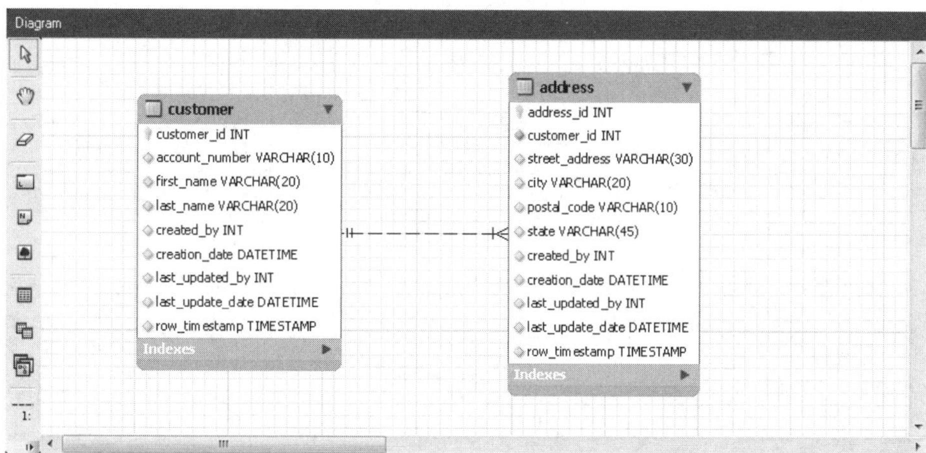

As discussed, you implement logical many-to-many relationships as two one-to-many relationships. Take, for example, the natural relationship between orders and items in a business model. An order may contain any item and more than one item per order, while an item may be part of one or more orders. This is a logical many-to-many scenario with relationships between many orders to many items.

The problem with a many-to-many relationship is that the table holding orders would need a foreign key from the table holding items for every item in an order, and likewise the items table would need to hold a foreign key from the orders table for every table that ordered the item. As discussed earlier, that's the physical reality of a primary key scalar data type column and a list column with multiple foreign key values. It isn't a relational model possibility. That's why an association table holds copies of the primary keys from both tables.

For example, you create an `ORDER_ITEM` association table between an `ITEM` table and `ORDER` table. The `ITEM` table donates a copy of its primary key to the `ORDER_ITEM` table for every `ORDER` that includes it, and the `ORDER` table donates a copy of its primary key to the `ORDER_ITEM` table for every `ITEM` on the order. This lets you create a customer order by associating any number of items with any number of orders because the association table holds the matching foreign key values. It holds one foreign key for the `ORDER` table and another for the `ITEM` table. A surrogate primary key may be added to the `ORDER_ITEM` table because it may hold shared attributes that describe neither the subject-fact of the `ORDER` nor `ITEM` tables. The composite natural key is the set of foreign key columns, and they should be uniquely constrained in any good design.

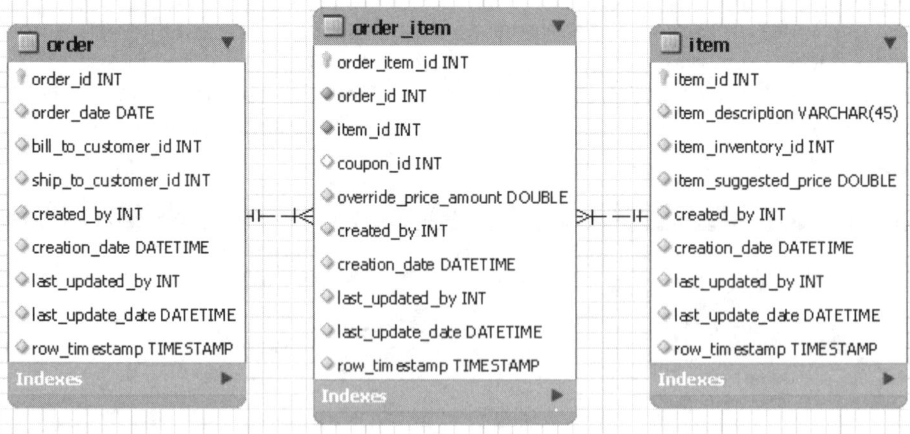

That was simple, but what happens when each order item holds both a suggested retail and actual price value for each item? You would typically capture the actual price from a `PRICE` table, but the actual price may be provided by a clerk through an override activity. That means the actual price belongs to the order for the item but doesn't belong to any subject-fact table. This is what's known as a shared attribute.

Shared attributes only have context in the midst of a relationship between two subject-fact tables.

Since clerks may assign actual prices that have no relation to anything in the data model, such prices would be raw entry at time of sale. That's why the foregoing model shows the `COUPON_ID` column as optional (null allowed or nullable) because a simple override price doesn't require a coupon. Alternatively, customers may present discount coupons that discount suggested-retail prices. The latter requires that you store the percentage and type of coupon presented. The percentage and coupon type become shared attributes in the `ORDER_ITEM` association table. While I'd love to leave it at that, there's one more twist that frequently occurs. Generally, the coupon type is set in a `COUPON` table or a `COMMON_LOOKUP` table, and the shared attribute is a foreign key to only one of those tables. My suggestion is that you should put the coupon information in a `COMMON_LOOKUP` table when you often use the same type of discount coupons and they change infrequently. If you often use coupons and they change frequently, put them in a `COUPON` table with temporal columns like `START_DATE` and `END_DATE`. This makes `COUPON` a coupon-only lookup table.

TIP

Never design a column that may hold a foreign key that belongs to one of two or more tables because it invariably leads to confusion and usage errors.

As discussed, there are different types of business rules that require shared attributes in association tables; and don't shy away from using association tables that may hold more shared attributes. The presence of shared attributes in an association table changes the natural key from the set of foreign keys to the set of foreign keys and all (one or more) of the shared attributes. That's something not immediately visible to new designers. The business reason for including the shared attributes in the natural key exists in a coupon scenario or a two-for-one sale where one item carries the discount and another doesn't.

An association table that supports coupons or two-for-one sales presents a challenge. It introduces the need for a `QUANTITY` column to support a two-for-one sale. Naturally, the `QUANTITY` column lets us track how many of a specific item are linked to an order, and it is always a mandatory column (containing an integer of 1 to any number of items) during an insert or update. Unfortunately, the `COUPON_ID` column is typically optional because the customer may or may not present a coupon.

There's a very subtle design trick here because some databases don't support unique constraints unless all columns are also not null constrained. It requires you to insert a full-price indicator in a coupon type shared attribute. I'd strongly recommend you always do this to ensure possible portability of ER Model designs. The two-for-one, three-for-one, or other ratio relationship should be stored in the `COUPON` or `COMMON_LOOKUP` table. The presence of a ratio relation column is a strong argument for a coupon-only lookup table.

While association tables typically don't require surrogate keys because the two foreign keys provide a unique natural key, they should always have a surrogate key when you have shared attributes in them. Shared attributes by themselves appear to be along for the ride in the association between the two tables, but sometimes shared attributes become transactional events—for example, when you need to generate an RMA for a customer who returns a single item from an order where two or more items were required for a discount. The value in the `QUANTITY` column of the `ORDER_ITEM` table and the ratio in the `COUPON` table (typically implemented as `MINIMUM` and `MAXIMUM` columns) let you resolve most returns but not all.

There are two patterns for storing shared attributes in an `ORDER_ITEM` table. One uses a quantity counter and the other creates two or more rows in the association table. The quantity counter is the easiest and preferred solution but doesn't work when the item sold has a serial number associated with it. You can resolve serial numbers by adding a `SERIAL_NUMBER` column to the association table while entering a value of 1 in the `QUANTITY` column. Inserting a serial number in the association table isn't a great idea, however, because it probably duplicates the serial number from your `INVENTORY` table.

In lieu of adding a `SERIAL_NUMBER` column, you should define an `INVENTORY_ID` column that holds a foreign key to the `INVENTORY` table. That way, you store the serial number in only one place in the database and eliminate the possibility of incongruent serial numbers in the two tables (that is, different values for the same serial number). A serial number fix like this promotes the association table solution from a two-table to three-table solution.

The RMA process would first check if two or more rows are involved in the purchase order for the same item and if they have serial numbers. The `SERIAL_NUMBER` column is typically an optional column in the `INVENTORY` table because not all merchandise has serial numbers. The RMA process would then authorize an RMA for the discounted price rather than the nondiscounted price and, in some cases, an average price.

Creating a surrogate key for all association tables is a best design practice because those without shared attributes may evolve to include them and those with shared attributes need them. Adding a surrogate key column to an association table is a low-cost design and development practice that may avoid higher modification costs during future application maintenance cycles.

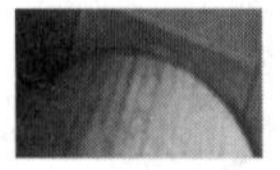

TIP

Always define a surrogate key for association tables because they may hold shared attributes and become data instead of relationship maps.

As shown in the serial number example, association tables between two tables become association tables between three or more tables. This occurs naturally when the foreign key of another table is stored as a shared attribute. A change like this promotes the binary association table to an n-ary association table, and they're covered in the next section.

N-ary Relationships

N-ary relationships are logical relationships that exist between more than two tables. They're resolved into a series of binary relationships like the many-to-many relationships. The key difference between the two is the number of foreign key columns in the natural key. A many-to-many binary relationship always has two foreign keys as a composite primary key. An n-ary relationship has *n* (the number of tables in the relationship) foreign keys in the composite primary key.

You should always define surrogate keys for association tables, and that rule becomes more important with n-ary association tables because they're more likely to include shared attributes. The problem with shared attributes in n-ary tables is more complex than in binary association tables. N-ary relationships are rare, and you should ensure that other simpler modeling solutions are carefully examined before adopting the complexity of n-ary relationships.

Notation Sets

There are several notation sets that represent relationships and tables. Since MySQL Workbench uses the Information Engineering model, the discussion focuses on the notation sets that led to it as the predominant notation set for ERDs. After describing the ones that help you use MySQL Workbench, there's a comparison of using UML for ERDs.

The notation sets explain how symbols enable you to read the cardinality of relationships between tables. Cardinality measures the minimum and maximum number of rows one table will be related to in another table. Check the "Cardinality" sidebar for more on the subject, which applies to columns, relationships, and the distribution of uniqueness in tables.

The book exposes you briefly to the main styles of ERD notation to ensure you can read older diagrams as you convert them into the EER Model of MySQL Workbench. The book covers Chen, Chen-Martin, and information engineering symbol sets. It excludes many others, like the DoD (Department of Defense) IDEF1X (Integration Definition for Information Modeling).

Cardinality

Cardinality comes from set mathematics and simply means the number of elements in a set. For example, in an arbitrary set of five finite values, a cardinality of [1..5] qualifies the minimum of 1 and the maximum of 5. This set expresses a range of five values.

(Continued)

In databases, cardinality applies to the following:

- The number of values in an unconstrained column within a row has a default cardinality of [0..1] (zero-to-one) for nullable columns. (The minimum cardinality of zero applies only to nullable columns, which are also known as optional column values.)
- The number of values in a `NOT NULL` constrained column within a row has a cardinality of [1..1] (one-to-one).

When there's no upward limit on the number of values in a column, it holds a *collection*. Collections typically contain one-to-many elements and their cardinality is [0..*] (zero-to-many). This type of zero-to-many cardinality can't exist in a relation model, but does exist in Object Relational Database Management Systems (ORDBMS), like Oracle and PostgreSQL.

Developers often describe the frequency of repeating values in a table as having low or high cardinality. *High cardinality* means the frequency of repeating values is closer to unique, where unique is the highest cardinality. *Low cardinality* means values repeat many times in a table, such as a gender column where the distribution is often close to half and half. A column that always contains the same value, which shouldn't occur, is the lowest cardinality possible.

Cardinality also applies to binary relationships between tables. Two principal physical implementations of binary relationships exist: one-to-one and one-to-many. The one-to-many relationship is the most common pattern. In this pattern, the table on the one side of the relationship holds a primary key and the table on the many side holds a foreign key.

Chen Notation

Chen notation has more value as a historical item than as a practical tool. It uses rectangles as the symbol for tables and ovals as symbols for columns (or attributes). A line between rectangles qualifies a relationship, and a diamond in the line indicates the type of binary relationship. The symbol sets in the diamond are 1:1 for a one-to-one relationship, 1:N for a one-to-many relationship, and N:M for a many-to-many relationship. These binary relations qualify the maximum number of rows in a relationship.

The Chen model didn't last long with the relationship cardinality inside the diamond. It removed the binary notation from the diamonds and replaced them with a keyword describing the relationship. Then, the number 1 or letter *n* was placed on the appropriate sides of the relationship description diamond.

The original Chen notation doesn't support the minimum cardinality of relationships, and that omission is why it's typically not used. The replacement Chen-Martin method does provide for both minimum and maximum relationship cardinality. The next illustration actually depicts a one-to-many cardinality with the *N* inside the diamond qualifying many and, at the same time, maximum cardinality.

While the foregoing illustration is a summary diagram, you would see a list of column names with the natural key columns underlined in a detail diagram. The modeling technique does not enable identifying the candidate keys—the natural and surrogate keys.

Chen-Martin Notation

As mentioned, Chen-Martin notation added minimum relationship cardinality to the drawing set. It did this by adding a single perpendicular line for a minimum cardinality of one and a zero (or oval) for a minimum cardinality of zero.

The change makes Chen-Martin a viable modeling symbol set, but the relationship description diamonds clutter diagrams. They make it hard to create large ERDs that conveniently fit on printed documents, even large poster boards. The Martin method, or information engineering, removes these diamonds and introduces a more streamlined notation symbol set.

Information Engineering Notation

Martin's method, which is also known as information engineering, drops the diamonds for what has become known as crow's-foot notation. Information engineering is probably the most widely used method for ERDs because many tools support it and it allows you to fit a lot on a single page.

The symbol set for relationships are

- One oval (or zero) and a perpendicular line across the relationship line indicate a minimum cardinality of zero and a maximum cardinality of one. This is the default because foreign key columns are typically unconstrained or null allowed columns. This means you may insert a row in the table holding the foreign key without providing a value to the foreign key column; and the table with the foreign key is unconstrained in the relationship to the table holding the primary key.

- Two perpendicular lines across the relationship line indicate a minimum cardinality of one and a maximum cardinality of one. This would be the relationship when the constrained (or dependent) table in a relationship can't insert a row until one exists in the unconstrained table with a primary key value. This relationship exists whenever the foreign key column is constrained as a `NOT NULL` column.
- One oval and a less than (<) symbol read left to right or one oval and a greater than (>) symbol read right to left indicate a minimum cardinality of zero and a maximum cardinality of many. Like the zero-to-one relationship, the foreign key would be nullable or optional when inserting a row in the table.
- One perpendicular line and a less than (<) symbol read left to right or one perpendicular line and a greater than (>) symbol read right to left indicate a minimum cardinality of zero and a maximum cardinality of many. Like the zero-to-one relationship, this relationship would make the foreign key value mandatory or required when inserting a row in the table.

Information engineering also moves the relationship qualifier outside of the diamond and next to the relationship line. While Chen and Chen-Martin let you qualify only one relation (half of a relationship), Martin's method lets you annotate the relationship line with verb phrases that let you read two relations in any relationship like English sentences (or whatever language you're using for ERDs).

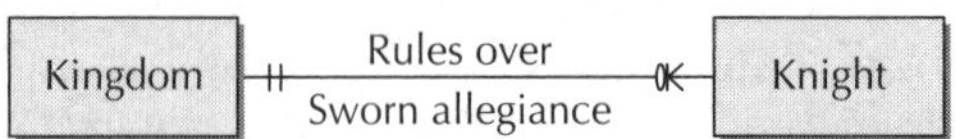

For example, you could read the relationship from `KINGDOM` to `KNIGHT` two ways because the minimum cardinality is zero. The first one qualifies that there may be *zero to many,* and the second uses *may* to qualify that the minimum cardinality is zero.

Any `KINGDOM` rules over zero to many rows of `KNIGHT`.

or, with the conditional *may* like this:

Any `KINGDOM` may rule over one to many rows of `KNIGHT`.

You can read the relationship back from the constrained `KNIGHT` table (assuming the foreign key is not null constrained) to the unconstrained `KINGDOM` table like this:

Any KNIGHT has sworn allegiance to one row of KINGDOM.

Information engineering covers all relationships patterns except one with rectangles. An ID-dependent relationship requires that you use a rectangle with rounded corners and an ordinary relationship line. It indicates that the table has no existence outside of the unconstrained table, and the unconstrained table holds the primary key. You can't implement an ID-dependent relationship easily in MySQL or relational databases. ID-dependent tables are typically implemented as nested tables—available in Oracle and PostgreSQL object relational databases.

UML Notation

UML (Unified Modeling Language) is an object-oriented analysis and design (OOAD) approach. There are only two differences worth noting.

One difference is that the rectangles have three subordinate rectangles. The top one is for the table name, the middle one is for the attributes of the table, and the bottom one is for any methods of the object (or table). The bottom one is the give-away that this doesn't work in relational databases but requires an object relational database like Oracle or PostgreSQL.

The other difference is that there are different symbols for the relationship line. One qualifies a non-ID–dependent relationship, which is the typical primary-to-foreign key relationship, and that symbol is an aggregation relationship line. The other qualifies the ID-dependent relationship, and it is the composition relationship line. An open (or unfilled) diamond represents aggregation, and a filled diamond represents composition.

This completes the data modeling system section.

Classic Normalization

Database normalization is the process of organizing data, as briefly discussed earlier in this chapter's "Primary, Surrogate, and Natural Keys" sidebar. There are a bunch of rules governing how you should do it, when you should undo it, and how you can't do it. My hope is to lay out what normalization means in Texas English, which means clear and simple.

There are now, as of 2010, seven or eight normal forms. They began when E.F. Codd first proposed the relational model in his *A Relational Model for Large Shared Data Banks* paper. There's also a concept of Domain-Key Normal Form (DKNF). According to some, this belongs between fifth and sixth normal forms. DKNF comes to us by way of Ronald Fagin, in his *A Normal Form for Relational Databases*.

Database normalization attempts to organize data in such a way as to prevent SQL statements from creating insertion, update, or deletion anomalies. As a practice, *third normal* form (3NF) is often considered normalized because most 3NF tables are free of insertion, update, or delete anomalies. The key word is most, not all.

Therefore, normalization design attempts to achieve the *highest normal* form (HNF) possible. A table is in HNF whether it meets or fails to meet any normal form definition. Oddly enough, any HNF may also be a *zero normal* (0NF) or *unnormalized normal* form (UNF). UNF means that a table contains one or more repeating groups.

Normalization is the process of organizing data into tables that act as single subject-facts when acted upon individually or through external relationships. As mentioned earlier in this chapter, a single subject-fact is also known as a domain.

First Normal Form

First normal form (1NF) exists when all columns, or attributes, of a table have a single data type and there are no repeating rows of data, which means rows are unique. 1NF requires that

- Column data types be atomic, which means columns shouldn't have repeating groups, comma-delimited groups, or other subatomic parts. This raises a question whether compound variables like Oracle's arrays, lists, and objects violate first normal form. Oracle's compound array and list columns do not violate the atomic design rule because they act like nested tables or ID-dependent tables—accessible only through the external table.
- Column names are unique in tables and arbitrarily ordered, which means their order doesn't impose any constraint on the table.
- Rows in a table have no implicit or explicit ordering required for their access and use.
- The collection of columns should define unique rows.

Moreover, first normal form modeling finds the nonrepeating row columns and moves them from a base table to their own table. It removes all trace of the nonrepeating row columns from the base table. It also puts a foreign key in the new table, and the foreign key points back to the primary key of the base table. The foreign key in the new table is functionally dependent on the primary key in the base table.

Atomic Data Types

Atomic column values are limited to scalar variables. Scalar variables only hold one thing at a time, like an integer. How I'd love to leave it at that!

Unfortunately, some MySQL designers create tables that store serialized strings in a single column, which introduces the concept of lists in a relational model. The only place lists belong is in an Oracle's database engine because it is an Object Relational Database Management System (ORDBMS) or Extended Relational Database Management System.

Likewise, some developers put numeric values separated by a delimiter that contain meaning; typically, the delimiter is a colon. This pattern is typical in the case of tickets, where the first, second, and third numbers map to the section, row, and seat. This force fitting of logic into a single column makes such a column nonatomic.

You should avoid putting more than one thing in any column. Likewise, you should try to use descriptive column names.

A table is in first normal form when all columns (or attributes) have a single data type and when there are no repeating rows or set of columns. The first two elements of this idea are generally understood and applied almost intuitively. The idea of a single data type is clear because most people understand any column can only have one data type at any given time. The idea of uniqueness makes sense because you generally only want to act on one copy of anything at a time.

The third point is sometimes misunderstood. The idea of not being able to have repeating groups of columns can confuse people because they often look at tables as a group of unique rows. Repeating groups of columns indicates that you've got multiple subjects in your single table design. The repeating row columns indicate the base table is on the one side of a one-to-many relationship. The columns of nonrepeating rows typically become a new table because they are on the many side of a one-to-many binary relationship.

The subsections present an example and two possible solutions. A third solution exists for object-oriented relational databases but isn't provided because the MySQL database doesn't support nested tables.

UNF-to-1NF Problem

The example in this section uses a sample address table to show you how to move a table from UNF, or an HNF of 0NF, to 1NF. It has a design that lets you violate first normal form whenever the `STREET_ADDRESS` column requires more than a single entry or more than one row.

This type of table design lets you violate the atomic rule of first normal form because the `STREET_ADDRESS` column may need to accommodate one or more street address values. Typically, many developers see no harm in putting multiple address lines into a column as comma-separated values. The data would look like the following:

```
+-----------------------------------+---------+-------+-------------+
| street_address                    | city    | state | postal_code |
+-----------------------------------+---------+-------+-------------+
| 1111 Broadway, Suite 500, MS-5045 | Oakland | CA    | 94604       |
+-----------------------------------+---------+-------+-------------+
```

Another type of table design lets you violate two rules of first normal form. It modifies the previous example by adding a second column to the primary key. The second column doesn't describe the subject-fact of the table, but introduces a way to order row results. Such a change makes the primary key a compound or composite key. The following provides an example of one record spread across three rows of such a table.

```
+------------+-------------+---------+----------------+---------+-------+
| address_id | customer_id | line_id | street_address | city    | state |
+------------+-------------+---------+----------------+---------+-------+
|          1 |           1 |       1 | 1111 Broadway  | Oakland | CA    |
|          2 |           1 |       2 | Suite 500      | Oakland | CA    |
|          3 |           1 |       3 | MS-5045        | Oakland | CA    |
+------------+-------------+---------+----------------+---------+-------+
```

The CUSTOMER_ID column links the row to the CUSTOMER table, and the LINE_ID column allows for multiple rows because the LINE_ID column lets you order rows. The CUSTOMER_ID and LINE_ID columns are a composite natural key in this scenario, notwithstanding that the CUSTOMER_ID is a foreign key (external reference) to the CUSTOMER table. Such a design creates a model where you have repeating column values, like CITY and STATE for each unique STREET_ADDRESS column value. This type of design violates the 1NF rule of no repeating group of columns, and the stored data mimics a denormalized result set that should be returned from a join between two tables.

You would create ADDRESS and STREET_ADDRESS tables to model this problem correctly. The ADDRESS table would hold one value of city and state for each unique address linked to a customer, and the STREET_ADDRESS table would hold the three rows related to the ADDRESS table's one row. The two tables would allow for unique results in a single subject-fact table, and the rows of the ADDRESS table are unique until you join them with the rows of the STREET_ADDRESS table.

Separating data into single subject-facts is the only proper way to achieve 1NF normalized results. Online transaction processing (OLTP) systems typically require normalized tables to avoid insertion, update, and delete anomalies. Interestingly, joining two normalized result sets yields a denormalized result set.

If you query the data with an INNER JOIN from these tables, the data will look very similar to the original problem data. As shown in this query:

```
SELECT   a.contact_id
,        a.address_id
,        sa.line_id
,        sa.street_address
,        a.city
,        a.state_province AS state
FROM     address a INNER JOIN street_address sa
ON       a.address_id = sa.address_id;
```

It generates the following as a result from the join. You should note that the one side of the one-to-many binary relationship is repeating, while the many side is unique. Joining tables always repeats copies of the columns on the one side of a one-to-many binary relationship for rows of columns from the many side of the relationship.

```
+------------+------------+---------+----------------+---------+-------+
| contact_id | address_id | line_id | street_address | city    | state |
+------------+------------+---------+----------------+---------+-------+
|          1 |          1 |       1 | 1111 Broadway  | Oakland | CA    |
|          2 |          1 |       2 | Suite 500      | Oakland | CA    |
|          3 |          1 |       3 | MS-5045        | Oakland | CA    |
+------------+------------+---------+----------------+---------+-------+
```

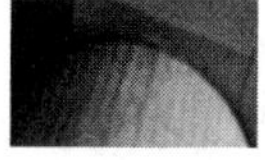

NOTE
You need to perform a nested join with a procedural language to get a match between one row and many rows into one structure.

It's important to note that almost every join result is in UNF. While that's not the way you store data to avoid insertion, update, and deletion anomalies, it is the way the end user consumes the information.

1NF Data Warehousing Solution Data warehousing models are online analytical processing (OLAP) systems. OLAP systems differ from OLTP systems in many ways, but the principal design difference is that you query data rather than insert, update, or delete data. This fact opens up a design pattern suited for queries that is not effective for transactions—flattening.

Flattening a nonrepeating column into a series of columns requires creating a column for every unique row that may occur. This means you replace the rows in the `STREET_ADDRESS` table with the `STREET_ADDRESS1`, `STREET_ADDRESS2`, and `STREET_ADDRESS3` columns.

The following is a definition of such a table:

```
+-----------------+------------------+------+-----+---------+
| Field           | Type             | Null | Key | Default |
+-----------------+------------------+------+-----+---------+
| address_id      | int(10) unsigned | NO   | PRI | NULL    |
| contact_id      | int(10) unsigned | NO   |     | NULL    |
| address_type    | int(10) unsigned | NO   |     | NULL    |
| street_address1 | varchar(30)      | NO   |     | NULL    |
| street_address2 | varchar(30)      | NO   |     | NULL    |
| street_address3 | varchar(30)      | NO   |     | NULL    |
| city            | varchar(30)      | NO   |     | NULL    |
| state           | varchar(30)      | NO   |     | NULL    |
| postal_code     | varchar(20)      | NO   |     | NULL    |
+-----------------+------------------+------+-----+---------+
```

The data in a flattened model appears like this:

```
+------------+-----------------+-----------------+-----------------+
| address_id | street_address1 | street_address2 | street_address3 |
+------------+-----------------+-----------------+-----------------+
|          1 | 1111 Broadway   | Suite 500       | MS-5045         |
+------------+-----------------+-----------------+-----------------+
```

It's got one obvious problem. When the data encounters a fourth street address value, you must change the structure of the table (a fact-table in a data warehouse). As rule, data warehouses understand the OLTP data and would never design without a complete set of columns, and that's why this type of solution works in data warehouse systems.

Second Normal Form

Second normal form (2NF) exists when a table is already in first normal form and all non-key columns depend on all of the key columns, where the list of key columns goes from 1 to n. The list of key columns makes up the natural key of a table, or the list of columns that makes any row unique in a table. A table that has only a single column as the natural key, like a vehicle identification number, is automatically in second normal form because there can't be a dependency on part of the key (or one column of a multiple column key).

A table that has two or more columns as a natural key may contain one or more non-key columns that has a partial dependency on one or a set of columns less than all the columns in the key (or primary key). This typically means you have created a table that contains two subjects. The following shows the definition of the 1NF `RENTAL` table before converting it to 2NF (and yes, it's a bad design):

```
+--------------------+------------------+------+-----+---------+
| Field              | Type             | Null | Key | Default |
+--------------------+------------------+------+-----+---------+
| rental_id          | int(10) unsigned | NO   | PRI | NULL    |
| customer_id        | int(10) unsigned | NO   |     | NULL    |
| check_out_date     | date             | NO   |     | NULL    |
| return_date        | date             | NO   |     | NULL    |
| item_barcode       | varchar(20)      | NO   |     | NULL    |
| item_type          | int(10) unsigned | NO   |     | NULL    |
| item_title         | varchar(60)      | NO   |     | NULL    |
| item_subtitle      | varchar(60)      | YES  |     | NULL    |
| item_rating        | varchar(8)       | NO   |     | NULL    |
| item_rating_agency | varchar(4)       | NO   |     | NULL    |
| item_release_date  | date             | NO   |     | NULL    |
+--------------------+------------------+------+-----+---------+
```

The preceding 1NF `RENTAL` table contains two subject-facts: one is the rental and the other is the item subject-fact. The natural key for the rental is a composite key of the `CUSTOMER_ID`, `CHECK_OUT_DATE`, and `RETURN_DATE` columns, and the natural key for the item is the `ITEM_BARCODE` column. Together the four columns could become the natural key for this table, but then the table would be in 1NF not 2NF.

The surrogate `RENTAL_ID` column maps to the four-column composite natural key. Unfortunately, all the other item columns depend on only part of the natural key, and this design limits a rental to a single item. You can move this table from 1NF to 2NF by dividing it into two subject-fact tables. Simply removing all the columns that start with item to a new `ITEM` table promotes the design from 1NF to 2NF.

Replacing those columns with an `ITEM_ID` foreign key provides an external reference to the `RENTAL` table, but limits rentals to a single item. While this type of resolution typically resolves one-to-one relationships between the subject-fact table and nested subject-fact table, it doesn't fix a one-to-many relationship between them.

Typically, business rules would support a rental of one to many items. That means you shouldn't add the foreign key to the `RENTAL` table to fix this problem.

You should create an association table that will hold a copy of the surrogate primary keys from the RENTAL and ITEM tables, like the following:

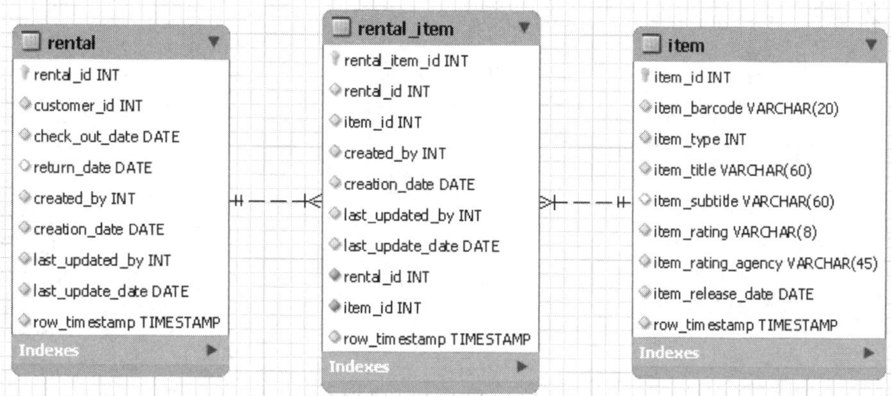

This section has explained how you fix partial dependencies by removing the nested subject-fact table and replacing it with a foreign key when there is a one-to-one relationship. It also explained how to fix a one-to-many relationship by removing the nested subject-fact table and creating an association table between the original and new tables.

Third Normal Form

Third normal form (3NF) exists when a table is already in second normal form and there are no transitive dependencies. A transitive dependency means a non-key column or set of columns is dependent on another column that generally isn't part of the natural key.

Since all non-key columns should be wholly dependent on the primary key, a transitive dependency exists when a column's functional dependency routes through another column or set of columns on its way to the primary key. This type of relationship indicates that there are at least two subject-facts in a table, but the dependency is not a column in the natural key.

Our example table for this section is the ITEM table from the previous example, as shown here.

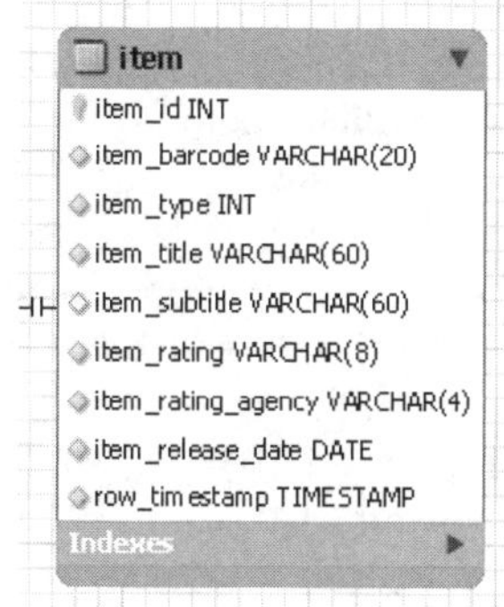

The ITEM_RATING column has a transitive dependency through the ITEM_RATING_AGENCY column. From a business perspective, a PG rating depends on a Motion Picture of America Association (MPAA) rating agency and an E10+ rating depends on the Entertainment Software Rating Board (ESRB).

You fix a transitive dependency by applying the same technique used to fix a partial dependency. You remove the two columns from the ITEM table and put them in their own table or a COMMON_LOOKUP table.

The transitive dependency in this instance is a one-to-one relationship between the subject-fact table and nested subject-fact table, which means you add a foreign key column that points back to the new `RATING` table. The solution is shown in the following illustration:

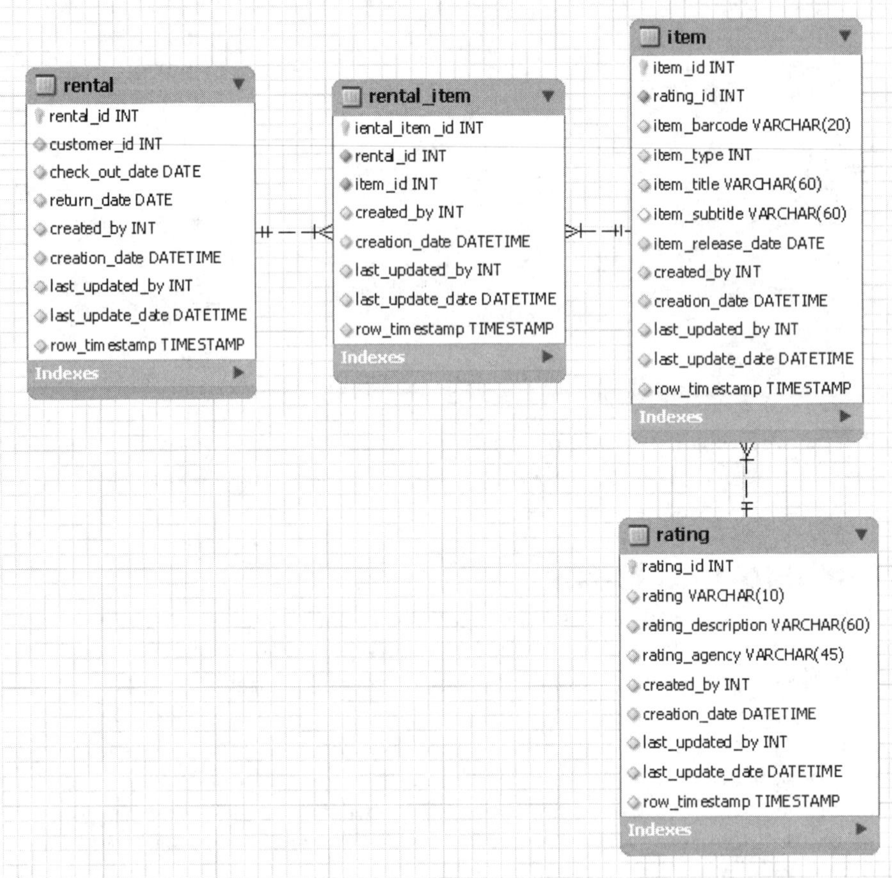

You should generally make the column or set of columns that acts as the intermediary column the natural primary key in a new table. The column or columns that had a transitive dependency on the intermediary column should also move to the new table. A `RATING_ID` foreign key column in the new table replaces the original columns, but allows access through joins to them. The following ER Model shows the fix to the problem.

Breaking the two subject-fact tables into one subject-fact table successfully promotes a 2NF table to a 3NF table. The foreign key links in the original table links the `RATING` and `RATING_AGENCY` column values to the base table.

This section has shown you how to migrate from 0NF to 1NF, 1NF to 2NF, and 2NF to 3NF. The key to the changes are ensuring that all tables contain a single subject-fact.

Summary

This chapter explained the basic of data modeling theory and systems, as well as normalization practices. You should be positioned to design database models.

Mastery Check

The mastery check is a series of true or false and multiple choice questions that let you confirm how well you understand the material in the chapter. You may check Appendix A for answers to these questions.

True or False:

1. ___External identifiers hold primary key columns.
2. ___Internal identifiers hold natural key columns.
3. ___External references hold foreign key columns.
4. ___Non-key data includes surrogate key columns.
5. ___Both surrogate and primary keys are candidate keys.
6. ___UNF is the same as HNF when a table is in 0NF.
7. ___HNF is only 3NF or higher.
8. ___A table is in 1NF when it has a partial dependency.
9. ___A table is in 1NF when it has a transitive dependency.
10. ___There is nothing higher than 3NF.

Multiple Choice:

11. MySQL Workbench uses which data modeling system?
    - **A.** Chen
    - **B.** Chen-Martin
    - **C.** Information engineering
    - **D.** UML
    - **E.** None of the above

12. Which relationship line models an ID-dependent relationship?

A. Aggregation line

B. Composition line

C. Inheritance line

D. Relationship line

E. None of the above

13. What type of relationship models a primary-to-foreign key association?

A. Unary

B. Binary

C. N-ary

D. Inheritance

E. Aggregation

14. What type of variable holds only one thing? (Multiple answers are possible.)

A. Compound variable

B. Composite variable

C. Scalar variable

D. Primitive variable

E. None of the above

15. Most relationships between tables are?

A. Independent

B. Dependent

C. ID-dependent

D. Non-ID–dependent

E. None of the above

CHAPTER 4

Creating and Managing Tables and Relations

n Entity Relationship Model (ER Model) or Entity Relationship Diagram (ERD) defines the tables, views, and relationships between them. MySQL Workbench uses the ER Model to describe these diagrams.

The relationships in ER Model diagrams show what's related to what and their cardinality. A 0..1 or 1..1 cardinality typically points to a table holding a primary key, and a 0..* (alternate syntax of *) or 1..* points to the table holding a foreign key.

MySQL Workbench treats ERDs as *Enhanced Entity Relationship Models (EERs)*. It's, as Shakespeare penned, much ado about nothing. Whether we use EER or ERD in the book, the concept is the same. I use EER from this point forward to simplify and align the language with the software.

You'll see how to create a simple EER Model in this chapter, as follows:

- Opening and saving files
- Creating tables and views
    - Add tables
    - Add columns
    - Add indexes
    - Add foreign keys
    - Add views
- Creating relationships

The three sections of this chapter have a number of illustrations that walk you through the process of creating an EER Model. It should be simple and straightforward as you understand the abbreviations and organizations of the software.

Opening and Saving Files

This chapter focuses on using the Data Modeling element of the MySQL Workbench software. It's in the middle of the form that opens when you launch the application. As you can see in the following screen shot, there's no existing model yet. An existing model displays inside the box below the *Open Existing EER Model* label.

You have four initial options with the Data Modeling element. You can open an existing EER Model when one exists, create a new EER Model, create a new EER Model from an existing database (known as backward engineering), or create a new EER Model from an existing SQL script.

The lack of an existing model means you'll need to click the file symbol with an overlaying plus symbol or the *Create New EER Model* link.

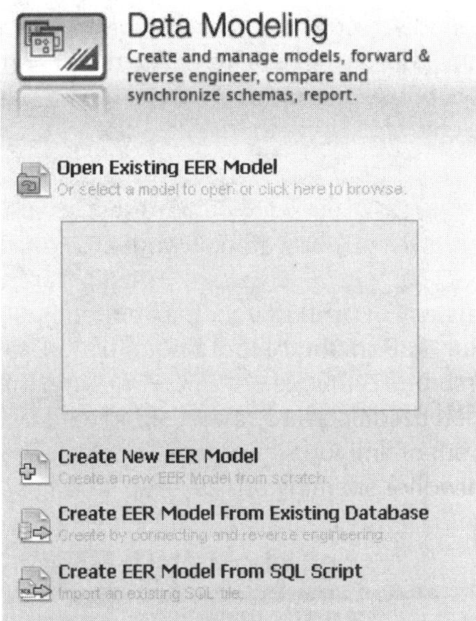

It launches the following screen, which is where you'll create an EER.

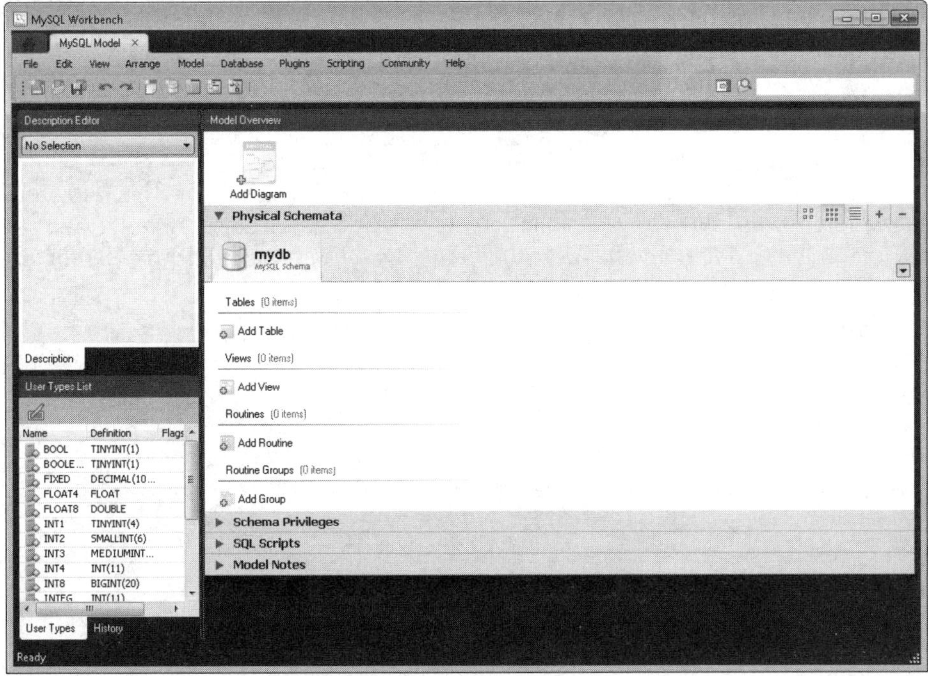

Whenever you work with software, the temptation is to just bang away on the keyboard, creating content, and then save it when you've got something meaningful. Succumbing to this natural tendency carries a risk. Sometimes the software fails to write the temporary file and you lose all the work you've done. I recommend that as soon as you open the file, you save it. Click the File menu item, and the following drop-down list appears. Choose *Save Model* to save the empty file. Alternatively, you can hold down the CTRL and S keys to save the file.

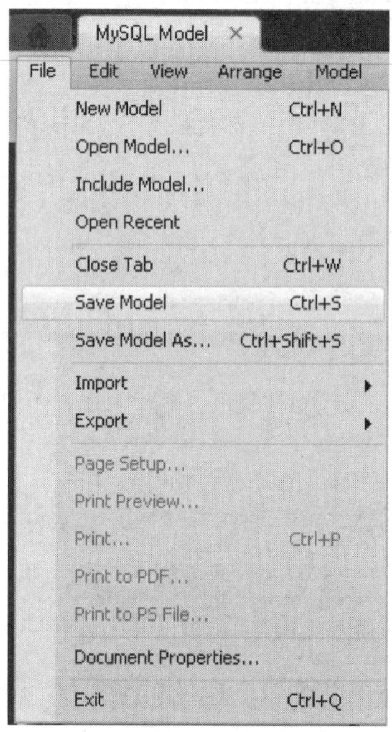

This file-choosing process opens a dialog to the operating system. The following illustration is from a Windows installation of the product. I'm saving the `MySQL.mwb` file in the C:\Program Files\MySQL5518\MySQL Server 5.5\data folder (or directory) by clicking the *Save* button.

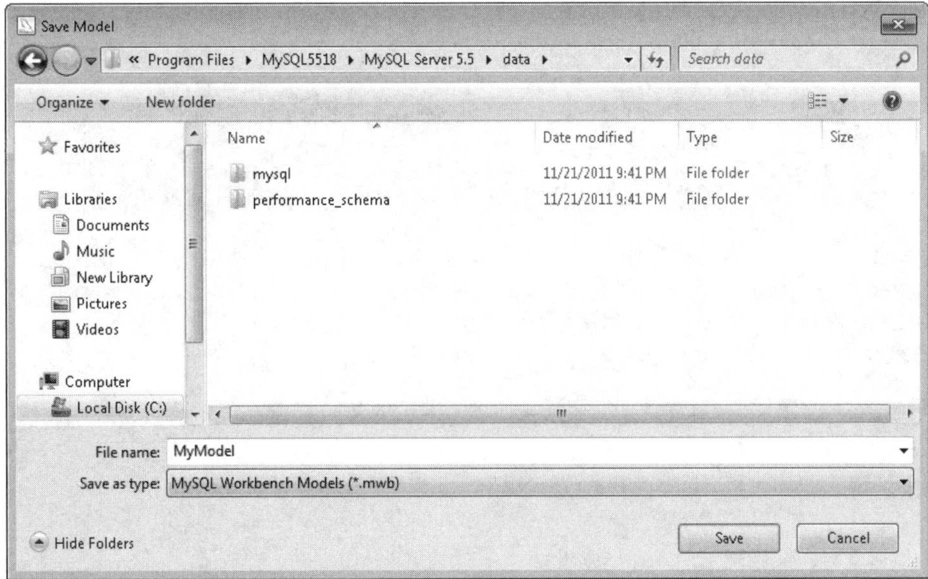

You now have a MySQL Workbench file, but it lacks any of the elements for an EER diagram. You reduce unexpected file loss by saving the container file. Taking this precaution, you can prevent the loss of any design work between opening a new file and saving the file, which does happen occasionally.

Creating Tables and Views

Before creating the new EER Model, you should inspect the MySQL Model menu bar in the following illustration. Scrolling through the drop-down menus gives you a quick idea about the many things that you may do with the MySQL Model component. Some options, like *Database, Plugins, Scripting, Community,* and *Help,* all contain enabled links. Other options, like *File, Edit, View,* and *Model,* have most options enabled, and the *Arrange* menu options are all gray-scaled because they're unavailable in an empty model.

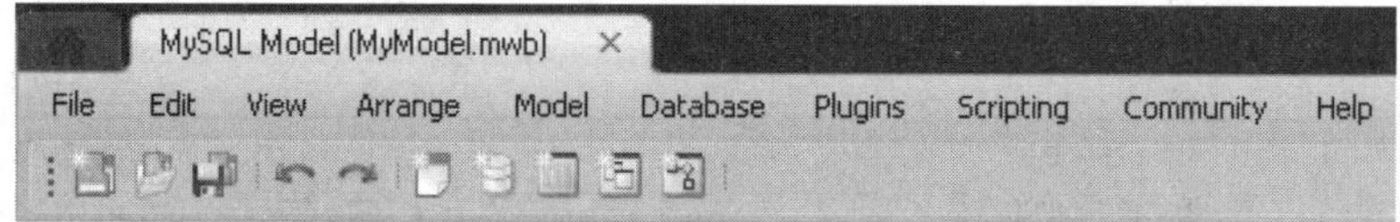

Most of your initial work is in the *Model Overview* panel, which is to the right of the *Description Editor* and *User Types List* panels shown in the next illustration. The menu has been stripped away from the illustrations so that you can focus on the area you're working in.

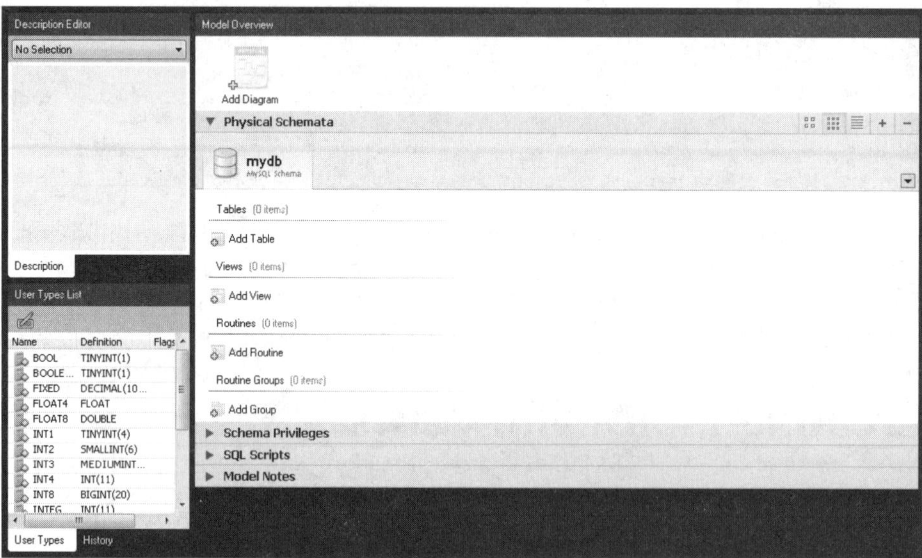

You have five activity options in the *Model Overview* panel. They are adding a diagram, managing the physical schemata (the oversized word for tables and views), schema (or database) privileges, SQL scripts, and Model Notes.

Add Tables

Click the *Add Table* option in the Physical Schemata section of the following illustration. It displays the next screen with placeholders for table name, collation, engine, and comments. The generic name is `table1`, and you should replace it with a lowercase string table name. You should accept the schema default (typically in a community edition, it's latin1) from the drop-down list unless you require a different collation method. The engine is preselected as InnoDB, and you should leave it that way unless you need to use another database engine. The comment field should hold a brief description of what the table holds.

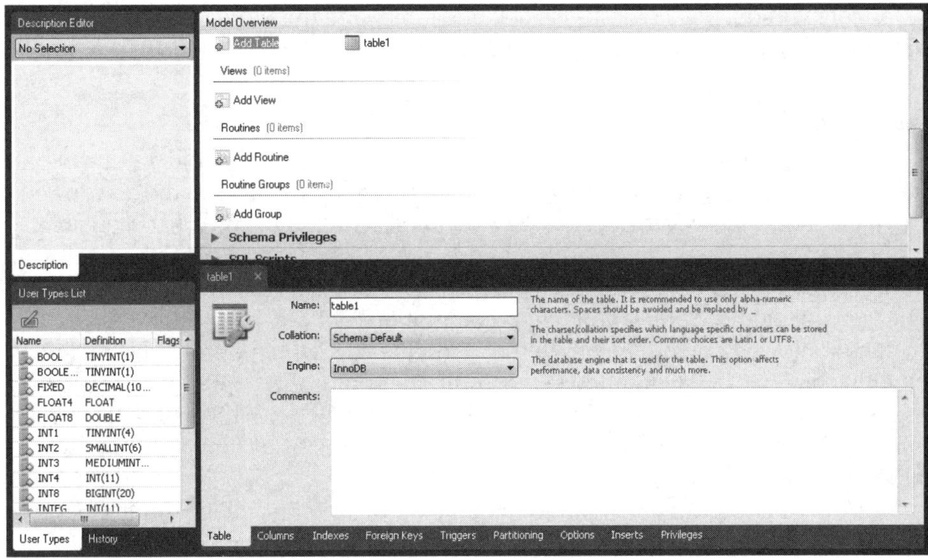

Use the following values shown in the next illustration to create the `application_user` table for this example. You should note that the topmost table tab changes to the new table name and you see a table added in the list of tables. Along the bottom of the table view, you have a series of options for the table, such as *Table, Columns, Indexes, Triggers, Partitioning, Options, Inserts,* and *Privileges*. The illustration is displaying the *Table* view of the selected `application_user` table.

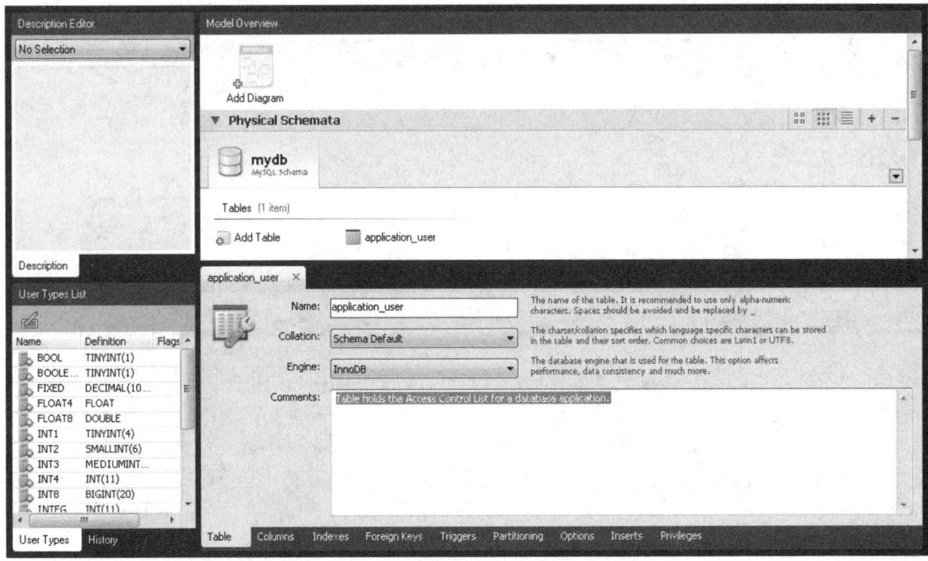

A table without any columns isn't a valid table, and therefore you should add at least one or more columns to the `application_user` table.

Add Columns

Columns are position specific at the time you create the table and hold a value of only one data type. You do have the option of moving them up or down in the drawing within the model, however, because the structure isn't set until you create the table.

The ANSI standard states all columns are *null allowed* or *nullable* by default, and only Microsoft SQL Server violates this practice. In the Microsoft SQL Server Management Studio (SSMS), you'll find columns are *not null* by default.

A null-allowed column means you can insert a row without providing a value for a nullable column. Null-allowed columns are often called optional because the insertion or update of values is at the user's (really developer's) discretion. Not-null columns are *mandatory,* which means any insert or update statement must provide values to those columns.

Click the bottom *Columns* tab to define columns for this table. You'll see the following:

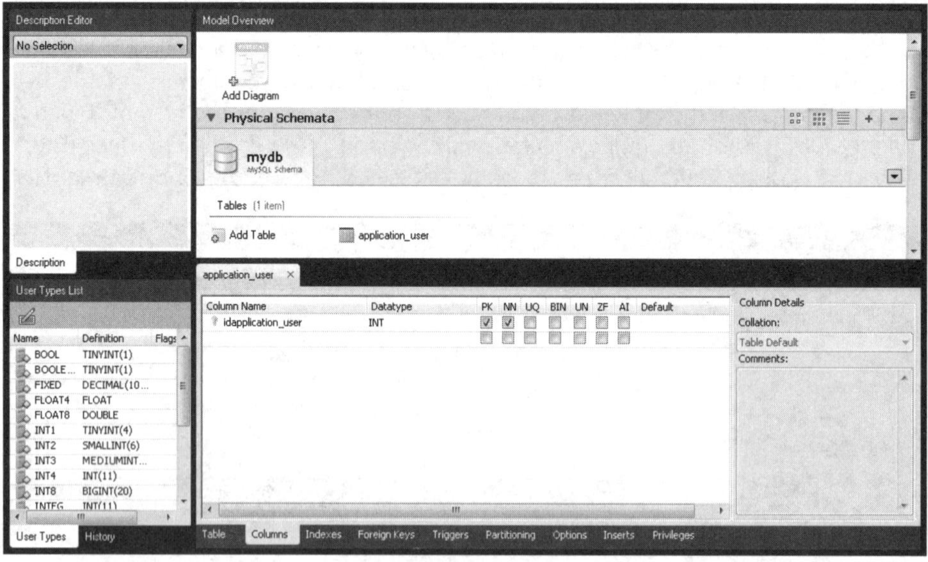

Originally, MySQL Workbench created the first column name automatically. The default column name combined a literal value of "id" and the table name. Most developers weren't fans of this convention and immediately changed the default column name to the table name plus an `_id` suffix, like the one shown in the following diagram. MySQL Workbench no longer provides a default column.

I recommend you create the first column with the table name plus `_id` suffix so that it holds a surrogate key value.

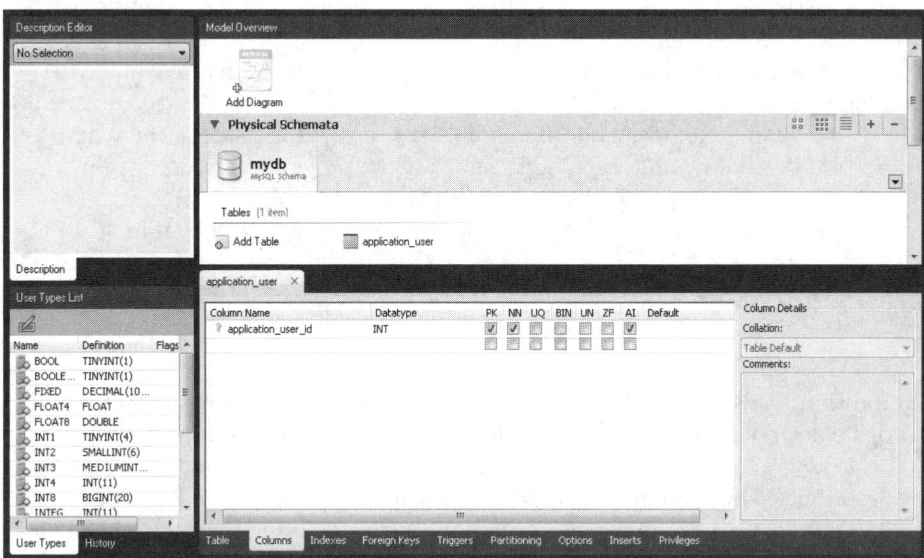

There are seven keys that you use in MySQL Workbench to designate the behavior of columns. Table 4-1 defines these keys.

Key	Meaning
PK	Designates a primary key column.
NN	Designates a not-null column constraint.
UQ	Designates a column contains a unique value for every row.
BIN	Designates a `VARCHAR` data type column so that its values are stored in a case-sensitive fashion. You can't apply this constraint to other data types.
UN	Designates a column contains an unsigned numeric data type. The possible values are 0 to the maximum number of the data type, like integer, float, or double. The value 0 isn't possible when you also select the PK and AI check boxes, which ensures the column automatically increments to the maximum value of the column.
ZF	Designates zero fill populates zeros in front of any number data type until all space is consumed, which acts like a left pad function with zeros.
AI	Designates `AUTO_INCREMENT` and should only be checked for a surrogate primary key value.

TABLE 4-1. *Column Attributes*

Who-Audit Columns

Who-Audit columns exist in tables to qualify when the data is created or last updated. At a minimum, there are four columns—two that hold foreign key values that point to the application's *Access Control List* (ACL) table, and two columns that hold timestamps.

Who-Audit columns can also qualify who ran a batch process and when. Two additional columns are added to track batch programs that update the row—they are the `batch_updated_by` and `batch_update_date` columns. Sometimes a designer adds a timestamp column to the table; it should always contain a timestamp value equal to the datetime value stored in the other Who-Audit date columns.

You should also check the AI check box when you change the name of the surrogate key column. The default leaves it unchecked, and that is unwise for surrogate keys in a MySQL database. You should also click the `UN` and `AI` check boxes for all surrogate key columns. The `UN` check box makes the surrogate key a positive number starting with 1, and the `AI` check box enables `AUTO_INCREMENT` behaviors.

You probably note the check boxes to the right of the column name—Table 4-1 qualifies their meanings. They may also have a default value. Default values are limited to strings or numbers.

Along with the key values you have column data types, listed under the *Datatype* column in the *Column* tab view for the table. You click the data type and have two options—auto-complete while typing the name of the data type and a drop-down box. All variable-length strings, or `VARCHAR` data types, have no default size value. You must provide a value by entering your desired size between the parentheses.

The next illustration shows how you highlight and select a `DATETIME` data type from the drop-down box. The `DATETIME` data type is ideal for Who-Audit columns like the `CREATION_DATE` and `LAST_UPDATE_DATE` columns. That's because they hold values within the time epoch and record the date-time stamp of inserts and updates.

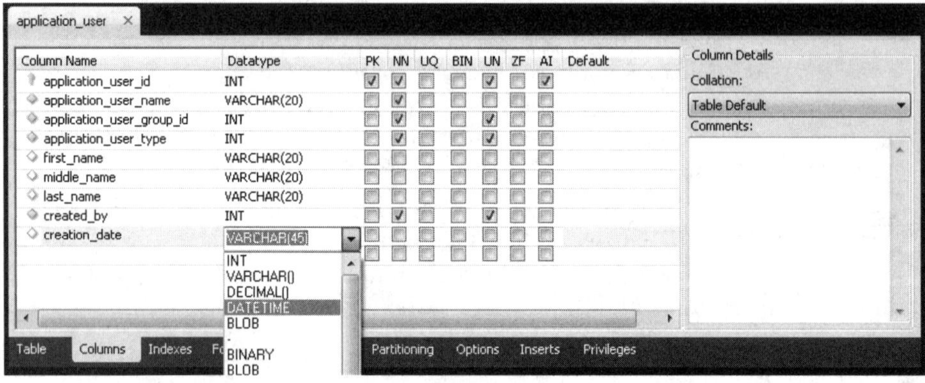

After checking all the correct key values for the table, you should see the following under the *Columns* tab:

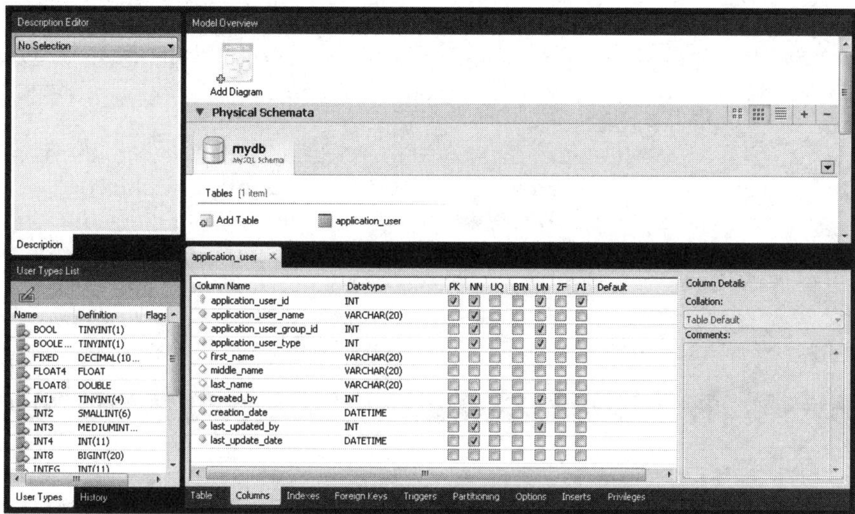

Having entered all the table's columns, you should now create indexes.

Add Indexes

Indexes enable you to search table data sets faster. There are restrictions on how to best use indexes, and the best-performing indexes are typically unique indexes.

When you click the *Indexes* tab at the bottom of the `application_user` table's model detail, you see the following screen. The `PRIMARY` index name relates to the primary key column or columns.

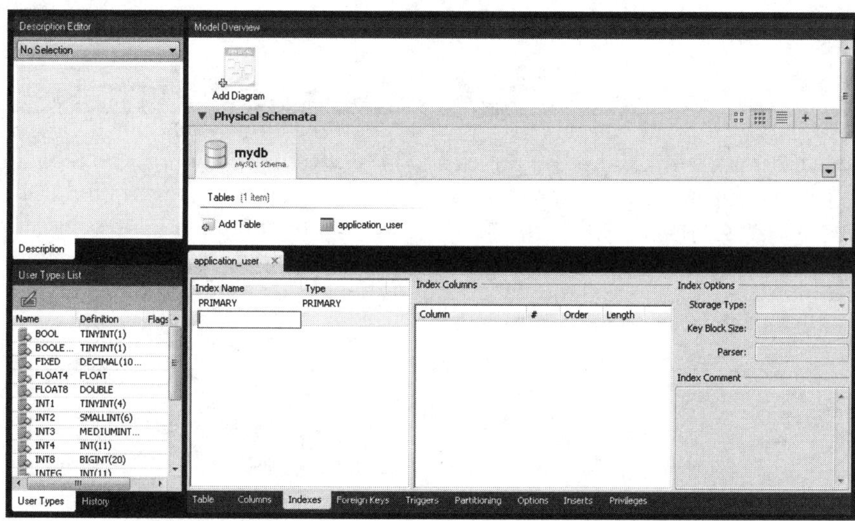

It is recommended that you always use surrogate keys as the primary key column, but the recommendation carries an assumption. As discussed in Chapter 3, the surrogate and natural keys should have a one-to-one mapping. The natural key supports queries and DML (Data Manipulation Language commands—`INSERT`, `UPDATE`, and `DELETE`) statements that work with unique rows, and the surrogate key should be chosen as the primary key. The single-column primary key serves as a reference for foreign key columns.

The next screen shows check marks next to the three natural key columns—`application_user_name`, `application_user_group_id`, and `application_user_type`. You should create an index by combining the surrogate key column with the three natural key columns. The surrogate key column should lead the index. You should also create another unique index of only the natural key. Together these keys ensure that queries and statements run effectively whether the `WHERE` clause uses the external or internal identifier to find the row.

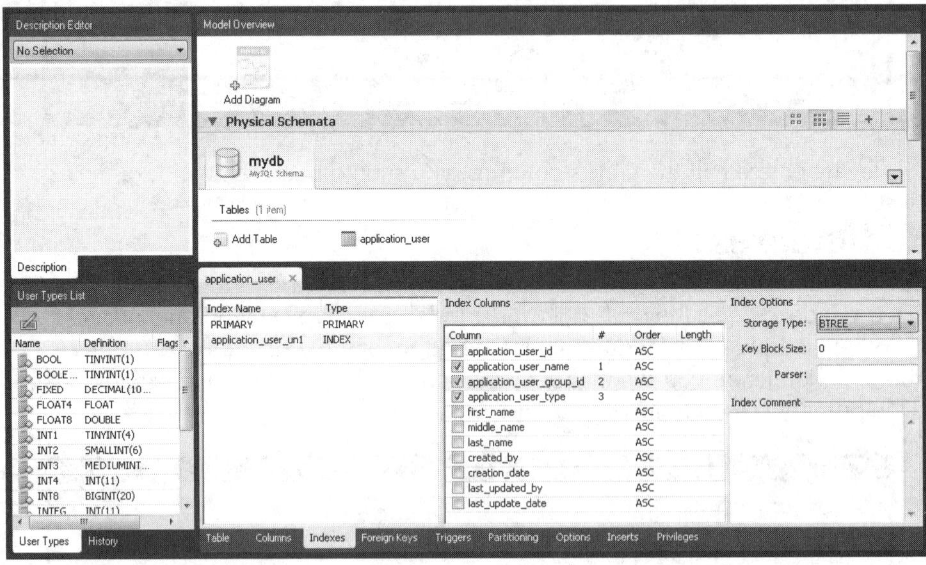

The first unique index speeds queries and DML statements that rely on the natural key columns. The second index optimizes the performance of joins run through matches of the primary key through a foreign key in another table.

This approach to table design assumes you know that MySQL uses an 80-character unique index. Sometimes you must choose substrings of the variable-length columns to ensure you can fit these in a single index.

A design like this gives you three unique indexes on the `application_user` table. Two serve key purposes in finding rows faster through the index than through a full table scan. The full table scan is expensive in both computing time and resources, and should be avoided whenever possible.

The `application_user` table is an ACL table, and a column like the `application_type` generally maps to a common lookup table. The following screen capture shows such a `common_lookup` table. This type of table resolves uniqueness by the combination of three values—a table name, column name, and type value. The respective columns are checked as a unique index for the table.

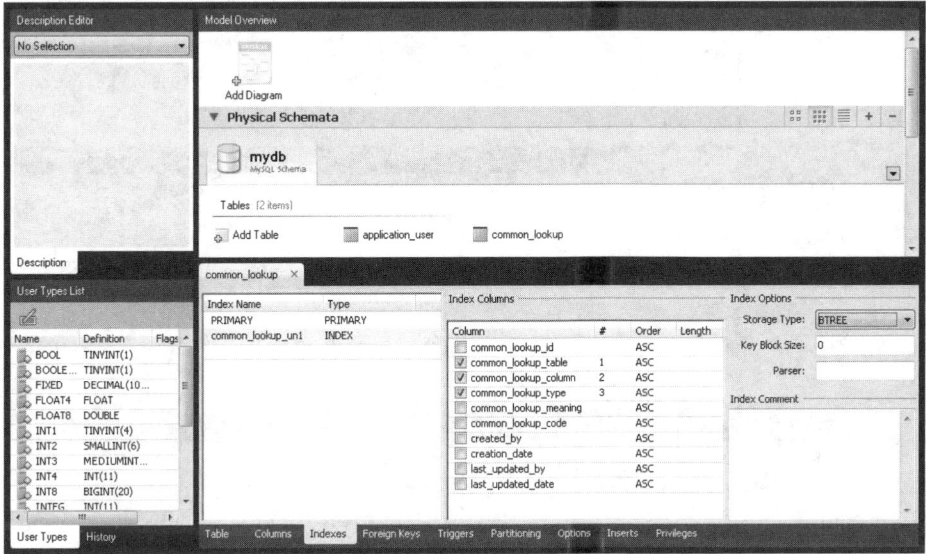

A lookup table is a generalization that holds lists of values that support end-user selections. The following example uses a combination of the `common_lookup_table` and `common_lookup_column` columns to identify sets of values for drop-down lists. The end user selects a value from the list to identify a unique row, which returns a `common_lookup_id` surrogate key value.

You would insert the `common_lookup_id` value as a foreign key in any table that wants to link to a descriptive value held by the `common_lookup` table. The foreign key links to the primary key, and through it to the description and vice versa. You'll use the `common_lookup` table as the reference table in the "Add Foreign Keys" section.

Add Foreign Keys

You click the *Foreign Keys* tab to add foreign key constraints, and you see the following displayed window. It's important to note that these types of constraints are not available in certain MySQL engines. They're clearly available in the MySQL 5.5 and forward InnoDB engine.

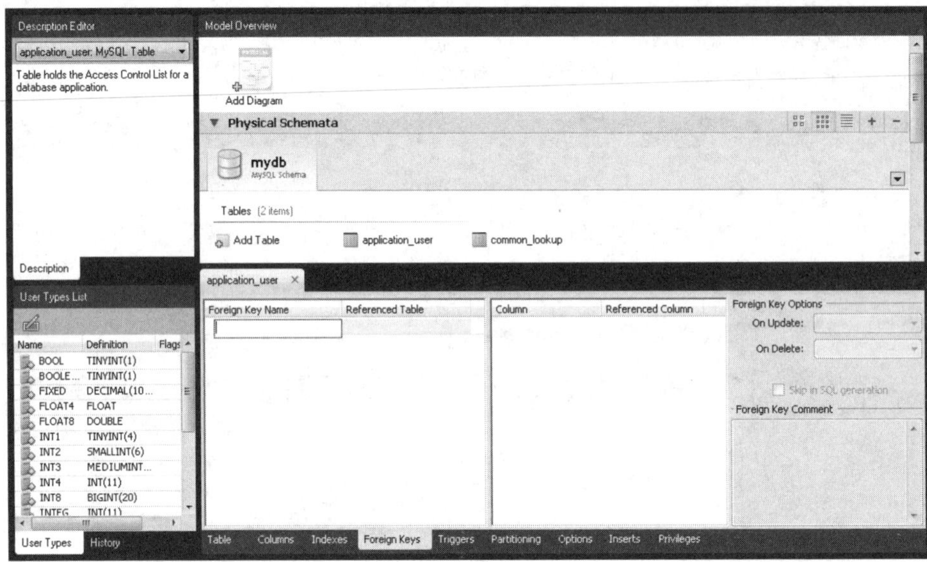

The first thing you do is enter a foreign key constraint name. The following example uses `application_user_fk1`, which lets us naturally handle more than one foreign key column in a table.

Next, you click the drop-down box and pick an available reference table, as shown in the following illustration. A reference table is where the foreign key column will look to find the primary key column. At this point you have two reference table options—the `application_user` and `common_lookup` tables.

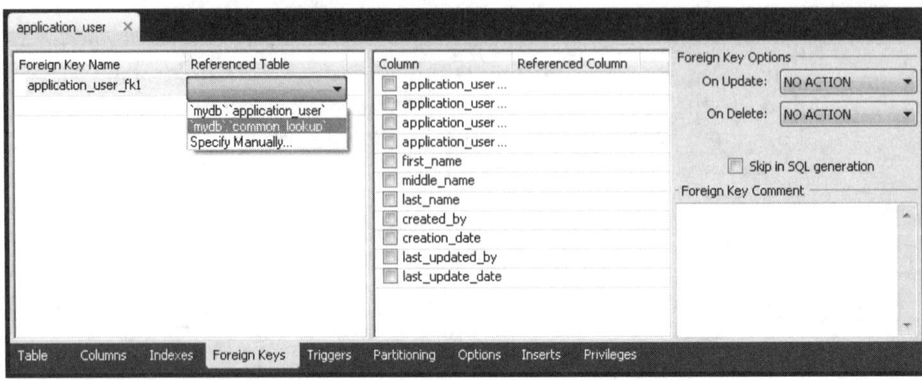

The example chooses the `common_lookup` table, which is represented by the `mydb` database name, a dot, and the `common_lookup` table name. `mydb` is the database where these designed tables exist.

After you pick the reference table, you need to check which column or columns hold the foreign key value. A foreign key is a column or set of columns that holds a copy of a primary key in another table, or a copy of the same table. A primary-to-foreign key match resolves equijoins (or, more naturally, equality joins) between tables and produces what you should know as a result set from a query.

The example uses single-column surrogate keys as the primary and foreign key columns. The `application_user_group_id` column holds the foreign key. The foreign key points to a single primary key column that holds the surrogate key value, and the primary key is found in the `common_lookup` table.

The next step requires that you pick the primary key column from the list of columns for the `common_lookup` table. The surrogate key column is the one with the table name followed by an `_id` suffix. As you can see in the next illustration, that is the `common_lookup_id` column.

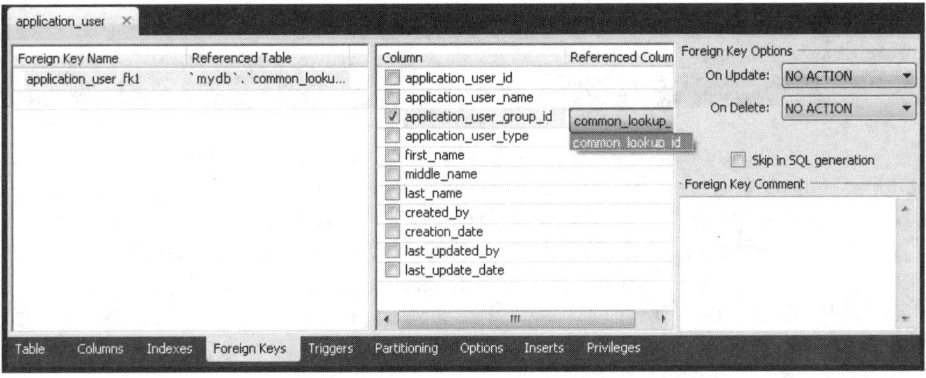

You would repeat the set of steps again for the `application_user_type` column, which also finds its parent (or primary key) in the `common_lookup` table. This is an *external reference relationship*. These two foreign keys point from a foreign key column in one table to a primary key in another table, and they're the most common type of foreign key constraint.

Alternatively, you can have a foreign key value that points to another column in the same table. This type of relationship is a *self-reference relationship*. You have two self-reference relationships in your `application_user` table. One maps the relationship of the `created_by` column to the `application_user_id` column, and the other maps the relationship of the `last_updated_by` column to the `application_user_id` column. The following illustration provides an example of a self-reference relationship.

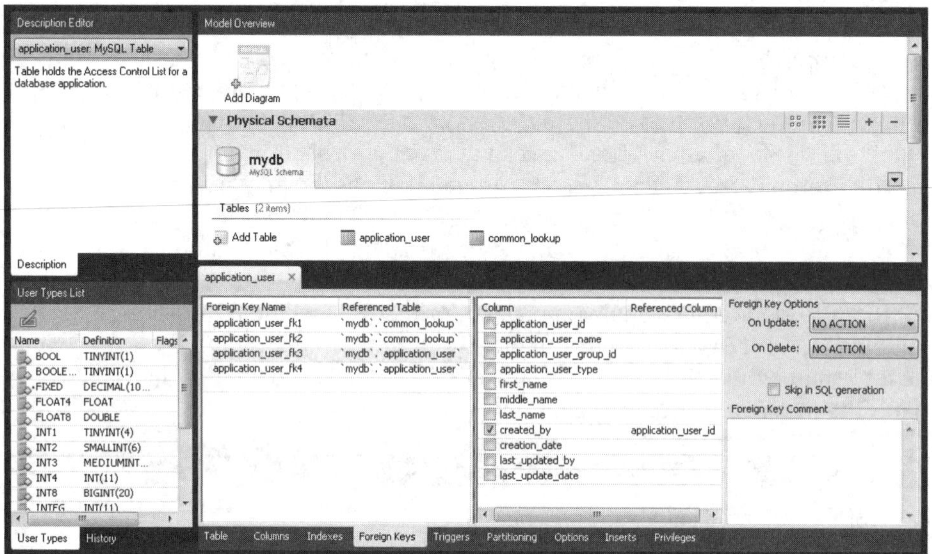

After creating the basic primary-to-foreign key mapping, you have the option of defining database triggers, partitioning designs, storage options, data insertions, and privileges. Database triggers require in-depth knowledge of how to write scripts that create SQL/PSM (Persistent Stored Modules) code blocks, and you can find those instructions in Chapters 14 and 15 of the *Oracle Database 11g and MySQL 5.6 Developer Handbook* (Oracle Press, 2011). Partitioning instructions can also be found in Chapter 6 of the same reference. Storage options and privileges are issues for the database architect.

Sometimes the data designer must seed data in the database model. In those cases, they may do so through the Inserts tab rather than write a separate script file. The reason is simple: MySQL Workbench supports creating an implementation script that includes inserting seeded data sets. The file is generated from the model into an independent script, which is covered in Chapter 11.

Creating Views

Views are stored queries or `SELECT` statements. They can return a subset of one table or a superset of several tables. They can include columns from tables or columns that are the result of expressions, such as string operations, numeric or date math results, or calls to built-in or user-defined functions. Some views are view-only (read-only), and others are updateable (read-write).

Immediate below the *Add Tables* icon in the *Model Overview* window, you have the *Add Views* icon. You can double-click the icon to add a view, and you get the following window.

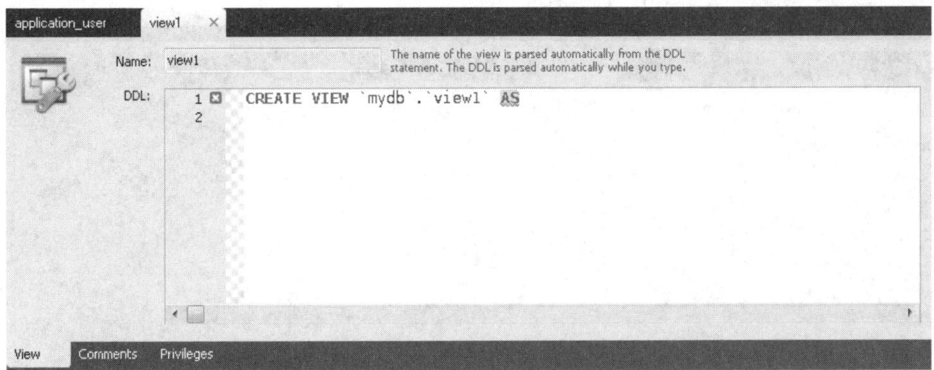

The name of the view in the dialog is set by the code in the window frame. This means that as you replace the generic `view1` with your view's name, the property name automatically updates, as you can see in the following illustration.

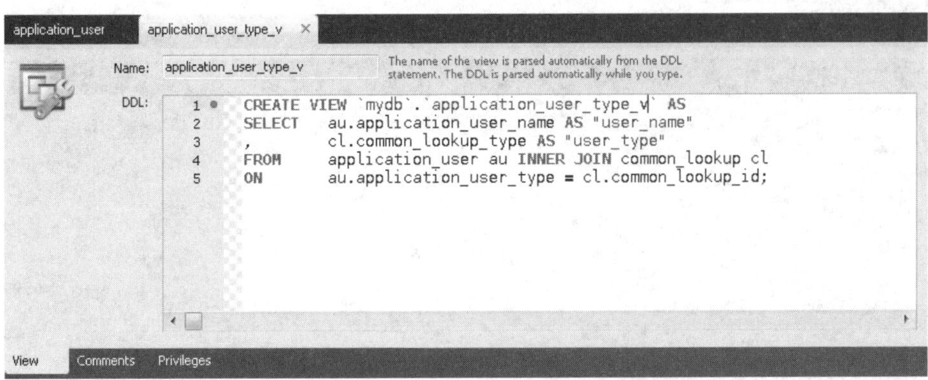

Views can contain joins between tables, views, or values from built-in functions, known as expressions. These, unfortunately, must be built manually with a knowledge of joins and views, which you may find in Chapter 11 of *Oracle Database 11g and MySQL 5.6 Developer Handbook*.

Creating Routines

Routines are stored functions and procedures. You add them by clicking the *Add Routines* icon in the *Model Overview* window. New routines look like the following screen shot, an empty shell.

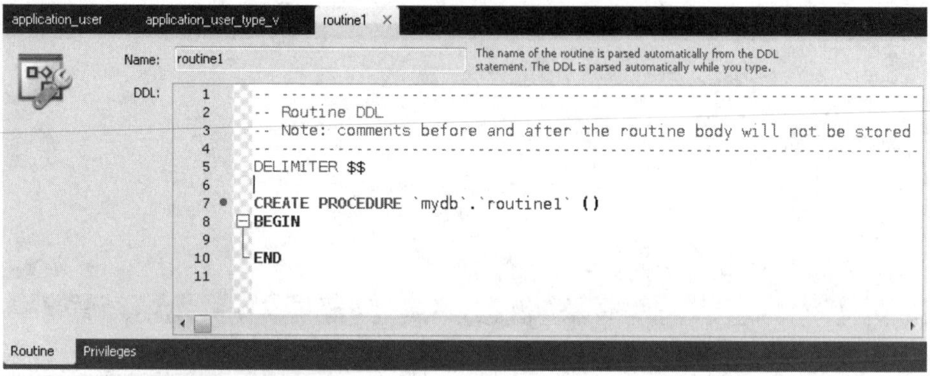

```
application_user   application_user_type_v   routine1 ×
Name: routine1
The name of the routine is parsed automatically from the DDL statement. The DDL is parsed automatically while you type.
DDL:
-- ----------------------------------------------------------------------
-- Routine DDL
-- Note: comments before and after the routine body will not be stored
-- ----------------------------------------------------------------------
DELIMITER $$

CREATE PROCEDURE `mydb`.`routine1` ()
BEGIN

END

Routine   Privileges
```

You must implement the routine by writing it in SQL/PSM-compliant syntax. An example of a simple function that returns a session-level variable follows in the next image.

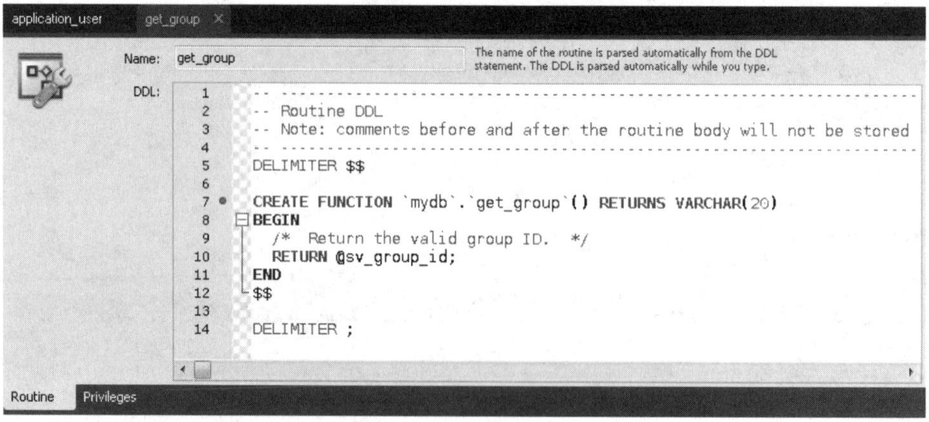

```
application_user   get_group ×
Name: get_group
The name of the routine is parsed automatically from the DDL statement. The DDL is parsed automatically while you type.
DDL:
-- ----------------------------------------------------------------------
-- Routine DDL
-- Note: comments before and after the routine body will not be stored
-- ----------------------------------------------------------------------
DELIMITER $$

CREATE FUNCTION `mydb`.`get_group`() RETURNS VARCHAR(20)
BEGIN
  /*  Return the valid group ID.  */
  RETURN @sv_group_id;
END
$$

DELIMITER ;

Routine   Privileges
```

After implementing the routine, you can add a view that uses the function inside it to create a striped view of the data, like the following:

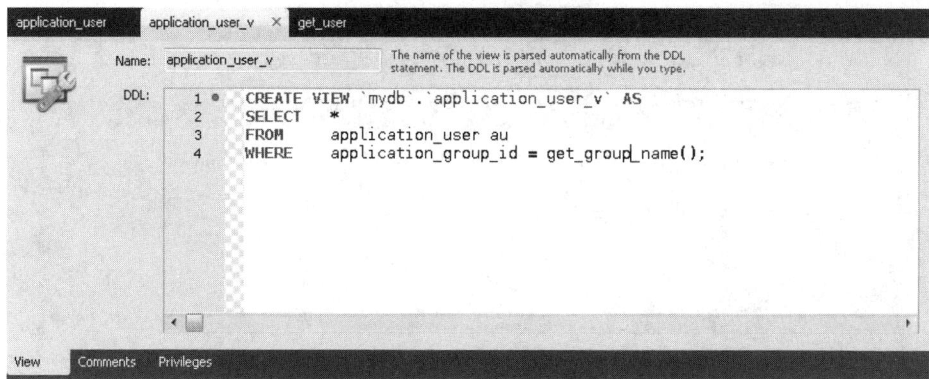

You've seen how to implement tables, views, and routines in this section. The next section teaches you how to graphically display relationships, like the primary-to-foreign key relationship described earlier in this section.

Creating Relationships

You define relationships by creating an association between primary and foreign key columns. These relationships fall into three logical binary relationships—they are one-to-one, one-to-many, and many-to-many. The many-to-many relationship can't have a physical implementation, and requires that you implement an intermediary table (known as an association or transaction table). The association table effectively holds a copy of the two tables' primary keys, and together these two foreign keys effectively map the many-to-many logical relationship by implementing two one-to-many relationships.

In a one-to-many relationship, the one side holds the primary key and the many side holds the foreign key. One-to-one relationships are slightly more complex because you must pick one to hold the primary key and the other a foreign key.

At the top of the *Model Overview* window, click *Add Diagram* to create an ERD. It launches an EER Diagram palette and canvas like the following:

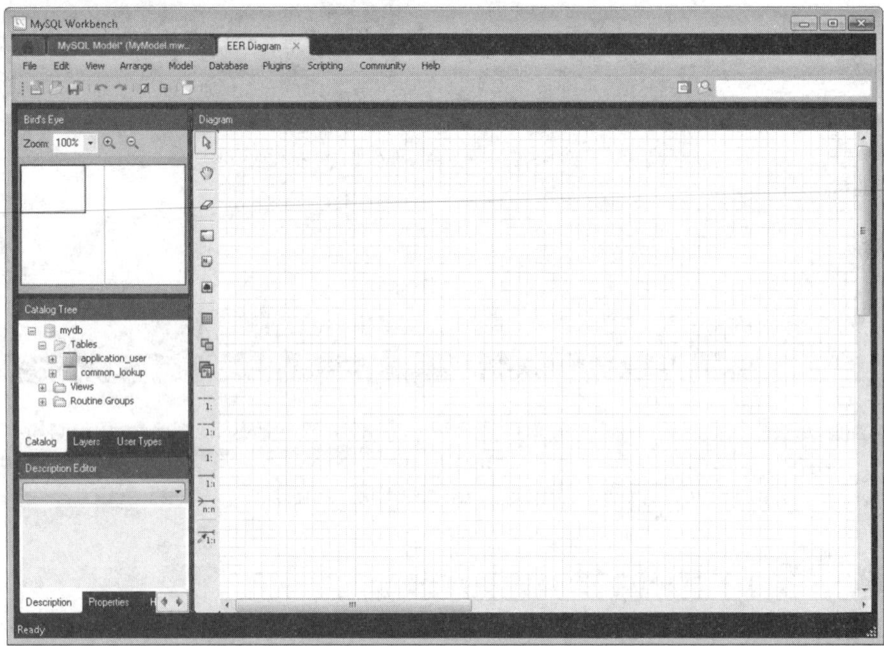

You can click the tables you want in the *Catalog Tree* window and drag them to the *Diagram* canvas. It's the easiest way to create an EER diagram like the following. Drag the `application_user` table to the *Diagram* canvas, like this.

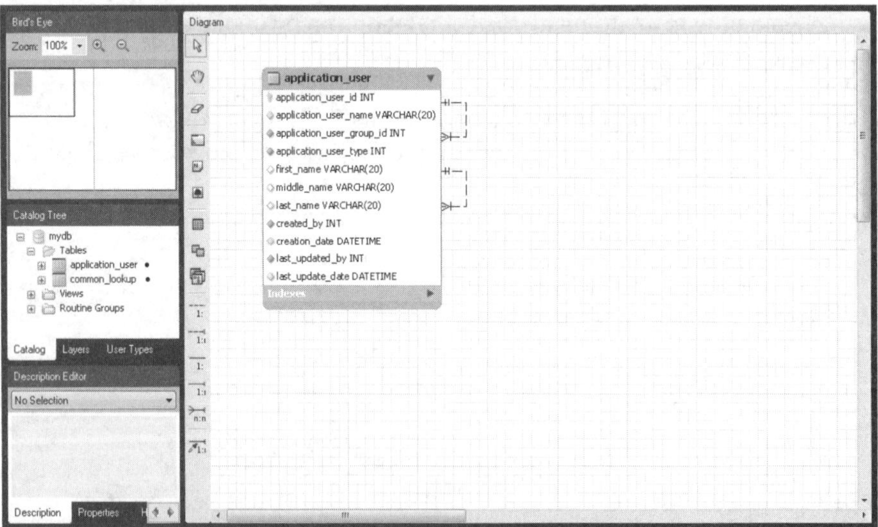

On the right of the `application_user` table, there are two dashed lines. Each dashed line represents a self-reference relationship. The side with two perpendicular lines has a cardinality of one to one, while the side with a perpendicular line and greater-than symbol has a cardinality of one to many. Essentially, the self-referencing relationship line would be read as any application user (found in one row) may create one to many instances (or rows) in the `application_user` table.

Dragging the `common_lookup` table from the *Catalog Tree* window to the *Diagram* canvas, you see one-to-many relationships between the `application_user` and `common_lookup` tables. The relationship between the two tables states that an application user's group ID references only one row in the `common_lookup` table and the application user's type is defined as only one row in the `common_lookup` table.

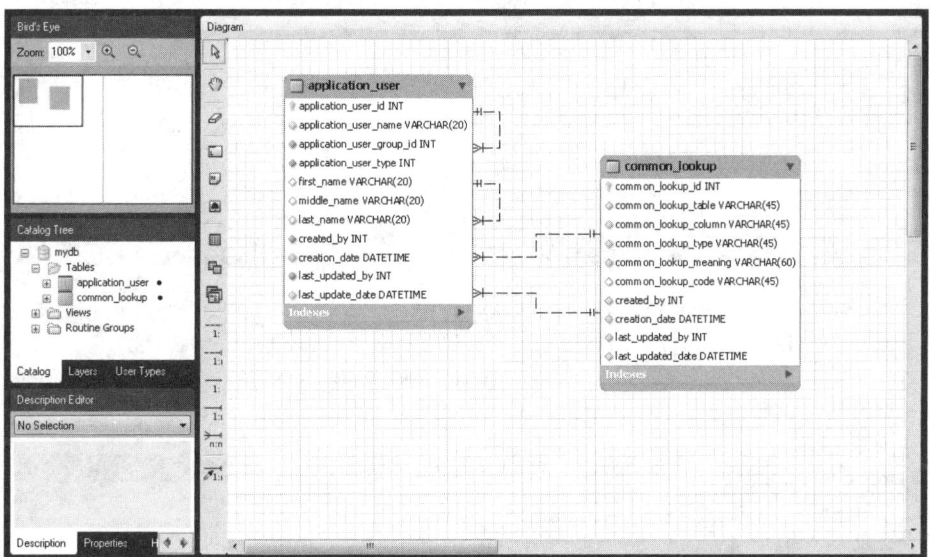

If you double-click any relationship, it displays a separate window for a foreign key constraint. For example, clicking the self-reference relationship at the top right of the `application_user` table highlights the relationship and displays a separate window for the foreign key constraint.

The constraint window has two tabs, and the default display is *Relationship*. In the *Relationship* tab of the constraint window, the *Fully Visible* radio button is checked, as shown in the following screen capture.

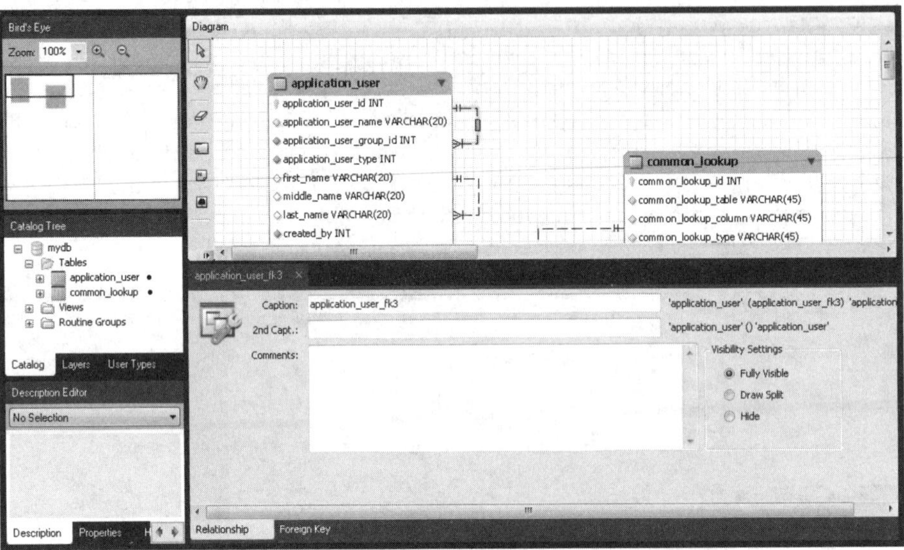

Sometimes the relationship lines are a distraction when you have too many tables in the Diagram canvas. Clicking the *Draw Split* radio button leaves the terminating elements of the relationship but removes the connecting lines, as shown in the next screen capture.

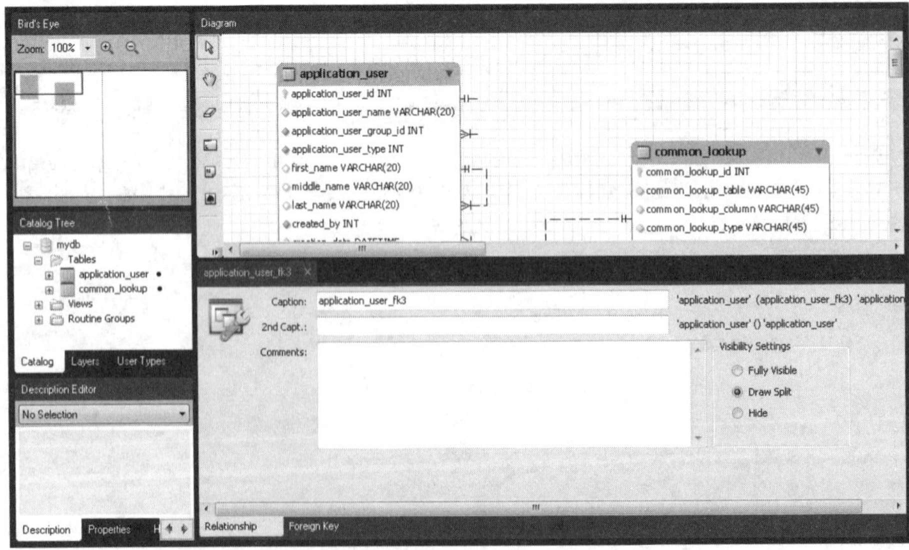

Clicking the *Foreign Key* tab of the constraint window displays the columns involved in the relationship. It also qualifies the referencing and referenced table. The referencing table always holds the foreign key, and the reference table always holds the primary key. The next illustration demonstrates this.

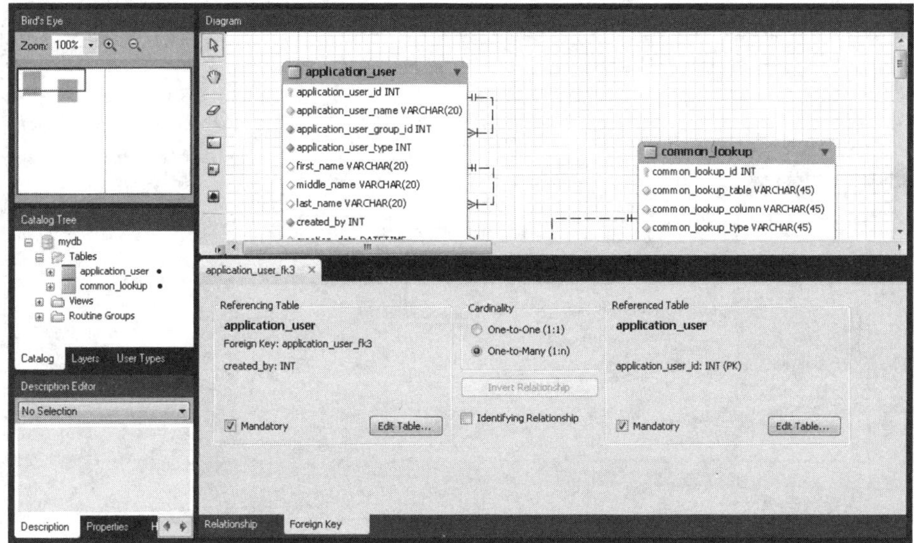

Adding foreign key constraints to the `common_lookup` table connects the Who-Audit columns to the `application_user` table's primary key. You would make the change by clicking the *Model* tab at the top of the application window, like those in the next screen shot.

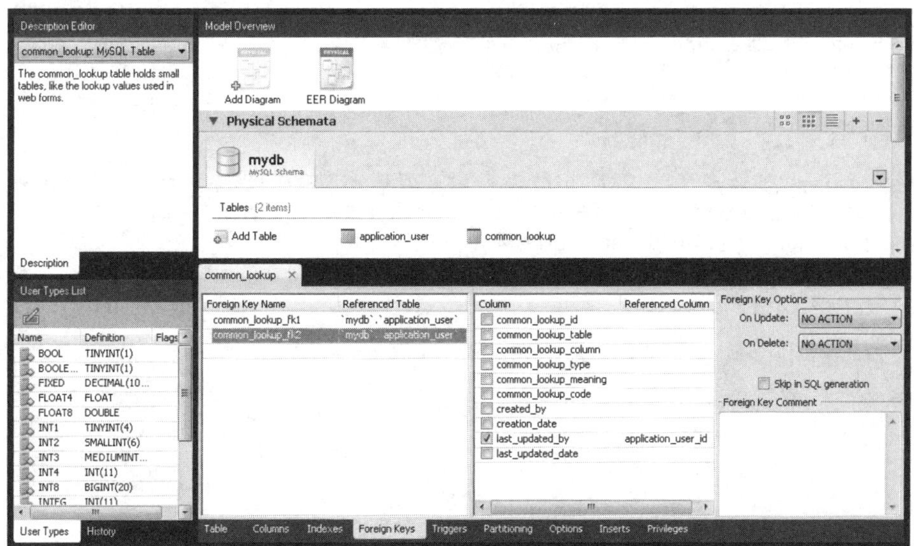

Clicking the *Diagram* tab again displays the modified EER. Clicking the two *Indexes* bars displays all indexes and relationships, as shown in the following screen capture.

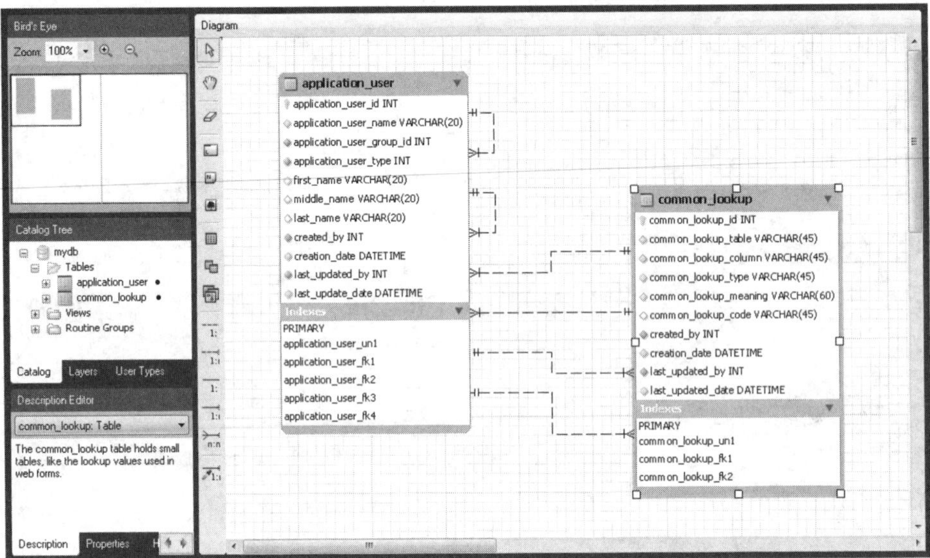

This segment has shown how to add and modify relationships.

Summary

This chapter explained how to open and save files, create tables and views, and create relationships through foreign key constraints. You should be positioned to use the tool to produce an EER diagram.

Mastery Check

The mastery check is a series of true or false and multiple choice questions that let you confirm how well you understand the material in the chapter. You may check Appendix A for answers to these questions.

True or False:

1. ___The `PK` key stands for a primary key column.
2. ___The `BIN` key stands for a case-insensitive column.

3. ___The `AI` key can only be checked for a primary key column.

4. ___The `UN` key represents a unique constraint.

5. ___The `NN` key represents a not-null constraint.

6. ___The Model Overview lets you add diagrams.

7. ___Each table in the Model Overview supports tabs for foreign keys.

8. ___The Model Overview lets you add tables.

9. ___The EER diagram has dashed lines to illustrate relationships between primary and foreign keys.

10. ___Relationships have two tabs, and the Foreign Key tab lets you set a self-identifying relationship.

Multiple Choice:

11. MySQL Workbench should use which of the following to set a primary key column with an unsigned integer or double? (Multiple answers are possible.)

    A. A `PK` key

    B. A `UQ` key

    C. A `UN` key

    D. An `AI` key

    E. A `NN` key

12. The diagramming tool supports which of the following? (Multiple answers are possible.)

    A. Column names

    B. Column types

    C. Relationships

    D. Cardinalities

    E. All of the above

13. Relationships may have which of the following cardinalities? (Multiple answers are possible.)

A. One-to-one

B. Zero-to-one

C. Zero-to-many

D. One-to-many

E. Many-to-many

14. What window displays the list of tables, views, and routine groups? (Multiple answers are possible.)

A. The Bird's Eye frame

B. The Catalog frame

C. The Description Editor frame

D. The Diagram frame

E. None of the above

15. The EER Diagram frame displays what? (Multiple answers are possible.)

A. Tables

B. Indexes

C. Routines

D. Non-ID-dependent relationships

E. All of the above

CHAPTER 5

Creating and Managing Routines

Routines are stored programs. Specifically, they're stored functions or procedures. There are three differences between functions and procedures in MySQL. Functions only take input or pass-by-value parameters, whereas procedures take input, input and output, and output-only parameters (any parameter with an output mode is a pass-by-reference parameter). Functions return a value and can be used inside queries or as right operands in assignments, but procedures can't do either. Procedures can contain `INSERT`, `UPDATE`, and `DELETE` statements, while functions can't.

MySQL Workbench assumes all routines are procedures and provides only that template when adding procedures. It also provides a procedure shell for definer rights program units, which are units that run inside a database, work with local data, and run with the privileges enjoyed by the user. The alternative to definer rights programs are invoker rights programs. Invoker rights programs work with the data in the current database rather than the same database, where they're defined and run with the privileges of the user calling them.

Invoker rights programs should be deployed in their own model, independently of the tables. You can create local views that point to the tables in another database, which lets you create the concept of synonyms (an Oracle database structure).

At present, there is only limited autocomplete functionality when writing stored routines. Therefore, it's recommended that you develop the routines externally, and then add them in their completed form. You can read more on writing MySQL routines in *Oracle Database 11g & MySQL 5.6 Developer Handbook*.

This chapter shows you how to create and modify routines, stored functions, and procedures. It shows you how to add, edit, and delete routines, and how to create, edit, and delete groups of routines. Rather than create separate sections for routines and groups of routines, they're in the same add, edit, and delete sections.

Adding a Routine

Adding a routine is very much like adding a table or view in the Model Overview. This section assumes that the USER table is in the ERD Model builder. You simply click the *Add Routine* option, as shown toward the bottom in the following illustration.

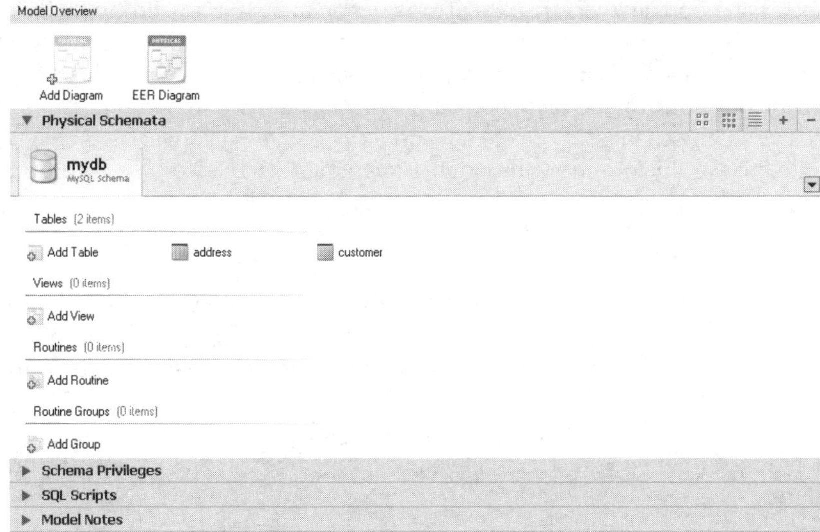

Adding a routine opens the Routine dialog box, as shown in the next illustration.

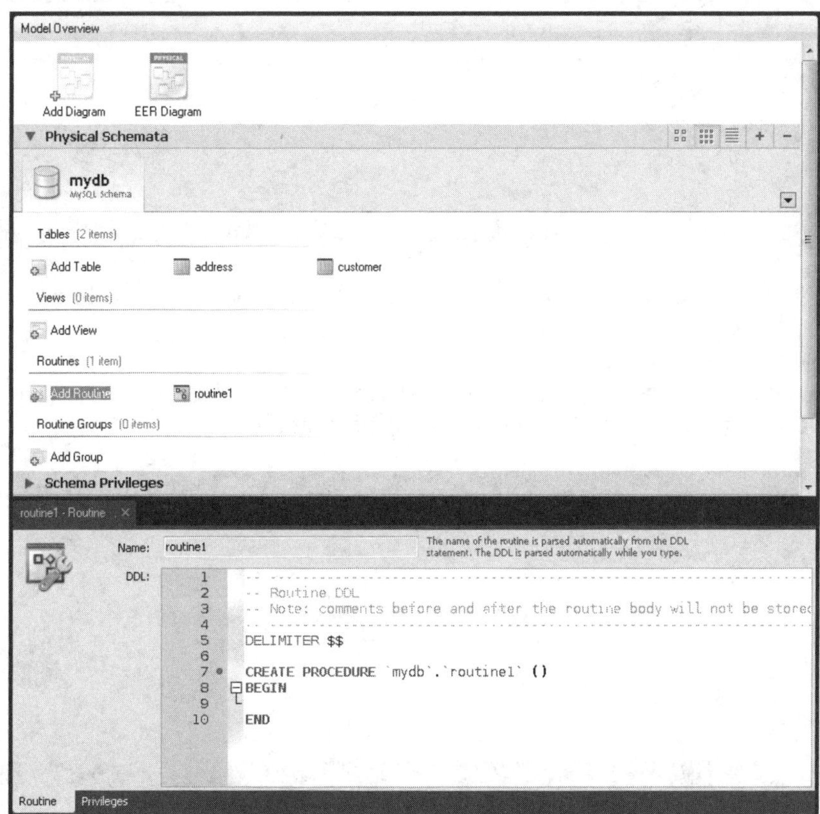

It seems appropriate to create a `HelloWorld` procedure as the first routine. Click in the *Name* field to enter a case-specific `HelloWorld`, and you'll immediately notice that you can't change the name there. You must click in the DDL field and change the name of the procedure in the definition, and then click anywhere outside of the DDL Field box to see the changes. Both the tab and routine names change.

While this would compile without any statements, it's best to provide at least one. Enter the following on line 9 in the `HelloWorld` – Routine DDL field:

```
SELECT 'Hello World!';
```

A drop-down list appears after you type the `SELECT` keyword for a list of functions. This behavior is a typical IDE (Integrated Development Environment) behavior known as auto-complete. It's available in any routine's DDL field for SQL statements.

After typing the `SELECT` statement, overwrite the *Routine* keyword in the comment line, and then you should have something like this as the HelloWorld procedure.

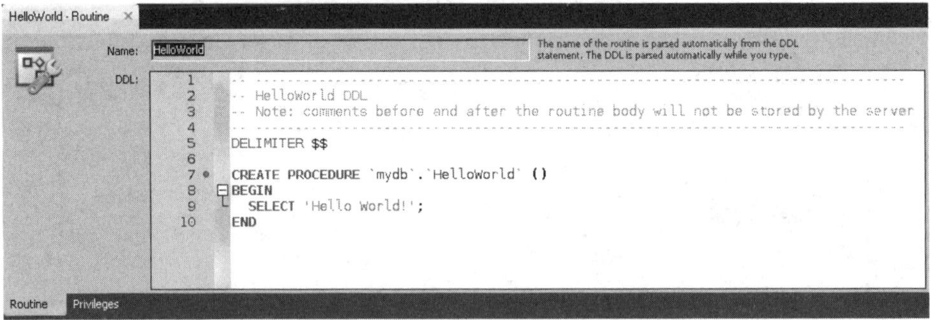

Other than writing the code modules, you only have the option to change the privileges for a stored routine. The process of managing users, groups, privileges, and roles is covered in Chapter 10.

Repeat the process by adding a `HelloThere` routine as a procedure. When you're done, it should look like the following illustration.

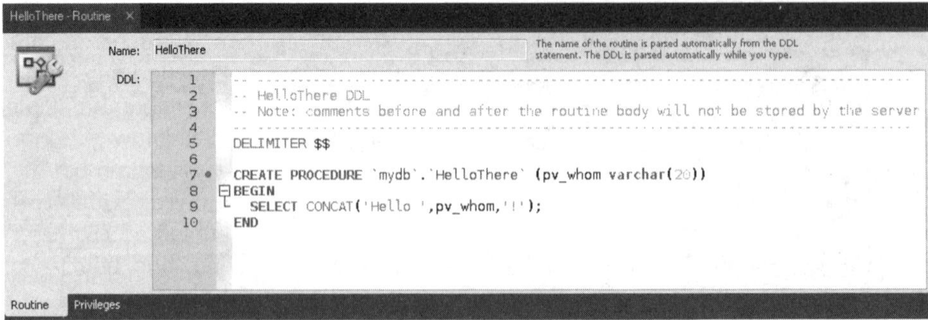

The difference between `HelloWorld` and `HelloThere` is that the latter takes a formal `pv_whom` parameter. The body of the procedure calls the MySQL `CONCAT` function to prepend a *Hello* and whitespace string and append an exclamation mark.

Both of these programs are trivial because they do very little of value. They do illustrate how to add and write procedure routines, and they help us when we create program groups.

You'll now create an additional table, two views, a procedure, and two related functions. The text for these is shown next. Inside the text you'll see the use of backward apostrophes (found below the tilde symbol on most keyboards). While the backward apostrophes aren't needed, they ensure things work well when you write script files, and they're automatically added by the MySQL Workbench in templates.

This section requires you to add the following table definition. Revisit Chapter 4 if you're not up to speed on doing so. This is an application user table:

```
CREATE TABLE 'application_user'
( 'user_id'  int(10) unsigned PRIMARY KEY AUTO_INCREMENT
, 'user_name'  varchar(20) NOT NULL
, 'user_role'  varchar(20) NOT NULL
, 'user_group_id'  int(10) unsigned NOT NULL
, 'user_type'  int(10) unsigned NOT NULL
, 'first_name'  varchar(20)
, 'middle_name'  varchar(20)
, 'last_name'  varchar(20)
, 'created_by' int(10) unsigned NOT NULL
, 'creation_date  datetime' NOT NULL
, 'last_updated_by'  int(10) unsigned NOT NULL
, 'last_update_date'  datetime NOT NULL
, CONSTRAINT natural_key UNIQUE (user_name)
) ENGINE='InnoDB' AUTO_INCREMENT=1 DEFAULT CHARSET='latin1';
```

You should seed it, eventually, with data. You'll add five rows when you get to Chapter 7, but if you can't wait, browse forward to it. These are the rows in a standard multiple-row `VALUES` clause (available in MySQL):

```
INSERT INTO 'application_user' VALUES
 ( null, 'potterhj', 'System Admin', 1, 1
 , 'Harry', 'James', 'Potter', 1, NOW(), 1, NOW())
,( null, 'weasilyr', 'Guest', 0, 1
 , 'Ronald', null, 'Weasley', 1, NOW(), 1, NOW())
,( null, 'longbottomn', 'Guest', 0, 1
 , 'Neville', null, 'Longbottom', 1, NOW(), 1, NOW())
,( null, 'holmess', 'DBA', 2, 1
 , 'Sherlock', null, 'Holmes', 1, NOW(), 1, NOW())
,( null, 'watsonj', 'DBA', 2, 1
 , 'John', 'H', 'Watson', 1, NOW(), 1, NOW());
```

It would be terrific to create only one view, but unfortunately, MySQL doesn't support SQL statements as views when they embed an inline query or runtime view in the `FROM` clause. That compels us as MySQL developers to create two views to have efficient code using the stored functions that we'll create later in this chapter.

The `function_query` view definition is what could have been written in a standard query as an inline view but can't be written in a view:

```
CREATE VIEW 'function_query' AS
SELECT    'get_login_id()' AS login_id
,         'get_group_id()' AS group_id;
```

The following view uses the other view inside it, which makes it dependent on the other view:

```
CREATE VIEW 'authorized_user' AS
SELECT   'au'.'user_id'
,        'au'.'user_name'
,        'au'.'user_role'
,         CONCAT('au'.'last_name'
          , ", "
          ,'au'.'first_name'," "
          , IFNULL('au'.'middle_name',"")) AS full_name
FROM     'application_user' au CROSS JOIN 'function_query' fq
WHERE    ('au'.'user_group_id' = 0
AND       'au'.'user_group_id' = 'fq'.'group_id'
AND       'au'.'user_id' = 'fq'.'login_id')
OR        'fq'.'group_id' = 1
OR       ('fq'.'group_id' > 1
AND       'au'.'user_group_id' = 'fq'.'group_id');
```

Having created the table and views, let's create the functions. Simply copy the following directly into a new routine. You should note that the semicolon is unnecessary after the `END` key word that terminates the program unit.

```
CREATE FUNCTION 'set_login'
( pv_login_name VARCHAR(20)) RETURNS INT UNSIGNED
BEGIN
  /* Declare a local variable to verify completion of the task. */
  DECLARE  lv_success_flag  INT UNSIGNED  DEFAULT FALSE;
  DECLARE  lv_login_id  INT UNSIGNED;
  DECLARE  lv_group_id  INT UNSIGNED;
  /* Declare a cursor to return an authorized user id. */
  DECLARE authorize_cursor CURSOR FOR
    SELECT   a.user_id
    ,        a.user_group_id
    FROM     application_user a
    WHERE    a.user_name = pv_login_name;
  /* Check whether the input value is something other than a null value. */
  IF pv_login_name IS NOT NULL THEN
    OPEN  authorize_cursor;
    FETCH authorize_cursor INTO lv_login_id, lv_group_id;
    CLOSE authorize_cursor;
    /* Set the success flag. */
```

```
    SET @sv_login_id := lv_login_id;
    SET @sv_group_id := lv_group_id;
    SET lv_success_flag := TRUE;
  END IF;
  /* Return the success flag. */
  RETURN lv_success_flag;
END
```

After creating the `set_login` function, you create the `get_login_id` and `get_group_id` functions. The functions return results that depend on session-level variables that are set by a prior call to the `set_login` procedure.

The `get_login_id` function is:

```
CREATE FUNCTION get_login_id() RETURNS INT UNSIGNED
BEGIN
  /* Return the success flag. */
  RETURN @sv_login_id;
END
```

The `get_group_id()` function is:

```
CREATE FUNCTION get_group_id() RETURNS INT UNSIGNED
BEGIN
  /* Return the success flag. */
  RETURN @sv_group_id;
END
```

You should now see the following in the Model Overview panel:

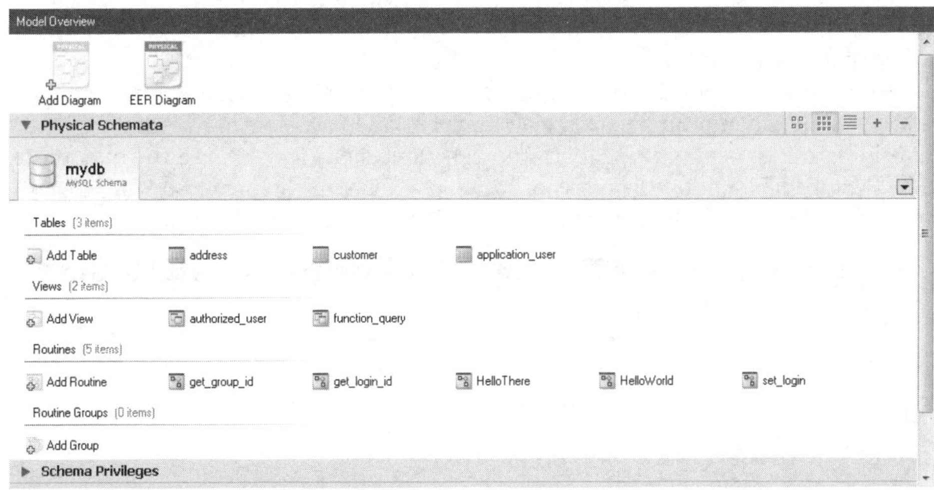

With the modules in place, you'll now create two groups. One is introductions, which contains the `HelloWorld` and `HelloThere` procedures. The other is security, which contains the `set_login`, `get_login_id`, and `get_group_id` functions.

Unlike the other objects, groups allow you to directly enter the group names in the field, as shown in the next illustration.

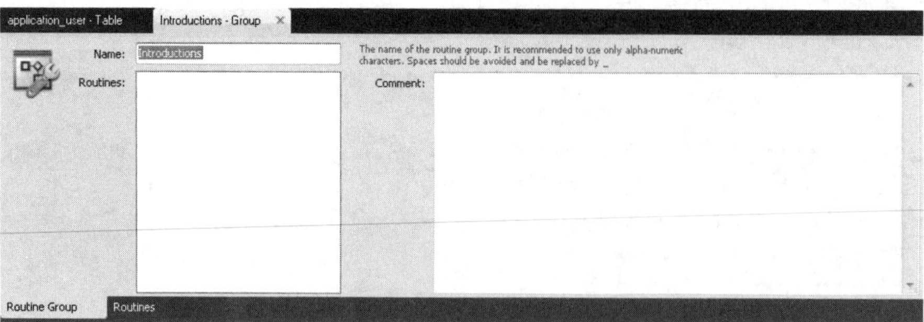

Nothing happens when you click in the routines field. That's because you need to click on the *Routine* tab to attach routines to a group. You copy the contents of the `HelloWorld` and `HelloThere` procedures into the routines section. The names are added to the routine group, and the routine name where the code was originally written is updated to the name of the stored function or procedure. That means once you copy the routine code into a routine group, there is still only one copy. Routine groups only hold a reference to the routines defined in the routine section.

Routine groups allow you to collect related stored programs. Any routine can be placed in one or more groups. Both groups then refer to the same program unit, and a change to the routine is thereby universal against all routine groups that hold a reference to it.

You may opt to place a routine group in its own database. The idea of storing routines in a different database makes their maintenance and backup schedule different from the transactional data.

It's generally a good idea to separate the user access point from the stored programs and stored programs from the data. Unfortunately, it's impossible to say what the best practice is at this point because there's no persistent cache for routines. The rumor is that MySQL will introduce a persistent cache in a future release, after MySQL 5.6.

The routine group should look like the following illustration.

Introductions - Group

```
-- ------------------------------------------------------------------
-- Introductions Group Routines
-- ------------------------------------------------------------------
DELIMITER $$

CREATE PROCEDURE `mydb`.`HelloWorld` ()
BEGIN
  SELECT 'HelloWorld';
END
$$

CREATE PROCEDURE `mydb`.`HelloThere` (pv_whom varchar(20))
BEGIN
  SELECT CONCAT('Hello ',pv_whom,'!');
END
$$
```

Routine Group | Routines

This now gives you a group of routines, and you can delete the individual ones created earlier, which you'll do in the subsequent section on deleting routines.

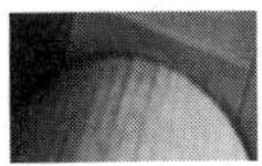

TIP

Forgetting the delimiter value of $$ at the bottom of the first or subsequent function or procedure raises an exception.

Some might think there's a problem with the Introductions routine group because it doesn't include syntax to conditionally drop the routines. There aren't any conditional drops of routines because MySQL Workbench manages that implicitly for you.

That means you shouldn't try to add conditional drop statements like those on lines 6 and 14 in the following screen capture. If you do add them as some audit of what's written, MySQL Workbench won't save them because it knows that it's already implicitly managing it for you.

Introductions - Group

```
1  -- ------------------------------------------------------------------------
2  -- Introductions Group Routines
3  -- ------------------------------------------------------------------------
4  DELIMITER $$
5
6  DROP PROCEDURE IF EXISTS `mydb`.`HelloWorld`$$
7
8  CREATE PROCEDURE `mydb`.`HelloWorld` ()
9  BEGIN
10   SELECT 'HelloWorld';
11 END
12 $$
13
14 DROP PROCEDURE IF EXISTS `mydb1`.`HelloThere`$$
15
16 CREATE PROCEDURE `mydb`.`HelloThere` (pv_whom varchar(20))
17 BEGIN
18   SELECT CONCAT('Hello ',pv_whom,'!');
19 END
20 $$
```

Routine Group | Routines

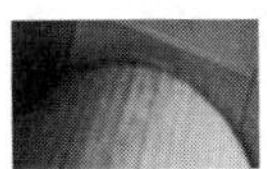

TIP

Conditional drop statements don't belong in routine groups.

Clicking the bottom *Routine Group* tab displays the list of routines in the group, as shown in the following illustration.

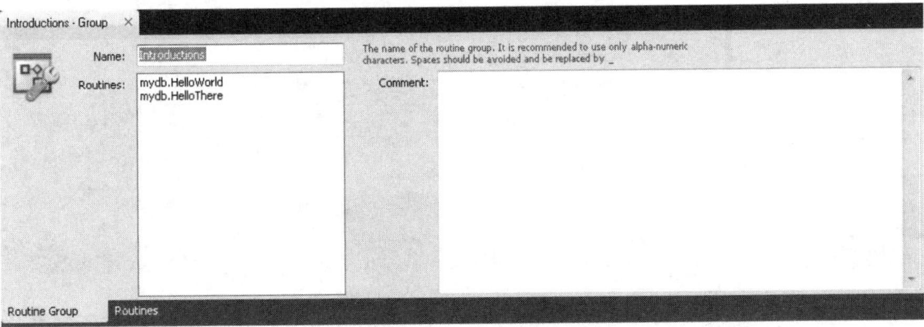

You should now move the `set_login` procedure and the `get_login_id` and `get_group_id` functions into a security group. This leaves you with the following in the Security routine group, as shown in the next illustration.

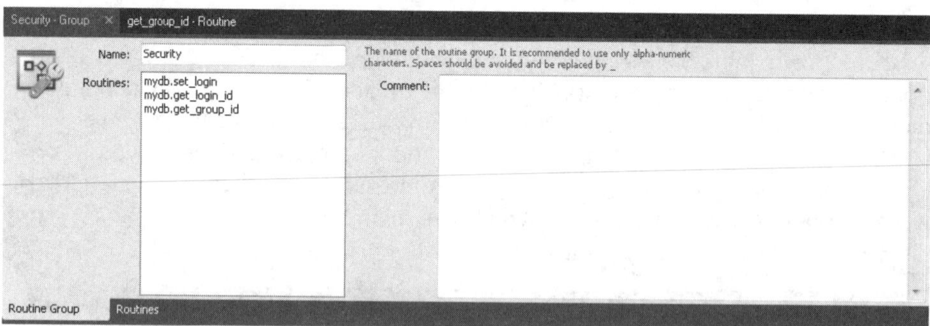

After making those changes, you should see the following in the Model Overview panel. You'll remove the stand-alone routines from the Model Overview in the "Removing a Routine" section later in the chapter.

You should see an illustration like the following when you click back on the Model Overview panel. It's important to understand that the MySQL Workbench architecture only maintains a single copy of any named routine in a model. That means you change all routine groups when you create, edit, or remove a routine assigned to one or more routine groups.

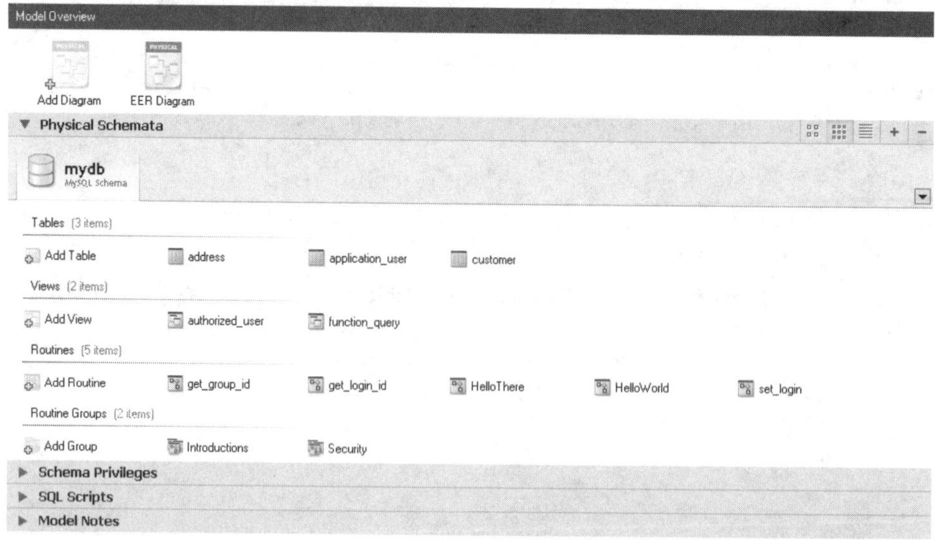

This segment has shown how to add routines, modify routine templates, and create groups of routines.

Editing a Routine

There are three ways to edit a routine after you've created it. You can double-click the routine to edit it. Alternatively, you can use the menu by navigating to the *Edit* option, or you can right-click the routine to use the floating menu. The menu option requires navigating to the Edit menu, where you choose *Edit Selected.* Choose *Edit Routine* from the floating menu.

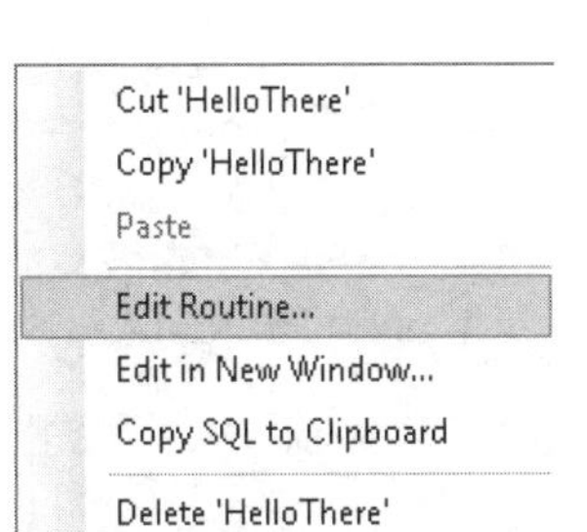

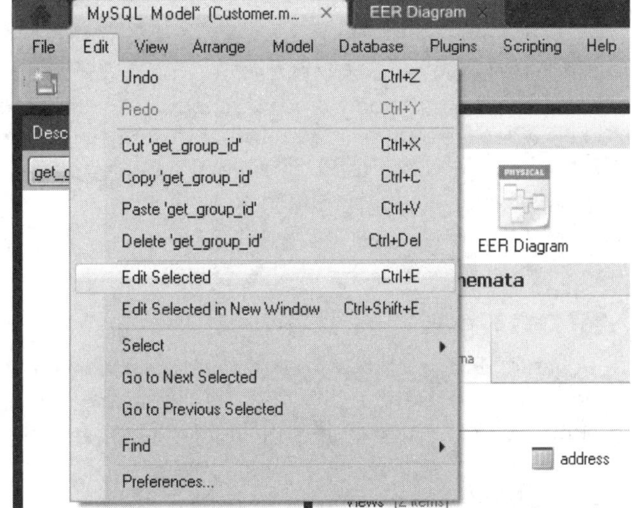

Closing the routine window saves any supported changes and surrenders control to the widget to remove an incompatible code. Since there's only one copy of the named function or procedure (routine), any change may impact all routine groups that hold a link to the routine.

The same rules apply to editing routine groups because it simply updates the routine with the name of the function or procedure. There is an exception in this behavior that's important to note. If you change a named routine from a function to a procedure or vice-versa, you create a new routine in the routine section rather than update the existing routine. The same behavior isn't true when you edit the routine in the routine section. Changing a function to a procedure or vice-versa in the routine section doesn't create a new block of code; it merely replaces what you had previously.

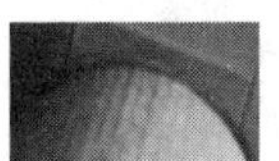

TIP

Make all modifications in the routines sections, add when you want to add, and remove when you want to remove. It provides better controls.

Removing a Routine

Like the three ways to remove a routine, you have three primary ways to delete a routine. You can click the routine and then press the DELETE key. Alternatively, you can use the menu by navigating to the *Edit* option. Right-clicking the routine lets you see the floating menu. Select the *Delete* option inside the drop-down or floating menu.

All of these methods permanently remove the routine from the model and from any routine group that referred to it. You also have a fourth way to remove a routine. This way requires you to delete the routine's text from the routine group. It automatically removes the routine if it isn't used by another group from the routine section. Moreover, you should always remove routines from the routine section when they exist in only one routine group. The only time you should delete the text of a routine from a routine group is when the routine is referenced by more than one routine group.

The same approach used to remove routines applies to removing a group, with one exception. Deleting a routine group deletes all referenced routines when they're not also referenced by another routine group.

Summary

This chapter explained how to open and save files, create tables and views, and create relationships through foreign key constraints. You should be positioned to use the tool to produce an EER diagram.

Mastery Check

The mastery check is a series of true or false and multiple choice questions that let you confirm how well you understand the material in the chapter. You may check Appendix A for answers to these questions.

True or False:

1. ___Routines can be added to any database.
2. ___A procedure is a routine.
3. ___A function isn't a routine.
4. ___Conditional drop statements should always be inside routine groups.
5. ___You should never use a backward apostrophe (`) symbol in a routine.
6. ___The Model Overview lets you add routines.

7. ___The Model Overview lets you delete routines.

8. ___The Model Overview lets you add tables.

9. ___Moving a routine into a routine group means you lose that functionality if you remove the stand-alone routine.

10. ___You must click the *Routines* tab to add, edit, or delete routines from routine groups.

Multiple Choice:

11. MySQL Workbench supports which of the following routines? (Multiple answers are possible.)
    - **A.** An object type
    - **B.** A user-defined data type
    - **C.** A function
    - **D.** A procedure
    - **E.** A nested inline view

12. Which of the following let you edit a routine? (Multiple answers are possible.)
    - **A.** The Edit menu followed by the *Edit Selected* option
    - **B.** The floating menu followed by *Edit Routine*
    - **C.** A right-click to launch a context menu and an editing session
    - **D.** A double-click to launch an editing session
    - **E.** Click the routine icon and use a hotkey combination of CTRL-E

13. Which of the following let you delete a routine? (Multiple answers are possible.)
    - **A.** Select the routine and then click the Edit menu followed by the *Delete routine_name* option
    - **B.** The Edit menu followed by the *Delete routine_name* option
    - **C.** A right-click to launch a floating menu, where you can delete a routine
    - **D.** Click the routine and then press the DELETE key
    - **E.** Click the routine icon and use a hotkey combination of CTRL-DELETE

14. What symbol must follow the `END` keyword of a routine? (Multiple answers are possible.)

    A. A semicolon

    B. A colon

    C. The character set that follows the `DELIMITER` keyword

    D. A semicolon and the character set that follows the `DELIMITER` keyword

    E. Nothing

15. Which of the following doesn't belong in a routine group? (Multiple answers are possible.)

    A. A `DROP` statement

    B. A conditional `DROP` statement

    C. Stored functions

    D. Stored procedures

    E. User-defined data types

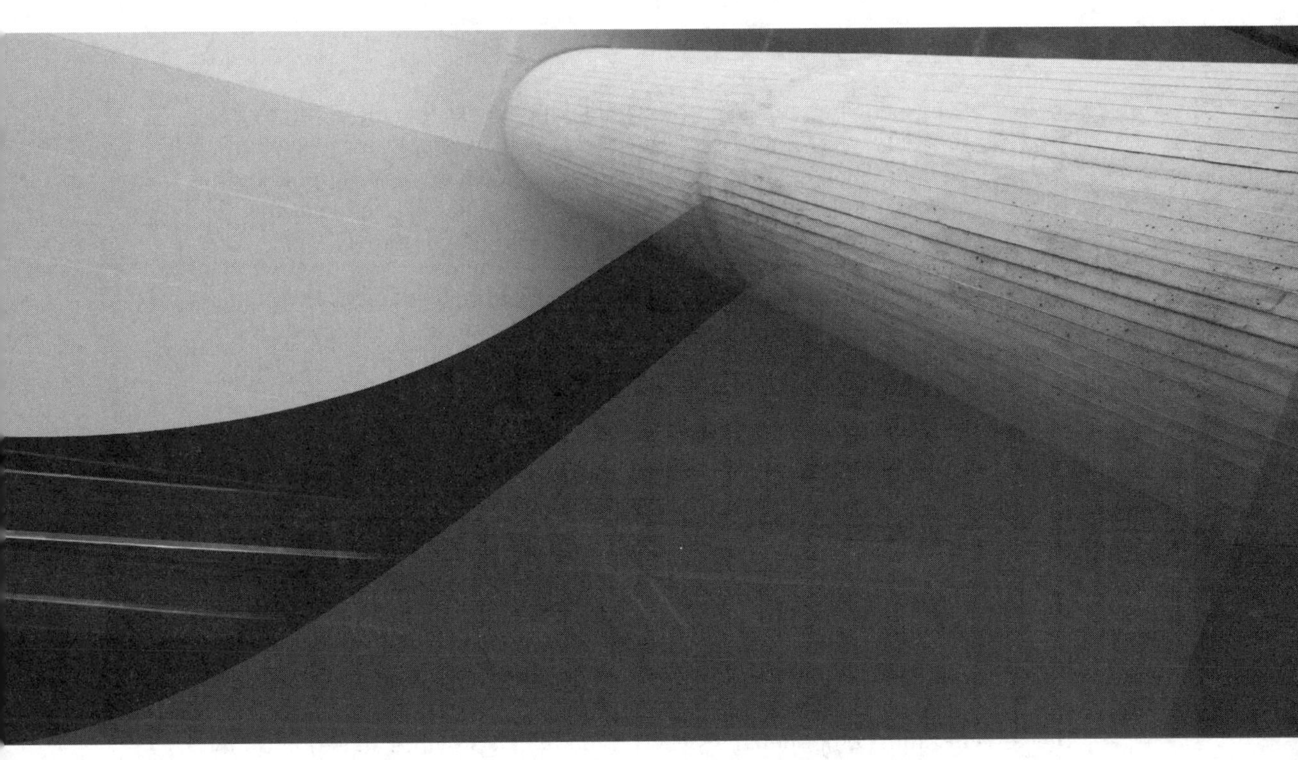

CHAPTER 6

Reverse Engineering

Reverse engineering is a process of taking an existing thing and using it to create a new thing. MySQL Workbench accomplishes reverse engineering by letting you take an existing database or script to build an Entity Relationship Diagram (ERD) of it. The ERD becomes the model of the original thing, which you can now improve upon.

You often look at examples before undertaking projects. Looking at a working ERD model of your business lets you find the things you like and dislike. MySQL Workbench builds the model for you and lets you accept the things you like and change the things you don't. It saves a great deal of time to work with something that already exists rather than creating it from scratch.

You reverse-engineer a database by capturing the definitions of tables, relationships, views, and routines. The definitions are stored in the MySQL database catalog, which is found in the `mysql` database (or schema).

MySQL lets you get this information two ways. One option lets you create an Enhanced Entity Relationship (EER) Model from a database directly, and the other lets you create an EER Model from a SQL script. Both of these options are in the Data Modeling component of MySQL Workbench. You export from a database to a new model using the Data Modeling tool, and you generate a script file to create a model using the Server Admin component.

The Server Admin component of MySQL Workbench provides an export utility. The export utility lets you read the contents of the database catalog and generates a script with the SQL statements that can create a copy of the database. The export tool can also grab a copy of the data and insert it in the new database, which would be like taking the fixtures and furniture from the original home to the new home.

Chapter 11 shows you how to use the MySQL Workbench export utility, and it may be advantageous to glance forward to that chapter before focusing on this one. While the earlier chapters in this section show you how to model data, this one focuses on using an existing database to create a model.

Modeling data from an existing model is much easier than building a complete model from scratch. You have two ways to avoid building a complete model from scratch—you can write a script to create a database, or you can analyze a database to write the script. Writing a script manually to build a database is *forward engineering*. Generating a script from an existing database is *reverse engineering*.

NOTE
A script is a file that contains a number of SQL statements in a specific sequential order.

Forward engineering occurs infrequently because it requires a substantial manual design process before developing the script. Forward engineering is the process of designing an ERD model and then generating a script from the design. If the design process is manual, the effort is daunting to write the script file, but if the design process uses a tool like MySQL Workbench, the tool generates the script from the design.

Reverse engineering is the more common case because all too often you come to work for a company with a database but no design that describes how it works. Reverse engineering from what you inherit in an existing database generally requires a tool that can generate a script that implements what you already have. MySQL Workbench lets you do just that; migrate or import a database into MySQL where you can generate a script file. The generated script lets you forward-engineer an EER Model.

This chapter covers both forward engineering and reverse engineering. The first part of the chapter shows you how to reverse-engineer with the tool, and the second part shows you how to forward-engineer.

Reverse Engineering a Database

The Data Modeling component is in the middle of the MySQL Workbench home page, and you click the *Create EER Model from Existing Database* link to reverse-engineer an existing database. The middle section of the MySQL Workbench home page follows to connect the text with the process.

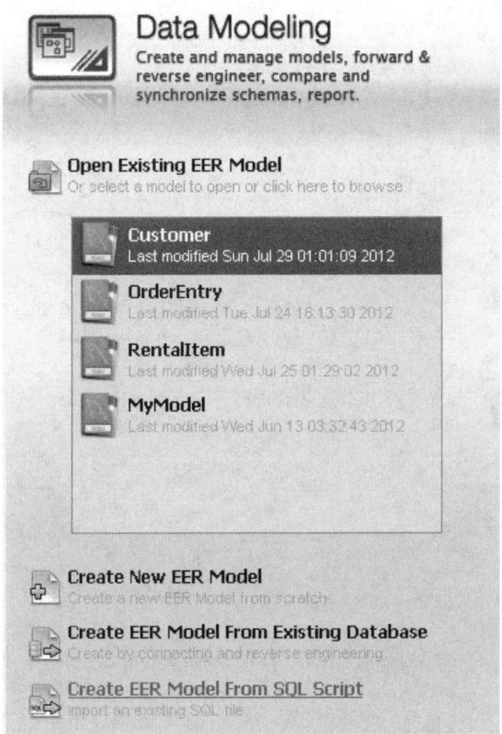

Clicking the *Create EER Model from Existing Database* link launches the *Reverse Engineer Database* wizard. Like other wizards, it depends on a pre-existing connection.

The example uses a non-super user account to demonstrate that the `root` (super) user isn't required when exporting a single schema (database). The connection can be to a local or remote server, and the wizard's functionality is completely independent of the location of the MySQL Server because the connection creates a level of abstraction.

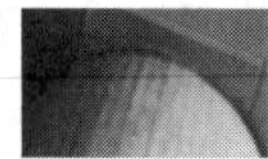

NOTE
Storing passwords in tools puts them in one additional place where they may be decrypted and used to marshal an attack on your database server.

You choose *Stored Connection* and *Username* in the Connection Options step. It is also possible to store the password in the *Vault,* but security fundamentals discourage doing so (that's why it isn't shown, if you're curious). The following screen shot shows you the *Parameters* view of the Connection Options step.

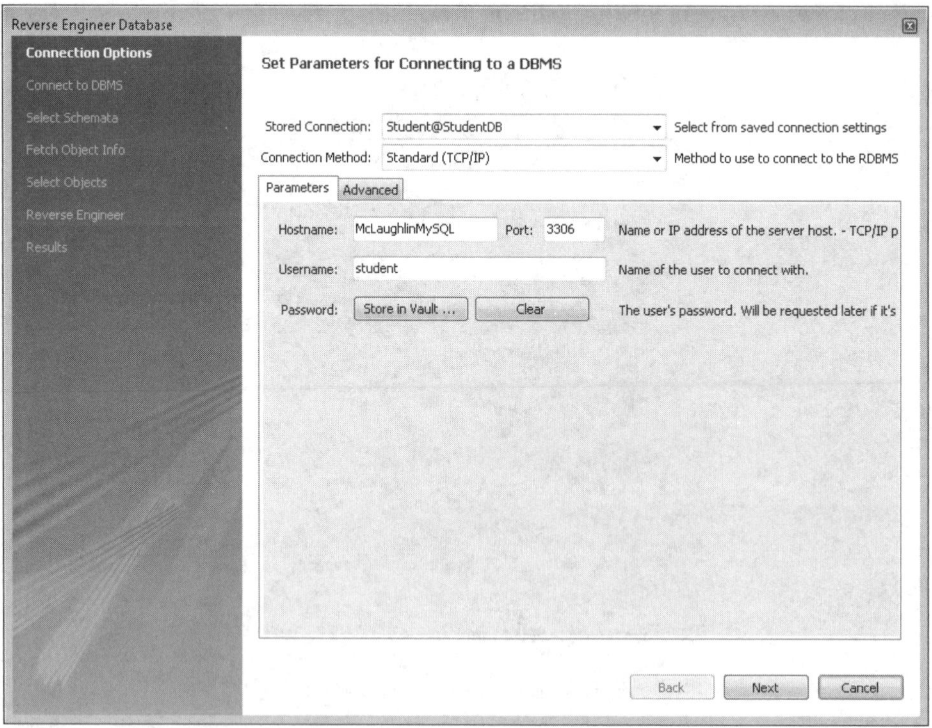

You can click the *Advanced* tab to see the entry form for secure shell (ssh) connections, which provides the Advanced view for the Connection Options step shown in the following screen capture.

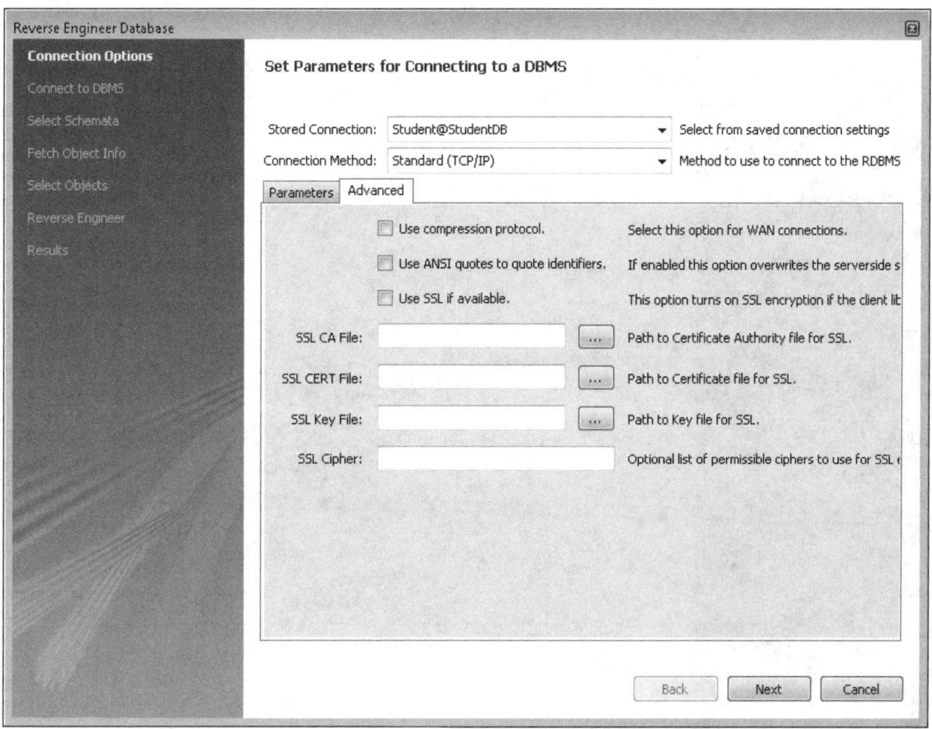

You can click the *Next* button to continue with the process after entering the connection and user name values. Alternatively, you can enter those values and click the Advanced tab to enter the ssh values before clicking the *Next* button. You now see the *Connect to DBMS* step's password entry dialog (unless you've stored that, against my advice, in the MySQL Workbench vault).

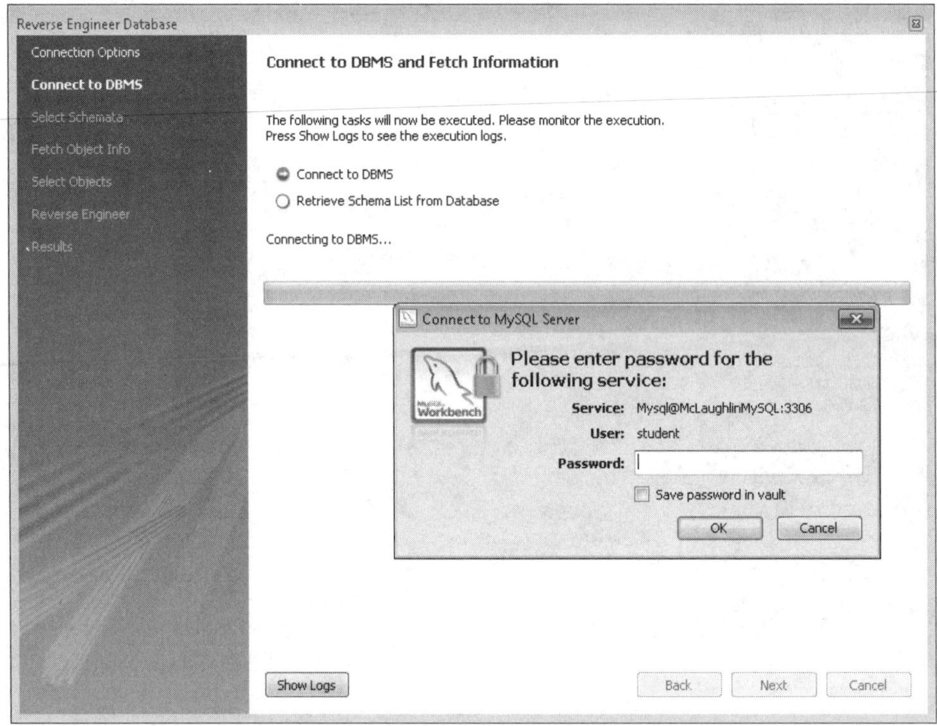

Enter the password for the `student` account, and you should see a verification form of the *Connect to DBMS* step, as shown in the next illustration. Click the *Next* button to proceed with the reverse engineering exercise.

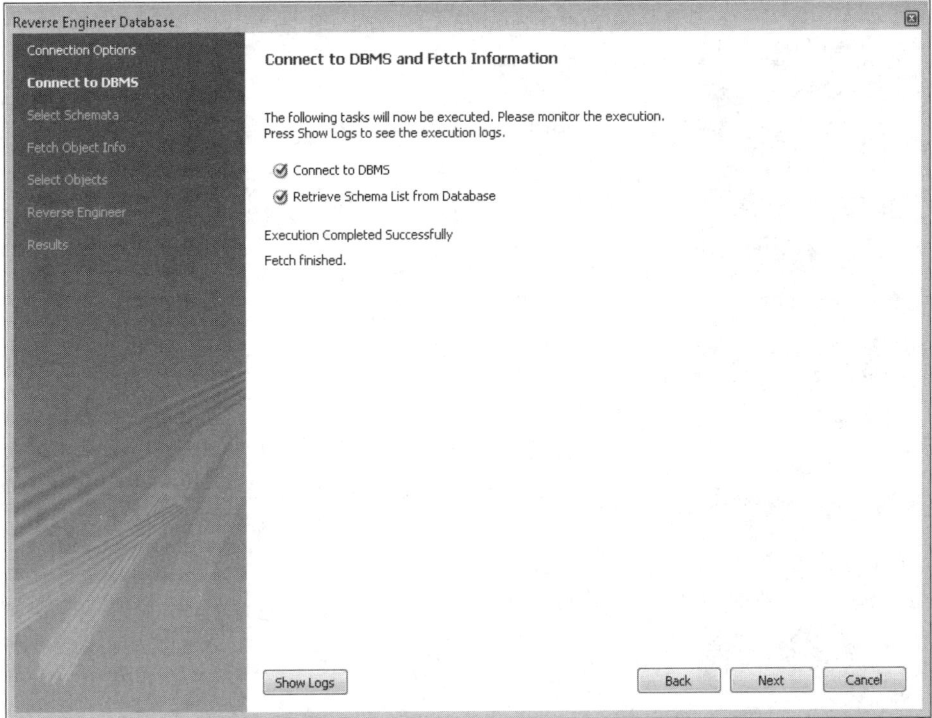

The next illustration is the *Select Schemata* step (that's a fancier word for the fancy word schema). The `student` user has access to four databases in this MySQL Server, and they're displayed in the view.

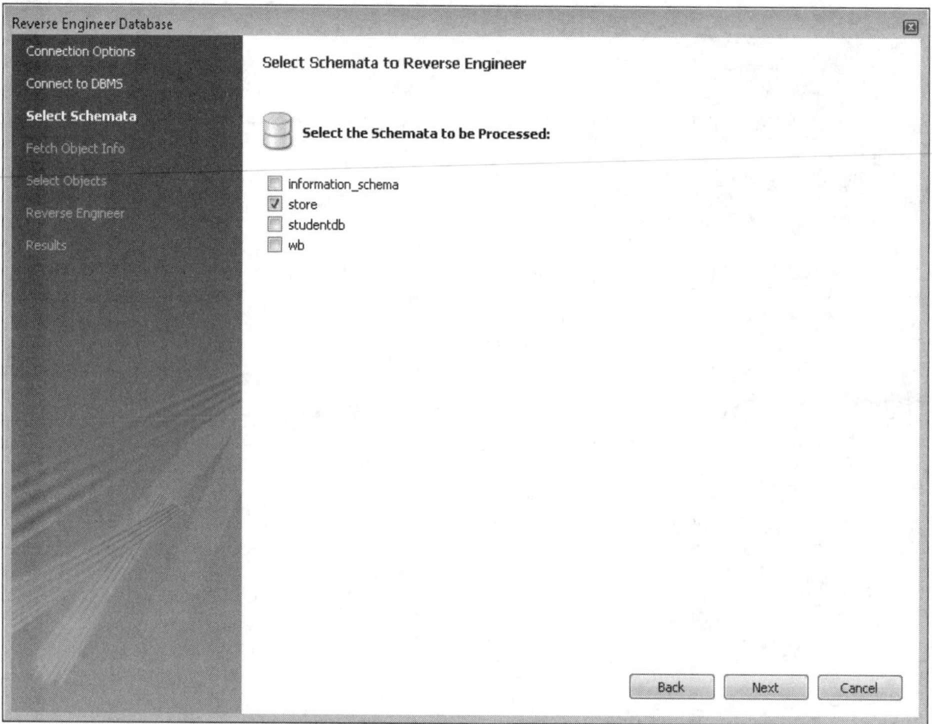

My example selects only the `store` schema (database) to reverse-engineer. Click the *Next* button to continue.

A reverse engineering process first audits whether you have access to everything you need to create a schema. This could include privileges to databases or parts of databases, like tables, views, or routines. When it finds shortfalls, some tools opt to create stubs for missing components.

Stubs are required when a component references other components that no longer exist in the instance. For example, a foreign key constraint may depend on a table in another database, and it would fail without the table and column that holds the primary key. This type of error occurs when you export only a database instead of a complete instance and your databases share dependencies. MySQL Workbench would add a `CREATE` statement for the missing table and column to the script to ensure it works.

As a rule, you should resolve anything that raises an error at this point before reverse engineering the database. This requires you to delete the incorrectly engineered components before you reattempt to reengineer the database.

The following *Retrieve Object Information* step displays missing information. Sometimes it returns errors, but most often it returns only a retrieval success message. If it returns an error, you should stop the process and investigate. If it returns a successful retrieval message, you should click the *Next* button to continue.

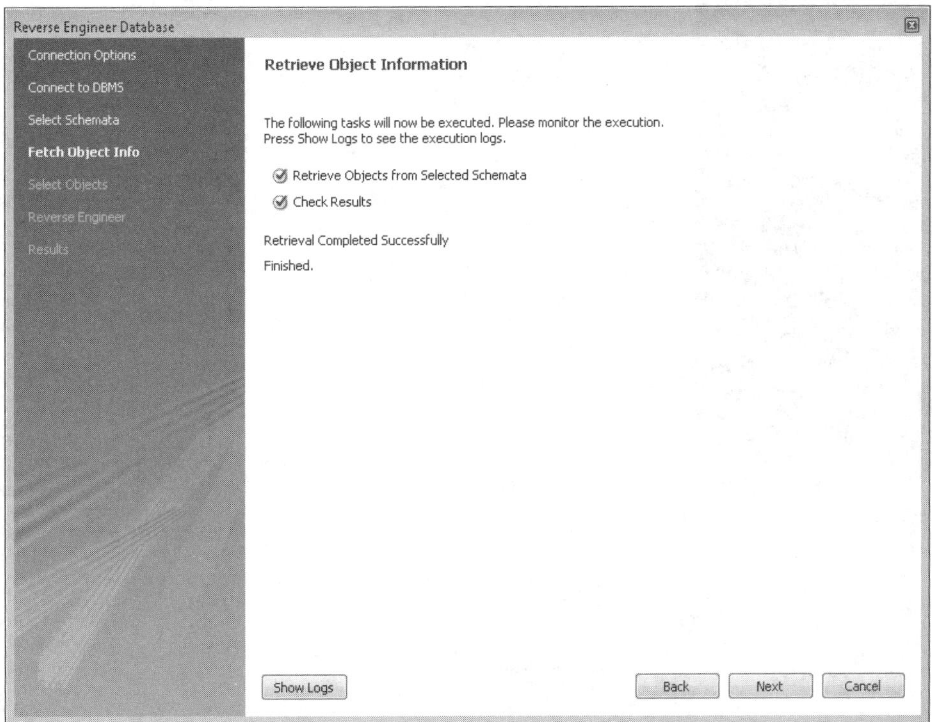

The *Select Objects to Reverse Engineer* step gives you a list of tables, views, and routines that you may want to select for the new EER Model. By default, all tables, views, and routines are selected from the databases you've chosen. Click the *Next* button in the following view of the *Select Objects to Reverse Engineer* step when you want all of the selected objects included in the new EER Model.

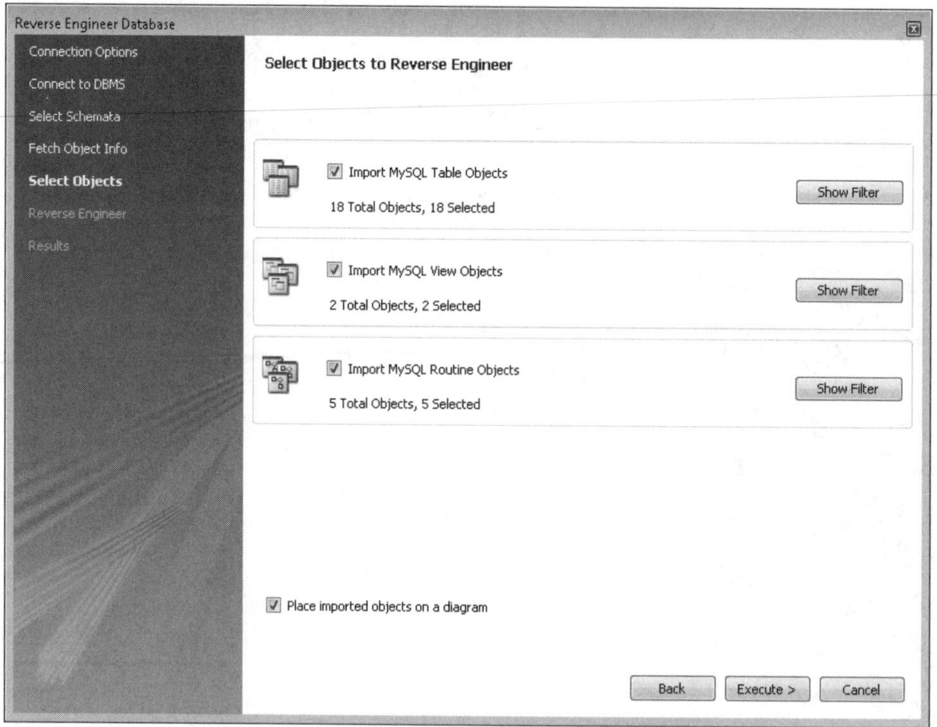

Click the *Show Filter* button in the next view when you want to exclude any objects from your selected databases for the reverse engineering process. Clicking any of the three displayed *Show Filter* buttons provides the following detailed view. You click items that should be deselected from the reverse engineering process and click the *Next* button to complete the generation of a MySQL script.

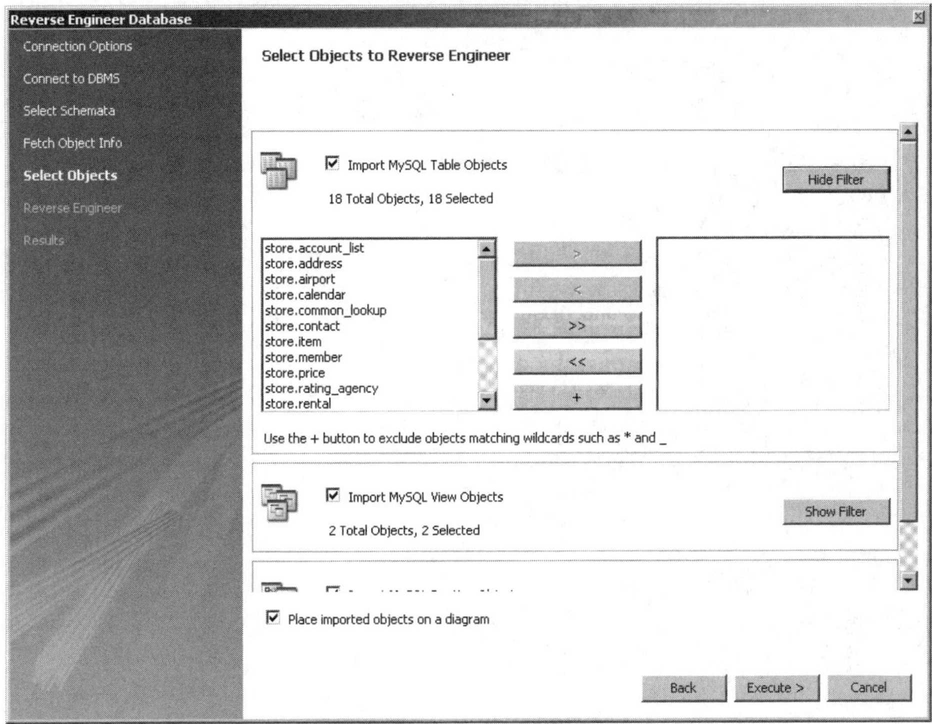

The *Reverse Engineering Process* step shows you whether reverse engineering worked and whether the objects were placed on an EER Model diagram. If you encountered errors during the process, you should delete the partially reengineered solution, resolve any errors, and start over. Repeat this until you have resolved all errors. Click the *Next* button to continue the process when you don't have any errors.

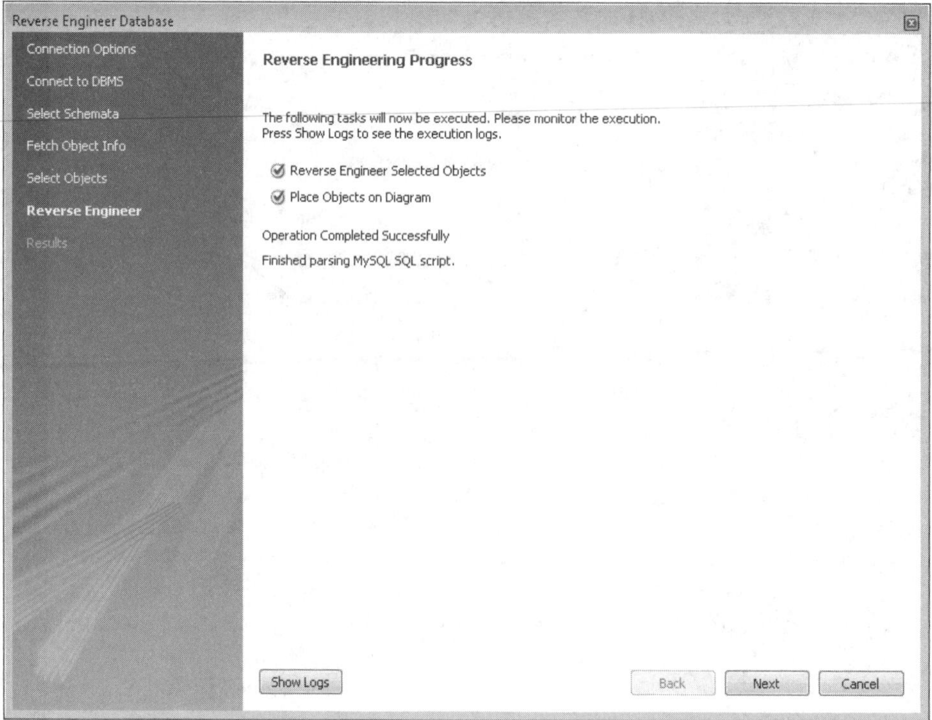

At this point, you have completed the reverse engineering process. You should see the final *Reverse Engineering Results* step as shown in the following illustration. It tells you that the 18 tables, two views, and five routines from the store schema are now in the `default_schema` EER Model.

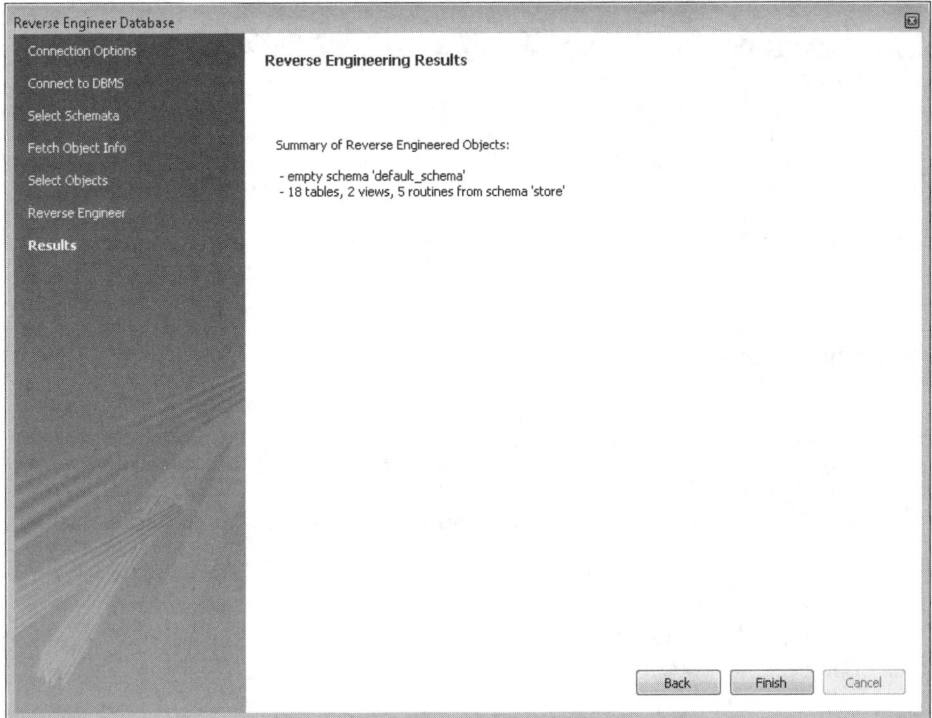

Click the *Finish* button to complete the reverse engineering wizard. It then displays the `default_schema` EER Diagram as the active view, as shown in the next illustration.

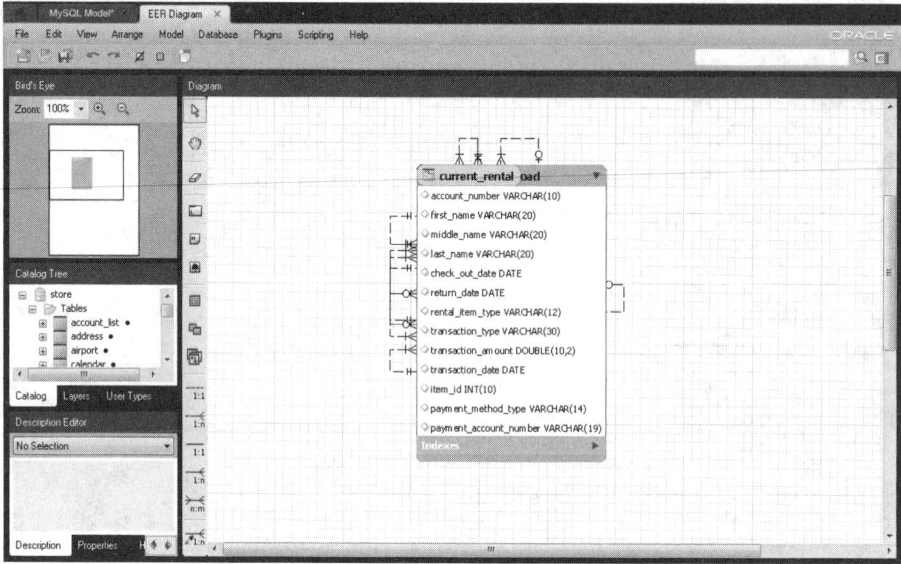

As you can see in the next illustration, the result looks like a table with a number of recursive, or self-referencing, relationships, although it's the collection of tables, views, and routines layered into a two-dimensional cake. More or less, the cake is a stack of objects that you need to drag apart and organize into a readable diagram.

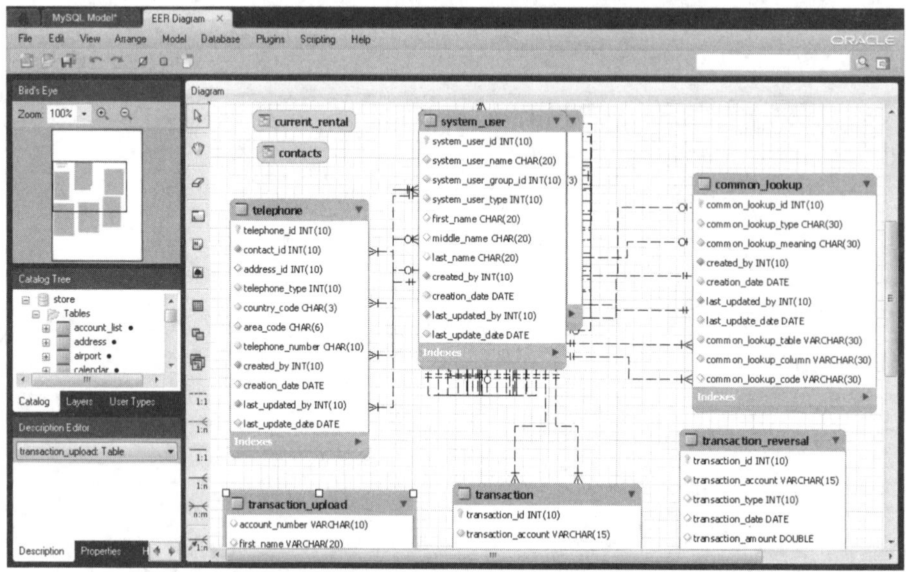

The grid area size is determined by the window frame you've allocated to MySQL Workbench. You can shrink or expand the objects inside the grid by using the plus or minus magnifying glass in the top-leftmost *Bird's Eye* window.

The names of views, such as "current_rental" and "contacts" shown in the previous illustration, appear with a yellow background. These are views and they don't natively have relationship lines because the SQL `SELECT` statement defines the relationships between tables as an equijoin or non-equijoin relationship.

NOTE
Equijoins are relationships resolved between the equality of values found in the primary and foreign keys, while non-equijoins are effectively a filtered cross-joins of sets based on an inequality or range comparison of values.

The prior illustration shows a few of the objects dragged off the two-dimensional stack in the *Bird's Eye* frame, although the diagram has become more readable. Click the *MySQL Model (default_schema)* tab, and you see a grid-like listing of objects by type of group.

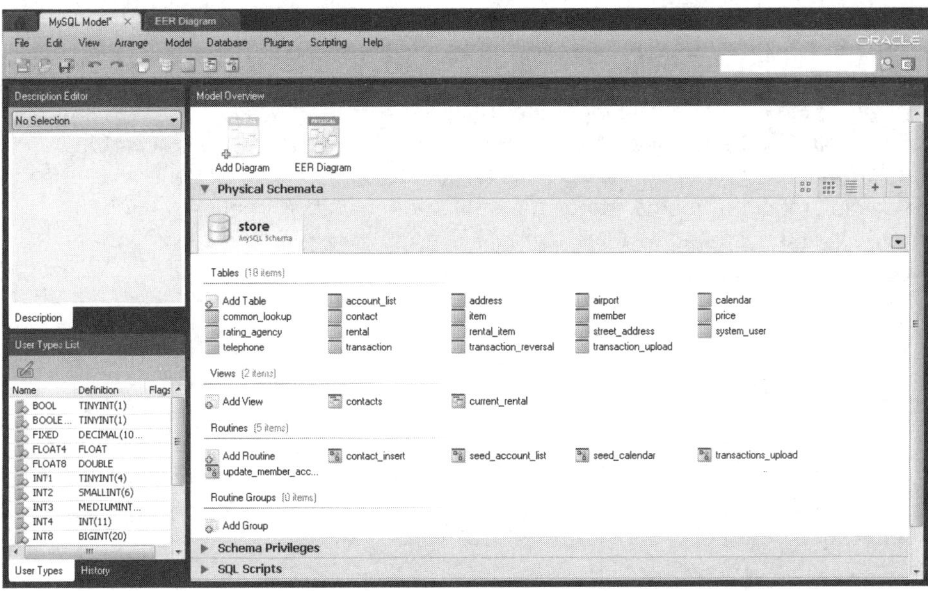

You should note that routines are visible in the model view but not in the EER Model Diagram. Check back to Chapters 4 and 5 for more detail on what's shown where.

This section has demonstrated how to reverse-engineer a schema (or database) into a new model. The next section shows you how to use a script to forward-engineer a database model.

Forward Engineering a Database

Forward engineering starts with a SQL script, where the SQL script contains the logic and commands to create tables, views, routines, and triggers in a database. This section starts by discussing how MySQL Workbench can generate such a script from an EER Model.

MySQL Workbench has two ways to generate a SQL script that can create the objects of a database. One is the Server Admin's export tool, and the other is Data Modeling's forward engineering tool.

Chapter 11 shows you how to create an export script, which can be used to forward-engineer a duplicate of another database. An export script may contain SQL that creates structures, routines, and triggers, with or without data.

While the export script can forward-engineer a new database, sometimes you need to make changes to some structures. For example, if you've exported a database from a MySQL Server and want to import that model, you should change the database name in the script. Effectively, this type of database name change creates a clone (that's a duplicate copy) of another database using a new name.

Reverse engineering gives you an EER Model Diagram of an existing database and an opportunity to reengineer it. The forward engineering process can include changes to tables, views, routines, and triggers.

MySQL Workbench provides two ways that you can forward-engineer. One starts from a menu option in an open EER Model and uses a script generated from an existing model. The other starts from a link in the Data Modeling section of MySQL Workbench's home page; it uses a script that creates and seeds (inserts preconfigured) data.

The next two sections cover MySQL Workbench's two approaches to forward engineering a database from an EER Model.

Forward Engineering from an EER Model

Forward engineering from an existing EER Model requires that you launch that model in MySQL Workbench. Then, you can click the *Database* menu item or use a CTRL-G hotkey sequence to launch the forward engineering wizard. Unfortunately, there is no way to activate a floating context menu with a right click of the mouse.

The following illustration shows using the main drop-down menu.

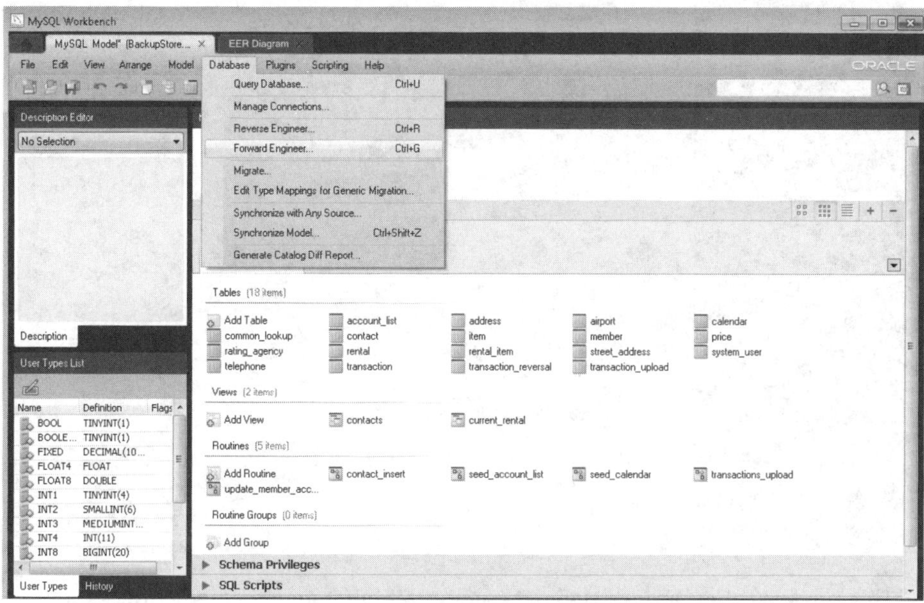

The *Connection Options* step, like so many of the other wizards, is the first step in the *Forward Engineering* wizard. Select the `Student@StudentDB` connection from the drop-down menu and enter the `student` user name in the *Username* field. Then, click the *Next* button in the following screen to continue the process.

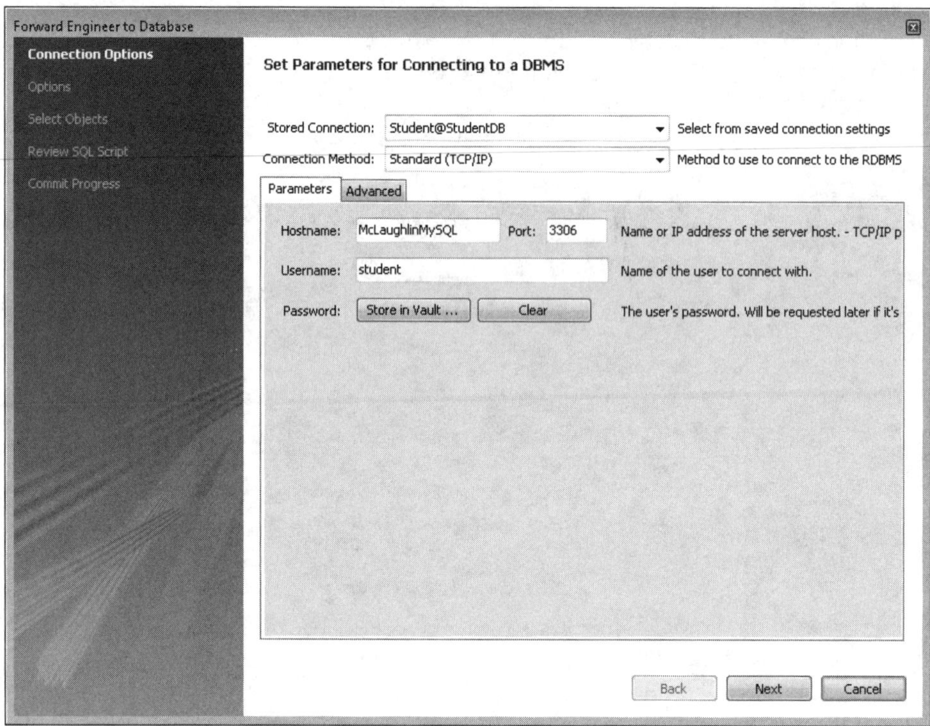

This launches the *Options* step. I'd recommend that you check the following option boxes:

- `DROP` Objects Before Each `CREATE` Object
- Generate `DROP SCHEMA`
- Generate Separate `CREATE INDEX` Statement
- Add `SHOW WARNINGS` After Every DDL Statement

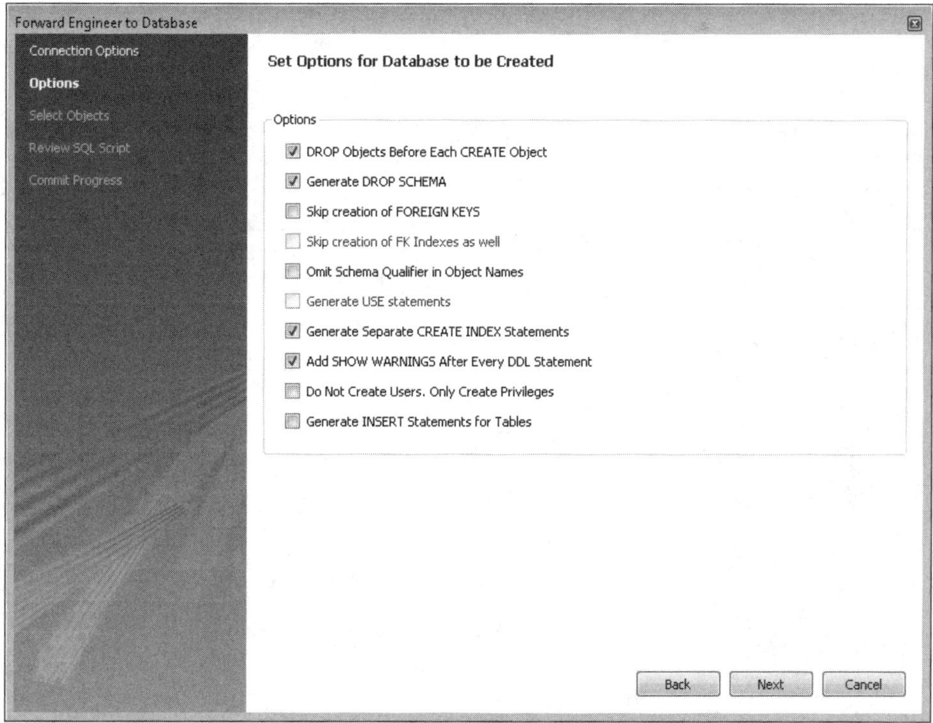

Before you click the *Next* button to proceed, you need to know that some versions (at the time of writing) raise an error when you create separate index statements. The errors occur only when you have self-referencing foreign-to-primary key relationships. As a rule, you should uncheck the box when you have self-referencing tables or confirm that it's not a problem with the version you're using.

You also want to check the *Generate INSERT Statements for Tables* option when you're forward engineering seeded data. Seeded data would mean any data previously exported when you created the script file. Click the *Next* button to proceed.

Here you are prompted for the `student` user's password, unless you've stored it in the MySQL Workbench's vault. Enter the password and click the *OK* button in the following dialog box.

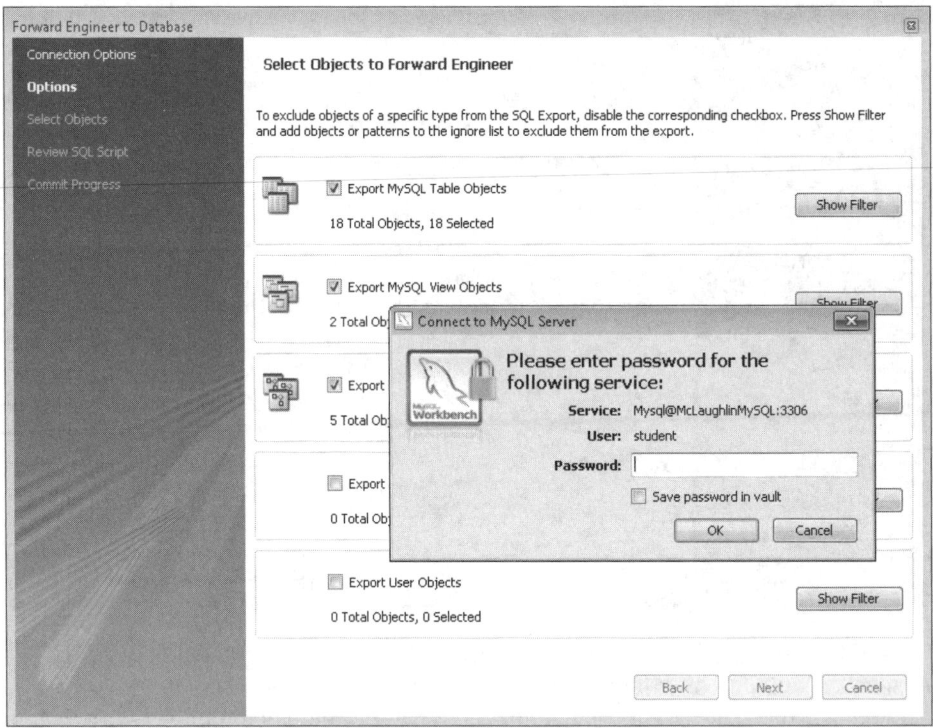

The *Select Objects* step lets you choose tables, views, routines, triggers, or objects. As shown in the "Reverse Engineering a Database" section, you can click any of the *Show Filter* buttons to get a list of tables, views, routines, triggers, or objects. You can click any of them to deselect them from the group (you need to flip back a few pages to see an illustration of that screen).

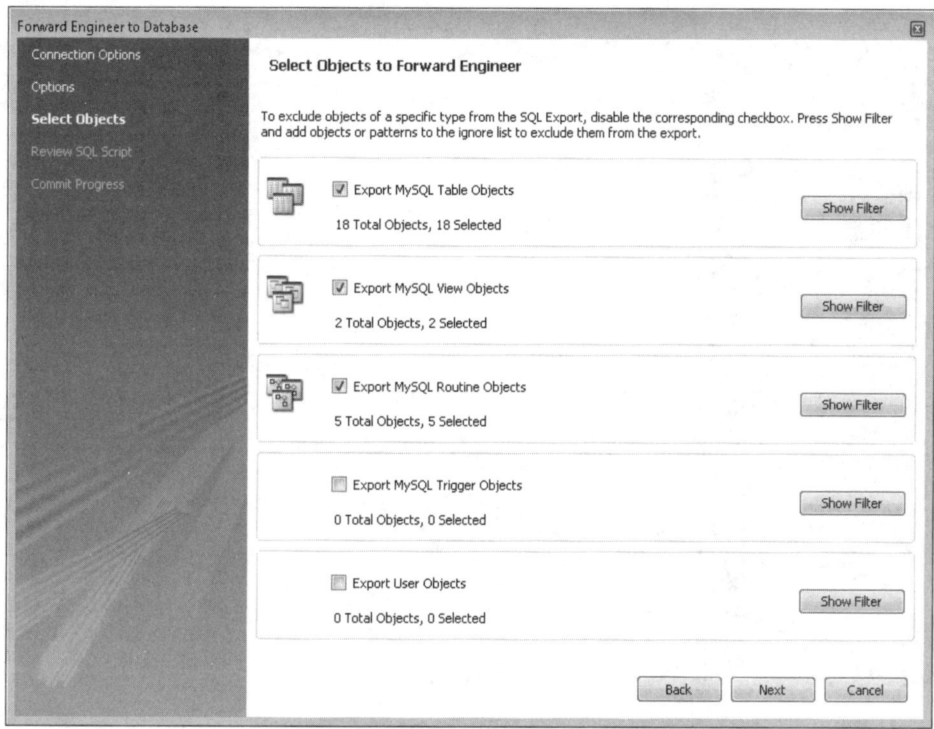

After you've made your selections and deselections from the *Select Objects to Forward Engineer* screens, click the *Next* button to continue with the wizard.

You should now see the *Review SQL Script* wizard step or *Review the SQL Script to be Executed* view. The script is displayed in a scrollable view pane. You can save the script to a file or copy the content to the clipboard, where you can paste it into a text editor of your choice.

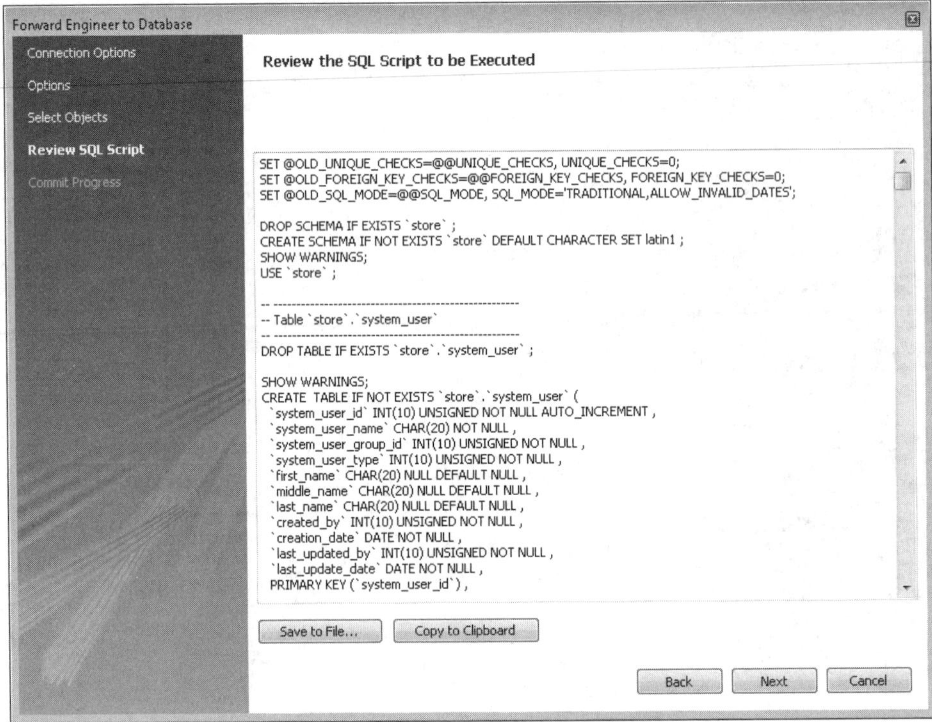

For this example, click the *Save to File* button, and you see the file chooser for the respective operating system. The default directory for the file chooser is the following on the Windows operating system (OS):

C:\Users\<*user_name*>\My Documents\dumps

You see dump files with a SQL extension in the following screen shot because I've already used MySQL Workbench's export feature to generate two export files. These dump scripts can also be used to forward-engineer a database.

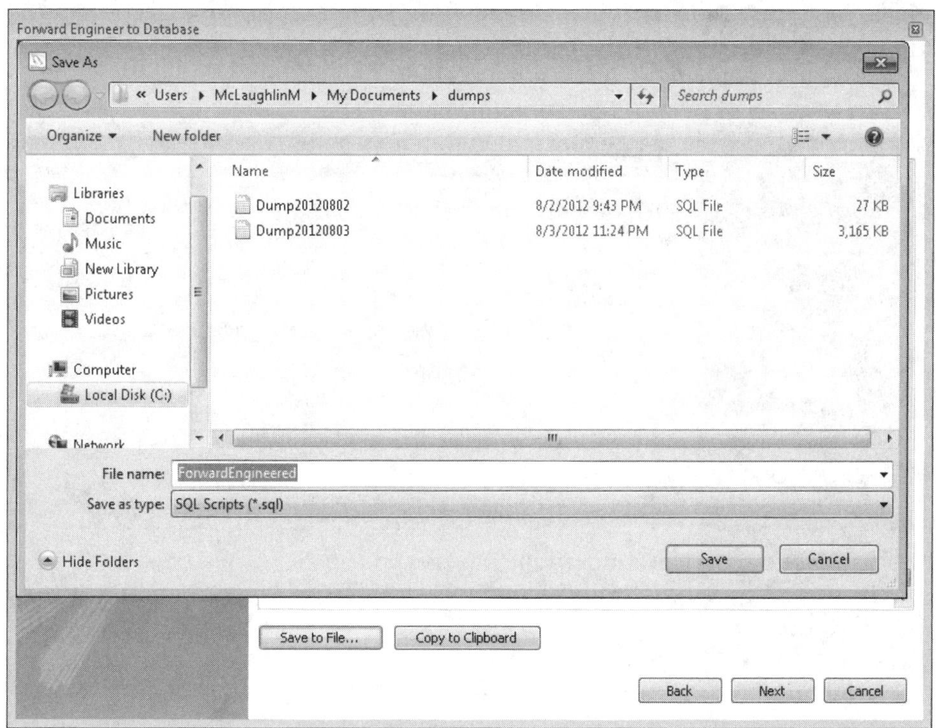

You should also note from the preceding screen shot that I'm saving the file as ForwardEngineering.sql in the dumps folder. Click the *Save* button to complete this step.

NOTE
You must have previously granted privileges to your user on the storedb database for this to work.

After saving the file, you're returned to the *Review SQL Script* wizard step or *Review the SQL Script to be Executed* view. Click the *Next* button to forward-engineer the database instance.

The next screen prompts you for the `student` user's password again. Enter the password and click the *OK* button in the following authentication dialog to continue.

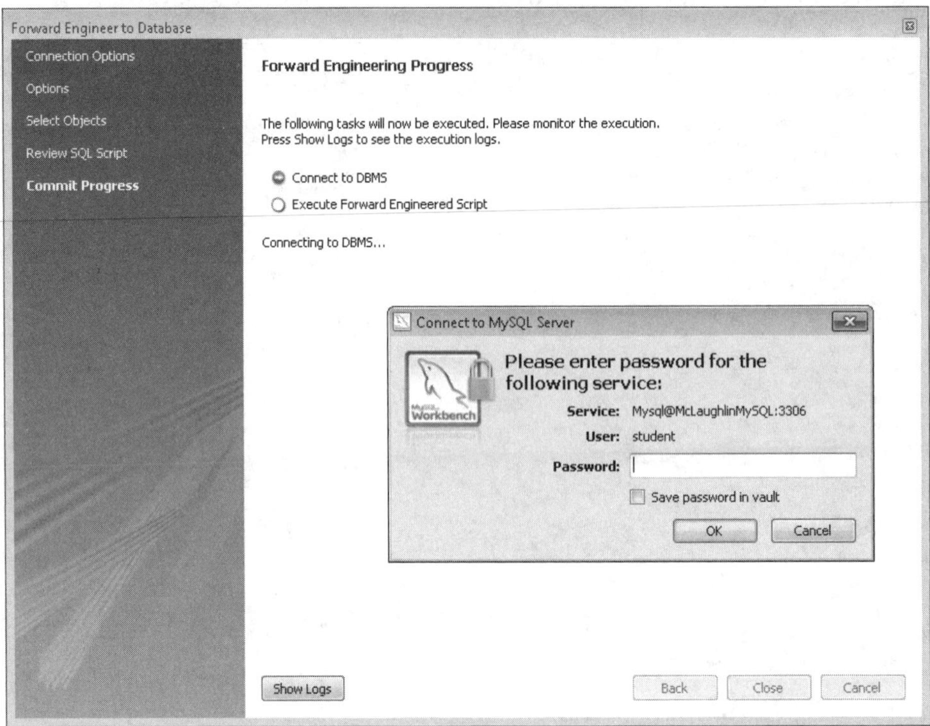

The *Commit Progress* step or *Forward Engineering Progress* view shows you that you were able to connect to the MySQL Server (or DBMS in the view) and run (execute) the forward engineering script. Click the *Close* button in the following screen to complete the *Forward Engineering* wizard.

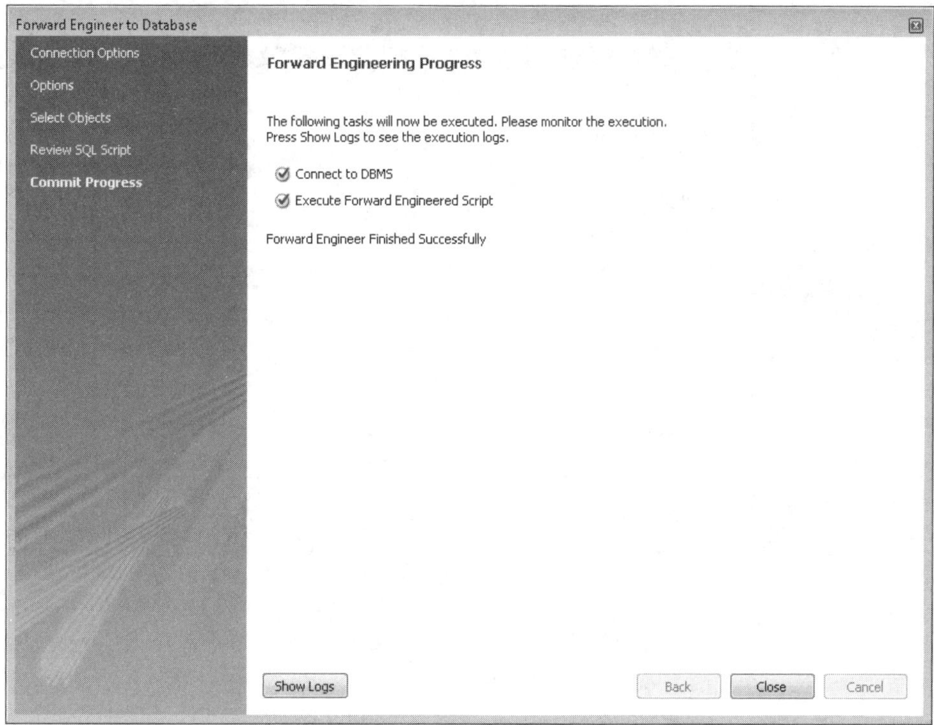

The wizard redisplays the following EER Model with any changes (deselections) you've made. The wizard also changes the EER Diagram to add or drop any schema objects that were added or removed, respectively.

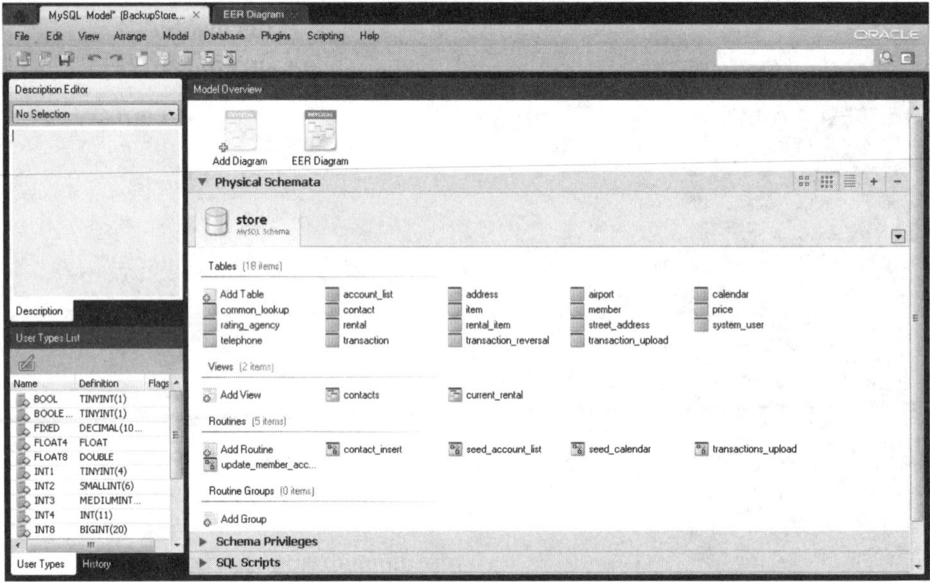

This subsection has shown you how to forward-engineer from a model to an existing database (or schema). The next shows you how to run a script to forward-engineer a database.

Forward Engineering from a Script

You don't need a MySQL Workbench model open when you start forward engineering with an existing script. If one is opened, you'll need to close it. MySQL Workbench only works with one open model at a time.

This process requires that you have a script that creates a database and potentially seeds (inserts preconfigured) data. There are many ways to create this type of script. You can create a script like this manually (ouch), or through the use of a CASE (Computer-Aided System Engineering) system like MySQL Workbench. The latter would be like the marketing campaign for Staples office supply—clicking the Easy button.

For this example, I ran several scripts that create and seed data in a database and then I exported them using MySQL Workbench (check Chapter 11) to a dump file. The example uses the dump file as the forward engineering script (you can find where it's located on the Web in the introduction). I also dropped down to the command line, connected as the `root` super user, and created a `newstore` database as the forward engineering target database with the following syntax:

```
mysql> CREATE DATABASE newstore;
```

Then, I granted all privileges on the `newstore` database to the `student` user with the following syntax:

```
mysql> GRANT ALL ON newstore.* TO student;
```

You don't have to use the command line because MySQL Workbench lets you perform these tasks. Chapter 10 show you how to use MySQL Workbench to accomplish the same thing.

As you'll see at the end of this section, you need to run a script manually or through the MySQL Workbench import tool to put the structures and data into the database. Forward engineering only puts the structure and data into a MySQL Workbench file. The existence of the `newstore` database helps show that.

You click the *Create EER Model from SQL Script* link in the *Data Modeling* section of the MySQL Workbench home page, as shown in the following screen shot.

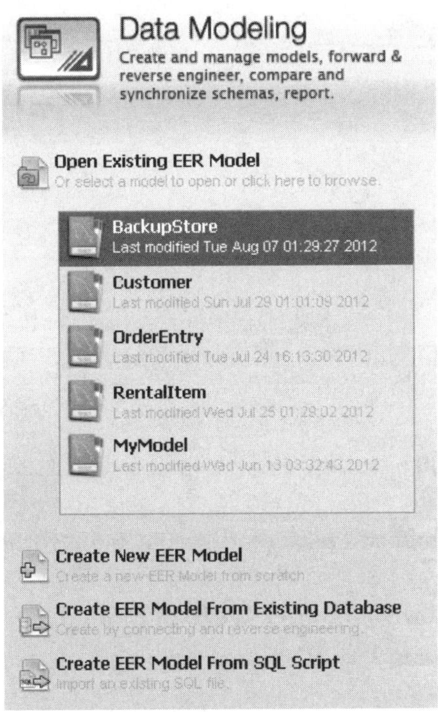

The following *Input and Options* step presents a view that lets you browse for a local file and run it. You also have the option of enabling the check box to import the objects from the script into a new EER Model Diagram.

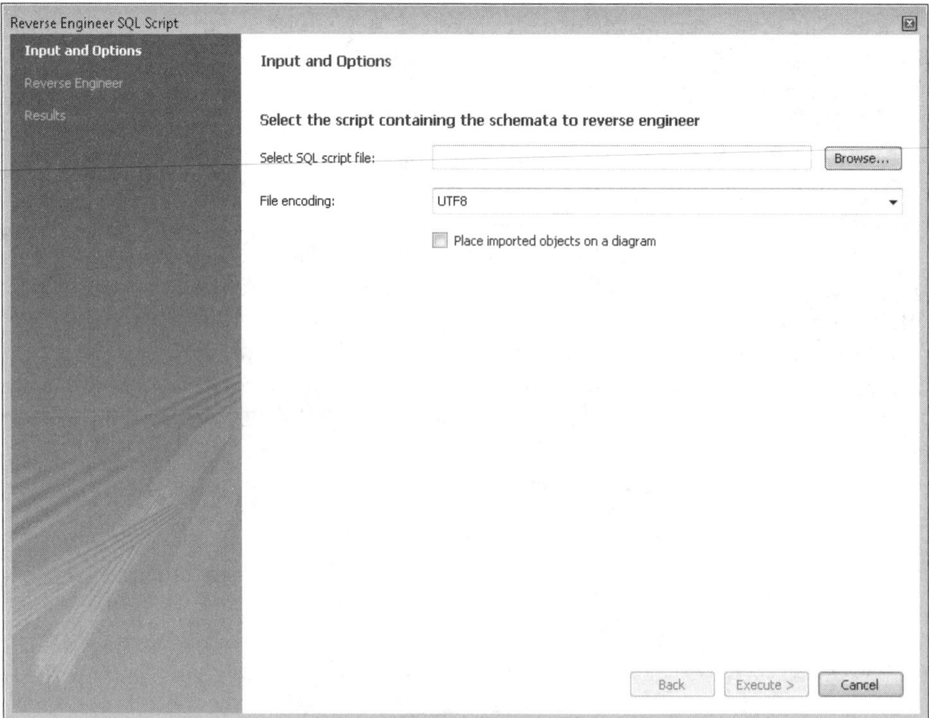

Before selecting the `ForwardEngineering.sql` script created from the file system (its location can be found in the introduction), you need to edit the file and replace the `store` schema name with a `newstore` text string. Open the file in a text editor of your choice or in MySQL Workbench's SQL script editor. Chapter 8 covers the MySQL Workbench SQL script editor.

When you open the file, you should find three instances of the `store` keyword in the file, as shown in the following NotePad++ screen shot. You can replace them individually or through a global find and replace. (NotePad++ is a free text editor for the Windows operating.)

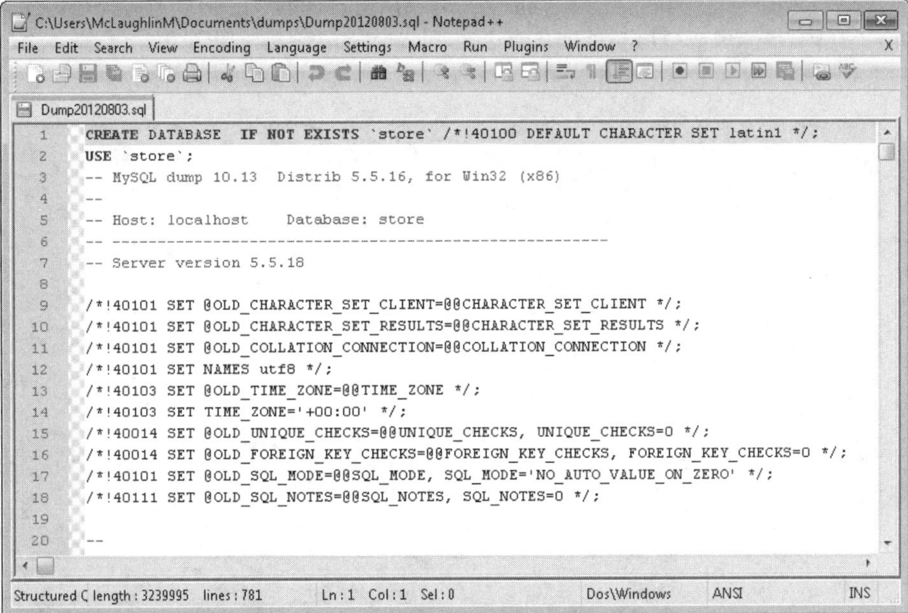

All editors have a global find and replace behavior and NotePad++. You click the *Search* menu item and then the *Replace* option. Enter the `store` string as the *find* argument and `newstore` as the *replace with* argument, as shown in the following NotePad++ example.

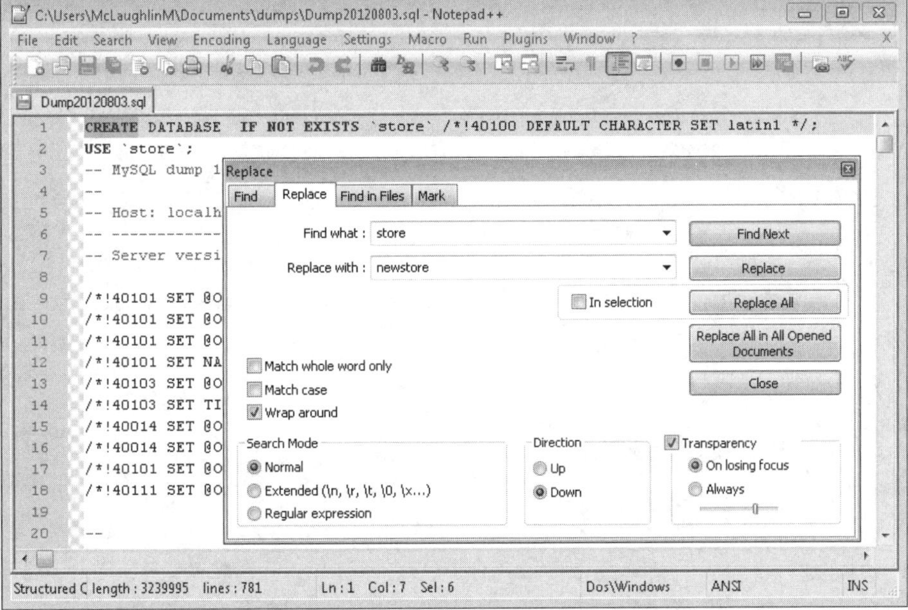

Having made the changes, you should save the file in the `dumps` folder mentioned earlier. Click the *Browse* button to find the file in the chooser, which should open the `dumps` folder by default, as shown.

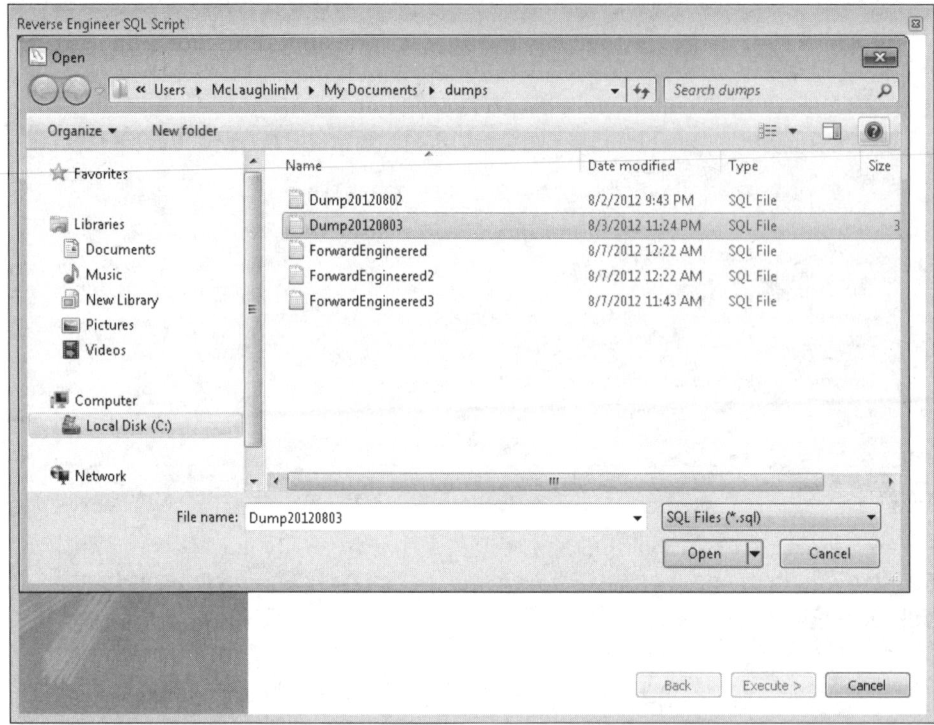

Clicking the *Open* button returns you to the *Input and Options* view, where you should click the *Place imported objects on a diagram* check box. In the following screen shot, you can see it is unchecked by default.

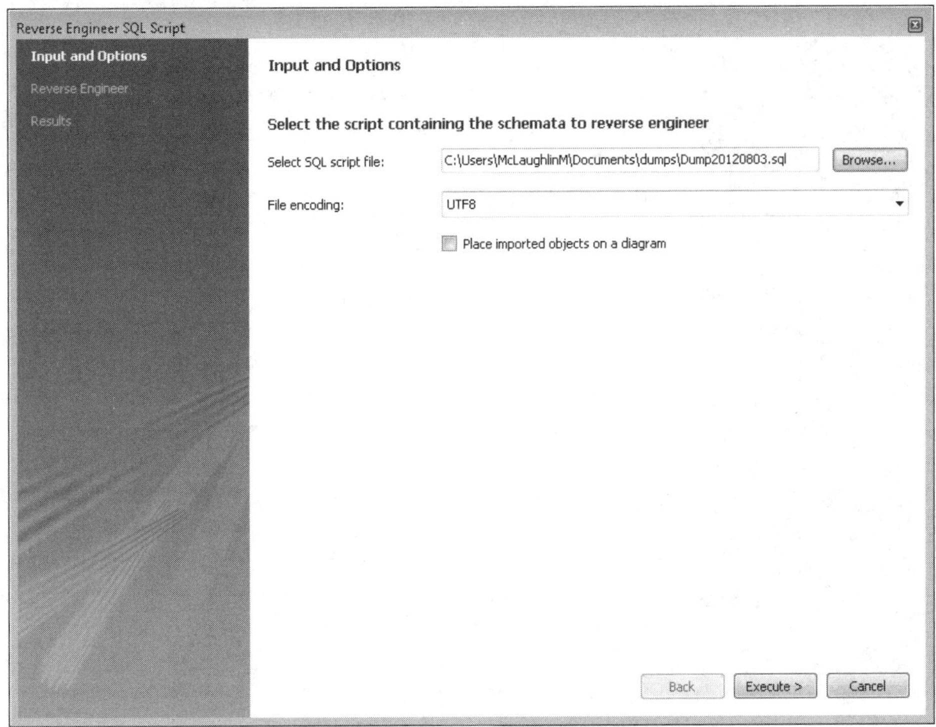

After enabling the check box, the *Input and Options* view should look like the following. Click the *Execute* button to continue.

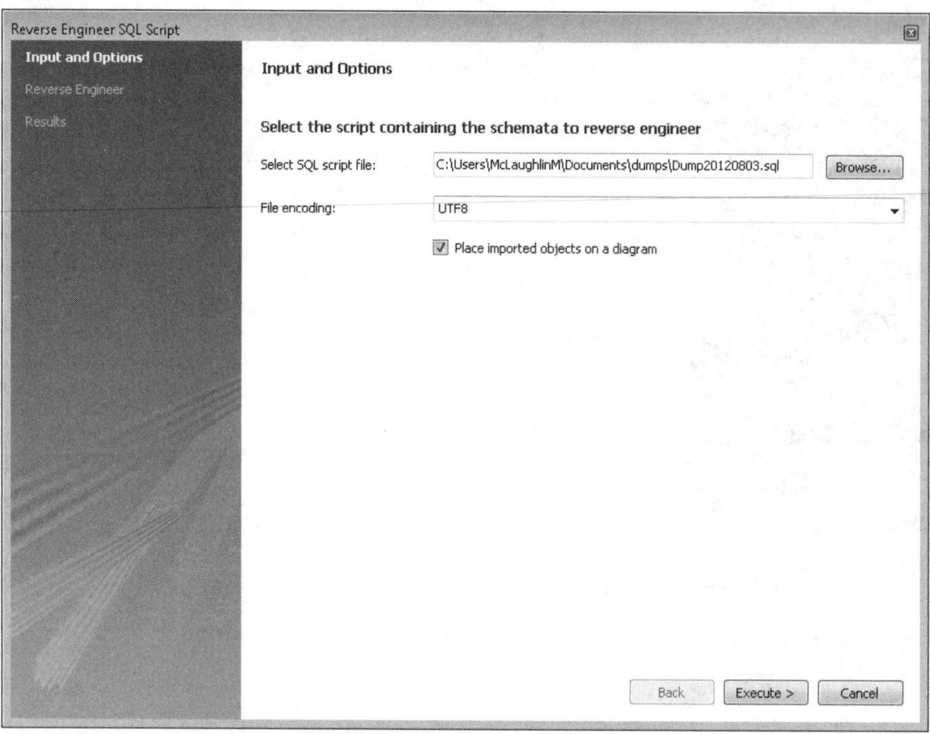

With a valid and working script, MySQL Workbench runs the reverse engineering script, verifies results, and places objects on a new EER Model. It displays successful results or raises errors.

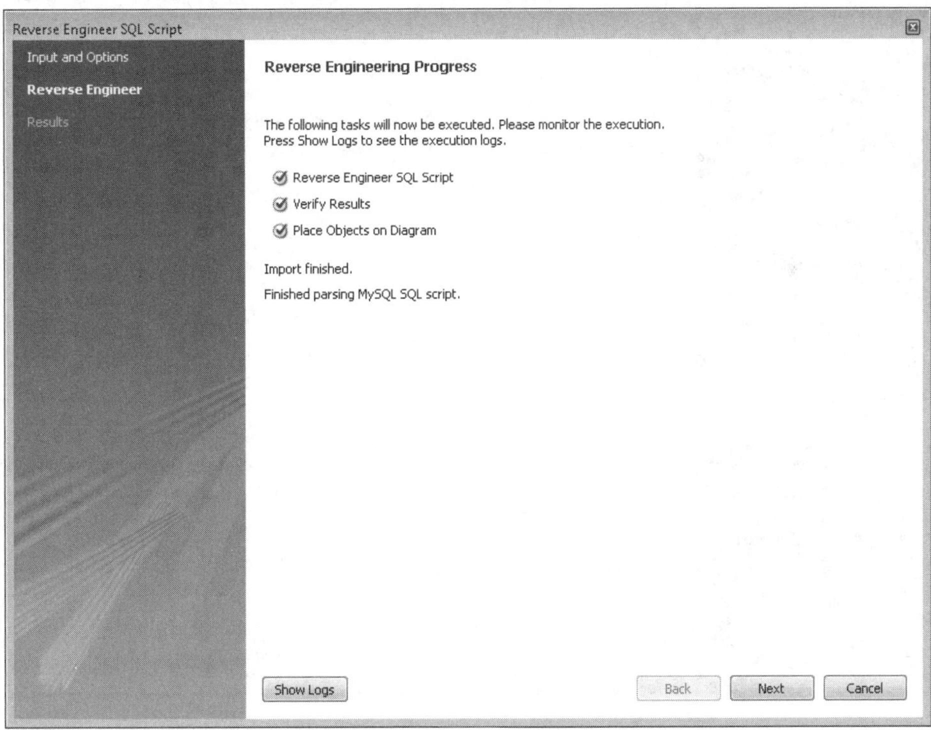

MySQL Workbench's forward engineering doesn't create any of the objects in the `newstore` database, which now appear in the diagram and model. That's because the MySQL Workbench files are separate from the MySQL Server's databases. You can verify that by using the command line to connect as the `student` user and run the following command:

```
mysql> use newstore;
```

After choosing to work in the `newstore` database, you can run the following command and see there are no tables in the database:

```
mysql> show tables;
```

Click the *Next* button to continue with the *Reverse Engineer SQL Script* wizard, and it displays the following *Results* step view.

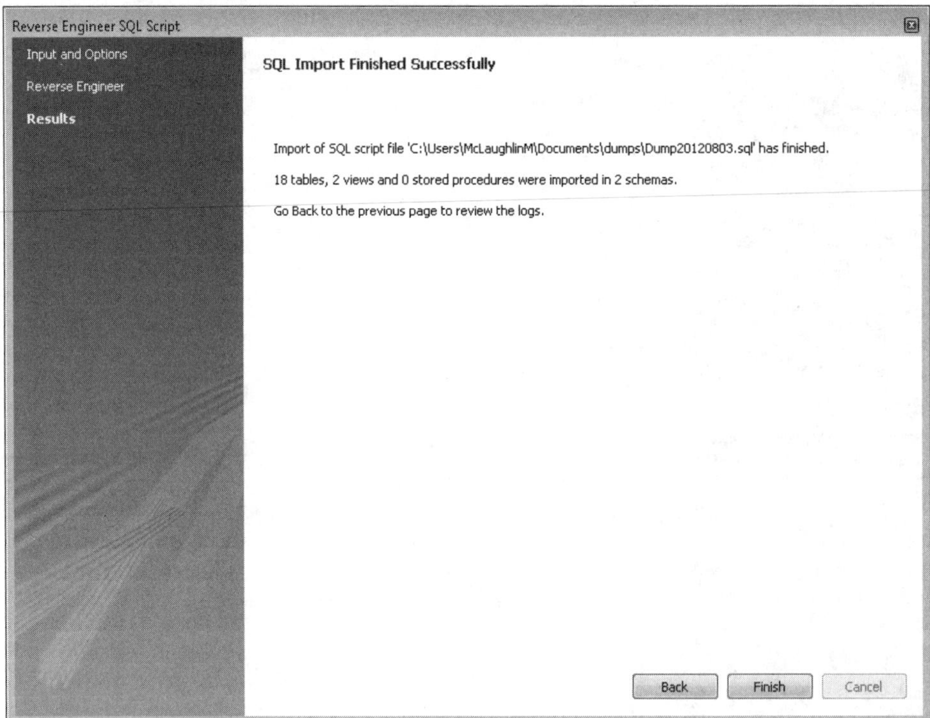

Clicking the *Finish* button completes the *Reverse Engineer SQL Script* wizard. It opens on a new EER Model Diagram, as shown in the following screen shot.

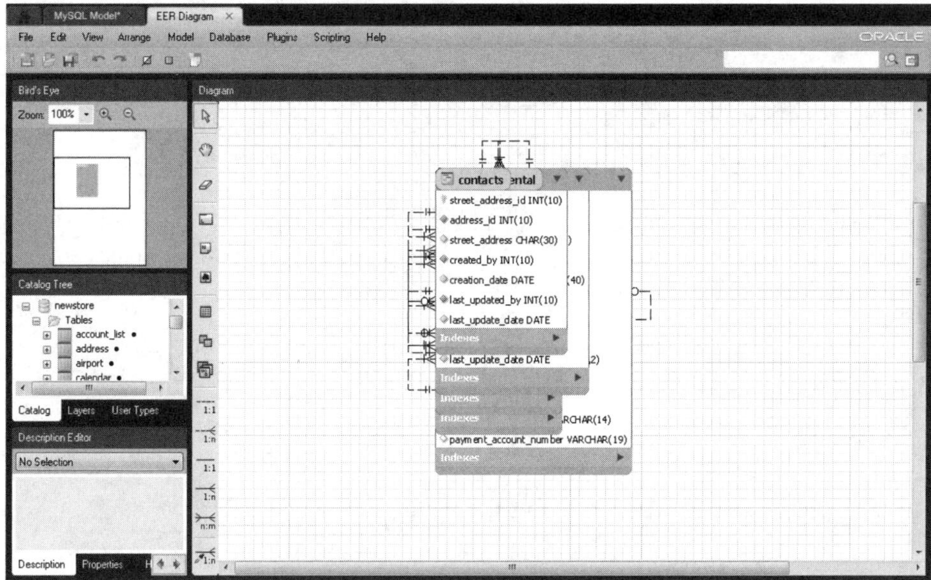

Click the *MySQL Model* tab, and you see the list of tables and routines that have been imported into a temporary *MySQL Workbench* document. Click the *File, Save As* option to save the file as `NewStore.mwb` in the following default folder:

C:\Users\<*user_name*>\My Documents\dumps

This subsection has shown you how to generate a new EER Model by using a previously generated script. It also explained how you forward-engineer a database into an EER Model file. Once in the file, you can now modify and add, change, or remove data that came with the script file. Chapter 7 shows you how to edit the data, and Chapter 8 shows you how to modify the script.

Summary

This chapter explained how to open and save files, create tables and views, and create relationships through foreign key constraints. You should be positioned to use the tool to produce an EER Diagram.

Mastery Check

The mastery check is a series of true or false and multiple choice questions that let you confirm how well you understand the material in the chapter. You may check Appendix A for answers to these questions.

True or False:

1. ___A forward engineering script can be written manually.
2. ___A forward engineering script can be generated from an EER Model.
3. ___A forward engineering script can be generated by using the MySQL Workbench export wizard.
4. ___Reverse engineering is the process of reading information from the data catalog to generate a SQL script that can re-create the database.
5. ___Forward engineering creates an EER Model and database instance in the MySQL Server.
6. ___Forward engineering creates a stack of objects in the EER Model Diagram view.
7. ___Forward engineering puts routine objects in the EER Model Diagram and displays them as yellow background objects with their routine name.
8. ___You need to change the schema (database) name in scripts with a text editor or the MySQL script editor.
9. ___You must open a MySQL EER Model to run forward engineering from the menu.
10. ___Reverse engineering requires an open MySQL EER Model.

True or False:

11. Forward engineering lets you choose which of the following types of objects for import to a new EER Model? (Multiple answers are possible.)

    A. Tables

    B. Views

    C. Procedures

    D. Functions

    E. Routines

12. Which of the following should you leave deselected when you have self-referencing foreign-to-primary keys in the same table? (Multiple answers are possible.)

    A. `DROP` Objects Before each `CREATE` Object

    B. Generate `DROP SCHEMA`

    C. Skip creation of `FOREIGN KEYS`

    D. Generate Separate `CREATE INDEX` Statements

    E. Generate `INSERT` Statements for Tables

13. Which of the following steps in the *Create EER Model from Existing Database* wizard lets you deselect objects for import? (Multiple answers are possible.)

    A. The *Show Filter* button

    B. The *Select Object* button option

    C. A *Show Filter* link

    D. A *Select Object* link

    E. An *Execute* button

14. What options do you have while reviewing the SQL script to be executed? (Multiple answers are possible.)

    A. Open the script

    B. Save the script to a file

    C. Copy the script to the MySQL Workbench Edit SQL Script wizard

    D. Copy the script to the clipboard

    E. None—you can only run (or execute) it

15. Which of the following is the default directory for files on the Windows operating system? (Multiple answers are possible.)

    A. C:\Program Files (x86)\MySQL\MySQL Workbench\data

    B. C:\Program Files\MySQL\MySQL Workbench\data

    C. C:\Users\<*user_name*>\My Documents\dumps

    D. C:\Program Files (x86)\MySQL\MySQL Workbench\models

    E. C:\Program Files\MySQL\MySQL Workbench\models

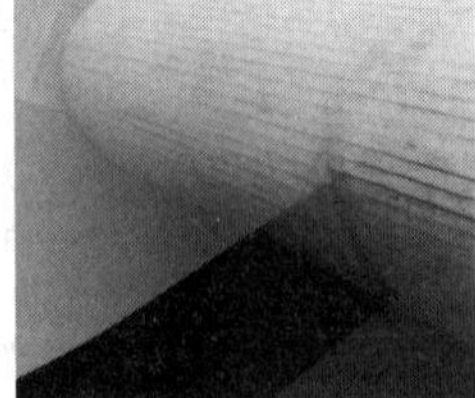

PART III

SQL Development

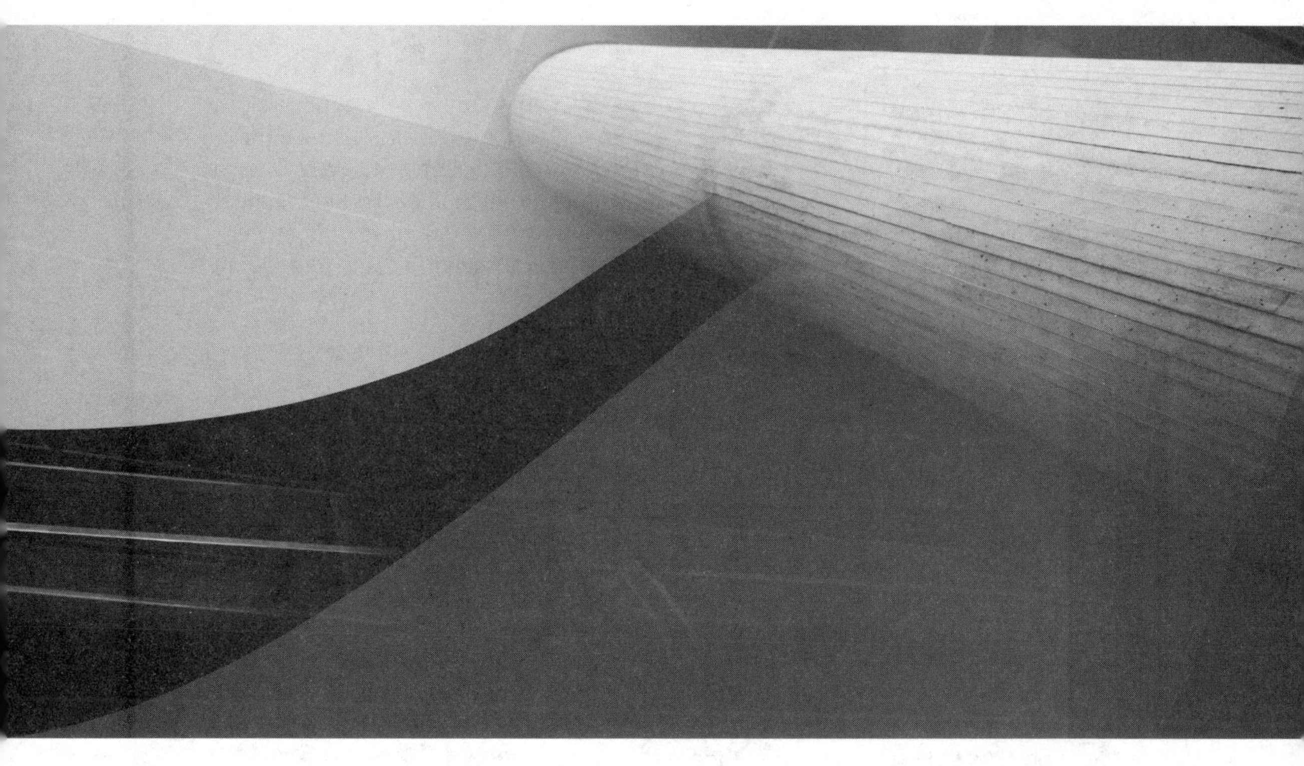

CHAPTER 7

Editing Data

The designer of a web form knows what you can do but not necessarily how you do it; likewise, a data modeler knows how to organize the data but may lack skills to enter or maintain data. MySQL Workbench provides a graphical user interface (GUI) tool that lets you interactively insert, update, and delete data from a MySQL database. It doesn't provide you with a tool to interactively edit seeded data in a model file.

NOTE
You can't edit data in your MySQL models.

You must already have defined a connection to the target database before you can edit the data. Refer back to Chapter 2 if you need to create a connection.

This chapter covers how you connect to edit data and how you insert, update, and delete data from a database.

Connecting to Edit Data

Editing data is part of the MySQL Workbench's SQL Development component. You can click the *Edit Table Data* link from the home page to insert, update, or delete data from a database, as shown in the following illustration.

SQL Development
Connect to existing databases and run SQL Queries, SQL scripts, edit data and manage database objects.
Open Connection to Start Querying
Or click a DB connection to open the SQL Editor.
localhost
User: root Host: localhost:3306
Student@StudentDB
mysqld@McLaughlinMySQL
localhost
New connection 1
New Connection
Add a new database connection for querying.
Edit Table Data
Select a connection and schema table to edit.
Edit SQL Script
Open an existing SQL Script file for editing.
Manage Connections
Modify connection settings or add connections.

After clicking the *Edit Table Data* link, you see the *Connection Option* step of the Edit Table Data wizard. Choose a valid stored connection and enter a user name in the Parameters tab view. You may also store the password in the MySQL Workbench vault, but for security reasons it isn't a good practice. Click the *Advanced* table when you're using Secure Shell (ssh) to connect to a Linux or Unix server, or click the *Next* button to continue with the installer from the following form.

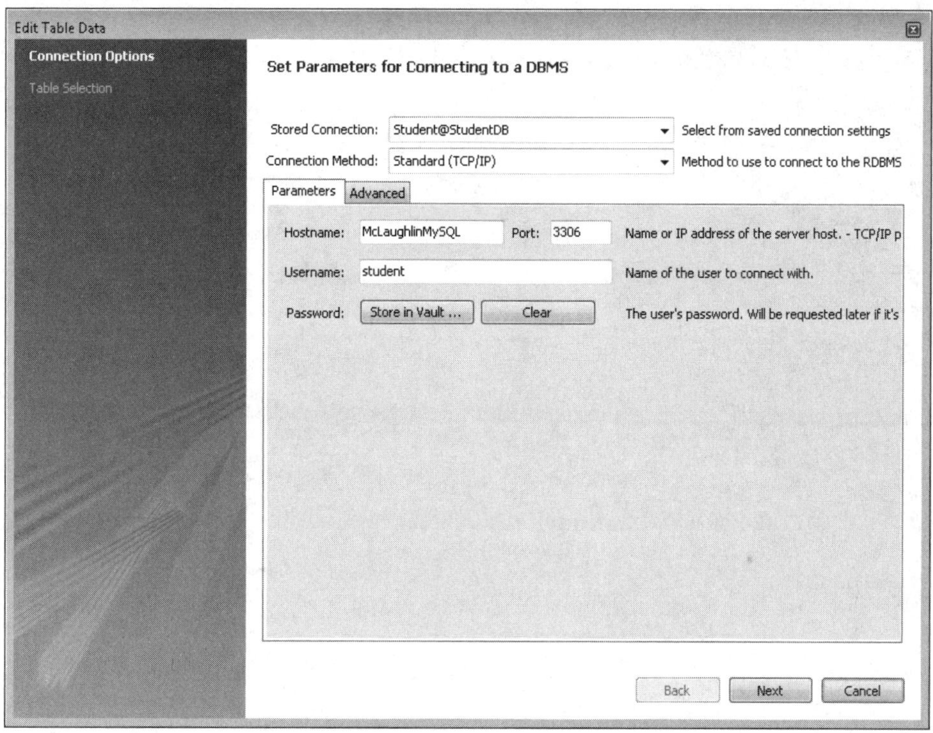

Unless the MySQL Workbench vault holds the password, you must enter the password in the *Connect to MySQL Server* dialog. Click the *OK* button to continue.

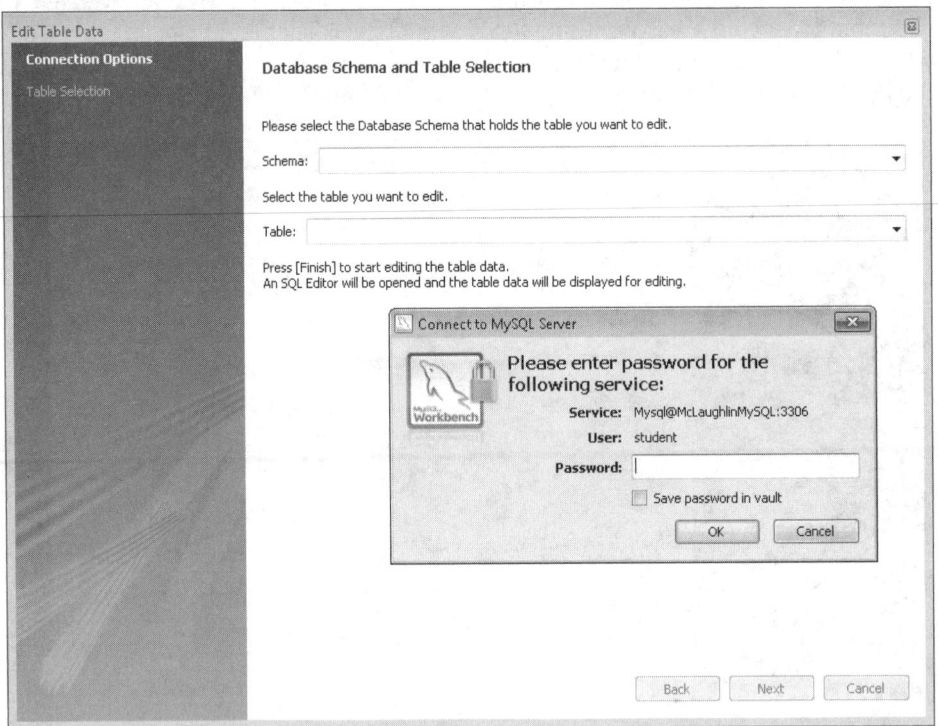

Choose a schema (or database) from the drop-down menu of the *Table Selection* step of the Edit Table wizard.

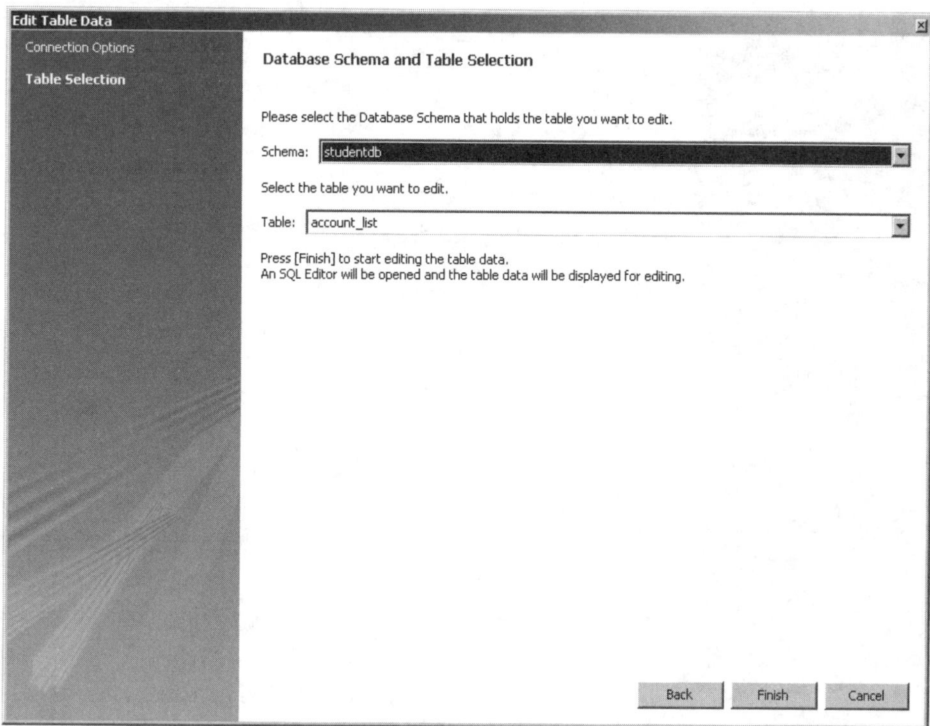

The `student` user selected the `storedb` schema or database. The choice of the `studentdb` enables the Table drop-down box to find all tables from that schema in the lower drop-down box. You can select a table from the list of possible values when the `student` user's privileges authorize access. The values in the drop-down box list table names in ascending order.

In the real world, most user accounts are narrow. That means you wouldn't have access to all the tables in a schema, although that's not true in this book because the `student` user enjoys full privileges on all objects in the sample databases or schemas.

Also, you can only work with tables. The Edit Table Data feature doesn't work with views. Views are excluded from the list of values in the drop-down list of options.

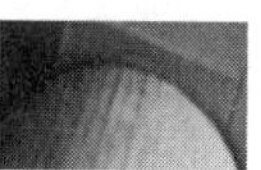

TIP

You can't use this tool to change the data in views.

You should select the `item` table, as shown in the next illustration, and click the *Finish* button to complete the connection wizard steps.

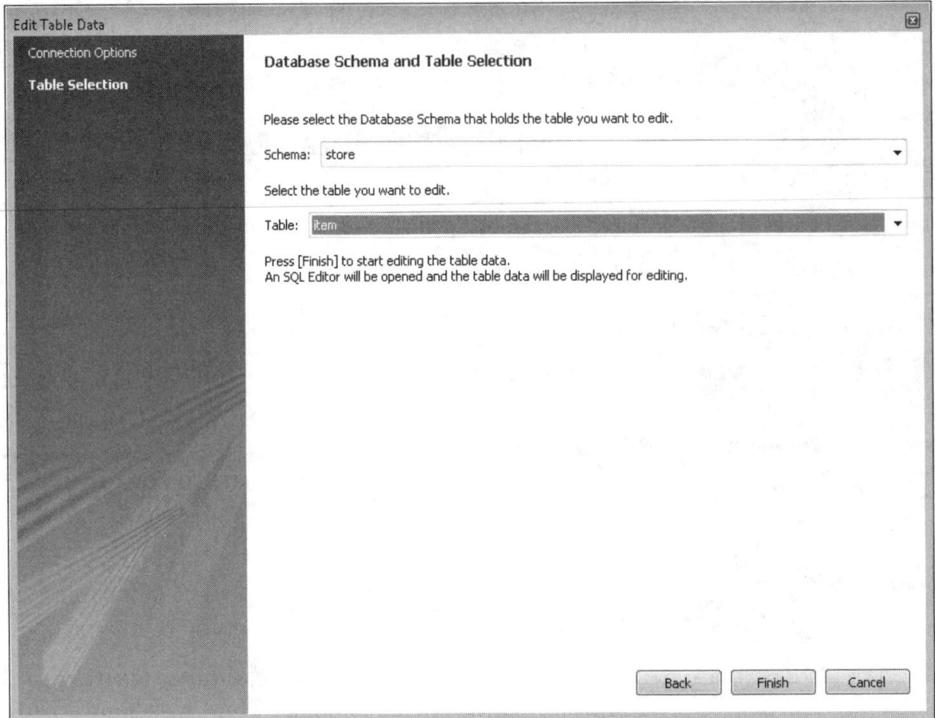

While probably annoying at this point, you're prompted for a password again. That's because the first connection let you find the table, and the second connection lets you edit the connection. The program simply doesn't share connections across the activities of the wizard (it's always possible that may change in later releases).

Enter the password again and click the *OK* button in the following dialog.

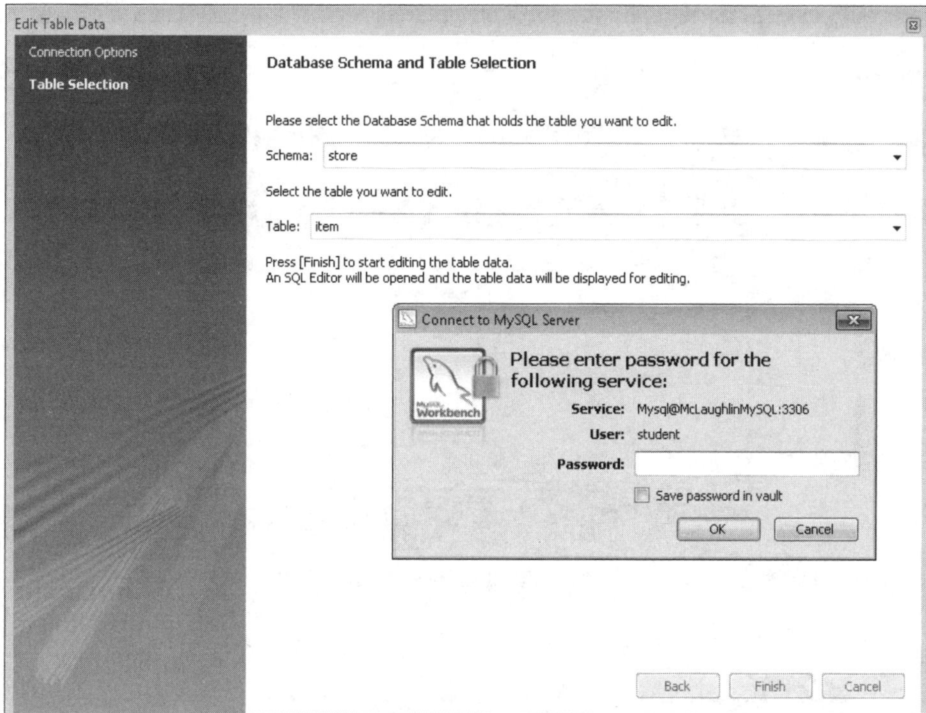

While you've opened only one tab, there's no limit on how many tabs you can open for editing different tables. Although it's probably a good idea to keep it at a small number so they're all displayed in your console.

This section has walked you through the Edit Table Data wizard. The next sections show you how to insert, update, and delete data, respectively. Then, you will learn how to perform group data edits.

Insert Data

The connection wizard walks you through opening a new tab. The *SQL Editor* tab always displays the name of the table in the tab, as you can see in the following illustration.

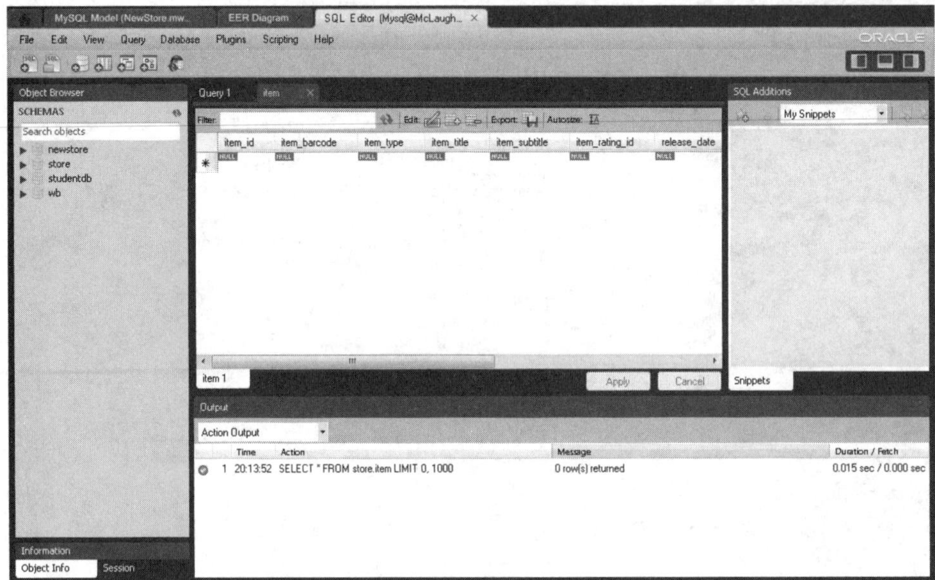

The preceding screen shot shows an item table without any data. The asterisk (*) appears next to the first row, and gray-scaled `NULL` values appear in all columns. Columns in any row can be null only when the column is null allowed, which is the ANSI standard. Null-allowed columns are more commonly called optional columns.

Refer back to Chapter 4 for how you enable `NOT NULL` column-level constraints, which make columns mandatory. The image shows nulls in all columns because no row exists in the table.

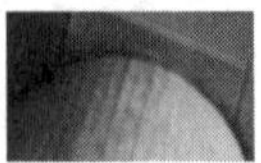

NOTE
Run the seed script from the introduction, then drop down to the command line and TRUNCATE the ITEM table to see this image.

After seeding the table with data (by running or rerunning the script found online at the publisher's web site), the screen should show the following *Refresh data from data source* message in the tab view.

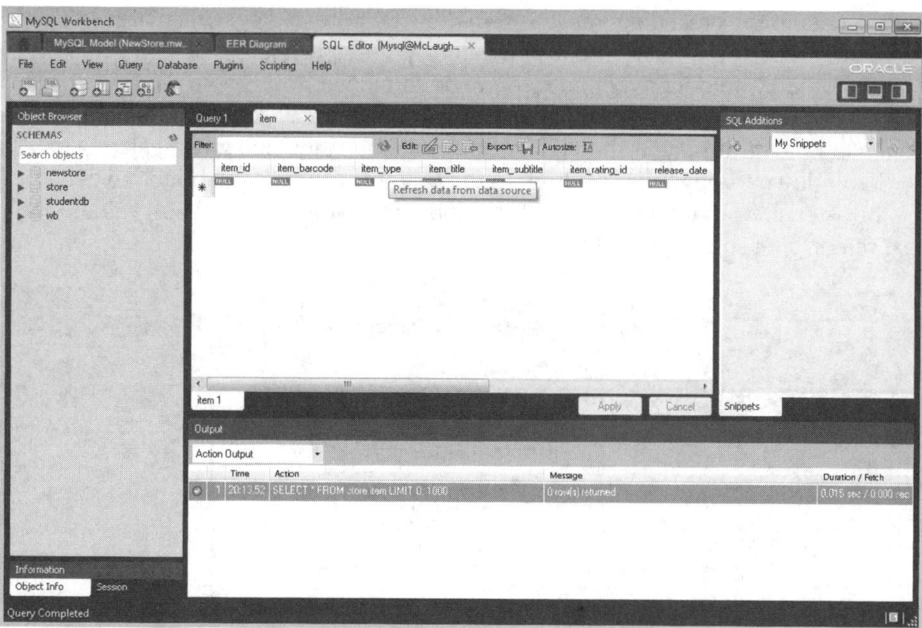

You can click the two blue curved arrows button in the tab's menu bar (at the left of the *Edit* keyword) to refresh the page. It now displays data that starts with the first row of the table, like the following screen shot.

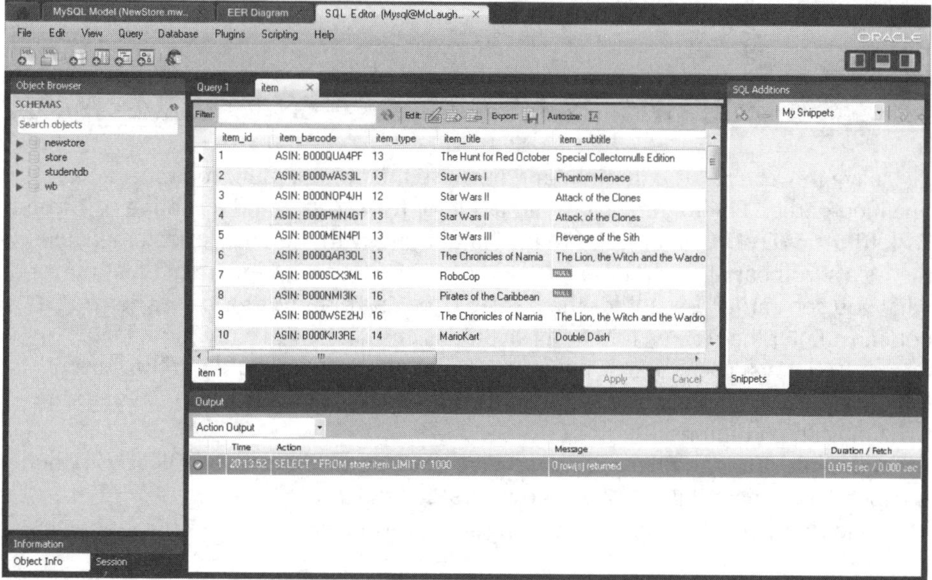

The data in the preceding image is sorted by the primary key, which is the `item_id` column. The `item_id` is also a surrogate key, and the values of a surrogate key are generated by auto-incrementing a numeric sequence. You should flip back to Chapter 3 if you're unfamiliar with the concept of a surrogate key. This is an important feature to note because you should leave that column value null when entering data.

Scroll down through the result set to the bottom. You're at the bottom when you see the asterisk (*) in the leftmost column and a row of gray-scaled null values. The next screen shot shows you what you should see at the bottom of the result set.

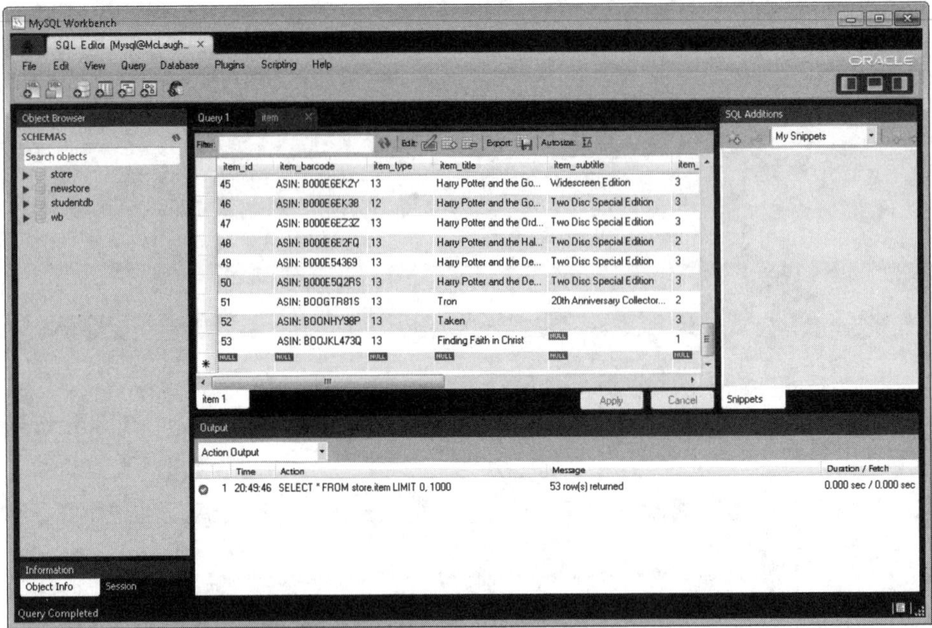

Leave the `item_id` column blank because the column auto-increments, as qualified earlier. Enter a new row with a title of **Iron Man 2** and a subtitle of **Three-Disk (Blu-ray/DVD Combo)**. You're not quite done with the entry of data because there's a scroll bar at the bottom. Scroll over to the right and enter data that mirrors what you see earlier, except for the `creation_date` and `last_update_date` columns. Enter the `now()` function (MySQL is case insensitive if you prefer uppercase letters) in those two timestamp columns, which would put the current timestamp from the operating system where the MySQL Server is running into the two timestamp columns.

You could enter another row, or several rows, at this point. MySQL Workbench is capable of generating a multiple-row `INSERT` statement.

It should now look like the following screen shot.

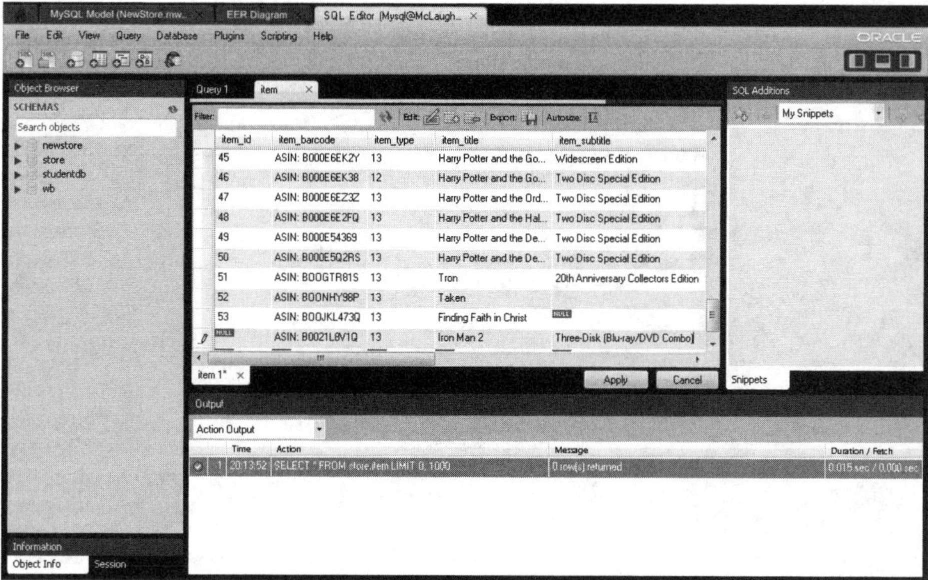

Click the *Apply* button to insert the new row. It presents the following dialog box, which is editable. It shows you the SQL for the `INSERT` statement to the item table.

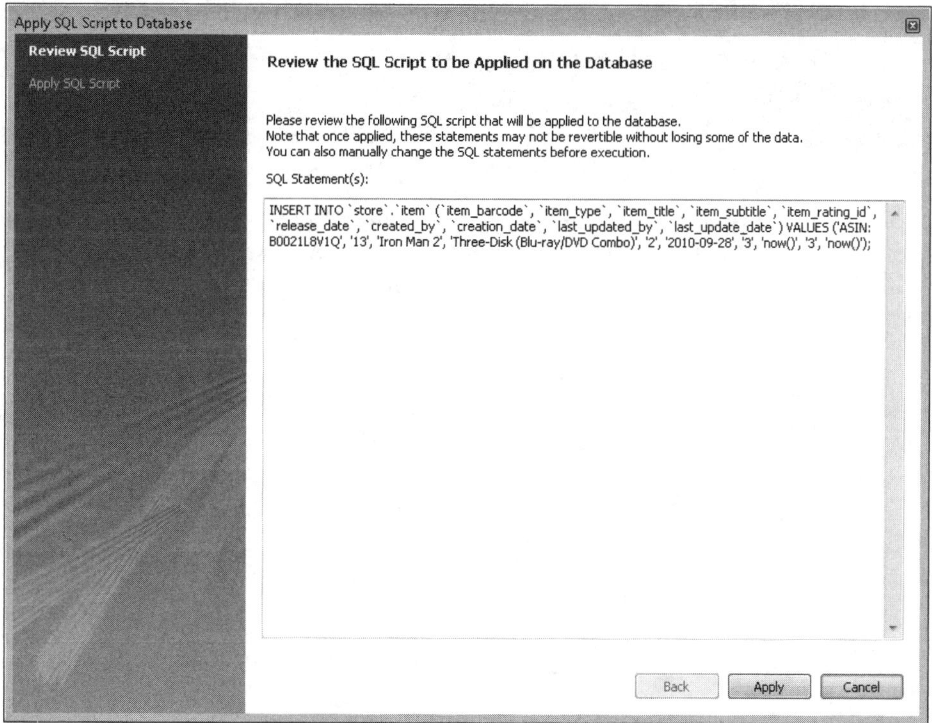

You should now see the following error message. It rejected the `now()` function calls. You can't use function calls in these statements because the interface doesn't support them. MySQL Workbench recognizes function calls and converts them as strings by enclosing them in single quotes.

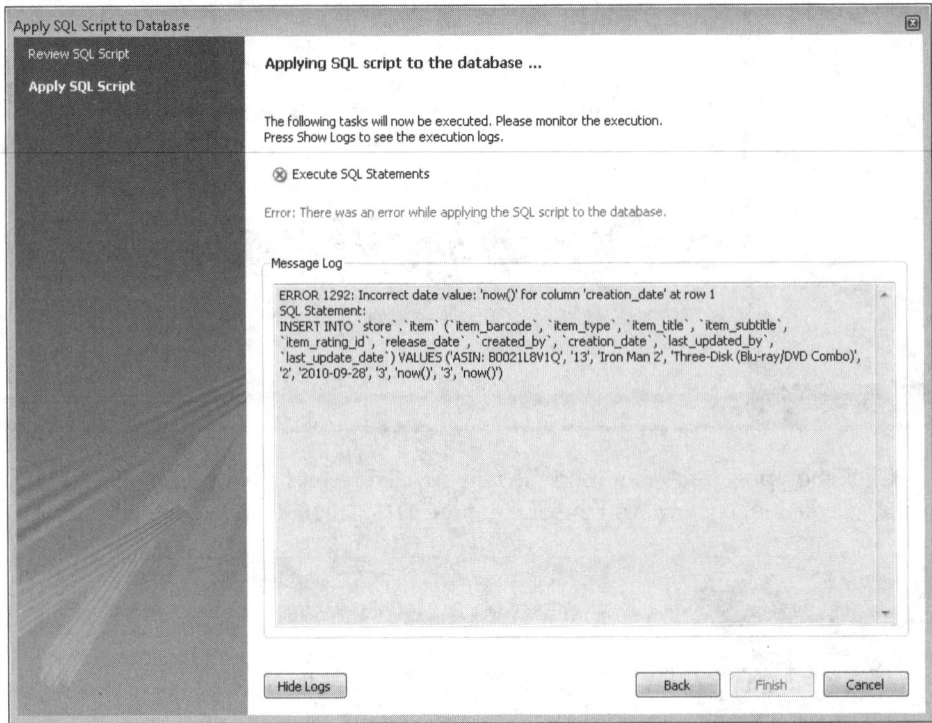

Click the back button and edit the `INSERT` statement by removing the single quotes around both of the `now()` function calls. You can make any number of changes in this editable console because it acts like a text editor.

NOTE
There's no limit on the number of edit changes you can make in the editable script window.

The screen should now look like the following screen shot before you click the *Apply* button again.

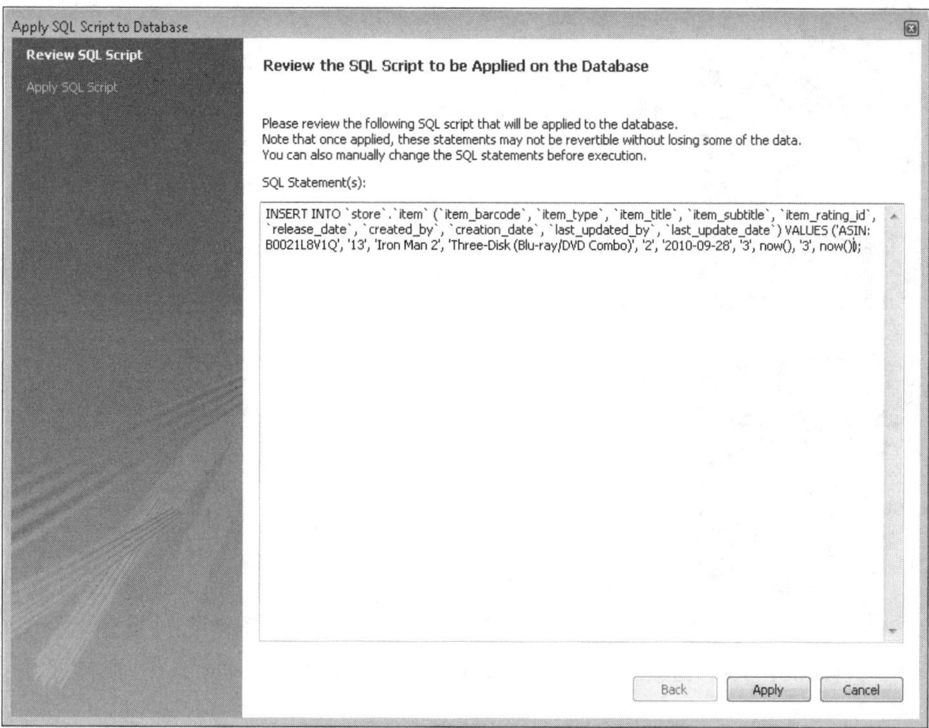

After rerunning the `INSERT` statement, you'll get a message like the following that tells you the SQL script was successfully applied to the database. That means you added a row to the table, which you can see by refreshing the screen.

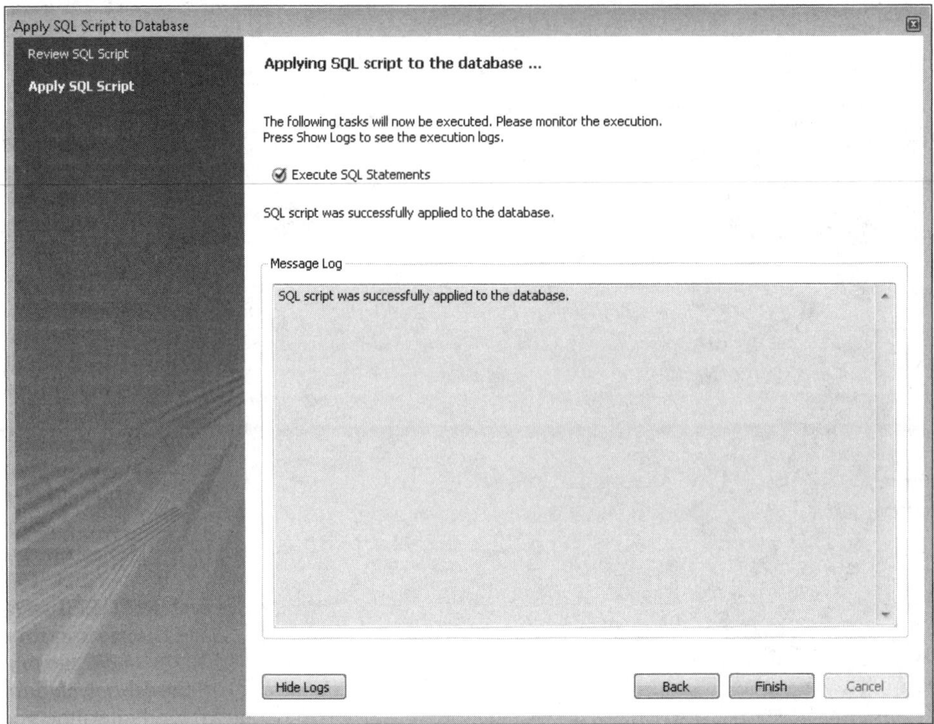

This section has shown you how to insert new data. The next section shows you how to update existing data.

Update Data

If you've just connected to the database and displayed the table for the first time, you're ready to proceed. However, if you've just inserted the new row, click the two blue curved arrows button in the tab's menu bar to refresh the page.

You can only update one row at a time. This means you can't use a multiple select and update a series of rows. You should do that with a SQL statement in a script file, which is covered in Chapter 8.

Assuming that you're using the sample data set, click the gray-scaled `NULL` value `item_subtitle` field for row 7. Enter **Special Edition** in the field. Then, click the `item_title` field for row 6. The *Apply* and *Cancel* buttons should no longer be gray-scaled, and you should see a screen that looks like the following screen capture.

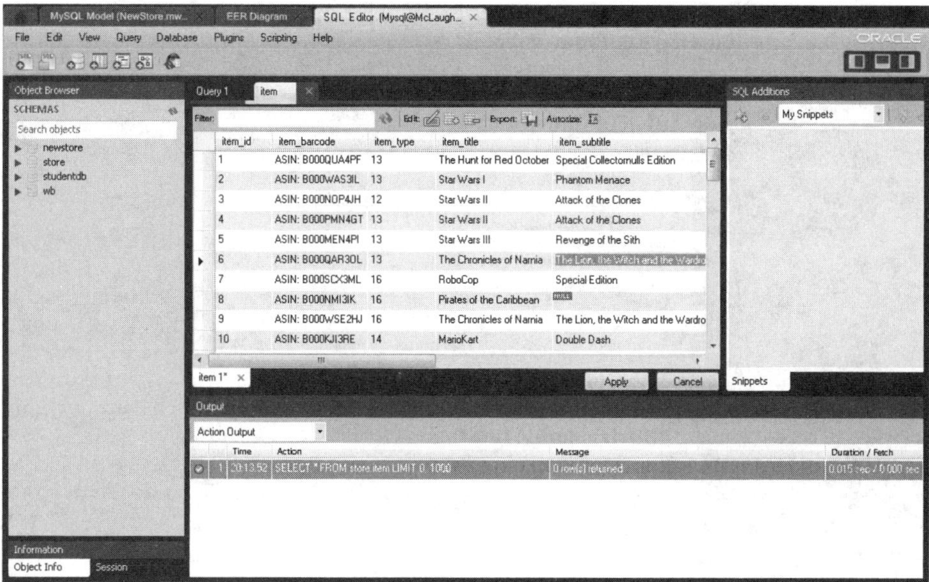

Click the *Apply* button, and you see the following editable script file for an `UPDATE` statement. You can click the *Apply* button to run the `UPDATE` statement.

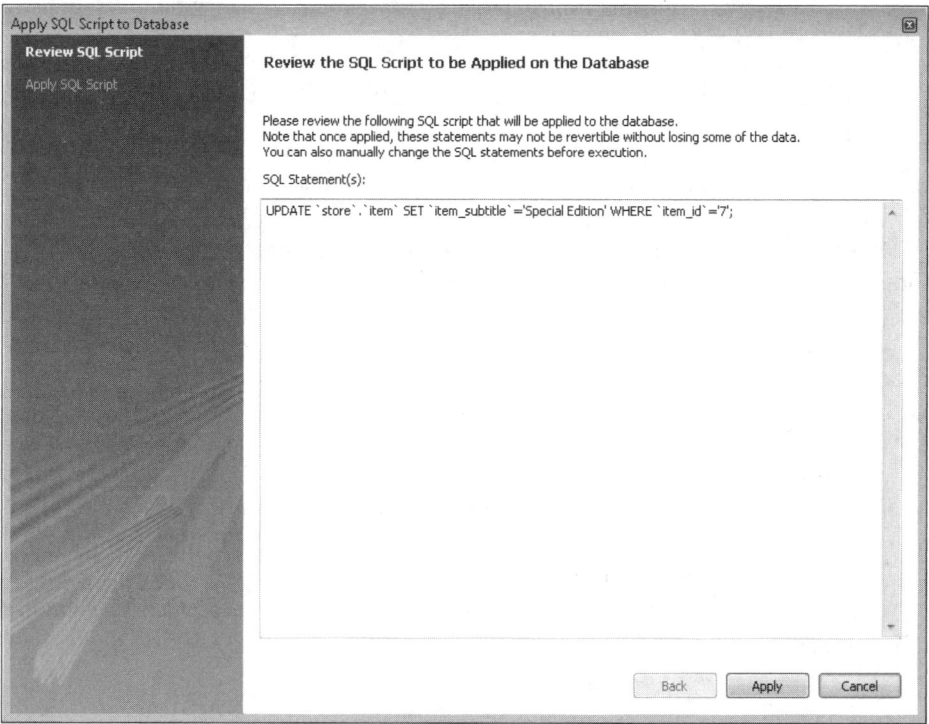

After running the statement, MySQL Workbench returns the following successful dialog prompt. If it weren't successful, you would have an error to fix.

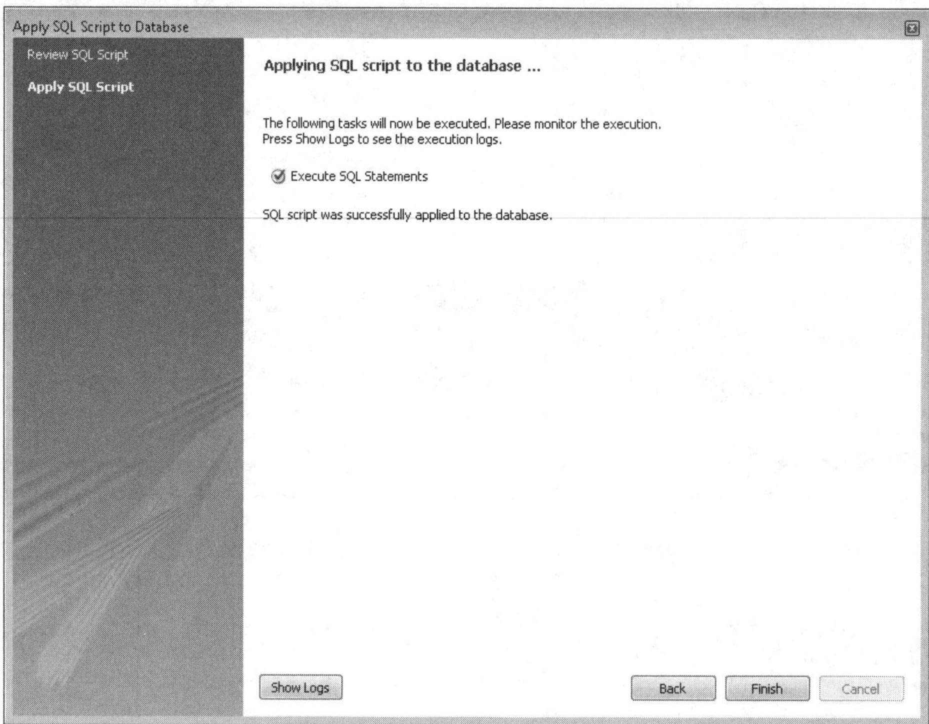

You should really go back and update the `last_update_date` timestamp column with the `now()` function, which applies what you learned in the preceding "Insert Data" section. You may also opt to leave the sample data unchanged.

This section has shown you how to update a field value for a row. However, you should make such updates sparingly. Updates should be managed by an application programming interface (API) set of components. The next section shows you how to delete a row.

Delete Data

Like the caveat that warned you to look out for a message in the "Update Data" section, you need to click the two blue curved arrows button in the tab's menu bar to refresh the table's data display page. At least you needed to do that when you inserted or updated data before you got to this section.

Deleting data is probably the simplest thing to do through the MySQL Workbench interface. You simply click a row and delete the data.

This example assumes you entered a row for Iron Man 2. Click that row, which is row 54 in the sample data set. The blue highlighting shows you're working with that row.

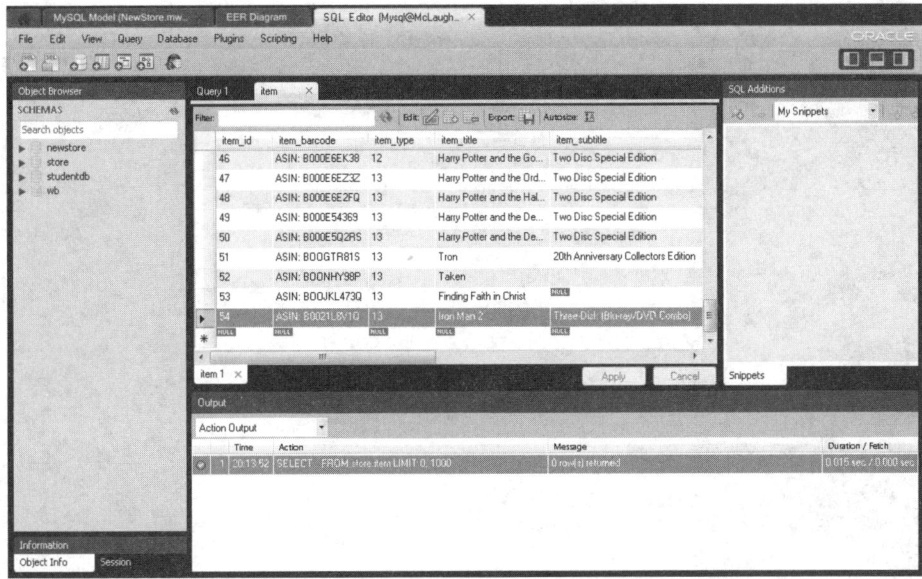

Right-click anywhere on the row, and the context dialog menu displays. Click the *Delete Row(s)* menu option to remove the row from the table's data set. Alternatively, you can press the DELETE key on your keyboard.

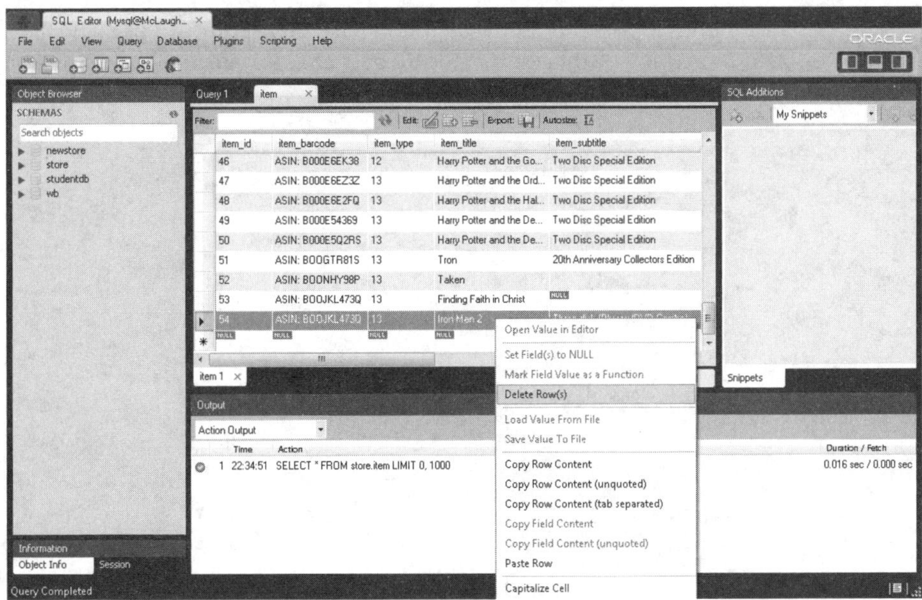

The editable dialog message shows you the DELETE statement that will be run. You can change anything you find wrong with it or click the *Apply* button to run it.

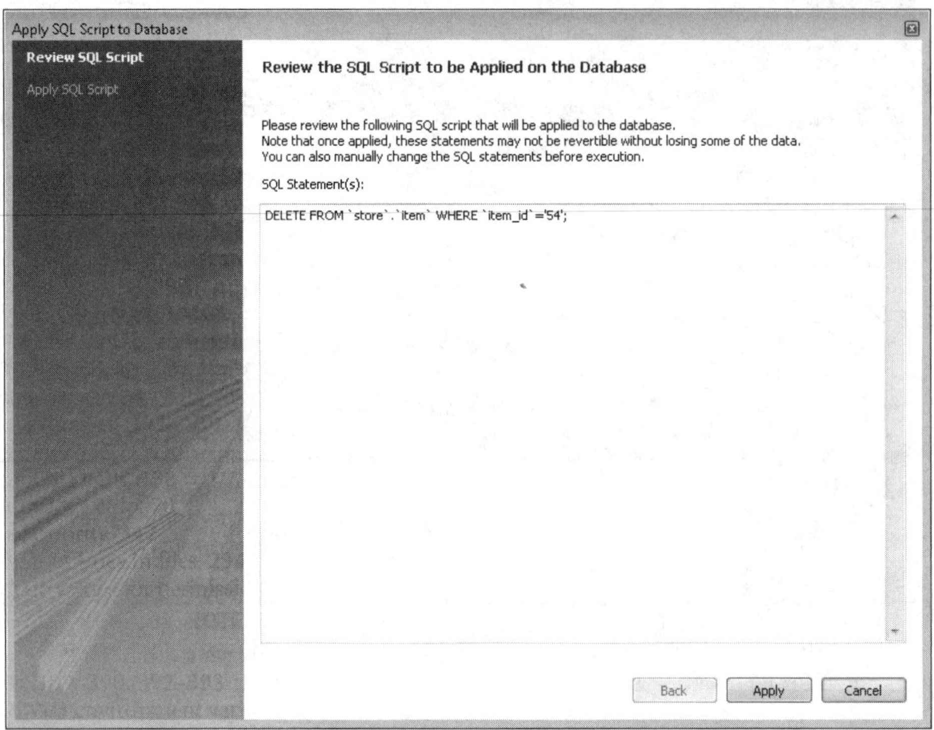

DELETE statements seldom fail because the WHERE clause always uses the primary key column, which in this case is the item_id column. You should see a confirmation dialog like the following.

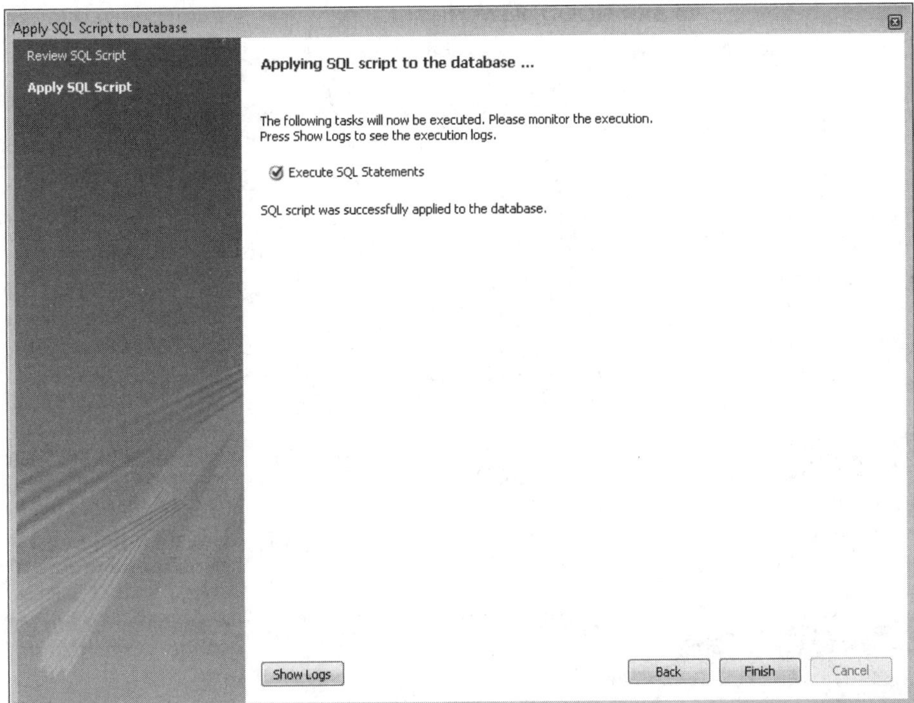

Refresh the page, if it doesn't auto-refresh, by clicking the two blue curved arrows button in the tab's menu bar, and then scroll to the bottom of the data. You should see that row 54 no longer exists, as shown in the following screen shot.

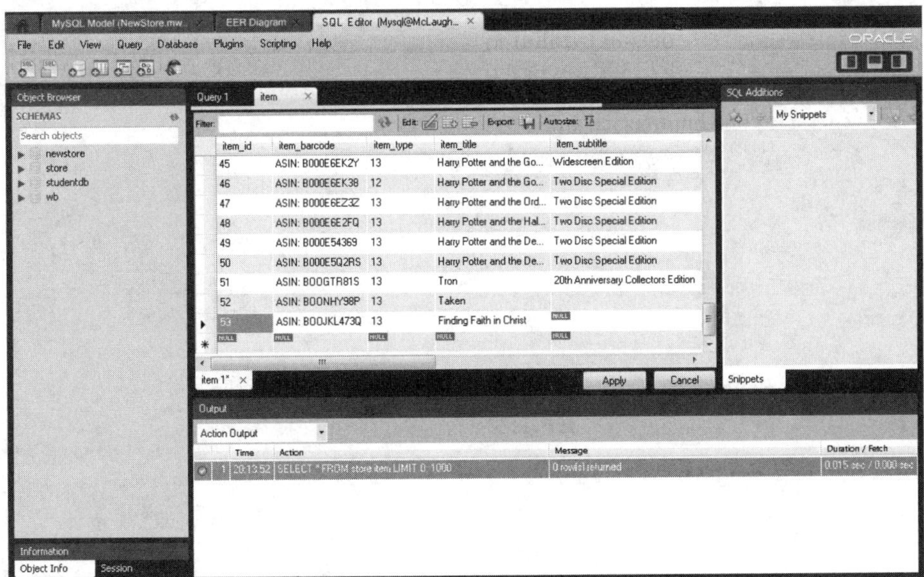

This section has shown you how to delete rows from the data set. The key here is not to forget the right-click because that is the easiest way to do it (except on the Mac OS X, where a two-finger track pad click does it).

The next section shows you how to make multiple edits to a data set at one time.

Multiple Data Edits

The Edit Table Data feature lets you make a combination of insert, update, and delete statements all at once. It simply generates all the changes into a dynamic script file. When you run it, the script makes all changes in the same sequence you made them in the model. The changes are made outside the scope of a transaction, which runs the risk of exposing partial changes before all changes are made.

For example, let's say the `DELETE` statement for row 54 hasn't been run before you notice that you need to update the `item_subtitle` field values for rows 52 and 53 with a "Two-disk Special" string. You enter the changes before applying the `DELETE` statement, and when you click the *Apply* button, you'll see an editable script file. Click the *Apply* button and you'll see the successfully applied dialog like the next screen shot.

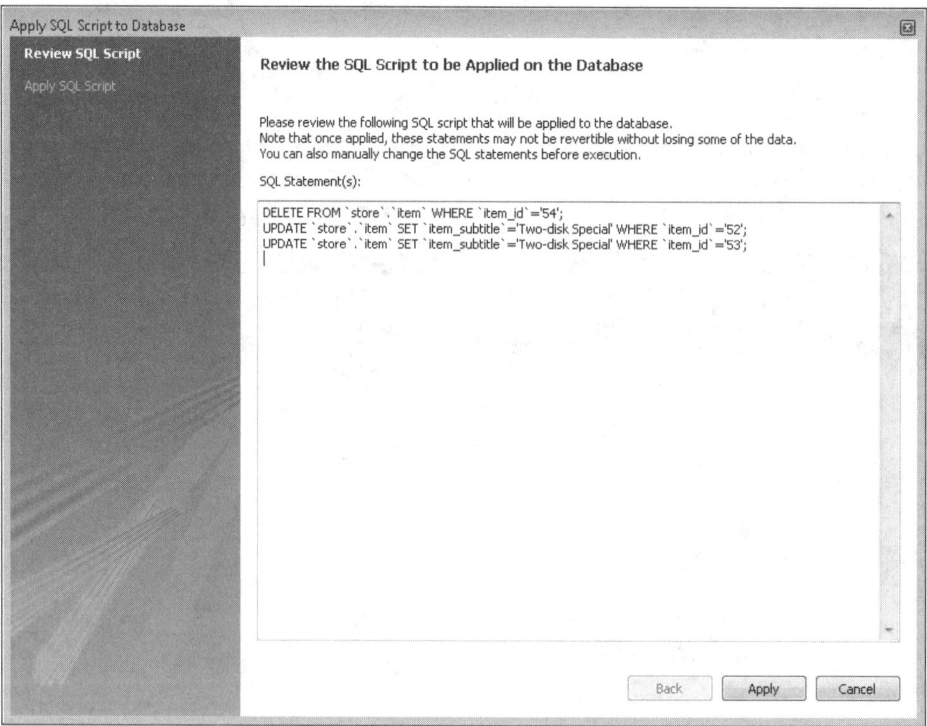

Click the *Finish* button to dismiss the following dialog window.

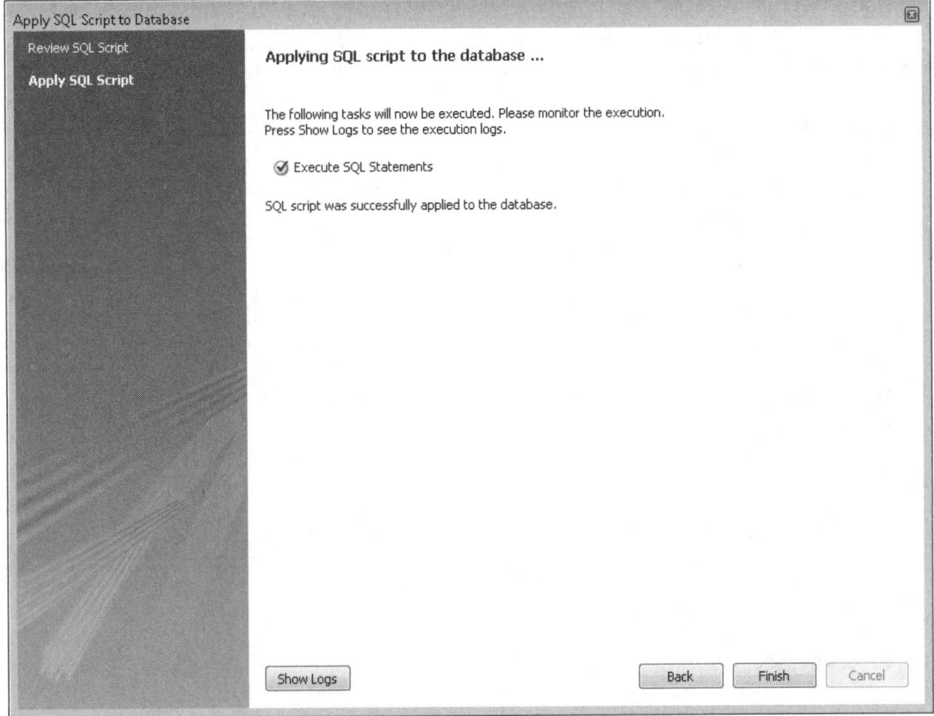

This section has shown you that you can make multiple edits to the same data set at the same time. The next chapter discusses how to work with script files.

Summary

This chapter explained how to edit data in MySQL Server database instances. You should be able to insert, update, and delete data one step at a time, or perform a combination of edits at once.

Mastery Check

The mastery check is a series of true or false and multiple choice questions that let you confirm how well you understand the material in the chapter. You may check Appendix A for answers to these questions.

True or False:

1. ___The editing feature is found in the Server Admin component.
2. ___The editing feature lets you change data in any database, with or without a connection.
3. ___The editing feature lets you change data in a MySQL Model, not a MySQL Server's database instance.
4. ___You can refresh the data set from the menu by clicking the two blue curved arrows button.
5. ___The asterisk points to the current row.
6. ___The blue highlighted cell is the one you're currently editing.
7. ___You can't insert more than one row at a time in the Edit Table Data feature of MySQL Workbench.
8. ___MySQL Workbench uses the primary key column in the `WHERE` clause to identify the proper row(s) to delete from the database.
9. ___You can't update more than one record at a time in the Edit Table Data feature of MySQL Workbench.
10. ___You can edit any generated SQL statement before the statement is run.

Multiple Choice:

11. You can perform edits on which of the following? (Multiple answers are possible.)
    - **A.** Tables
    - **B.** Views
    - **C.** Procedures
    - **D.** Functions
    - **E.** Triggers

12. How many rows can you edit at one time?

A. One

B. Many

C. Any number you can select

D. All

E. None of the above

13. How many tables can you open in tabs for concurrent editing at one time?

A. 1

B. 2

C. 8

D. 16

E. No stated limit

14. How many edits can you make with a script file before applying it? (Multiple answers are possible.)

A. 1

B. 64

C. 256

D. No stated limit

E. None

15. How many rows can you update at one time?

A. 1

B. 64

C. 128

D. 256

E. No stated limit

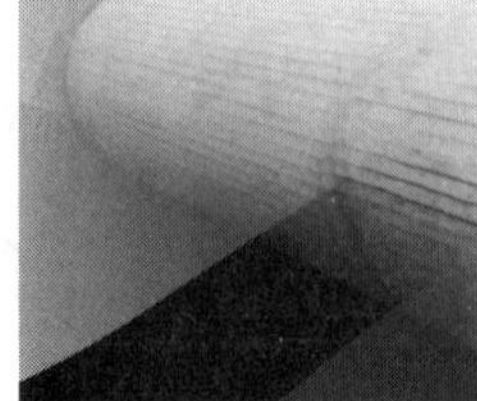

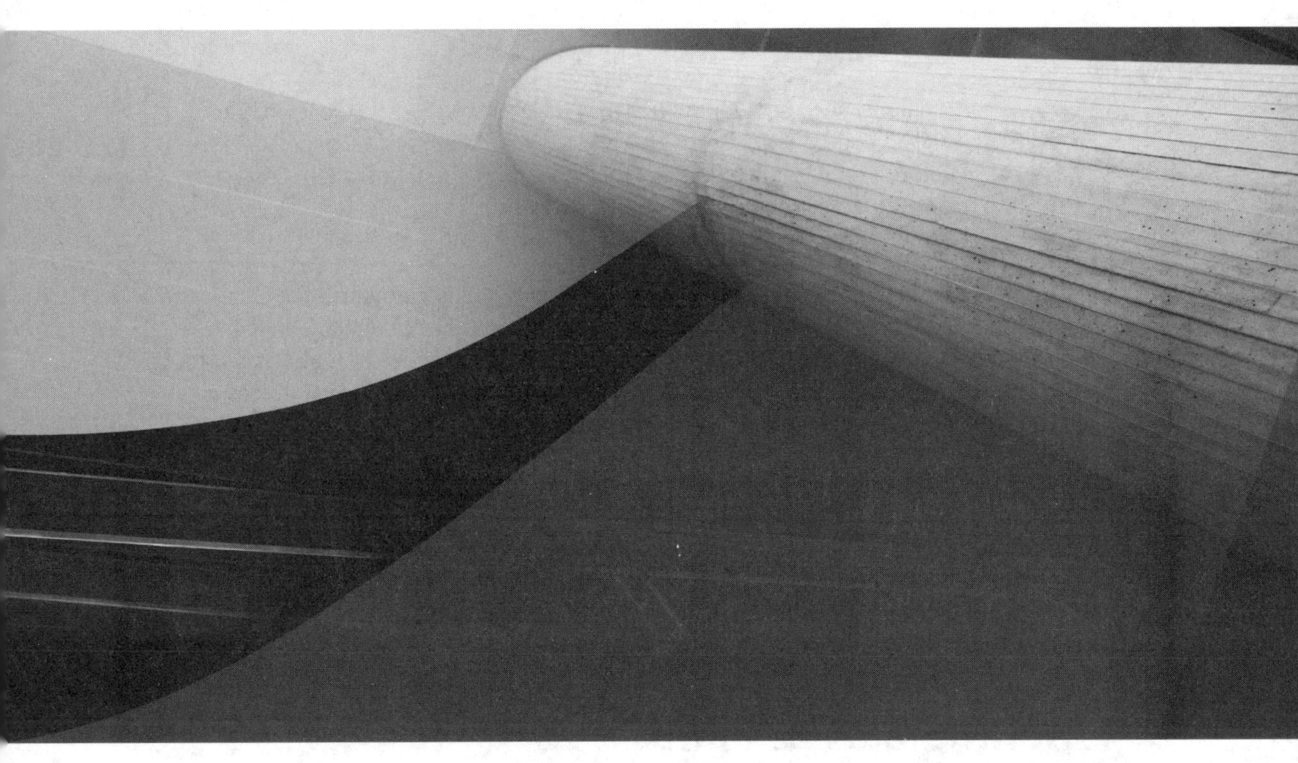

CHAPTER 8

Managing SQL Scripts

T

his chapter shows you how to manage SQL scripts in MySQL Workbench. It shows you how to work with MySQL Workbench's *SQL Editor.* Lua and Python scripting don't work in SQL Editor, and you'll find a full discussion demonstrating Python scripts in Appendix B.

MySQL Workbench's SQL Editor lets you work with SQL statements, like Data Definition Language (DDL), Data Manipulation Language (DML), Data Control Language (DCL), and Transaction Control Language (TCL) commands. It also supports MySQL stored programs—SQL/PSM (SQL Persistent Stored Modules). That means you can run scripts that create stored functions or procedures.

You may also use the `SET` command to address variables, and both `@` and `@@` for session and global variables, respectively, which work like MySQL Monitor. You can refer to *Oracle Database 11g & MySQL 5.6 Developer Handbook* (Oracle Press, 2011) for more information on the MySQL Monitor features.

The following sections show you how to open a file, edit the file, run the file, and check the output logs. It's presented in two sections—opening a SQL file and running a SQL file.

Opening a SQL File

There are two ways to open, edit, and run SQL scripts from the SQL Development component of MySQL Workbench. One way lets you create a new SQL script or edit an existing SQL script file, and the other lets you open an existing file. Whether you opt for the former or latter, both let you create new and edit existing SQL scripts when you open a *SQL Editor* pane.

You can click any connection in the *SQL Development* section, shown here, and open a *SQL Editor* pane by default. It's important to note that the connection is to the MySQL Server, not any specific database inside the server.

SQL Development
Connect to existing databases and run SQL Queries, SQL scripts, edit data and manage database objects.
Open Connection to Start Querying
Or click a DB connection to open the SQL Editor.
localhost
User: root Host: localhost:3306
Student@StudentDB
User: student Host: McLaughlinM...
New Connection
Add a new database connection for querying.
Edit Table Data
Select a connection and schema table to edit.
Edit SQL Script
Open an existing SQL Script file for editing.
Manage Connections
Modify connection settings or add connections.

Inside the *SQL Editor* pane, you click the SQL with file folder overlay button (second from the left on the button panel) to open a preexisting SQL file. You may also write a query, statement, or set of statements in the query pane, and then click the folder button (on the far left of the query window) to save what you've written in a file.

Clicking the *Edit SQL Script* link, as shown in the preceding illustration, launches a two-step wizard that lets you select and open a SQL file.

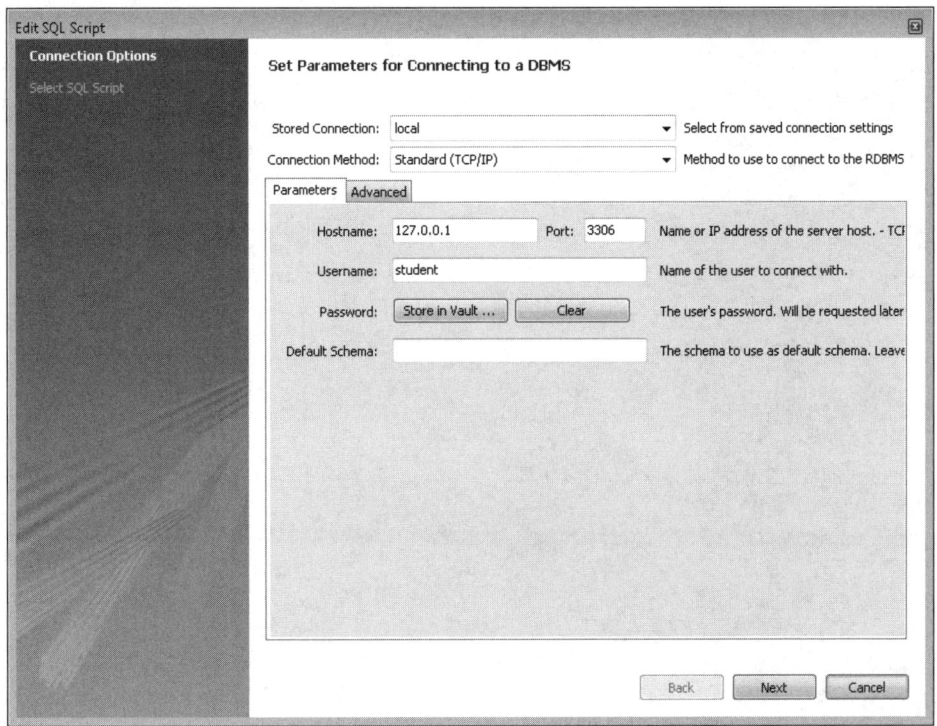

The next dialog is the *SQL File Selection* dialog. Click the *Browse* button to find a file you want to open.

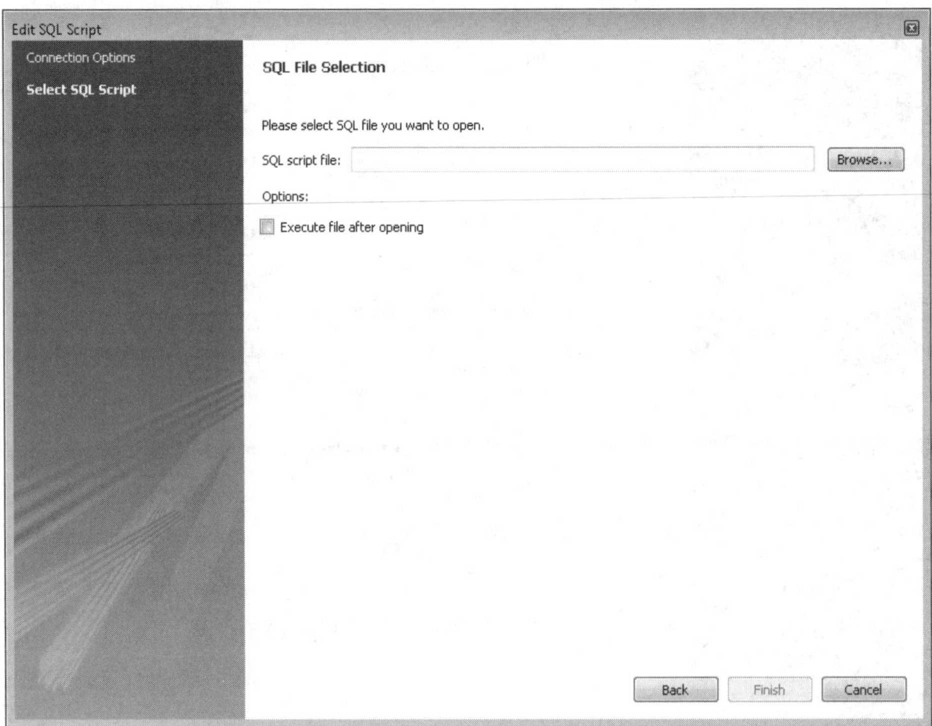

The prior step launches a *File Chooser* window. Select a SQL file that you want to open, edit, or run. After navigating the folder structure and clicking a file, click the *Open* button to see the script.

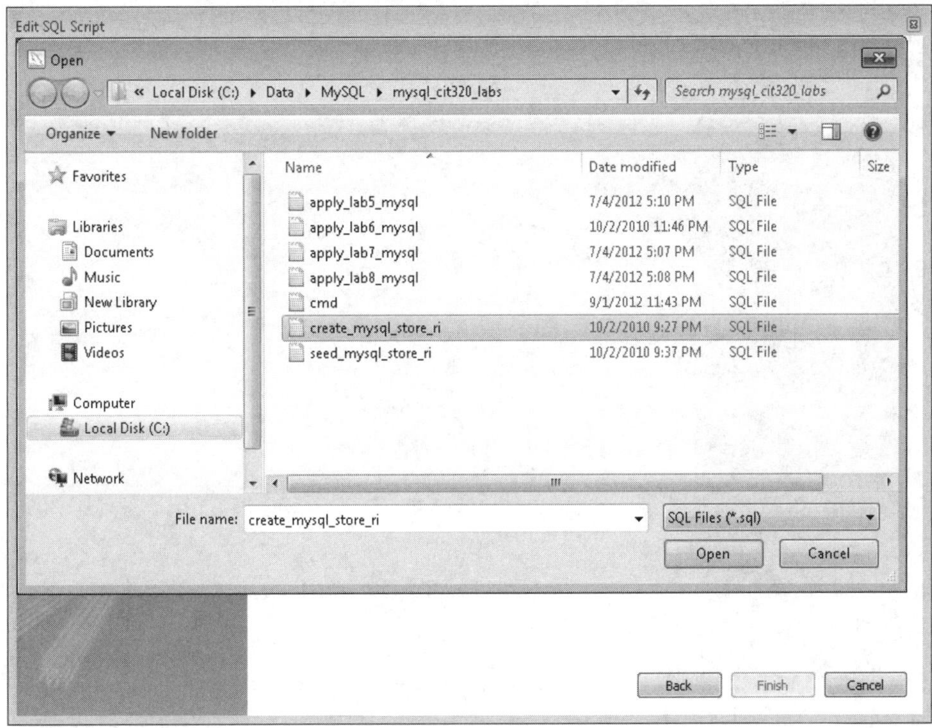

Having selected the file, you return to the *SQL File Selection* dialog. Click the *Finish* button, shown in the next illustration, to open the file.

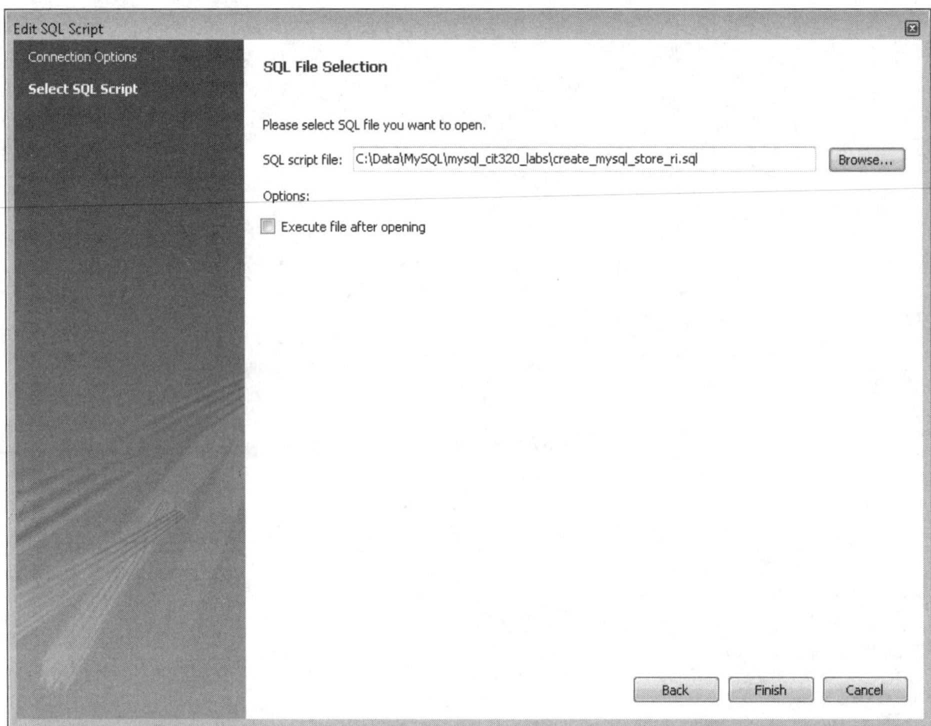

It launches a *SQL Editor* pane and prompts you to connect to the database. You don't have the ability to write or edit SQL script files unless you're connected to a database in the MySQL Server. The next illustration shows you the connection dialog as an overlay to the *SQL File Selection* screen. This should look familiar by this point in the book. Click the *OK* button after entering the valid user password in the following screen shot.

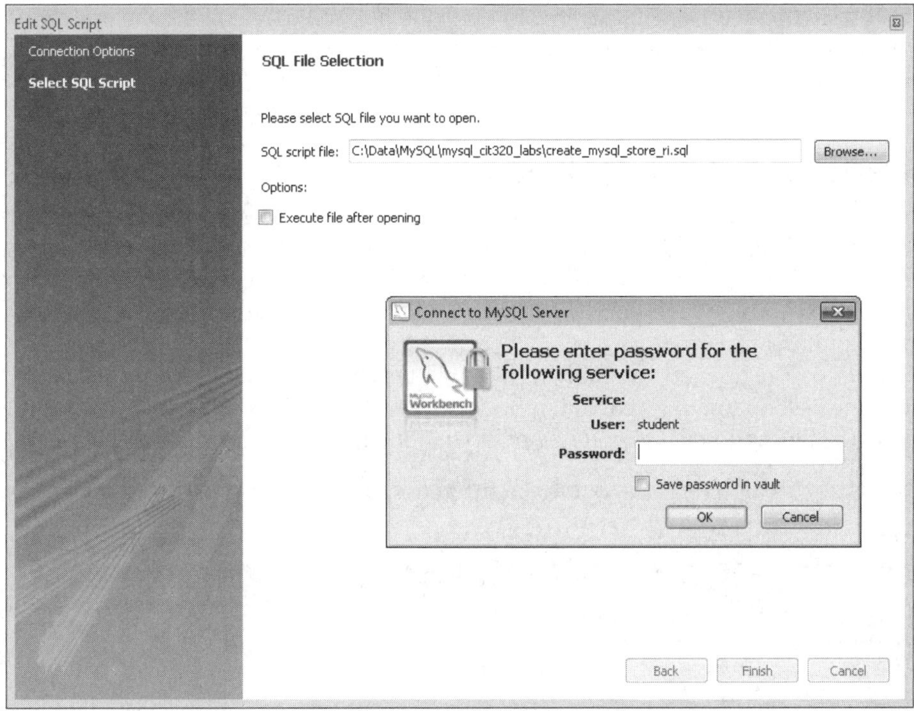

You should see a script editing pane after clicking the *OK* button. It should look like the one shown in the next illustration. This interactive panel lets you run, edit, or save the SQL script file.

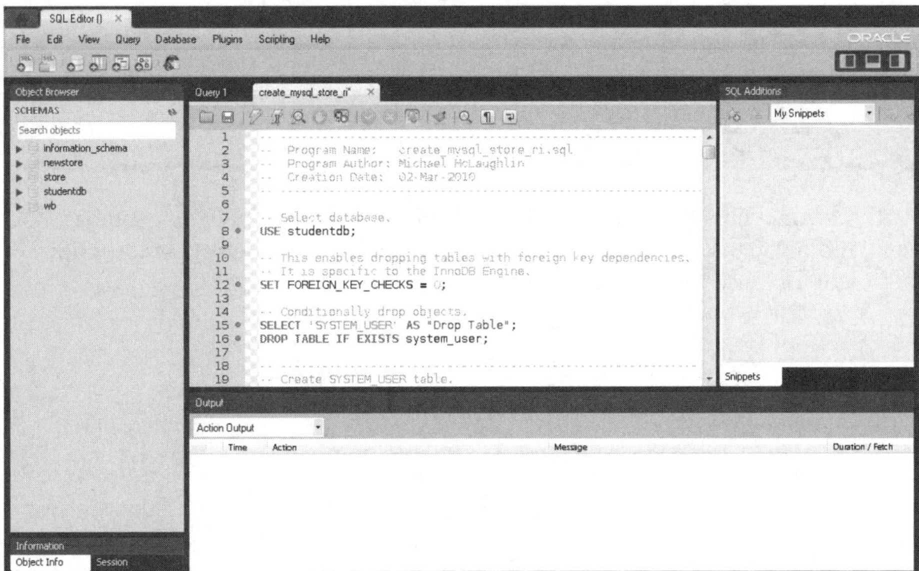

This section has shown you how to open the file. You may edit the file and then save the changes by clicking the disk icon button. The next section describes running the SQL script file.

Running a SQL File

Running a SQL script file is straightforward when you know what must be inside a SQL script file for MySQL Workbench. You must include a `USE` statement that selects a database in each script you're going to run from within MySQL Workbench. You raise an exception when you forget to include a `USE` *`database`* statement in your scripts.

After you've opened a complying script in the *SQL Editor* pane, you click the lightning bolt button to run a SQL script statement. You might see an error like the following illustration when you neglect to include the `USE` *`database`* statement.

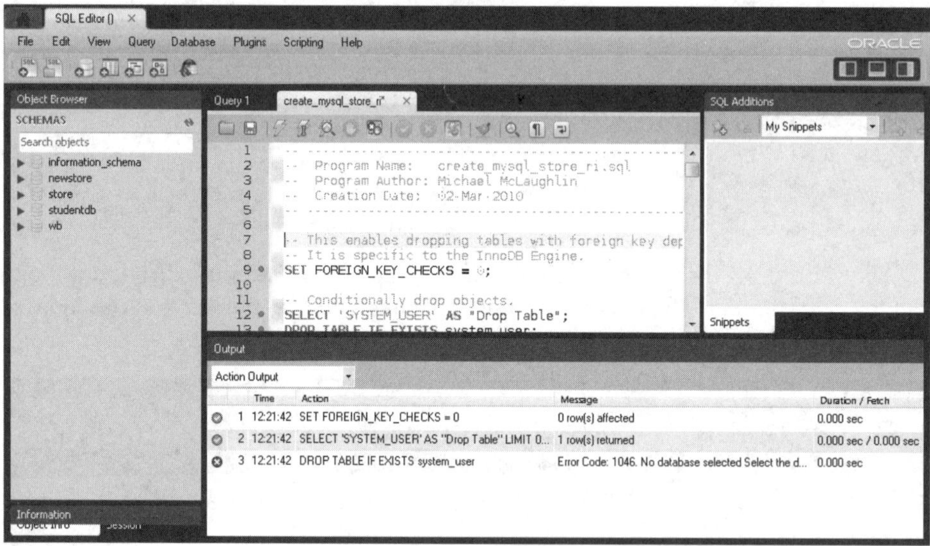

This error occurs because the SQL script file doesn't specify which database to use. The omission is a common practice in SQL script files when a master script calls them, because the master script selects the database.

Showing you this type of error lets me explain a governing assumption about SQL script files that work in MySQL Workbench. The assumption is that all scripts stand alone and qualify which database they work with when they include DDL and DML statements. You qualify the database by selecting it with the `USE` command, like this:

```
USE studentdb;
```

The `USE` command refers to a `studentdb` database. The semicolon isn't required, but it doesn't cause a problem. Using semicolons is a good practice because they're generally required in MySQL Monitor, which interprets the SQL submission from MySQL Workbench.

Another element of `USE` command assumption is that no script will call another script when run from inside MySQL Workbench. This precludes including a `SOURCE` or `\.` (a backslash and dot symbol set is shorthand for `SOURCE`) command in a SQL script file.

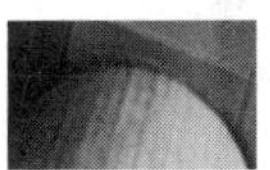

NOTE
The TEE and NOTEE commands are also disallowed in MySQL Workbench because logging is managed inside the application software.

While MySQL Workbench currently disallows running scripts that call other scripts, which would be the production-ready approach, this limitation means that final deployment can't be tested in MySQL Workbench. In addition, the final deployment must occur inside a single SQL script or tested outside of the MySQL Workbench tool. A new feature request to use the `SOURCE` command was pending at the time of writing.

TIP
Check for the status of the new feature request (bug) 63999.

The *Action Output* pane now contains the error, and there isn't a convenient button to clear it. You must right-click the *Action Output* pane to see a context menu with a *Clear* option. Click the *Clear* option to reset the *Action Output* pane, as shown in the following illustration.

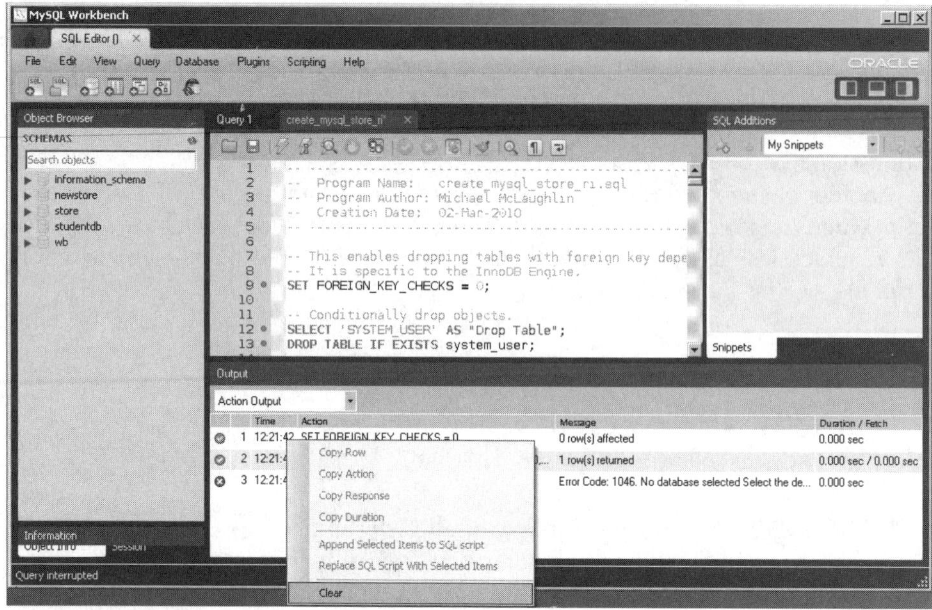

The SQL script runs successfully when you add a `USE` command to the SQL script file. Unfortunately, it doesn't automatically save that change to the file. You must click the disk icon button to save the change in the file.

Any query results or `SHOW` statements in the script display as results to the console. The following shows that the sample script displays 23 results. You must click on and close all result sets before you can see your script file.

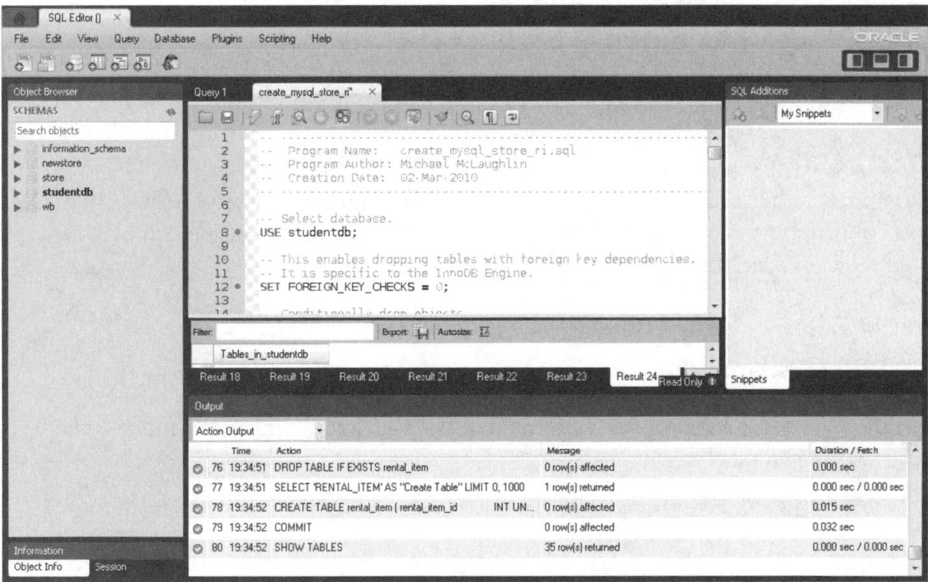

After you clear all the result sets, you can save your changes to this script by clicking the disk icon button. It shows you a file chooser where you save the file.

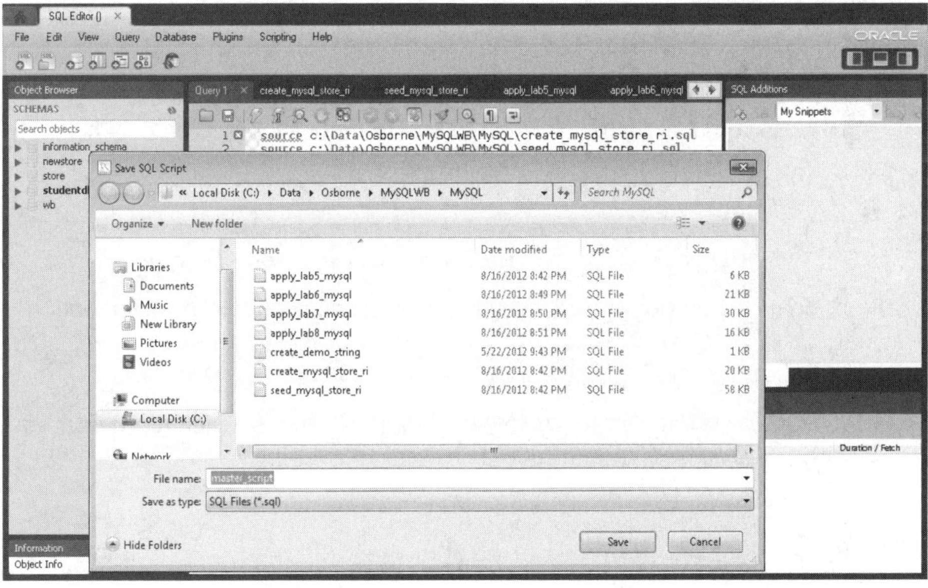

This section has shown you how to run SQL scripts from the MySQL Workbench tool.

Summary

This chapter explained how you manage SQL scripts in MySQL Workbench.

Mastery Check

The mastery check is a series of true or false and multiple choice questions that let you confirm how well you understand the material in the chapter. You may check Appendix A for answers to these questions.

True or False:

1. ___MySQL Workbench lets you write new SQL scripts from scratch.
2. ___MySQL Workbench automatically saves any changes you make to an open script.
3. ___MySQL Workbench provides two ways to open script files from the *SQL Editor* pane.
4. ___Opening any connection provides you with a *SQL Editor* pane.
5. ___All SQL scripts must include a `USE` statement when they run DDL or DML SQL statements.
6. ___You can `SOURCE` another script from within a SQL script that you run from MySQL Workbench.
7. ___You can't use the `\.` (a backslash and dot symbol set) in lieu of the `SOURCE` command when you run the script from MySQL Workbench.
8. ___You clear the output screen by clicking a *Clear script* button in the *SQL Editor* pane.
9. ___MySQL Workbench provides context menus for some features.
10. ___Some features of MySQL Workbench don't have buttons or menu options.

Multiple Choice:

11. MySQL Workbench connects to which of the following when it provides you with a *SQL Editor* pane? (Multiple answers are possible.)

    A. MySQL database

    B. MySQL Server

    C. MySQL Monitor

    D. MySQL ODBC

    E. MySQL JDBC

12. Which of the following SQL commands require a MySQL database connection? (Multiple answers are possible.)

    A. TCL

    B. DDL

    C. DML

    D. DCL

    E. None—they only require a MySQL Server connection

13. Which of the following MySQL Monitor commands fail in MySQL Workbench while running a SQL script? (Multiple answers are possible.)

    A. `TEE`

    B. `SOURCE`

    C. `\.`

    D. `NOTEE`

    E. None—they all work

14. Which of the following types of scripts run in MySQL Workbench's *SQL Editor*? (Multiple answers are possible.)

    A. PHP

    B. Python

    C. SQL

    D. SQL/PSM programs

    E. Lua

15. Which of the following are usable in SQL scripts run from within MySQL Workbench? (Multiple answers are possible.)

    A. Global variables

    B. Session variables

    C. Stored procedures

    D. Stored functions

    E. Shell variables

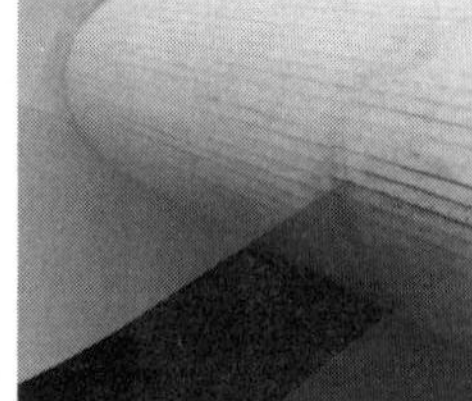

PART IV

Server Administration

CHAPTER 9

Instances

This chapter leads the discussions of using the server administration features of the MySQL Workbench. You have the ability to administer instances, create local or remote instance managers, manage import and export processes, manage user security, and manage the server instance managers.

The following illustrates the portion of the MySQL Workbench's home page for server administration. It shows an existing instance administration link to a Microsoft Windows–based MySQL instance. The Server Administration list is empty until you create an instance manager.

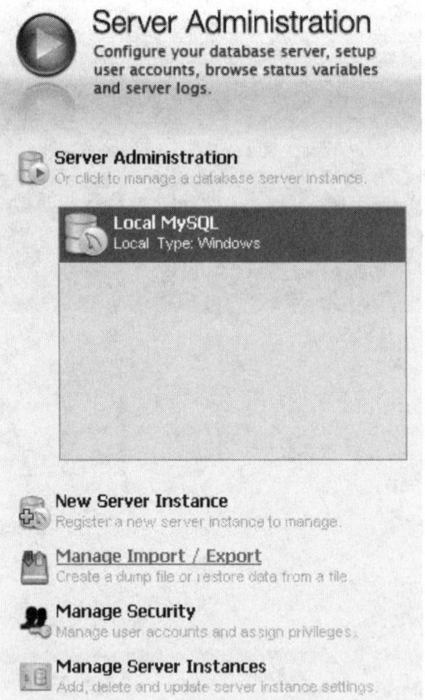

A local instance manager allows you to start, stop, and manage operation of the MySQL database on the same server. MySQL Workbench provides these instance management services. The remote instance manager allows you to likewise start, stop, and manage operation of a MySQL instance running on a different server.

Instance managers support utilities that manage the database, including backup and recovery tools. The full set of MySQL utilities is available through the MySQL Workbench. Many utilities, such as migration from external databases, are delivered as wizards inside the MySQL Workbench.

This chapter shows you how to create local and remote instances, start and stop local and remote instances, view and edit status and system variables, view error logs, and maintain existing instance managers. There's also some introductory discussion to the Windows Management Instrumentation (WMI) and Secure Shell (ssh) connections that enable remote management of the MySQL services.

Create a Local Instance Manager

You create an instance manager by clicking the *New Server Instance* icon shown in the preceding image. It launches a wizard that lets you create and register the instance manager.

As you can see in the following illustration, there are 11 steps in the wizard. The first step specifies the host machine for the instance manager. You have the option of creating a local or remote host and leveraging parameters from an existing database connection. You can refer back to Chapter 2 for a refresher on connections.

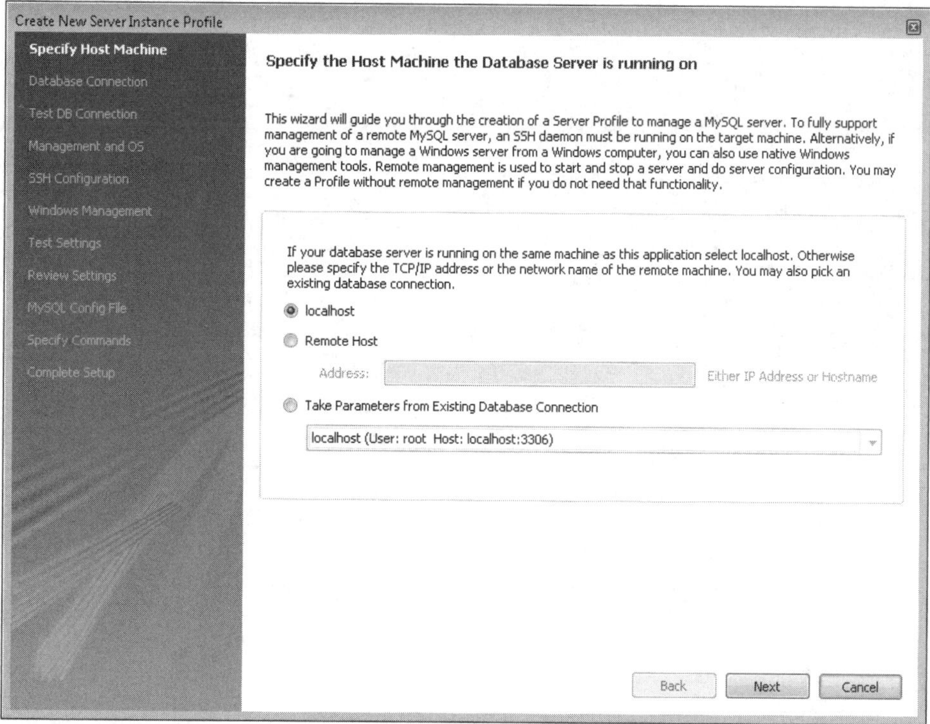

The first example creates a local host connection. You don't need to select a radio button because `localhost` is the default. Click the *Next* button to continue with the wizard.

The database connection is the next step in the wizard. It presents two components—the parameters and advanced configuration screen. The local host configuration only requires setting the parameters, but the advanced settings enable Secure Shell (ssh) for remote instance management.

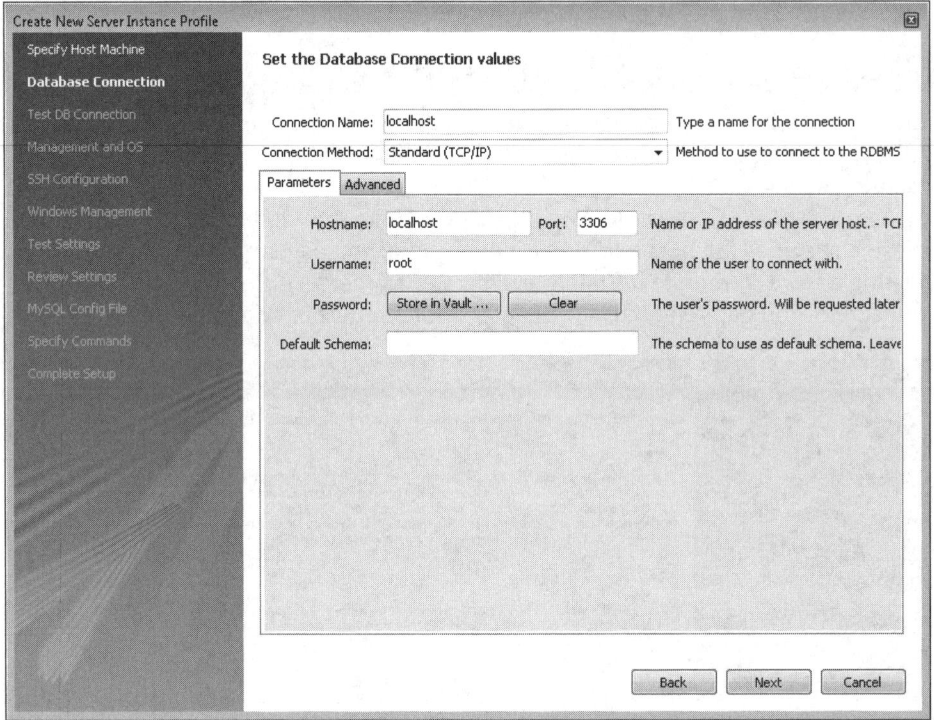

You can leave the `localhost` connection name or replace it. That's a decision for you to make. Update the connection name field with your preferred choice.

Click the *Next* button to move forward in the wizard. The next illustration shows that the wizard tests the database connection and prompts for a password. Enter the root user's password and click the *OK* button to continue with the wizard.

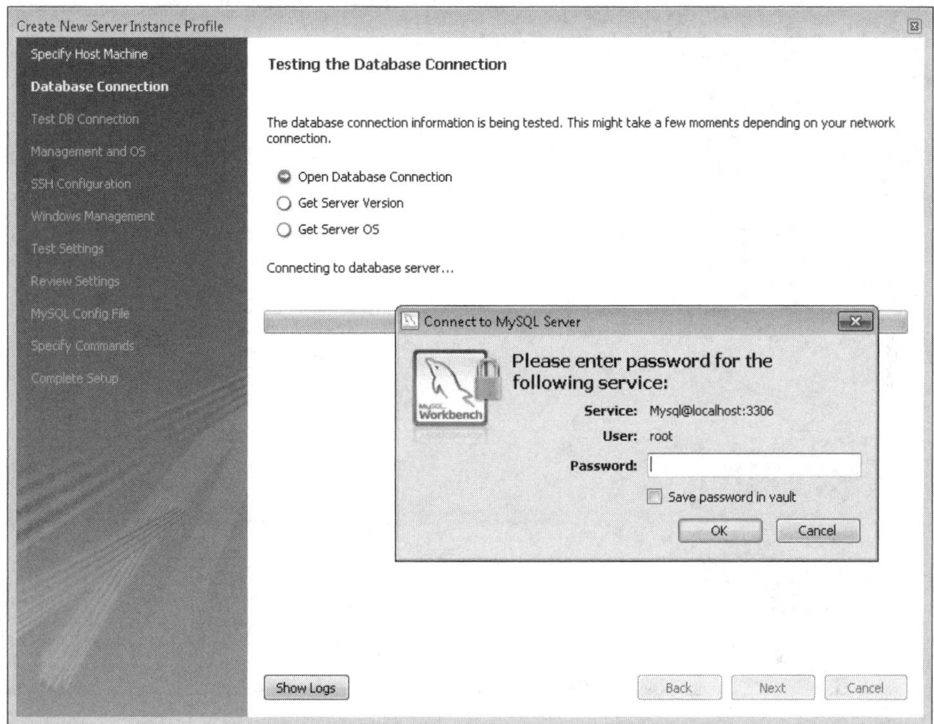

If the database connection can be opened, it verifies the version and operating system before acknowledging a successful test. It displays the following screen.

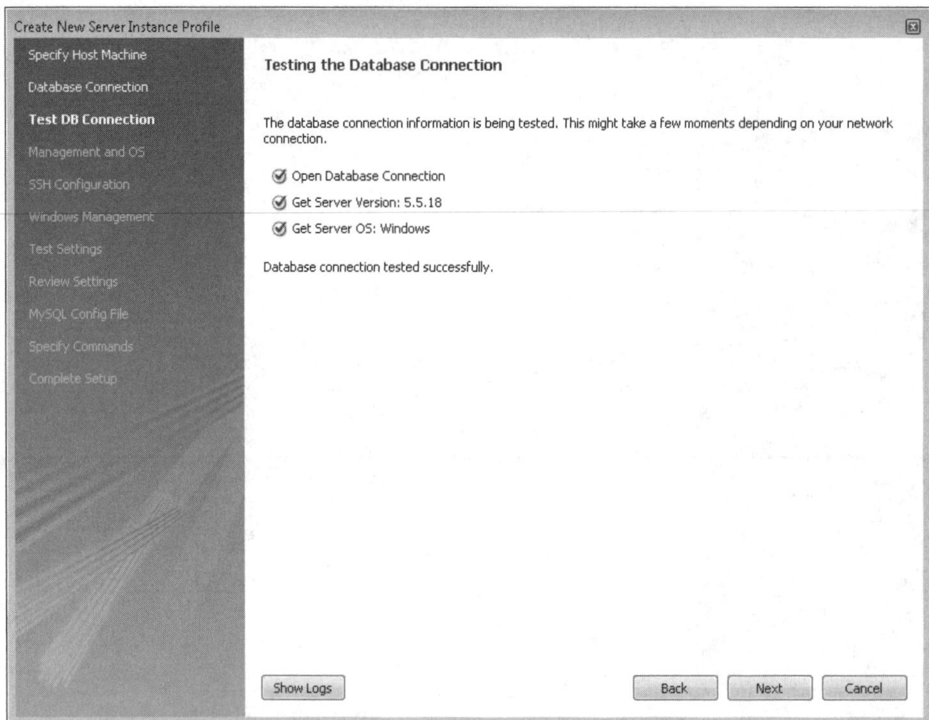

You have prerequisite steps when configuring a remote instance manager. The next screen lets you choose the service from the native operating system, which you needed to configure before beginning this step.

You specify the path of your remote service here. In a fully authorized remote connection, you would also perform these steps. You must configure WMI for a Windows operating system or ssh for a Linux or Unix operating system before you'll get the opportunity to perform these tasks. Naturally, the machine where you deploy

MySQL Workbench and the MySQL Server must be connected across a network using Transmission Control Protocol/Internet Protocol (TCP/IP).

Remote MySQL Connection

It's always wise to install MySQL on the same platform that you'll run MySQL Workbench because it has both a client and server software component. The MySQL Monitor client software lets you connect to a local machine or remote machine.

The syntax to make a remote connection using MySQL is

```
mysql -uroot -p -P3306 -hmclaughlinxp32.techtinker.com
```

You should test this before you begin the WMI or ssh configuration, because it must work across TCP/IP before the other can work. Connecting as the root user does require that you configure the host aspect of the root user as `%`, a `hostname`, IP address, or subdomain. This configuration is less secure than a root super user account that accesses a local instance with a `localhost` authorization. The best recommendation is to limit access to the subdomain of your servers, which is typically behind the corporate firewall.

There are many arguments about what's appropriate as the host value for a root user. My opinion is rather conservative. I believe you should use a `hostname` or subdomain within the corporate intranet. The decision is ultimately yours, but remember as a database administrator (DBA), your primary role is to protect the data.

Start mode is most often set to automatic, but the location of the `my.ini` file on Windows or `my.cnf` file on Linux or Unix isn't guaranteed. You need to figure that out before you create an instance manager. Refer back to Chapter 1 for configuration locations on Fedora and Mac OS X.

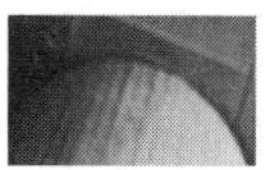

NOTE

There's no problem when you configure the my.ini in a nontraditional location, but most DBAs don't do this.

The following example is a nontraditional location because it qualifies the subdirectory (or folder beneath) the Program Files directory by the MySQL version number. The default subdirectory is MySQL and the actual one is MySQL5518. Click the *Next* button to continue with the wizard.

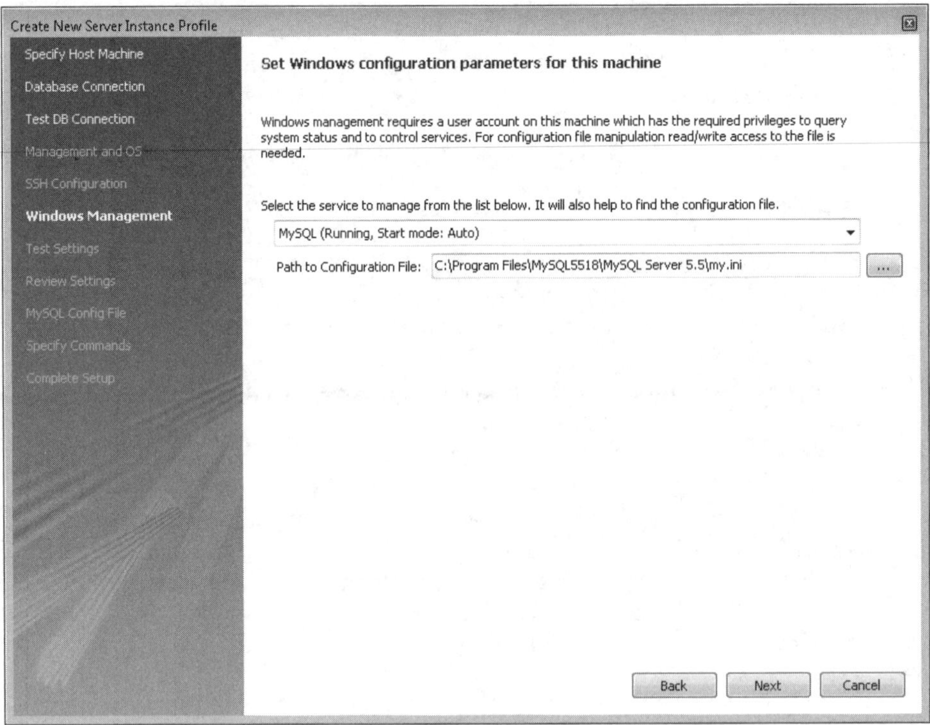

The wizard's next screen verifies that it found a valid MySQL configuration file. It displays that message, and you should click the *Next* button to continue.

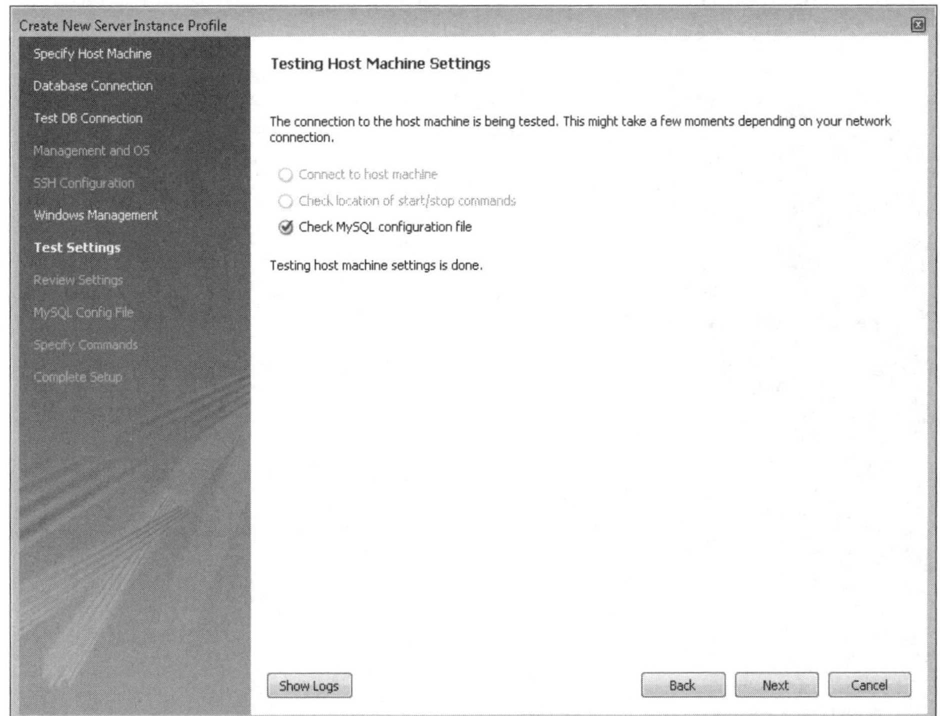

The next screen lets you know that your remote configuration passed the review process. You're also given a last chance to accept or change the settings before you proceed. This presents an overlay dialog to ask whether you want to continue or review the settings again. You click *Continue* to press forward with the wizard.

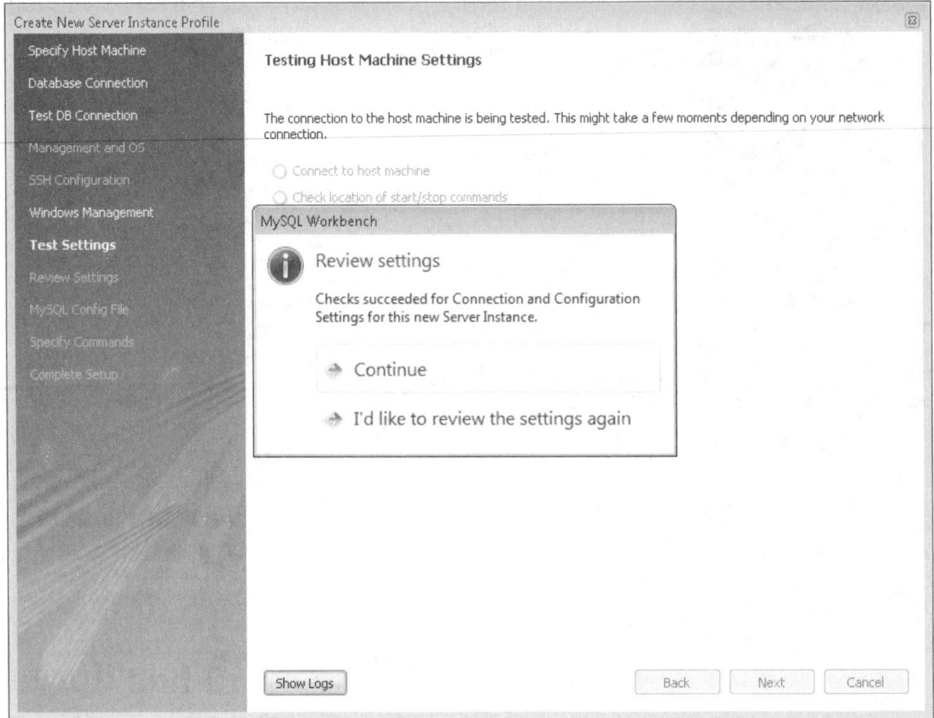

This is where you create the name that displays in the Server Administration list of server instance managers. You need to choose a unique name and then click the *Finish* button to complete the creation of an instance manager. A general recommendation for an instance manager name is mysqld@servername.

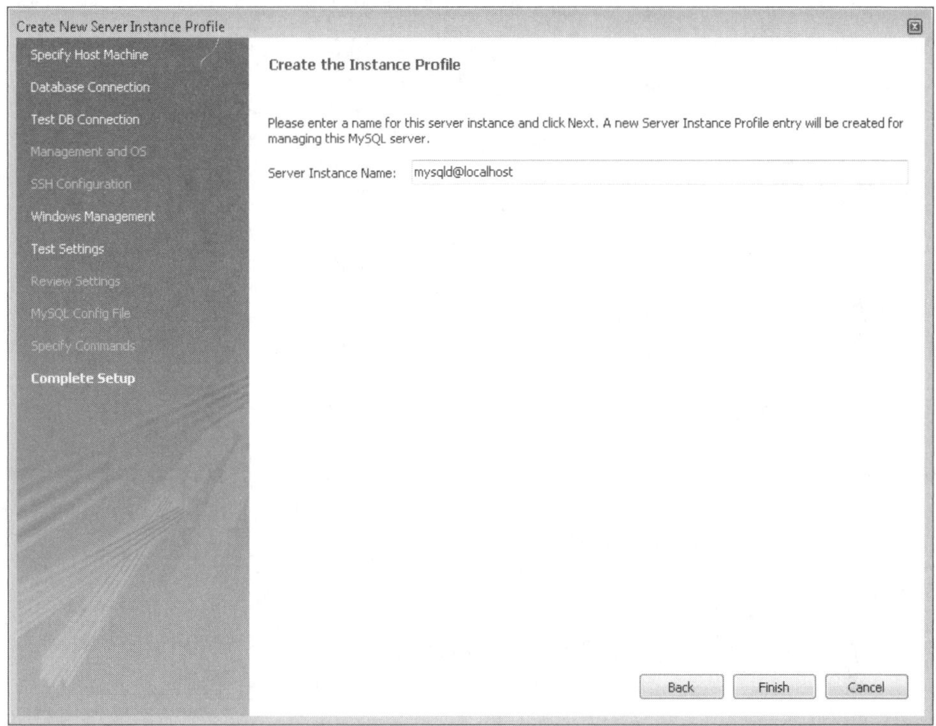

After running the wizard, MySQL Workbench returns you to the home page. You should see the *mysqld@localhost* instance manager in your list, as shown in the following illustration.

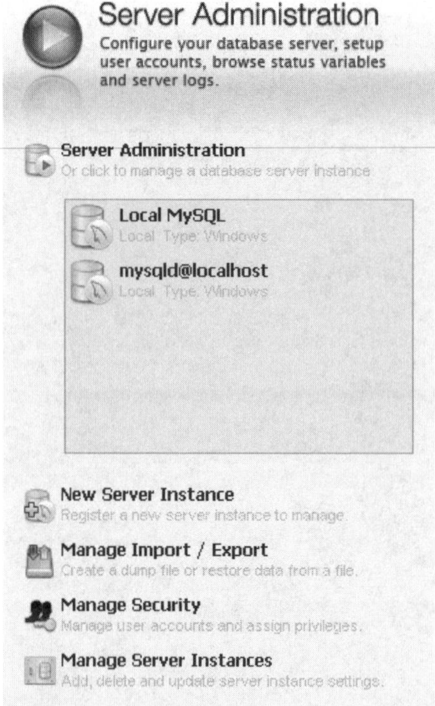

This section has shown you how to create a local instance manager. The next section shows you how to create a remote instance manager for a restricted user.

Create a Remote Instance Manager

A remote instance manager can work with a super user account, like the `root` user, or a restricted account. A `root` authorized user requires that you set up WMI when the remote instance runs on a Windows server. It also requires ssh when you want to control the ability to start and stop services.

The setup for WMI differs between versions of Windows, as does the configuration of ssh across Linux distributions. You should configure WMI or ssh before you try to create a remote instance manager.

This example uses a restricted user because WMI setup and ssh configuration differ from release to release. The skipped elements of the wizard are already shown for the local instance manager. A restricted instance manager is more or less limited to seeing a user and their schemas. That means a restricted instance manager only holds the ability to manage a database running inside the remote server, whereas an unrestricted instance manager holds the ability to manage any database on the server and to start up or shut down the remote MySQL Server.

You should click the *Home Screen* tab to create a new instance. Like the local instance, the wizard prompts you for the host. The default is the local host. You must click the *Remote Host* radio button when you want to create a remote instance manager, as shown in the following illustration.

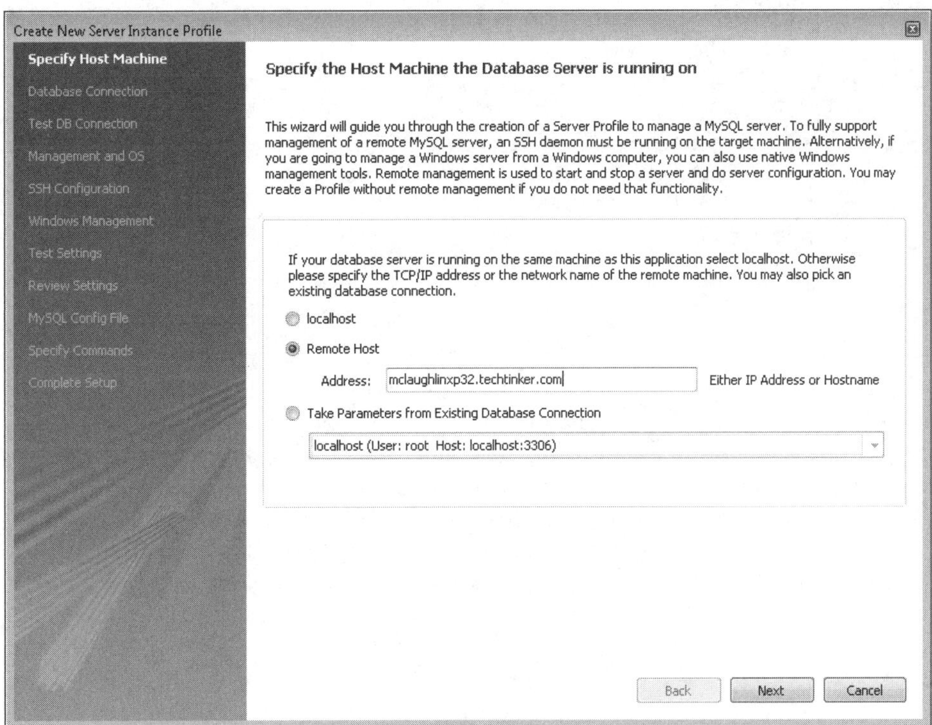

The database connection is always set to a default of the `root` user, as shown in the following illustration.

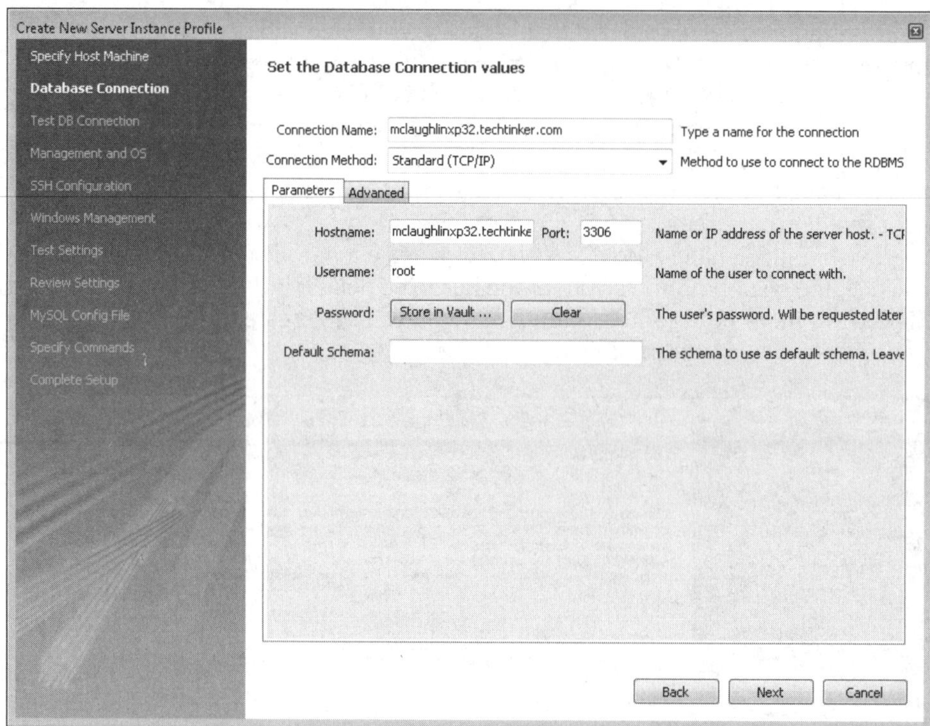

You need to change the user name from `root` to `student` and for this example. While an unrestricted `root` user can change any of the databases and is the more frequent choice, a restricted `student` user only has privileges to act on a set of databases. I've opted to demonstrate with a limited privileged `student` user.

If you're new to the MySQL database's user configuration, you can turn to Chapter 10 to add the user and assign privileges, or you can refer to *Oracle Database 11g & MySQL 5.6 Developer Handbook* (Oracle Press, 2011) for instructions.

You can enter the password and store it in MySQL Workbench, but that's not the best practice from a security perspective. If you choose to enter the password, make sure entry to the native operating system requires validating credentials from an authorized DBA.

A MySQL `root` user is the super user. You don't assign a default schema to a `root` super user, but in this case, the `student` user, you may want to assign a default schema. This is one of the reasons for using the `student` user. Assign `studentdb` as the default schema for the `student` user, as shown in the following illustration. Click the *Next* button to proceed.

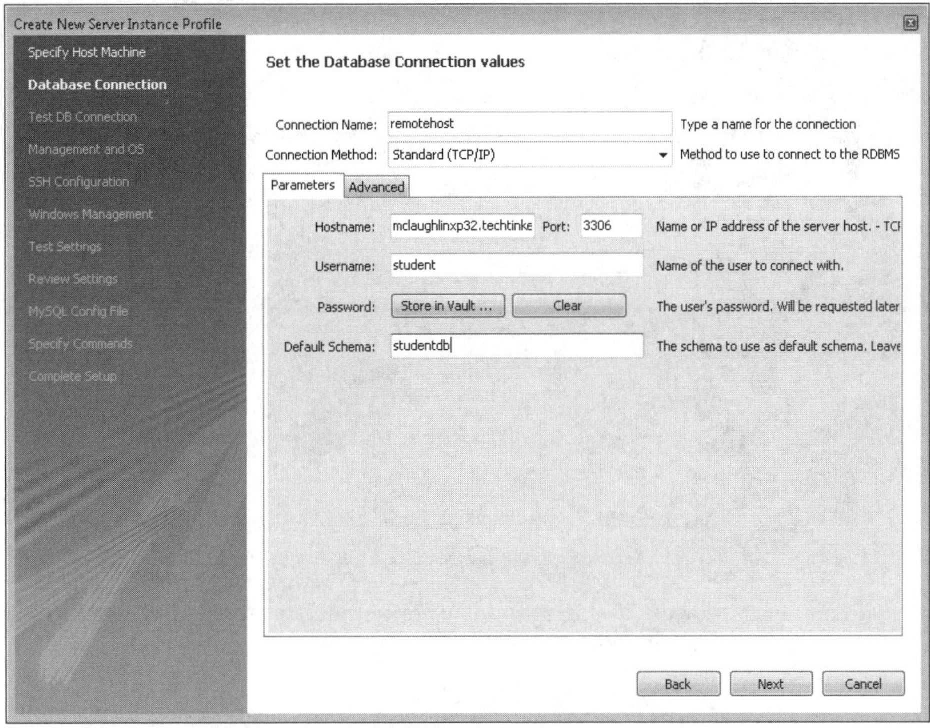

While the WMI configuration for Windows doesn't require ssh configuration, Linux and Unix remote servers do sometimes require it. You could click the *Advanced* tab to configure the Secure Sockets Layer (SSL), as shown in the next screen shot. Click the *Next* button to continue with the wizard.

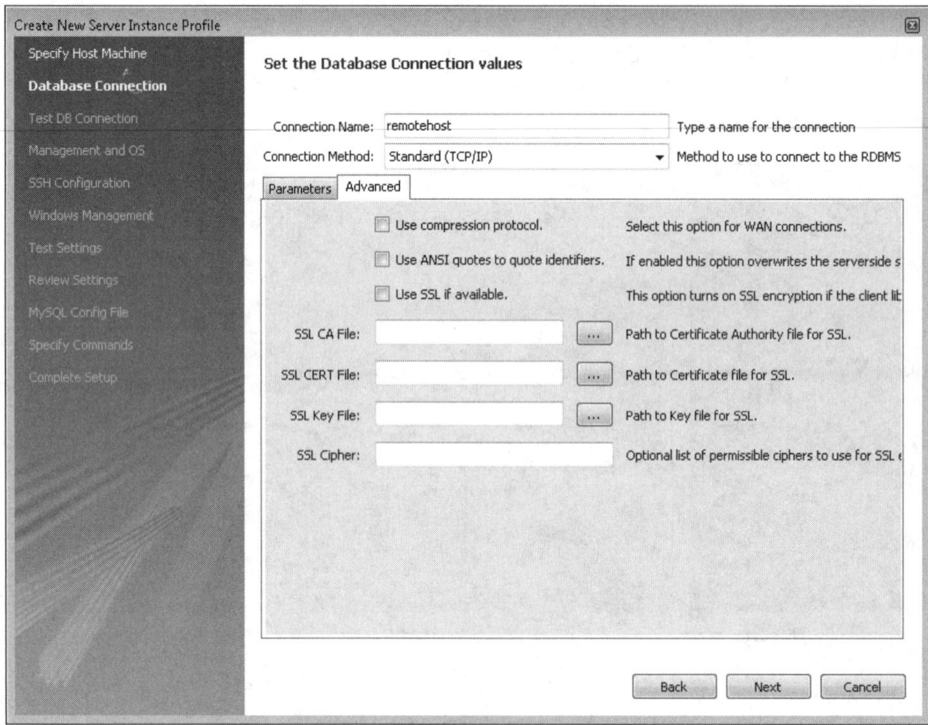

Rather than overlay the dialog again, you're prompted for the MySQL `student` user's password. Enter it and click the *OK* button to proceed.

The wizard progresses to confirm the connection. The next screen shot shows the results of testing the database connection. After reviewing the details, click the *Next* button to continue with setting up the instance configuration.

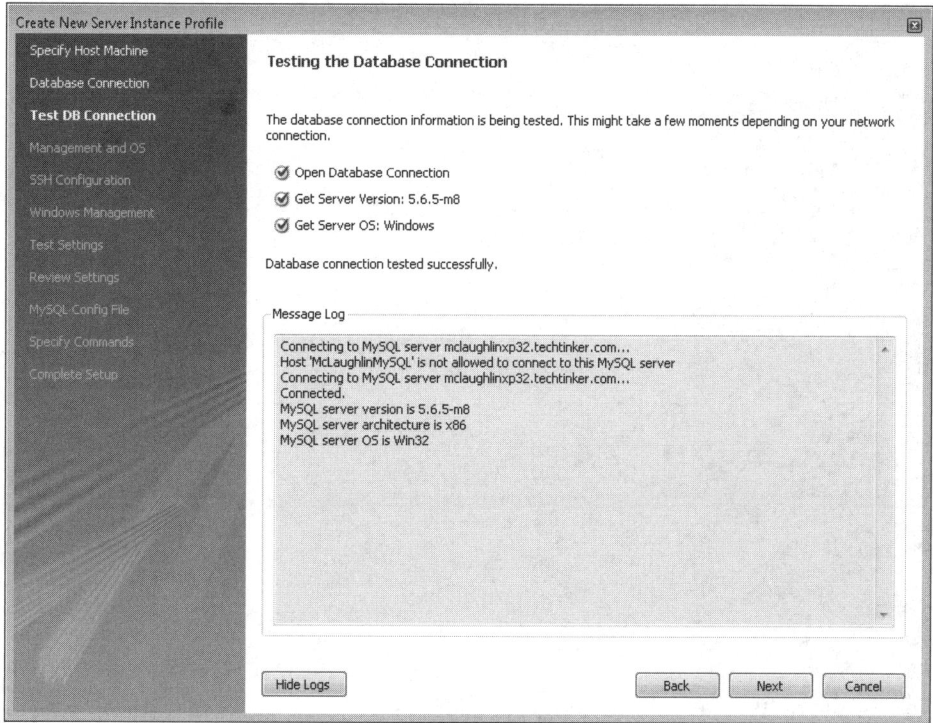

This screen lets you choose whether you want to use remote management. Remote management in this context refers to an instance manager for an unrestricted `root` super user, not a restricted user. Since we haven't configured WMI or ssh, accept the default radio button and click the *Next* button to continue.

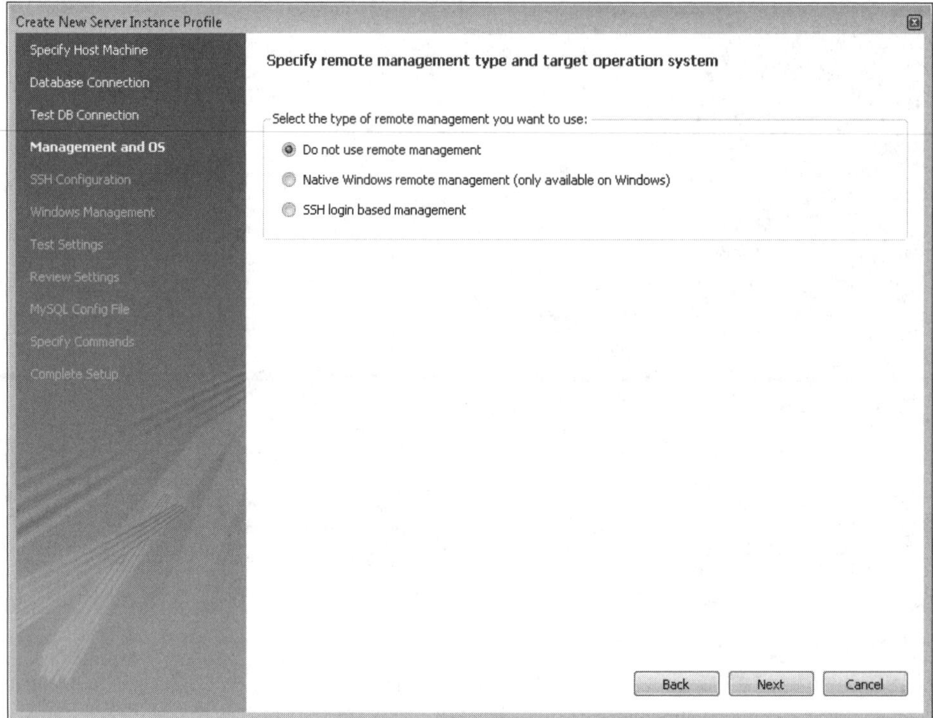

Remote Management

Remote management only occurs with an operating system user that's fully authorized to start and stop the MySQL service. This requires WMI for Microsoft Windows and ssh for Linux or Unix operating systems.

When creating a MySQL `root` super user, it prompts you for the remote operating system's user name and password. The remote operating system's user requires privileges adequate to start and stop the MySQL Server.

That screen looks like a standard user and password dialog box where you enter those values and click the *OK* button to proceed.

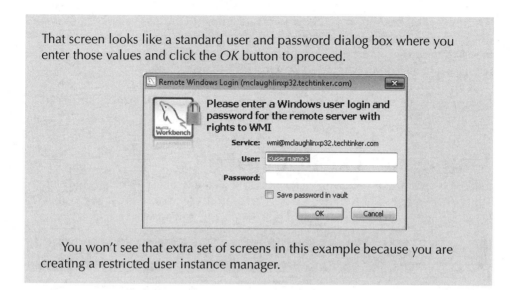

You won't see that extra set of screens in this example because you are creating a restricted user instance manager.

The last screen of the wizard asks you to confirm the server instance name, which is the remote hostname. Click the *Finish* button to complete a remote restricted instance manager, as shown in the following illustration.

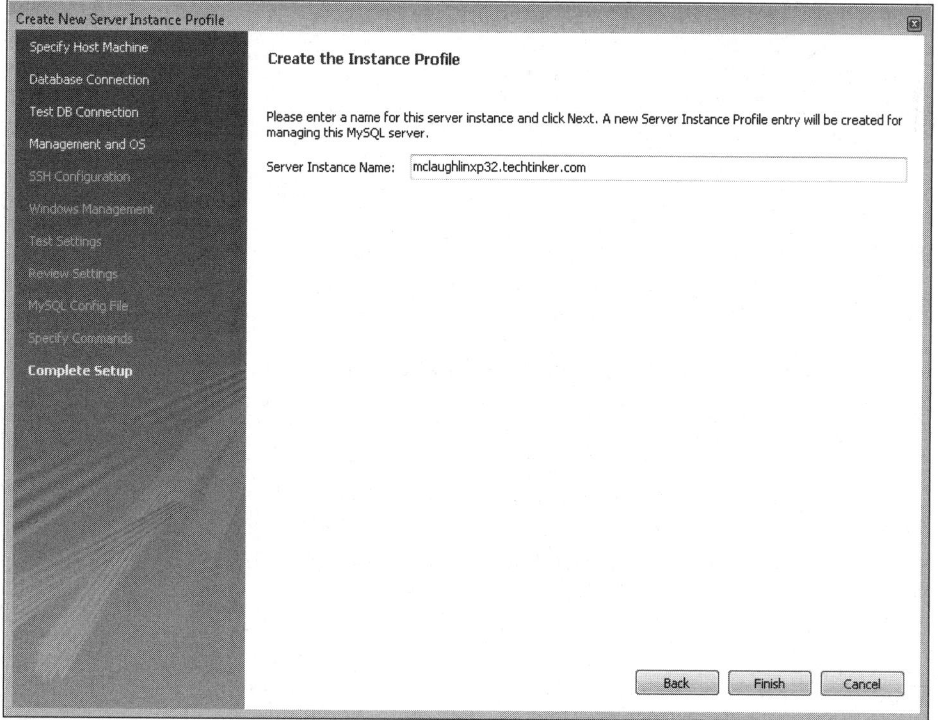

This section has shown you how to create a remote instance manager for a restricted user. The differences for a remote manager that can start, stop, and monitor the MySQL Server mirrors the identification of the MySQL service and configuration file shown in the earlier "Create a Local Instance Manager" section.

Only an unrestricted MySQL `root` user–managed instance manager has the ability to see, allocate, and monitor resources. Likewise, the unrestricted user can start and stop the remote MySQL Server.

Manage an Existing Instance

Once you create an instance manager, you can click it to manage the target instance. The following illustration shows the *Service Status* screen for a local Microsoft Windows instance manager in the Server Administration view.

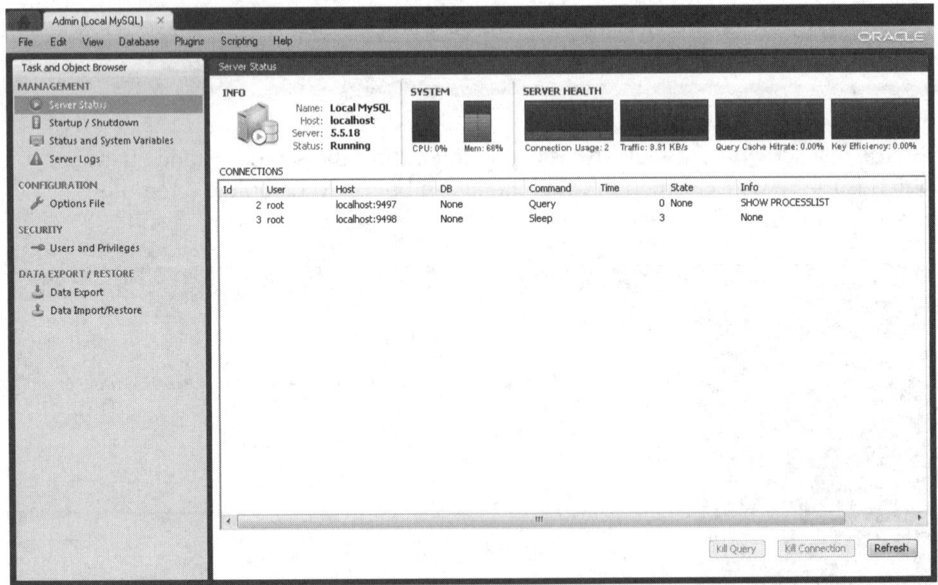

In the frame on the left, you start up or shut down a local or remote instance, check the values of status and system variables, check the log files, and inspect the configuration file options.

When configured as an unrestricted MySQL `root` user, clicking the *Startup / Shutdown* link in the left frame displays the following dialog when the MySQL service is alive and running. You can click the *Stop Server* button to shut down the server. This is typically needed when you've changed a parameter and want that parameter to take effect in the active server.

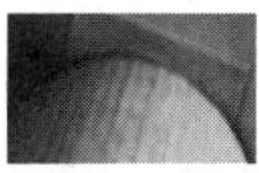

NOTE

Shutting down the server does terminate any open connections and should only be performed during periods of downtime.

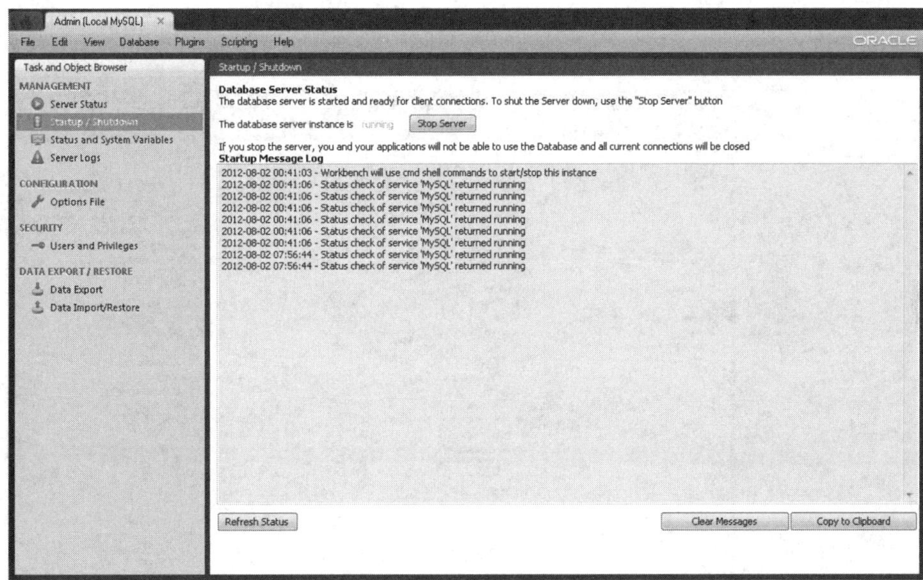

After stopping the MySQL service, the frame on the right changes to the following. You restart the MySQL service by clicking the *Start Server* button.

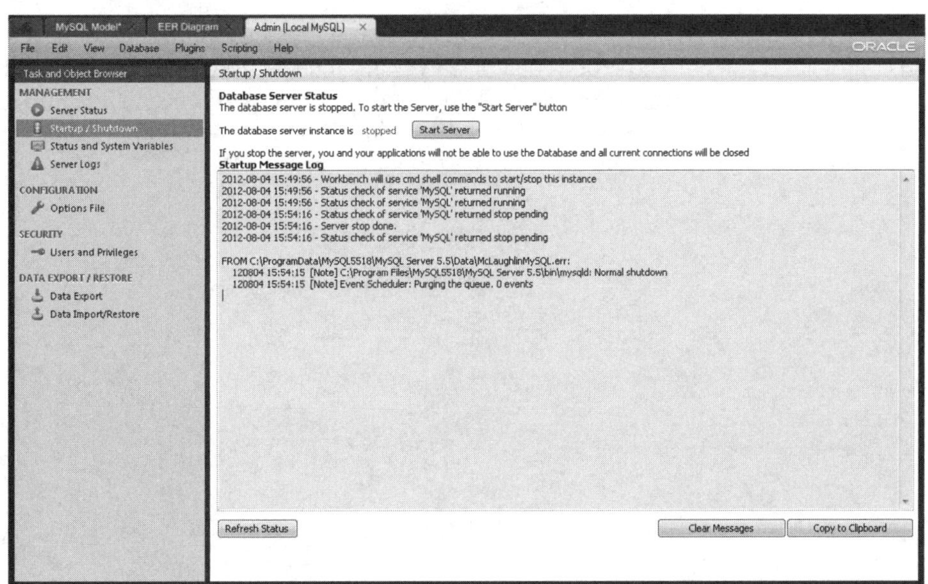

Clicking the *Status and System Variables* link in the left frame displays status variables by default. Status variables advise you of the current working status of the global and session elements of the MySQL Server. You have the ability in this frame to search for them or look only at certain subsets of values, like the binlog, replication, Ndb, Server, Merge, Innodb, or other status variables.

The following screen shot displays the default appearance of the status variable frame.

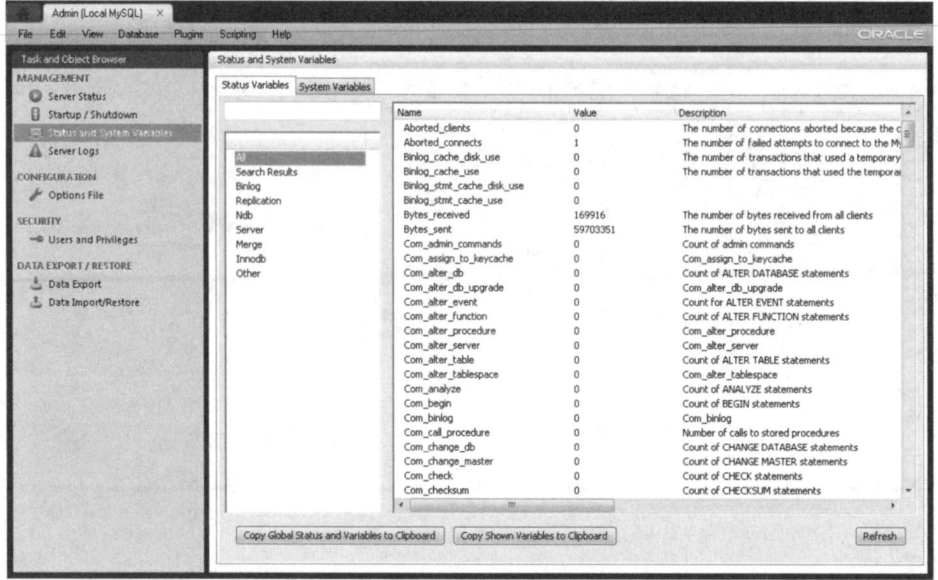

You can click the *System Variables* tab to see them. System variables maintain the configuration information for a MySQL Server instance. Unfortunately, the default behavior for the *System Variables* window doesn't display any system variables. You must first click a value from the list of possible values. The following screen shot results from clicking the *All* choice in the nested frame on the left.

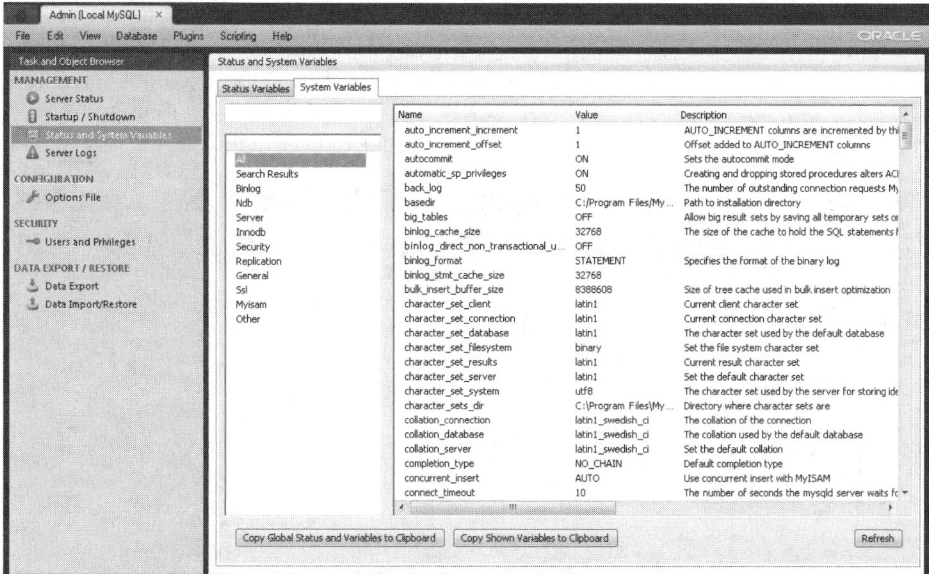

Clicking the *Server Logs* link in the left frame yields a list of error log entries. The next illustration shows an example of what you should see.

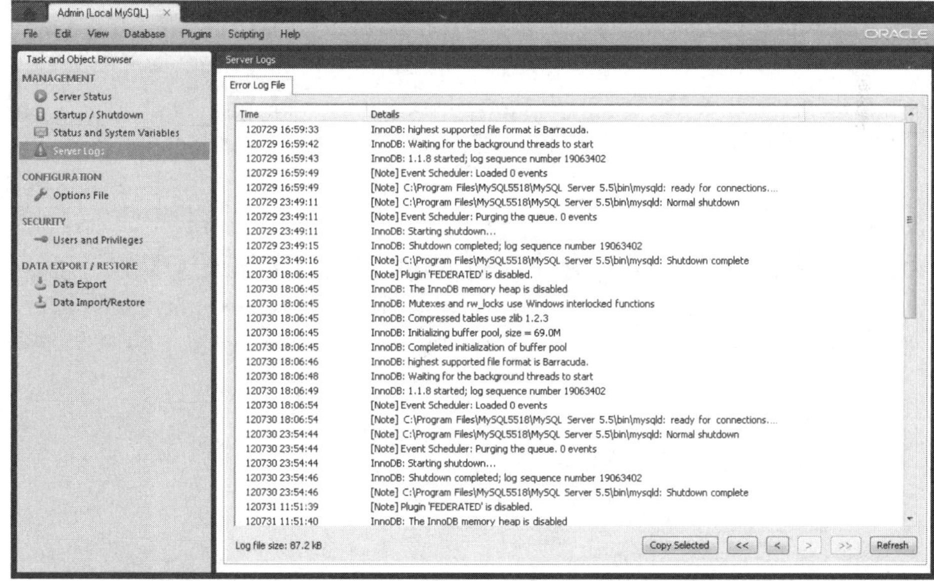

You also have the ability to configure the server instance by clicking the *Option File* link. This gives you the ability to edit `my.ini` (on Windows) or `my.cnf` (on Linux or Unix) in a visual interface. The following illustration shows only the initial *General* tab. You can navigate through the tabs easily by choosing a tab and then scrolling through the list when you've configured an unrestricted remote instance manager.

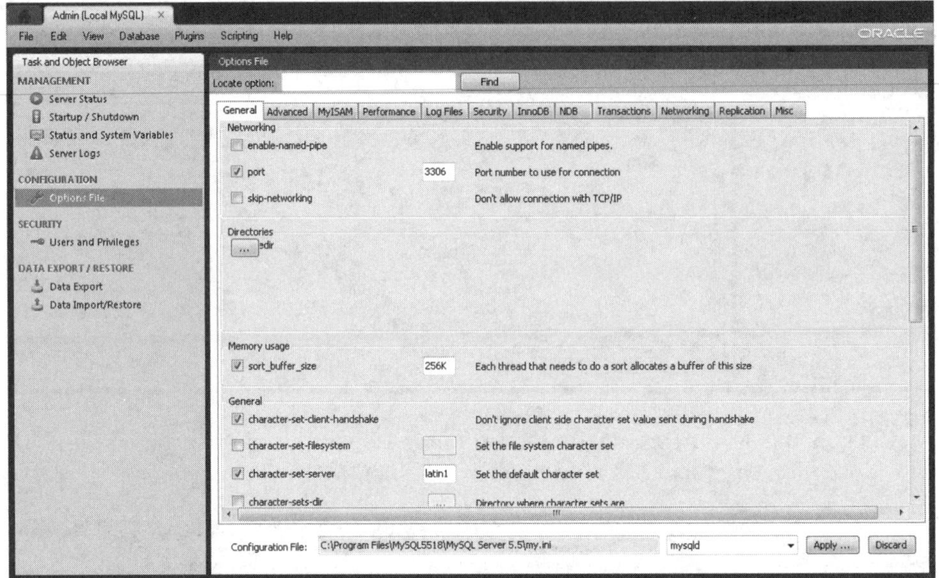

This section has shown you the options that instance management delivers. It's a great graphical tool to assist you in managing a MySQL instance when you have an unrestricted remote instance manager.

Maintain Existing Instance Managers

MySQL Workbench's Server Administration also provides you with the ability to manage instance managers. You click the bottom option to manage existing managers and see the following window.

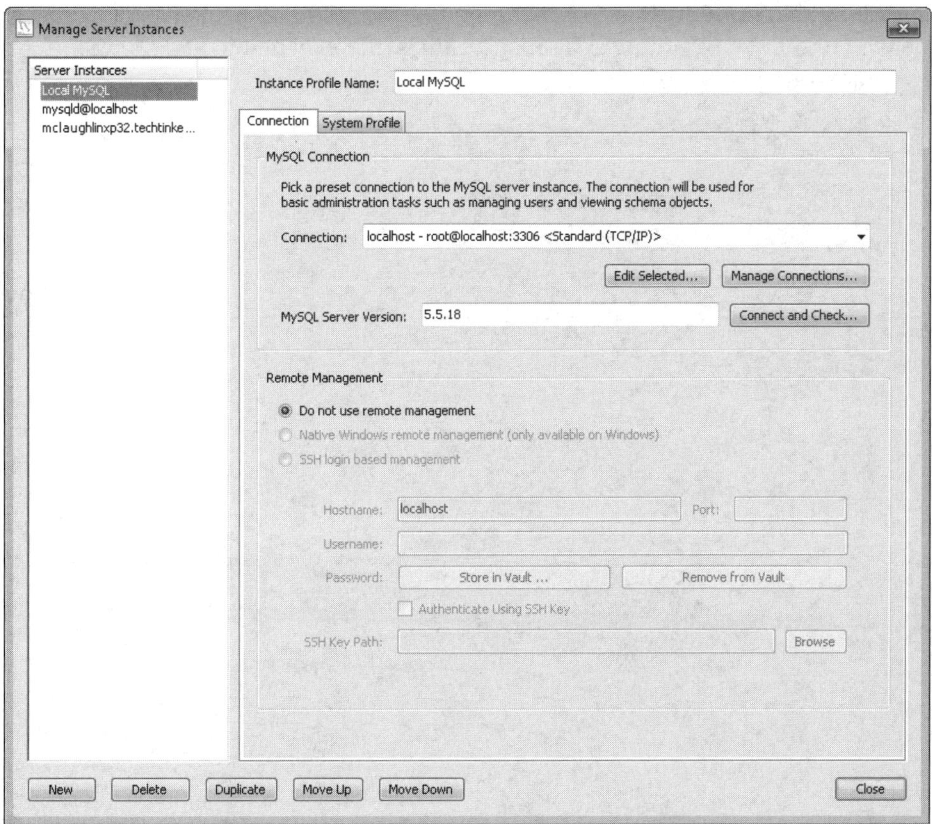

You choose the instance you want to manage in the left frame and manage the connection settings in the Connection tab, which is active by default. The Connection tab also lets you check whether or not the connection works.

The System Profile tab takes you to the following frame, where you manage the type of remote operating system and path to the executable and MySQL configuration file.

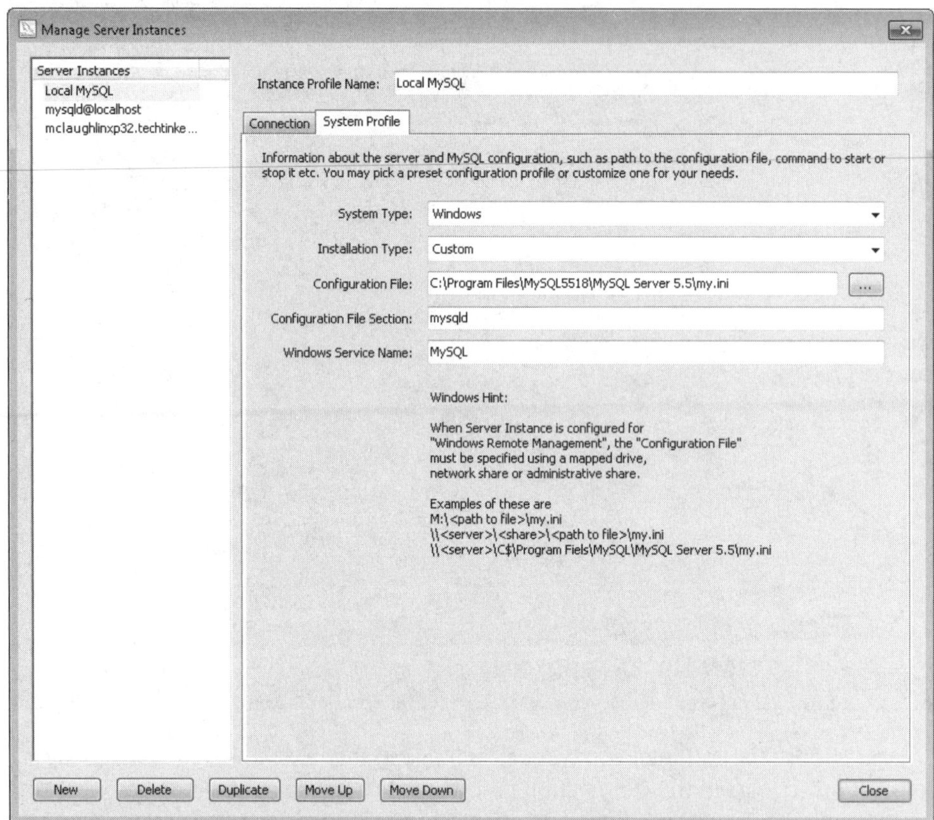

This last tool gives you the ability to fix mistakes made when creating instance managers. It's always best to edit rather than delete instance managers, because unique naming conventions can sometimes find conflicts in the MySQL Workbench file.

Summary

This chapter explained how to create local and remote instance management tools, how to start and stop the MySQL service, how to view and change status and system variables, how to view error logs, and how to maintain instance managers.

Mastery Check

The mastery check is a series of true or false and multiple choice questions that let you confirm how well you understand the material in the chapter. You may check Appendix A for answers to these questions.

True or False:

1. ___MySQL instance managers must have access to privileged operating system users on remote nodes.

2. ___Full access to the MySQL instance manager only requires access to the `root` super user account.

3. ___MySQL instance managers can work with less privileged database users than the `root` super user.

4. ___A local instance manager can start the MySQL Server.

5. ___A remote instance manager can start the MySQL Server by using ssh on a Microsoft Windows operating system.

6. ___WMI is a useful Linux utility.

7. ___Remote host privileges must be configured on the remote machine before you can create and test instance managers.

8. ___Installing MySQL on the same machine as MySQL Workbench is strongly discouraged.

9. ___The MySQL Monitor client software is natively installed with MySQL Workbench.

10. ___MySQL Workbench provides a tool to maintain instance managers.

Multiple Choice:

11. MySQL Workbench connects through which of the following? (Multiple answers are possible.)

    A. Secure Shell (ssh)

    B. TCP/UDP

    C. TCP/IP

    D. Windows Management Instances (WMI)

    E. Windows Management Instrumentation (WMI)

12. Which of the following are *Option File* tabs? (Multiple answers are possible.)

    A. General

    B. Advanced

    C. Performance

    D. Networking

    E. Other

13. Which of the following are displayed as server status values? (Multiple answers are possible.)

    A. Binlog

    B. Replication

    C. Myisam

    D. Innodb

    E. Other

14. Which of the following are subsets of system variables? (Multiple answers are possible.)

    A. Binlog

    B. Ndb

    C. Miscellaneous

    D. Myisam

    E. Security

15. Which of the following belong to the server system variables? (Multiple answers are possible.)?

    A. Com_show_fields

    B. Com_show_open_tables

    C. Com_show_status

    D. Sort_merge_passes

    E. Uptime

CHAPTER 10

Creating and Managing Users and Roles

Users are distinct from work areas, like databases (also known as a schema). Whether you create users or databases first is an awesome question, and I'm not sure of the right answer. While I'll argue both cases in the next paragraph, databases should generally precede users beyond the `root` super user.

There's value to the argument that you should define databases before you create users, because a user without grants to act in a database can't do much. Likewise, there's value to the argument that you should create users first as part of the data modeling or design process, but then you have to create databases before you grant privileges to the users. It becomes a vicious circle.

This book presents how you create and manage users and roles first, and in Chapter 11 how you create and manage instances. Readers may want to flip back and forth as they use the book, but on initial read, understanding how to create and manage the user first adds more to the discussion of database design and deployment.

This chapter describes how you use the Server Administration feature of MySQL Workbench to create and manage users. You grant system-level or schema-level privileges to MySQL users after you create them.

MySQL Workbench lets you grant roles, which are groups of related privileges, to users. However, roles don't exist in the MySQL database. MySQL Workbench maps the roles to actual privileges and then assigns those privileges to the user. You assign system-level privileges without referring to a MySQL database (or schema). Likewise, you assign schema-level privileges by referring to a MySQL schema (or database).

Privileges provide the right to act on objects in the database. System privileges can be global or database-level privileges. Global privileges let you act on any type of object in any database of the MySQL Server, while database privileges let you act on any object in a specific database. There are also object privileges and they extend privileges to users to alter, create, and drop objects; execute routines; or transact against the database with insert, update, or delete statements.

The chapter shows you how to create a user and assign, change, or revoke system-level roles, and how to assign schema-level privileges to users and how to revoke them from users. This chapter also provides examples that let you verify the status of users and privileges in the `mysql` database, which is the metadata schema or database catalog of the MySQL database.

Adding a User

After opening the MySQL Workbench, you will focus on *Database Server Administration.* Server Administration is where you add, edit, and drop users. Adding a user is straightforward, like adding a table in the section on Entity Relationship Diagram (ERD) modeling. Many developers don't find the user interface very intuitive when looking at it the first time. You can judge that for yourself in the following illustration.

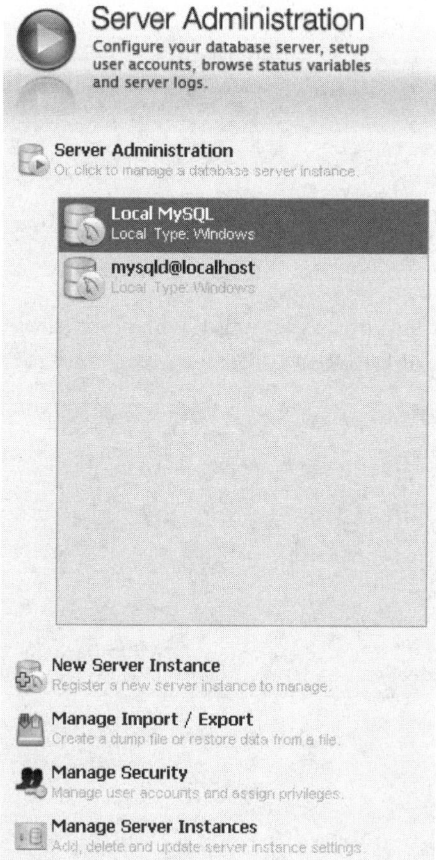

You click *Manage Security* to add, edit, or drop a user from MySQL. Managing users should be restricted to local connections, but you can do it across the network. Many administrators frequently configure multiple connections within the confines of the local intranet.

After clicking the *Manage Security* link, you'll see the following screen when you have more than one connection. Choose a server to work with by clicking it; then click the *OK* button to proceed.

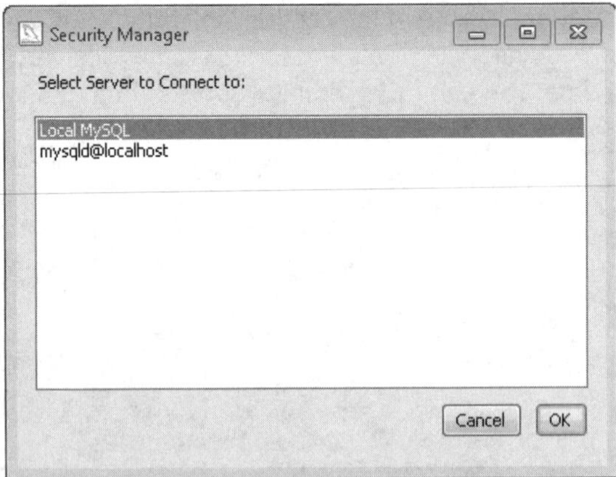

The next dialog box requires a password, which you should enter before clicking the *OK* button to work with users or roles.

After validating your login credential, you see the following server's Admin console. Some parts are grayed out, but that's because you haven't chosen a user to modify or signaled you want to add a new user.

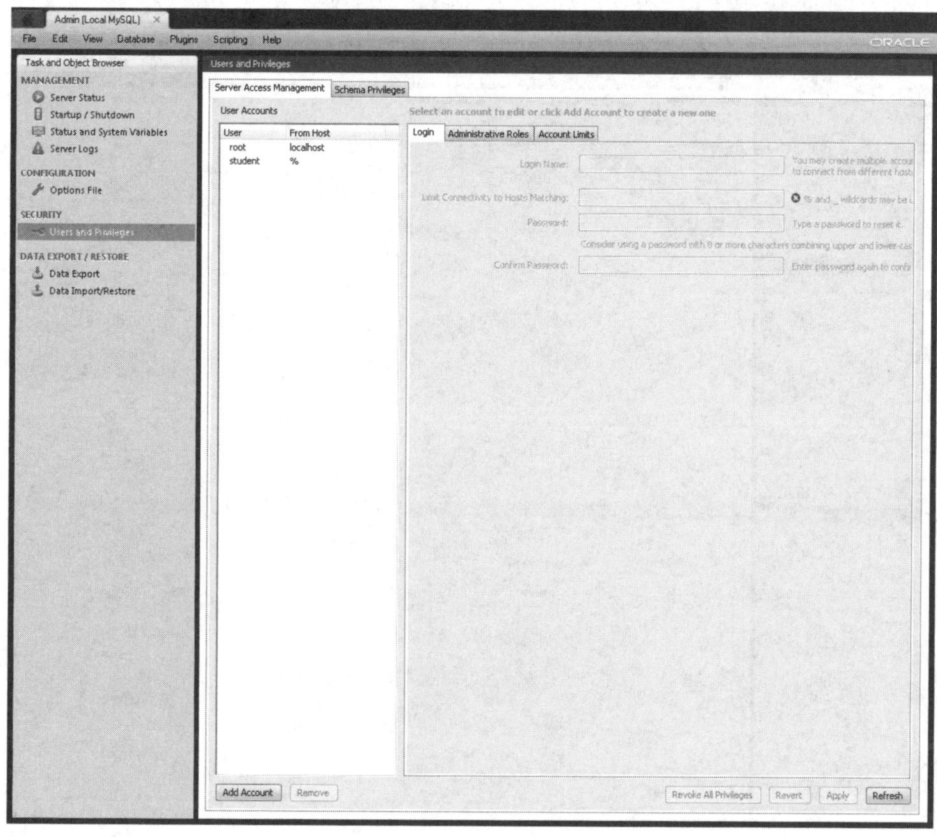

Click the *Add Account* button in the *Users and Privileges* frame to add a new user. Replace the `newuser` entry in the Login Name field with `dba`, enter the same password twice, and click the *Apply* button. Those activities change the user name in the User Account list. You should see the following after applying the changes.

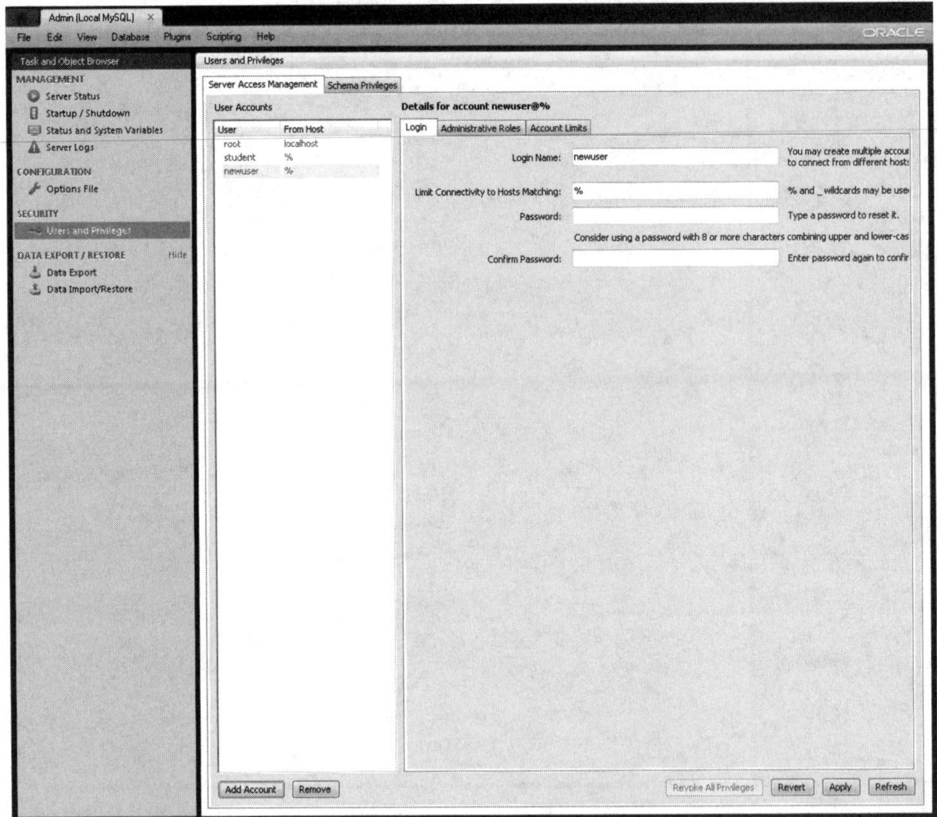

After applying the change you should see the following in the *User and Privileges* frame. You should note the `dba` user connects from any device, as represented by the `%` as the host identifier.

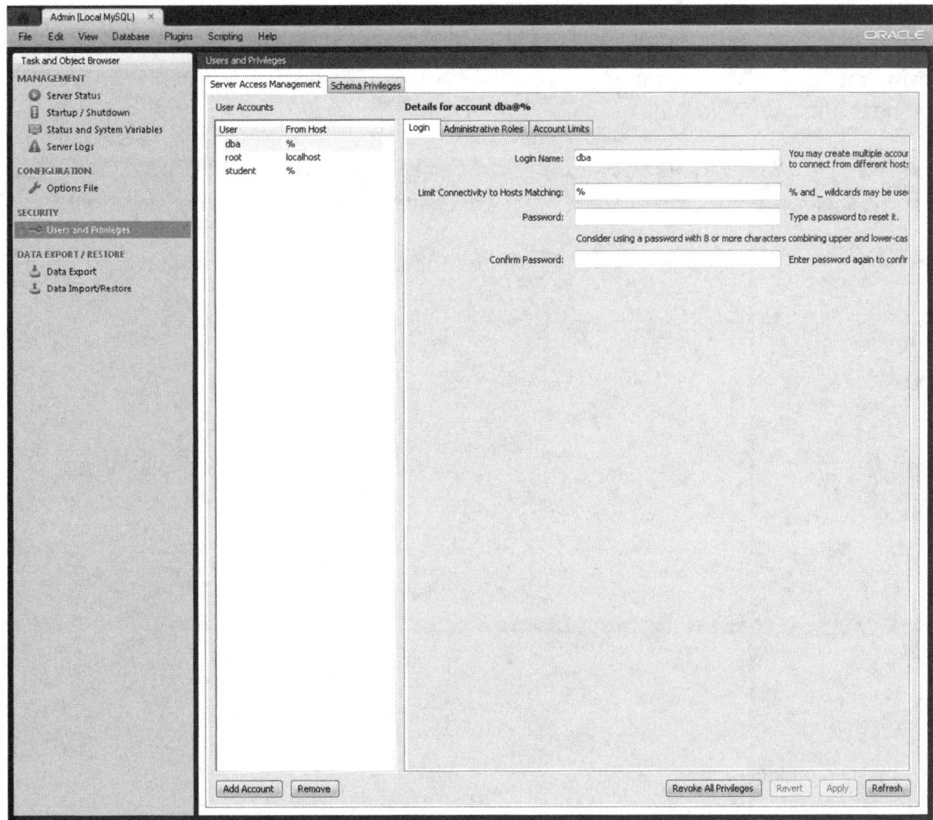

NOTE

MySQL qualifies unique users by a composite primary key of their user and hostname.

The dba user has been created at this point in the process, which you can confirm by connecting to the database through the MySQL Monitor, where this query:

```
USE mysql;
SELECT user, host FROM user WHERE user = 'dba';
```

returns the following:

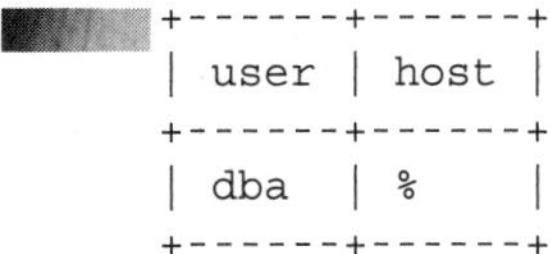

```
+------+------+
| user | host |
+------+------+
| dba  | %    |
+------+------+
```

At this stage, the `dba` user doesn't have any privileges to act in the database. You grant privileges in MySQL Workstation by clicking the *Administrative Roles* tab inside the Server Access section of the User and Privileges frame. As you can see in the next illustration, you have the option of selecting a role or individual privileges.

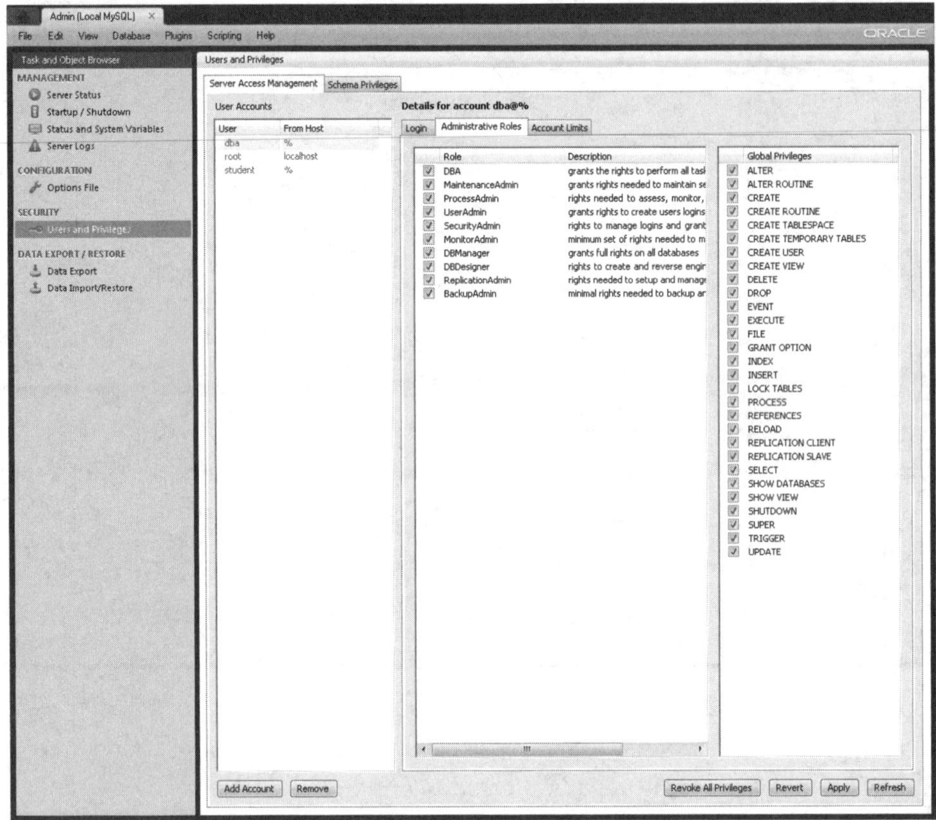

Roles are a collection of individual privileges. MySQL, unlike Oracle, doesn't support roles natively in the database. MySQL Workbench roles are internal relationships, and they map to actual privileges. The roles aren't assigned to users; only the related group of privileges is assigned to MySQL database users. Table 10-1 lists the preconfigured roles delivered by MySQL Workbench.

Role	Description	Privileges
DBA	Grants the rights to perform all tasks.	ALTER, ALTER ROUTINE, CREATE, CREATE ROUTINE, CREATE TABLESPACE, CREATE TEMPORARY TABLE, CREATE USER, CREATE VIEW, DELETE, DROP, EVENT, EXECUTE, FILE, GRANT OPTION, INDEX, INSERT, LOCK TABLES, PROCESS, REFERENCES, RELOAD, REPLICATION CLIENT, REPLICATION SLAVE, SELECT, SHOW DATABASES, SHOW VIEW, SHUTDOWN, SUPER, TRIGGER, UPDATE
MaintenanceAdmin	Grants rights needed to maintain server.	EVENT, RELOAD, SHOW DATABASES, SHUTDOWN, SUPER
ProcessAdmin	Grants rights needed to assess, monitor, and kill any user process.	RELOAD, SUPER
UserAdmin	Grants rights to create user logins and reset password.	CREATE USER, RELOAD
SecurityAdmin	Grants rights to manage logins and grant and revoke server privileges.	CREATE USER, GRANT OPTION, RELOAD, SHOW DATABASES
MonitorAdmin	Grants minimum set of rights needed to monitor server.	PROCESS
DBManager	Grants full rights on all databases.	ALTER, ALTER ROUTINE, CREATE, CREATE ROUTINE, CREATE TEMPORARY TABLE, CREATE VIEW, DELETE, DROP, EVENT, GRANT OPTION, INDEX, INSERT, LOCK TABLES, SELECT, SHOW DATABASES, SHOW VIEW, TRIGGER, UPDATE

(continued)

TABLE 10-1. *MySQL Workbench Roles and Privilege Map*

Role	Description	Privileges
DBDesigner	Grants rights to create and reverse-engineer any database schema.	ALTER, ALTER ROUTINE, CREATE, CREATE ROUTINE, CREATE VIEW, INDEX, SHOW DATABASES, SHOW VIEW, TRIGGER
ReplicationAdmin	Grants rights needed to set up and manage replication.	REPLICATION CLIENT, REPLICATION SLAVE, SUPER
BackupAdmin	Grants minimal rights needed to back up any server.	EVENT, LOCK TABLES, SELECT, SHOW DATABASES
Custom	Grants custom role.	ALTER, ALTER ROUTINE, CREATE, CREATE ROUTINE, CREATE TABLESPACE, CREATE TEMPORARY TABLE, CREATE USER, CREATE VIEW, DELETE, DROP, EVENT, EXECUTE, FILE, GRANT OPTION, INDEX, INSERT, LOCK TABLES, REFERENCES, REPLICATION CLIENT, REPLICATION SLAVE, SELECT, SHOW DATABASES, SHOW VIEW, SHUTDOWN, TRIGGER, UPDATE

TABLE 10-1. *MySQL Workbench Roles and Privilege Map (continued)*

After creating the user and assigning privileges, you have the option of constraining the maximum number of queries, updates, connections, or concurrent connections by clicking the *Account Limits* tab in the Server Access Management window. These are powerful features because they set hard limits that may cause users to alter how they work with the database. Setting them too low may trigger questions as to why this is the case. This increases the workload for the DBA.

The next illustration shows the Account Limits tab's view.

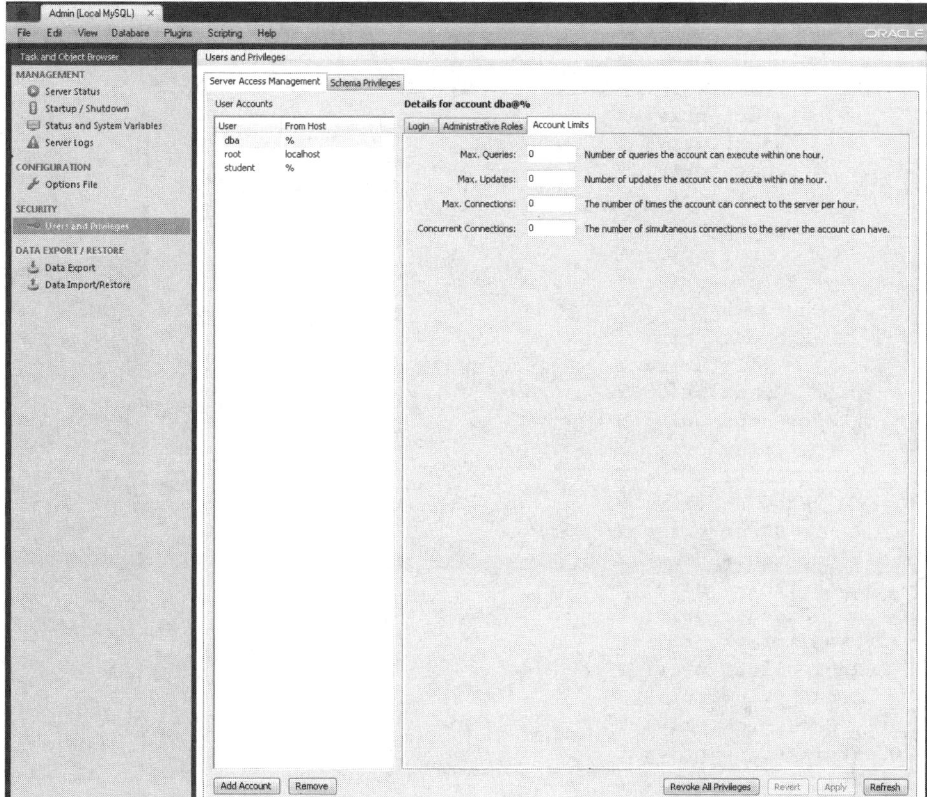

Click the *Apply* button to assign the privileges to the `dba` user. You should ensure that your system-level rows are only assigned to DBAs, specialized tasks (like replication and backup designees), or developers with responsibilities across the entire instance. Developers who manage a specific application (application developers) or set of applications shouldn't receive system-level privileges.

You can query the user table to find the assigned privileges with the `\G` option to display the column name on the left and value on the right.

```
SELECT * FROM user WHERE user = 'dba'\G
```

It displays:

```
*************************** 1. row ***************************
                  Host: %
                  User: dba
              Password: *F7C12736973F0D71DE85272915099A4429EB
           Select_priv: Y
           Insert_priv: Y
           Update_priv: Y
           Delete_priv: Y
           Create_priv: Y
             Drop_priv: Y
           Reload_priv: Y
         Shutdown_priv: Y
          Process_priv: Y
             File_priv: Y
            Grant_priv: Y
       References_priv: Y
            Index_priv: Y
            Alter_priv: Y
          Show_db_priv: Y
            Super_priv: Y
 Create_tmp_table_priv: Y
      Lock_tables_priv: Y
          Execute_priv: Y
       Repl_slave_priv: Y
      Repl_client_priv: Y
      Create_view_priv: Y
        Show_view_priv: Y
   Create_routine_priv: Y
    Alter_routine_priv: Y
      Create_user_priv: Y
            Event_priv: Y
          Trigger_priv: Y
Create_tablespace_priv: Y
              ssl_type:
            ssl_cipher:
           x509_issuer:
          x509_subject:
         max_questions: 0
           max_updates: 0
       max_connections: 0
  max_user_connections: 0
                plugin:
 authentication_string: NULL
```

You can edit a role to remove privileges from the list or include them. Generally, you should only edit the custom role. MySQL Workbench doesn't let you dynamically create your own roles, unless you count modifying existing roles as creating a role. I'm not counting it because the role retains the same name. Altering the privileges of these predefined roles is not advised.

This section has shown you how to create a user and grant them privileges that are system-wide. Few users receive system-level privileges. Most users receive schema-level privileges, and that's covered in the next section.

Adding Schema Privileges

A schema is synonymous with a database, which means it's a work area. You add schema-level privileges for a user's account by clicking the *Schema Privileges* tab in the Users and Privileges window. Only users with system-level privileges are super users. Most users don't have system-level privileges and are sometimes called nonprivileged users, which really means they don't have broad authority to act in the database.

Some users have access to only one schema, and others to more than one schema. Frequently, the scope of access varies for users between databases. That means a user may have some privileges to one database that it lacks for another database. This is a natural outcome because users typically don't require like privileges across schemas unless they're an administrative user.

This is the section of the MySQL Workbench that most application DBAs use most frequently because they're responsible for assigning and monitoring privileges to users within schemas. The *Schema Privileges* tab displays the following initial screen.

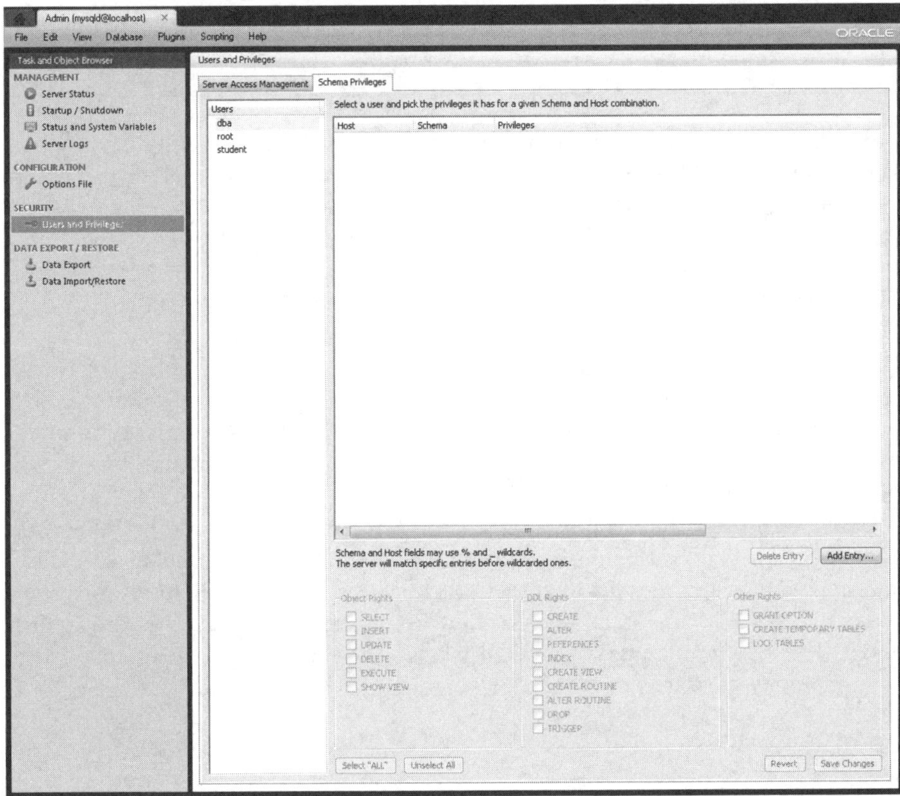

By default, there aren't any granted schema privileges. You click the *Add Entry* button at the bottom right to add a schema privilege. It launches the following dialog box.

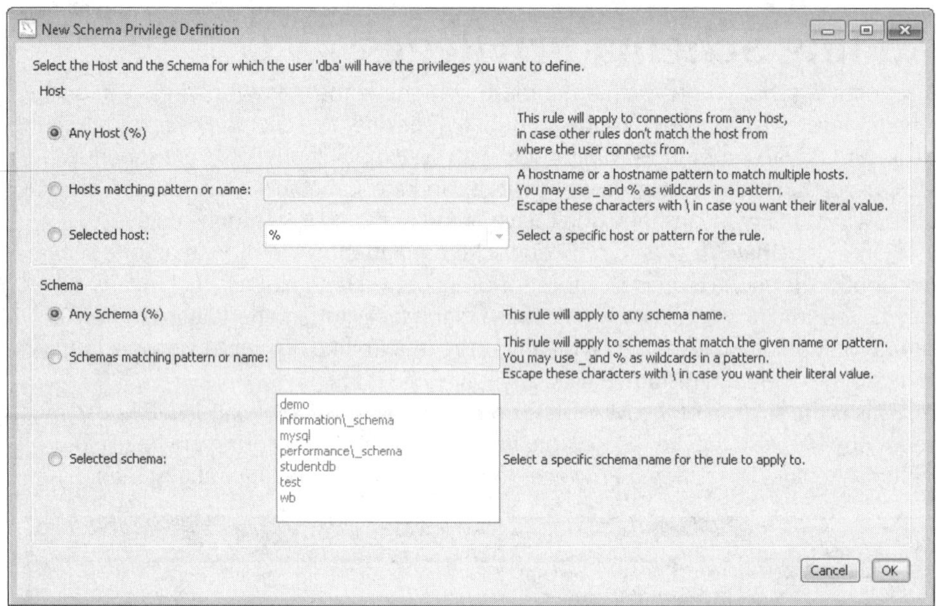

As a rule, the host setting is appropriate as any host (or a %). Assigning any host access means a user may connect from any machine, which presents the possibility of a security risk. The risk presented by this approach is a man-in-the-middle attack where the user credentials have been intercepted by a network sniffer.

You should consider whether users require broad access, like any host. Most users connect through the corporate intranet—at least that's true for highly privileged users, like administrators. If you create any host user, it should be given web user access, and that information is stored inside an Access Control List (ACL). ACLs are typically information stored in a table within the database. When a web user authenticates to the server, it gains privileges to an application programming interface (API). The API acts with a database user's privileges that would be set as schema-level privileges.

A business design that combines an API and ACL is well suited to granting users intranet-only host access or an even more restrictive subdomain-only access. This means the web user comes through the Apache server using HTTP and is forwarded from an intranet IP to the database server, where its credentials are checked against the ACL. The forwarded message typically calls a programming language like PHP, which references a stored set of database credentials to access the MySQL Server.

Defining MySQL Users

MySQL users are defined by two key attributes: the user and host (or access point of origin) names. The user name is stored as a plain-text string. The access point origin, known as `host`, designates the permitted origin of communication with the MySQL database. The options for hostname are `localhost`, `hostname`, IP address, domain, or subdomain address or a wildcard, which is the percent (`%`) character.

The most generic way to create a user in MySQL excludes reference to the access point of origin, which means a `%` (the wildcard for any point of origin). You would use the following syntax to implicitly create a user that can connect from anywhere:

```
CREATE USER 'some_username' IDENTIFIED BY 'some_password';
```

Alternatively, you could create the same user by qualifying anywhere, like this:

```
CREATE USER 'some_username'@'%' IDENTIFIED BY 'some_password';
```

When you want to link an access point through a Domain Name Service (DNS) server lookup, you would qualify the user with the following syntax. This is the easiest configuration when you know the hostname and IP addresses are provided through Dynamic Host Configuration Protocol (DHCP) licenses that can change over time.

```
CREATE USER 'some_username'@'hostname.company.com'
IDENTIFIED BY 'some_password';
```

You can exclude the hostname and substitute an IP address to accomplish the same task. That's possible when user machines are assigned static IP addresses.

```
CREATE USER 'some_username'@'192.168.1.124'
IDENTIFIED BY 'some_password';
```

Limiting connections to machines within your company's domain is a common configuration for limiting developer connections. You would substitute a `%` as the wildcard for hostname before the domain name as the access point of origin to accomplish this, like so:

```
CREATE USER 'some_username'@'%.company.com'
IDENTIFIED BY 'some_password';
```

(Continued)

Another option lets you limit access points of origin to a subdomain within a company. Two options are available for that. The first uses the % wildcard operation, and the other the IP number and netmask. Here's the wildcard subnet syntax:

```
CREATE USER 'some_username'@'192.168.%'
IDENTIFIED BY 'some_password';
```

Here's the more complex IP number and netmask:

```
CREATE USER 'some_username'@'10.0.0.0/255.255.255.0'
IDENTIFIED BY 'some_password';
```

This matches the first 24 bits of its IP number, which maps to 10.0.0. It lets a specified user connect from any host in the subnet 10.0.0!

The most restrictive connection is `localhost`, which means the user can connect only from the server where the MySQL database is installed. A user with only `localhost` as an access point of origin can't connect through a web server. Here's the syntax for a server-only connection:

```
CREATE USER 'some_username'@'localhost'
IDENTIFIED BY 'some_password';
```

Other, more advanced ways of creating users can be used as well. Specifically, it's possible in MySQL to create a user with the same name but different hosts and passwords. When you choose to do this, it means all subsequent grants of privileges must include the user, password (through the `IDENTIFIED BY` clause), and host.

As a result of that web-based architecture, granting schema privileges across all databases in the server isn't typically done for ordinary or restricted users. It can be done for super users where you have replication running. As a rule, you select schemas in this screen.

The selection process includes two steps. Clicking the *Selected schema* radio button in the following window removes the gray scaling from the list of schemas (or scheme if you prefer) and lets you choose one or more schemas. The second step chooses one or more schemas by clicking them.

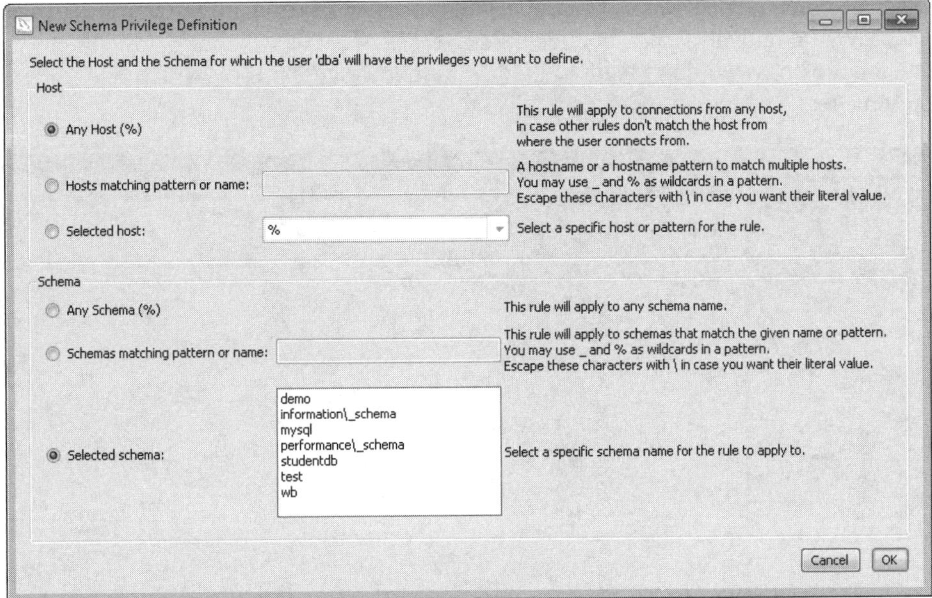

After clicking the `studentdb` schema (or database), you then click the *OK* button, shown in the following screen shot.

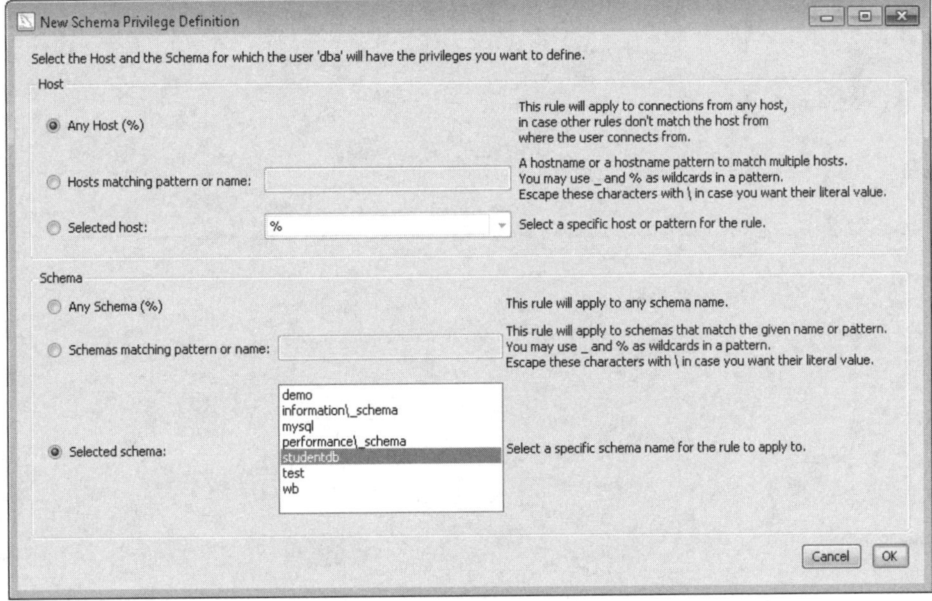

Now you can click the individual privileges you want to grant in the following window. Alternatively, you can click the lower-left *SELECT "All"* button and then unclick the ones you don't want to grant. Your choice depends on which one presents less clicking.

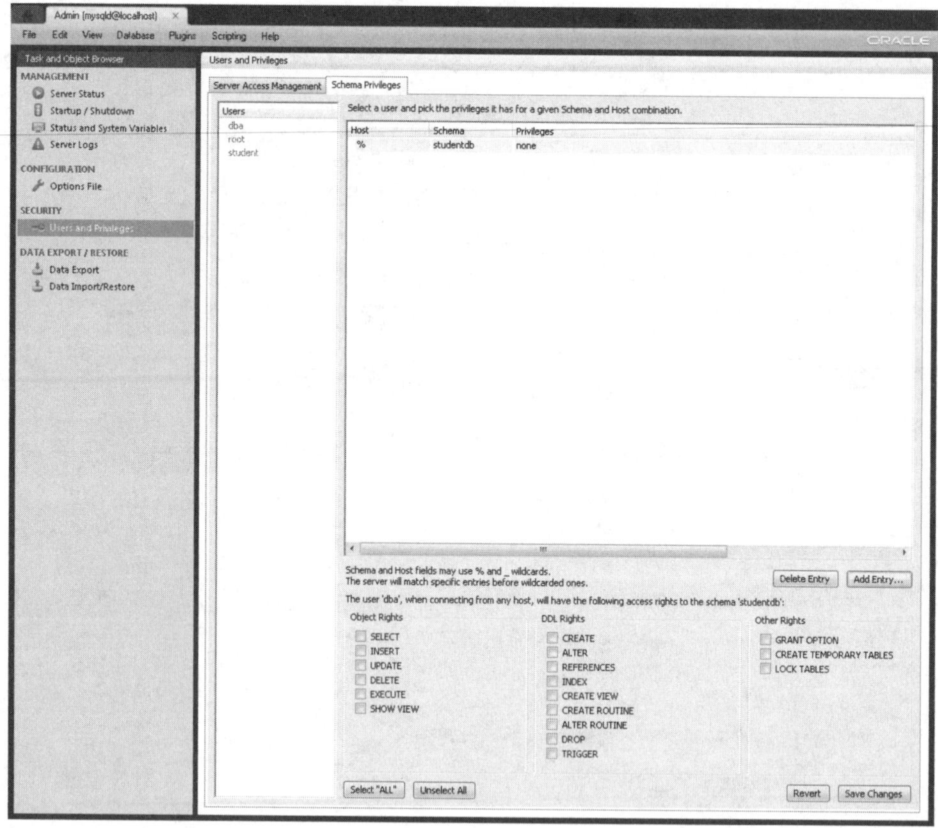

Since these privileges are for the `dba` user, and the `studentdb` is a learning rather than production database, click the *SELECT "All"* button in the lower-left corner, and you will see the following results.

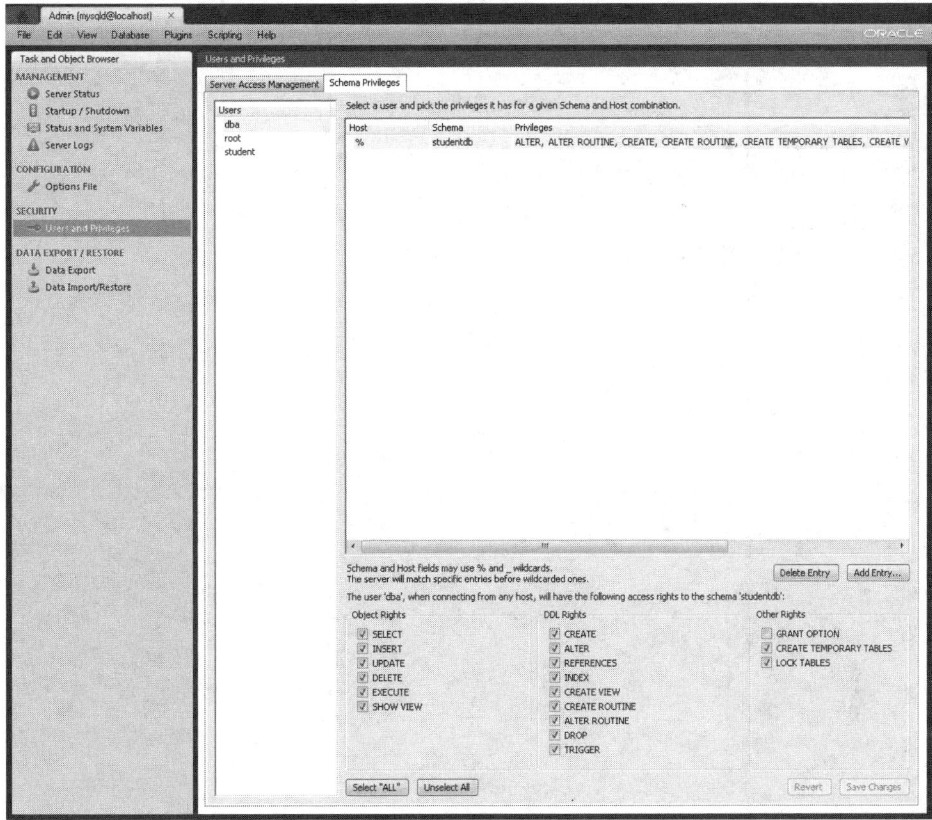

Click *Save Changes* to make those grants in the database server. You can now connect as the DBA and have full access to the `studentdb` database.

You can revoke privileges by clicking any selected privilege to deselect it. Then, you click the *Save Changes* button in the lower-right side of the window in the following illustration.

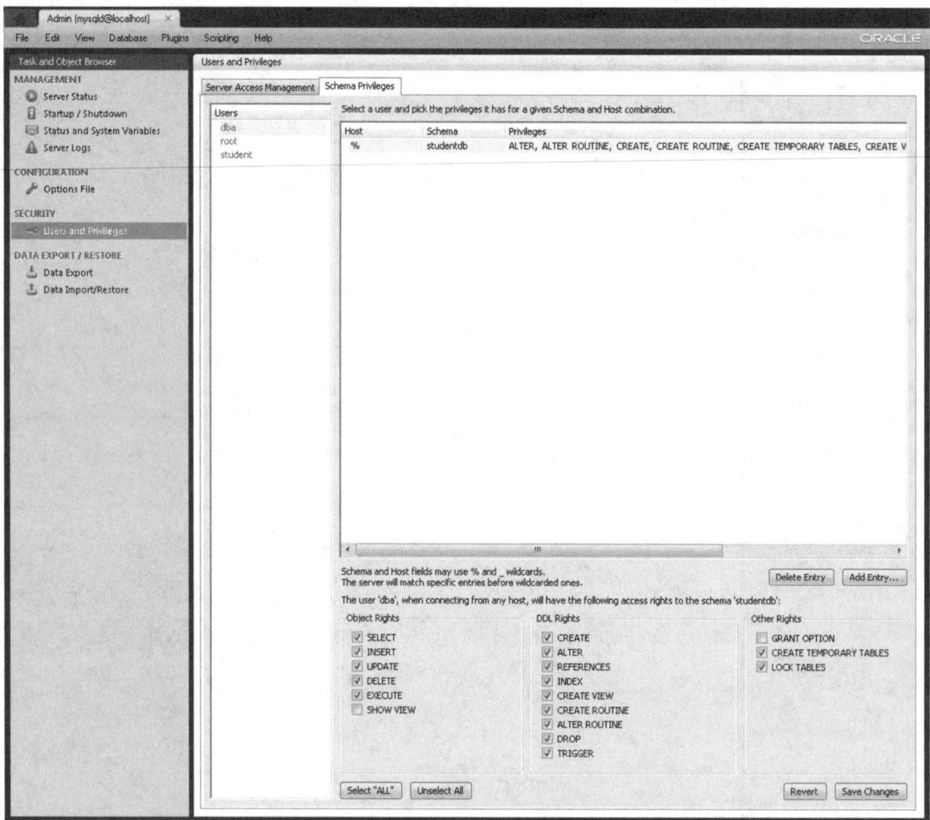

The last illustration deselected the `SHOW VIEW` privilege, and the change of selected privileges activates the buttons on the lower left. They leave you with the option to undo or save changes.

This section has shown you how to grant privileges to users for specific schemas.

Summary

This chapter explained how to create users and grant them system-level or schema-level privileges.

Mastery Check

The mastery check is a series of true or false and multiple choice questions that let you confirm how well you understand the material in the chapter. You may check Appendix A for answers to these questions.

True or False:

1. ___Roles in MySQL Workbench map to roles in the MySQL Server's database instance.
2. ___A database is synonymous with a schema.
3. ___System-level privileges should be limited to administrative or super users.
4. ___Non-privileged users are only granted schema-level privileges.
5. ___The `SUPER` privilege is part of the *BackupAdmin* role.
6. ___The DBA role enjoys the most privileges of any role.
7. ___The *ProcessAdmin* role grants privileges to create users.
8. ___The *ReplicationAdmin* role grants privileges to lock tables.
9. ___The *SecurityAdmin* role grants the `SHOW VIEW` privilege.
10. ___Users are identified by a unique user name and hostname.

Multiple Choice:

11. MySQL Workbench supports which of the following roles? (Multiple answers are possible.)

    A. DBA

    B. DatabaseManager

    C. Custom

    D. ReplicationAdmin

    E. DesignerAdmin

12. Which of the following are object-rights? (Multiple answers are possible.)

    A. INSERT

    B. UPDATE

    C. DELETE

    D. EXECUTE

    E. RUN

13. Which of the following are DDL rights? (Multiple answers are possible.)

    A. CREATE

    B. DROP

    C. UPDATE

    D. TRIGGER

    E. EXECUTE

14. Which of the following are other rights, not object-rights or DDL rights? (Multiple answers are possible.)

    A. EXECUTE

    B. INSERT

    C. GRANT OPTION

    D. CREATE TEMPORARY TABLES

    E. UNLOCK TABLE

15. Which type of user should receive system-level privileges? (Multiple answers are possible.)

    A. A DBA

    B. A replication manager

    C. A developer

    D. An application user

    E. A guest user

CHAPTER 11

Imports and Exports

mports and exports are key elements of being a DBA. MySQL Workbench makes exporting and importing databases easy. These processes are part of the Server Administration features of MySQL Workbench.

Exporting a database means you take a copy of it and store it somewhere. That somewhere can be a propriety file structure or a SQL script. SQL scripts are files that contain one or more SQL statements to perform a task in the database. After you have a copy of an export, you can import that copy and create a new database.

This chapter shows you how to export an existing database and import it into a new database. It opts to show the process using a SQL script because it lets you inspect it with a text editor or manage it as a script file in MySQL Workbench.

Exporting a Database

The export functionality is part of the *Manage Import/Export* option under Server Administration on the MySQL Workbench home page. As shown in the following image, you click the *Manage Import/Export* link to start the process.

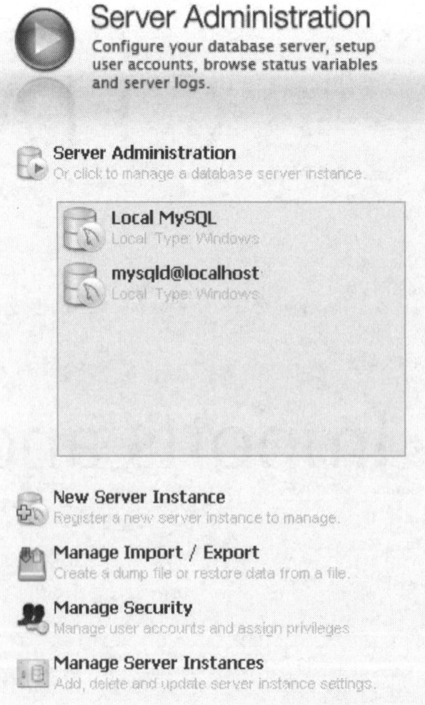

Clicking the *Manage Import/Export* link launches a chooser dialog where you choose a server to work with by clicking the instance manager (covered in Chapter 9). After choosing a server, click the *OK* button to proceed.

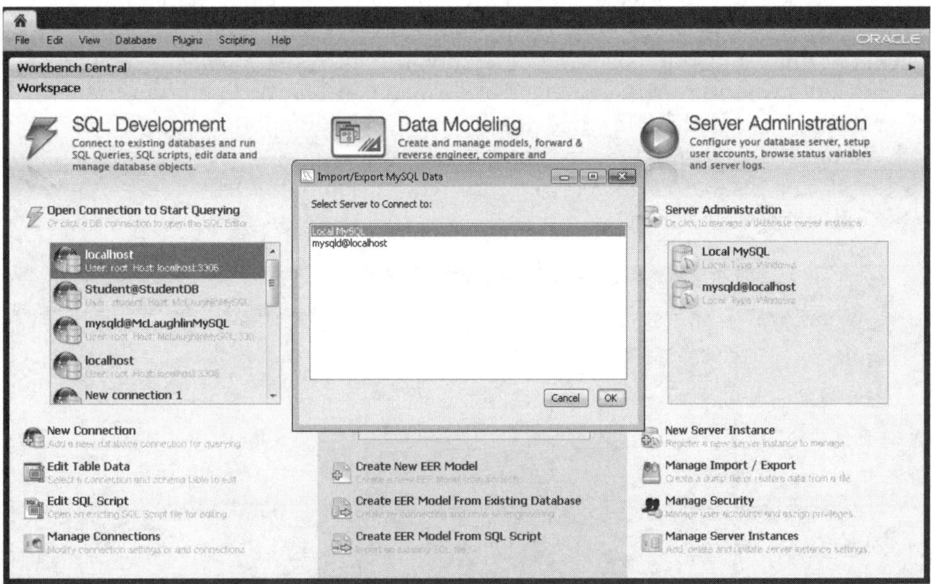

You need to authenticate with the password, unless you stored it in MySQL Workbench when you created the instance manager. Enter the password and click the *OK* button to continue.

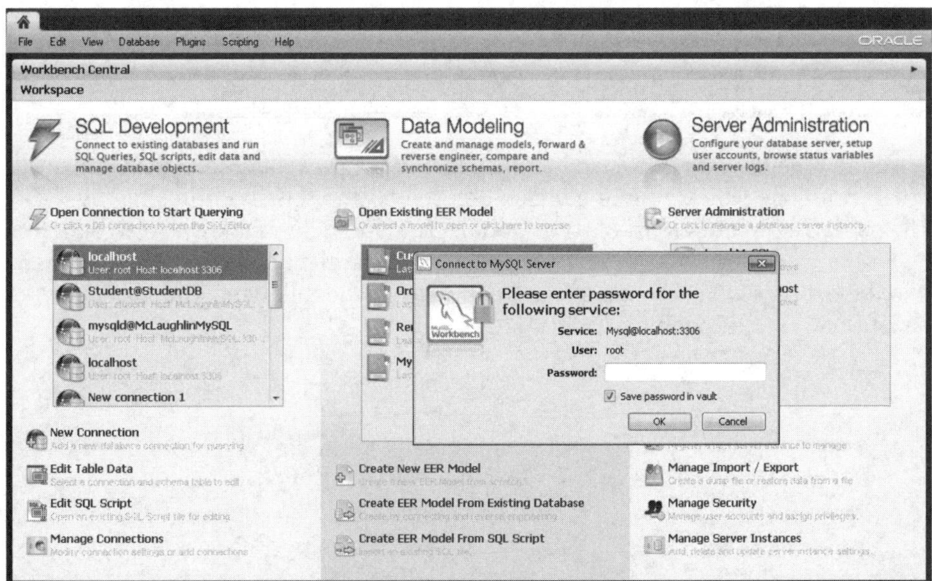

This is the Admin window introduced in Chapter 9. Click the *Data Export* link in the left frame to export data. It then lists the databases available in the MySQL Server instance in the *Select Database Objects to Export* scrollable multiple select list. You can select a database by clicking in the check box to the right of the database name.

You also have the ability of selecting only one or a set of objects from any schema during the export process. The ability to select only some schema objects is convenient when structural changes or data changes have occurred to only some tables, but not all tables, because you export and import only those tables with changes to their structure or data.

The `store` database is the only one that you export in this example, as shown in the following screen shot.

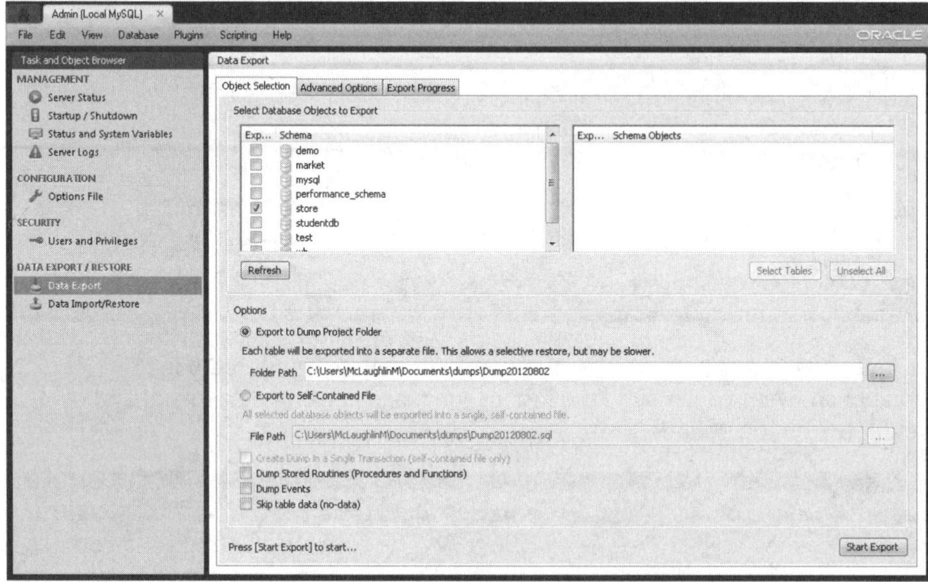

At the time of writing, clicking the check box behaves differently than clicking the object name. Clicking in the check box selects the schema. Clicking the schema name provides a list of schema objects in the right window. It also enables the *Select Table* and *Unselect All* buttons. You can deselect objects to exclude them from the export of the schema, as has been done in the following screen shot for the `common_lookup` table.

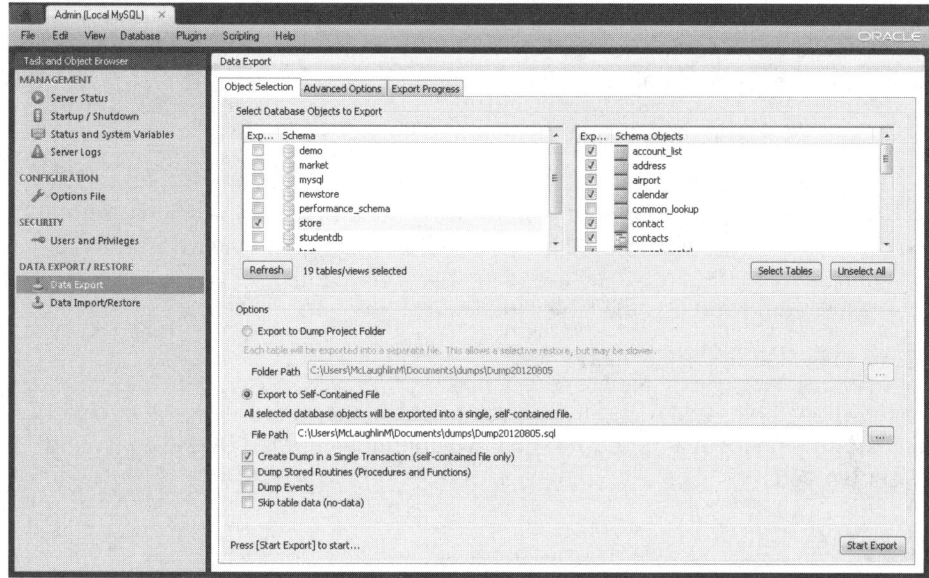

The default option in the bottom half of the current view lets you choose to export each table to a separate SQL file in a target directory (labeled *Folder Path* in the view). You can click the *Export to Self-Contained File* radio button to export all definitions to a single file. It's generally the easier and more manageable solution.

The next screen shot shows you the difference between displays when you check the *Export to Self-Contained File* radio button. You should notice that the gray scaling switches between the *Folder Path* and *File Path* selection fields.

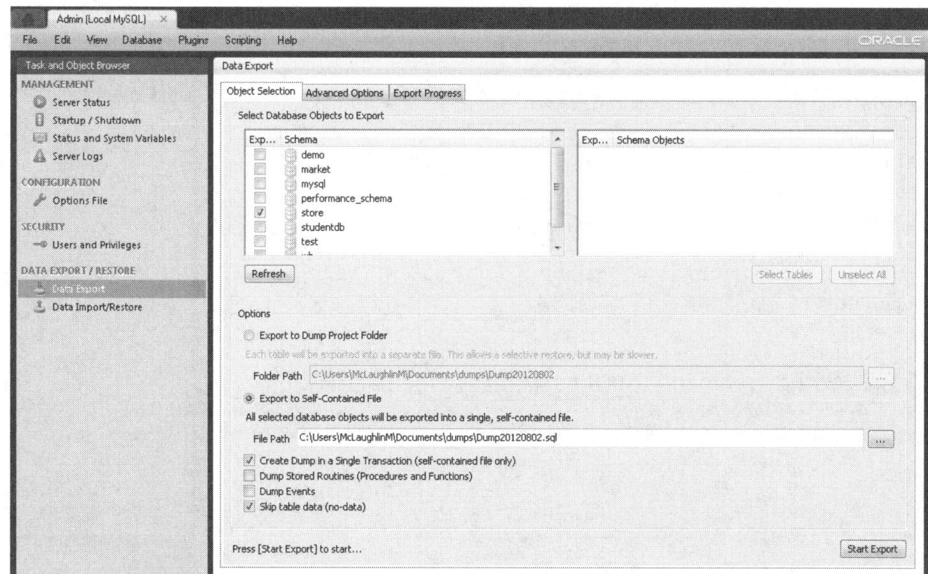

You should make note of the file's path because you'll need it when you want to use the file as an importing source SQL script. By default, MySQL Workbench puts the file into the following directory:

C:\Users\user_name\Documents\dumps\Dump20120802.sql

The name of the file always starts with the keyword Dump and is followed by the date of the export in four-digit year, two-digit month, and two-digit day format. You can also confirm what should be exported by logging into the MySQL Server and connecting to the store database to run two commands.

The first command lists the tables in the database:

```
mysql> show tables from store;
```

The show tables command from `store` lists all tables found in the `store` database in alphabetical order. The first five columns returned by the command are shown here:

```
+---------------------+--------+---------+------------+-------+
| Name                | Engine | Version | Row_format | Rows  |
+---------------------+--------+---------+------------+-------+
| account_list        | InnoDB |      10 | Compact    |   200 |
| address             | InnoDB |      10 | Compact    |    15 |
| airport             | InnoDB |      10 | Compact    |     6 |
| calendar            | InnoDB |      10 | Compact    |    12 |
| common_lookup       | InnoDB |      10 | Compact    |    34 |
| contact             | InnoDB |      10 | Compact    |    15 |
| contacts            | NULL   |    NULL | NULL       |  NULL |
| current_rental      | NULL   |    NULL | NULL       |  NULL |
| item                | InnoDB |      10 | Compact    |    53 |
| member              | InnoDB |      10 | Compact    |     9 |
| price               | InnoDB |      10 | Compact    |   367 |
| rating_agency       | InnoDB |      10 | Compact    |    12 |
| rental              | InnoDB |      10 | Compact    |  4313 |
| rental_item         | InnoDB |      10 | Compact    | 10595 |
| street_address      | InnoDB |      10 | Compact    |    15 |
| system_user         | InnoDB |      10 | Compact    |     4 |
| telephone           | InnoDB |      10 | Compact    |    15 |
| transaction         | InnoDB |      10 | Compact    |  5356 |
| transaction_reversal | InnoDB |      10 | Compact    |  1221 |
| transaction_upload  | MEMORY |      10 | Fixed      |     0 |
+---------------------+--------+---------+------------+-------+
```

The second command lists the routines in the database:

```
mysql> show procedure status where db = 'store';
```

It should display the following first four columns:

```
+-------+-----------------------+-----------+-----------+
| Db    | Name                  | Type      | Definer   |
+-------+-----------------------+-----------+-----------+
| store | contact_insert        | PROCEDURE | student@% |
| store | seed_account_list     | PROCEDURE | student@% |
| store | seed_calendar         | PROCEDURE | student@% |
| store | transactions_upload   | PROCEDURE | student@% |
| store | update_member_account | PROCEDURE | student@% |
+-------+-----------------------+-----------+-----------+
```

After selecting the databases you want to export, click the *Advanced Option* tab to see what rules govern your export. Leaving the defaults unchanged works for many users, but you do have the option of making many configuration choices in this form, as listed in Table 11-1.

Option	**Description**
Add-locks	Surround each table dump with `LOCK TABLES` and `UNLOCK TABLES` statements.
Complete-insert	Use complete `INSERT` statements that include column names.
Extended-insert	Use multiple-row `INSERT` syntax that includes several `VALUES` lists.
Insert-ignore	Write `INSERT IGNORE` statements rather than `INSERT` statements.
Replace	Write `REPLACE` statements rather than `INSERT` statements.
Delayed-insert	Write `INSERT DELAYED` statements rather than `INSERT` statements.
Lock-tables	Lock tables for read. Disable if user has no `LOCK TABLES` privilege.
Dump-date	Include dump date as "Dump completed on" comment if comments are given.
Flush-logs	Flush the MySQL Server log files before starting the dump.
Delete-master-logs	On a master replication server, delete the binary logs after performing the dump operation.
Hex-blob	Dump binary columns using hexadecimal notation (for example, "abc" becomes 0x616263).

(continued)

TABLE 11-1. *Data Export Options*

Option	Description
Compress	Use compression in server/client protocol.
Flush-privileges	Emit a `FLUSH PRIVILEGES` statement after dumping the mysql database.
Disable-keys	For each table, surround the `INSERT` statements with statements to disable and enable keys.
Force	Continue even if we get a sql-error.
Order-by-primary	Dump each table's rows sorted by its first unique index.

TABLE 11-1. *Data Export Options (continued)*

The following displays the *Data Export* tab with the default selections.

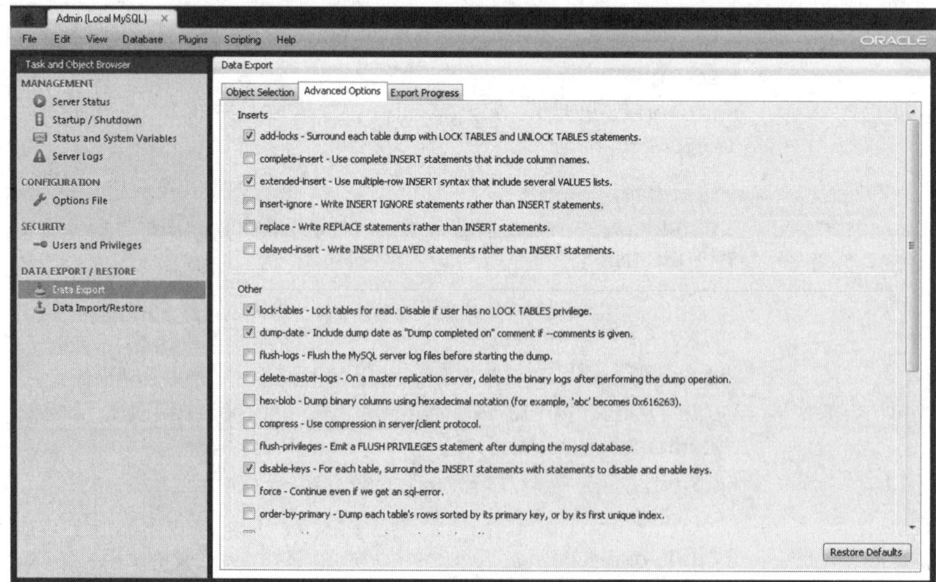

You must click the *Object Selection* tab to start the export by clicking the *Start Export* button. It will take you to the third *Export Progress* tab view, and that view should look like this before starting the process:

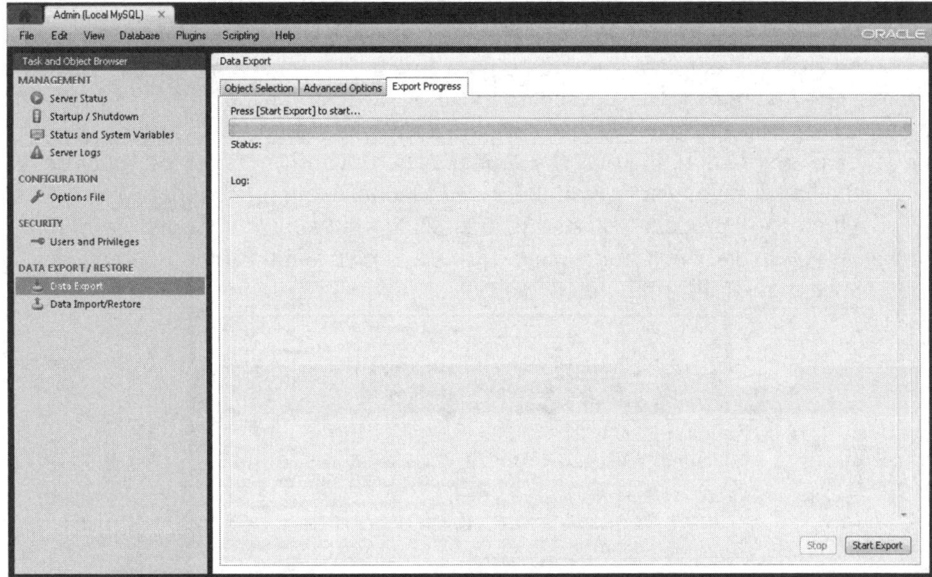

After the export completes, you'll see a log file describing the export status. If there are no errors, the export process will look like the following screen shot.

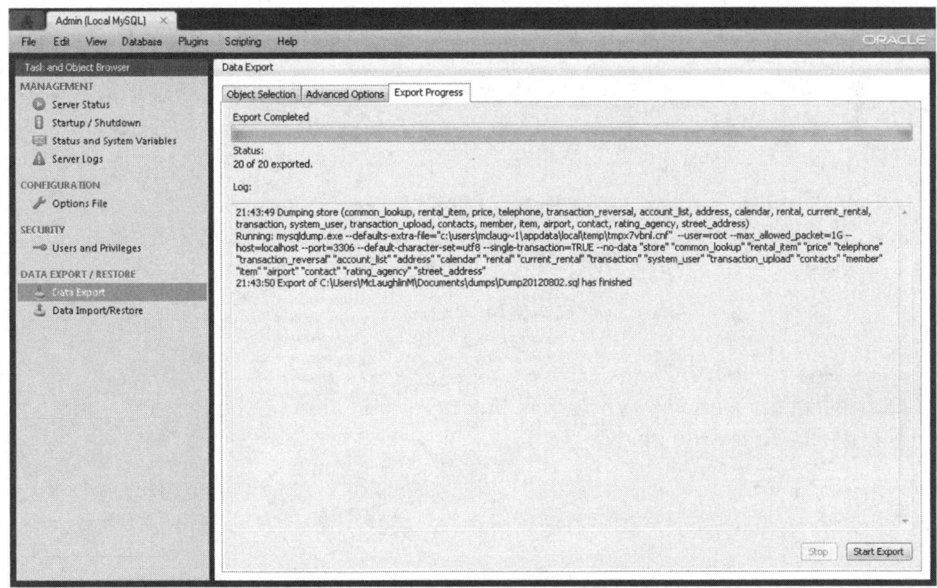

This completes the export process. It was straightforward and gives you a file that can serve as an import source in the next section.

Importing a Database

Importing a database from a script file is convenient with MySQL Workbench for two reasons. The tool makes the import easy to accomplish, and it can also creates an ER Model for the new database by following the instructions found in Chapter 6. You have the option of importing only the structures (tables and views) or the structures and data. Likewise, you can import the stored functions and procedures (routines).

Like the export process, you start with clicking the *Manage Import/Export* link on the MySQL Workbench home page. This is a Server Administration option, as you can see in the following illustration.

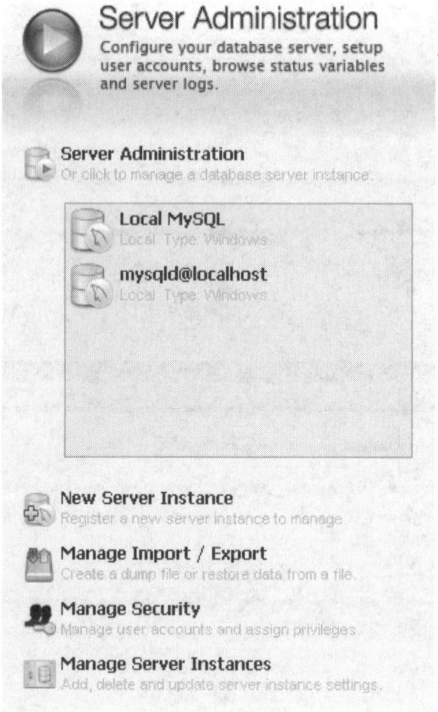

You select the *Data Import/Restore* link from the frame on the left, and you should see the following image.

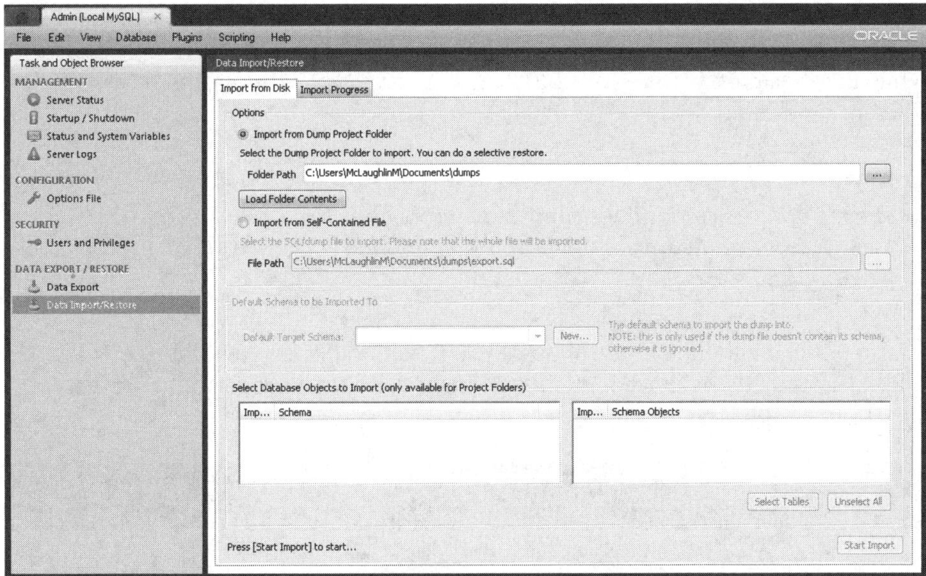

Like the export process, you can take a series of scripts from a data dump directory or you can run a self-contained file. The export example creates a self-contained file, and this import example will use the file.

You should click the *Import from Self-Contained File* radio button and then the *Ellipsis* (that's a set of three dots or periods) button to select a file for the import. The *Ellipsis* button is on the far right of the *Import from Disk* tabbed frame as an extension of the File Path field.

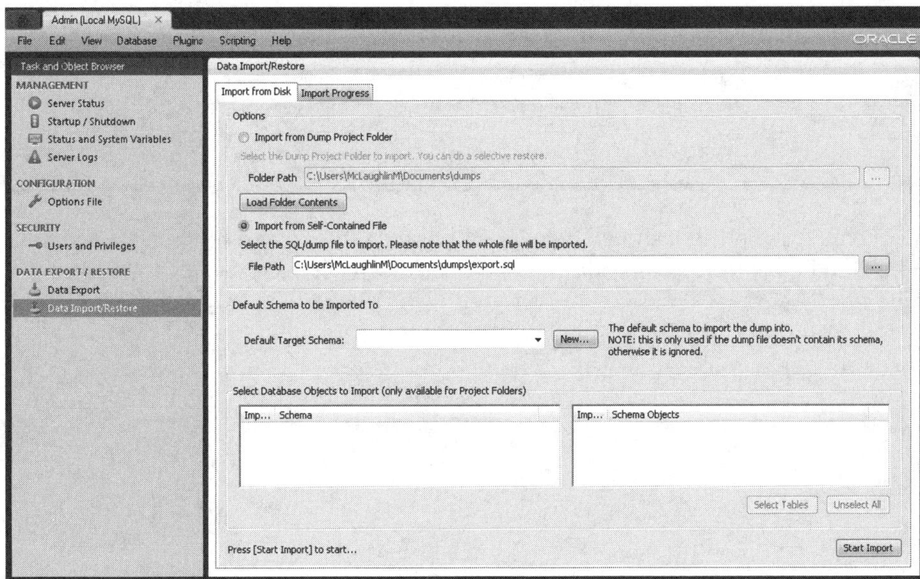

Clicking the *Ellipsis* button raises an overlay file chooser menu for the user's dump folder. Click the self-contained file generated by the earlier export file. While the illustration shows `Dump20120802.sql`, your file should have a different timestamp.

NOTE
The file chooser finds all files in this directory, which means you need to ensure the file chosen has a SQL file extension.

After clicking the file in the chooser list, it will be displayed in the *File Name* field. Click the *Open* button in the file chooser dialog, and you should see a screen shot like the following.

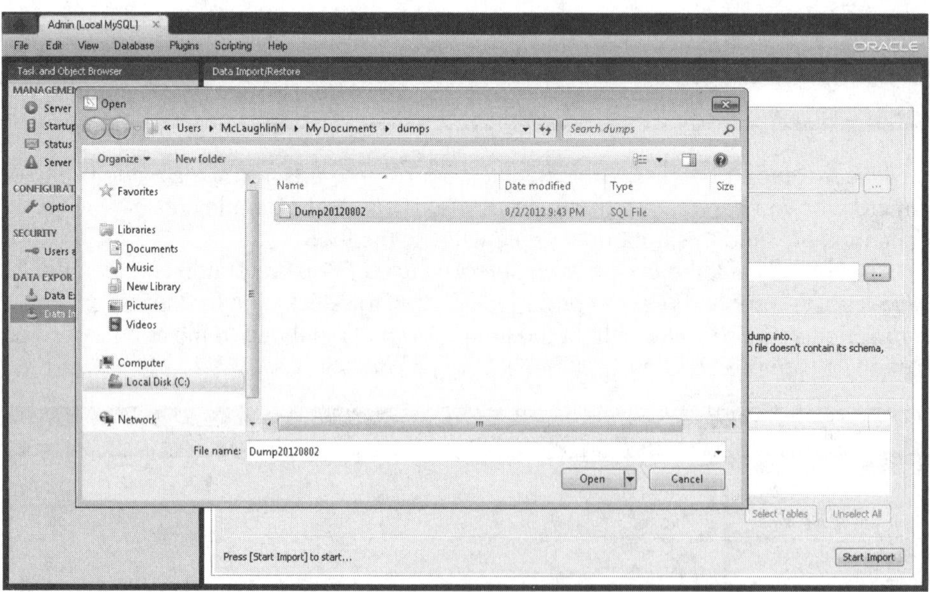

The new screen shot shown here should display the chosen file in the *File Name* field. Don't click the *Start Import* button yet because you're not ready to begin the import process.

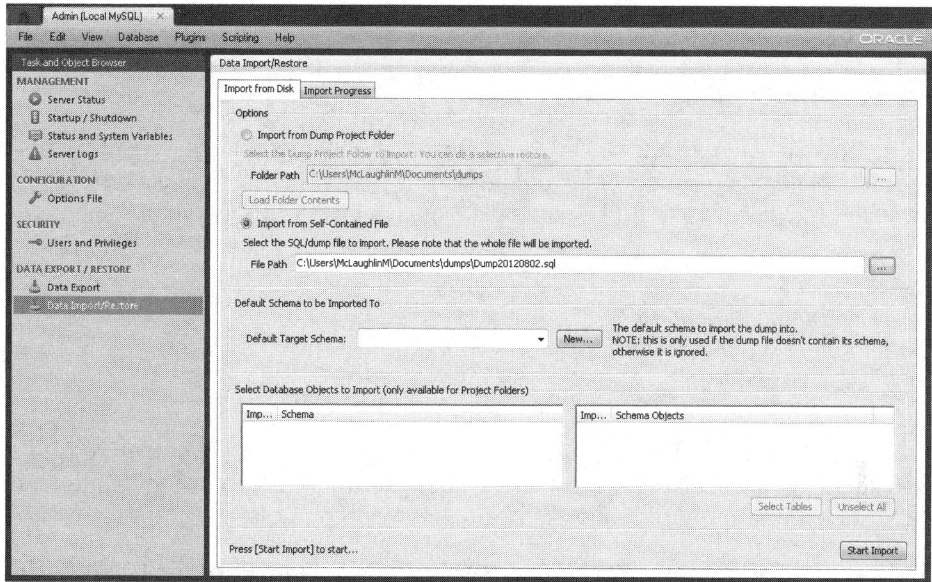

You must choose a *Default Target Schema* (remember that's a database) or create a new schema by clicking the *New* button. You get a Create Schema dialog message when creating the target schema ad hoc (on the fly) during the import process. The *Create Schema* dialog message is shown in the next illustration, but I cancelled that choice for the rest of the example.

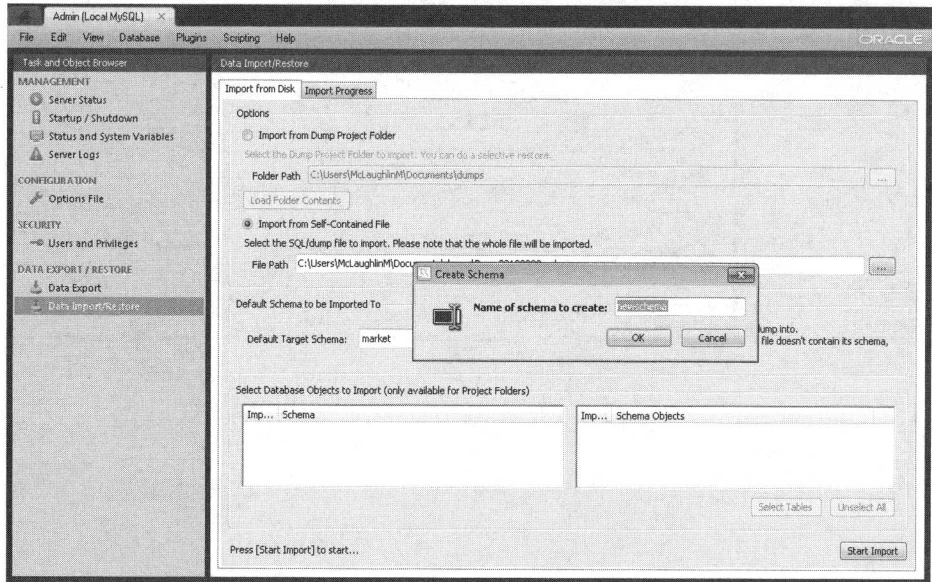

You need to drop out of MySQL Workbench and create a `market` database, which you can do with the following command:

```
CREATE DATABASE market;
```

A `market` database has already been created as the import target schema. It's generally better to create the target before starting this process. The select drop-down menu lets me pick it from the available databases in this MySQL Server instance.

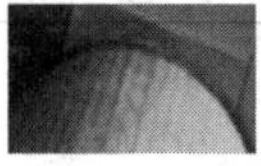

TIP
It's recommended that you create a target database before performing an import process with the MySQL Workbench tool.

The new screen shot shown here should display the chosen file in the *File Name* field and highlight a valid target schema where you want to place the structures and data. Click the *Start Import* button to begin the import process.

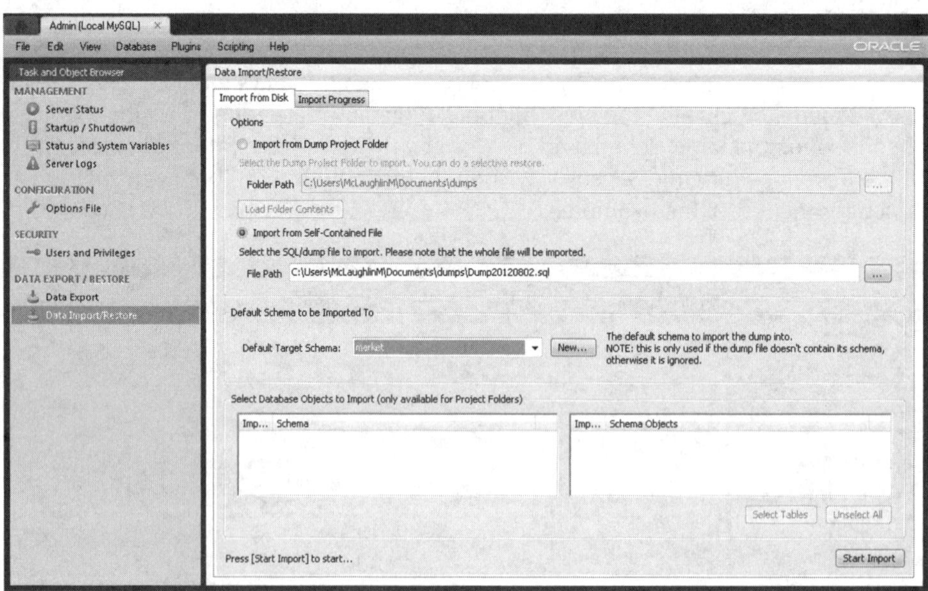

The import process launches the *Import Progress* tab. If everything imports successfully, you should see a screen like the following.

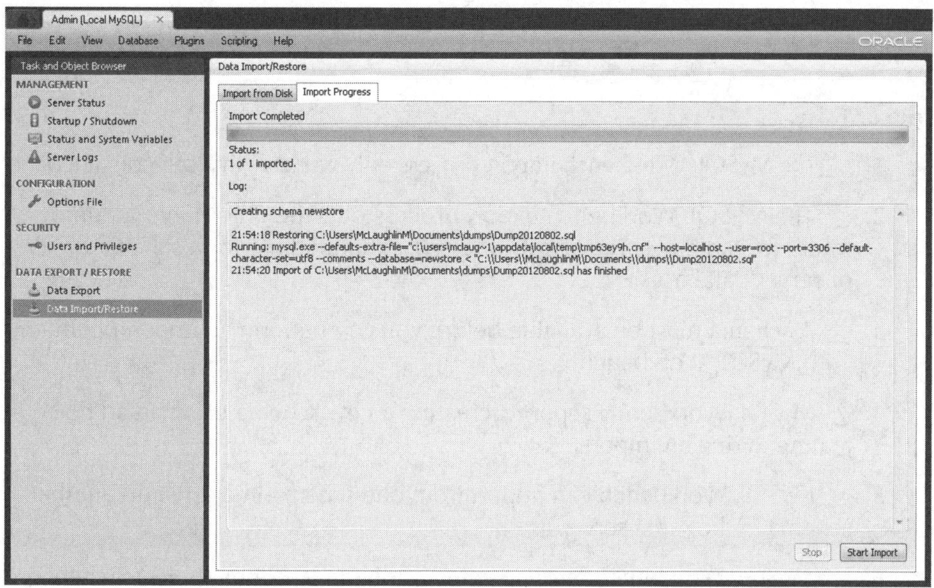

The log shows errors and warnings when everything doesn't work correctly. You can generally assume warning messages haven't interfered with the import, but you should do a comparison between the old and new schemas.

Any error message indicates you should remove the target schema, fix the source file, and try the import again. While you should be able to empty the database, dropping it and re-creating it guarantees a fresh container when you re-create the database.

This section has shown you how to import structures and data into a new MySQL schema. Although the example has simply moved the data from one schema to another in the same instance, you can, and generally do, move these from one server to another.

Summary

This chapter explained how to export and import database instances.

Mastery Check

The mastery check is a series of true or false and multiple choice questions that let you confirm how well you understand the material in the chapter. You may check Appendix A for answers to these questions.

True or False:

1. ___The MySQL Workbench import process only works with a self-contained file.
2. ___The MySQL Workbench export process puts the output into a dump folder for table-specific scripts or a self-contained file for a schema or set of server databases.
3. ___A schema must be available before you can perform an import operation with MySQL Workbench.
4. ___MySQL Workbench supports creating a new schema using an ad hoc feature during an import.
5. ___MySQL Workbench can import from one schema in a server to another schema in the same server.
6. ___MySQL Workbench lets you select individual schema objects when performing an export.
7. ___The import progress view shows warnings and errors.
8. ___Clicking the database object name in the object selection process displays the physical objects of the selected database.
9. ___The export progress view shows warnings and errors.
10. ___The file chooser looks only for files with a SQL extension.

Multiple Choice:

11. MySQL Workbench supports which of the following exports? (Multiple answers are possible.)

    A. All schemas and objects

    B. Some schemas and all objects for the selected schemas

    C. One schema and all of its objects

    D. One schema and some of its objects

    E. All schemas and some of their objects

12. MySQL creates which of the following in a dump project folder? (Multiple answers are possible.)

    A. A self-contained file

    B. A file for each table

    C. A file for each view

    D. A file for each routine

    E. A file for all synonyms

13. Which are valid options for a self-contained file? (Multiple answers are possible.)

    A. Create dump in a single transaction

    B. Dump stored procedures

    C. Dump events

    D. Skip table data

    E. Dump stored routines

14. Which are valid options for a dump project folder? (Multiple answers are possible.)

    A. Create dump in a single transaction

    B. Dump stored procedures

    C. Dump events

    D. Skip table data

    E. Dump stored routines

15. Which are valid options for `INSERT` statements? (Multiple answers are possible.)

    A. Add-locks

    B. Complete-insert

    C. Extended-insert

    D. Insert-ignore

    E. Replicate

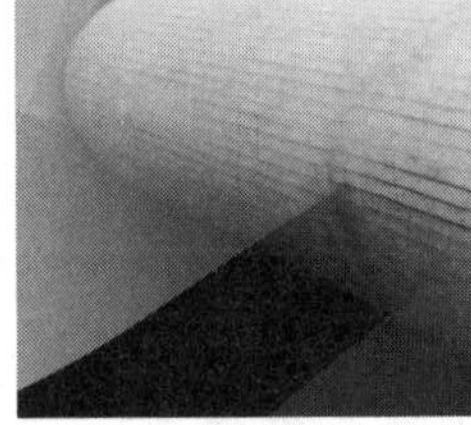

CHAPTER 12

Migrating Databases

ySQL Workbench supports migrating databases to MySQL 5.6. Migration lets you take a structure and data set from one database into another. The tool takes care of changes between the different database structures.

MySQL Workbench currently provides a migration facility that lets you move a MySQL 5.1 database to a MySQL 5.6 database. At the time of writing, it also lets you move a SQL Server 2000, 2005, 2008, or 2012 database to a MySQL 5.6 database. By the time this book releases, MySQL Workbench should support migrating Sybase 15.7 and Postgres 9.1 to MySQL 5.6 too.

This chapter shows you how to migrate from a Microsoft SQL Server 2012 database to a MySQL 5.5 database. It shows all the necessary steps, and you can refer to Appendix C if you'd like to set up a Microsoft SQL Server 2012 instance to test it.

Exporting a Database

The migration functionality isn't part of any of the three major MySQL Workbench components. You find it by opening MySQL Workbench and navigating through the menu. Click Database | Migrate to launch the migration wizard, as shown in the following illustration. Migrations can be on local or remote servers. Click the *Migrate* option to launch it.

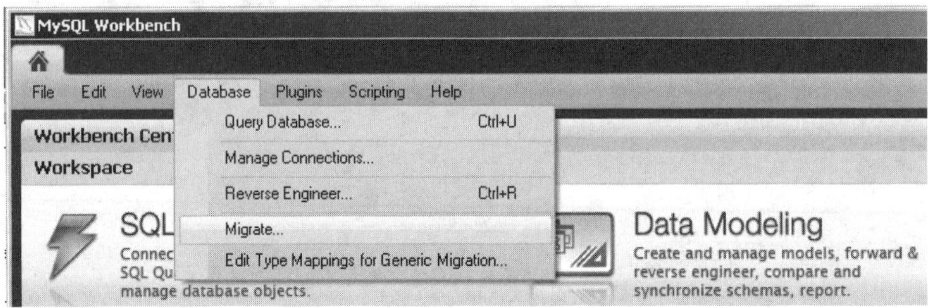

The Welcome screen opens, and you have three choices. The *Start Migration* button starts the migration wizard, which is what you'll focus on in this chapter. The *Open ODBC Administrator* button launches the *Windows ODBC Data Source Administrator* button, which is covered in Appendix C. The *View Documentation* button launches a web page for Chapter 10 of the MySQL Workbench documentation.

Click the *Start Migration* button to start the migration wizard.

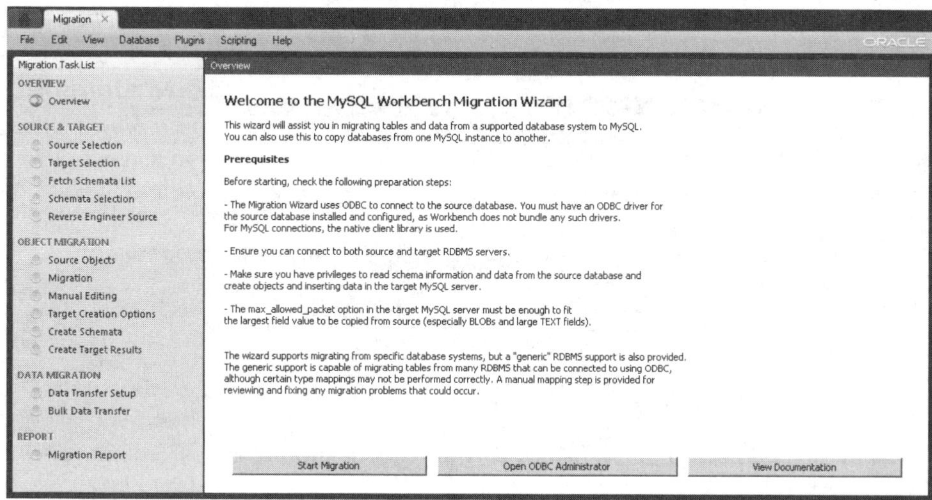

You see the following default *Source Selection* screen. You need to change the *Database System* and *DSN* values (shown in a later illustration). Both of these values are set by default to a MySQL instance.

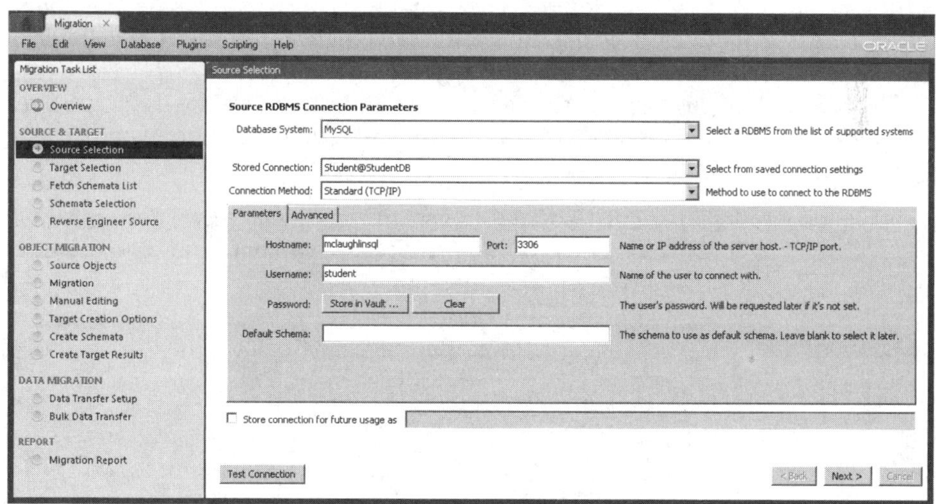

The next screen illustrates the values in the drop-down box at the time of writing. The choices in this box will change over time as the tool becomes capable of working with new databases. For this example, select the *Microsoft SQL Server* menu option in the *Database System* option.

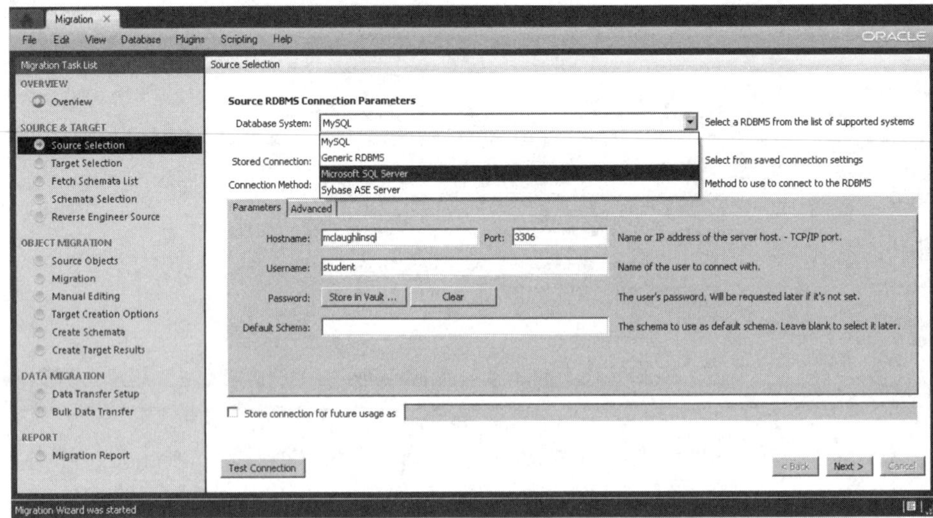

The selection of *Microsoft SQL Server* updates the *Connection Method* with the *ODBC Data Source* value. This selection is required to enable the MySQL Workbench tool to read an external database.

The next screen illustrates the selection of a *SQL Server ODBC for the SQL Server Native Client 11.0* from the *DSN*. This is the second required step to identify the source database.

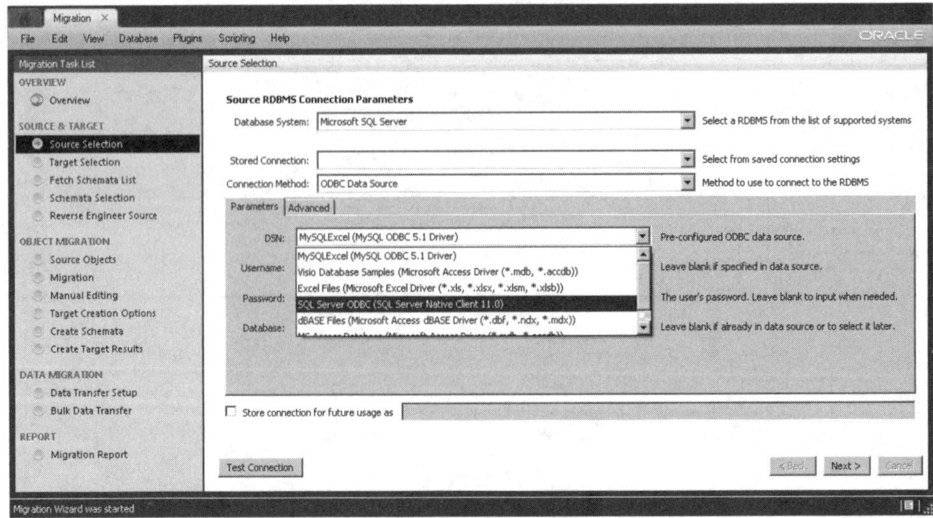

After making those selections, you should see the following illustration. It does have options, such as choosing a database. You want to leave the Database field empty when you migrate the server instance. Click the *Next* button to continue working with the wizard.

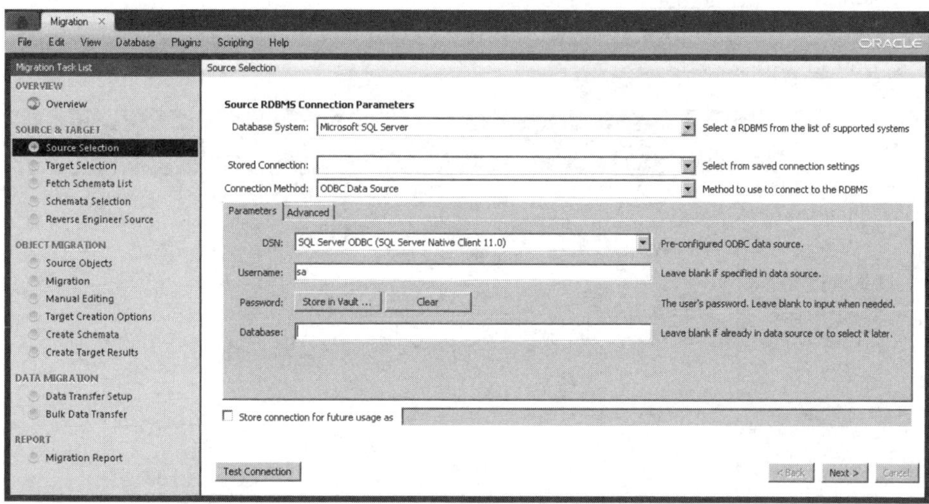

This takes you to the *Target Selection* step of the wizard. The *Stored Connection* value comes from the definitions you've defined for the SQL Development component of the MySQL Workbench. You need to connect with the MySQL `root` user when you migrate an instance.

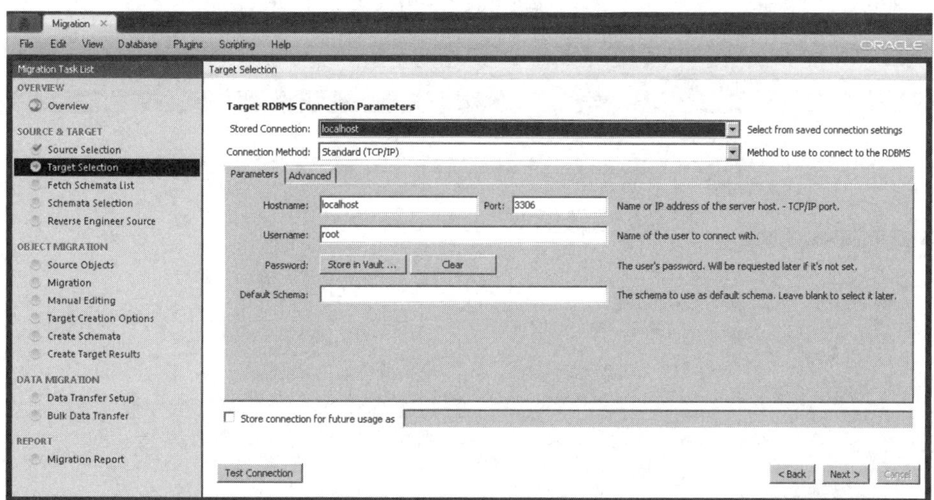

The *Fetch Schemata List* wizard step is automatic, unless it encounters an error. It connects to the source database, validates the target database, and retrieves the schema list from the source database.

Click the *Show Logs* button when you encounter an error. The logs should show you what may have caused the failure.

After everything works, you should see a screen like the following. Click the *Next* button to proceed.

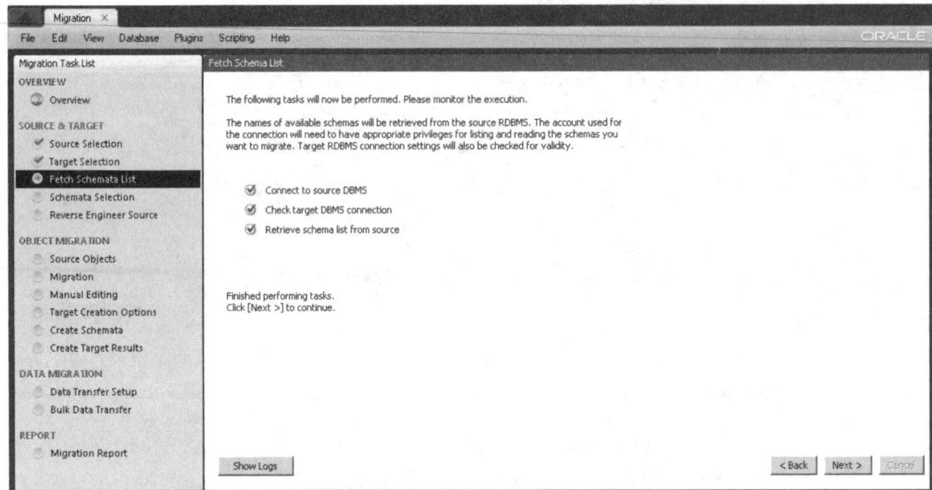

The next step, *Schemata Selection,* shows you the available schemas. You can click any of the empty boxes in the *Include* column on the left.

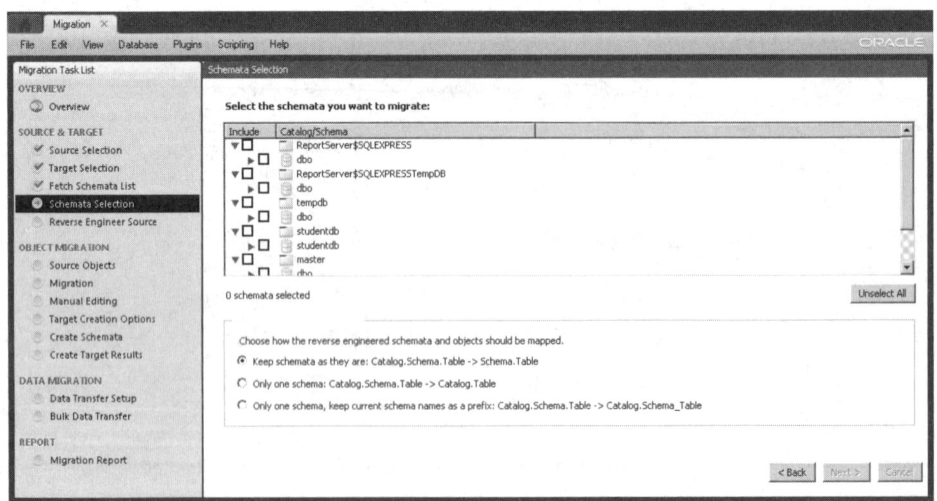

You would click all other desired schemas, as shown, in an actual migration. Naturally, there's a problem when application tables in a Microsoft SQL Server share the DBO schema with the data catalog.

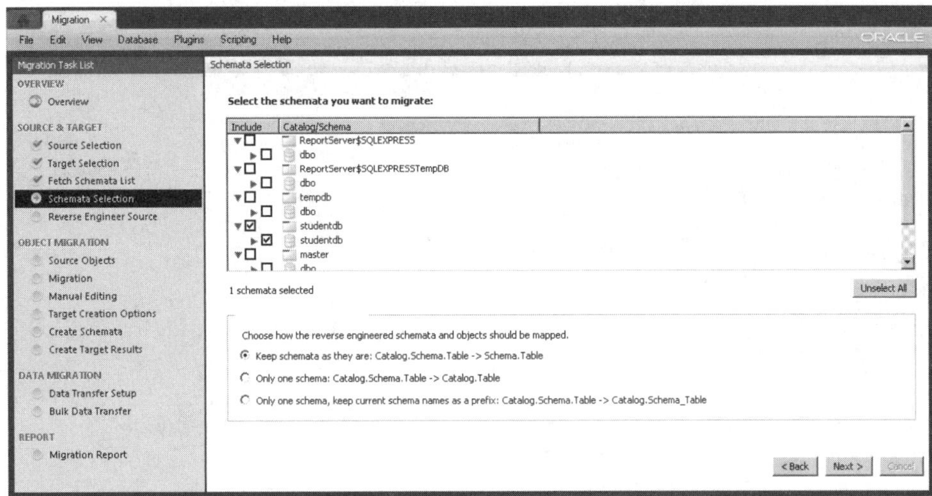

The *Reverse Engineer Source* step acts like the *Fetch Schemata List* step. The connect to the database, reverse-engineer selected schemata, and post-processing of reverse-engineered schemata steps run automatically unless they encounter an error.

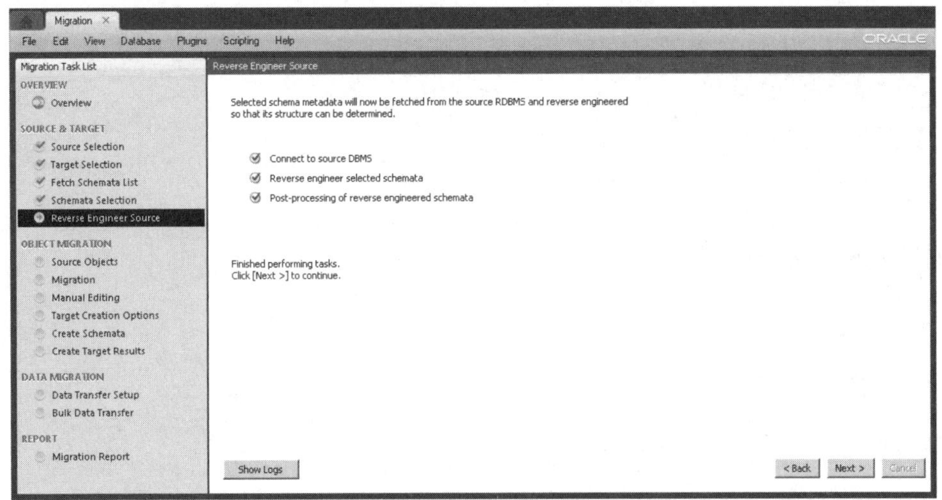

Click the *Show Logs* button when you encounter an error. The logs should show you what may have caused the failure. When everything works, click the *Next* button.

The prior section detected the source and target databases. This section migrates objects. The first screen in this section asks you to confirm that you want to migrate the objects that you previously selected. Click the *Next* button to proceed.

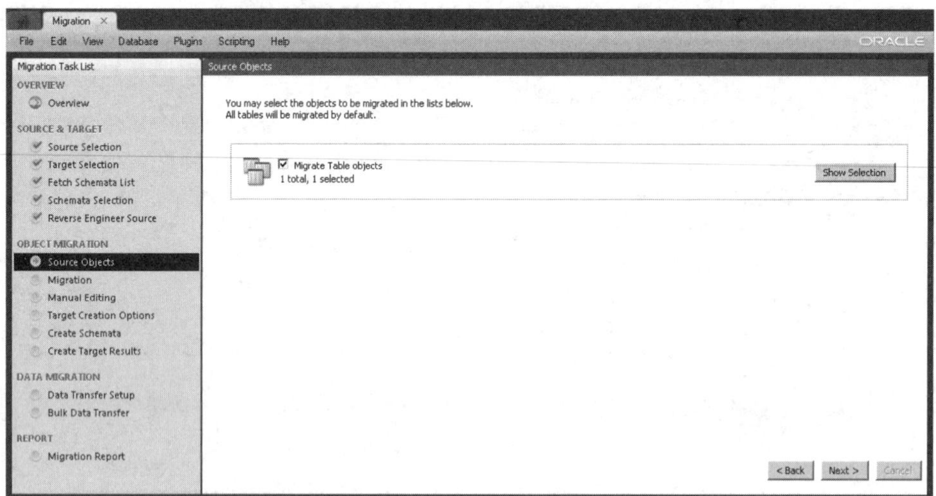

If you don't remember what you selected, click the *Show Selection* button to display your previous choices. The next screen shows you the choices made during this example.

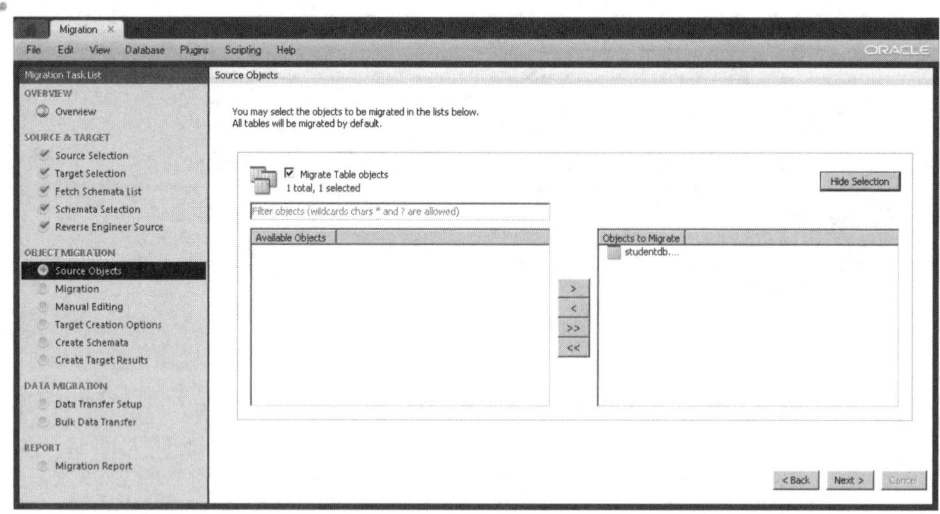

After inspecting the choices, click the *Next* button to proceed.

By default, the *Migration* step acts like the *Reverse Engineer Source* and *Fetch Schemata List* steps. The *Migration* step migrates the selected objects and generates the SQL creation statements. You also have the ability to click the *Show Logs* button to check for errors when everything doesn't work as it should.

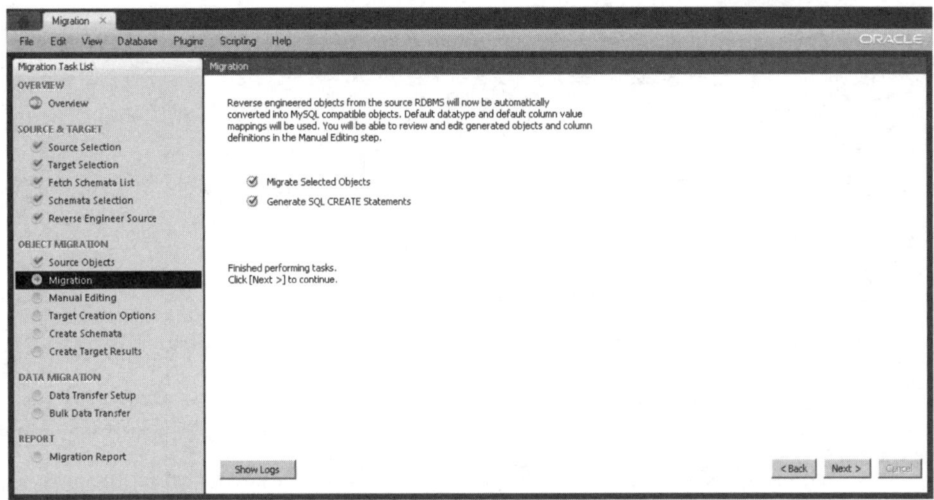

Assuming all steps are complete, you should click the *Next* button to proceed.

The *Manual Editing* step shows that there weren't any mapping problems in the following screen shot. There are three views at this stage of the migration. The default and initially displayed value is the *Migration Problem* view.

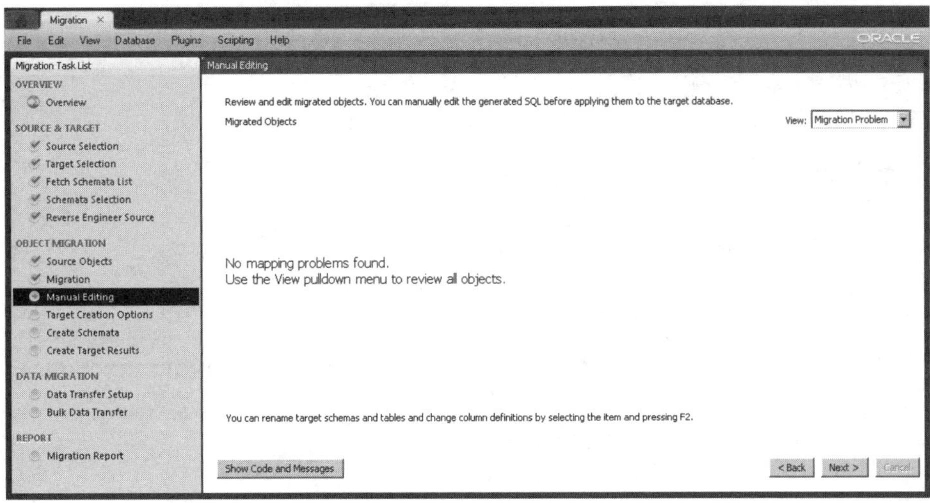

By clicking the *View* drop-down list, you can choose the *All Objects* option. It displays the objects selected for migration, as shown in the next illustration.

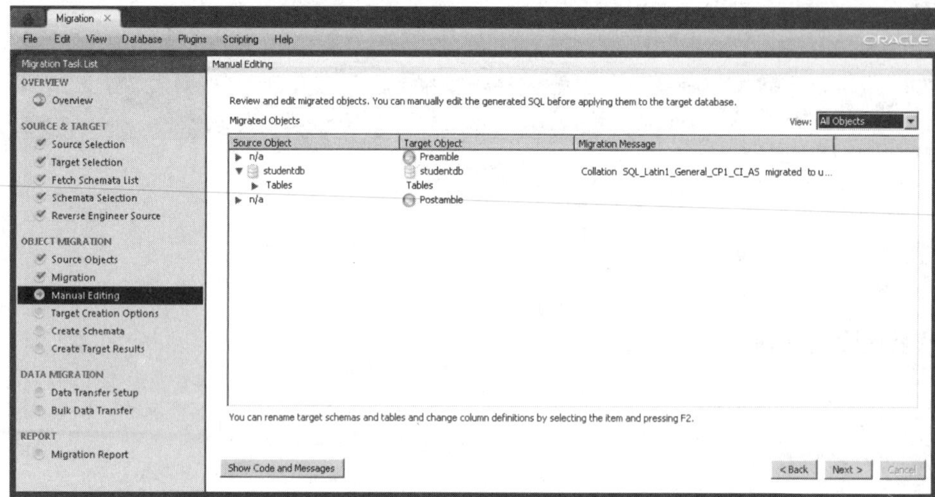

The *Column Mapping* view option displays the source schema and tables, as you see in the next illustration. Click the *Next* button to proceed with the migration.

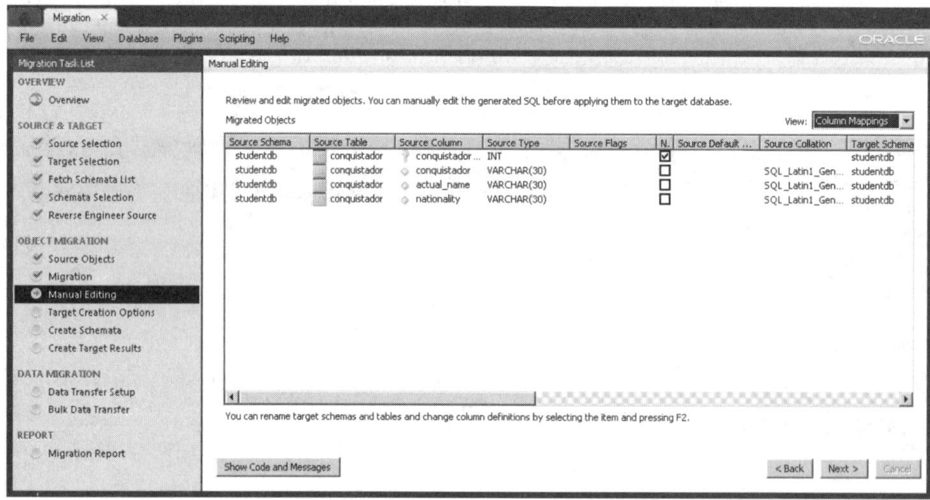

The default behavior of the *Target Creation Options* step creates a schema in the target Relational Database Management System (RDBMS). The screen should look like the following illustration.

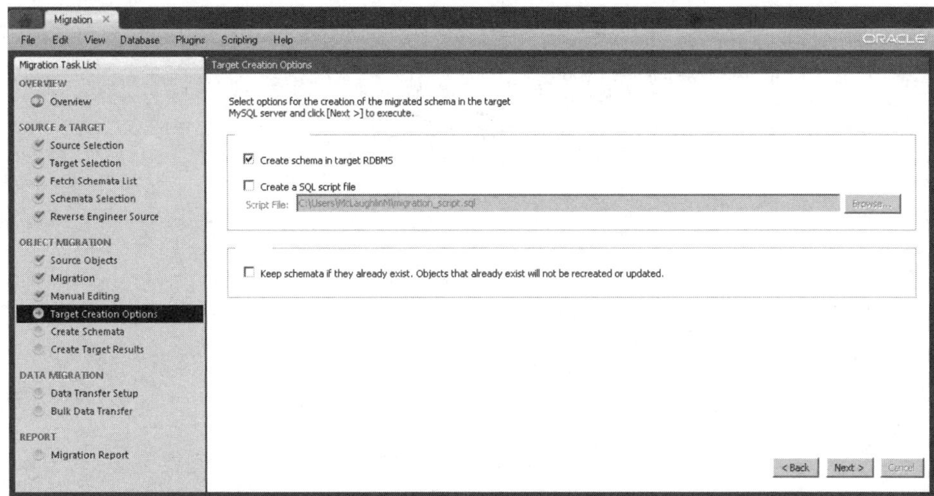

Generally, migrations have many phases. The first phase requires testing the software, like you're doing in this chapter. The second phase may use the tool to perform the migration or a script generated by the migrating tool.

During the migration, you generate a script file by clicking the *Create a SQL script file* check box. It's prudent to enable the SQL script file so that you can examine what happens during the migration.

The following screen shot shows the enabled check box. Click the *Next* button to proceed.

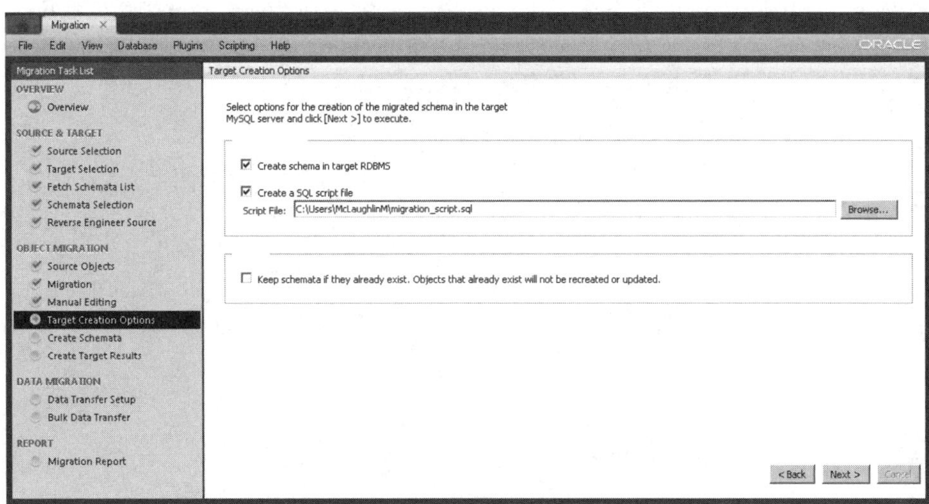

The following is the script generated when migrating only the single table from the `studentdb` schema of the Microsoft SQL Server 2012 database. You should change the schema name in the script before running it.

```
-- ----------------------------------------------------------------
-- MySQL Workbench Migration
-- Migrated Schemata: studentdb
-- Source Schemata: studentdb
-- Created: Wed Oct 10 23:00:29 2012
-- ----------------------------------------------------------------

SET FOREIGN_KEY_CHECKS = 0;

-- ----------------------------------------------------------------
-- Schema studentdb
-- ----------------------------------------------------------------
DROP SCHEMA IF EXISTS `studentdb`;
CREATE SCHEMA IF NOT EXISTS `studentdb`
  COLLATE utf8_general_ci;

-- ----------------------------------------------------------------
-- Table studentdb.conquistador
-- ----------------------------------------------------------------
CREATE  TABLE IF NOT EXISTS `studentdb`.`conquistador` (
  `conquistador_id` INT NOT NULL AUTO_INCREMENT ,
  `conquistador` VARCHAR(30) NULL ,
  `actual_name` VARCHAR(30) NULL ,
  `nationality` VARCHAR(30) NULL ,
  PRIMARY KEY (`conquistador_id`) )
COLLATE = utf8_general_ci;
SET FOREIGN_KEY_CHECKS = 1;
```

When you've generated the `migration_script.sql` script previously, you raised a *Create Script File* dialog message. The following illustration shows the exception dialog message.

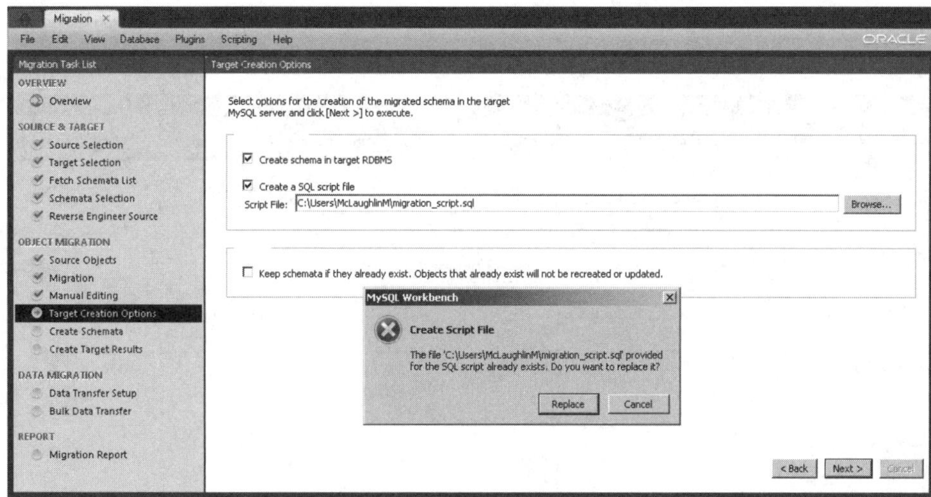

By default, the *Create Schemata* step acts like the *Migration, Reverse Engineer Source,* and *Fetch Schemata List* steps. This step creates a script file, connects to a target database, performs checks in the target database, and creates the schemata and objects. Like the other steps, the *Show Logs* button lets you inspect any errors.

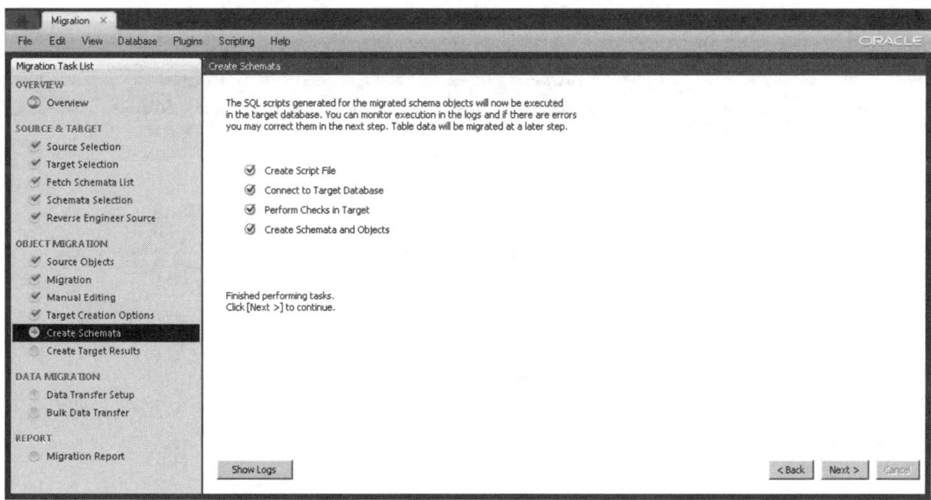

Click the *Next* button to proceed.

The *Create Target Results* step shows the structures created in the target MySQL database. Click the *Next* button to proceed.

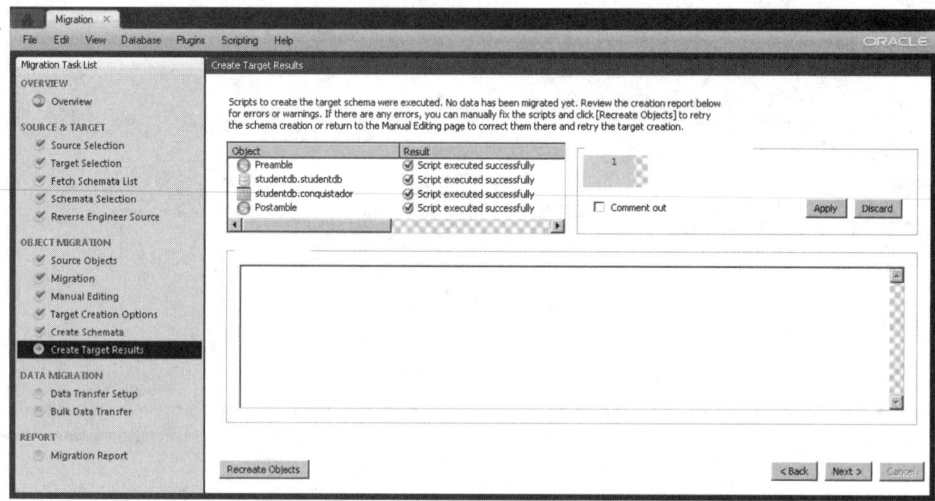

This concludes the migration of objects. The next screen shot displays a screen result like the *Data Transfer Setup* step. The default option simply migrates the data, like the prior *Target Creation Option* step migrates structures.

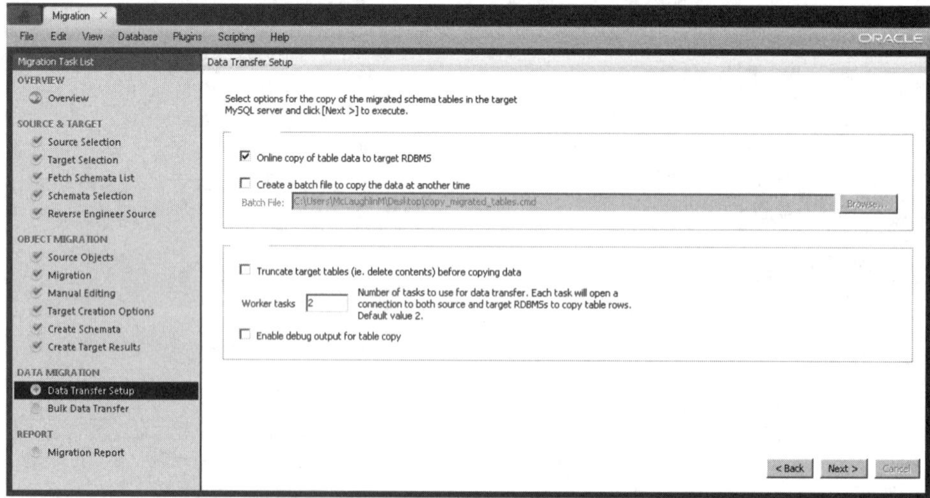

Check the *Create a batch file to copy the data at another time* check box to create a command shell script, as shown in the following screen shot. Click the *Next* button.

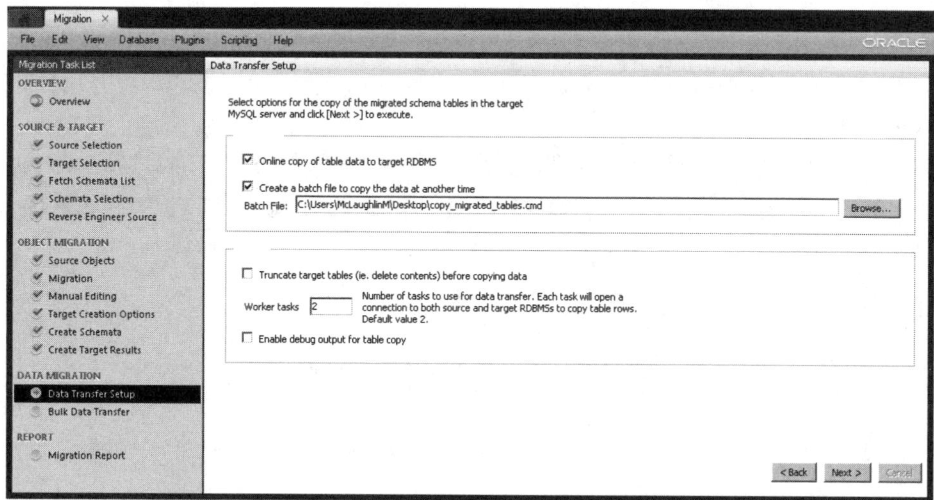

It generates the following command script in our test case:

```
REM Workbench Table Data copy script
REM
REM Execute this to copy table data from a source RDBMS to
REM MySQL. Edit the options below to customize it. You will
REM need to provide passwords, at least.
REM
REM Source DB: Mssql@SQL Server ODBC (Microsoft SQL Server)
REM Target DB: Mysql@mclaughlinsql:3306

REM Source and target DB passwords
set arg_source_password=cangetin
set arg_target_password=student
REM Uncomment the following options according to your needs

REM Whether target tables should be truncated before copy
REM set arg_truncate_target=--truncate-target
REM Enable debugging output
REM set arg_debug_output=--log-level=debug3

wbcopytables.exe
--odbc-source='[DSN=SQL Server ODBC;DATABASE=studentdb;UID=sa]'
--target=student@mclaughlinsql:3306
--source-password=%arg_source_password%
--target-password=%arg_target_password% %arg_truncate_target%
  %arg_debug_output%
--table '[dbo].[ORGANIZATION]' '`studentdb`' '`ORGANIZATION`'
```

You need the sa user's password, which you set when you installed Microsoft SQL Server 2012. Appendix C provides instructions for installing Microsoft SQL

Server 2012. The `sa` super user in Microsoft SQL Server is equivalent to the `root` super user in MySQL.

Enter the Microsoft SQL Server `sa` user's password and click the *OK* button to proceed.

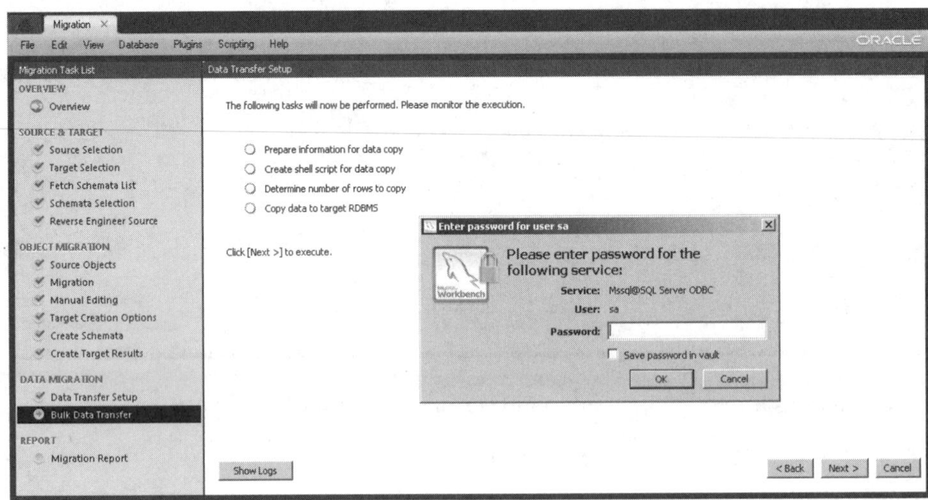

By default, the *Bulk Data Transfer* step acts like the *Create Schemata, Migration, Reverse Engineer Source,* and *Fetch Schemata List* steps. This step prepares information for data copy, creates the shell script for data copy, determines the number of rows to copy, and copies the data to the target database. Like the other steps, the *Show Logs* button lets you inspect any errors, which display a red *X* in the round button before any step.

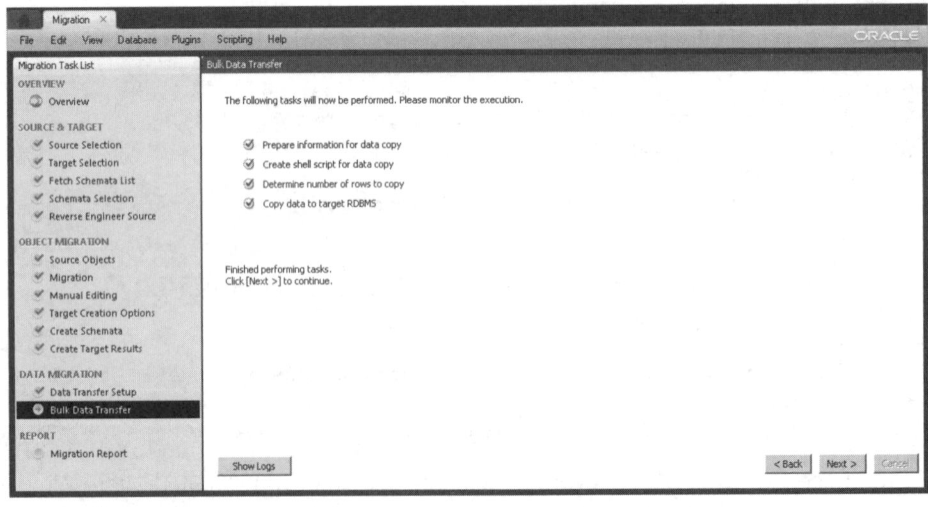

Click the *Next* button to proceed.

The last step shows the migration report. It tells you what you've migrated. It's a scrollable dialog, as shown in the following illustration.

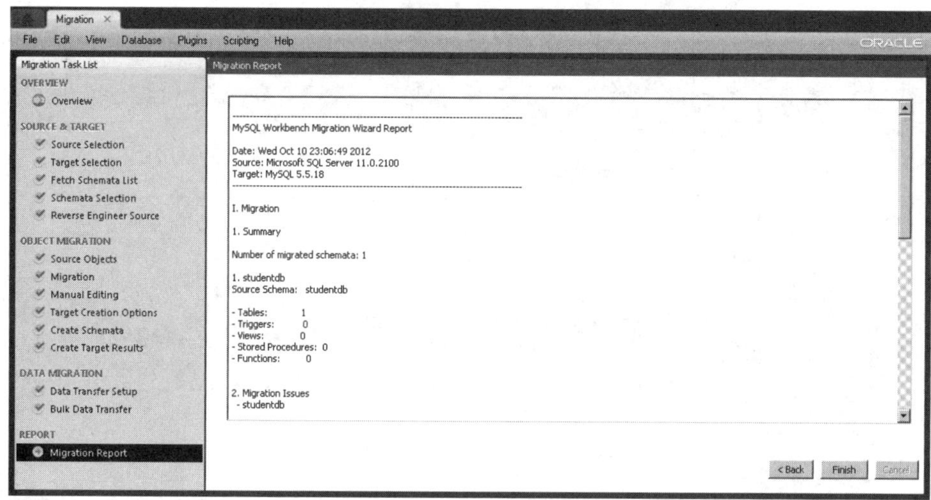

You can confirm the results by opening a new connection to the database from the SQL Development component by choosing *Edit Table Data* or *Edit SQL Script*. Click either of those two links in the SQL Development column of command options.

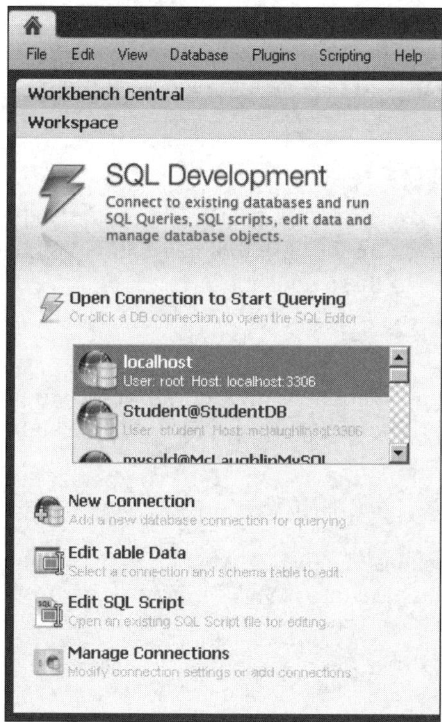

Write a USE statement and query to check whether the database values have migrated, like those shown in the following screen shot.

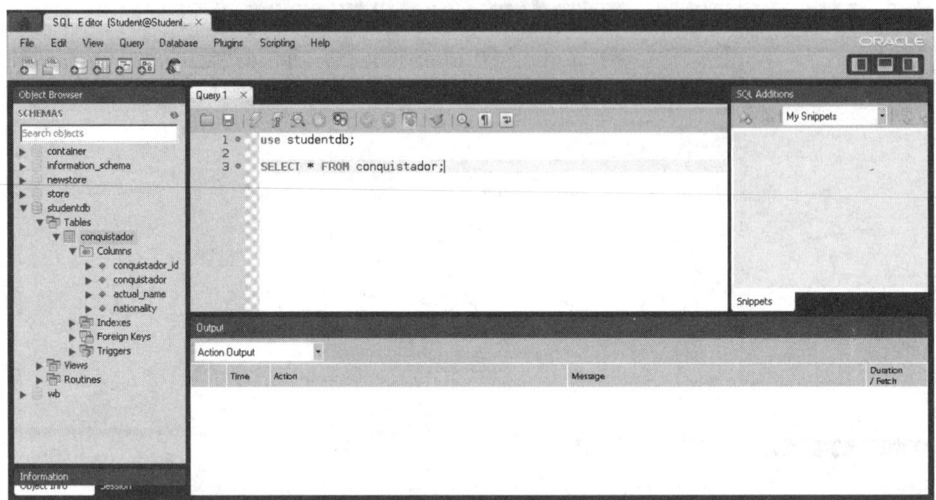

This concludes showing you how to migrate a Microsoft SQL Server 2012 instance into MySQL. It certainly makes it quite easy to move from one to the other.

Summary

This chapter explained how to migrate a foreign database into a MySQL 5.5 database.

Mastery Check

The mastery check is a series of true or false and multiple choice questions that let you confirm how well you understand the material in the chapter. You may check Appendix A for answers to these questions.

True or False:

1. ___The MySQL Workbench migration tool lets you migrate a Microsoft SQL Server 2012 database into a MySQL 5.5 database.
2. ___At the time of writing, the MySQL Workbench migration tool lets you migrate a Postgres 9.1 database into a MySQL 5.5 database.
3. ___In the future, the MySQL Workbench migration tool will let you migrate a Sybase 15.7 database into a MySQL 5.5 database.

4. __The MySQL Workbench migration tool requires super user accounts for both users in all cases.

5. __MySQL Workbench can migrate one or more databases from a server instance.

6. __MySQL Workbench lets you select individual schema objects when performing a migration.

7. __The migration steps show success or failure and provide a *Show Log* button when errors occur.

8. __Clicking the database object name in the *Object Selection* step displays the physical objects of the selected database.

9. __You don't have an option during migration with MySQL Workbench to write scripts, because it only supports interactive migrations.

10. __The *Manual Editing* step provides you with an *All Objects* view as the default.

Multiple Choice:

11. MySQL Workbench supports which of the following source database servers? (Multiple answers are possible.)

    A. IBM DB2

    B. MySQL 5.1

    C. MySQL 5.0

    D. Postgres 9.1

    E. SQL Server 2012

12. MySQL creates which of the following if you enable creating script files? (Multiple answers are possible.)

    A. A data catalog query of the target data dictionary

    B. A set of statements to migrate the structure of tables and views from the source database server

    C. A set of statements to generate the structure of tables and views in the target database server

    D. A data catalog query of the source data dictionary

    E. A master log file for all elements of the migration wizard

13. Which are valid tasks for the *Create Schemata* step? (Multiple answers are possible.)

   A. Create dump in a single transaction

   B. Create script file

   C. Connect to source database

   D. Connect to target database

   E. Create schemata and objects

14. Which are valid tasks for the *Bulk Data Transfer* step? (Multiple answers are possible.)

   A. Create dump in a single transaction

   B. Create shell script for data copy

   C. Determine number of rows to copy

   D. Copy data to target RDBMS

   E. Prepare information for data copy

15. Which are valid tasks for the *Data Transfer Setup* step? (Multiple answers are possible.)

   A. Online copy of table data to target RDBMS

   B. Create a batch file to copy the data at another time

   C. Migrate selected objects

   D. Truncate target tables

   E. Enable debug output for table copy

PART V

Appendixes and Glossary

APPENDIX A

Mastery Check Answers

This appendix contains the answer key to Mastery Check questions from the chapters in the book. Brief explanations supporting the answers follow each question. It is organized by chapter.

Chapter 1

True or False:

1. You use a Linux socket by default in a Linux MySQL Server after the default installation.

   True. The default installation uses a socket. You must convert it to use a network port.

2. You configure a listening port when you use the MySQL Windows configuration tool.

   True. The MySQL Windows configuration tool lets you choose and configure a listening port.

3. The default service name for Windows is `mysql`.

   True. The default service name for a MySQL Windows installation is `mysql`, but you may also choose any of the other options presented in the drop-down menu. You can't manually enter a value. Note that some older versions let you manually enter a value, but it isn't used when setting up the Windows service for MySQL.

4. The default service name for Linux is `mysqld`.

   True. The default service name for a Linux installation is `mysqld`. The ending d stands for Daemon (pronounced dee-*muhn*). Daemons are background processes and are most often referred to as services.

5. You should check the *Include Bin Directory in Windows Path* check box when you want to install two or more MySQL Servers on a Windows platform.

   False. When you want to install two or more versions of the database, you would leave the `bin` directory check box unchecked. However, MySQL 5.6 disallows multiple installations from the MSI file at the time of writing.

6. You can create aliases in a `.bash_rc` file in Mac OS X, and they're read every time you open a Terminal session.

   False. You need to make the change in the `.bash_login` file or it won't be read when you start a command-line or terminal session.

7. You can create aliases in a `.bash_login` file in Linux, and they're read every time you open a Terminal session.

   False. You need to create the alias in the `.bash_profile` file in Fedora Linux.

8. The look and feel of MySQL Workbench's initial dialog menu differs between the Linux, Mac OS X, and Windows platforms.

   False. The look and feel of MySQL Workbench is the same, regardless of platform, other than the differences between rendering component frames.

9. The Linux installation of MySQL Server lets you dynamically choose where to install the MySQL product.

   False. The Linux install automatically deploys the MySQL Server files into the `/usr/bin` and the MySQL daemon is stored in the `/etc/init` directory.

10. The MySQL Workbench installation puts a menu choice in the Application | Programming menu of the GNOME interface.

    True. Installation menus are installed on Linux.

Multiple Choice:

11. Which platform provides a configuration wizard that manages the product setup?

    A. Linux

    B. Mac OS X

    C. Windows

    D. All of the above

    E. None of the above

    C is correct. The Windows platform provides an automatic configuration wizard.

12. Which platform supports running the `mysql_secure_installation` script without modification?

A. Linux

B. Mac OS X

C. Windows

D. All of the above

E. None of the above

A is correct. The Linux platform runs the `mysql_secure_installation` script without modification. The other platforms require modifications.

13. Which platform supports loading a customized package for the MySQL Server?

A. Linux

B. Mac OS X

C. Windows

D. All of the above

E. None of the above

A is correct. While each port of the MySQL Server requires customized compilation, only the Linux distribution ships in both `.rpm` and `.deb` formats. The nature of Linux requires two different approaches to package installations.

14. Which platform supports a Linux or Unix pipe or socket for communication? (Multiple answers are possible.)

A. Linux

B. Mac OS X

C. Windows

D. All of the above

E. None of the above

A and **B** are correct. They both support a Linux or Unix pipe or socket for communication, but Windows supports a non-Linux or non-Unix pipe.

15. Which are the generic ports for a MySQL installation? (Multiple answers are possible.)

    A. 3306

    B. 3307

    C. 3308

    D. 3309

    E. All of the above

    A, **B**, and **C** are correct. They represent the default port assignments for the MySQL Server.

Chapter 2

True or False:

1. The Linux installation adds a menu option to launch MySQL Workbench under the Application | Other menu path.

   False. The menu option is under the Application | Programming menu path for MySQL Workbench.

2. You can configure a SQL Development connection that only allows access to a specific schema (or MySQL database).

   True. You do so by choosing a default database.

3. The `localhost` keyword is a valid hostname.

   True. You can use the `localhost` keyword when you are connecting to the local server from an account on the local server.

4. The `127.0.0.1` IP address is a valid hostname.

   False. The MySQL Workbench installation automatically substitutes `localhost` for the `127.0.0.1` loop back protocol IP address.

5. The machine's `hostname` value is the only valid hostname.

   False. The `localhost` can also be a valid hostname even when the machine has a DNS-assigned DHCP or static IP address because the loop back network works for MySQL Workbench local installations.

6. You launch MySQL Workstation from a drop-down menu in Mac OS X.

   False. No, you launch MySQL Workstation from Spotlight (the Mac OS X finder application). It's also found in the Applications folder like other software applications on the Mac OS X platform.

7. SQL Development connections depend on the values in the hosts file on all platforms.

   True. This is correct because the hosts file either identifies the IP address or references a DHCP address.

8. The look and feel of MySQL Workbench is virtually identical across Linux, Mac OS X, and Windows platforms.

   True. This is generally true, but there are some slight overlay differences made possible by .NET libraries on the Windows platform.

9. Editing the hosts file on Windows 7 requires the ability to work with restricted directory paths and open an editor as the administrator.

   True. This is part of the security precautions inherent in the Microsoft Windows operating system.

10. MySQL Workbench lets you start and stop MySQL Server instances on local and remote servers.

    True. This is correct. You can start and stop any MySQL Server that you can access via a TCP/IP connection. This typically means within the corporate intranet.

Multiple Choice:

11. Which SQL Development connection features are available in the context menu? (Multiple answers possible.)

    A. Move up

    B. Move down

    C. Edit

    D. Delete connection

    E. Delete all connections

    A, **B**, **D**, and **E** are correct. Only the Edit option isn't a feature.

12. Which SQL Development connection feature lets you change configuration options of a SQL Development connection from the MySQL Workbench menu?

    A. Manage

    B. Configure

    C. Edit

    D. All of the above

    E. None of the above

    A is correct. You select Manage Connections to change connection configuration options.

13. On the Windows 7 platform, what is the default hostname for a SQL Development instance?

    A. 127.0.0.1

    B. localhost

    C. hostname

    D. All of the above

    E. None of the above

    B is correct. `localhost` is the default when installing the client tool on the server.

14. Which platform preconfigures a SQL Development connection and Server Administration to a local instance?

    A. Linux

    B. Mac OS X

    C. Windows

    D. All of the above

    E. None of the above

    D is correct. All preconfigure the connection to the local MySQL Server.

15. Which of the following is the standard deployment port?

A. 3306

B. 3307

C. 3308

D. 3309

E. All of the above

A is correct. The default standard port is `3306`.

Chapter 3

True or False:

1. External identifiers hold primary key columns.

True. The external identifier is always the primary key and may be composed of one to many columns, but is typically a single-column surrogate (or stand-in) key.

2. Internal identifiers hold natural key columns.

True. Internal identifiers are the columns that uniquely identify the subject of the table, and those columns, by definition, are the natural key of the table.

3. External references hold foreign key columns.

True. External reference columns hold foreign keys, which are copies of primary keys and the principal way to resolve value-based joins between tables.

4. Non-key data includes surrogate key columns.

False. A non-key data element or column holds something that is unnecessary to uniquely identify a single row in the table. It is more or less data that provides a supplemental description of the subject. Non-key data can't hold a surrogate key because that would make it a key column.

5. Both surrogate and primary keys are candidate keys.

True. A surrogate key is always unique and an automated sequence value, which makes it a candidate key. A primary key must also be a candidate key because you choose a primary key from the available candidate keys.

6. UNF is the same as HNF when a table is in 0NF.

   True. UNF (un-normalized normal form) is the HNF (highest normal form) when the table is in 0NF (zero normal form).

7. HNF is only 3NF or higher.

   False. HNF (highest normal form) is the highest form of the table, regardless of what level the table achieves.

8. A table is in 1NF when it has a partial dependency.

   True. A partial dependency can't exist unless the table is in 1NF (first normal form) because all rows must be unique and columns contain atomic values before you fix a partial dependency on only part of the natural primary key.

9. A table is in 1NF when it has a transitive dependency.

   False. A transitive dependency can't exist until you've resolved any partial dependency, which automatically promotes the table's design to 2NF (second normal form).

10. There is nothing higher than 3NF.

    False. There are several higher forms of normalization beyond 3NF (third normal form), and they are Boyce-Codd, fourth, fifth, and sixth normal forms.

Multiple Choice:

11. MySQL Workbench uses which data modeling system?

    A. Chen

    B. Chen-Martin

    C. Information engineering

    D. UML

    E. None of the above

    C is correct. Information engineering uses a crow's-foot method for displaying cardinality between tables.

12. Which relationship line models an ID-dependent relationship?

    A. Aggregation line

    B. Composition line

    C. Inheritance line

D. Relationship line

E. None of the above

D is correct. The relationship line is typically an ordinary relationship line, but in certain derivative methods a dashed line represents the relationship where the relationship may be optional.

13. What type of relationship models a primary-to-foreign key association?

A. Unary

B. Binary

C. N-ary

D. Inheritance

E. Aggregation

B is correct. A binary relationship represents the link between a primary and foreign key, which are generally in separate tables but may be in different columns of the same table.

14. What type of variable holds only one thing? (Multiple answers are possible.)

A. Compound variable

B. Composite variable

C. Scalar variable

D. Primitive variable

E. None of the above

C and **D** are correct. Scalar is the descriptor in database modeling, but primitive may also be used since the evolution of Java in database applications.

15. Most relationships between tables are?

A. Independent

B. Dependent

C. ID-dependent

D. Non-ID–dependent

E. None of the above

D is correct. Non-ID–dependent relationships are ordinary relationships and the most common type of binary relationship.

Chapter 4

True or False:

1. The PK key stands for a primary key column.

   True. The PK key represents the primary key.

2. The BIN key stands for a case-insensitive column.

   False. The BIN key stands for a case-sensitive column.

3. The AI key can only be checked for a primary key column.

   True. The AI key represents auto-increment, and it may only be checked for a primary key column.

4. The UN key represents a unique constraint.

   False. The UN key represents an unsigned integer or double.

5. The NN key represents a not-null constraint.

   True. The NN key represents a not-null value.

6. The Model Overview lets you add diagrams.

   True. You can add diagrams through the Model Overview.

7. Each table in the Model Overview supports tabs for foreign keys.

   True. You have a tab to monitor foreign keys for any table.

8. The Model Overview lets you add tables.

   True. You can add a table from the Model Overview.

9. The EER diagram has dashed lines to illustrate relationships between primary and foreign keys.

   True. The ERD has dashed lines between entities.

10. Relationships have two tabs, and the Foreign Key tab lets you set a self-identifying relationship.

    True. There are two tabs, and the Foreign Key tab lets you manage a self-identifying relationship.

Multiple Choice:

11. MySQL Workbench should use which of the following to set a primary key column with an unsigned integer or double? (Multiple answers are possible.)

A. A `PK` key

B. A `UQ` key

C. A `UN` key

D. An `AI` key

E. A `NN` key

A, **C**, and **D** are correct. The `PK`, `AI`, and `UN` keys together identify a primary key using auto-incrementing, which requires an unsigned integer or double data types.

12. The diagramming tool supports which of the following? (Multiple answers are possible.)

A. Column names

B. Column types

C. Relationships

D. Cardinalities

E. All of the above

E is correct. Column names and types are supported, as well as relationships and their cardinalities.

13. Relationships may have which of the following cardinalities? (Multiple answers are possible.)

A. One-to-one

B. Zero-to-one

C. Zero-to-many

D. One-to-many

E. Many-to-many

A, **B**, **C**, and **D** are correct. One-to-one, zero-to-one, one-to-many, and zero-to-many relationships are supported by the model because they're physical relationships. A many-to-many relationship is a logical relationship that is implemented by using a translation or association entity and two zero-to-many or one-to-many relationships.

14. What window displays the list of tables, views, and routine groups? (Multiple answers are possible.)

A. The Bird's Eye frame

B. The Catalog frame

C. The Description Editor frame

D. The Diagram frame

E. None of the above

B is correct. The Catalog frame is where the navigating list of tables, views, and routines is displayed.

15. The EER Diagram frame displays what? (Multiple answers are possible.)

A. Tables

B. Indexes

C. Routines

D. Non-ID-dependent relationships

E. All of the above

A and **D** are correct. It displays tables and relationships.

Chapter 5

True or False:

1. Routines can be added to any database.

True. You can add routines to any database.

2. A procedure is a routine.

True. A procedure is a routine, and so is a function.

3. A function isn't a routine.

False. A function is a routine. A function returns a value, whereas a procedure doesn't. In most cases, a procedure would be a routine, function, or method that returns a void type, and a function is a routine that returns a physical value at runtime.

4. Conditional drop statements should always be inside routine groups.

   False. You can't, at the time of writing, include a conditional drop statement in a MySQL Workbench routine.

5. You should never use a backward apostrophe (`) symbol in a routine.

   False. You can use backward apostrophe in a routine.

6. The Model Overview lets you add routines.

   True. You can add routines in the Model Overview.

7. The Model Overview lets you delete routines.

   True. You can delete routines in the Model Overview.

8. The Model Overview lets you add tables.

   True. You can add tables in the Model Overview.

9. Moving a routine into a routine group means you lose that functionality if you remove the stand-alone routine.

   False. You simply remove the stand-alone duplicate routine.

10. You must click the *Routines* tab to add, edit, or delete routines from routine groups.

    True. You click the *Routines* tab to add, edit, or delete routines from routine groups.

Multiple Choice:

11. MySQL Workbench supports which of the following routines? (Multiple answers are possible.)

    A. An object type

    B. A user-defined data type

    C. A function

    D. A procedure

    E. A nested inline view

    C and **D** are correct. You can define a stored function or procedure.

12. Which of the following let you edit a routine? (Multiple answers are possible.)

A. The Edit menu followed by the *Edit Selected* option

B. The floating menu followed by *Edit Routine*

C. A right-click to launch a context menu and an editing session

D. A double-click to launch an editing session

E. Click the routine icon and use a hotkey combination of CTRL-E

A, **B**, **D**, and **E** are correct. You can edit a routine one of four ways. First, you can click the routine and then choose the *Edit Selected* option from the Edit menu. Second, you can right-click and select the *Edit Routine* option. Third is double-clicking the routine option. Fourth is a context click on the routine and a hotkey combination of CTRL-E.

13. Which of the following let you delete a routine? (Multiple answers are possible.)

A. Select the routine and then click the Edit menu followed by the *Delete routine_name* option

B. The Edit menu followed by the *Delete routine_name* option

C. A right-click to launch a floating menu, where you can delete a routine

D. Click the routine and then press the DELETE key

E. Click the routine icon and use a hotkey combination of CTRL-DELETE

A, **C**, and **E** are correct. You can delete a routine one of three ways. First, you can click the routine and then choose the *Delete routine_name* option from the Edit menu. Second, you can right-click and select the *Edit Routine* option. Third is double-clicking the routine option. Fourth is a context click on the routine and a hotkey combination of CTRL-E.

14. What symbol must follow the `END` keyword of a routine? (Multiple answers are possible.)

A. A semicolon

B. A colon

C. The character set that follows the `DELIMITER` keyword

D. A semicolon and the character set that follows the `DELIMITER` keyword

E. Nothing

E is correct. Nothing is required after the `END` keyword.

15. Which of the following doesn't belong in a routine group? (Multiple answers are possible.)

    A. A `DROP` statement

    B. A conditional `DROP` statement

    C. Stored functions

    D. Stored procedures

    E. User-defined data types

    B is correct. A conditional `DROP` statement can't be used in a routine.

Chapter 6

True or False:

1. A forward engineering script can be written manually.

   True. You can write a forward engineering script manually or develop it with another tool.

2. A forward engineering script can be generated from an EER Model.

   True. You can create a forward engineering script from a capable EER Model.

3. A forward engineering script can be generated by using the MySQL Workbench export wizard.

   True. You can create a forward engineering script from the MySQL Workbench export wizard.

4. Reverse engineering is the process of reading information from the data catalog to generate a SQL script that can re-create the database.

   True. This is a correct definition of reverse engineering. Reverse engineering does depend on database constraints to map primary-to-foreign key relationships.

5. Forward engineering creates an EER Model and database instance in the MySQL Server.

   True. Forward engineering with the MySQL Workbench does create an EER Model, but forward engineering can simply be generating the tables, views, routines, and data in a new database.

6. Forward engineering creates a stack of objects in the EER Model Diagram view.

   True. MySQL Workbench automatically overlays all objects, and you must manually shift them to create a readable drawing.

7. Forward engineering puts routine objects in the EER Model Diagram and displays them as yellow background objects with their routine name.

   False. Views placed on the drawing canvas appear as yellow background objects. The view name is displayed in the yellow background highlighted objects.

8. You need to change the schema (database) name in scripts with a text editor or the MySQL script editor.

   False. You would only need to change the database name in the script file when you export a database from a MySQL Server and re-import it into the same MySQL Server.

9. You must open a MySQL EER Model to run forward engineering from the menu.

   False. You have access to the menu without having to open an EER Model view.

10. Reverse engineering requires an open MySQL EER Model.

    False. You don't need an open MySQL EER Model to reverse engineer a database.

Multiple Choice:

11. Forward engineering lets you choose which of the following types of objects for import to a new EER Model? (Multiple answers are possible.)

    A. Tables

    B. Views

    C. Procedures

    D. Functions

    E. Routines

    A, **B**, and **E** are correct. You can choose table, view, routine, and trigger objects. Functions or procedures are simply types of routines.

12. Which of the following should you leave deselected when you have self-referencing foreign-to-primary keys in the same table? (Multiple answers are possible.)

A. `DROP` Objects Before each `CREATE` Object

B. Generate `DROP SCHEMA`

C. Skip creation of `FOREIGN KEYS`

D. Generate Separate `CREATE INDEX` Statements

E. Generate `INSERT` Statements for Tables

C is correct. Self-referencing foreign keys trigger an error during the reverse engineering process. You have to make these changes manually.

13. Which of the following steps in the *Create EER Model from Existing Database* wizard lets you deselect objects for import? (Multiple answers are possible.)

A. The *Show Filter* button

B. The *Select Objects* button option

C. A *Show Filter* link

D. A *Select Object* link

E. An *Execute* button

B is correct. You check or uncheck table, view, routine, trigger, or user objects in the *Select Objects* step of the wizard.

14. What options do you have while reviewing the SQL Script to be executed? (Multiple answers are possible.)

A. Open the script

B. Save the script to a file

C. Copy the script to the MySQL Workbench Edit SQL Script wizard

D. Copy the script to the clipboard

E. None—you can only run (or execute) it

B and **D** are correct. You can save the script to a file or copy the script to the clipboard before clicking the *Next* button to continue with the wizard.

15. Which of the following is the default directory for files on the Windows operating system? (Multiple answers are possible.)

A. C:\Program Files (x86)\MySQL\MySQL Workbench\data

B. C:\Program Files\MySQL\MySQL Workbench\data

C. C:\Users\<*user_name*>\My Documents\dumps

D. C:\Program Files (x86)\MySQL\MySQL Workbench\models

E. C:\Program Files\MySQL\MySQL Workbench\models

C is correct. It automatically writes the reverse engineering script into a dump file in the C:\Users\<*user_name*>\My Documents\dumps folder.

Chapter 7

True or False:

1. The editing feature is found in the Server Admin component.

False. The editing feature is in the SQL Development component.

2. The editing feature lets you change data in any database, with or without a connection.

False. The editing feature requires that you connect to the database to make a change in the database. The only local access is the MySQL Workbench file, and the editing feature works with live database connections.

3. The editing feature lets you change data in a MySQL Model, not a MySQL Server's database instance.

False. The editing feature is designed to work with live databases through a valid TCP/IP connection.

4. You can refresh the data set from the menu by clicking the two blue curved arrows button.

True. This refreshes the data and undoes any uncommitted changes that you would have made with the data.

5. The asterisk points to the current row.

False. The asterisk points to a new row where you may insert a new row of data.

6. The blue highlighted cell is the one you're currently editing.

   True. The highlighted cell is the one you are editing or are poised to edit.

7. You can't insert more than one row at a time in the Edit Table Data feature of MySQL Workbench.

   False. The editing tool lets you enter as many new rows as you would like to at one time. It generates separate `INSERT` statements for each new row. You may also exclude entering values in auto-incrementing primary key columns.

8. MySQL Workbench uses the primary key column in the `WHERE` clause to identify the proper row(s) to delete from the database.

   True. MySQL Workbench generates `DELETE` statements by using the primary key column in the `WHERE` clause.

9. You can't update more than one record at a time in the Edit Table Data feature of MySQL Workbench.

   False. MySQL Workbench generates UPDATE statements for any pending changes in the editing panel, which means you can update more than one record at a time.

10. You can edit any generated SQL statement before the statement is run.

    True. MySQL displays all SQL statements before running them and lets you edit them.

Multiple Choice:

11. You can perform edits on which of the following? (Multiple answers are possible.)

    A. Tables

    B. Views

    C. Procedures

    D. Functions

    E. Triggers

    A is correct. The editing feature is designed to support single table edits.

12. How many rows can you edit at one time?

A. One

B. Many

C. Any number you can select

D. All

E. None of the above

D is correct. **A**, **B**, and **C** all work, and that means all of the above are correct. You can select one or any number (many) of rows to edit at any time.

13. How many tables can you open in tabs for concurrent editing at one time?

A. 1

B. 2

C. 8

D. 16

E. No stated limit

E is correct. You must start the process from the *Edit Table Data* link on the main page, but you may enter as many tables as you'd like to edit at one time. The tables may be in the same or different MySQL databases on the same MySQL Server or on different MySQL Servers.

14. How many edits can you make with a script file before applying it? (Multiple answers are possible.)

A. 1

B. 64

C. 256

D. No stated limit

E. None

E is correct. The *Edit Table Data* link doesn't support you running script files.

15. How many rows can you update at one time?

    A. 1

    B. 64

    C. 128

    D. 256

    E. No stated limit

    E is correct. There is no stated limit. Naturally, when you make many changes at once, the MySQL Workbench tool may not be the best solution.

Chapter 8

True or False:

1. MySQL Workbench lets you write new SQL scripts from scratch.

   True. MySQL Workbench lets you edit existing script files directly, but you must open a new window for running a SQL statement, write the script in that window, and then save the file to write a new SQL script from scratch.

2. MySQL Workbench automatically saves any changes you make to an open script.

   False. MySQL Workbench lets you save a file by using the *File* menu option or by clicking the blue disk icon in the toolbar.

3. MySQL Workbench provides two ways to open script files from the *SQL Editor* pane.

   True. MySQL Workbench lets you open a file by using the *File* menu option or by clicking the blue folder icon in the toolbar.

4. Opening any connection provides you with a *SQL Editor* pane.

   True. Opening any connection provides you access to the generic menu, which lets you open existing SQL files for editing. It also lets you open an empty window and create a new SQL script file.

5. All SQL scripts must include a `USE` statement when they run DDL or DML SQL statements.

   True. All SQL scripts must include a `USE` statement when you run them because that determines where they are run.

6. You can `SOURCE` another script from within a SQL script that you run from MySQL Workbench.

   False. At the time of writing, you can't source another script file from within a script run in MySQL Workbench. In the future, this may be possible, but the MySQL Workbench team could not confirm this while writing this book.

7. You can't use the `\.` (a backslash and dot symbol set) in lieu of the `SOURCE` command when you run the script from MySQL Workbench.

   True. At the time of writing, you can't source files from within a script run in MySQL Workbench. The `\.` is a sourcing command and therefore disallowed. This type of feature may be added in future releases.

8. You clear the output screen by clicking a *Clear script* button in the *SQL Editor* pane.

   True. This is one way to clear the output screen. The other requires a right-click on the output screen. The right-click raises a context-sensitive menu that lets you clear the output screen.

9. MySQL Workbench provides context menus for some features.

   True. MySQL Workbench has a number of context menus, which you access by right-clicking while dwelling on a selected visual object.

10. Some features of MySQL Workbench don't have buttons or menu options.

    True. These features are only accessible through context menus accessed by right-clicking while an object is selected in the window. In the future, options may be added to the menu for these tasks.

Multiple Choice:

11. MySQL Workbench connects to which of the following when it provides you with a *SQL Editor* pane? (Multiple answers are possible.)

    A. MySQL database

    B. MySQL Server

    C. MySQL Monitor

    D. MySQL ODBC

    E. MySQL JDBC

    A and **B** are correct. Connections are through the MySQL Server, but to a database, and some view these as interchangeable concepts.

12. Which of the following SQL commands require a MySQL database connection? (Multiple answers are possible.)

A. TCL

B. DDL

C. DML

D. DCL

E. None—they only require a MySQL Server connection

A, **B**, **C**, and **D** are correct. Any SQL statement requires a MySQL Server connection.

13. Which of the following MySQL Monitor commands fail in MySQL Workbench while running a SQL script? (Multiple answers are possible.)

A. `TEE`

B. `SOURCE`

C. \.

D. `NOTEE`

E. None—they all work

A, **B**, **C**, and **D** are correct. MySQL Workbench, at the time of writing, disallows the use of logging mechanics with the `TEE` and `NOTEE` and sourcing commands with the `SOURCE` or `\.` commands.

14. Which of the following types of scripts run in MySQL Workbench's *SQL Editor?* (Multiple answers are possible.)

A. PHP

B. Python

C. SQL

D. SQL/PSM programs

E. Lua

C and **D** are correct. Only SQL files, with or without embedded SQL/PSM program units, run as SQL scripts.

15. Which of the following are usable in SQL scripts run from within MySQL Workbench? (Multiple answers are possible.)

    A. Global variables

    B. Session variables

    C. Stored procedures

    D. Stored functions

    E. Shell variables

    A, **B**, **C**, and **D** are correct. Global and session variables are supported in MySQL Workbench SQL scripts, as are stored functions and procedures.

Chapter 9

True or False:

1. MySQL instance managers must have access to privileged operating system users on remote nodes.

   True. You must have the credentials for a privileged operating system account, and in the case of Windows, you must configure WMI (Windows Management Instrumentation).

2. Full access to the MySQL instance manager only requires access to the `root` super user account.

   False. You must have access to the `root` super user account on MySQL and a privileged operating system account with full rights to act on the MySQL Server to use all the features of the MySQL Workbench instance manager. You may see schema if all you possess is the MySQL `root` super user account.

3. MySQL instance managers can work with less privileged database users than the `root` super user.

   True. The MySQL instance manager can work with less privileged users, but in turn, you have restricted access to information and actions.

4. A local instance manager can start the MySQL Server.

   True. MySQL Workbench can start and stop the MySQL Server when it has the proper OS (operating system) credentials.

5. A remote instance manager can start the MySQL Server by using ssh on a Microsoft Windows operating system.

   False. A remote instance manager requires WMI (Windows Management Instrumentation) to effect full control, and at present `ssh` isn't a possibility with Windows Server.

6. WMI is a useful Linux utility.

   False. WMI (Windows Management Instrumentation) is an exclusively Windows operating system feature.

7. Remote host privileges must be configured on the remote machine before you can create and test instance managers.

   True. Privileges for the operating system users must be configured on the native servers.

8. Installing MySQL on the same machine as MySQL Workbench is strongly discouraged.

   False. It's encouraged to install a copy of MySQL Workbench on the server where you've deployed the MySQL Server.

9. The MySQL Monitor client software is natively installed with MySQL Workbench.

   False. The MySQL Monitor is only installed when you deploy it on a server, and is deployed anytime you install the MySQL Server.

10. MySQL Workbench provides a tool to maintain instance managers.

    True. MySQL Workbench delivers a tool to manage and maintain instance managers..

Multiple Choice:

11. MySQL Workbench connects through which of the following? (Multiple answers are possible.)

    A. Secure Shell (ssh)

    B. TCP/UDP

    C. TCP/IP

D. Windows Management Instances (WMI)

E. Windows Management Instrumentation (WMI)

A, **C**, and **E** are correct. You can use TCP/IP, but it's not advised because credentials are transmitted in clear text. Secure Shell (ssh) is the preferred communication protocol, and you must also enable WMI on the Windows Server.

12. Which of the following are *Option File* tabs? (Multiple answers are possible.)

A. General

B. Advanced

C. Performance

D. Networking

E. Other

A, **B**, **C**, and **D** are correct. The Other label isn't a valid tab option. Misc is the catch-all option tab.

13. Which of the following are displayed as status variables? (Multiple answers are possible.)

A. Binlog

B. Replication

C. Myisam

D. Innodb

E. Other

A, **B**, **D**, and **E** are correct. Myisam is a system variable, not a status variable.

14. Which of the following are subsets of system variables? (Multiple answers are possible.)

A. Binlog

B. Ndb

C. Miscellaneous

D. Myisam

E. Security

A, **B**, **D**, and **E** are correct. There's no Miscellaneous system variable value.

15. Which of the following belong to the server system variables? (Multiple answers are possible.)

    A. Com_show_fields

    B. Com_show_open_tables

    C. Com_show_status

    D. Sort_merge_passes

    E. Uptime

    A, **B**, **C**, and **E** are correct. The Sort_merge_passes belongs to the Merge system variable.

Chapter 10

True or False:

1. Roles in MySQL Workbench map to roles in the MySQL Server's database instance.

   False. There are no roles in MySQL Server. The roles from MySQL Workbench map to a collection of privileges maintained by the MySQL Server.

2. A database is synonymous with a schema.

   True. A database is synonymous with a schema, and a schema is officially an alias for a database in MySQL Server.

3. System-level privileges should be limited to administrative or super users.

   True. System-level privileges should be limited to administrative or super user accounts.

4. Non-privileged users are only granted schema-level privileges.

   True. The definition of a non-privileged user is typically that they don't enjoy anything other than schema-level privileges.

5. The `SUPER` privilege is part of the *BackupAdmin* role.

   False. The `SUPER` privilege is not a privilege mapped to the *BackupAdmin* role.

6. The DBA role enjoys the most privileges of any role.

   True. The DBA role has the most default privileges of any role in the MySQL Workbench.

7. The *ProcessAdmin* role grants privileges to create users.

   True. It grants those privileges through the `SUPER` privilege.

8. The *ReplicationAdmin* role grants privileges to lock tables.

   True. It grants those privileges through the `SUPER` privilege.

9. The *SecurityAdmin* role grants the `SHOW VIEW` privilege.

   False. The *SecurityAdmin* role does not hold the `SHOW VIEW` privilege.

10. Users are identified by a unique user name and hostname.

    True. Users are defined by a unique user name and hostname.

Multiple Choice:

11. MySQL Workbench supports which of the following roles? (Multiple answers are possible.)

    A. DBA

    B. DatabaseManager

    C. Custom

    D. ReplicationAdmin

    E. DesignerAdmin

    A, **B**, **C**, and **D** are correct. The DesignerAdmin role doesn't exist in the MySQL Workbench application.

12. Which of the following are object-privileges? (Multiple answers are possible.)

    A. INSERT

    B. UPDATE

    C. DELETE

    D. EXECUTE

    E. RUN

    A, **B**, **C**, and **D** are correct. The `RUN` privilege doesn't exist. The valid privileges are object-level privileges that let you add, modify, or remove data from structures in the database.

13. Which of the following are DDL privileges? (Multiple answers are possible.)

A. CREATE

B. DROP

C. UPDATE

D. TRIGGER

E. EXECUTE

A and **B** are correct. A DDL privilege creates, alters, drops, or modifies a structure in the database.

14. Which of the following are other rights, not object-rights or DDL rights? (Multiple answers are possible.)

A. EXECUTE

B. INSERT

C. GRANT OPTION

D. CREATE TEMPORARY TABLES

E. UNLOCK TABLE

C and **E** are correct. The `GRANT OPTION` and `UNLOCK TABLE` rights are system-level privileges.

15. Which type of user should receive system-level privileges? (Multiple answers are possible.)

A. A DBA

B. A replication manager

C. A developer

D. An application user

E. A guest user

A and **B** are correct. A DBA and replication manager (a limited-privileged DBA) should hold system-level privileges. As a rule, developers, application users, and guest users shouldn't.

Chapter 11

True or False:

1. The MySQL Workbench import process only works with a self-contained file.

   True. The import process works with a self-contained file, like the export process.

2. The MySQL Workbench export process puts the output into a dump folder for table-specific scripts or a self-contained file for a schema or set of databases.

   True. The export process places the scripts to create the data structures and inserts the data into a single file. It's convenient if you want to edit it for changes.

3. A schema must be available before you can perform an import operation with MySQL Workbench.

   False. A schema may or may not exist before you perform the import process. If one doesn't exist, you need to check a box during the import that this is a new schema. The tool will then create the schema during the import process.

4. MySQL Workbench supports creating a new schema using an ad hoc feature during an import.

   True. The ad hoc feature is a button that you check when you need to create a new schema for the imported database.

5. MySQL Workbench can import from one schema in a server to another schema in the same server.

   True. You can export one schema, modify the dump file by providing a new schema name, and import the dump file into a new database in the same server.

6. MySQL Workbench lets you select individual schema objects when performing an export.

   True. You can opt to export a complete database or only certain schema objects.

7. The import progress view shows warnings and errors.

   True. The MySQL Workbench import progress view shows warnings and errors that occur during the import process.

8. Clicking the database object name in the object selection process displays the physical objects of the selected database.

   True. The object selection process provides a view of all available objects.

9. The export progress view shows warnings and errors.

   True. The export process shows warnings and errors.

10. The file chooser looks only for files with a SQL extension.

    True. The file chooser looks for files with the SQL extension.

Multiple Choice:

11. MySQL Workbench supports which of the following exports? (Multiple answers are possible.)

    A. All schemas and objects

    B. Some schemas and all objects for the selected schemas

    C. One schema and all of its objects

    D. One schema and some of its objects

    E. All schemas and some of their objects

    A, **B**, **C**, and **D** are correct. You get all objects from all schemas when you elect to choose all schemas. You get all the objects in the selected schemas when you choose a set of schemas. However, you get the option to pick all or some objects when you choose a single schema.

12. MySQL creates which of the following in a dump project folder? (Multiple answers are possible.)

    A. A self-contained file

    B. A file for each table

    C. A file for each view

    D. A file for each routine

    E. A file for all routines

    A, **B**, **C**, and **E** are correct. The export process generates a single self-contained file.

13. Which are valid options for a self-contained file? (Multiple answers are possible.)

    A. Create dump in a single transaction

    B. Dump stored procedures

C. Dump events

D. Skip table data

E. Dump stored routines

A, **B**, **C**, and **D** are correct. The dump stored routines is fabricated. You'll find the list of valid values in the Object Selection view.

14. Which are valid options for a dump project folder? (Multiple answers are possible.)

A. Create dump in a single transaction

B. Dump stored procedures

C. Dump events

D. Skip table data

E. Dump stored routines

B, **C**, and **D** are correct. The create dump in a single transaction becomes unavailable when we choose to dump the content into a project folder.

15. Which are valid options for `INSERT` statements? (Multiple answers are possible.)

A. Add-locks

B. Complete-insert

C. Replicate

D. Insert-ignore

E. Extended-insert

A, **B**, **D**, and **E** are correct. These are found under the Advanced Option tab. The replicate option doesn't exist.

Chapter 12

True or False:

1. The MySQL Workbench migration tool lets you migrate a Microsoft SQL Server 2012 database into a MySQL 5.5 database.

True. You can migrate a Microsoft SQL Server 2000, 2005, 2008, and 2012 database into a MySQL 5.5 database.

2. At the time of writing, the MySQL Workbench migration tool lets you migrate a Postgres 9.1 database into a MySQL 5.5 database.

   False. At the time of writing, you can't migrate a Postgres 9.1 database. This is an envisioned feature that may be available as you read the book.

3. In the future, the MySQL Workbench migration tool will let you migrate a Sybase 15.7 database into a MySQL 5.5 database.

   True. At the time of writing, the development team is working on migrating a Sybase 15.7 database, and it should be available before the book publishes.

4. The MySQL Workbench migration tool requires super user accounts for both users in all cases.

   True. You require a super user account for the source and target databases. Only a super user account guarantees adequate privileges to effect the migration.

5. MySQL Workbench can migrate one or more databases from a server instance.

   True. The MySQL Workbench lets you migrate the entire instance or individual databases (schemas).

6. MySQL Workbench lets you select individual schema objects when performing a migration.

   True. You can select individual schema objects during the migration process by clicking the relevant check boxes to enable them.

7. The migration steps show success or failure and provide a *Show Log* button when errors occur.

   False. While the migration steps do show success or failure, they provide the *Show Log* button, regardless of success or failure.

8. Clicking the database object name in the *Object Selection* step displays the physical objects of the selected database.

   True. Clicking the database object name enables the object selection of individual physical objects in the database.

9. You don't have an option during migration with MySQL Workbench to write scripts, because it only supports interactive migrations.

   False. You do have the option of generating a script. The script can only be run with the MySQL Workbench tools. Interactive migration is also supported.

10. The *Manual Editing* step provides you with an *All Objects* view as the default.

    True. The *Manual Editing* step provides only an *All Objects* view. Interactive migration gives you more options.

Multiple Choice:

11. MySQL Workbench supports which of the following source database servers? (Multiple answers are possible.)

A. IBM DB2

B. MySQL 5.1

C. MySQL 5.0

D. Postgres 9.1

E. SQL Server 2012

B, **C**, and **E** are correct. MySQL Workbench currently supports MySQL 5.0, MySQL 5.1, and SQL Server 2012.

12. MySQL creates which of the following if you enable creating script files? (Multiple answers are possible.)

A. A data catalog query of the target data dictionary

B. A set of statements to migrate the structure of tables and views from the source database server

C. A set of statements to generate the structure of tables and views in the target database server

D. A data catalog query of the source data dictionary

E. A master log file for all elements of the migration wizard

E is correct. The script file is a single master log file that you can use to generate a duplicate of the source database.

13. Which are valid tasks for the *Create Schemata* step? (Multiple answers are possible.)

A. Create dump in a single transaction

B. Create script file

C. Connect to source database

D. Connect to target database

E. Create schemata and objects

B, **D**, and **E** are correct. The four steps for creating a schemata are: (1) Create script file; (2) Connect to target database; (3) Perform checks in target; and (4) Create schemata and objects.

14. Which are valid tasks for the *Bulk Data Transfer* step? (Multiple answers are possible.)

A. Create dump in a single transaction

B. Create shell script for data copy

C. Determine number of rows to copy

D. Copy data to target RDBMS

E. Prepare information for data copy

B, **C**, **D**, and **E** are correct. The four steps for bulk data transfer are: (1) Prepare information for data copy; (2) Create shell script for data copy; (3) Determine number of rows to copy; and (4) Copy data to target RDBMS.

15. Which are valid tasks for the *Data Transfer Setup* step? (Multiple answers are possible.)

A. Online copy of table data to target RDBMS

B. Create a batch file to copy the data at another time

C. Migrate selected objects

D. Truncate target tables

E. Enable debug output for table copy

A, **B**, **D**, and **E** are correct. They can be seen in the *Data Transfer Setup* step of the wizard. The Migrate selected objects option is made up.

APPENDIX B

Extending MySQL Workbench

his chapter demonstrates the extension and scripting system that lets you extend the behaviors of MySQL Workbench. You develop extensions in the Lua or Python programming languages.

MySQL Workbench provides the GRT, or Generic RunTime, which is a collection of libraries that let you automate tasks in the tool. With these tools, you could develop a plug-in that lets you add traditional who-audit columns.

Many readers won't have the Lua or Python (release 2.7) scripting skills to use these, but seeing the basics may encourage you to learn one of those two languages. I've opted to use Python for the examples because it's more likely readers have been exposed to its syntax.

Lua vs. Python

Lua is not as well known as Python among all programmers generally, but most programmers using either know about the other. These languages have their respective strengths and weaknesses.

Python is the broader language, with a more comprehensive set of libraries. Python also has extensive Unicode support, high-performing numeric computing, built-in binary operators, extensive tools to slice strings, whitespace sensitivity, and a remote debugger. It has a strong set of online documentation resources that help beginning, intermediate, and advanced programmers.

Lua started as a configuration language and has some neat syntax when creating games. It has a smaller footprint (uses less memory) than Python, a faster interpreter, and a simple but very powerful syntax. Lua is not whitespace sensitive, which makes errors easier to create and harder to find. It is the preferred choice when writing threaded applications. Unfortunately, there is very little documentation to help beginners learn how to write Lua.

This appendix covers how you create and run a script, module, and use the command-line shell interface. Their order lays the quickest foundation to understanding how they work. Plug-ins require substantial coding experience, and as a result of that, only the monitoring screen is shown in the appendix.

These features are only accessible through the Scripting menu option. As you'll discover reading the appendix, you can't edit everything within the interface, and you may have to remove files from the operating system to start over.

Scripts

You create scripts that run steps as a processing group. Many programmers write scripts first to understand the logic of what they want to accomplish before migrating the scripts to modules. Modules are library methods. They are also the basic level of functions or methods in Python.

While you can create the files in an editor and then copy them to the target directory, it's much better to use a good programming editor to write generic code. You should use the MySQL Workbench Scripting tool to write, test, and save your Python modules when working with the MySQL Workbench GRT libraries, although developing Python scripts externally works well for advanced programmers.

Beginners should develop their code in the MySQL Workbench window because it tends to reduce errors and speed development of automation scripts and modules.

Python File Conventions

Python uses two types of file extensions. A `.py` file extension represents interpreted scripts and modules because Python is an interpreted language. A `.pyc` file extension represents compiled Python programs, and these are typically modules.

MySQL Workbench leaves scripts as interpreted `.py` file extension files and compiles all `.py` file extension files at initialization (a fancy word for when you launch the program). If you don't find a program gets recompiled at application startup, you should delete the `.pyc` file, which forces compilation of a new Python source file.

You create a new script file by clicking the *Scripting* menu option and then selecting *New Script*, as shown in the following illustration. Let's get started by building a MySQL Workbench extension as a new script file.

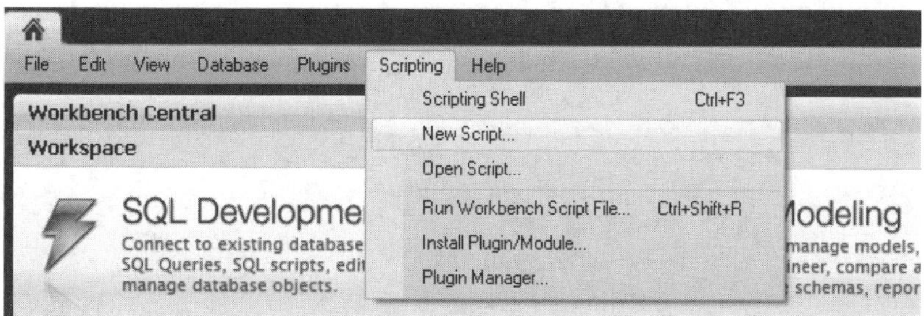

This prompts you with a dialog to choose whether you're creating a Python script, Python plug-in, Python module, or Lua script. For this example, choose the *Python Script* radio button and enter `ReadFile.py` in the *Script File Name* text field before clicking the *Create* button. You should choose the correct one, because the editor coordinates behavior on the file's extension.

If you're following along, your dialog should look like the following screen capture.

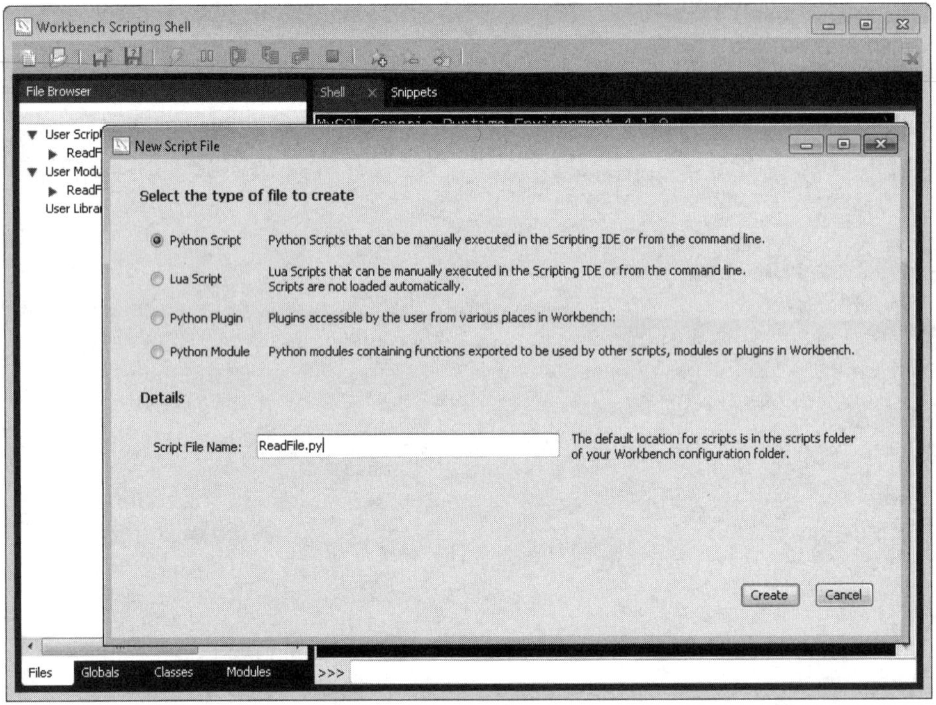

Clicking the *Create* button gives you an editing console for the `ReadFile.py` script file. It shows two default libraries. One is the `grt` (Generic RunTime library), and the other is the `mforms` library. The `mforms` library is needed when you want your plug-in displayed in the MySQL Workbench interface. The initial form should look like the following screen capture.

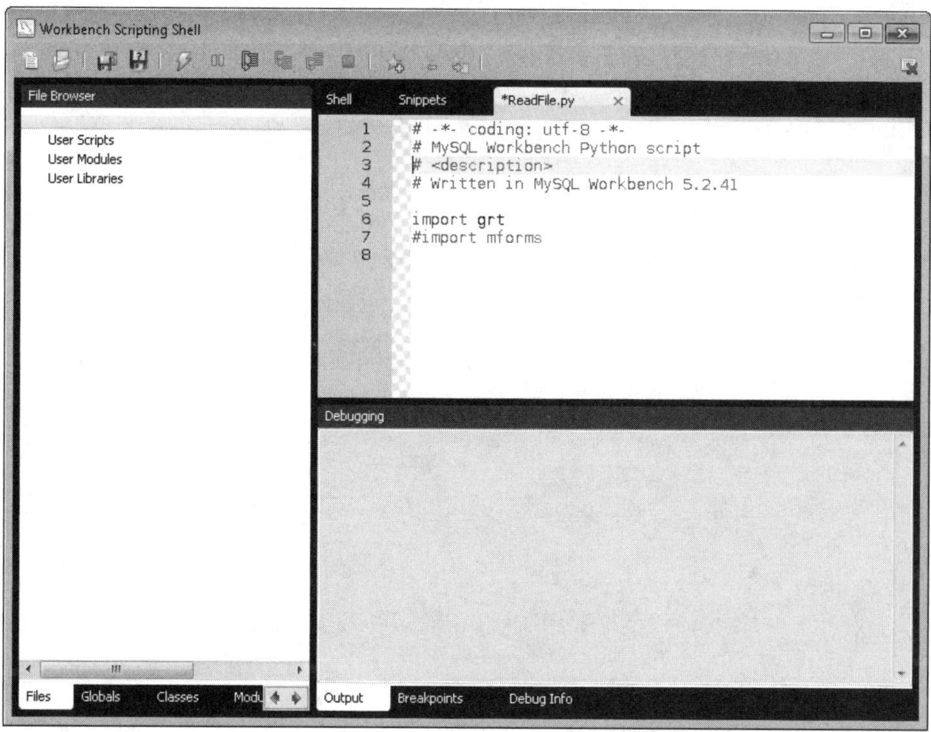

The sample Python script file will read a static file from a Microsoft Windows directory. That means you need to create the directory, subdirectory, and file before testing this program. (I'm assuming you stopped and created them because the balance of this appendix assumes their existence.) The code doesn't have any error handling, with the hope of keeping it as simple as possible to those new to Python. You'll find an improved version with error handling in the "Modules" section.

For the following demonstration of how you read a file from the file system, you need to perform a couple of steps outside MySQL Workbench. You need to prepare a `query.sql` file and store it in the `C:\Data\MySQL` directory of the local file system. Naturally, the directory path changes when you're on Linux or Mac operating system.

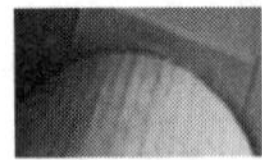

NOTE
Don't put a white space in the filename or you will have problems unless you backquote it.

The example program includes one import statement of two libraries, then the logic to read a program and print it line by line:

```
import grt, os
f = open("c:\\Data\\MySQL\\query.sql",'rU')
while True:
    line = f.readline()
    print(line),
    if not line:
        print
        break
```

The sample program opens a `query.sql` file, reads the file line by line, and prints each line to the console. The `print(line),` isn't a typo. The trailing comma is required to suppress an extra line return in the result displayed for Python 2.7. The equivalent `print(line, end = '')` works in Python 3.x.

NOTE
Change the `print(line)` *to* `print(line, end = '')` *when you're testing this in Python 3.*

You should see a console like the following after typing the code into the editing window.

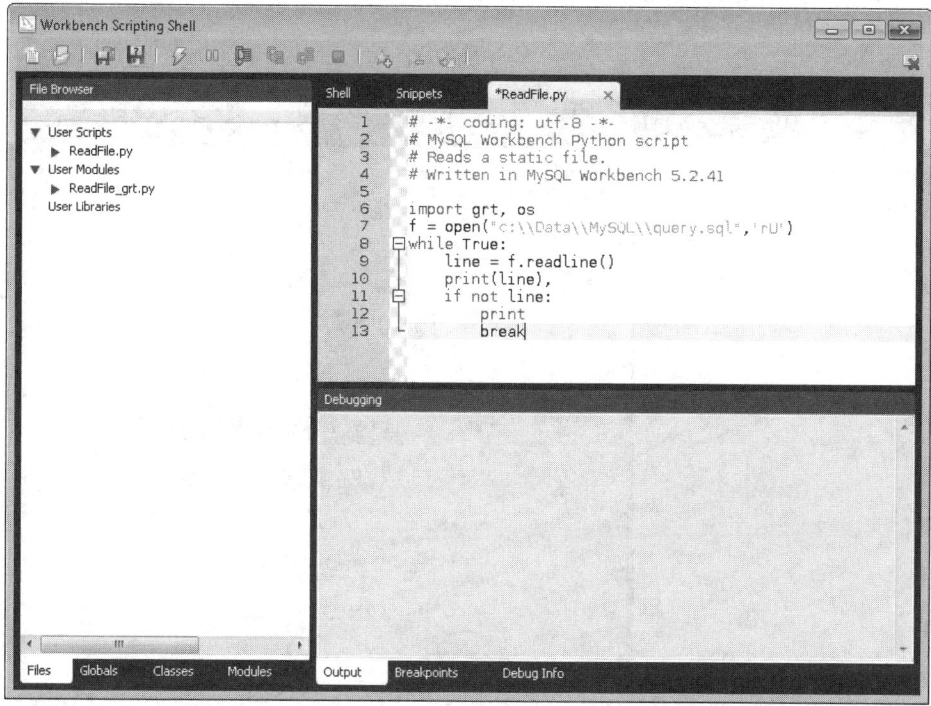

Click the blue disk icon to save the file before running it. Click the yellow lightning bolt icon in the button panel to run the script file. You should see the following results when you create the directories and file beforehand.

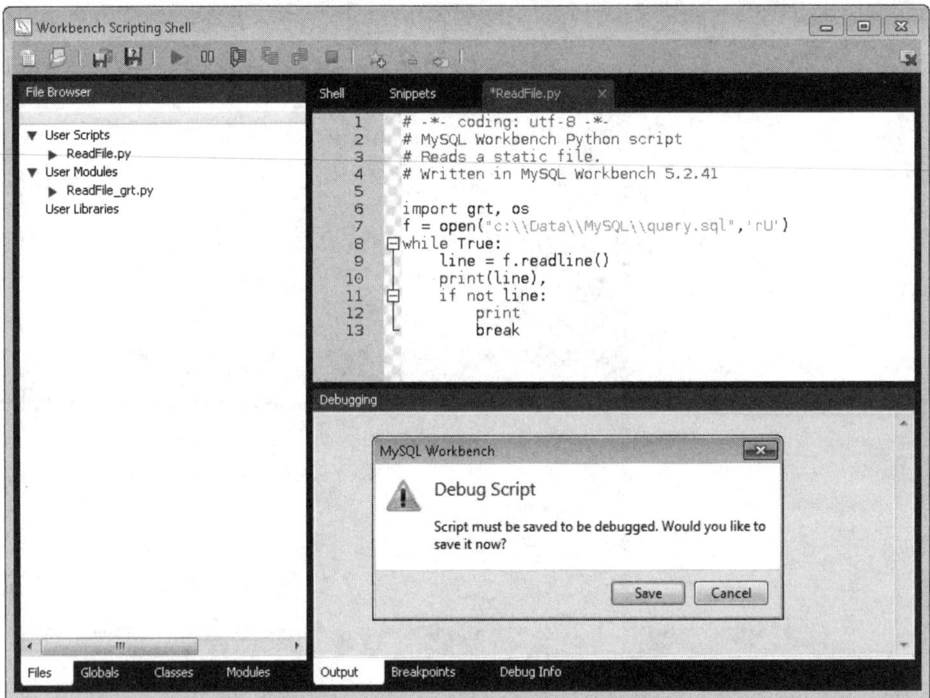

If you forget to save the file before clicking the lightning bolt button, you get the following Debug Script dialog prompt. Click the *Save* button to proceed if you see this dialog.

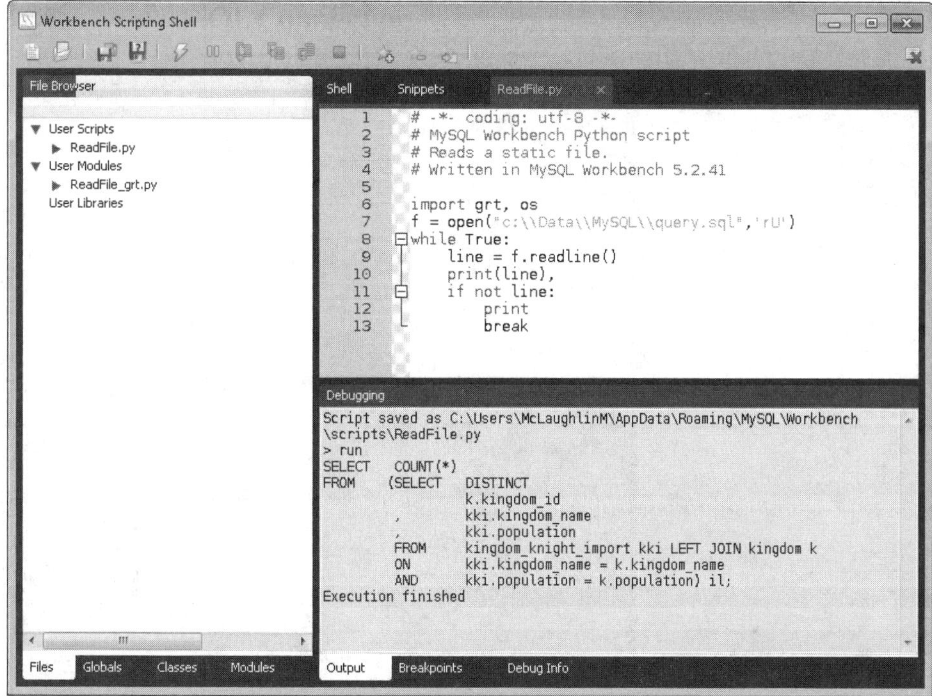

While unlikely, it's possible that you could have tried this once and it failed. Re-attempting the process when the file exists isn't possible. You get the following dialog when the file exists.

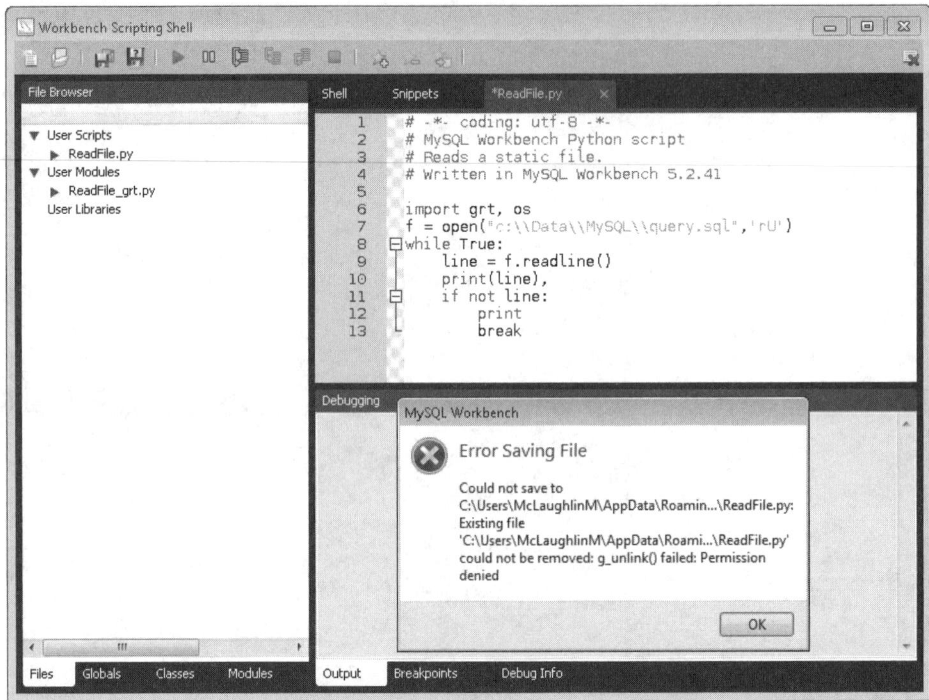

There are only two ways to fix this. Copy the contents of your new file to a text editor or other text-based program. Then, close MySQL Workbench and manually delete the file from the following directory in Windows. This is a protected directory, which means you can't simply navigate by pointing and clicking. You must edit the directory line to include `AppData\Roaming\MySQL\Workbench\scripts` to get to the directory using Windows Explorer (not Internet Explorer, right).

```
C:\Users\<user_name>\AppData\Roaming\MySQL\Workbench\scripts
```

Alternatively, you can close the MySQL Workbench scripting shell, navigate to the *Scripting* menu option, and choose *Open Script*.

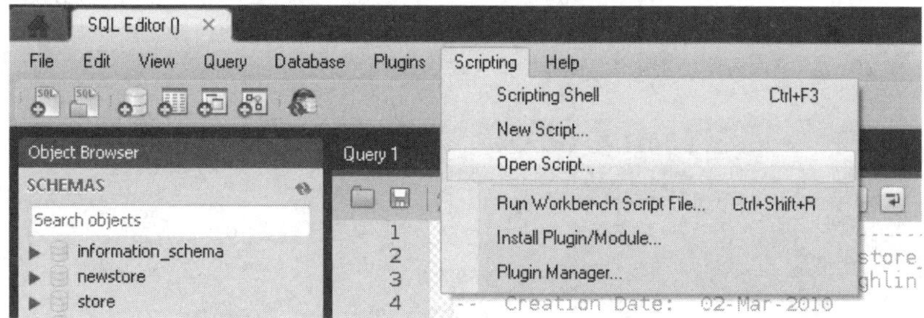

This opens a file chooser. You should navigate to the correct directory (noted earlier) to open the existing `ReadFile.py` file, edit it, and save it. Then reopen the file and make a change to check the typical cycle of script creation and maintenance.

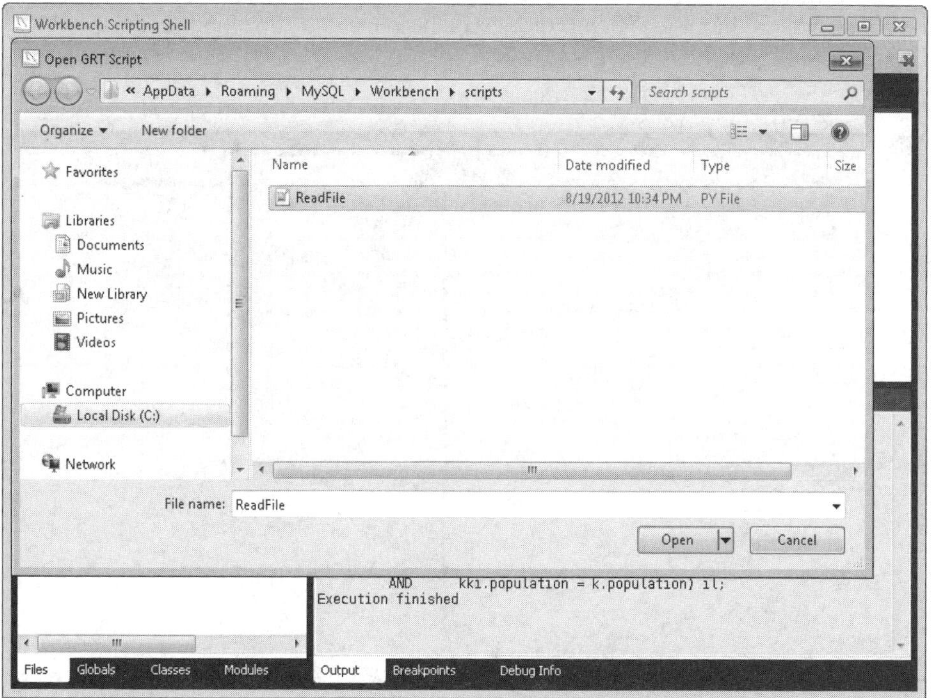

Click the filename, and it displays in the *File Name* field. Click the *Open* button to continue with editing an existing file.

Once you have scripts written and tested, you can simply run them from the same menu by clicking *Run Workbench Script File* in the menu list for the *Scripting* menu option, as shown in the following screen capture.

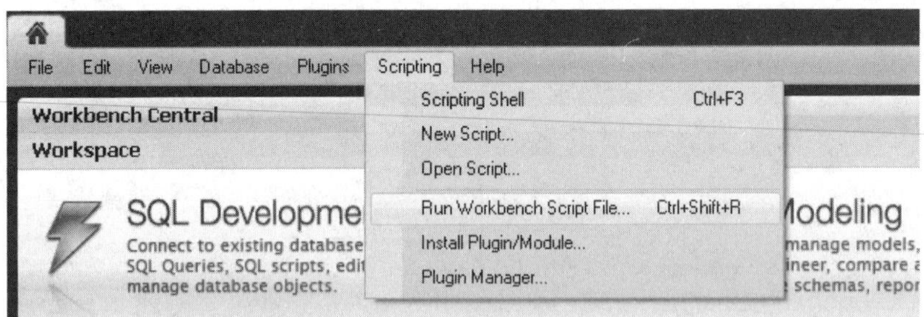

Clicking the *Run Workbench Script File* opens the chooser, shown earlier. Click the filename and then the *Open* button, which opens and runs the file. It should display a result like the following shows.

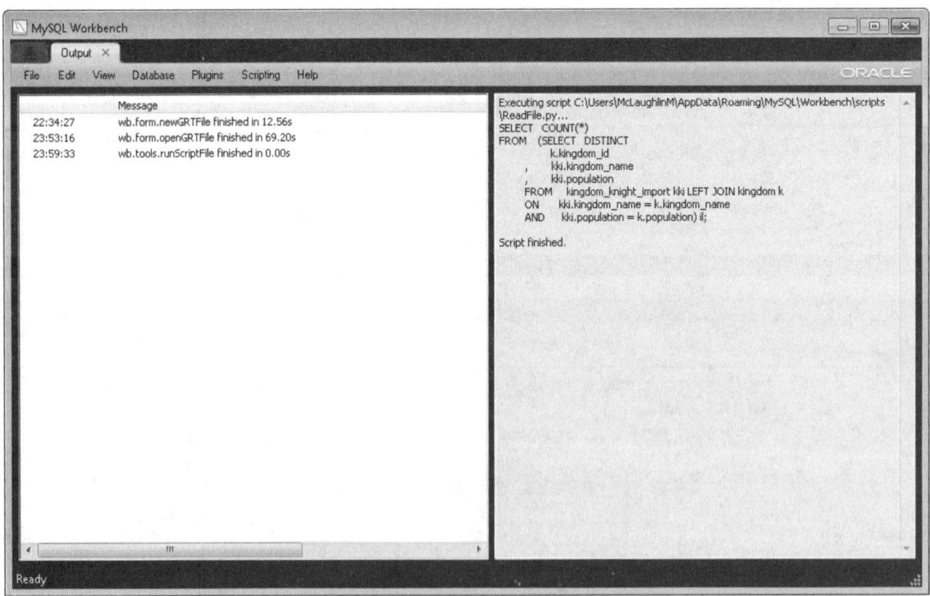

This section has shown you how to work with script files. The next one shows you how to work with modules.

Modules

Modules differ from scripts because they're named library objects, like stored functions and procedures in the MySQL Server. You should test your modules' logic in scripts before migrating them to modules.

Unfortunately, there's no way to simply write new modules on the fly, like script files. You can edit them after they're created and imported into MySQL Workbench.

For this example, create the following file in a text editor and save it as `ReadFile.py`. While that's the same name as the previously created script file, don't worry about it. All modules should have `_grt` appended to the filename, and MySQL Workbench performs that task for you automatically during import.

```
# -*- coding: utf-8 -*-
# MySQL Workbench Python Module
# ReadFile_grt.py
# Written in MySQL Workbench 5.2.41

# Provide a method name.
def print_file(fname):
  import os, sys
  try:
    f = open(fname,'rU')
    while True:
      line = f.readline()
      # Suppress line return from print() function.
      print(line),
      if not line:
        print
        break
  except IOError as e:
    print "I/O error({0}): {1}".format(e.errno, e.strerror)
  if __name__ == '__main__':
    print_file(fname)
```

Click the *Scripting* menu option and choose *Install Plugin/Module*.

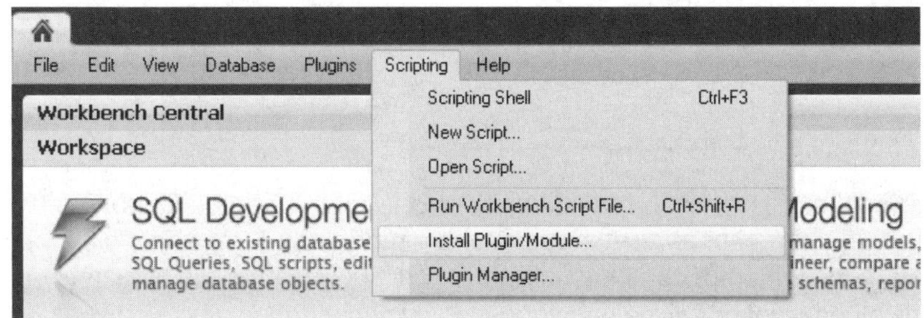

It opens a chooser where you select your file that will become a module. Let's assume you fixed the `ReadFile.py` script so that it can be used as a module. You can now select it in the file chooser, like the following shows.

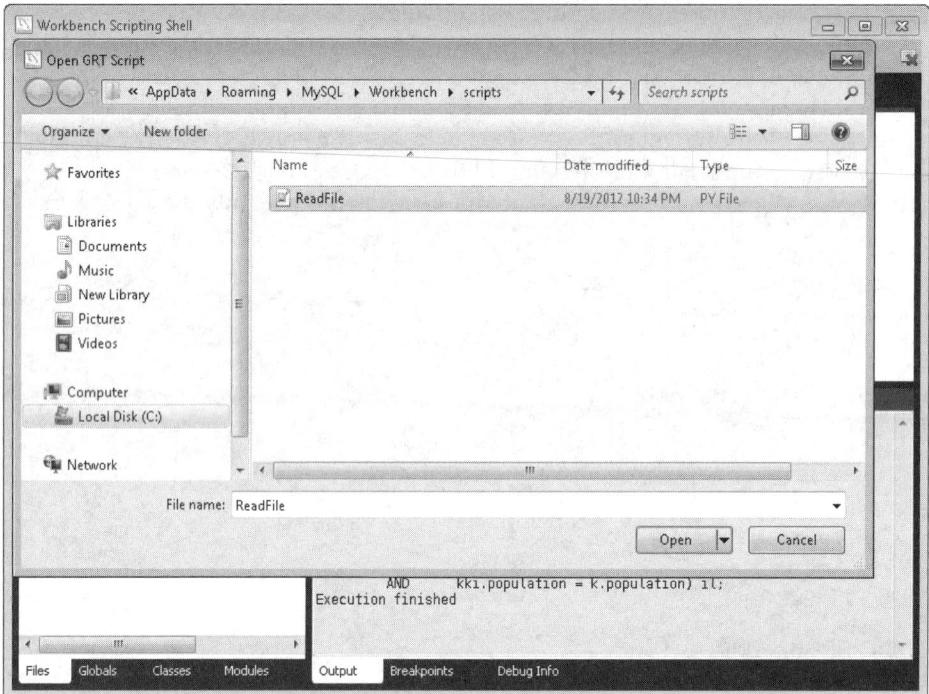

You get the following dialog message when successful. Click the *OK* button to dismiss the dialog, and then you must stop and restart MySQL Workbench.

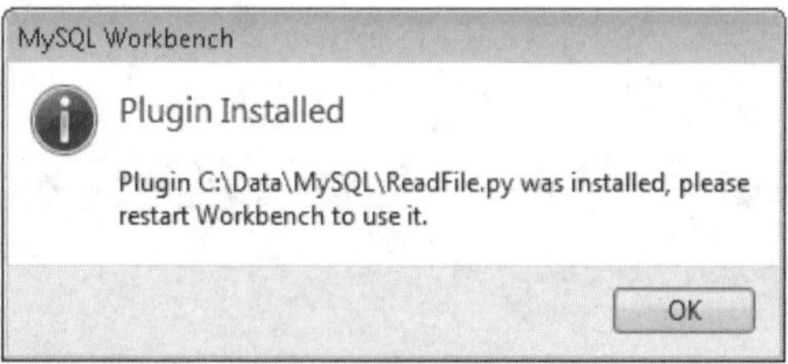

During the restart, MySQL Workbench checks your module directory and compiles or recompiles all user modules. User modules are recognized by their location in the following directory and the `_grt` suffix within the filename:

```
C:\Users\<user_name>\AppData\Roaming\MySQL\Workbench\modules
```

Sometimes the modules may already exist and you want to import a new version. MySQL Workbench allows for that possibility. You get the dialog message shown here when the module already exists.

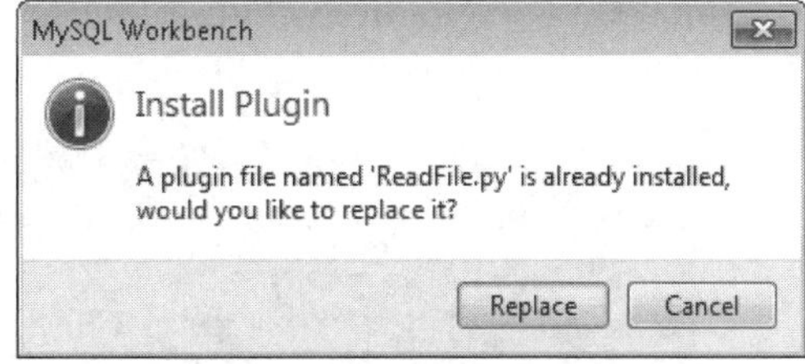

After importing the module, you can edit it. You use the *Open Script* selection from the *Scripting* menu option. Point the file chooser to your module directory, and you should see the plain text and compiled Python programs.

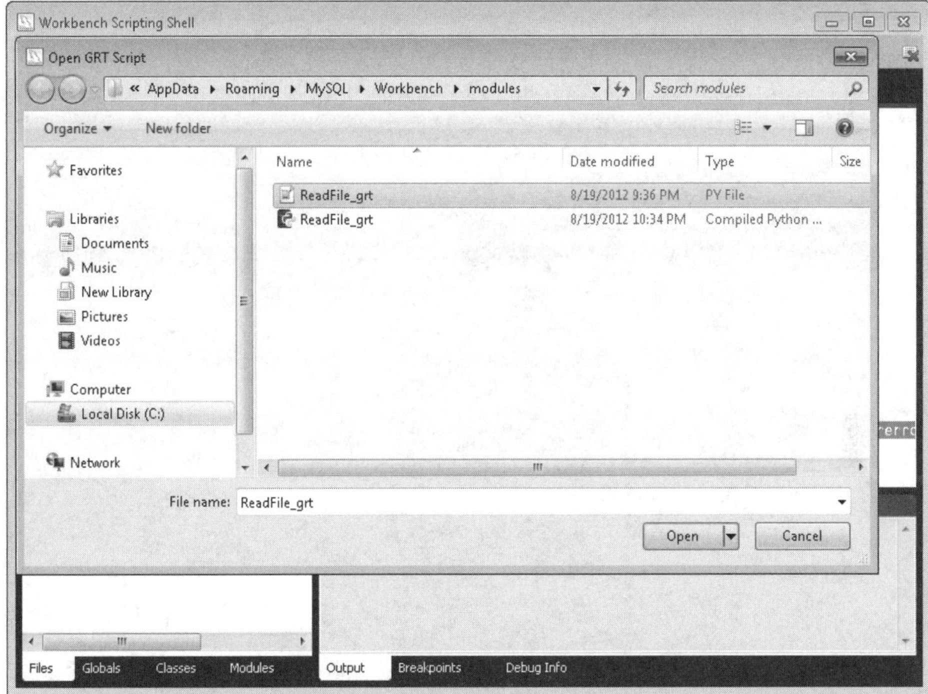

Open the plain-text Python version of the program to edit it. Just remember that you need to save it and restart MySQL Workbench to force a compilation of the program file. MySQL Workbench runs the compiled version, and in the next section you discover how to run those modules in the MySQL Workbench Scripting Shell.

Shell

The MySQL Workbench Scripting Shell is like a Lua or Python interactive interpreter. The only problem, at least at the time of writing, is that there were a few open bugs with interactive use of Python commands.

You open the shell by clicking *Scripting Shell* under the *Scripting* menu option, as shown in the following screen capture.

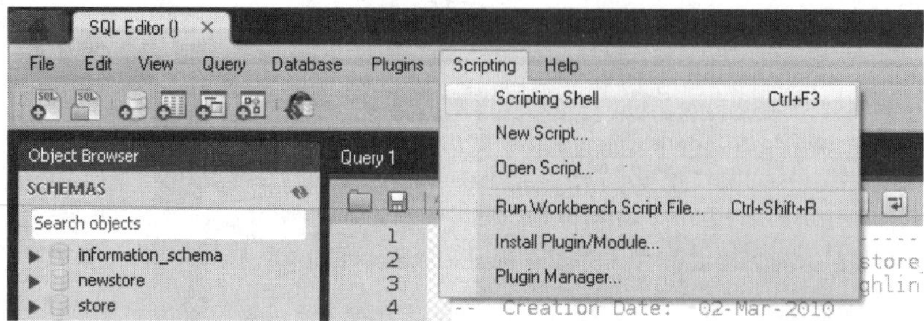

The Scripting Shell is initially blank, but retains all errors and code run until you stop and restart MySQL Workbench. It looks like the following when first started during a running session of the product.

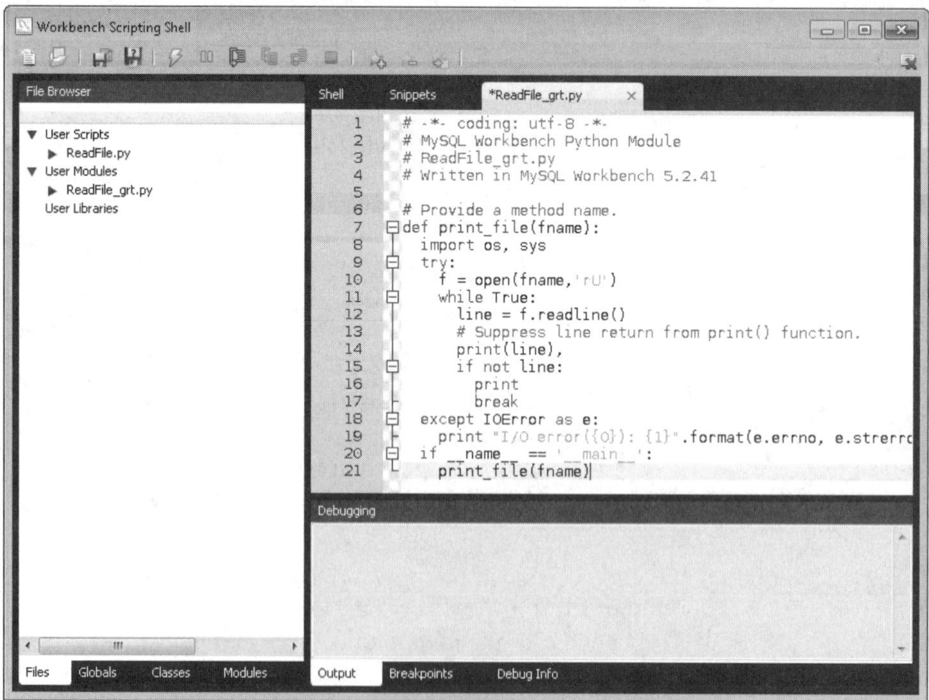

It's fun to show you how you use the Shell to discover things about your working MySQL Workbench environment. The following screen capture shows you how to find the Python version and Python internal system path.

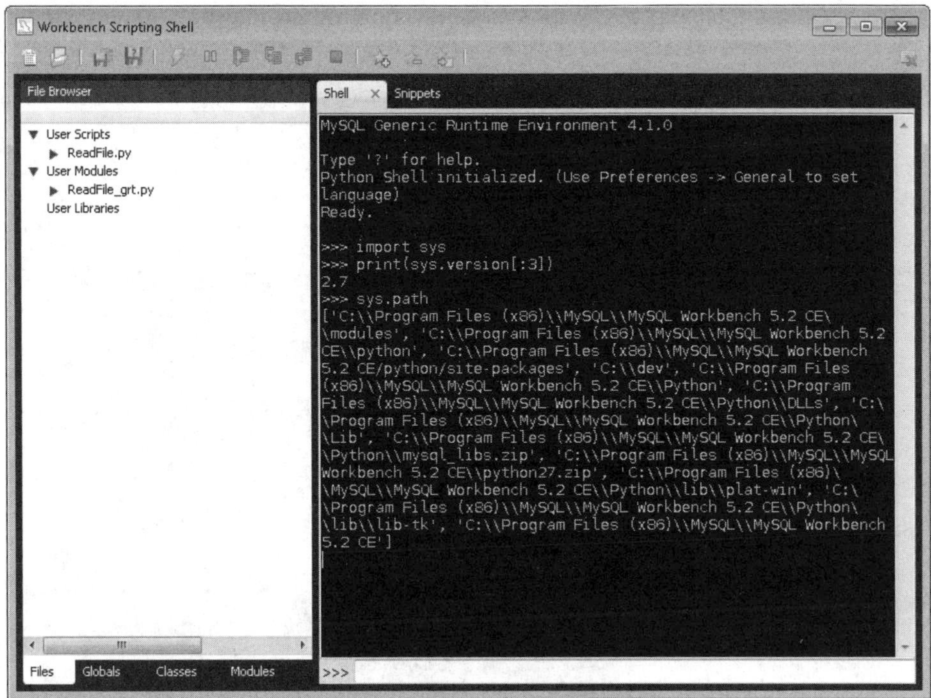

You import the sys module and then run the following command to get the Python version:

```
>>> print(sys.version[:3])
```

The directory search path, as shown in the previous image, can be discovered by the following command syntax:

```
>>> sys.path
```

There's much more that you can do with the Shell, but it requires a solid working knowledge of Python. I'd recommend *The Quick Python Book* by Vernon L. Ceder (Manning Publications, 2010) as a great place to start if you're new to Python.

Refreshing the Shell, let's examine how you source and run the module you created. You source the `ReadFile_grt.py` module like this:

```
>>> import ReadFile_grt.py
```

You call the `print_file()` function like this, provided the directory, subdirectory, and file exist:

```
>>> ReadFile_grt.print_file("c:\\Data\\MySQL\\query.sql")
```

That displays the text of the file, but changing the filename to one that's nonexistent generates an error and tests the module's exception handling:

```
>>> ReadFile_grt.print_file("c:\\Data\\MySQL\\queries.sql")
```

All of these commands and output are shown in the next screen capture.

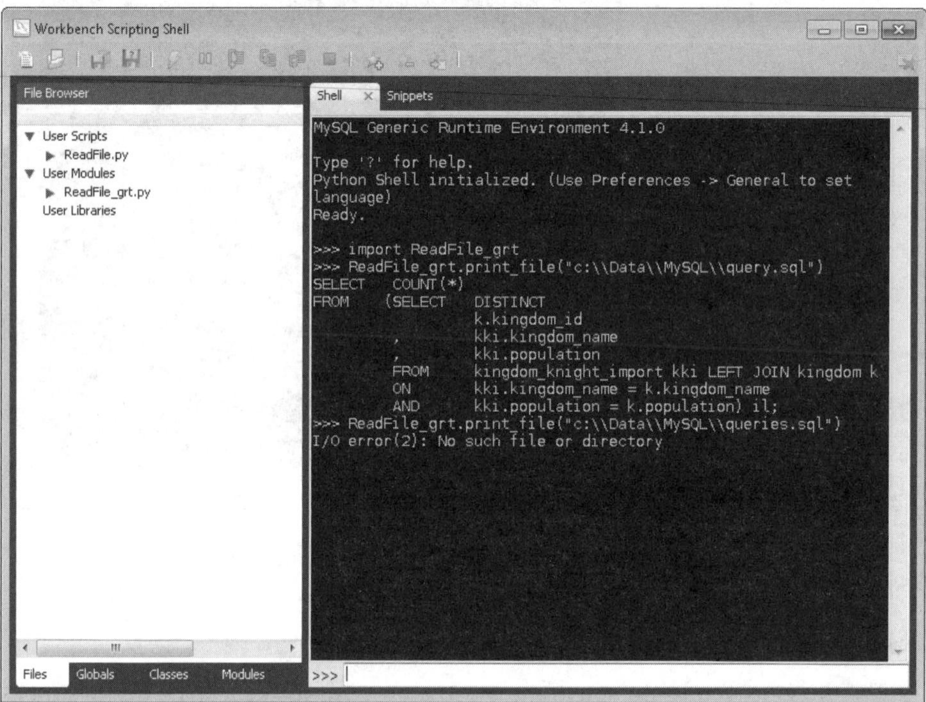

This concludes the demonstration of how to deploy and call your own modules. The last option under the *Scripting* menu option allows you to manage plug-ins. Unfortunately, that requires larger code modules and a broader discussion of how you extend MySQL Workbench and leverage Python or Lua programming environments.

Summary

This appendix explained how to create scripts and modules to automate tasks in MySQL Workbench. It served as a quick introduction to how the interface works and where you deploy and call these modules.

APPENDIX C

Setting Up SQL Server

This appendix demonstrates how to install, configure, and create a small database in Microsoft SQL Server 2012 to test the MySQL Workbench migration utility. My examples use Microsoft SQL Server 2012 Express Edition because that version is free to download and deploy with a database instance of up to 8GB. You can also use the commercial version of the product.

This appendix is divided into the following four parts:

- Installing SQL Server
- Fixing the SQL Server command-line interface
- Configuring a user schemata
- Creating and seeding a database

If you already have Microsoft SQL Server 2012 installed, you can move to fixing its command-line interface, or skipping that, simply configure, create, and seed a database.

Installing SQL Server

I've skipped showing the images for a software download or designating the location of the web site because downloading is the same for a Microsoft product as it is for an Oracle product and the download web sites at Microsoft change over time.

After you download and double-click the MSI (Microsoft Software Installer) icon, it launches the Microsoft SQL Server Installation wizard. Click the *New SQL Server stand-alone installation or add features to an existing installation* link at the top of the right side of the wizard to start the installation, as shown in the following screen shot.

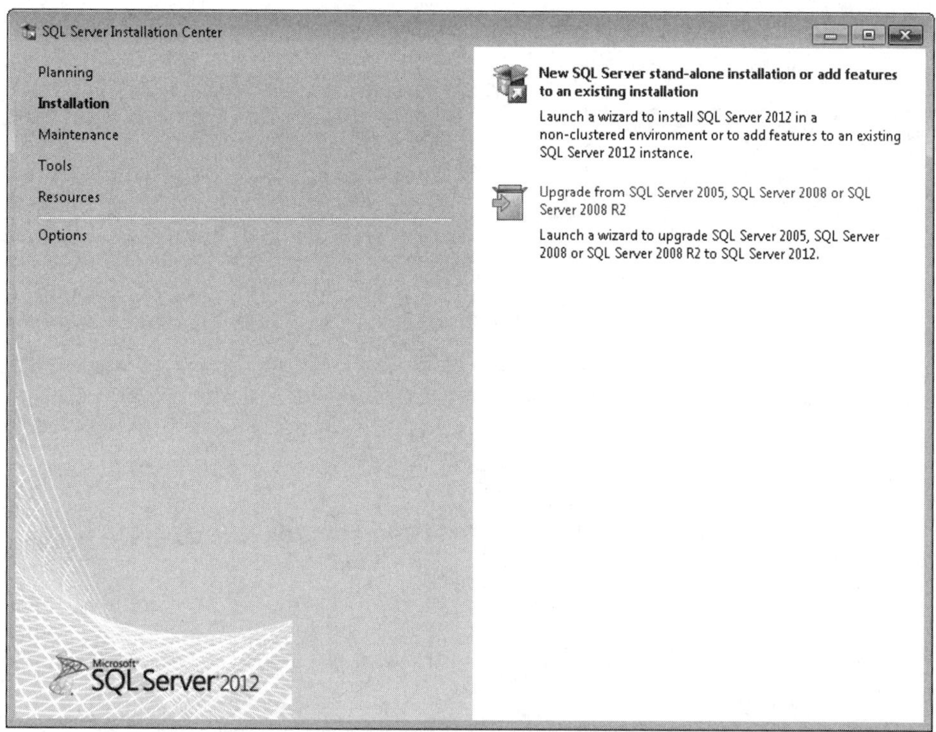

The first step is accepting the licensing agreement. You can't proceed without accepting it, but you should read it. The next screen shot shows the *License Terms* dialog page. Click the *I accept the license terms* check box and if you'd like, the check box that sends your selected features to Microsoft before you click the *Next* button to proceed with the installation.

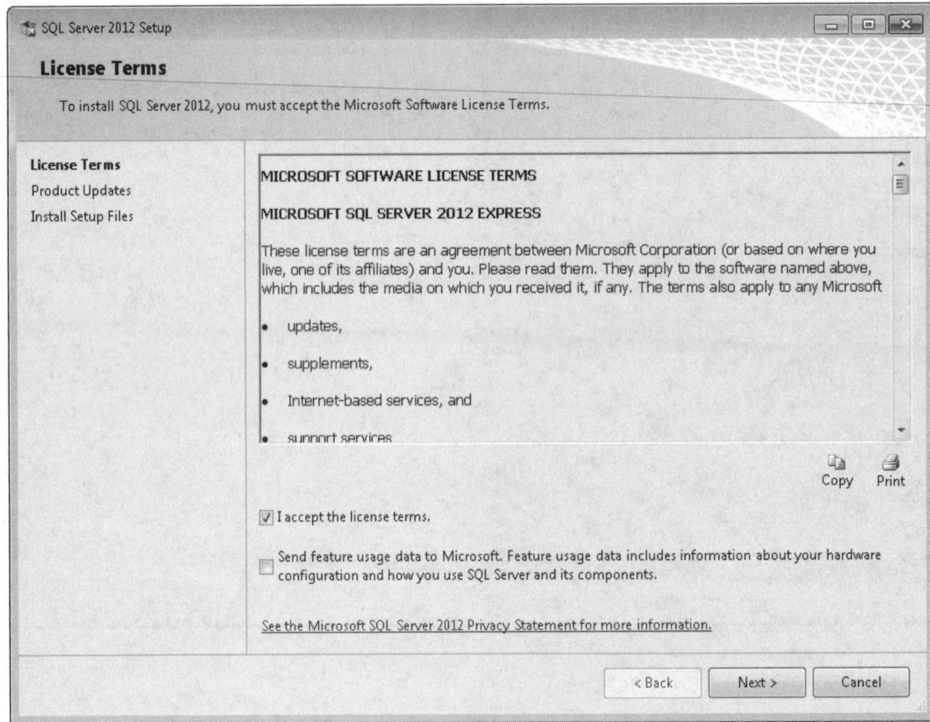

Typically, the *Product Updates* section runs so quickly you won't see the screen long enough to bother with it. After it completes checking for updates, you see the Install Setup Files dialog shown in the following screen shot.

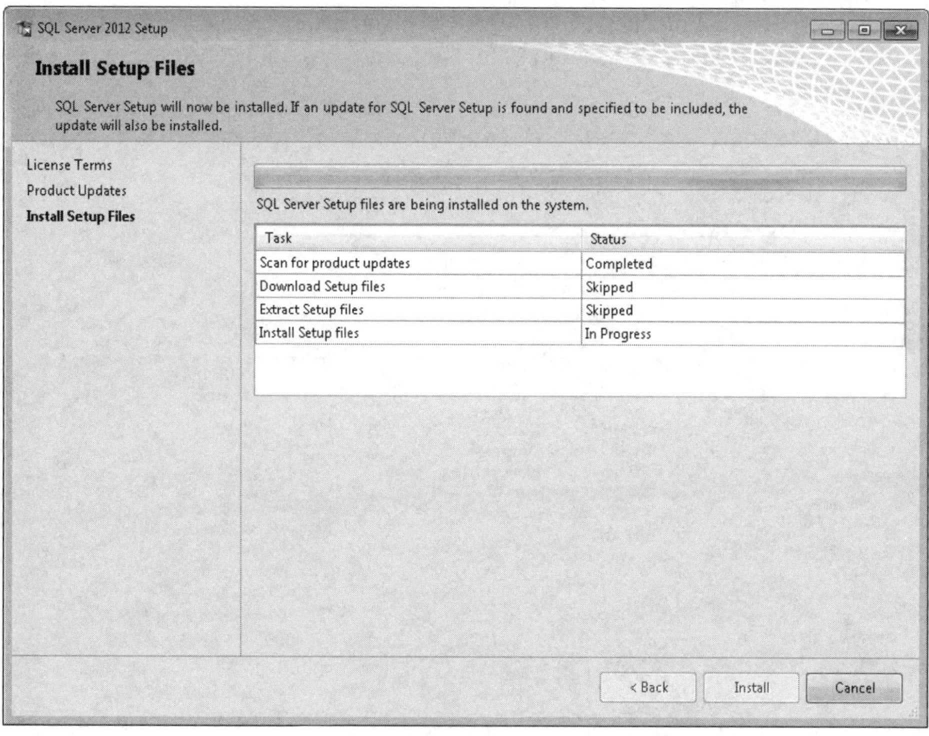

The product update scan should show completed unless you need to download and extract new files. The latter only occurs when you download the product some time before installing it. I'd recommend you download the current version whenever possible because sometimes patches may cause problems in the installation.

After installing all the files, the dialog automatically advances to the following Feature Selection dialog. You should note that *LocalDB* is unchecked in the default set of options.

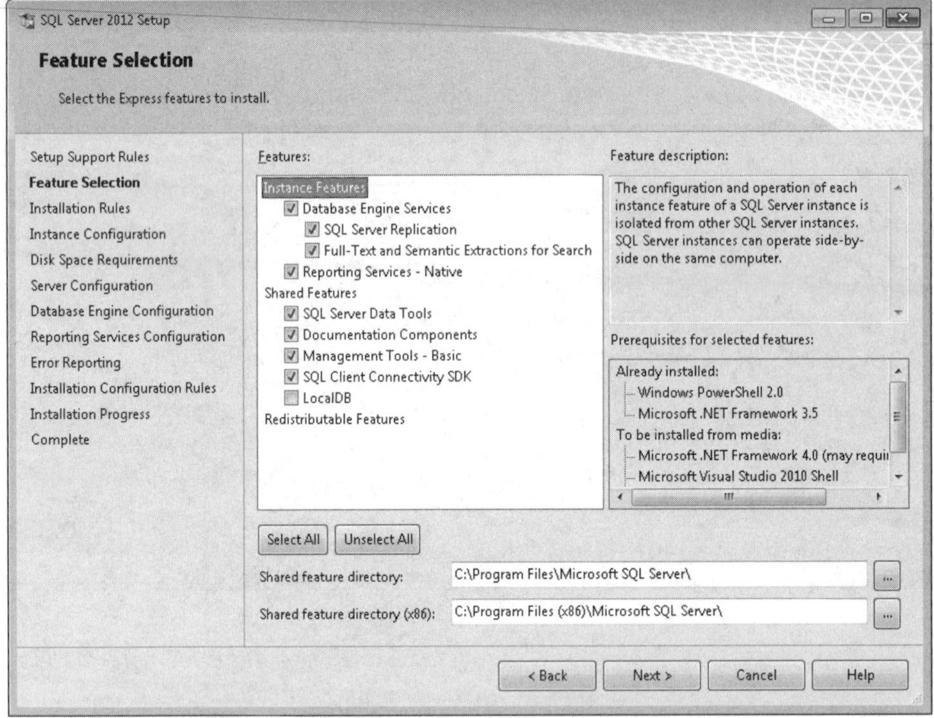

Check the *LocalDB* check box and verify the shared feature directories. Please note that SQL Server installs components in both the 32-bit and 64-bit segments of a 64-bit Windows environment. Click the *Next* button after you've selected the *LocalDB* feature, as shown in the following screen shot.

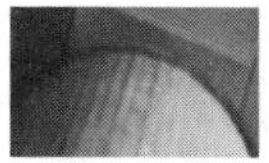

NOTE

This box is already checked and can't be unchecked when the LocalDB is installed separately.

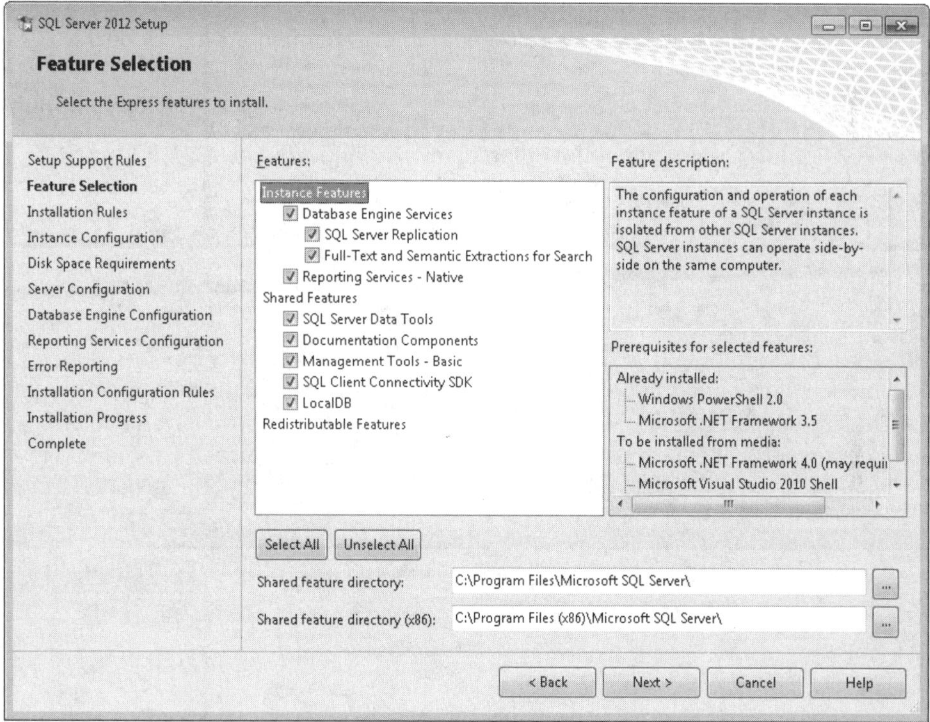

A default installation installs the *Default instance,* which is not what you should do. Click the *Named instance* radio button to install `SQLExpress`, as shown in the following screen shot. Once you've made that choice, click the *Next* button to continue with the installation.

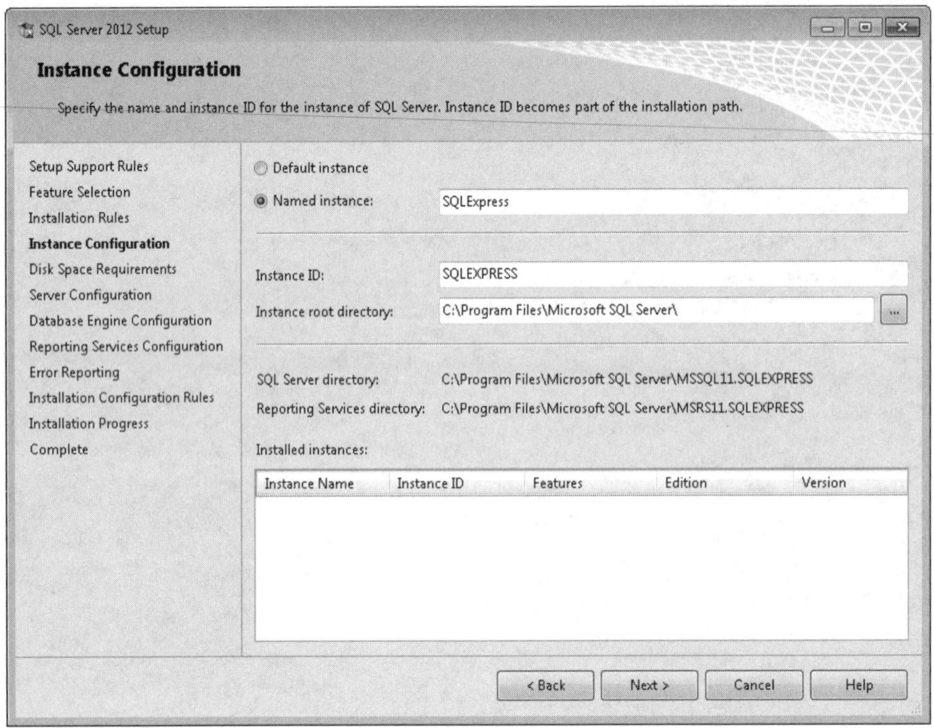

The *Server Configuration* page displays three automatic startup services. The *SQL Full-text Filter Daemon Launcher* is set to *Manual*. Unless you plan to use the feature, leave it as is, and click the *Next* button, shown in the next screen shot, to proceed.

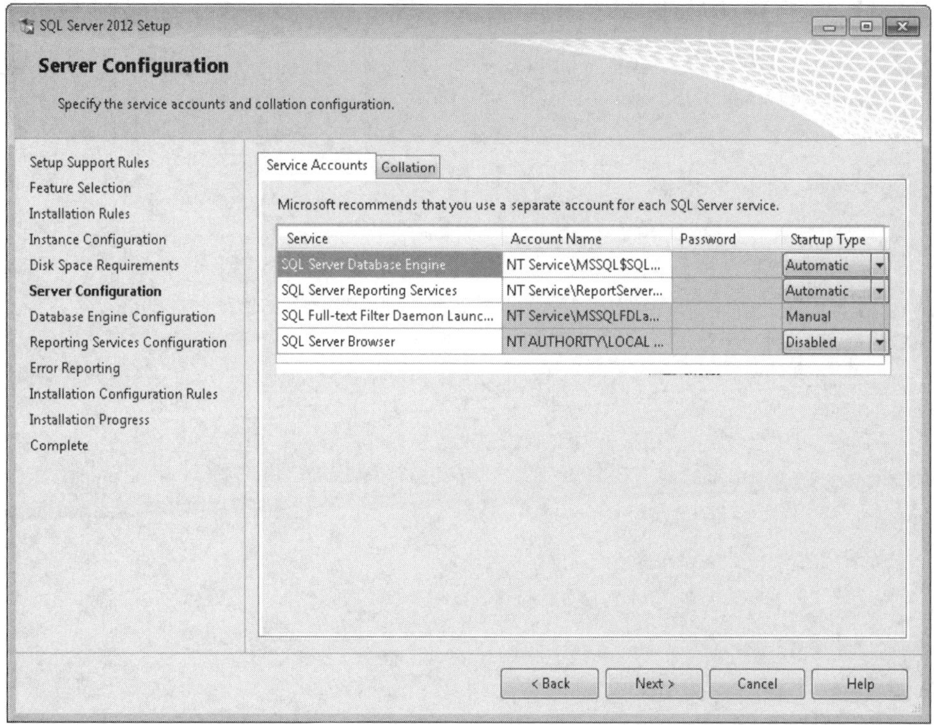

The next *Database Engine Configuration* dialog has four tabbed components, as you can see in the screen shot. This is a critical dialog form for you and requires important action when you want to access SQL Server 2012 from MySQL Workbench.

SQL Server 2012, like prior releases, assumes you want to use Windows authentication mode. Leaving the default selection intact will cause a problem with the MySQL Workbench migration tool.

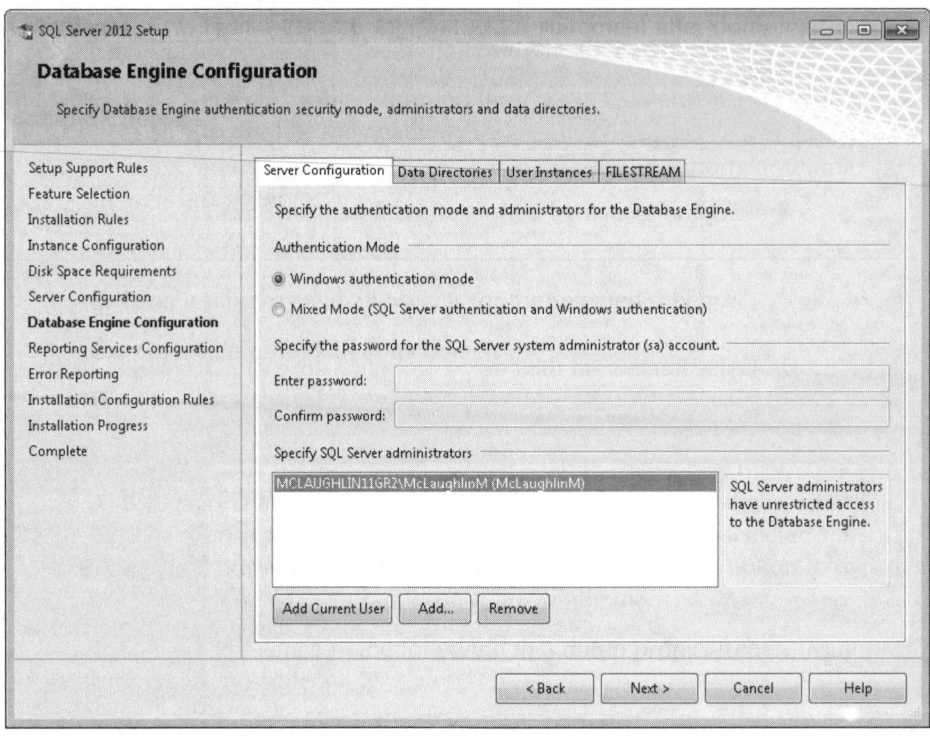

Click the *Mixed Mode* radio button and enter a password twice for the super user. It's your choice what to use, but for simplicity in a test situation like this, use something you won't forget.

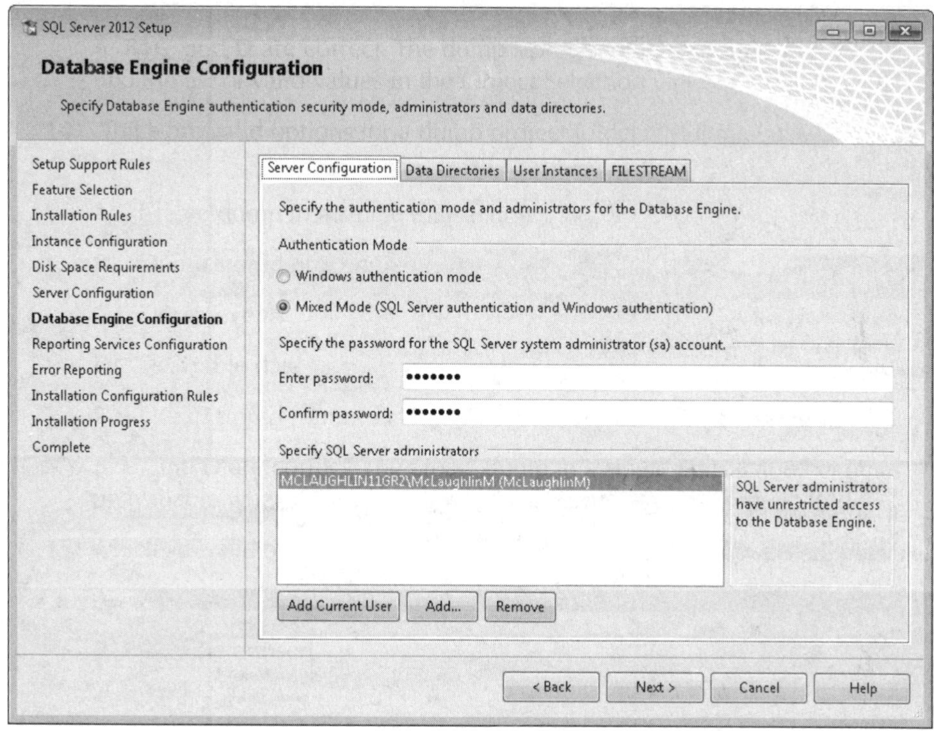

The next screen shot is the *Reporting Services Configuration* dialog. Leave the default *Install and configure* radio button selected and click the *Next* button to continue.

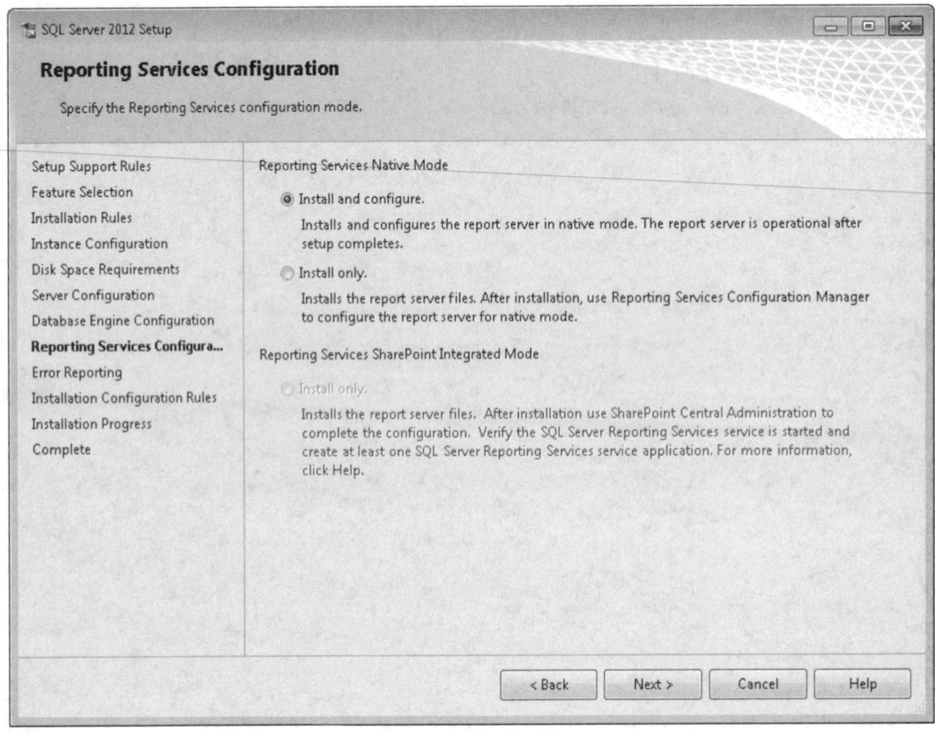

Like the Reporting Services dialog, you can leave the *Error Reporting* dialog unchanged, as shown in the following screen shot. Click the *Next* button to continue.

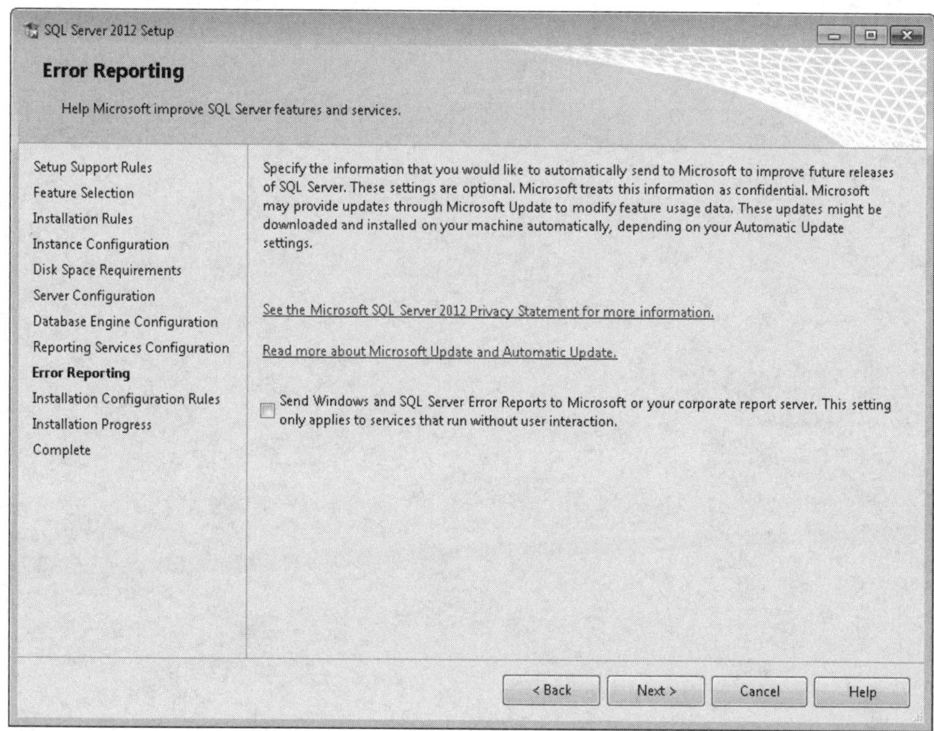

The Installation Progress dialog will take some time, and it's a good place to break and stretch your legs a moment. Having installed various versions dozens of times, I've never run into an error at this point with a fresh download. The following screen shot is provided for your reference, but at the conclusion of the installation it will advance without any required action.

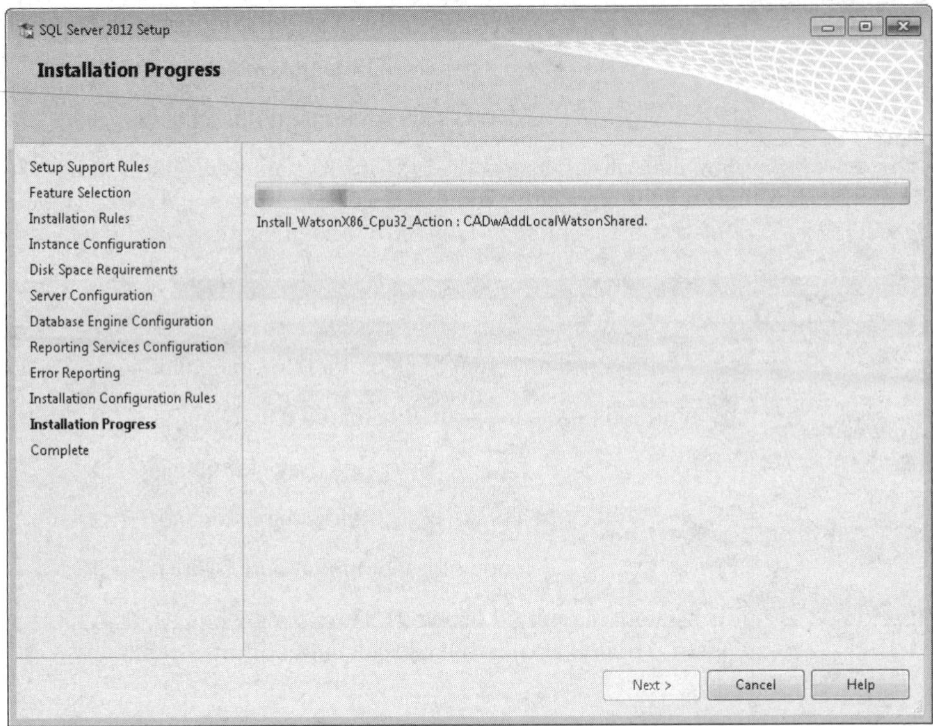

The following *Complete* dialog shows you what's installed. Inspect what you installed to ensure it all worked. Then, click the *Close* button to dismiss the installation wizard, and you've completed the installation.

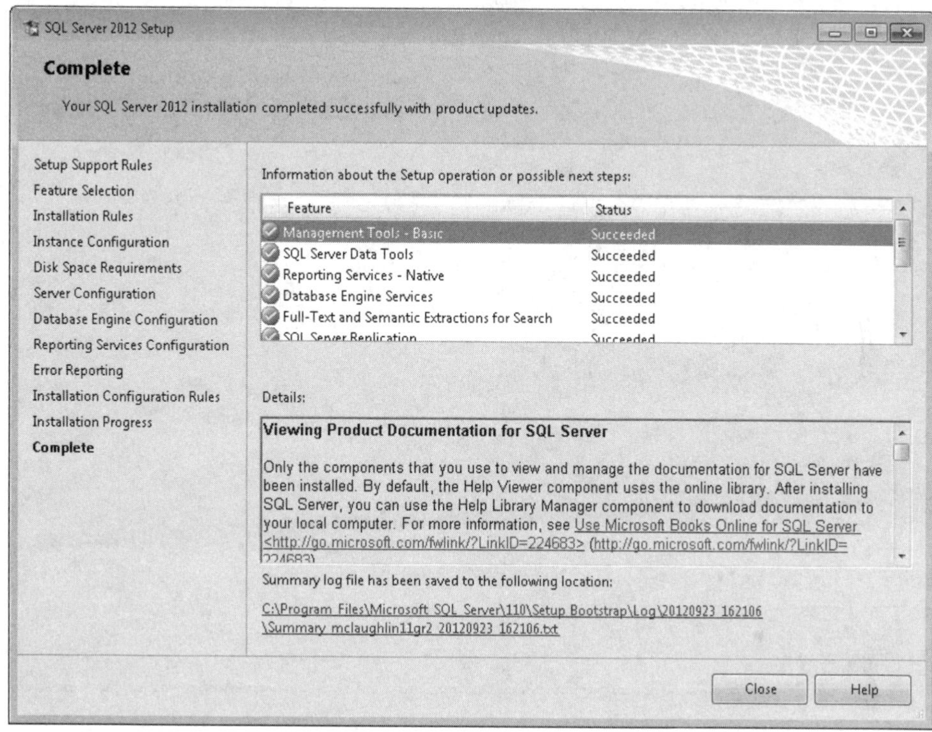

The completion of the wizard returns you to the original launch page shown next. Click the X in the upper-right corner to dismiss the installation page.

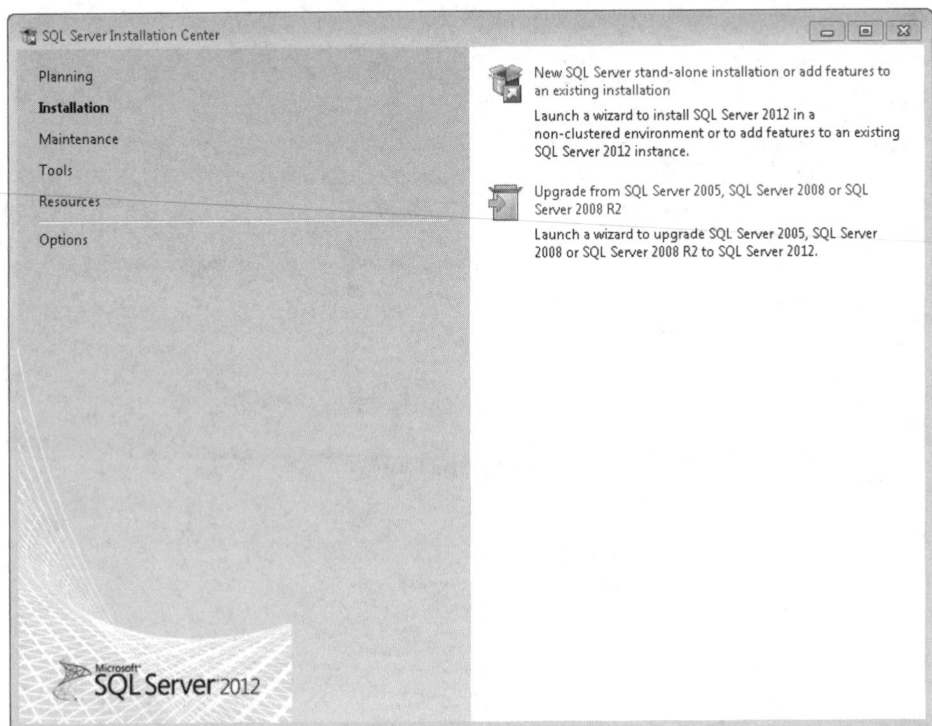

The next section shows you how to configure a feature that's typically disabled by the installation program.

Fixing the SQL Server Command-line Interface

Microsoft SQL Server automatically disables the internal pipe that allows you to run script files from the operating system. This choice limits your access to the SQL Server Management Studio (SSMS), which may be what Microsoft intends.

Clicking the Windows *Start* button launches the program menu. Click the *Microsoft SQL Server 2012* folder, and inside that folder, click the *Configuration Tools* folder. In the *Configuration Tools* folder, click the *SQL Server Configuration Manager* program, as shown in the following screen shot.

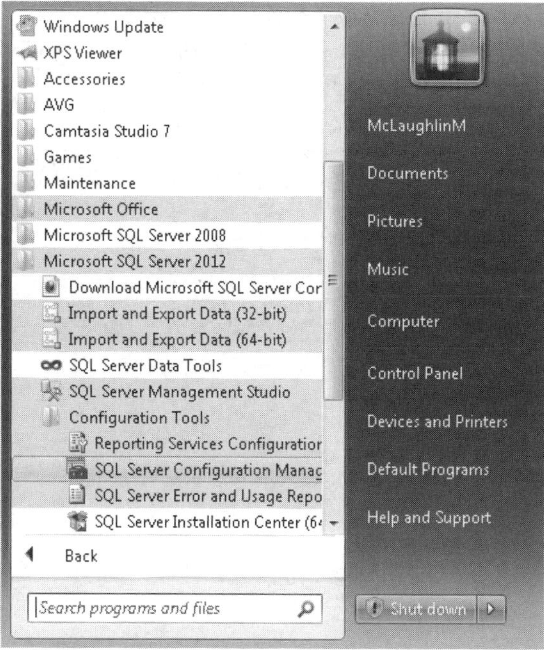

The SQL Server Configuration Manager lets you manage configuration of the Microsoft SQL Server instance, including networking setup. The following initial dialog screen shot is what you see when you launch the SQL Server Configuration Manager.

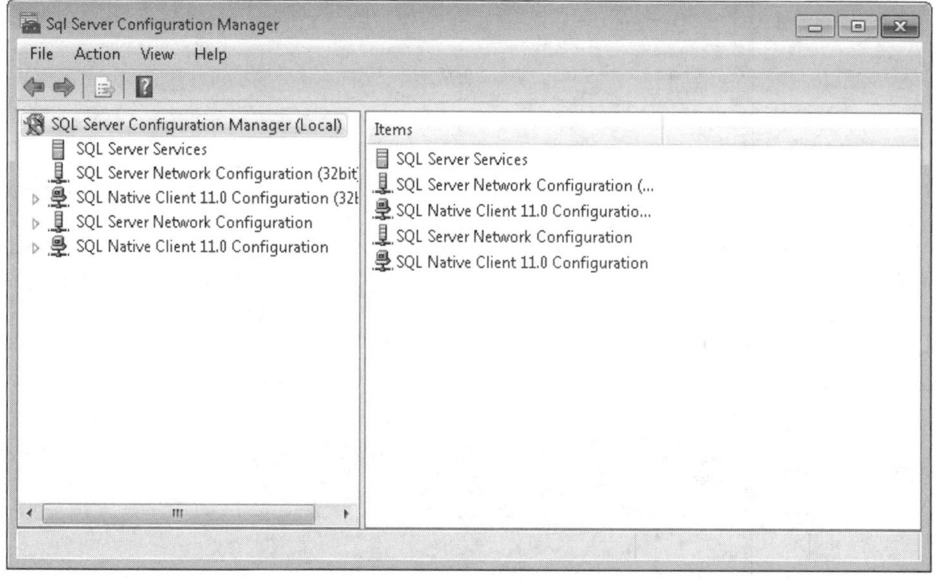

You click the *SQL Server Network Configuration* option, and then the *Protocols for SQLEXPRESS* option. After double-clicking (or right-clicking and opening) the protocols option, you see the shared memory, named pipes, and TCP/IP protocols, as shown in the following illustration.

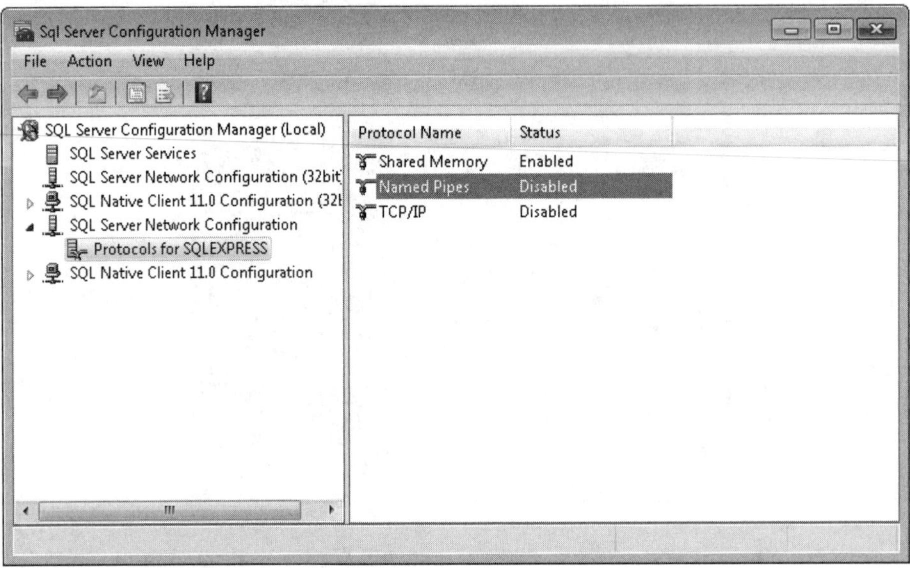

Click the *Named Pipes* option and you see the following dialog.

It lists the default value of the default pipe name:

```
\\.\pipe\MSSQL$SQLEXPRESS\sql\query
```

Click the pipe name definition and edit the default value as follows:

```
\\.\pipe\sql\query
```

This change to the pipe name leaves you with the following display. Click the *OK* button to save the change.

Your change prompts you with the following warning. It requires you to restart the SQL Server 2012 service. Click the *OK* button to dismiss the warning dialog message.

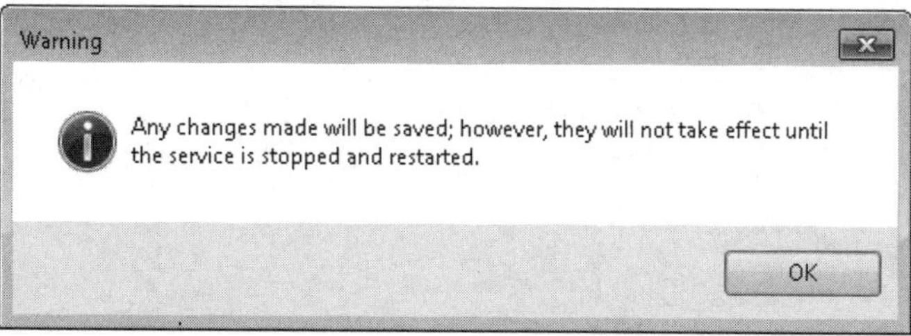

Back on the default dialog, click the green semicircular arrow to restart the Microsoft SQL Server service, which is the forth button from the left. Click the X in the dialog screen to close the SQL Server Configuration Manager.

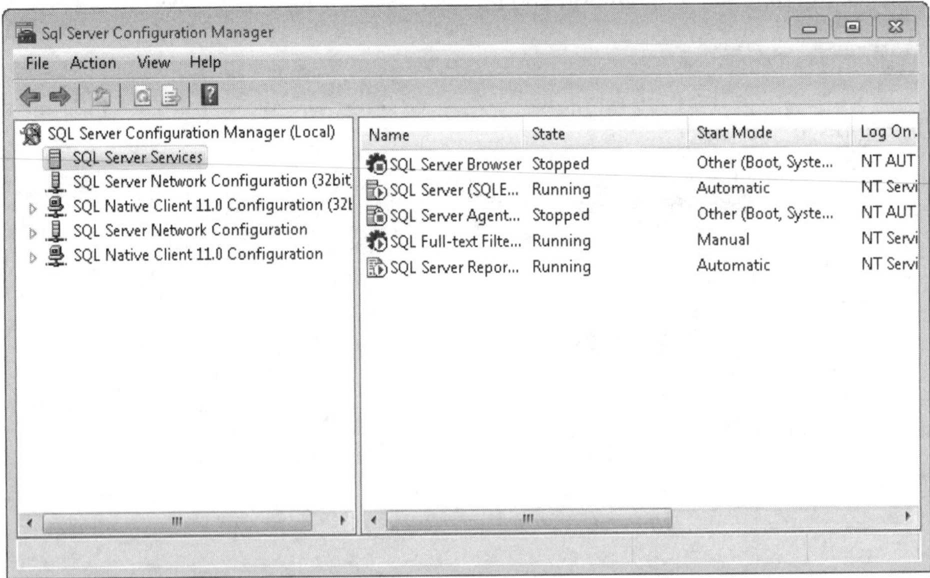

These steps enable the SQL Server command-line interface and let you run script files from the operating system.

Configuring a User Schemata

The next step in the process of setting up Microsoft SQL Server requires that you create a database user and schemata. These steps are easiest to perform by using the SQL Server Management Studio.

Click the *Microsoft SQL Server 2012* folder, and launch the SQL Server Management Studio. You are prompted to connect using Windows Authentication. Click the *Connect* button in the following dialog to connect to the database as the super user.

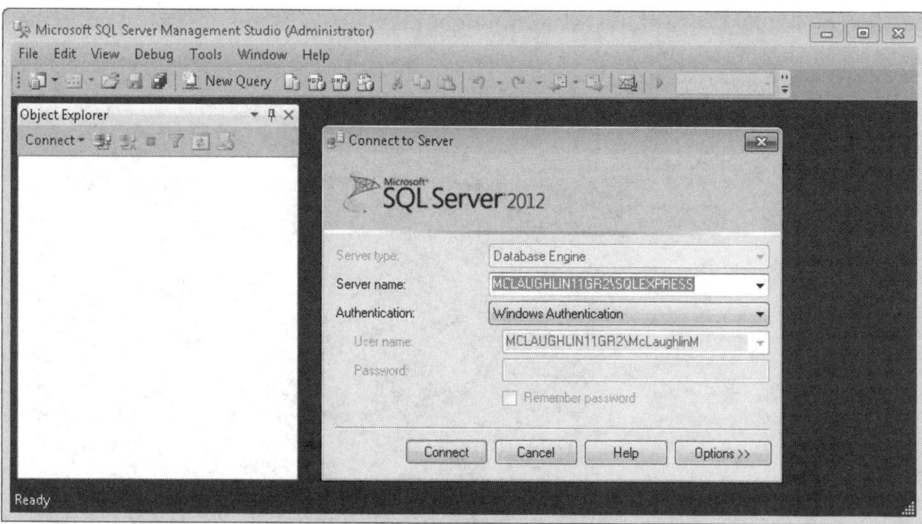

Once you connect to SQL Server 2012, you see the following dialog. Right-click the *Databases* folder.

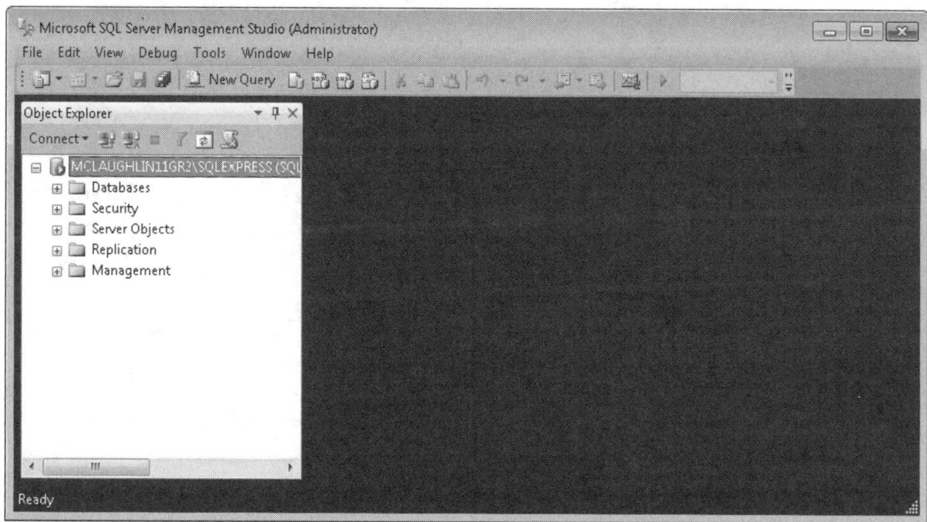

The context menu displayed with the right-click presents the options seen in the next screen shot. Click the *New Database* menu option.

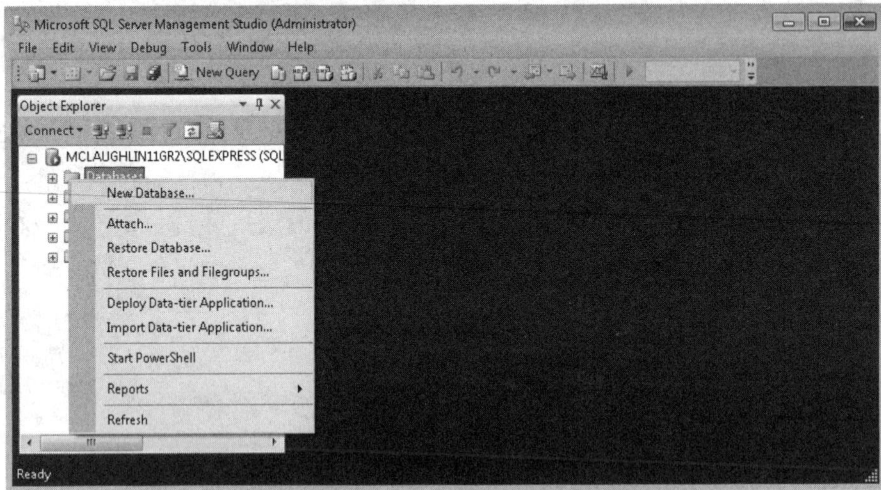

The first dialog prompts you for a database name, which you need to enter to proceed. I've entered `studentdb` as the new database name.

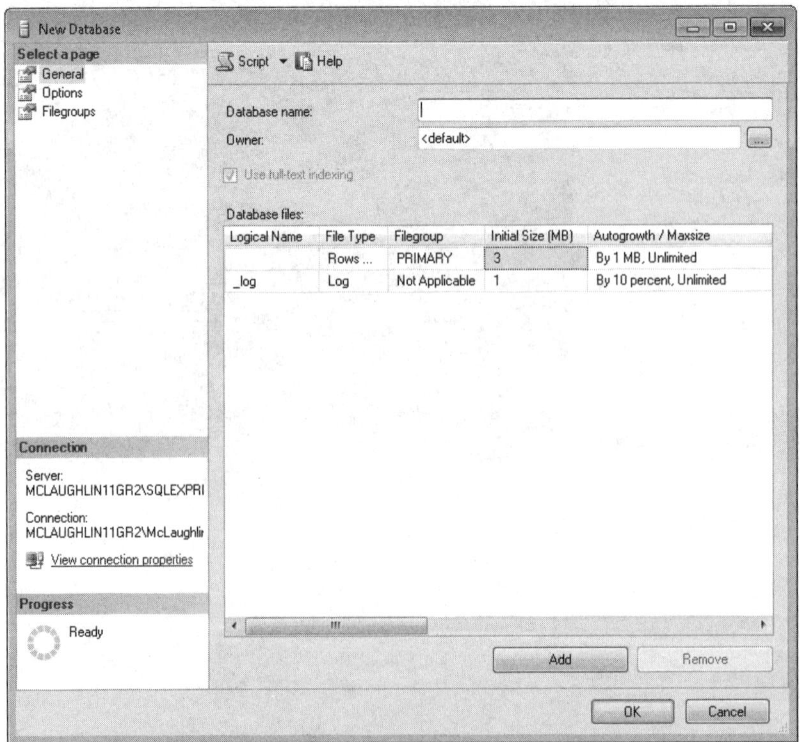

The entry of the `studentdb` value is shown in the following screen shot. Click the *OK* button to complete setting up the database.

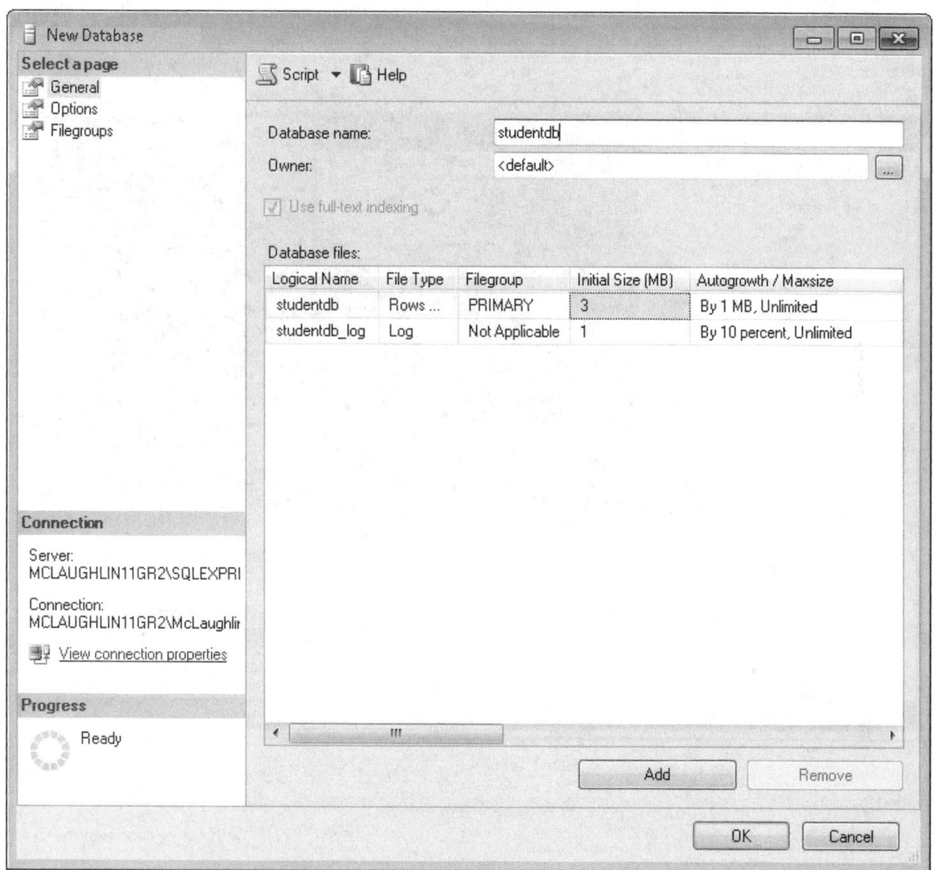

It returns you to the SQL Server Management Studio (SSMS). Click on and expand the *Security* folder and then right-click the *Logins* folder. It launches the following context menu, as you can see in the next screen shot. Choose the *New Login* option.

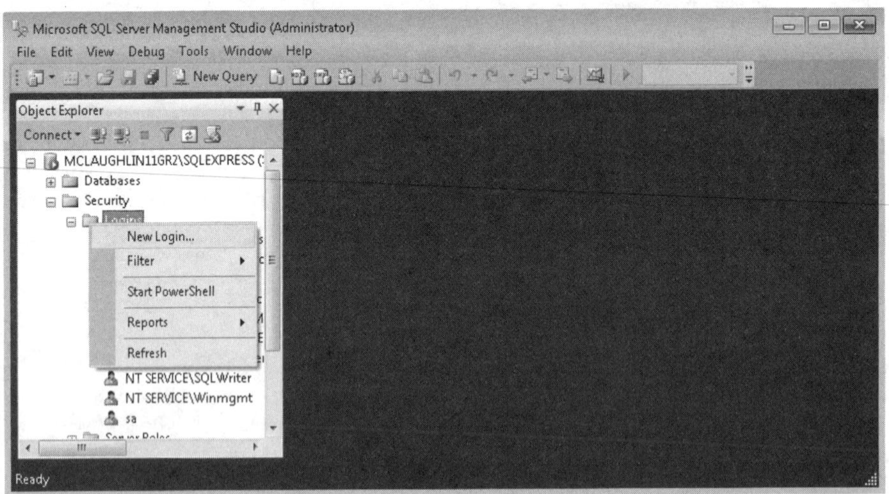

The following dialog appears.

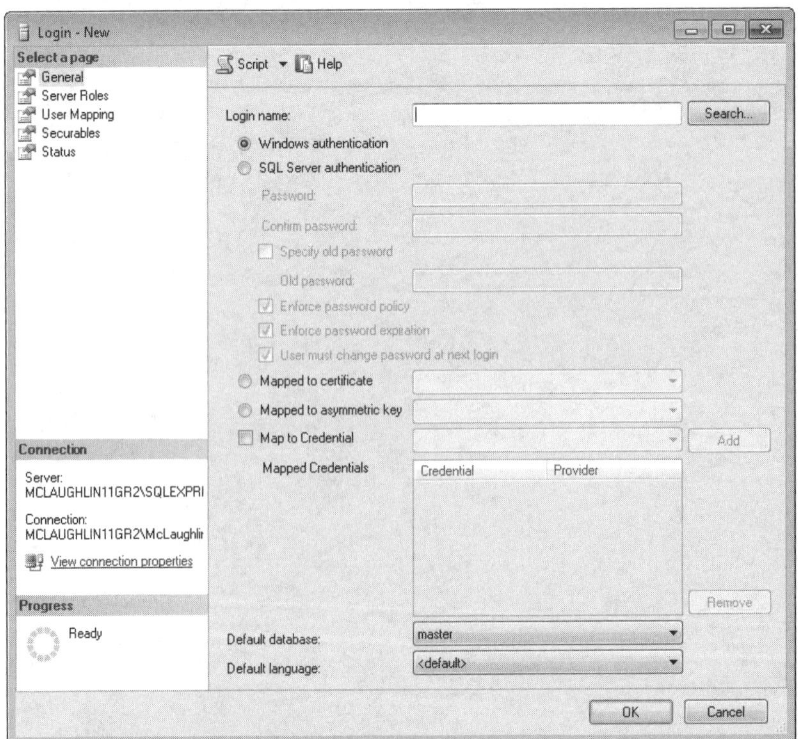

On the *General page* enter a *Login Name,* change Windows authentication mode to SQL Server authentication and choose a default database. The following screen shot uses student as the login name, uses SQL Server authentication with the passwords entered during the installation, and sets the default database to the `studentdb` created earlier.

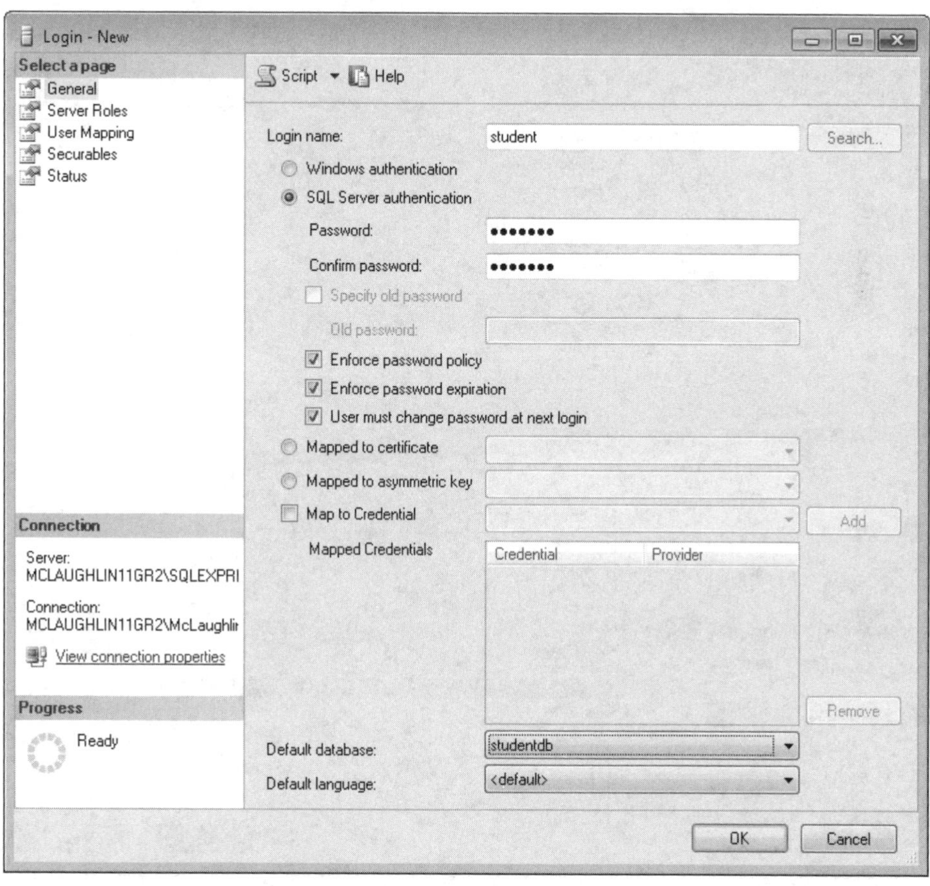

Click the *User Mapping* page to set the `studentdb` as the default schema. Also, confirm that the database, user, and schema values are defined properly (typically done by default). Then, give the role *db_owner* to the student user that you're creating, as shown in the next screen shot. Click the *OK* button when you complete all the tasks.

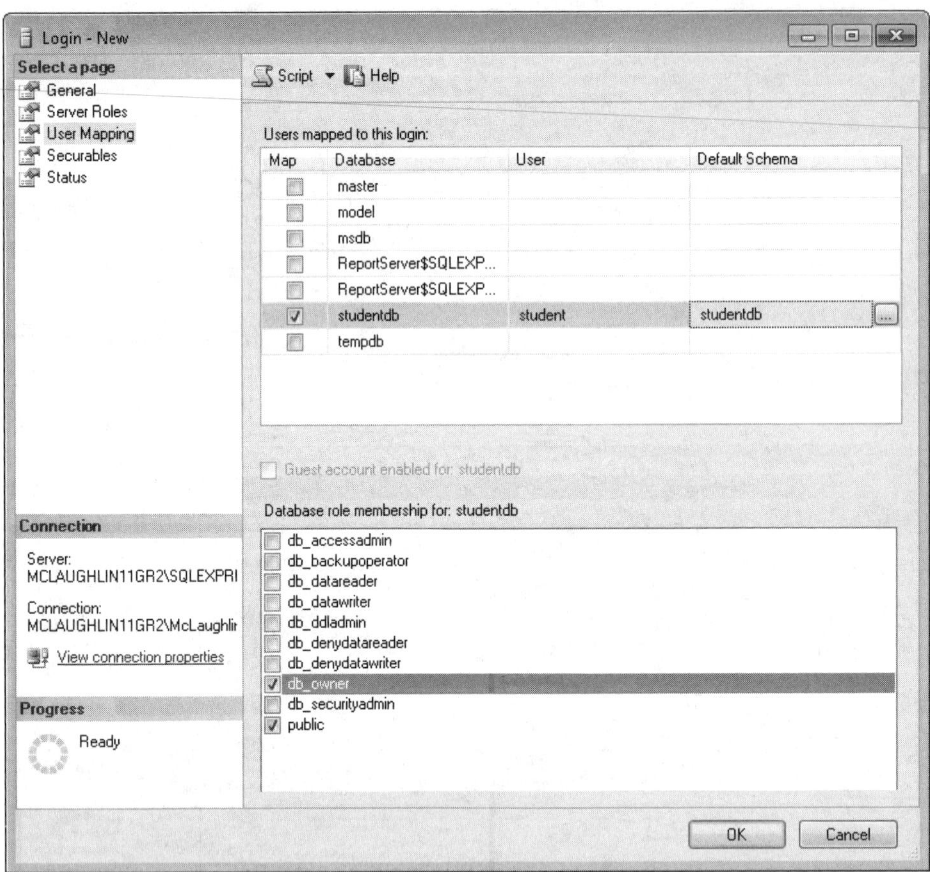

This returns you to the Object Explorer, where you should confirm that you now have a `student` login value. You expand the *Security* folder and *Logins* folder to see whether the `student` user has been successfully created.

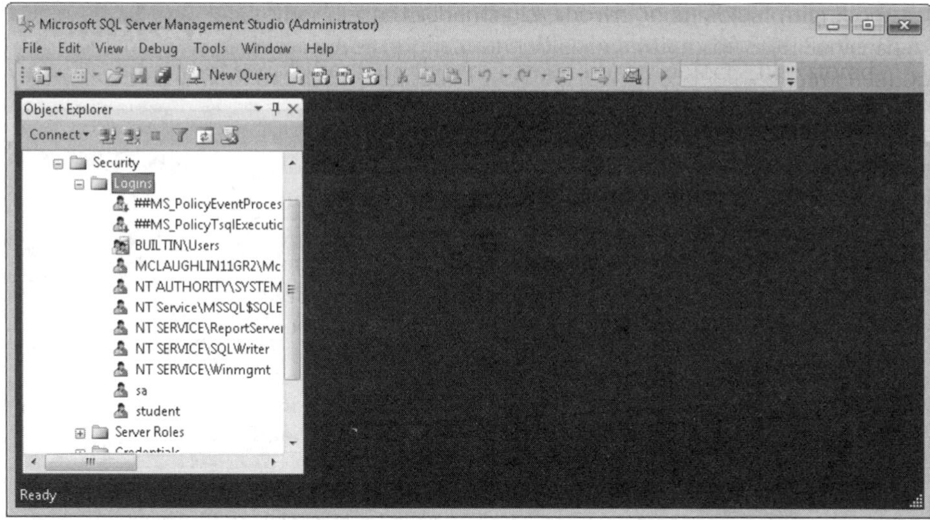

In the Object Explorer of SQL Server Management Studio, open the *Databases* folder, and then right-click the `studentdb` database. In the following context menu choose the *Properties* option.

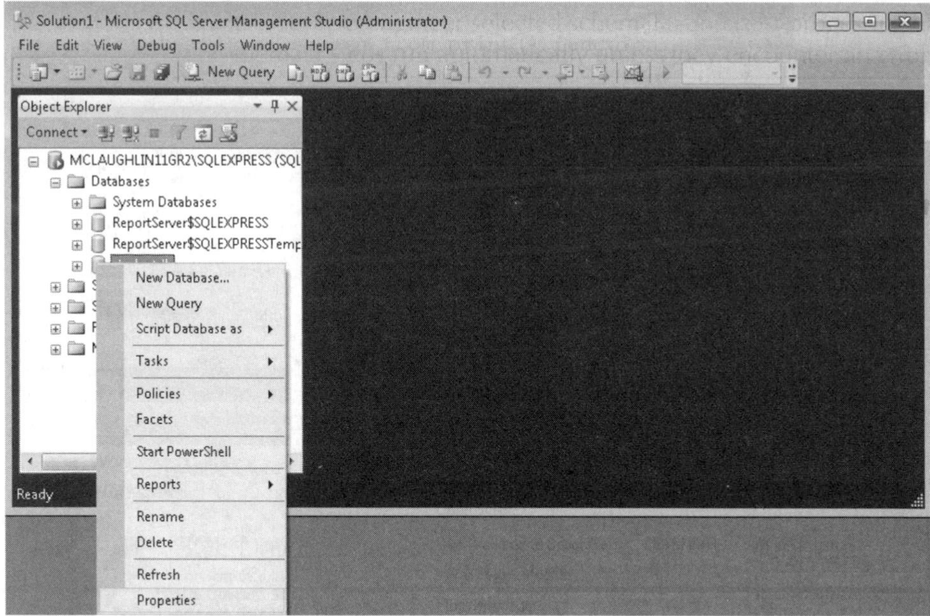

You should see the following initial *General* page after choosing the *Properties* option. Click the permissions object to verify that you've properly assigned the `studentdb` schema.

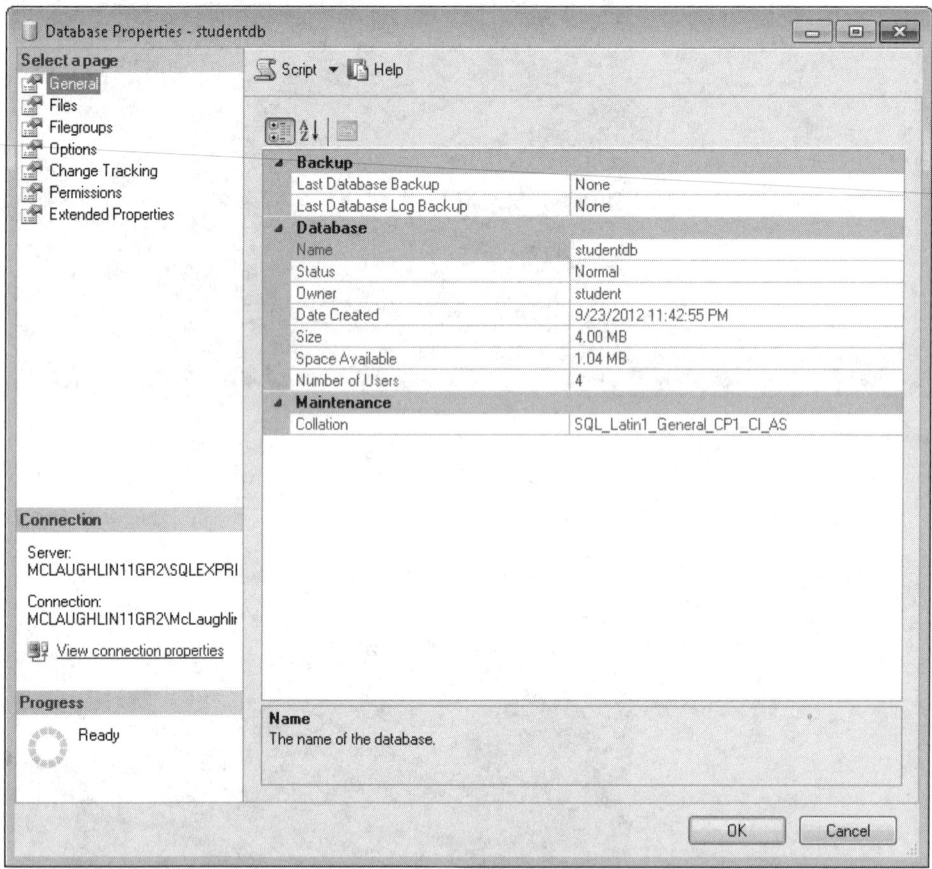

The Permissions page should show you that the `student` is the primary user of roles for the `studentdb` schema. The following screen shot shows you that you've configured the `studentdb` schema correctly.

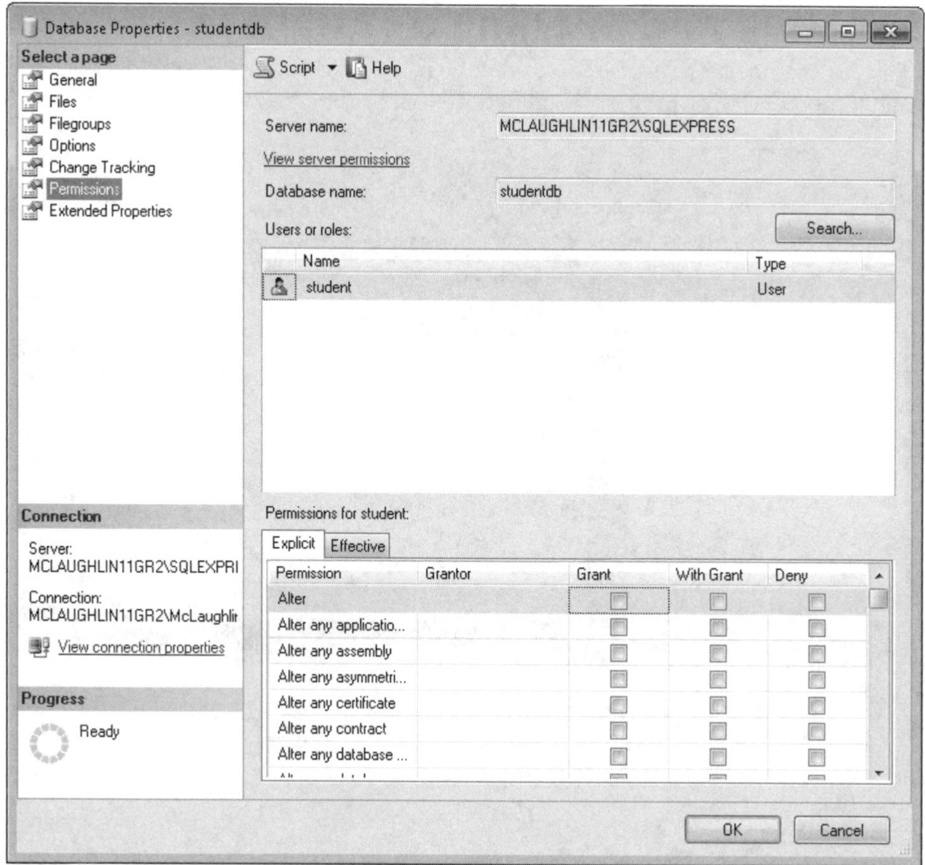

At this point, you need to log out as the super user. You click the *File* menu option and choose the *Logout* option. In the next section, you'll see how to create a table in the `studentdb` schema and populate the table with data.

Creating and Seeding a Database

Click *File | Connect Object Explorer* from the menu, and you open a connection. The default prompt shows a Windows authentication, as shown in the next screen shot.

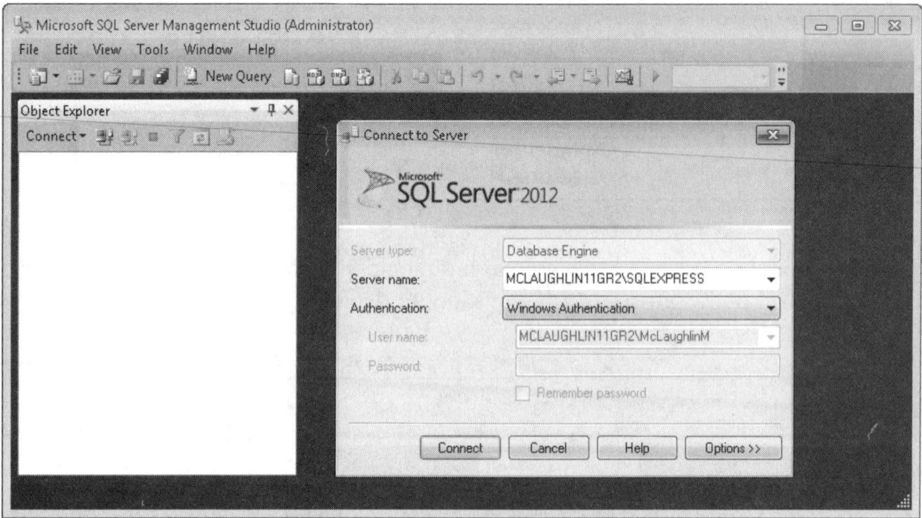

Click the *Authentication* drop-down list, choose *SQL Server Authentication,* and then enter the student login and password. Click the *Connect* button to connect to the database, as shown in the following screen shot.

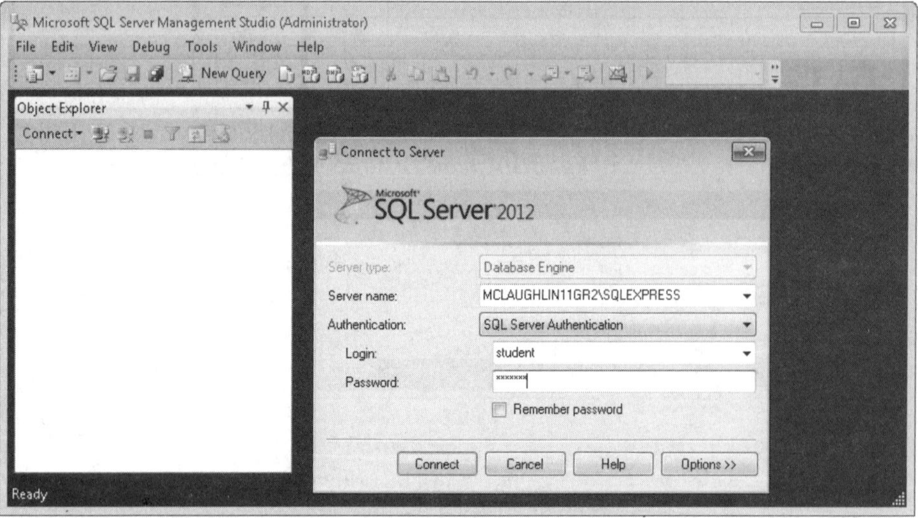

The system prompts you to enter a new password the first time you log in as a new user. You must enter the password twice and click the *OK* button, as shown in the next screen shot.

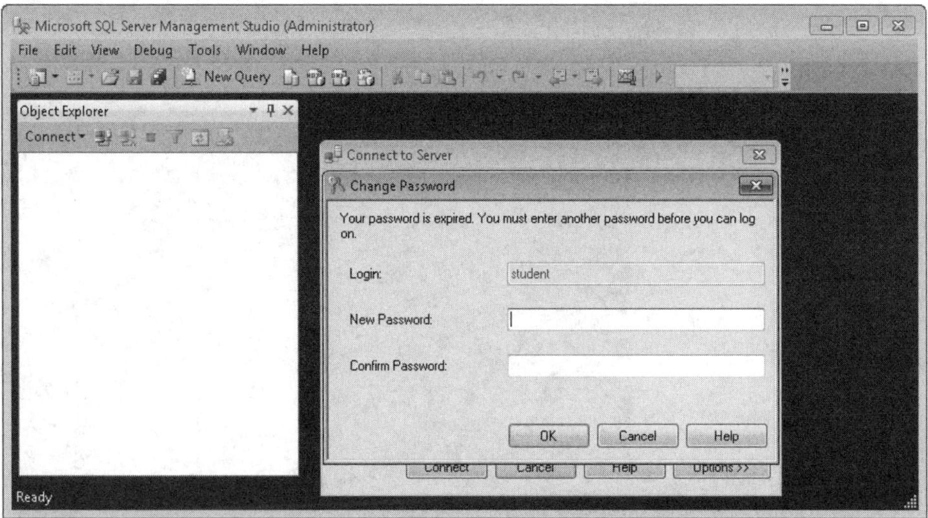

After validating the `student` user, you see the following in the *Object Explorer*.

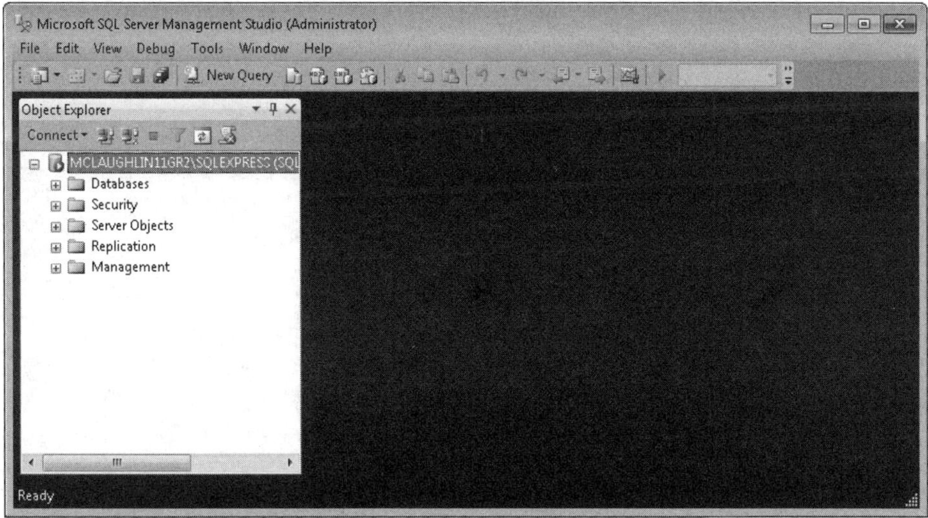

Click the *Databases* folder to expand it, and you see the following dialog. Click the `studentdb` database, and then click the *New Query* button from the toolbar below the menu.

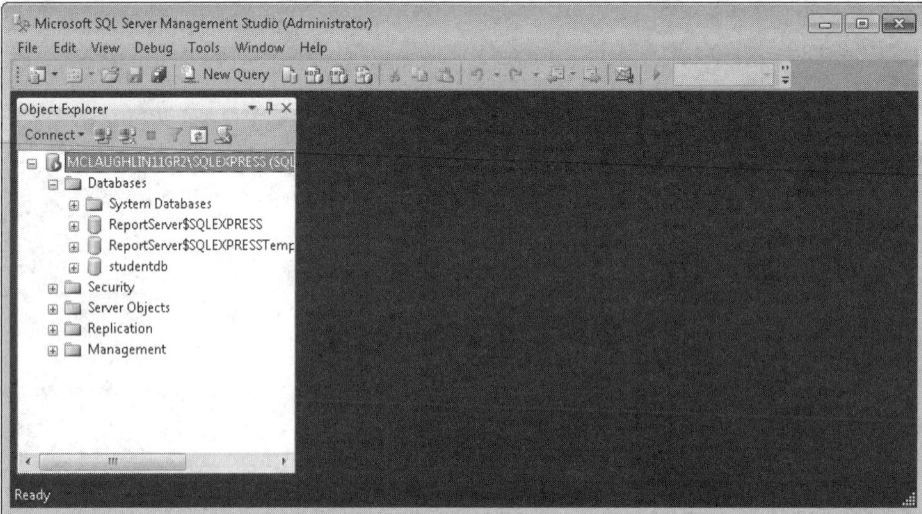

The *New Query* button brings up the *SQL Query* pane and a *Properties* pane as shown in the next dialog box.

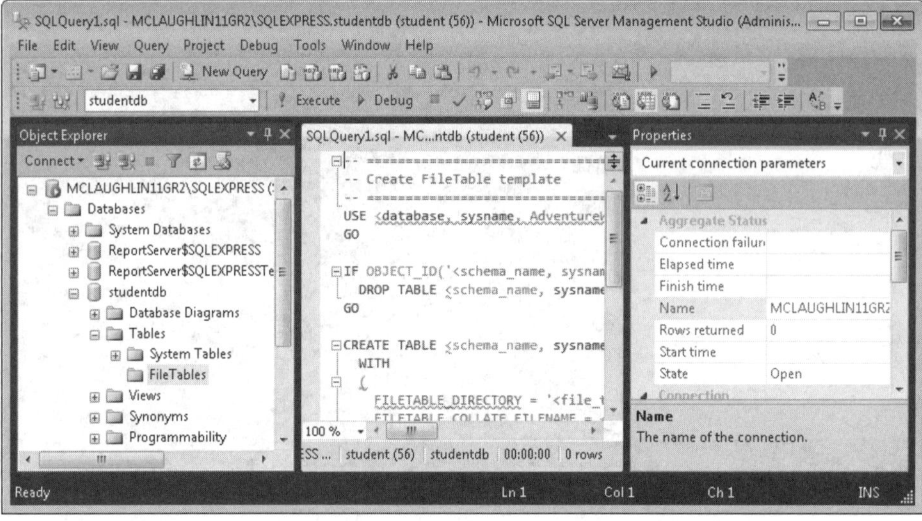

Inside the SQL Query, insert the following:

```
IF OBJECT_ID('studentdb.conquistador','U') IS NOT NULL
  DROP TABLE studentdb.conquistador
GO

CREATE TABLE studentdb.conquistador
( conquistador_id   INT  NOT NULL  IDENTITY(1,1)
  CONSTRAINT pk_conquistador PRIMARY KEY
, conquistador      VARCHAR(30)
, actual_name       VARCHAR(30)
, nationality       VARCHAR(30))
GO

INSERT INTO conquistador
VALUES
 ('Juan de Fuca','Ioánnis Fokás','Greek')
,('Nicolás de Federmán','Nikolaus Federmann','German')
,('Sebastián Caboto','Sebastiano Caboto','Venetian')
,('Jorge de la Espira','Georg von Speyer','German')
,('Eusebio Francisco Kino','Eusebius Franz Kühn','Italian')
,('Wenceslao Linck','Wenceslaus Linck','Bohemian')
,('Fernando Consag','Ferdinand Konšcak','Croatian')
,('Américo Vespucio','Amerigo Vespucci','Italian')
,('Alejo García','Aleixo Garcia','Portuguese')
GO
```

After copying the script contents into the SQL Query pane, click the *Execute* button on the second toolbar to run the code. You've now successfully created the tiny database schema that you can migrate with the instructions from Chapter 12. Just one catch; it's in Unicode by default in the Microsoft SQL Server and when you migrate it to MySQL, the target database should be set to a UTF8 character set.

Summary

This appendix has explained how to install, fix, configure, and deploy a database inside Microsoft SQL Server 2012. It supports Chapter 12, where you migrate a database from a SQL Server 2012 database.

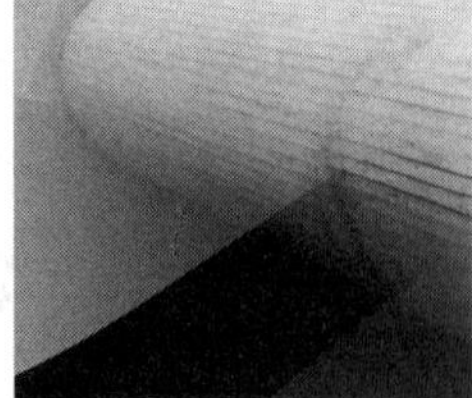

GLOSSARY

Database Modeling Terms

his is a list of terms that support database modeling in practice and theory. Some of these terms have varying meanings in mathematics and computer science, and these are their database management system definitions.

0NF An acronym for zero normal form (0NF). An *0NF* table describes the normalization level as not normalized. This means that the collection of columns may result in non-unique rows and that any column may contain non-atomic values. Non-atomic values are composites of two or more values.

1NF An acronym for first normal form (1NF). A *1NF* table describes a table that has columns that only hold atomic values and rows that are unique because the list of all columns guarantees unique rows.

2NF An acronym for second normal form (2NF). A *2NF* table describes a table that meets 1NF rules and contains no partial dependency. A partial dependency exists when the table has a composite primary key (made up of two or more columns and chosen from possible candidate keys as a natural primary key), and exists when any non-key column in the table depends on only part of the composite primary key. The presence of a partial dependency in a table's design establishes it as a 1NF table. Moving a table from 1NF to 2NF typically requires that you divide a table into two tables, because the partial dependency indicates that the initial table's design contains more than a single subject-fact or theme.

After removing the column from the composite natural primary key, you should check whether the natural key truly resolves uniqueness with the remaining columns. The remaining columns should describe uniqueness of the table's single subject-fact or theme. If it does, you have a good natural key for the table from a design perspective. While a valid natural key becomes a candidate key that you may select as the primary key, you should always add a surrogate key column as the primary key.

3NF An acronym for third normal form (3NF). A *3NF* table describes a table that meets 2NF rules and contains no transitive dependency. A transitive dependency exists when the table has a non-key column that depends on another non-key column for context. The presence of a transitive dependency means the table is in 2NF. Moving a table with a transitive dependency from 2NF to 3NF requires removing the transitive dependency. Like the process of changing a table with a partial dependency, you remove both the dependent column and the column that it is dependent on. The column through which the transitive dependency exists should become the natural key of a new table, and the dependent column should become a non-key column in that new table.

During early design, there may be more than one transitive dependency. You should repeat the process for all transitive dependencies.

anomaly An *anomaly* is a deviation from the common rule, type, arrangement, or form; or an incongruity or inconsistency.

association table An *association table* is designed to hold two or more foreign keys and enables resolving logical relationships into physical relationships. An association table is also a translation table, and the terms are interchangeable.

attribute An *attribute* is a specification that describes an object or element, and in database modeling and theory, attribute refers to a column in a table. Attribute (or column) describes elements in the row, where the row also can be called a tuple or object instance. (See *column* for more information on the importance of attributes.)

attribute domain An *attribute domain* is the possible values that fit within an attribute. The domain of male and female represents the classic choices in a traditional gender column, while male, female, or other (third gender) represent the choices in a more modern gender column. The possible choices (or values) define the domain of column, and you can restrict the domain values through database-level constraints.

binary relationship A *binary relationship* is a reciprocal set of relations between two things. In databases, the two things are tables, and the relation is between rows (or instances) of tables or views (where views are semi-permanent result sets or temporary result sets).

There are two physical binary relationships. The one-to-one and one-to-many binary relationships are physical relationships between two tables, or two rows in the same table for recursive relationships.

A one-to-one binary relationship between tables really means one row in one table relates to one row in another table through a relationship. One row holding a primary key column qualifies half the relationship, and a copy of the primary key column's value, a foreign key column, qualifies the other half. In a one-to-one binary relationship, it doesn't technically matter which one holds the primary key. However, if you choose the wrong one, changing it later when the relationship evolves to a one-to-many relationship can be expensive in time and resources.

A one-to-many binary relationship between tables means one row holds a primary key column and another row holds multiple copies of the same primary key values as a foreign key column. In essence, the one side donates a copy of itself to enable a join on the equality of values—an equijoin. Some describe the primary-to-foreign key relationship as the one side donating a copy to the many side (although the many side can, in rare cases, be the other one side of the relationship).

It is also possible to have a recursive or self-referencing relationship between two copies of the same table. Such a relationship exists within a single table when it holds columns for both the primary key and recursive foreign key. This lets any row match to one or more rows in the same table when you use table aliases in a join statement.

NOTE
A self-referencing relationship may resolve between two different rows or two copies of the same row.

There are also many-to-many relationships, but they're logical binary relationships because neither can be implemented as a physical binary relationship. All many-to-many relationships require intermediary tables that hold copies of the respective primary keys in the same row. The row provides the mapping between the related rows of the two subject-fact or theme tables.

candidate key A *candidate key* is a unique key that you may choose as a primary key. Unique keys are one or more attributes (or elements) of a row that uniquely identify a tuple (or object instance).

Chen notation *Chen notation* was the first take at data modeling. It put relationships into diamonds and failed to capture minimum cardinality in relations.

Chen-Martin notation *Chen-Martin notation* was the second take at data modeling. It added the idea of minimum cardinality to the drawings but kept binary relationships in the diamond.

column *Column* is an alternative name for an attribute or element of a tuple, row, or object instance. It describes a vertical element in a two-dimensional table. It comes into the database lexicon from spreadsheets, where a column defines the vertical axis of data.

Columns may or may not contain a value in any row. A column that allows a null value is an optional column and has a `0..1` cardinality, which means zero to one attribute (or element) per tuple, row, or object instance. A column that disallows a null value is a mandatory column and has a `1..1` cardinality. A mandatory column means every row requires a not-null value in the column or attribute. Databases let you allow or disallow a null value when you create or modify a table by assigning a column-level constraint.

composite key A *composite key* is made up of two or more columns. A composite key can be applied to many different types of keys, and composite keys are interchangeable with compound keys. Some reference materials use composite key, while other reference materials use compound key. The composite key takes its meaning from composite materials, like fiberglass.

compound key A *compound key* is made up of two or more columns, like a composite key. The terms are interchangeable. The compound key takes its meaning from a chemical compound.

data structure A *data structure* describes the definition of a type of data, like a collection of elements. The elements can be a group of attributes (or elements), like integers, dates, or strings. The data structure can also become the base *user-defined type* (UDT) of a collection, where a collection is a set of rows characterized as a list or an array. This type of data structure can be the basis of a nested object instance.

delete anomaly A *delete anomaly* occurs when the data model's design is flawed. It means you may delete the wrong data. Like insertion and update anomalies, deletion anomalies occur when you fail to ensure that a table has a single thing, theme, or subject. It generally occurs when non-unique keys fail to find the correct set of rows or a natural key fails to find a unique row.

determinant A *determinant* is the thing that decides meaning or context of another variable (see *functional dependency* in the glossary for an example). A determinate may be part of a composite natural key or a single-column natural key. A single-column natural key (also called a candidate key) determines uniqueness in a table about a single thing, theme, or subject, and is a positive indicator of a good design. A determinate inside a composite natural key identifies a set of possible values that only have context with the determinate, and indicates that the table is less than second normal form.

domain A *domain* is a set of related things, like the set of integers or real numbers. This definition describes the domain of possible values in a column. It is also possible to apply the term to instances of a thing, theme, or subject. That makes the domain the possible unique rows in a table.

entity An *entity* is a container, most often a table in a relational database.

Enhanced Entity Relationship (EER) Model An *Enhanced Entity Relationship (EER) Model* is the label MySQL Workbench uses to describe their rendering of an ER Model.

Entity Relationship (ER) Model An *Entity Relationship Model* is a symbolic drawing that shows a collection of tables and their connecting binary relationships.

equijoin An *equijoin* is a join between two tables or instances of one table based on the equality of values in the primary and foreign key columns.

field A *field* describes an attribute (or element) of a primitive or user-defined data type. A field is one element of a row and one instance of the column's data type. A field can have a fixed or variable size. The field descriptor belongs with the record descriptor for rows of a table.

file A *file* holds data. The data can be a set of characters or binary values, and it holds information like an image, program, or document.

file system A *file system* manages files, which are data repositories. Typically, file systems manage the storage, access, and retrieval of files.

foreign key A *foreign key* can be one or a set of attributes (or elements) that maps to a primary key made up of one or a set of attributes (or elements). The primary key is typically in another table, but it can be in the same table as the foreign key.

This type of relationship is a one-to-many binary relationship. The table holding the primary key is the one side of the binary relationship, and the table holding the foreign key is the many side of the binary relationship. A self-referencing one-to-many relationship exists when both the primary and foreign keys exist in the same table.

forward engineering *Forward engineering* is the process of using a SQL script to create an ER (Entity Relationship) Model. ER Models are symbolic representations of how tables are connected in a relational database.

functional dependency A *functional dependency* exists when an attribute or a set of attributes (or elements) depends on exactly one other unique attribute or set of attributes. For example, a movie rating of PG by the Motion Picture Association of America is an example of a functional dependency because the PG rating is wholly dependent on the rating body. This is shown as a functional dependency with the following notation:

Rating Agency → Rating

The expression says the rating agency determines the rating. The variable on the left of this type of expression is called the determinant (the thing that decides meaning or context of the variable on the right).

HNF An acronym for *highest normal form* (HNF). *HNF* is the normalization level of any table at a point in time, and may refer to zero, first, second, third, and so forth normal forms.

information engineering notation *Information engineering* is the formal name for the notation system developed by Martin. It removed the diamonds and put all notations along the relationship lines. The use of perpendicular lines, greater than or less than symbols, and zeros gave rise to a notation system that was easy to read and didn't waste space when printed. MySQL Workbench uses the information engineering notation symbols.

insertion anomaly An *insertion anomaly* means that you can insert duplicate or incorrect data. It typically occurs when your data modeling design fails to ensure that a table focuses on a single thing, theme, or subject. More often than not, it means rows aren't unique if the table's highest normal form is first normal form, and it means the primary key fails to *determine* the uniqueness of rows in second normal form.

instance An *instance* is a collection of databases managed by a Database Management System (DBMS). A MySQL Server instance is the set of databases it manages.

key A *key* may be a unique or non-unique attribute or set of attributes that identifies rows in a table. Unique keys identify a unique row, and non-unique rows identify one or more rows in a table.

Keys serve different purposes in tables. They may identify the column or set of columns that uniquely qualify a row, and such a key qualifies as a candidate key.

logical relationship A *logical relationship* is a binary or n-ary relationship that has no physical implementation without an intermediary table. Logical relationships enable modeling patterns to accommodate the real-world business problems. The logical relationship is always implemented by creating an association or translation table that maps the relationship between the two tables' primary keys. A mandatory column may have a `0..*` (zero-to-many) cardinality when the column uses the MySQL `SET` data type.

mandatory column A *mandatory column* requires a value when inserting a row or updating that specific column. It has a `1..1` cardinality during design and most often has a not-null database constraint to guarantee the insertion or update of a valid value.

many-to-many binary relationship A *many-to-many binary relationship* is a non-specific relationship between two tables where one row in one table may map to zero to many rows in the other and vice versa. Naturally, you must resolve this type of logical binary relationship to a physical binary relationship. The one-to-many and one-to-one (infrequently implemented) are the only physical binary relationships. You resolve the logical many-to-many binary relationship by creating a third table that holds the foreign key from both tables in the same row. The third table is typically an association or translation table.

Martin notation *Martin notation* refers to information engineering notation. Please see that entry in the glossary.

n-ary relationship An *n-ary relationship* is a non-specific relationship between three or more tables. Like the logical many-to-many binary relationship, an n-ary relationship doesn't have a physical implementation by itself. You map the three or more tables by using another table that holds foreign keys from all of the other tables in a single row. This intermediary table is typically an association or translation table.

The other table is known as an association or translation table too. Typically, all of the original tables have a one-to-many relationship to the association table, and all relationships resolve through the association table.

natural key A *natural key* is a unique key that identifies a row of data, or instance of data. A natural key may be one or more attributes (or elements) that uniquely identify a tuple (a row) or object instance. Natural keys are typically a set of attributes that uniquely identify each row in a table.

A natural key is automatically a candidate key that you may choose as the table's primary key. All other columns in the table should enjoy a direct and full functional dependency on all attributes in the natural key.

A surrogate key varies only in one regard—a surrogate key needs to map to one and only one natural key. A surrogate key should never be added to the natural key in order to achieve unique rows. This means the surrogate key plus the natural key should never become the natural key, because that means attributes that describe the table's single subject don't do so uniquely.

NOTE
If you adopt a surrogate key for joins, the surrogate key plus the natural key should become a unique index to speed searches through the table.

nominated key A *nominated key* is the candidate key you choose to nominate as the primary key. At some point, the nominated key simply becomes the primary key, the nomination becomes history, and nobody cares about it.

The only subtle difference is that some people use nominated keys to indicate the candidate key they've tentatively chosen before making a final decision, and others substitute the nominated key for the candidate key. This secondary use should be discouraged.

non-key A *non-key* is an attribute (column) or set of attributes (columns) that contain a descriptive set of values that identify rows as unique, but provides a characteristic to a row of data. All non-key columns should have a full functional dependency on the natural, or primary, key.

non-specific relationship A *non-specific relationship* is a logical or reciprocal set of relations between two things. Non-specific relationships are many-to-many and n-ary relationships.

Non-specific relationships create situations where rows in two tables have no way to establish a relationship between the two rows. That's because you can't donate one copy of the primary key to the other row without breaking the many-to-many relationship pattern. Logical non-specific relationships are thereby mapped through association or translation tables, and decomposed into specific one-to-one or one-to-many binary relationships.

normalization *Normalization* is the process of breaking a table with more than one thing, theme, or subject into a set of tables. The goal of normalization is to have tables with one thing, theme, or subject because they're not going to suffer from insertion, update, or delete anomalies.

object instance An *object instance* is a data structure or row of data inserted into an object type, which is like a hybrid table in an Object Relational Database Management System (ORDBMS). Moreover, an object instance is a row in any table. The row contains only attributes in a relational database.

object type An *object type* in the context of a relational database is a data structure, or the definition of a table. Definitions of tables are stored in the database catalog and built upon preexisting data types. Some databases support user-defined types (UDT), which include attributes and methods. The pattern of a table is a generalization of a table, and rows are instances of an object type.

one-to-many binary relationship A *one-to-many binary relationship* is a physical relationship, which is characterized by one table holding a primary key and the other a foreign key. The primary key can be one or more attributes, and the foreign key is a copy of values from the primary key attribute(s).

The one side of the relationship holds the primary key, while the many side holds one to many copies of the primary key as the foreign key. The tables resolve or map rows from one to the other by comparing the values of the primary and foreign key columns.

one-to-one binary relationship A *one-to-one binary relationship* is a physical relationship. It is also a specialized or subtype of a one-to-many relationship. The one side holds the primary key value(s), and the other one side holds a copy of the primary key as the foreign key value. It is possible to choose either table as the one with the primary key, but if you choose wrong, the re-engineering cost is high. That's because the one side holding the single copy of the primary key as a foreign key should never become the table that holds the primary key in the relationship between the tables.

optional column An *optional column* doesn't require a value when inserting a row or updating that specific column. It has a `0..1` (zero-to-one) cardinality during design and is typically unconstrained. An optional column may have a `0..*` (zero-to-many) cardinality when the column uses the MySQL `SET` data type.

partial dependency A *partial dependency* exists when the primary key is a composite or compound key (of two or more columns) and one or more non-key columns depends on less than all of the columns of the composite or compound primary key. Hence, the non-key column is partially dependent on the primary key.

primary key A *primary key* may be a surrogate key, which is an artificial numbering schema or a natural key made up of one to many columns of the table.

record A *record* describes a horizontal element in a table, like a row or tuple. Traditionally, a record is made up of fields. It comes from file systems, which predate databases. Therefore, a record is a row of data, or an instance of a defined data structure, such as a table.

reverse engineering *Reverse engineering* is the process of using an existing database to generate a SQL script capable of generating an ER (Entity Relationship) Model. ER Models are symbolic representations of how tables are connected in a relational database.

routine A *routine* is a subroutine, stored program unit (that is, a stored function or procedure), or programming language function or method.

row A *row* describes an instance of an object, where the object is the table or an instance of a data structure. It also describes a horizontal element in a table. It comes from spreadsheets, where a row defines the horizontal axis of data. A row is also an instance of the data structure defined by a table definition, and the nested array of a structure inside an ordinary array.

specific relationship A *specific relationship* is a reciprocal set of relations between two things where one row in a result set finds one row in another result set. Another example is where one row in a result set finds many matches in another result set. These binary relationships are, respectively, one-to-one and one-to-many.

Specified relationships have equijoin or non-equijoin resolution. The first matches values, like the process in a nested loop, and the second matches values through a range or inequality relationship. Equijoins typically have a primary and foreign key, and the one side holds the primary key while the many side holds a foreign key. In the specialized case of a one-to-one relationship, you must choose which table holds the primary key that becomes a functional dependency as a foreign key in the other.

subdomain A *subdomain* is a subset of related things, like negative, zero, and positive integers are subsets of the set of integers. This definition describes the subdomain of possible values in a column based on the column's data type. It is also possible to apply the term to instances of a like set of rows in a table. The easiest example would be using a gender column to find the men or women in a set of people.

subroutine A *subroutine* is an alternative description for a routine. Like routines, subroutines are stored program units (that is, stored functions or procedures) or programming language functions or methods.

super key A *super key* identifies a set of rows, like a gender column that lets you identify males or females in your data model.

surrogate key A *surrogate key* isn't related to the subject of the table and as an attribute provides no characteristic of the subject except uniqueness.

Every surrogate key should map to one unique natural key. Using the natural key and surrogate key together to define uniqueness means the natural key isn't unique and therefore is not a natural key.

symbol set A *symbol set* is a group of drawing symbols that let you tell a story—for example, when you use a rectangle to depict a table or line when you show a relationship between two tables. Unified Modeling Language (UML) is a common symbol set, and it uses two cardinal numbers separated by two dots to represent a longhand (wordy) cardinality between relationships, like 1..* for one-to-many. While a one-to-many has no shorthand version, a zero-to-many may be shown with an asterisk (*), or in MySQL Workbench with an infinity symbol (∞).

table A *table* is a two-dimensional structure defined by the data structure of the columns and rows of the data structure.

transitive dependency A *transitive dependency* exists when a column depends on another column before relying on the primary key of the table. It may exist in tables with three or more columns that are in second normal form.

translation table A *translation table* is designed to hold two or more foreign keys and enables resolving logical relationships into physical relationships. A translation table is also an association table, and the terms are interchangeable.

tuple A *tuple* describes a row in a table. It comes from relational algebra, where a column is an attribute and a row is a tuple.

unique key A *unique key* is a column or set of columns that uniquely identify a row of data.

update anomaly An *update anomaly* occurs when the data model's design allows incorrect changes to data. Like insertion anomalies, update anomalies occur when you fail to ensure that a table has a single thing, theme, or subject. It generally occurs when non-unique keys fail to find the correct set of rows, but also can occur when a natural key fails to find a unique row.

user-defined data type (UDT) A *user-defined data type* is created by a user in an Object Relational Database Management System (ORDBMS), like Oracle. UDTs don't exist in MySQL.

Index

B

C

D

E

F

G

H

I

J

K

L

M

N

R

S

T

Z